MW01285464

Apartheid Remains

Apartheid Remains

ERRANTRIES
A series edited by Simone Browne, Deborah Cowen,
and Katherine McKittrick

Series Editorial Advisory Board   Jacqueline Nassy Brown, Ruth Wilson Gilmore,
Paul Gilroy, Gayatri Gopinath, Avery Gordon, Richa Nagar, AbdouMaliq Simone,
Françoise Vergès, and Bobby Wilson

SHARAD CHARI

DUKE UNIVERSITY PRESS
Durham and London 2024

© 2024 DUKE UNIVERSITY PRESS

This work is licensed under a Creative Commons Attribution-
NonCommercial-NoDerivatives 4.0 International (CC BY-NC 4.0)
License, available at https://creativecommons.org/licenses/by-nc/4.0/.

Printed in the United States of America on acid-free paper ∞
Project Editor: Michael Trudeau
Designed by Courtney Leigh Richardson
Typeset in Warnock Pro and Helvetica Inserat
by Westchester Publishing Services

Library of Congress Cataloging-in-Publication Data

Names: Chari, Sharad, author.
Title: Apartheid remains / Sharad Chari.
Other titles: Errantries.
Description: Durham : Duke University Press, 2024. | Series: Errantries |
Includes bibliographical references and index.
Identifiers: LCCN 2023034802 (print)
LCCN 2023034803 (ebook)
ISBN 9781478030416 (paperback)
ISBN 9781478026174 (hardcover)
ISBN 9781478059455 (ebook)
ISBN 9781478094005 (ebook other)
Subjects: LCSH: Apartheid—South Africa—Durban. | Durban (South
Africa)—Race relations—History. | South Africa—Social policy. |
BISAC: SOCIAL SCIENCE / Ethnic Studies / African Studies |
SOCIAL SCIENCE / Black Studies (Global)
Classification: LCC DT2405.D8857 C44 2024 (print) |
LCC DT2405.D8857 (ebook) | DDC 968.4/5505—DC23/ENG/20240130
LC record available at https://lccn.loc.gov/2023034802
LC ebook record available at https://lccn.loc.gov/2023034803

Cover art: *Wentworth Blues,* circa 2004. © Peter McKenzie. Courtesy of
the artist.

Publication made possible in part by support from the Berkeley
Research Impact Initiative (BRII) sponsored by the UC Berkeley Library.

for ismail

CONTENTS

Part II: Remains of Revolution

ILLUSTRATIONS

Figures

ANC	African National Congress
ASH	Association for Self-Help
BC	Black Consciousness
BCP	Black Community Programmes
BPC	Black People's Convention
CEIWU	Chemical, Engineering and Industrial Workers Union
COSAS	Congress of South African Students
CPSA	Communist Party of South Africa
CRU	Community Research Unit
DAR	National Archives of South Africa, Durban Archives Repository
DHAC	Durban Housing Action Committee
FOSATU	Federation of South African Trade Unions
FRELIMO	Frente de Libertação de Moçambique
IFCH	Institute of Family and Community Health
IIE	Institute for Industrial Education
IPRC	Internal Political Reconstruction Committee, or "the Internal"
IRA	Irish Republican Army
JMC	Joint Management Centre of the National Security Management System
JORAC	Joint Rent Action Committee
LAC	Local Affairs Committee (Indian or Coloured)

LHM	Local History Museum Archive, Durban
MEC	minerals-energy complex
MHQ	Military Headquarters of MK
MIRA	Merebank Indian Ratepayers Association
MJK	Mandla Judson Kuzwayo Unit
MK	uMkhonto we Sizwe, armed wing of the ANC
MRA	Merebank Ratepayers Association
NAB	National Archives of South Africa, Pietermaritzburg Archives Repository
NCI	Natal Chamber of Industries
NEC	National Executive Committee of the ANC
NIC	Natal Indian Congress
NMA	Natal Manufacturers Association
NOW	Natal Organisation of Women
NUSAS	National Union of South African Students
PMC	Politico-Military Council
RC	Revolutionary Council
RPMC	Regional Politico-Military Council
SACP	South African Communist Party
SACTU	South African Congress of Trade Unions
SADF	South African Defence Force
SAHA	South African History Archive
SAHO	South African History Online
SANF	South African Naval Force (neighborhood in Wentworth)
SAPREF	South African Petroleum Refineries
SASO	South African Students' Organisation
SASOL	Suid-Afrikaanse Steenkool-, Olie- en Gas Maatskappy (South African Coal, Oil, and Gas Corporation)
SDCEA	South Durban Community Environmental Alliance
SPRO-CAS 2	Special Project on Christian Action in Society
TRC	Truth and Reconciliation Commission
TUCSA	Trade Union Council of South Africa

UCC	United Committee of Concern
UCM	University Christian Movement
UDF	United Democratic Front
UND	University of Natal, Durban (later UKZN)
UDW	University of Durban-Westville (later UKZN Westville campus)
UKZN	University of KwaZulu-Natal
WDF	Wentworth Development Forum

PRELUDE: What Remains?

OCCUPATION

FIGURE P.1 Playing soccer, Highbury Ground, Wentworth, 1995. © Cedric Nunn.

It sits in the middle of Wentworth like an occupying power. Cedric Nunn's photograph at apartheid's end captures perfectly the contrast between corporate power and community vitality. Blink, and the soccer players will have run off the frame while the smokestacks are frozen in time. Fermented rot of ages, the devil's excrement that we cannot get enough of, oil conjures petrodollars and oil wars, ruined environments and hopes of untold wealth. Oil encapsulates corporate imperialism digging its heels into every reserve on land and sea, under glacial ice and desert sand, foreclosing democratic energies that may have led elsewhere. Places proximal to the promise of oil wealth have a particular pathos, in oceanic rigs, oil-saturated water tables, children playing around lagoons of crude, and neighborhoods stuck next to oil refineries. In this seventh century of imperial crossings, the empire of oil lurks in the background. Detritus of our living planet, charred remains of our collective dreams.

SITTING

FIGURE P.2 Sitting, Wentworth, 1995. © Cedric Nunn.

And yet it sits in the middle of the neighborhood surrounded by the bustle of life. They call it the ship that never sails, its fumes billowing from silhouetted smokestacks. On certain nights the smell is so obvious that it goes without comment, and yet bodies remember, curtains remember. Refineries and other polluting industry surrounding the neighborhoods of Wentworth and Merebank saturate daily life to such an extent that they seem inviolable. Photographers like Nunn have been exemplary critics of what remains painfully unsaid as people sit, smoke, walk, talk about work, go to church, scope out sexual possibilities, make an angle, crack a joke, wait for a *kombi* (shared taxi), or shout at the kids. Wentworth is an exceedingly vibrant place; its edgy, transgressive poetry borne by daily contrasts of power and inequality has produced jazz singers, dance troupes, soccer players, and everyday dreamers. In the shadows of smokestacks, this young man sits, lost in a daydream.

THE DISTRICT

FIGURE P.3 *Alabama.* Wentworth, 2003. © Jenny Gordon.

There is something expansive about *the District,* the relatively small, walkable square mile of Wentworth, with its low homes, little hills, and micro-neighborhoods, next door to the equally walkable neighborhood of Merebank with its lanes, temples, mosques, and backyard churches. Wide skies do not advertise pollution but rather hide it, shifting its pain into the interiors of homes, into uncounted forms of chronic suffering. Jenny Gordon's wide-angle "environmental portraiture" awes and inspires while subtly suggesting slow and pervasive suffering. This image was taken from the Alabama Road flats, from the home of a man who also repairs cars and fridges on the road outside. The photographer looks out to the former green "buffer zone" between the former Coloured Group Area of Wentworth and the former white area on the horizon beyond. From this vantage, the hustle-bustle of life entwines with refinery smokestacks. This is the District, where the sky remains wide and beautiful. At night, all is quiet. The quiet release of pollutants, the smell of dreams.

FIGURE P.4 *Hafiza Reebee.* Merebank, 2003. © Jenny Gordon.

Embodied remains of corporate waste. Gordon photographs Hafiza Reebee with her inhaler in her home in Merebank in a series that documents how people live with toxic suffering. Reebee passed away after many years of asthma attacks, the consequence of nocturnal emissions from the refinery. Another gentle man who ran a *spaza* shop (informal convenience store) in Assegai is now gone. And another person, another brother, another sister. There are no statistics of a long history of ill health. The apartheid regime did not keep records linked to Black people's addresses, so journalists like Tony Carnie battled to document slow death in South Africa's cancer alley. Capital makes people workers and consumers, and also repositories for industrial waste. Yet embodied life slips the grasp of power. Her eyes. Her expression. One arm outstretched, holding on.

FIGURE P.5 Waiting, Wentworth, 1995. © Cedric Nunn.

The refinery is also a sign of prized labor. Wentworth men have been compelled to aspire to be industrial artisans waiting for periodic employment as
boilermakers, pipe fitters, or fitters and turners, particularly when the refinery shuts down for maintenance. However, living in a neighborhood surrounded by industry has never guaranteed them work. City hall plays the
"race card" when workers from surrounding neighborhoods protest; it is
expedient to portray them as Coloureds and Indians fighting against African jobs. In the eclipse of Black Consciousness politics, the city manager is
complicit with a deepening mire of political corruption in Durban and in the
African National Congress (ANC). Here, Nunn photographs young people in
Wentworth standing, leaning, sitting, smoking. A year after the democratic
elections, we might ask what they are waiting for. We might ask when this
time of waiting will end.

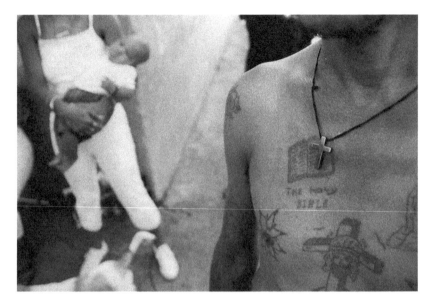

FIGURE P.6 Tattoos, Wentworth, circa 2004. © Peter McKenzie.

When I tell an interlocutor from Wentworth that I finally have a book title, *Apartheid Remains*, he nods. "How true." Pausing, he wonders if affirmative action is a kind of apartheid. I deflect, shifting to the ambiguities of various things that remain. He humors me. As elsewhere in South Africa, race is un-relenting. Peter McKenzie carefully photographs marks on the body, etched in the psyche. Frantz Fanon famously described the horror with which a white child saw him, but he realized as a psychiatrist treating victims and perpetrators of colonial violence that this was the tip of the iceberg. Of the Algerian Revolution, he warned that any successor regime would also inherit the protracted psychic, embodied, and spatial effects of colonial violence. Any attempt to think against the relentlessness of race stumbles on the ri-gidities of categories, archives, subjectivities, stories, songs, feelings, hopes, skins, and dreams. As we write with hope about a shared future, the Hydra of race returns, shifting its face and form, sneaking into the hand held out in solidarity. In McKenzie's image, the living mind-body remains, tattoos of survival pointing to the beauty of life beyond race.

FIGURE P.7 Young people in conversation, Wentworth, 1983. © Cedric Nunn.

These young people photographed by Nunn in 1983 did not yet, perhaps, know that they were going to sign up for the revolution. Robert McBride, in the middle, remains vilified for his role in blowing up two beachfront bars. His father, the late Derrick McBride, incarcerated on Robben Island, recalled suggesting to Chris Hani, popular leader of uMkhonto we Sizwe (MK), the armed wing of the ANC, that he could blow up all the oil tanks along the airport in South Durban, to which, apparently, Hani gently replied, "We want to inherit this country, not blow it up." The aging militant recalled this with a specific irony, as it is his restraint that is important in this biblical warning of "the fire next time." This gesture calls forth wider echoes and kindred spirits across centuries of revolutionary politics. Derrick McBride, an aging community activist when we met, thought resolutely against forms of knowledge in his neighborhood, as well as in the country and the world at large. The implicit care and caution in his warning provides a moment of emotional solidarity with the arcane, priestly work of academic writing and pushes for a space of learning beyond it.

FIGURE P.8 Looking out, Wentworth, circa 2004. © Peter McKenzie.

Social science was not always so venerated. To most people it continues to
be weird and inaccessible. Who can argue with so many dates and citations,
big words and claims to really know how the world works? Scholarly labor
involves its own preoccupations, but there are some consolations, including
that many things can make it into the written record. Look around at the
many moments of arrested science that hold open the possibility of learning from less privileged people facing the conditions of their social domination. Each man in McKenzie's photograph offers a different view. The central
figure dares to look directly into our uncertain future; the others are more
guarded. This is not just a book about what specific populations think, nor
is it a township study about life after apartheid, nor is it about degradation
in a toxic sink in a time of jobless growth. While these are unavoidable aspects of the problem of life in the shadows of oil refineries, what remains on
these pages are living energies that continue to strive, under conditions not
of their choice, for a future in which nothing of racial capitalism, nothing of
apartheid, remains.

FIGURE P.9 *Wentworth Blues*, circa 2004. © Peter McKenzie.

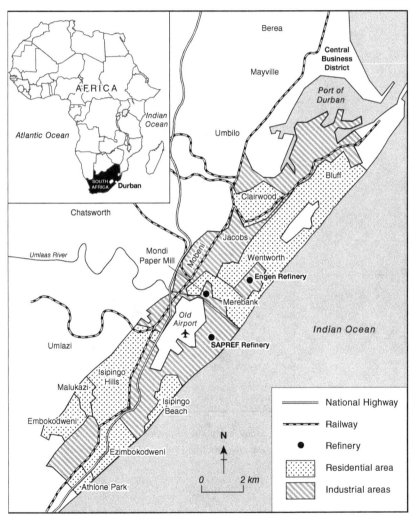

MAP 1 South Durban: An industrial-residential space. Credit: Mina Moshkeri,
LSE Design Unit, 2012.

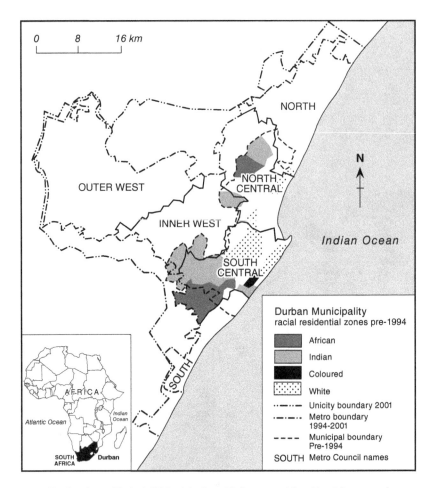

0   8   16 km

NORTH

N

OUTER WEST

NORTH
CENTRAL

INNER WEST

Indian Ocean

SOUTH
CENTRAL

AFRICA

Indian
Ocean

Atlantic Ocean

SOUTH
AFRICA   Durban

SOUTH

Durban Municipality
racial residential zones pre-1994

African

Indian

Coloured

White

·—·—·— Unicity boundary 2001

·—··—·· Metro boundary
1994-2001

– – – – Municipal boundary
Pre-1994

SOUTH   Metro Council names

MAP 2 Durban (now eThekwini) Municipality with former racial residential zones and
political boundary changes, pre-1994, 1994–2001, and 2001. Credit: Mina Moshkeri,
LSE Design Unit, 2012.

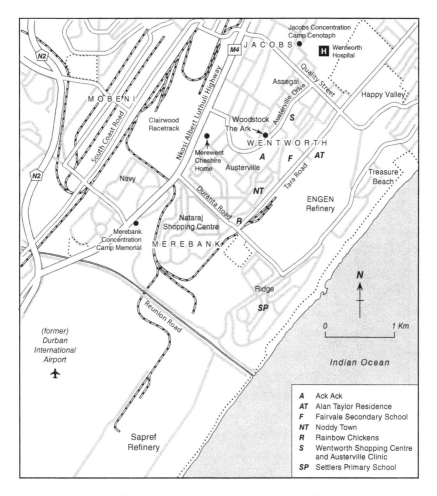

MAP 3 Merebank and Wentworth: key sites, 2012. Credit: Mina Moshkeri, LSE Design Unit, 2012.

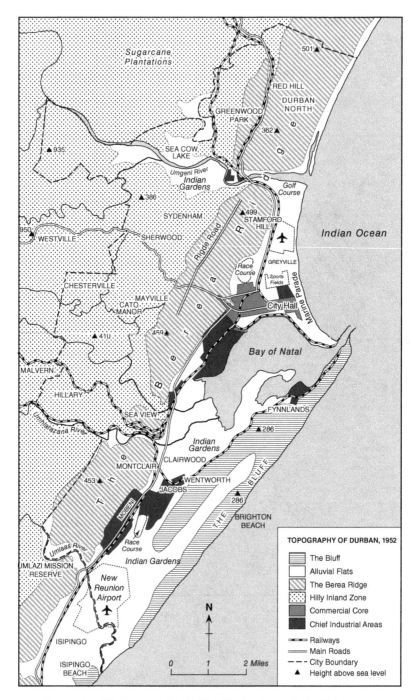

MAP 4 *Topography of Durban, 1952.* Credit: Mina Moshkeri, LSE Design Unit, 2012, redrawn from *Durban Housing Survey,* 1952.

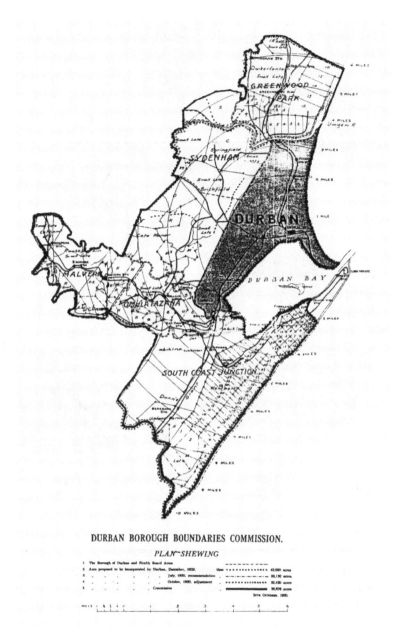

MAP 5 *Durban Borough Boundaries Commission Plan*. Credit: Durban Borough Boundaries Commission, 1929.

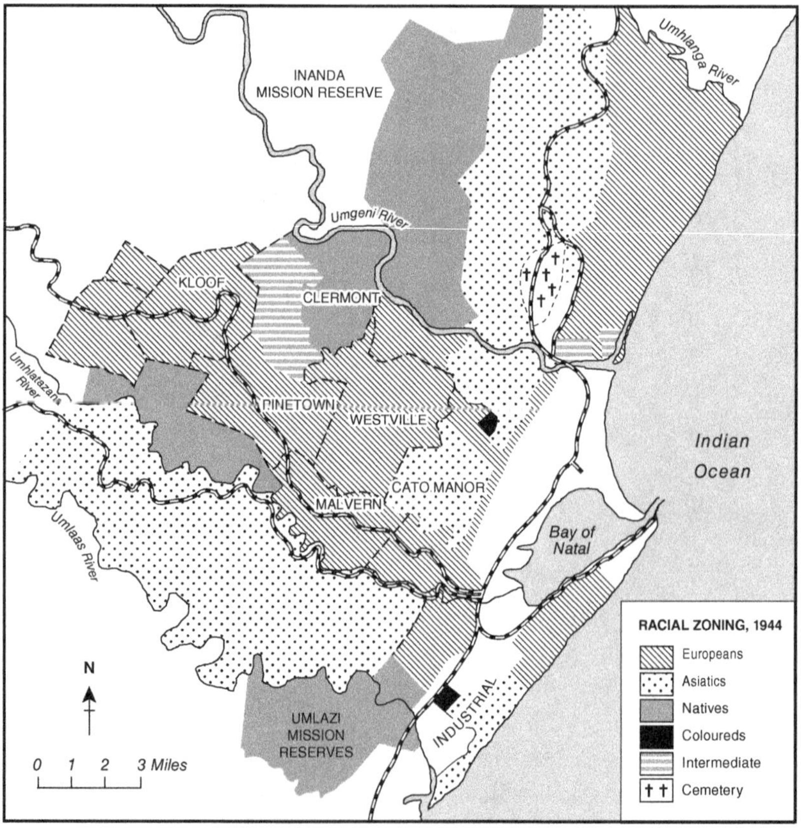
INANDA
MISSION RESERVE
Umhlanga River
Umgeni River
KLOOF
CLERMONT
Umhlatazana River
PINETOWN
WESTVILLE
Indian
Ocean
CATO MANOR
MALVERN
Umlaas River
Bay of
Natal
RACIAL ZONING, 1944
Europeans
Asiatics
Natives
Coloureds
Intermediate
Cemetery
N
INDUSTRIAL
UMLAZI
MISSION
RESERVES
0 1 2 3 Miles

MAP 6 *Racial Zoning, 1944*. Credit: Mina Moshkeri, LSE Design Unit, 2012, redrawn from *Durban Housing Survey*, 1952.

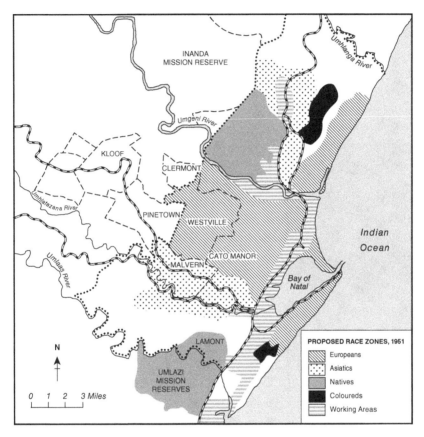

MAP 7 *Proposed Race Zones, 1951.* Credit: Mina Moshkeri, LSE Design Unit, 2012, redrawn from *Durban Housing Survey,* 1952.

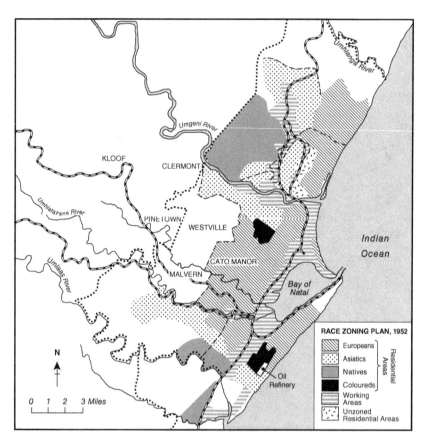

MAP 8 *Race Zoning Plan, 1952*. Credit: Mina Moshkeri, LSE Design Unit, 2012, redrawn from *Durban Housing Survey*, 1952.

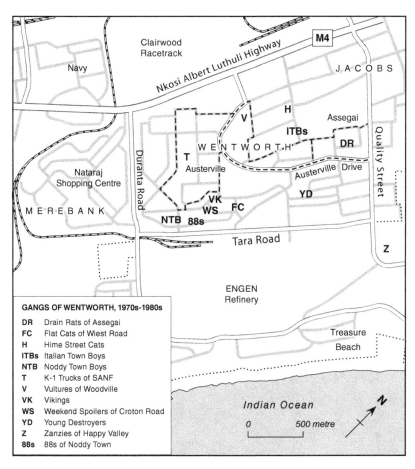

MAP 9 Street gang turf, Wentworth, 1970s–1980s. Credit: Mina Moshkeri, LSE Design Unit, 2012.

Detritus in Durban, 2002–2008

I'm not worried about the environment. All I want is my piece of oxygen!
—"JANE," Wentworth, 2003

Abandoned places are also planned concentrations—or sinks—of hazardous materials and destructive practices that are in turn sources of group-differentiated vulnerabilities to premature death (which, whether state-sanctioned or extralegal, is how racism works). . . . People in forgotten places who lack social or economic mobility, or who simply don't want to move away, act within and against the constraints of capital's changing participation in the landscape and the government's multiscalar and sometimes contradictory struggle to relegitimize state power. . . . *Constraints* does not mean "insurmountable barriers." However, it does suggest that people use what is available to make a place in the world.
—RUTH WILSON GILMORE, "Forgotten Places and the Seeds of Grassroots Planning"

I remain absorbed by Jane's demand.[1] We sat at her new doorstep in the section of the Woodville Road Flats that she called "the ghetto within the ghetto." I had come to meet Jane to find out about how a group of women had occupied flats left vacant too long, in defiance of community leaders dragging their feet with the Provincial Housing Department while securing deals for local contractors. We sat facing a field, beyond which lay the engineering workshops of the Jacobs industrial area.

We could not see the oil refinery from this vantage. What we could see was a more prosaic view of life in the formerly, and still primarily, Coloured neighborhood of Wentworth, next to the formerly, and still primarily, Indian neighborhood of Merebank.[2] Map 1 shows Wentworth and Merebank hemmed in by industry, including two oil refineries (Engen, formerly owned by Mobil and now by Malaysian Petronas, and SAPREF [South African Petroleum Refineries, a joint venture of Shell-SA and British Petroleum-SA]), a pulp and paper mill (Mondi Merebank, unbundled from the Anglo American conglomerate), a waste-treatment plant, the industrial areas of Jacobs and Mobeni, and the Durban International Airport, closed in 2010 and the site of the planned Durban Dug-Out Port expansion of the Port of Durban, delayed to the 2030s in response to prolonged political-economic crisis and local resistance.

I had been coming to Durban for four to six months of each year between 2002 and 2012. More than four years in Durban, aggregated, gave me the luxury of scholarly community alongside periodic field revisits to Wentworth and Merebank, particularly between 2002 and 2008. I spent considerable time at the Durban Depot of the National Archives and other repositories and interviewed a large number of figures connected to events in this book, many of whom had lived in Wentworth and Merebank and had since moved on, some to the heights of corporate and state power.

When I arrived, the 2001 census allowed broad comparison of Wentworth and Merebank, with populations of twenty-seven thousand and twenty-one thousand respectively, and individual monthly incomes in the range of R1,600–R3,200 (approximately $8–$16 per day.)[3] Wentworth had a substantially higher unemployment rate of 34 percent, while Merebank had markedly higher household monthly incomes. Male occupations in Wentworth concentrated in industrial work, and there were significantly more single-headed households in Wentworth, headed by men or women. Comparison with African townships including nearby Lamontville and Umlazi, and with former white areas like Musgrave and Kloof, showed Wentworth and Merebank roughly in the middle of Durban's income spectrum.[4]

Map 1 shows Wentworth and Merebank roughly at the center, near the coast, and the corresponding areas on map 2 show that Merebank was a small part of a dispersed geography racialized Indian, while Wentworth is a concentrated site racialized Coloured. This resonates with the way in which

Merebank is generally perceived as part of Indian Durban, while Wentworth is seen as a distinct working-class Coloured township. Map 2 shows the location of apartheid-era racial areas within municipal boundaries, and the expanding boundaries of eThekwini Municipality, which incorporated peri-urban white and African areas in the hope of forging a democratic "unicity."[5]

Sharply contrasting with this hope, postapartheid Durban has been a study in contrasts. Verdant bungalows, many now dilapidated, look out from the Berea Ridge with a hesitant Englishness. For more than a century, the central business district, port, and beachfront have witnessed a complex jostling of municipal employees, dockworkers, itinerant traders, subsistence fishers, shopkeepers, city officials, professionals, long-distance migrants, and working-class commuters transiting through the heart of Durban's Warwick Triangle to segregated townships or to the fragmented geographies that comprised the KwaZulu "homeland."[6]

Twenty-first-century Durban continues to be transformed by racial capital flight to the coastal north, African township sprawl into the hinterland, and shack settlement in precarious interstices. South Durban has been a singular space in which people have been consigned to living in a patchwork industrial-residential valley in which the benefits of proximity to industrial work and the city center have remained largely unrealized. Instead, the South Durban Industrial Basin has long trapped pollution and foisted the burden of ill health on its denizens, who cannot or will not move elsewhere. To paraphrase Ruth Wilson Gilmore, they have found ways to confront geographic constraints as instruments of place-making as well as, periodically, of opposition.

South Durban has witnessed sustained struggle over housing, services, limited-duration industrial labor, health care, and social services, and it has seen the rise of one of Southern Africa's most vibrant community-based environmental justice movements, led by the South Durban Community Environmental Alliance (SDCEA) and its affiliates, including the Wentworth Development Forum (WDF), the Merebank Ratepayers Association (MRA), and groundWork. In Gilmore's terms, residents have refused to abandon themselves to premature death in a toxic valley.[7]

As we spoke in the winter of 2003, Jane framed her act of seizing a home of her own within a multifaceted account of communal suffering. In the early 2000s, I encountered similar narratives of township life freighted by precarious work, violence against women and children, homelessness (in Jane's rendition, a group of children living collectively in an abandoned warehouse), sex work, drug trade, substance abuse, "gangsters" in and out of prison, and rampant theft and resale of stolen objects that made suspects of friends and lovers.

Against stock tales of criminalization and degeneration, Jane praised God for her survival as she looked out wistfully at her neighborhood. When I asked why the environmental movement had not galvanized a community of resistance, she chuckled at my naivete and exclaimed, "I'm not worried about the environment. All I want is my piece of oxygen!"

Jane described the evening before, when a group of women of Woodville Road defied the authority of the WDF as representative of the community. They held hands late in the night and prayed to the Holy Spirit for the strength to act. By the next morning, they had occupied the flats and could not be dislodged. Furious, the WDF called a public meeting at the Austerville Community Centre to censure this group of women for defying their leaders. Prominent Durban struggle veteran Fatima Meer rebuked them for breaking rank. Jane's impromptu public statement on her decision to act is a tour de force: "I woke up one morning, and I said to myself, 'What is it that depresses me so much about living here?' And when I looked around, I looked at the flat, and I said, 'My God! It looks like the walls are closing in on me!' So, if we failed somewhere along the way, we are so sorry. You know, when we needed some men around, there were no men available, so we took it upon ourselves to get in there and take on the task."[8] Playing on familiar tropes of impossible intimacies in overcrowded flats, Jane performed the betrayal of a proper sexuality. But there is more to her narrative of gendered claustrophobia than meets the eye. God, Malthus, and family values allowed her to focus her polemic on the political inactivity of the men around her. Pentecostalism, pervasive in Wentworth's backyard churches, added an emotional intensity to her call for the fruit of this world. While referencing neither the oil refineries nor local government, her demand points to a regeneration of politics itself.

As I replay her public speech, I imagine Jane as Walter Benjamin's Angel of History, heaping the debris of capitalism in the middle of the Austerville Community Centre.[9] In Jane's hands, environmental injustice is an inadequate explanation of degraded life in Wentworth. There is a dialectical openness to her enigmatic words "All I want is my piece of oxygen," a far-flung response to Frantz Fanon's rejection of "a world without spaciousness," as well as Eric Garner's "I can't breathe" from US racial capitalism.[10] Jane's enigmatic demand for oxygen points to all that blunts life in this productive landscape, including all the elements portrayed so vividly by the photographers in the prelude: from short-term respiratory ill health to the slow violence of cancer, from racialization that sticks to the skin to the slow afterlife of apartheid's infrastructures.[11]

In award-winning reporting in the *Mercury* in 2000, environmental journalist Tony Carnie wrote of a "cancer cluster" in Merebank with child leukemia rates 24 percent over the national average; he likened South Durban to what environmental justice activists called Louisiana's "cancer alley."[12] Carnie's findings were from an informal neighborhood survey, interpreted with public health scholars. The evidence was dismissed as circumstantial. There were no peer-reviewed studies. The Department of Health had not been collecting statistics to demonstrate long-term exposure through the apartheid period. The Cancer Association of South Africa responded that vehicular traffic was just as likely as industry to be the primary cause. The refineries picked up this convenient script. As in other parts of South Africa, routine ailments remain trapped in official denialism and dissimulation.

The Settlers School Study by researchers from the University of Natal Medical School and the University of Michigan School of Public Health between 2000 and 2002 found 53.3 percent of students at the Settlers Primary School in Merebank between the Engen and SAPREF refineries suffering from asthma and other respiratory problems, and 26 percent suffering from persistent asthma.[13] The dynamic model took into consideration air flows from the range of industries, and it found that 85 percent of sulfur dioxide emissions were from Engen, SAPREF, and Mondi. In other words, it named culprits. In the face of this seemingly incontrovertible evidence, both the municipality and the corporations denied the facts of exposure. After the Settlers School Study, residents like Jane suffered a kind of environmentalism fatigue.

In the wake of official dissimulation, South Durban residents turned to other ways of signifying degraded life. During this period I witnessed a routine circulation of horror stories of sex, drugs, and crime. President Thabo Mbeki was regaled with similar tales of moral and social decay in Wentworth on the election circuit in 2005. Contagion talk infiltrated local debates about whether to accept corporate social responsibility funding or whether tainted money made people complicit with hegemony. While *Apartheid Remains* seems a melancholy title for a book that interrogates this moment, what drew me to these neighborhoods in 2002 was political hope.

A Rising Tide of Livelihood Struggles:
South Durban, 2001–2006

In 2001 something exceptional took place in South Durban, an activation of solidarity across environmental justice, labor, and community activism. Over the prior decade, the Merebank Ratepayers Association had steadfastly lobbied the municipality to attend to air pollution in South Durban. In 1995 activists in Wentworth formed the South Durban Community Environmental Alliance to reorient civic organizations across South Durban's racial divides to fight the polluters.[14] Bobby Peek from Wentworth formed the environmental justice organization groundWork in 1999 to widen the focus to pollution from chemical industries, health care waste and incineration, and hazardous waste.

Together, this alliance of organizations connects activism from "fence-line communities" living cheek by jowl with polluting industry to pressure city, provincial, and national governments and to work with transnational advocacy networks. The many heads of the alliance enable a diversity of tactics including research, advocacy, campaigning, legal activism, political pressure, and direct action.[15] A persisting challenge remains mass organizing, including popular collection of evidence of pollution-related ill health. Since relocation has never been desirable for residents or the refinery, residents were consigned to life and struggle in this toxic valley. Environmental justice activists tried to turn this into an opportunity to link the violence of the present with the endurance of apartheid's corporate occupation.

Paralleling environmental activism, Wentworth witnessed the emergence of militant labor unionism led by limited-duration industrial artisans. Wentworth men had long been recognized as skilled boilermakers, pipe fitters, and fitters and turners who built and retrofitted refineries across the country and the continent. Artisans from Wentworth were employed at the coal-to-oil SASOL (South African Coal, Oil, and Gas Corporation) refineries in Sasolburg and the SASOL 2 and SASOL 3 refineries in Secunda, which promised the apartheid regime energy self-sufficiency. Wentworth men had participated in wildcat strikes in all of these refineries since the 1970s. Sterling, a Wentworth artisan who worked at several refineries, recalls the army called in at a strike in 1982. He also recalls the refineries, beginning with SASOL 2, shifting to internal contracting during annual maintenance shutdowns. The shutdown system enabled some artisans to become labor brokers; one of them said, "In 1982–1983 everybody wanted to be a labor broker; everybody who wanted to make a buck." The older white-led craft union, the South African Boilermakers Society, did not oppose the shutdown system or labor brokering, so a group of artisans connected in complex ways to labor brokering organized into what became the Chemical, Engineering and Industrial Workers Union (CEIWU).

For about a decade until the late 1990s, CEIWU operated as an independent labor union for limited-duration contract workers striking during Engen's annual shutdown for parity between them and permanent employees, and in response to the turn to outsourcing to circumvent the postapartheid Labour Relations Act of 1995. In 2001 about a thousand limited-duration contract workers led by CEIWU struck at the beginning of the annual shutdown. They were supported by local environmental activists organizing against an oil pipeline that would pass through the neighborhood. Community activists came to their mutual support. When the refinery tried to continue its shutdown work without CEIWU labor, the strike turned militant. The result was an extended refinery shutdown whose effects were felt in fuel shortages across the country during the winter of 2001.

Ashwin Desai's primer on postapartheid struggles uses this and other events to argue for a brewing movement across South Africa.[16] Desai's analysis, and his introductions to community activists, brought me to Wentworth in 2002 to research how, between peaks of protest, members of the community reflected on their praxis, their theory-in-action.[17] My initial observation was that between the high points of activism, when the male activists were gone, what came into view was a women-led space of theory and action that was not seen as political at all. My hypothesis was that this domain of "community work" is precisely a site of nurturing political hope.

This hope would prove necessary. In response to the 2001 strike, Engen shifted to partial and unscheduled shutdowns, and it began to outsource fabrication to Gauteng. Jambo, one of CEIWU's founders, argued that the refineries had been illegally blacklisting activist workers, and he was sure that he was one of them: "I've lost my car, I've lost my wife, I've lost my house, I find myself in the situation where my lights are being cut, and I'm being evicted because I stand for justice for workers."

In a key legal struggle in 2004, CEIWU fought against the unfair dismissal of 176 limited-duration contract workers. The court ruled that these industrial workers could not be considered "limited duration" as their contracts referred to benefits, leave, overtime, and other conditions of service; it also ruled that striking workers could not be terminated either for insubordination or for operational requirements without following due procedure, a reversal of the landmark 2002 judgment in *Fry Metals (Pvt. Ltd.) v. NUMSA* (National Union of Metalworkers of South Africa). The 2004 ruling altered the terms of labor struggle for artisans in the petrochemical sector, and the case became a resource for contract labor across South Africa. On the tails of this victory, CEIWU sought to consolidate its base in the South Durban Industrial Basin; it broadened its remit to scaffolders and cleaners and began representing unprotected workers on very short-term contracts; and, finally, it sought to federate with a large labor union federation.

During the 2001 strike, CEIWU garnered strong community support. Yet its members were painfully aware that with about a third of Wentworth's population unemployed, households were reliant on social grants and on various kinds of criminalized or stigmatized informal activity that further devalues lives. They also knew the value of unwaged community work, primarily that of women who care for the young, infirm, and injured and who redistribute minimal material remuneration, including grants, donations, cups of tea, and surplus food from a prominent grocery store. Most important, community work offered poor women a domain of dignity and resolve.[18] In the immediate context of blacklisting, and with declining possibilities of a racialized artisanal labor regime, CEIWU had to confront its relationship to community work.

This opportunity came in 2002 when a group of unemployed artisans from CEIWU launched an experiment in worker cooperatives. Jambo explained that rather than continue to bear the intimate burdens of migrant labor, he had decided to stay and fight for an alternative future. To this end, he and others formed a metalworkers' cooperative, mostly male, with support from a German labor union federation. In parallel, a group of women retrenched from the clothing industry started an all-female sewing cooperative. Together, they pitched the Wentworth Poverty Alleviation Programme (WEPAP) to the German funder and to eThekwini Municipality. Their initiative predates the 2003 Presidential Growth and Development Summit, which posed cooperatives as a mechanism of job creation, as well as the 2005 Cooperatives Act. Kate Philip, former organizer of cooperatives for the National Union of Mineworkers, argues that South African producer cooperatives have tended toward contestation at the expense of productivity.[19] Mirroring this diagnosis, Wentworth's co-ops were quickly in conflict. The sewing co-op was led by a mother and daughter with connections in the clothing industry who appeared to run it as a contract production unit. Jambo exclaimed, "They are offering big businesses cheap labor. That's exploitation." A heated public debate clarified that members of the two co-ops were deeply divided in their understanding of producer cooperatives, amplified by gender and class and by divergent histories of politicization.

At another meeting community members invited the municipality's Poverty Alleviation Programme to hear the Wentworth Poverty Alleviation Programme's comprehensive response to the many issues facing Wentworth. Taken aback by his outspoken interlocutors, the soft-spoken city official praised Wentworth for bucking the "level of demobilization in civil society" after apartheid. He introduced the municipality's new indigent registers to identify households below the poverty line that might qualify for special programs. Well before the formation of the National Integrated Social Information System in 2006, would-be beneficiaries were offered a glimpse into the imagination of municipal reform. As he spoke, the city official drew a pyramid with small entrepreneurs in the middle, to be targeted by the Economic Development Department, and the poor at the bottom, to be targeted by Poverty Alleviation. Jambo responded in his slow and booming voice, "We have come up with these ideas ourselves. We have done research, and we have workshopped most of these ideas, and we have done a pyramid like yours and found we are on the bottom." Another member said, "People are already starving here, and there are competent organisations here, like Women of Wentworth, so how can the city help?" Others followed with more questions. The city official made brief remarks before beating a hasty retreat.

To people in attendance, this was confirmation that Wentworth had been left out of the city's priorities as a constituency of little value to the ruling alliance and to municipal coffers. What was striking was that some residents presented themselves as professionalized civil society experts, ready to research, workshop, and "liaise telephonically." Over time, I found that most people involved in community work hedge their bets by walking a fine line between those who dispense betterment and those, often in quite similar material circumstances, in need of it. At the edges of poverty, these figures earn the right to some remuneration through the theater of community work. As we will see, they act under conditions not of their making (chapter 1).

This gendered domain of community work appeared ever more important as postapartheid social movements flowed and then ebbed by the mid-2000s, with the important exception of the shack-dweller movement Abahlali baseMjondolo, with deep roots in the Durban region, as well as the Treatment Action Campaign, and municipal "service delivery" protests mediated by the politics of infrastructure, as Antina von Schnitzler argues.[20] Gillian Hart calls this the time of "movement beyond movements," which seemed to revive forms of everyday assertion that Anne-Maria Makhulu calls "a politics of presence."[21] However, the brewing storm envisioned by Desai failed to challenge the hegemony of the ruling alliance. The rot had sunk in deeper than expected.

In South Durban, community work remained effaced from these portrayals of rising and falling movements, even though, I would argue, this largely unseen domain has been key to the endurance of political hope. As I delved deeper into the historiography of racial capitalism and struggle to understand the conjuncture of the mid-2000s, I realized that I was thinking in the wake of Shireen Hassim's powerful argument that women activists of the 1950s had forged novel ways of stitching together overtly political and seemingly apolitical forms of praxis, as well as Kumari Jayawardena's expansive account of women's agency in anti-imperialist struggles of the nineteenth and early twentieth centuries.[22] Was this a conservative formulation? Absolutely, and in a positive sense. Debates about postapartheid activism evaded precisely how people, most often Black women, women of color, and gender-nonconforming people, refused in varied ways the remains of apartheid through critical sensitivities that are uncertain and, in Grant Farred's prescient formulation, "not (yet) counterpartisan."[23] While the confluence of labor, environment, and community struggles in South Durban faced major limits, residents remained undefeated.[24] This book explains the conditions of possibility of this situation.

The Argument, in Apartheid's Remains

Apartheid Remains argues that across the twentieth century, attempts at fixing the crisis tendencies of South African racial capitalism through the production of racial space, also by biopolitical means, only sowed new contradictions and forms of struggle, the limits and possibilities of which are powerfully discernible through Black Marxist feminist critique. I detail each element of this argument in this section. However, it would be a mistake to think of this as an abstract argument for which all that remains is empirical support in the chapters that follow. Concrete elaboration is everything. The usefulness of theory is only borne in the labor of working through material of various kinds, drawing liberally from the tools of the ethnographer, historian, cultural critic, and geographer. The palimpsestic form allows the reader to see how elements of the argument emerge within specific conjunctures of power and protest, leaving their remains behind as conjunctures shift.

Here I lay out the three broad lines of thought that converge across this book. The first concerns capitalism's search for a spatial and racial fix to its immanent contradictions, and the ways in which any such fix remains elusive. The second concerns the ways in which the racial state and capital seek to harness biopolitical discourse, intervention, and subjectivation to this futile quest, which produces periodic rounds of what I call "biopolitical struggle," raced and gendered class struggle over the conditions of life. These inconclusive struggles take us to Black Marxist feminist politics, including cultural politics, that reach beyond biopolitical struggles and their racial/spatial domestication, for the possibility of an actual world in common.

On the Racial-Spatial Fix

Capitalism is necessarily growth oriented, technologically dynamic, and crisis prone. One of the ways it can temporarily and in part surmount crises of overaccumulation of capital . . . is through geographical expansion. This is what I call the "spatial fix" to capitalism's contradictions.

—DAVID HARVEY, *Justice, Nature, and the Geography of Difference*

Prisons are partially geographical solutions to political economic crises, organized by the state, which is itself in crisis.

—RUTH WILSON GILMORE, *Golden Gulag*

I begin with the argument that Gilmore's conception of the "prison fix" can be read as a Black Marxist revision of David Harvey's notion of capital's futile quest for a "spatial fix."[25] To appreciate this, it is important to note that both thinkers build on key aspects of Karl Marx's critical method. Marx understood that what seems like an eternal law or logic immanent to capital is prone to crisis and breakdown, revealing its "logic" to be grotesquely illogical and violent. Marx also thought that people at the coalface of crisis have recognized this in mystified but collective ways. From his early writings to his very last letters, Marx was concerned with forms of difference and mutuality that might be repurposed toward the abolition of capitalism and the construction of a different organization of collective life.[26]

Harvey's historical-geographical materialism works this imperative through Henri Lefebvre's triadic dialectics of space and time, which Harvey usefully explicates as encompassing "space and time" in the absolute sense as separable and known through cadastre and clock, "space-time" in the relative sense as linked through routinized circuits of capital or spatial practice, and "spacetime" in the relational sense as indivisible and freighted with affect.[27] Lefebvre also attends to geographical difference in two senses: as "induced" through the capitalist co-optation of some forms of mutuality, for instance, in place branding, but also as "produced" through the ongoing bodily production of "differential space" that prefigures a future after capitalism.[28] While Lefebvre had nothing to say about racism as intrinsic to capitalism, we can read his insights on difference and capitalism precisely for this purpose.[29] We have no recourse but to force Lefebvre into the clarity of Black Marxist method.

In his Lefebvrian reworking of Marx's crisis theory, Harvey theorizes capital's attempt at a spatial fix to crisis either through the export of surplus capital to make new geographies or through the techno-organizational transformation of spatial relations. Either route produces "new territorial divisions of labor and concentrations of people and labor power, new resource extraction activities and markets," and consequently an elaboration of geographical differentiation in which "'difference' and 'otherness' are produced in space through . . . uneven capital investment, a proliferating geographical division of labor, an increasing segmentation of reproductive activities and the rise of spatially ordered (often segregated) social divisions."[30] Indeed, Harvey realizes all too well that the spatial fix utilizes Lefebvrian induced difference to segment and segregate capitalist geographies.

Harvey also insists that the spatial fix is speculative, crisis-prone, and inevitably impossible; it is really a theory of unfixing. Speculation turns capital against itself, feeding competition between places over induced difference, between different fractions of capital, and ultimately the contradiction "between place-bound fixity and spatial mobility of capital erupts into generalized crisis."[31] At this point, tellingly, Harvey shifts from the positive to the normative, from what is actually happening to what must happen: "The geographical configuration of places must then be reshaped around new transport and communications systems and physical infrastructures, new centers and styles of production and consumption, new agglomerations of labor power, and modified social infrastructure. . . . Old places . . . have to be devalued, destroyed, and redeveloped while new places are created. The cathedral city becomes a heritage center, the mining community becomes a ghost town, the old industrial center is deindustrialized, speculative boom towns or gentrified neighborhoods arise on the frontiers of capitalist development or out of the ashes of deindustrialized communities."[32]

Harvey's narrative form mirrors capital's immanent tendencies; it conveys that any attempt at resolving capital's contradictions through the production of space will be a mirage. But there is always a break between the old and the new, an indeterminacy that implies that the "fix" as solution also gets "in a fix," as in a quandary, a laced turn of phrase to match Marx's "free labor." And since the fix as quandary must be legible to its denizens, the problematic of the spatial fix cries out for a materialism attentive to struggles over representation as necessary to its immanent dialectic.

This is the point at which Harvey's explanation of geographical differentiation diverges from Gilmore's, which also draws from Antonio Gramsci, Stuart Hall, and Cedric Robinson an attentiveness to forms of consciousness and to renovations of the past.[33] Hence, Gilmore reads Robinson's term *racial capitalism* as a reminder that capitalism always draws on and revises prior power relations in the attempt at enshrining the differentiation that capital produces.[34]

There is a third sense of the fix to consider if we think with Robinson's insight that racial regimes "wear thin over time."[35] Racial capitalist geographies, it follows, are always in a state of protracted degradation. This prompts a third sense of the "fix" as a drug-induced free fall into a virtual reality of induced difference, a mass hallucination with its own possibilities of creativity and critique within the world remade by racial capitalism. Robinson's focus is on the "masquerades" of motion pictures and their racist misapprehensions of Black life.[36] We might turn to Walter Benjamin's hashish-induced tracing of Ariadne's thread through the urban sensorium as particularly appropriate to the collective intoxication of racism.[37] Consider, in this light, Stuart Hall and colleagues' *Policing the Crisis* as a critique of a degrading form of crisis management premised on the fear and loathing of young Black British men who in turn refuse their racist interpellation by conserving the energies of a waning tradition of Black Power. Nothing is quite what it seems in this racial free fall.

Gilmore is distinctive for attending to the way in which people actively engage both induced and produced difference to forge new solidarities while opposing the racial-spatial fix, under conditions not of their making.[38] Through her work with Mothers Reclaiming our Children (Mothers ROC) in Los Angeles, which had formed to respond to the incarceration of male kin in the wake of deindustrialization, criminalization, aggressive policing, gang violence, and deepening social crisis, Gilmore shows that there is always a possibility of articulating collective will in opposition to what she characterizes as the state's attempts at using capital to save capital from capital. Cutting through the hallucination that prison building in California had produced a radical spatial fix that can continue to articulate surplus labor, land, finance, and state capacity, Ruthie and Craig Gilmore joined broader political organizing on various fronts across rural and urban California in solidarity with unemployed or precariously employed, dehoused, and encaged people who refuse to become surplus people. Ananya Roy's work with the After Echo Park Lake research collective in *(Dis)Placement* is a parallel initiative that refuses another racial-spatial fix after state-led displacement of unhoused communities in Los Angeles.

Across this book, we will see strikingly similar forms of collective praxis in the wake of attempts at engineering a racial-spatial fix before, during, and after apartheid. This takes us to the specific forms of biopolitical regulation of imperial-capitalist crises in the late nineteenth and early twentieth centuries, and the struggles in their wake.

On Biopolitics, Capital, and Biopolitical Struggle

English doctors are unanimous in declaring that where the work is continuous, 500 cubic feet is the very least space that should be allowed for each person. . . . The sanitary officers, the industrial inquiry commissioners, the factory inspectors, all harp, over and over again, upon the necessity for these 500 cubic feet, and upon the impossibility of wringing them out of capital. They thus, in fact, declare that consumption and other lung diseases among the workpeople are necessary conditions to the existence of capital. —KARL MARX, *Capital*

Biopower was without question an indispensable element in the development of capitalism; the latter would not have been possible without the controlled insertion of bodies into the machinery of production and the adjustment of the phenomena of population to economic processes. —MICHEL FOUCAULT, *The History of Sexuality*

In 1977 Maynard Swanson published a foundational essay on the origins of urban segregation in South Africa, scarcely two years after Michel Foucault's lectures on biopolitics as central to state racism across Western liberal capitalisms, fascisms, and state socialisms.[39] Swanson argued that infectious disease provided the pretext for the exclusion of Africans from Cape Town from 1900 to 1904 and that this "sanitation syndrome" set a precedent for urban segregation to come. Swanson was prescient in addressing a blind spot in the prevailing Marxist historiography of segregation, the role of scientific expertise in national and urban spatial politics.[40]

As is evident in his Collège de France lectures, Foucault had for some years been working on a conception of biopolitical governmentality alongside transformations in capital, law, sovereignty, sexuality, medicine, punishment, and so on in the making of bourgeois society.[41] Foucault's insights remain bold, provocative, and incomplete. He did not pose biopolitical governmentality in state-centric terms. Rather, he conceived of biopower and discipline emerging as counterforces to sovereignty, subsequently drawn into specific articulations with it, with dire consequences. Biopolitical government harnessed by sovereign power in Western capitalist and Soviet socialist states, he argued incisively, resulted in "state racisms" that cut the social body into populations subject differentially to biopolitical intervention or exposure to death. We can only wonder how he might have revised his formulation, as he often did in interrupting his accounts of regimes of truth, by forms of *parrhesia*, or fearless speech.

Foucault's method afforded him the capacity to make long-term historical claims about, for instance, the remaking of forms of exclusion from medieval plague regulation to medical campaigns against epidemics and endemics since the eighteenth century, recasting historical process through his particular genealogical method.[42] Given his attention to the world beyond France, and his enthusiasm about the Iranian Revolution of 1978, it is surprising that he did not attend to the imperial career of biopower, particularly in late-Victorian settler colonies and in movements that rose in opposition to them.[43] Scholarly works on biopower are legion, but much work remains to be done on the tenuous articulation of biopolitics, sovereignty, and capital that Foucault discerned but did not fully elaborate.[44] Furthermore, the divide in treatments of biopower between an abstract approach that poses biopower ontologically and a historical approach that is only concerned with empirical operations misses the opportunity to think about concrete and abstract in relation.[45] Not fortuitously, Foucault developed his biopolitics concept alongside advocacy for the rights of French prisoners; the radical political milieu of his concept work has much to offer a reconsideration of biopolitics for our time.[46]

A historical approach, considered dialectically and genealogically, helps us attend to the colonial and postcolonial career of biopolitics. Keith Breckenridge insightfully reads Foucault's concept through histories of North Atlantic Progressivism between the 1870s and 1920s, and across the imperial world, to note a resonance between biopolitics and Progressivism, as well as a distinctive class politics.[47] Read with histories of North Atlantic Progressivism, biopolitics appears as a class project peopled by middle-class experts in what they called "social politics," who responded to spiraling social crisis through knowledge and intervention in public health, urban planning, workingmen's insurance, immigration controls, cooperative farming, and rural reconstruction.[48] Progressives varied according to context, but they shared a focus on the state, on statistical social scientific methods, on policy-relevant expertise, and on social engineering; both eugenics and segregation were very much a part of their toolbox.[49] Critical of the plutocrats, Progressives forced them into philanthropy, creating some of the key foundations of the North Atlantic world, and they kept a distance from the militancy of anarchists and communists who argued for deeper structural change.

In much of colonial Africa, the metropolitan presumptions of Progressivism—middle-class experts, acceptance of social scientific expertise and its calculative tools, and political expediency for state intervention in broad-based welfare—remained presumptions.[50] Most African colonies subject to what Sara Berry calls "hegemony on a shoestring" could hardly afford to regulate the various aspects of life, sex, work, or movement that biopolitics implies.[51] Scholars of the colonial world show us that the hope of biopolitical government was typically fraught.[52] Where biopolitical intervention did become important was precisely in settler colonies in which the consent of white working classes became a pressing issue for imperial control.[53] Hence, British settler colonies witnessed fierce debate over immigration controls, fingerprinting systems, labor regulations, agrarian transformation, and urban cleanup, as they tensely balanced ideals of responsible self-government with instruments to delimit populations deemed incapable of exercising democratic rights.[54]

Metropolitan theory presumes too much about the smooth workings of biopower.[55] Rather than presume that biopolitical government works as a cohesive whole, I build on Breckenridge's cue to disaggregate biopolitics into tools of biopolitical knowledge, intervention, and subjectivation, which do not work in unison and are prone to periodic breakdown.[56] Disaggregating biopolitical tools is important. Too often, "the biopolitical" is depicted as a unitary monster, like the reading of Hannah Arendt's notion of "the social" in Hanna Pitkin's *The Attack of the Blob*. There are substantive differences between biopolitical expertise in public health, urban planning, and population control, let alone in how this expertise is deployed or how people might become subjects of biopower. While state and capital might attempt to instrumentalize specific tools of biopolitical government, and while this attempt might confirm Foucault's hypothesis that biopolitical sovereignty tends to racism, we ought to approach these attempts *as attempts*. Indeed, the point of Foucault's genealogies is that governmental efforts routinely fail to do what they purport to do and that people subject to their blunt edge often refuse to be subjects of power/knowledge.

We should likewise expect that capital's attempt at a biopolitical fix, like any other racial-spatial fix, produces new geographies of struggle. Twentieth-century capitalist and state-socialist societies across the Global North and South witnessed powerful popular struggles to disarticulate the tools of biopolitics from the imperatives of state racism. Refusing the inevitability of necropolitics, these struggles over the content of biopolitical expertise and its concrete deployment in public health, public education, public housing, urban planning, social insurance, or regional development turned expert knowledge into a terrain of popular struggle, or what I call "biopolitical struggle."[57] The ties that bind biopower, capital, and racial sovereignty run deep, and transforming their articulation is no easy matter, but that has not deterred the hope of popular and ecological determination of biopower in the service of planetary flourishing. We must imagine this possibility, not after the end of the world, but after the end of capitalism.

After apartheid, South Africa has been a crucial site of biopolitical struggle in the the movement for access to HIV/AIDS medication and in widespread protests over housing, services, land, health care, livelihoods, and public higher education, amplified in our time of multiple crises.[58] South African realities push us to ask how biopolitical instruments have been deployed in struggles over unequal means of life to produce what Didier Fassin calls "bio-inequalities" but also to call them into question.[59] We might think in parallel with scholarship on struggles over biopolitical expertise in contexts ranging from the compromised "biological citizenship" of Chernobyl survivors, to the suppression of health risks associated with asbestos mining, to breast cancer activism and radical AIDS activism in the United States, as well as present and future research on the unraveling of biopolitical sovereignty.[60] The question is how variously dehumanized subjects imagine a popular biopolitics in the ruins of biopolitical sovereignty.

Throughout this book we see the racial state's repeated attempts at fixing the racial-spatial borderlands of South Durban, by any biopolitical means necessary, only to turn biopolitics into a field of struggle. While this terrain is grappled with in a range of ways, I turn next to why the confluence of Black, Marxist, and feminist critique pushes biopolitical struggle beyond limits set by racial capitalism and sovereignty.

On Black Marxist Feminism and the Risk of Conjuncturalism

Black. Marxist. Feminist. These three categories do not always line up. Often they are posed as antithetical for reasons that have more to do with broken promises of solidarity. Hopes of material benefit through whiteness or masculinism were often central to these failures of solidarity, but so were unfinished promises of Black liberation. When the three categories have lined up, the combination has been explosive. Radical anti-capitalist, antipatriarchal, and anti-racist critique pushes beyond the ruse of a biopolitical resolution to racial capitalist crises. This was the promise of the Combahee River Collective and of a host of radical Third World feminist and worker collectives forged across the world in the 1970s and 1980s, also in South Africa, often as an explicit critique of masculinist and militarist forms of putatively radical politics that had not interrogated their reliance on sovereignty.[61]

In our time of often bewildering uncertainty, radical traditions of materialist feminist, postsocialist, postcolonial, oceanic, and ecological critique across the planet converge in profound unease with respect to political hope for a substantially altered world of collective flourishing. Forty years and more of neoliberal crisis management in the capitalist world portends continued political-economic volatility, deepened by states' inability to respond to challenges of grotesque inequality, pandemics, and climate change. There are no consolations in nostalgia for a mid-twentieth-century golden age of welfare capitalism or state socialism, which were committed to varieties of racism, sexism, and imperialism. We can discern political hope precisely where the ruses of counterpower offered by racial capitalism and sovereignty have been laid bare. This has been key to the postcolonial predicament from a materialist perspective, as well as to its specific iteration in South Africa after the ascent to political power of the dominant alliance of the African National Congress (ANC), the South African Communist Party (SACP), and the Congress of South African Trade Unions (COSATU). Black, Marxist, and feminist traditions remain central to this ongoing challenge.

South African radical scholarship anticipates this moment in decades of research through Marxist social history and political economy, on regionally differentiated processes of social change before, during, and after apartheid.[62] Much of this work attends to geographic differentiation.[63] In an important study, Hein Marais diagnoses South Africa's "limits to change" since apartheid, provoking questions about how these limits have taken root differently.[64] More recently, Black scholars have argued for attention to "the Black register," as Tendayi Sithole puts it; or to "the Black intellectual's work," as Farred puts it; or to the insights of South African Black feminism, as Pumla Dineo Gqola and Gabeba Baderoon argue.[65] This work questions whether radical scholarship of the past was attentive enough to the archives of Blackness and Africanity in a society still trapped by vestiges of colonialism and apartheid. These critiques mirror those of earlier generations of Black thinkers committed to liberation, who might have anticipated disenchantment in a postapartheid racial capitalism to come.

The thinkers who are particularly instructive in this regard have not shied away from productive tensions across Black, anti-colonial, Marxist, and feminist radical traditions. Among them, Stuart Hall is indispensable for his practice of reading across traditions in the face of political revanchism, attentive to Black expressive forms that might shift the public conversation. I offer a brief excursus through Hall's method to show how his "conjuncturalism" informs how this book approaches people and places racialized Indian and Coloured through Black Marxist feminist critique, with a special place for critique from documentary photographers (see the prelude).

In the late 1970s, Hall fundamentally revised his understanding of racism and capitalism through the collective work of the Centre for Contemporary Cultural Studies at Birmingham, at a moment that Arun Kundnani aptly characterizes as Britain on the verge of neoliberalism but still actively shaped by anti-colonial Black community and labor struggles.[66] Through interaction with South African exiles, and with debates on the relationship between capitalism and apartheid, Hall arrived at a focus on "the concrete historical 'work' which racism accomplishes under specific historical conditions—as a set of economic, political and ideological practices, of a distinctive kind, concretely articulated with other practices in a social formation."[67] A methodological internationalist, Hall refined his argument about South Africa alongside a critique of the British state's crisis management through the criminalization of young Black men.[68] In Britain, Hall could do what he could not do in South Africa, which was to directly understand what young people made of their own racial condition. This deepened his famous formulation that "race is . . . the modality in which class is 'lived,' the medium through which class relations are experienced, the form in which it is appropriated and 'fought through.'"[69]

In subsequent decades, Hall deepened his engagement with the final phrase, on appropriation and "fighting through," drawing from Gramsci, Benjamin, Fanon, and C. L. R. James.[70] These would prove perfect interlocutors for neoliberal times, each thinker doggedly invested in critique in the face of political defeat. Hall's thought transformed through feminism, the Black Arts Movement, Black popular culture, the culture wars of the Thatcher years, and a new generation of Black British scholars redefining cultural studies in internationalist, feminist, and anti-essentialist ways.[71] Hall argued that the 1990s marked "the end of the innocent notion of the essential black subject" that sought to unify multiple histories of oppression and expression on the ground of a particular Black masculine subject; Roderick Ferguson offers the corollary that Black feminist and queer art and critique made this "end of innocence" possible.[72]

Committed to the multiplicity of Black representation, Hall notes the importance of a political rather than anthropological conception of Blackness, one attentive to the multiplicity of forms of Black life and to the broader work they might do. This is an important shift, germane to this book. Political Blackness in Britain as in South Africa was not without its own risks, its own forms of "innocence." Perhaps the only way to hold on to the possibilities of solidarity enabled by political Blackness is to engage the questions it prompts. In South Durban the primary questions are, What is to be made of Indian and Coloured townships composed of some people who signed up for radical Black politics but many who did not? What does this landscape propose for Black politics, including cultural politics, in a city at the confluence of the Black Atlantic and the Indian Ocean? These are questions that recur in the background of this book.

Paralleling questions concerning a political Blackness that spoke to some people who signed up for Black politics to liberate everyone, and many who did not, is the significance of feminist critique of processes of place-making and opposition, which were exceedingly masculinist. As we saw in the livelihood struggles in South Durban in the early 2000s in the previous section, male leadership routinely ignored the centrality of women's political work. As we turn to the past, we find a long history of effacement of Black women's praxis. However, historical effacement need not alter political and theoretical commitment to the centrality of gender and of Black women's praxis. What I attempt in this book is to diagnose the entry of feminist insight when it punctures specific conjunctures, as well as when it is disciplined into the margins of the dominant political imagination.

By the 2000s Hall had transformed his notion of "articulation" into a "conjuncturalism" that linked the acuities of Marxist political economy with Black expressive arts, with anti-racist, feminist, and queer critique folded in. Consider this powerful methodological statement from a piece on Black diaspora artists:

> Thinking conjuncturally involves "clustering" or assembling elements into a formation. However, there is no simple unity, no single "movement" here, evolving teleologically. . . . I try to assemble . . . "moments" in their fused but contradictory dispersion. . . . By "moment" then, I mean the coming together or convergence of certain elements to constitute, for a time, a distinct discursive formation, a "conjuncture," in a Gramscian sense. This is always "a fusion of contradictory forces"; or as Althusser once put it, a "condensation of dissimilar currents, their ruptural fusion of an accumulation of contradictions" whose "unity" is necessarily over-determined.[73]

The intellectual is now in the frame rather than observing dispassionately from on high; they think conjuncturally at the scene of representation, assembling moments that are contradictory, dispersed, and ruptural. The "moment" here is not purely temporal, as in the primary definitions in the *Oxford English Dictionary*, as short duration, definite period, stage, turning point, or opportune point in time.[74] Rather, moments are spatiotemporal. The intellectual assembles dissimilar and contradictory moments to clear space for critique. This act is always a wager; it comes with no guarantees that representing the conjuncture in this way will be consequential, and yet it might be. This is the political hope with which the chapters that follow assemble dissimilar and contradictory elements as they come together, conserving remains for future formations of critique.

The dominant ideological means that the ANC, and the multiracial political coalition it led called the Congress Alliance, has claimed to conserve political hope has been through "nonracialism." David Everatt notes that this category has been called the movement's "unbreakable thread" even while it has remained fragile and ill defined; Raymond Suttner defends nonracialism as an anti-essentialist concept that can attend to race as social and historical, yet Suttner cannot imagine Blackness doing similar work.[75] Victoria Collis-Buthelezi thoughtfully suggests that "non-racialism, at its best, is more indicative of a future time at which we have yet to arrive, a time in which it is possible to shed race as a category of experience or study," and that, like Christina Sharpe's "wake work," attention to the devaluation and destruction of Black lives is a necessary part of the journey to such a future.[76]

Read through Collis-Buthelezi and Sharpe, Hall's conjuncturalism is precisely a form of "wake work" that prompts a reading of South African radical scholarship of the past while attending to the challenges posed by Black intellectual and political work today. Hall's approach questions "innocent" claims to nonracialism by Marxist social history unreflective of its whiteness, and also "innocent" claims to Africanity and coalitional Blackness that claim general admission while erecting barriers to entry.[77] The emphasis on Blackness as a political rather than anthropological category makes it available not just to specifically racialized people but to the planet as a whole. If, as Achille Mbembe prophesies, "Blackness and race . . . [are] two sides of a single coin, two sides of a codified madness" increasingly generalized to a planetary condition, a "becoming Black of the world," what remains is the hard work of tracing the multiple itineraries through which a world for all might still take form.[78] *Apartheid Remains* carries this hope of Blackness, in relation to anti-colonial, Marxist, feminist, and other radical traditions, as a beacon of planetary futurity.[79]

On Racial Risks and Spatial Histories

With this political aim in mind, it is possible to state axiomatically that the use of racial categories is never innocent. I do not use quotation marks around *race* as a distancing mechanism. The Blackness in Black politics referred to here is a proper noun for a political coalition paid for with intimate sacrifices. This does not exhaust all senses of Blackness, and there is nothing sacrosanct in this choice; scholars whom I respect have made other choices.[80] While a coalitional conception of Black politics circulated in South Durban in the 1970s, I use the term anachronistically as well to refer to people who did or do not affirm it. I do so willfully for its promise of universality that we cannot do without in another century of racial imperialism. The question remains as to whether and how a nonanthropological conception of Blackness might help undo the capitalist basis of racial embodiment and territoriality through the production of induced/produced spatial difference.

There is more to be said about the specific risks that follow the racial categories in this book. Coloured in South Africa is often premised by an apology, written and spoken "so-called Coloured," but there are no apologies for "so-called Indians" also descended from oceanic migrants creolized in Africa. There are also linguistic "false friends" to be wary of, as the Indian in South Africa is not the Indian of South Asia, Fiji, or Mauritius, although people readily assume their kinship. I leave *white* uncapitalized, as the unmarked background category across a set of settler capitalisms, although it is also a transnational abstraction with its own protracted half-life. The task, as I see it, is to diagnose racial abstractions as they surface in their specificity, proclaiming their trans-historicity even as they fade, or so we might continue to hope.[81]

The racial state might have hoped for neat racial separations and gradations of privilege, as in its attempts to make Indian and Coloured "buffer zones" between white and African space. Ground realities, as we will see, remained messy. Racial terms twisted and changed over time and space.[82] "Coloured" transformed considerably across the twentieth century from marking anxieties about "mixed bloods" and "race mixture" to distinguishing Africans who were divisible into tribes from "non-whites" who were not, with implications for residence, work, and franchise; it named a "race group" under the Population Registration Act of 1950, subdivided in 1959 into Cape Coloured, Cape Malay, Griqua, Indian, Chinese, Other Asiatic, and Other Coloured populations, all subject to race determination tests in everyday racial statecraft; Indian and Coloured are closely intertwined categories, although this is rarely noted in scholarship or popular consciousness.[83]

Circulation of the Coloured category accelerated in Durban in the 1940s, after "mixed-race" tenants were expropriated and located in residentially segregated areas like Wentworth, but its ambiguities index a persisting quandary. Grant Farred argues that South African Colouredness rests on a denial of a prelapsarian moment that might enable a "retreat into a mythic precolonial innocence" and that "Coloured difference is . . . insufficiently different" for people "to conceive of themselves as anything but South African."[84] This formulation speaks directly to events in Wentworth in which residents voiced an inability to affirm the breakdown of racial authentication. Living with "insufficient difference," these residents often repeat well-worn accounts of parents unable to help their child complete assignments on "Coloured culture," or they offer variations on "We weren't white enough then; we're not black enough now."[85] While race trouble in Wentworth appears to confirm Farred's argument, Indians in Merebank, as elsewhere in South Africa, appear ever ready to authenticate race as "culture." Whether in overt practices of communal affiliation or in engagement with the differentiated commodity cultures of the Indian diaspora, Indianness is inexorably transnational but also, as we will see, perennially exposed to xenophobia.[86]

This contrast, well after the 1991 repeal of apartheid's Group Areas Acts that marked Wentworth and Merebank as separable Coloured and Indian townships, would seem to require that this book take the form of a comparative township study, an established tradition in South Africa.[87] The challenge in this form is that it risks reifying racial and spatial difference rather than explaining these differences as products of complex geographical histories. A comparative township study would typically not apprehend that Merebank's residents have access to a wider archipelago of Indian Durban, while Wentworth's residents find themselves stuck in this working-class Coloureds township. Ashwin Desai negotiates this carefully in his study of soccer as a means of attending to proximity across people racialized Indian and Coloured in Durban.[88] Township studies have an uncomfortable proximity to segregated histories, despite conscious efforts to push against apartheid's archives and forms of consciousness. A productive approach shifts the frame from locality to circulation, as Mark Hunter does in an exemplary study of race and schooling across Durban.[89]

Apartheid Remains foregrounds the spatial histories that frame Merebank and Wentworth in counterpoint, through processes of dispossession, settlement, livelihood, planning, and struggle that link these neighborhoods to broader social forces in different and linked ways.[90] In brief, Merebank was an old village of ex-indentured Indian peasant-workers on the urban fringe, taken apart and remade into an apartheid township. Despite a rich and multilayered history of opposition to apartheid, former activists have been able to move up and out after apartheid, some to the highest levels of political-economic power. On the other side of Duranta Road, Wentworth was created as a Coloured township to house a large number of mixed-race tenants thrown out of informal backyard tenancies in Indian homes through preapartheid waves of dispossession in the 1940s. While Wentworth men have been South Africa's preeminent industrial artisans, they have returned between jobs to a neighborhood saturated by a sense of isolation from the city around it. In the mirror of Merebank, Wentworth's introversion comes into sharp relief.

Narrating this as a tale of two townships would replicate the persisting problem shared by people racialized Indian and Coloured: that they are not generally regarded as African, even when they have lived for generations in South Africa and are committed to Black politics. Part of the reason is that the relative privilege of these intermediate race-class groups in South African society often serves to fortify their ongoing racialization and antipathy to a future shared with the Black majority.

Might the inclusion of a Black African township and its residents in this study have resolved this issue? I suggest it would not have. Instead, it may have staged an alibi that hides the difficult problem that anti-racist solidarity is never guaranteed. There is another reason that bringing a Black African township into the mix would have been inadequate. The specificity of Wentworth and Merebank is that these racial and spatial borderlands constituted a zone of experimentation in biopolitical statecraft and struggle, including in the global circulation of "social medicine" and "environmental justice." African townships, including neighboring Lamontville, were subject to brutally invasive repression rather than the kind of biopolitical concern and intervention meted out to intermediate racial groups. This is why, as we will see, a particularly opportune moment arose when a Black medical student residence for African, Indian, and Coloured students was set up in the middle of Wentworth, to became a crucible for a new, coalitional form of political Blackness (chapter 6). The political hope at the center of this book emerges from this fleeting moment of solidarity.

Bringing the Argument Together: Theory, Politics, Form

Apartheid Remains elaborates the argument that the racial-spatial fix is always an intoxicating ruse and fantasy, that in deploying biopolitical tools it creates new geographies of biopolitical struggle, and that a Black Marxist feminist lens helps us interpret forms of praxis, both action and reflection, that survive the violence of biopolitical sovereignty.

I elaborate this argument in the palimpsestic form of this book. The palimpsest resists linear historical narrative for the accumulation of detail that weighs on the living. I reiterate that it would be a mistake to see this detail as simply empirical corroboration of a conceptual argument laid out fully here. This is not meant to be a "theory section" in the genre of positivist social science. Critical "elaboration" is the labor of diagnosing the spatial-historical conjuncture, to contribute to the collective political will necessary to abolish, and to build the new.[91] If readers are drawn to theoretical arguments that bubble up at various moments in the text, for instance, on the submergence of Indian Ocean pasts (chapter 2) or on the elective affinity between racial segregation and the developmental state (chapter 3), I mean these arguments to emerge where they do, in relation to the material that prompts a particular line of thought. Relatedly, the approach to the Marxist critique of political economy I take is genealogical.[92] Chapters bring together constellations of spacetimes to convey the recursive and ongoing violence of racial statecraft and its fantasy of a racial-spatial fix to crises. Each conjuncture transforms the urban fabric as it coheres for a period, then comes apart, leaving a trail of remains behind, well into the present.

In a strict sense, the ethnographic present in which the book begins and ends is 2008, but the remains explored here have by no means disintegrated. In addition, the conjunctures sometimes clarify Black women's praxis but often occlude it; they sometimes reveal Indian and Coloured solidarity with the Black majority and often occlude it as well; and they sometimes disclose moments in which Black feminist proletarian solidarity emerges, even when the possibility seems foreclosed. As conjunctures shift, some people return to certain remains, leaving others for future acts of critical assembly, until there is no more "wake work" to be done.[93]

As we have seen in the livelihood struggles of the early 2000s, residents living in conditions of multifaceted injustice struggled to find efficacious means to represent their plight through the domains of environmental justice, contract labor, or community work. The point of departure of *Apartheid Remains* is that in the face of political intransigence, they confronted a set of limits to struggle inherited from multiple pasts.

Part 1, "Racial Palimpsest," diagnoses layered conjunctures in South Africa's twentieth century as seen through transformations in South Durban, where various people occupied and transformed a marshy commons just beyond municipal control. As denizens of an expanding city were drawn into a segregated urban capitalism, the Durban City Council innovated forms of racial control, imagining fulfilling its fantasy image of building a white city on the Southern African Indian Ocean, and yet it pursued this vision at various moments with very thin knowledge of ground realities, instead fomenting waves of struggle over race and space.

Chapter 1, "Remains of a Camp: Biopolitical Fantasies of a 'White Man's Country,' 1902–1904," rethinks community work in Wentworth in light of late-Victorian biopolitical fantasies of gendered whiteness and racial government that arrived in the marshlands south of Durban through Anglo-Boer War concentration camps. While the camps of South Durban are forgotten in Merebank and Wentworth, the circulation of biopolitical expertise around them returns at various moments in conjunctures to come.

Chapter 2, "Settlements of Memory: Forgeries of Life in Common, 1900–1930s," turns to spatial histories of dispossession and settlement in Durban's interstices and peripheries, where Indian peasant-workers collectively re-fashioned selves and landscapes to forge a tradition and geography of Indian progressivism (not capitalized since its architects did not call themselves Progressives) that Indians could rely upon at various times and in various ways. In contrast, the search for Coloured pasts leads to a radically nomadic and impermanent sense of attachment, without the forms of racial-communal progressivist "uplift" that have become second nature to Durban Indians. Considered dialectically, memory conventions from Indian Merebank and Coloured Wentworth clarify the spatial basis for enduring racial differences in collective life and politics. Yet residents have come to share a repression of Indian Ocean histories of forced movement not as easily affirmed as the legacies of the Black Atlantic, with implications for their relationship to Black politics to come.

Chapter 3, "Ruinous Foundations of Progressive Segregation, 1920s–1950s," returns to city hall's intensified racial biopolitical fantasy of a white city through the forging of a contradictory space of industrialization and residential segregation. Seen through a series of commissions culminating in racial planning during World War II, the city council continued its coercive form of biopolitical government with little knowledge on the ground, a process perfectly suited to what is euphemistically called "capitalist development" through a local "developmental state" that produced the toxic landscape of South Durban, a microcosm of our poison-soaked industrial planet. When the local state began to use visual means, including the race zoning map that prefigured apartheid's spatial planning, it did so as an index, not of the power of its hegemonic vision, but rather of its protracted decay.

Chapter 4, "The Birth of Biopolitical Struggle, 1940s," revisits the violent failures of biopolitical territorialization through the insights of Black radical feminist critique also emergent in this conjuncture. The articulation of racial biopolitics and capital only sowed more suffering and strife, but this provoked new and inventive forms of what I call *biopolitical struggle* in landscapes primed for industrial transformation, like South Durban. Black working-class women were central figures in this groundswell of struggle, as they continue to be after apartheid, and this sheds powerful light on the genealogy of biopolitical struggle.

Chapter 5, "The Science Fiction of Apartheid's Spatial Fix, 1948–1970s," shows how the apartheid state's attempt to engineer a science fiction reality of forced estrangement, even in its "golden years," intensified a police form of biopolitical government, but this could not overwhelm forms of conviviality central to life in Durban's peripheries and interstices. As the racial state "fixed" townships by the same measure that it "unfixed" Black people, waves of dispossession produced new spaces of perversion and conviviality, particularly in places like Wentworth and Merebank that were shaped by submerged Indian Ocean pasts. Rather than fixed Group Areas, Wentworth and Merebank were becoming dialectical townships whose denizens experienced the forgeries of racial planning powerfully, and in markedly different ways.

Part 2, "Remains of Revolution," turns to how people opposed the accumulation of contradictory remains through four distinct, overlapping moments in South Africa's revolutionary 1970s and 1980s. This was a revolution that was and was not, which is why a geographically differentiated perspective is key to its diagnosis. Residents from Wentworth and Merebank participated in trying to shatter the racial palimpsest that was the apartheid city, while still shaped by distinct spatial histories that brought them into "the Struggle" differently. Reading oppositional politics in these neighborhoods in counterpoint offers a window into a genealogy of the anti-apartheid revolution in four conjunctural moments—all of which are spatiotemporal and overlapping—the theologico-political, the insurrectionist, the urban revolutionary, and the disqualified. Different facets of the same complex period, considered as spatiotemporal and not in temporal sequence, none of these conjunctural moments is ever overcome. All of them leave remains of revolution in our contradictory time.

Chapter 6, "The Theologico-Political Moment, 1970s," turns to what is popularly called the Durban Moment, a confluence of industrial labor, student, Black Consciousness (BC), and Natal Indian Congress (NIC) activism, in a period of intense political reinvention that worked differently through Merebank and Wentworth, including through a gendered strike in the church. I interpret what I call, after Benjamin, the *theologico-political moment* as an interconnected set of leaps of faith into the political unknown that produced a "flashing up" of the abolition of apartheid's racialization of personhood and territoriality, as well as of a Black politics disinterested in accumulation or sovereignty and committed instead to a biopolitics of life in common. Brutally suppressed, this fleeting conjuncture leaves specific remains behind.

Chapter 7, "The Insurrectionist Moment: Armed Struggle, 1960s–1980s," turns to imagined military struggle, through a group of primarily young men from Merebank drawn into NIC and underground activity, then into exile to join the External Mission of the ANC, where they had to confront what they already knew, which is that the External Mission had not been the impetus for the revolts of the 1970s, including the Durban Moment, BC, and the Soweto Uprising. The irony is that just as apartheid statecraft proceeded with very limited knowledge about ground realities, the External Mission operated with a conception of revolution by remote control with very limited understanding of struggles in South Africa. Merebank activists could work with these limitations in unique ways, as they had forged a web of underground and aboveground activity linking the township to networks in exile. As the movement was increasingly infiltrated by the apartheid security apparatus, the moment of insurrection felt the strains of a particular vision of armed struggle, but the Merebank activists imagined a new moment of interconnection of political and military action to come.

Chapter 8, "The Moment of Urban Revolution, 1980s," focuses on attempts by a small vanguard primarily of Indian men who sought to bring together the communitarianism of the first moment and the militancy of the second in a concerted strategy of urban revolution. Internal critics of this moment, particularly from feminist and workerist perspectives, saw the limits of this vanguardism, and yet it continued to engage the intricate web of political activism that took hold in Merebank. As this moment drew on the remains of BC communitarianism, it drew biopolitical tools into urban struggle through the United Democratic Front (UDF) and its affiliates, also in Wentworth and Merebank. This civic biopolitics held the possibility of popular determination of urban government, a project left by the wayside as other imperatives took center stage, as some movement leadership began negotiating with fractions of capital and the state, and as others staged the External Mission's most daring possibility of insurrectionism in what was called Operation Vula. Merebank was drawn into these dynamics in key ways.

In contrast, chapter 9, "The Moment of the Disqualified, 1980s–2000s," turns to a unique underground cell from Wentworth excluded from the expertise of revolution and drawn into other kinds of militancy, most significantly through spectacular acts of sabotage, including a car bombing, after which these activists could never completely transition from "terrorist" to "struggle hero." I read this cell alongside others from their milieu, including Black documentary photographers who tried to shoot back in other ways at apartheid's end. I argue that both forms of praxis reflect "the moment of the disqualified" for their direct engagement with the relation among Blackness, negation, and revolution. Both the saboteurs and the photographers engaged psychic wounds of racial capitalism in a way that neither the Congress nor BC activists quite did. Relatedly, both engage enduring questions about the racial ontologization of territory and personhood. In this sense, their praxis is key to reckoning with the actual negation of apartheid's remains. I conclude with the first decade of the twenty-first century in Wentworth and Merebank, and the emergence of environmental struggle as another attempt to bring into the domain of political consciousness something "disqualified" by both the state and its revolutionary opposition, now sublated (both canceled and preserved) in the state of the 2000s. As Jane's demand at the beginning of this introduction demonstrates, actual environmental justice remains a form of disqualified knowledge as well.

Apartheid Remains begins and ends with the palimpsestic thinkers central to this book, documentary photographers whose critical view through the lens and darkroom allows us to think beyond the damaged political discourse of the recent past. Palimpsestic artisans in their own right, these photographers have been central interlocutors for their skill with representing layered pasts. Their practice is precisely about conserving political hope when the limits of struggle come into view and while new horizons of possibility seem distant. We will see this in the work of Cedric Nunn, Peter McKenzie, Jenny Gordon, and Omar Badsha. Marijke du Toit's collaboration with Gordon in their photobook *Breathing Spaces* and a series of exhibitions and photography workshops with youth from Wentworth, Merebank, and Lamontville are an important inspiration that this book is in conversation with as well. As with Hall's engagement with Black arts, thinking with these photographers allows us to consider what it means to assemble critique at the scene of the crime, in the wake of biopolitical struggle, to imagine the forms that new struggles might yet take. By this book's end, I elaborate on why it is important to read this photographic work as part of a blues tradition that links the traditions of the Black Atlantic to the submerged legacies of the Indian Ocean. On Durban's shores, this audiovisual blues tradition points to other pasts still palpably present, other futures waiting to emerge.

Racial Palimpsest

PART I

Remains of a Camp

Biopolitical Fantasies of a "White Man's Country," 1902–1904

Never before have women and children been so warred against. England, by the hands of Lord Roberts and Lord Kitchener, adopted the policy of Spain, while improving upon her methods. She has placed her seal upon an odious system. Is it to be a precedent for future wars, or is it to be denounced not merely by one party, but by every humane person of every creed and every tongue, denounced as a "method of barbarism" which must never be resorted to again—the whole cruel sequence of the burning, the eviction, the rendering destitute, the deporting, and finally the reconcentrating of the non-combatants of the country, with no previous preparation for their sustenance?

—EMILY HOBHOUSE, *The Brunt of the War and Where It Fell*, 1902

Reforming Wentworth, 2007

I begin with a provocation, before we know who Emily Hobhouse was and how and why she traveled to South Africa to bear witness to the cruelties visited on Afrikaner women and children by the British government, including in the places that would become Wentworth and Merebank: the forms of knowledge that this late Victorian brought to bear on early 1900s South

Africa cast a long shadow into the early twenty-first-century milieu of "community work" in South Durban (see the introduction).

Consider that on the many occasions I stopped by her home, Patricia was always planning. There were meetings to be held, proposals to be written, people to be connected, families to be intervened in, disputes to be resolved, children's rights to be defended, youth dance groups to be organized, and yet more meetings to be planned. Patricia is one of a set of key figures in the world of community work in Wentworth, each with their turf and strong personalities. This domain, as I suggest in the introduction, is almost entirely peopled by women invested in reforming Wentworth. As is the case with others engaged in community work, Patricia faces detractors and admirers, and she deals with both as part and parcel of working through the fiction of "community" for incremental change.

I attended meetings at which Patricia spoke with passion about the problems facing Wentworth. I read proposals that she had written to the surrounding corporations for social responsibility funding, attempts that risked accusations of tainted money. I witnessed her press the official from eThekwini Municipality's Poverty Alleviation Programme on what the city was going to do, until he left the meeting in haste. Despite her brother's high-ranking job in the municipality, and her siblings' involvement as "comrades" in the 1980s, Patricia remained rooted in the everyday and the communitarian, in micropractices of regeneration. In the face of multifaceted suffering in Wentworth, she had fashioned herself as a social reformer with a particular concern for women and children, and this position lent her a moral authority that appeared obvious to her and those in her network. I argue in this chapter that this locus standi is premised on an authoritative discourse forged in the early 1900s across wide-ranging sites and with important implications, then and still.

On one occasion, Patricia promised to take me to a place where she said children were being sold into sexual slavery in collusion with parents or guardians. This was just one of several situations in which shock-and-horror poverty talk circulated in the neighborhood. On another occasion, I walked around with her to a set of homes and noted the resolve with which she walked right into people's intimate spheres to observe children she considered "at risk." On one occasion, in responding to sexual violence among young men, she opted not to press charges against the offenders, which she defended in moral terms as safeguarding privacy for all concerned. This act could be interpreted as symptomatic of widespread homophobia, but I suggest it is one of many moments in which, as Michel Foucault put it, the discourse of sexuality is a "dense transfer point" in relations of power/knowledge: a conduit to express anxieties about problems difficult to address, or redress.[1] As we will see repeatedly, knowledge and power are not so easily conjoined in past and present South Africa as Foucault's compound term implies.[2]

Another aspect of Patricia's community work was its location within informal economic activity. Patricia and her medically boarded husband ran a small *spaza* (convenience) shop next to their home, which she continued to run after her husband passed away with leukemia. Like other working-class neighborhoods in South Africa, Wentworth and Merebank have several such *spaza* shops selling generic commodities bought in bulk and resold to neighbors. Patricia combined this informal trade with an ability to reach out to various charitable sources. She received surplus or recently out-of-date food from a major grocery retailer and dispersed packages to people in her networks, keeping some for her family. Marginal gains from commodity and charitable circuits allowed her to set herself up as a self-made broker in moral and material improvement. In this, her work appears as part of a broader world of informality and improvisation in African societies, in which African women have often been key political and economic intermediaries in the wake of neglect by state and capital.[3] This improvisation forced Patricia to constantly confront norms of difference and inequality, as she attempted to secure the possibility of improvement for some.

In her site visits, Patricia presented herself as fundamentally different from fallen community members. Fissures in this binary logic appeared as I interacted with some of the unemployed women around her. These women marked complex histories of pain without getting into too much detail, and I did not press for more.[4] While revealing a more general disinclination to recall specifics about painful pasts, these women sometimes referred to a turning point, often divinely inspired, through things appearing of their own accord, or a stranger bringing groceries to the door. The temporal break helps separate past selves from a future in which God is on their side. Against a sense of despair in their inability to find meaningful waged work, these narratives bolster the regenerative possibilities of unwaged community work.

In contrast to Patricia, another prominent figure engaged in community work, whom I call Jacob, turned to me after a long and spirited conversation, to confess that reforming Wentworth requires sacrificing some part of the population. He took out a piece of paper and diagrammed a pyramid of types of residents in Wentworth, as if to show me how neat and scientific the process of separating the wheat from the chaff could be. At the bottom, in his neat diagram, were a class of people who would have to be sacrificed.

The argument of this chapter is that the praxis of Jacob, Patricia, and the unemployed women surrounding them is powerfully shaped by a persisting authoritarian discourse, shadows of a Victorian discourse of deserving and undeserving poor that accompanied the journey of biopolitics to South Africa.

A palimpsestic method helps us interpret what seem like merely coincidental objects and events as artifacts of different times with critical possibilities for the present. What, then, are the buried genealogies of this discourse of expert and disqualified knowledge, or improvable and sacrificial life, that continue to shape today's community work? And what better place to look for things buried than in the local graveyard?

Dead Camps

The Merebank Concentration Camp Memorial took some searching for.[5] After driving around aimlessly for a while, we were directed by a priest at the Tamil temple, in Tamil, to the cemetery on the eastern side of the Southern Freeway on the edge of Merebank. We wandered through the empty graveyard until we came on a promising enclosure. The site was desolate but maintained. I knew that barbed wire had ringed the monument following the defacing of a mural in 1986.[6] The barbs were still there, but the security gate was ajar. As we approached the obelisk erected in 1930 to mark the concentration camp cemetery, we encountered this disclaimer dated 1999: "Of the 453 inhabitants who died in the Merebank Concentration Camp, 412 were buried here, including seven people of colour. Those who died after the declaration of peace as well as the people of colour are not honoured on the monument. Of those buried here, 358 were children under the age of 12."

The Garden of Remembrance was dedicated in 1970. Walking around its heavy symbolism forty years later was a surreal experience. Three tents made of concrete slabs and a mural represent the camp cemeteries at Jacobs, Isipingo, and Mobeni (figure 1.1). A mural on one wall depicts the austerity of the camps, with, at its center, the captured Afrikaner woman (figure 1.2). British imperial discourse was obsessed with Afrikaner women as the backbone of resistance as the British army faced agrarian commandos in a guerrilla war. The stylized form looks today like a work of science fiction. During the apartheid era, the Burger Graves Committee of Durban's Dutch Reformed Church had the site deproclaimed as part of the Indian Group Area of Merebank and reproclaimed as a "white island" surrounded by an Indian graveyard.[7]

FIGURES 1.1 AND 1.2 Merebank Concentration Camp Memorial Garden, 2010.
© Sharad Chari.

FIGURE 1.3 Jacobs Concentration Camp Cenotaph, 2010. © Sharad Chari.

Map 3 shows the sites of the Merebank Concentration Camp Memorial and the Jacobs Concentration Camp Cenotaph, as well as the Merewent Cheshire Home and the Ark, which we encounter later in this chapter. The site of the Wentworth Concentration Camp was just off this map to the north, along the railway lines that run parallel to today's M4 highway.

The layout of the Garden of Remembrance, with its encircling wall and lookout point, was clearly meant to convey what the camp was like. An amphitheater at the center suggests instruction, perhaps of schoolchildren to be taught about the costs of war and the necessary birth of Afrikaner nationalism.[8] As we left the desolate site, I thought of this hapless *lieu de mémoire*, a site of memory overloaded with symbolism, where even intended lessons remain unlearned.[9]

Not far off lies a less dramatic memorial in the very different setting of the Jacobs industrial area bordering Wentworth. The site of the Jacobs Concentration Camp is downhill from Wentworth Hospital on map 3, just beyond the large Dudley Street Cemetery. A modest cenotaph sits on one side of an empty field minimally maintained by the city (figure 1.3). This site is open to the streets around it. People regularly cut across the field in a buzzing factory landscape that appears oblivious to the diminutive obelisk. There is no trace of any attempt to proclaim this a white area, nor of pedagogical value to be

FIGURE 1.4 *First Boers Leaving Camp for Homes*, Wentworth, 1902.
© Local History Museum, Durban.

utilized in an official site of memory. What remains puzzling is why the plot
has not been usurped by industry and why it persists as another stubborn
monument to forgetting.

A final remnant of the South Durban camps is a photograph taken at the
dissolution of the Wentworth Concentration Camp near the Wentworth
Railway Station yards, an industrial no-man's-land. There is no *lieu de mémoire* of a declarative kind here. All we have is this photograph archived in
the Local History Museum. The photography of British supremacy during
the war, focusing on new technologies of camps and barbed wire, and on
backward "Boers" on the verge of agrarian devastation, merits close study in
its own right. However, this photograph, patched and filed without further
comment, is specifically poignant (figure 1.4). On the face of it, the image
documents women and children leaving the Wentworth camp when it was
dismantled in 1902. A group of people in the distance appear to be standing by a train full of people that appears, from its headlights, to be shunting
backward. Some people are in motion; others are still, perhaps as onlookers.

Some watch from behind a barbed fence on the right. A group of children sit in the foreground, their backs facing the photographer, and it is unclear whether they are Afrikaner, white, or Black, recent detainees or spectators. At the geometric center, a lone figure looks from a distance at the photographer, and at us, with their hands on their hips, but there is no way to say that this is a gesture of defiance.

The carefully ordered frame presumes what Ann Laura Stoler calls a colonial education in sentiment, with railways, key symbols of British imperial benevolence, ferrying people from camps on the verge of closure.[10] The caption of this very ambiguous photograph, *First Boers Leaving Camp for Homes*, marks a cruel irony that the inmates' homes were very likely to have been razed, their farms burned to the ground, their livelihoods destroyed, and their Afrikaner Republics lost. Many of the children would return to cities in decades to come as part of the "poor white problem." How might we understand these remains of camps, if precisely not for a recuperative project of heritage? How might this debris of history—a Garden of Remembrance, a lone obelisk in the Jacobs industrial area, and a photograph of the dissolution of the forgotten Wentworth camp—speak to South Africa's turbulent past and present?

The first and third of these were pedagogical objects: a place for visitors to reflect on Afrikaner suffering and endurance, and a photograph to teach British imperial benevolence. In both, the camp is conscripted into ethnonationalist narratives. The Jacobs obelisk might have begun with pedagogical possibilities that were set aside when it was surrounded by a mixed industrial area abutting a Coloured township. A racially partitioned politics of memory make it an unlikely site of commemoration. That it still exists in a small park maintained by the city speaks to the importance of something other than property values in determining uses of space, or else the land would surely have been usurped by industry.

After circuiting through the history of British imperial reformism with respect to these camps, this chapter concludes with sites that refer neither to the Anglo-Boer War nor to actual concentration camps. Victorian imperial reformism allows a palimpsestic reading of these sites as well as the domain of community work that I begin this chapter with, as differently legible through the long shadows of humanitarian reform of dishonored or devalued populations.[11] I hope to elaborate how biopolitical expertise brought to bear on these specific camps of the South African War continues to shadow degraded life in the ruins of apartheid.

Historical Camps and Possible Futures

As we turn from dead camps to the discovery of civilian concentration camps by British social reformers in the early twentieth century, it is important to clarify the historiographical argument. To those steeped in the revisionist social history of South Africa, the camps of the South African War might seem unnecessary to rehearse. In doing so, my intention is not to juxtapose an abstract understanding of camps as biopolitical instruments with the rough-and-tumble of historical process. I attempt a relational reading of camps as historical exceptions and also as archetypal political technology gathering momentum over the century, differently across space, well into our time.

In a brilliant intervention, Jonathan Hyslop shows how the journey of the concentration camp from Cuba, Southern Africa, and the Philippines to its more murderous forms after German South-West Africa centered on "the response of new, professionalized military cultures to the challenges of guerrilla warfare," fueled by "media wars" enabled by the telegraph and by new forms of print media.[12] The camps of the South African War fit into these circuits as sites that presented the possibility of managing detained populations not to maximize civilian fatalities but to limit them. Aidan Forth clarifies that British imperial camps differed from Spanish, American, or German camps and that the camps of the Anglo-Boer War "were less instruments of military counterinsurgency than humanitarian responses to the hunger, disease, and social chaos unleashed by modern war"; they were, as he puts it, "kindred products" of Victorian biopolitics across Britain and its colonies.[13] I have come to a parallel view. However, Forth's formulation begs more questions about biopolitical expertise across an "empire of camps." Colonial authorities may have been forced by public concern about rising mortalities in Boer camps to draw from plague and famine camps in British India, but what did they thereby accomplish?[14] Like other colonial designs "in the conditional mode," as Stoler puts it, camps were "nodes of anxious, uneasy circulations, settlements that are not settled at all."[15] Dialectical reading of the history of these camps requires us to dwell in the conflictual minutiae, to discern their stakes and latent potentialities.

I argue that early twentieth-century discourse concerning the camps is important for three reasons. First, we can see in retrospect that it experimented with the possibility of biopolitical segregation, or the state-sanctioned use of biopolitical instruments to selectively intervene in the lives of people. We will see how, in South Africa, the interregnum of war broadened the realm of possibility in the state's deployment of biopolitical tools, for instance, after the arrival of the plague. After the 1899 Hague Convention's protection of the boundaries among combatants, prisoners of war, and civilians, discourse about the camps fomented questions concerning imperial violence and the protection of humanity.[16] Sentiment was central to these debates, not in opposition to reason but as a means of handling contradiction. As we will see, even the radical reformer Emily Hobhouse found it difficult to escape the pathos of colonial violence, because debating the semantic values of imperialism was quite different from playing into its pragmatics.[17]

The second way in which camp discourse matters has to do with diagnosing remains. Biopolitical discourse circulating through camps brought to the fore questions concerning infrastructures of vitality and their constitutive gradations of supported and disqualified life, well before the hardening of racial segregation. To claim that this was portentous is not to say that what happened around the camps was simply determinative of the future. Rather, it is to ask how the camps were part of a conjuncture that brought the contradictions of British imperial benevolence into view, opening a set of possible futures in its immediate aftermath.

Forms of knowledge circulating through the camps continue to have a spectral presence more than a century later. We might theorize this spectral quality, as Ian Baucom does, as the "reiterative temporality" of a truth event, its becoming-present through retrospective naming that points to "the global abnormality of the system as such."[18] The category "concentration camp" might appear to require such teleological expectations, through its loaded retrospective significance after Nazism. Yet for the actual camps of the South African War to bear such a theoretical burden is to assume far too much. The ghostly afterlife of these camps is far more uncertain, its effects dialectical in a nonteleological and conjunctural sense.

The spectral and hauntological qualities of the camp, visible to us in retrospect, help us see biopolitical sovereignty as a long-standing statist fantasy of segregation and industrialization.[19] By this, I do not mean that the state suffered from paranoid delusions. Rather, the spectral and fantastic point to the work of hauntology as willing into being a possible future, however implausible it might seem; it is a commitment in the subjunctive mood to that which seems utterly implausible but might yet be: a "white city" or a "white man's country," after a "white man's war."[20] While South Africa has transformed in innumerable ways in more than a century since the South African War, the continued precariousness of Black life in democratic times, most notably in the struggle over preventable mass death through HIV/AIDS in the first democratic decade, or preventable death since, brings the fantasy of biopolitical sovereignty squarely into our time.

This takes us to a third way in which debates about the camps matter. The key protagonist, Hobhouse, was precisely inside/outside British imperial discourse, a border figure not unlike Patricia in Wentworth today. Excluded from the official commission on the conditions in the camps, she pushed at the edges of this commission before, during, and after its formulation of truth, and in so doing, she "activated the colonial archive . . . brought back into circulation promises not kept, resolutions shelved."[21] Despite her own biographical limitations, she is an archival boundary figure dwelling in the subjunctive mood a reminder to refuse to repeat the atrocities that befell Afrikaner inmates on the broader Black population. Her activation of the past in the service of possible futures remains a call for a historical ethnography of the possible.

The South African War or Second Anglo-Boer War, of 1899–1902 as a war between British and Afrikaner colonialisms was a site for debate over ideologies and techniques of empire. The ensuing decade of reconstruction involved a rearticulation of whiteness in a putatively unified South Africa.[22] Black people were always in the background of the war, signaled by the retrospective disclaimer at the Merebank Garden of Remembrance. At the start of the war, Lord Milner and Joseph Chamberlain discussed whether to employ and arm African subjects for the war effort and decided instead that this would be a "white man's war." In practice, Black people performed a variety of armed and unarmed labor for both sides. African farmers and manual laborers sustained the wartime economy and maintained its infrastructure. African tenants and rural laborers displaced by war, along with Afrikaner women and children, were interned in segregated camps in which many died of disease; one estimate is that of 45,000 camp deaths, 25,000 were Afrikaners, and anywhere between 14,000 and 20,000 were Africans.[23] Despite the important work of revisionist historians over the past forty years to document African experience of the war and its camps, with very limited archival means, Black concentration camps have fallen almost entirely out of popular historical consciousness, as they certainly have in today's Wentworth and Merebank.[24]

However, Shula Marks argues that the "white man's war" was neither white nor male; rather, it was gendered in new ways, whether in the employment of British nurses in large numbers or in the expertise of Victorian social reformers surveying the conditions of Afrikaner women and children in the camps, or indeed in anxieties about whiteness, manhood, and nationhood reflected in the writings of Jan Smuts.[25] There is a vast and important body of scholarship on the lives of Victorian women reformers and on the ways in which they ventured cautiously into the poorer districts of their great and unequal cities, just as they ventured into the colonial world. Thanks to gender history, we know quite a bit about eighteenth- and nineteenth-century gendered class struggles over "breadwinner wages" and "separate spheres"; about nineteenth- and early twentieth-century British feminists and their negotiations of whiteness, "social imperialism," and middle-class respectability; about imperial masculinities and femininities in need of rescue, submission, or, occasionally, solidarity; and about social and sexual nonconformity with bourgeois values afforded by travel and dislocation.[26] Several of these themes recur in the historiography of the South African War.[27]

In a colorful rendition, Queen Victoria, a keen observer of military developments in South Africa who apparently followed blown-up maps to counter her cataracts, was particularly concerned about what she thought was the frivolous adventurism of British society women in South Africa.[28] In fact, Victorian British women with access to new discourses of social welfare and humanitarianism were from varied class positions, and they forged professional lives with considerable independence and freedom. As we will see, they used these possibilities in different ways and were by no means destined to become apologists for colonial violence.

With respect to the South African War, two Victorian women stand out. The remarkable Emily Hobhouse traveled from Britain to document the human costs of war. She stumbled on the existence of the camps and broke it to the press. Hobhouse was then sidelined by the British government, as the War Office appointed a more controllable commission chaired by the eminent Millicent Fawcett, and it published a series of Blue Books to deal with the public fallout following Hobhouse's reports. Most important of these was Command Paper 893, the Concentration Camps Commission: Report of the Concentration Camps of South Africa by the Committee of Ladies, also called the Fawcett Commission or the Ladies Commission.[29]

As we trace the journey of expert knowledge following the "discovery" of concentration camps, we find experts venturing through the ideological minefields of imperial patriotism and military humanitarianism. We will also find that this British experiment with socio-technical intervention quite literally stalled in its tracks in the swamps of Merebank.[30] The swamp aggravated the problems that beset displaced and confined populations to such an extent that the Ladies Commission deemed the site inhospitable for habitation, even for concentration camps.

Discovering Camps, 1901–1902

I call this camp system wholesale cruelty. It can never be wiped out from the memories of the people. It presses hardest on the children. They droop in the terrible heat. . . . Thousands, physically unfit, are placed in conditions of life which they have not the strength to endure. In front of them is blank ruin. . . . Will you try somehow to make the British public understand the position and force it to ask itself what is going to be done with these people? . . . In one of two ways the British Public must support them, either by taxation through the authorities or else by voluntary charity. . . . If only the English people would try to exercise a little imagination and picture the whole miserable scene. Entire villages and districts rooted up and dumped in a strange bare place. To keep these camps going is murder for the children. Still, of course, by more judicious management they could be improved; but do what you will, you can't undo the thing itself. —EMILY HOBHOUSE, *Report of a Visit*, 1901

With her emotive style and subject matter, including appeals to the "British Public" for "improvement" but not the seditious call to abolish the camps, Hobhouse was very much of a piece with Victorian reformism.[31] She was born in 1860 in Cornwall, where she lived until her thirties, taking care of her ailing father. When he died in 1895, Hobhouse followed the migration of Cornish miners to the United States, to social welfare work in Minnesota and in mining communities in Virginia. A short engagement to a Virginian businessman took her to Mexico, where both the relationship and his speculative venture failed. She returned to England in 1898 and worked in the Women's Industrial Committee, where she gained expertise in conducting large-scale investigations of need, the kind of fact generation that Foucault had in mind as biopolitical expertise. She researched the history of factory children before the 1833 Factory Act and wrote a novel on the topic, which she then destroyed. In her thirties Hobhouse had gained a range of skills and insights, and a remarkable capacity to think comparatively about the plight of subaltern people.[32]

At the inception of the Second Anglo-Boer War in late 1899, Hobhouse became honorary secretary of the women's branch of the South African Conciliation Committee. Following a set of Boer victories, Frederick Roberts became commander-in-chief of British forces in South Africa in 1900. The key architect of the strategy of scorched-earth warfare to combat the guerrilla tactics of Boer militias, Roberts advocated farm burnings and concentration camps for enemy populations.[33] His successor, H. H. Kitchener, intensified this brutal war of attrition by burning farmhouses, slaughtering livestock, destroying crops, and displacing Afrikaner farm families and African tenants, while Afrikaner strategy turned decisively to guerrilla warfare.[34]

Early on in this sequence of events, Hobhouse organized a women's protest against the war and became increasingly interested in the plight of Afrikaner women bearing the brunt of counterinsurgency. She created a nonpolitical, nonsectarian distress fund for South African women and children and left for South Africa at the end of 1900.

In October the first camps opened in Bloemfontein; another in Pretoria was moved southwest to Irene; the camp outside Mafeking was described as "primitive"; women labeled "undesirables" for either supporting commandos or firing on British troops were sent to camps in the Orange River Colony or to Pietermaritzburg in Natal. Very little was known about the camps in the public sphere until Hobhouse began her investigations.[35]

Before her intentions were publicly known, "Miss Hobhouse" was granted a meeting alone with Alfred Milner, high commissioner for Southern Africa and governor of the Cape Colony. Hobhouse questioned him directly about civilian war casualties, to which Milner responded that he had seen women refugees and that it was "rather terrible."[36] With limited support, Hobhouse planned her trip to the camps. She collected stories of destroyed homes, arduous journeys, broken families, insufficient food, water and fuel shortages, and unhygienic conditions leading to sickness and death.[37] In short, her evidence showed that the camps were premised on widespread destruction of the means of life and that the scale of disaster in concentrating detained civilians could have been mitigated through the emerging field of public health.[38]

Defying orders from Kitchener not to venture beyond Bloemfontein, Hobhouse traveled to camps in the Orange River and Cape colonies, returning to Britain with stories about farm burnings and conditions in the camps to shock British public opinion.[39] Hobhouse's testimonies are grounded in the details of a scarred landscape. Hobhouse begins *The Brunt of the War and Where It Fell* with the many violations by the occupying power, with the horrors of farm burnings, looting of livestock, destruction of grain stores, and eviction of women and children. She is cognizant that narrative means cannot suffice to bear witness to the depth of devastation: "From January onwards, helpless families have been wandering homeless, captured, exiled, deported hither and thither on foot, in trucks, trolleys, wagons and trains. It may be long before they can fully speak or write the story of that twelve months."[40] She nevertheless collected, translated, and compiled testimony, and continued to give evidence to the government and the press. Her collection of women's letters includes the remarkable account by A. M. Van den Bergh on her farm's destruction; on being "jeered" en route by "Kaffirs, English and Coolies"; on the indignity of being called "refugees" after having been torn from their homes; on "Kaffir police" preventing contact between inmates and new arrivals at the camp; on hunger and the loss of children; and on English visitors coming to see "wild Boers" in captivity.[41] Hobhouse concludes with Afrikaner general Louis Botha visiting the camp to commend women for having suffered and died in large numbers while "weak men" turned to the other side.[42] While these themes have been well documented and analyzed in the historiography of the war, what is important is Hobhouse's attention to problems of writing amid ruination. Whether she actually inspired imprisoned women to write their own testimonials or not, a woman at a camp in Kroonstad was questioned for writing letters "in Miss Hobhouse's style."[43]

A chapter of *The Brunt of the War* details the accumulating resentment in the Cape Colony among the relatives of dispossessed burghers in the besieged Afrikaner Republics. Hobhouse details the horror of fragmentary knowledge obtained alongside expulsions, through "a stray letter, a traveler from the north, or a soldier's story . . . bits and scraps of news, worse in their effects than a whole knowledge of the truth would have been."[44] Her writing conveys the immediacy of wartime devastation, and the risks of sympathy with the enemy, not least by reproducing an official report from Afrikaner general Jacobus "Koos" de la Rey in late 1901: "Our land is one heap of ruins. . . . Nothing remains but the walls of buildings, except where even these were blown up with dynamite. Nothing has escaped this destruction. The properties of neutrals as well as of burghers killed in battle, and of those who are now prisoners of war, and of the widows and orphans—everything has been destroyed. . . . The treatment of women and children, defenceless creatures, is really the darkest page among the many dark pages of this sad war."[45] Hobhouse repeats the terms of Victorian discourse on gendered sympathy, charity, and improvement.[46] Within the ferment of patriotism in England at the turn of the century, the lead writers of the *Times* castigated her as a naive "Boer-sympathizer" woefully ill equipped to understand either Afrikaner society or the necessities of war. A correspondent from Cape Town representing "matured colonial opinion" shared her sympathy for the suffering inmates but castigated her for besmirching the name of England.[47] In a subsequent report, this correspondent mocks her English presumptions:

> Miss Hobhouse dilates upon the misery of overcrowding, as though it were something unknown before in the lives of the inmates in the camps. I do not for a moment wish to say that life in these concentration camps has all the comforts of a sojourn in a stone-built house,

but it must be remembered that the climate of South Africa is a most genial one, and it is the only one, perhaps, where it is possible to live in the open air all the year round without much risk of illness. That there are hardships, and terrible hardships too, I cannot deny, nor indeed, do I wish to, but these hardships are the result of war.[48]

And, it follows, the camps are a military necessity. The correspondent concludes that "Miss Hobhouse" remains "unaware of how well the Boer women have served, and are still serving, the commandos as intelligence officers, spies and even as decoys" and that "they cannot appeal to sympathy on the plea of harmless womanhood, for they have proved themselves to be very dangerous enemies."[49]

In the imperial imagination, to have left Afrikaner women and children in the countryside would have meant starvation and exposure to the Black majority. When Jan Smuts uses a similar argument near the end of the war in response to the arming of "Natives and Coloured" men by the British in what should have been "a war between the white races," Marks argues that the deeper issue was that the war had intensified a sense of loss of control over Black people in the countryside.[50] *Swart gevaar*, or "black peril," was sentimental ballast to the suspension of rights in the name of security, and a key element in the grammar of imperial liberalism.

The administration of the camps was also a battleground between the War Office and the Colonial Office. Milner took effective control of the camps, introducing civilian camp superintendents, doctors, nurses, and sanitary inspection, but Kitchener retained military control through the war years. What actually ensued on the ground depended on what kinds of sanitary labor Boer men and women would consent to.[51] Hobhouse is cognizant of this distinction of civil and military power, as she carefully suggests that her argument was for intervention to ameliorate suffering in civilian camps, not for their abolition: "I have never, and do not now, put forward any criticism of the policy (be it military or civil) which led to the formation of these camps. Seeing, however, that it is a new departure in our own history to have placed 93,000 white women and children (besides 24,000 natives) in camps after total destruction of their homes, it is also for us a new as well as difficult problem to learn how to carry out so serious an undertaking without undue suffering and loss of life."[52] In the appendix to *The Brunt of the War*, Hobhouse admits that she was unable to visit "native camps" "for lack of time and strength," prefiguring the whitewashing of camp historiography.[53] However, Hobhouse's attention to the figure of the Boer woman clarifies her critique of imperial benevolence: "Other critics admit the high mortality, but lay the whole blame upon the Boer mothers. That is singularly unfair. A Boer woman brought to camp, smarting under the recollection of what she has just undergone, the sight of her burning home, her lost goods, her ignominious captivity, looks at first, naturally enough, on the khadi-clad officials of the camp as 'the enemy.' It is so difficult to us as a nation to realize that we are regarded as 'the enemy' by others, being so sure of our best possible intentions for the welfare of all."[54]

The Ladies Commission

Since 1890, the South African Republic and its gold-mining industry, producing about a fifth to a quarter of the world's gold, was central to Britain's financial, trade, and military interests, particularly after India switched to the gold standard; while access to gold was not a singular determinant of the South African War, it was central to the stability of international trade in a global financial regime centered on sterling.[55] Gold was to this war as oil has been to our time, the strategic commodity key to imperial power.[56] Hobhouse's sentimental critique of British barbarism hit a vein in imperial ideology without reference to any of these material forces, and it is in this light that we can interpret why the British government felt compelled to appoint a commission to investigate conditions in the camps.

The commission was headed by feminist and suffragette Millicent Fawcett, also a critic of Hobhouse. Fawcett sought to neutralize Hobhouse's critique of camp suffering, drawing it into a narrative of necessity and determination during wartime. Fawcett's liberalism was undergirded by faith in the British Empire; she also sought common cause between her work for women's suffrage in England and the demand for the vote by British *uitlanders* (foreigners) in the Boer Republics. As the defense of the *uitlander* was the pretext for British aggression in the first place, this was a calculated political move. Fawcett realized early on that white women's suffrage might be gained precisely at the frontiers of settler colonialism, where their consent was necessary to colonial expansion. There was therefore a mutuality of interest in her leadership of the War Office's inquiry into conditions in the camps.

Meanwhile, Hobhouse was denied permission to go to South Africa, boarded a ship all the same, was not allowed to disembark, and was deported from Cape Town under martial law. However, her ideas had already set the grounds of debate. The Ladies Commission appointed by the War Office comprised six middle- to upper-class women, all of whom had distinguished themselves in the cause of women's domestic social and political struggles. Apart from Fawcett, Alice Knox was a Scot who thought the Boer population was at the same stage as the Scottish two hundred years earlier, Lucy Deane was one of the first British women factory inspectors, and Jane Waterston was the first British woman physician, who saw the British military caring more for these most ungrateful Afrikaner women than Afrikaner men. There are echoes here of British colonial fantasies of "white men saving brown women from brown men," with Boer women coded as racially inferior; Hobhouse was violently rejected for refusing this script.[57]

The commission was given complete access to the camps and was advised about discretion and the advantages of working with the authorities.[58] Hobhouse was rarely mentioned, but the report of the commission added to her findings of "overcrowding, poor and inadequate rations, polluted water, neglect of the elementary rules of hygiene, a shortage of beds and mattresses, sick children sleeping on the ground, failure to isolate contagious diseases."[59]

At Merebank Camp: The Swamp Strikes Back

The Ladies Commission visited the Burgher Camp at Merebank on December 6 and 7, 1901. The camp had opened in September 1901 with 24 "refugees" from Pretoria, and numbers increased rapidly to 5,154 by December, of which 534 were men, 2,145 women, and 2,475 children.[60] They were forced to use a single bathhouse, with ten baths for women and two each for men and boys.[61] The arrival of five hundred people with measles scarcely two days after the camp opened, followed by three weeks of unrelenting rain, lent much to the view that the Merebank camp was inhospitable from the outset. Rain, marsh, and bog permeate the commission's rendition of this swampy landscape:

> The camp . . . lies at the foot of a low hill, the water from which drains into it. The flat, swampy ground on which the camp is pitched slopes slightly from both sides towards a central drain or little stream into which all surface water from wash-basins etc. runs, and which flows slowly into a large mere from which there is no outlet. On the Durban side of the camp there appears to be a big morass which drains towards the camp. The newly built mortuary in the centre of the 4 sections is approached through boggy ground and in making graves in the cemetery . . . it is impossible to dig more than 4½ft without reaching water. The Commission saw water being bailed out of a child's grave before the funeral arrived.[62]

The commission describes the water supply, bathhouses, sanitation manned by "coolie" staff with an Indian "Sirdar" (foreman), rubbish disposal, slop water, a dump, various forms of housing (wood and iron huts, wood and canvas huts, bell tents, and marquees), meager rations, and inadequate hospital facilities, but also a functional school whose "children looked clean and cheerful."[63] The Merebank camp would become the largest of all the camps, with relatively better accommodation, access to the local beach, and "fruit and vegetables more readily available" from Indian smallholders nearby (chapter 2).[64]

These interventions aside, the swamp returns in the problems that beset camp life.[65] The commission's main concern was what they saw as inmates' disregard of hygiene in preferring to use a polluted river rather than wells, in not boiling water, and in reusing dirty puddles for washing clothes, as well as the poor sanitation and lack of disinfection in the hospitals: all swampy matters. To the authorities, they recommended care with overcrowding, better food, and hospital care, and, urgently, "the removal of the camp to another more suitable site," a point that Milner refused, as the land had been cleared by the military.[66]

The official response was that "though the camp was near marshland, the town of Durban was also practically surrounded by marshes," that malaria was rare, that "the site was open to cleansing winds from east to west," and that it was deemed healthy by "several doctors."[67] The governor, Henry McCallum, assured Milner that "the Ladies Report had exaggerated the disadvantages having seen the camp at its worst after two days of non-stop soaking rains" and that in the event of flooding, inmates could be held temporarily in the Jacobs camp without abandoning Merebank.[68] The debate ended when the Boer Republics surrendered to the British empire at the Treaty of Vereeniging on May 31, 1902. The numbers in the Merebank camp had swelled to 8,350 by March of that year, but things changed quickly in the ensuing months, when inmates were repatriated, and the Merebank camp emptied by December 1902.

Representing Camps

Command Paper 893, the Concentration Camps Commission: Report of the Concentration Camps of South Africa by the Committee of Ladies of 1902 generally corroborates Hobhouse and argues for charitable funds to be used to improve sanitation, water, housing, provisions, and "discipline and morals."[69] Hobhouse welcomed that the Ladies Commission had confirmed her initial reports, but she strongly criticized the presumption that Afrikaner women's ignorance and superstition lay behind the lack of order and hygiene and that they were naturally "dirty" or beset by "dirty habits."[70] To put it differently, Hobhouse saw the power of biopolitical intervention, but she refused its moralistic racialization.

The obvious difference between Hobhouse and Fawcett is that the former faced imperial government as an irritant, the latter as a benefactor. The Fawcett Commission presumes that civilian concentration camps must be militarized, and movements must be strictly regulated to reduce risks of disease and immorality.[71] Needless to say, the Ladies Commission did not investigate African camps, inmates, or workers at all. Hobhouse noted this failure alongside her own guilt for not deciding "to investigate the conditions or personally carry relief to the native camps."[72] Hobhouse tried to gain the support of her Cape Town colleagues for the cause of "sickness and destitution" in "native camps," to no avail.[73] Her letters to her brother indicate an interest in African suffering, but she was also complicit with the racism of her Afrikaner interlocutors like Smuts in cautioning against the use of African camp guards; she wrote to the *Times* that "considering the growing impertinence of the Kaffirs, seeing white women thus humiliated, every care shall be taken not to put them in places of authority."[74]

Brian Roberts laments that there was no Sol Plaatje to document African dispossession as British scorched-earth warfare intensified, nor conditions in African labor camps along railway lines in the Transvaal and the Orange River Colony.[75] The problem of African refugees became acute in 1901 following Kitchener's sweeps of the countryside, and African concentration camps were becoming apparent to some white observers; Hobhouse reported on one of the first "Kaffir camps" in February 1901.[76] By June a separate Native Refugee Department was established in the Transvaal to secure mine workers to replace men who had been forced to move from gold mines to the army and to house African women and children. Disease rates soared in the African camps, including over eight thousand deaths in the first half of 1901.[77] Only after the war were the miserable conditions improved by breaking these camps into smaller units with land for crops and cattle, a mechanism that may have reduced Black fatalities dramatically. But many Africans allied with the British felt a profound sense of betrayal of British secretary of state for the colonies Joseph Chamberlain's promise of citizenship in a postwar order; this was Plaatje's actual complaint, that the postwar order prevented the consolidation of a progressive African middle class.

Hobhouse's reports may well have given the Liberal Party fodder as the opposition in the House of Commons.[78] The British government was very concerned with international public opinion when William Jennings Bryan of Nebraska decried the US government's lack of official support for the Afrikaners and when the governor of Illinois began to speak of "death camps." But these were not Nazi or Stalinist death camps built to exterminate imagined enemies.

Victorian concern about these camps shows, on the one hand, a profound erasure of Black suffering and, on the other hand, concern for racialized "Boers" through sentimentality, morality, and a technical concern with deficiencies in infrastructure and services. Clearly, the camps were mismanaged and beset by problems of sanitation, food shortage, overcrowding, and insufficient medical facilities, all of which exposed confined populations to what Ruth Wilson Gilmore calls modern racism: "the state-sanctioned and/or extralegal production and exploitation of group-differentiated vulnerability to premature death."[79]

This brings us back to Milner's response to camp mortalities through biopolitical intervention, which may have worked to limit mortalities while also, as Hyslop puts it, making respectable the idea of the "'good' or 'well run' concentration camp . . . as a legitimate technique for managing populations."[80] Indeed, the Milner regime responded to the Fawcett Commission by drawing on famine and plague camp expertise from British India. Forth surmises from this that "camp reform reached its pinnacle" in the coastal camps near East London, King Williams' Town, Port Elizabeth, Merebank, and elsewhere around Durban and that "sanitation" in these camps was aimed at particularly recalcitrant inmates for whom isolation from the *platteland* was meant to be "an object lesson in British power."[81] However, Forth repeats the hope of imperial power that "in the process, they rendered Boer inmates governable subjects, who . . . became as easy to manage as 'any English crowd.'"[82] That imperial biopolitics actually accomplished its aims in producing governable subjects is far-fetched. My argument is that its failure to do so cast a very long shadow.

The dialectics of the camp illuminate the varied uses of the Progressivist ambitions of late-Victorian biopolitical expertise, then and now. In retrospect, the attempt to forge a "white man's country" in the aftermath of a "white man's war" was hopelessly futile. At the heart of this futility is the paradox that attempts to limit mortality may have helped make a particular form of racial biopolitical intervention respectable in imperial eyes, and only in imperial eyes. While "the camp" was not an archetype of things to come, this paradox of making racial biopolitics respectable took multiple forms across the racial palimpsest of twentieth-century South Africa.

Proximal Remains: Circulations of Urban
Segregation, Early 1900s

While modern ideas of race, class, and nation took particular form in the revolutionary Atlantic and again in the crisis-ridden late-imperial North Atlantic, the mania for urban segregation emerged from the late-Victorian Indian Ocean.[83] Carl Nightingale's history of segregation shows how Calcutta and London were connected through imperial administration but also through "reformist gadflies" like Hobhouse, including "doctors, medical researchers, and public health experts (later, housing reformers, architects, and town planners)" who would gain influence after the movements of the cholera bacillus.[84] The story of cholera in London is well known, but we now have better accounts of interconnected histories of "social politics" across the great cities of the late-Victorian world, as networks of Progressivists thought alongside and against each other about the possibilities of urban reform.[85]

London was also the first city to use the state-sanctioned legal means of restrictive covenants to protect the entitled and propertied West End from "Outcast London"; at the turning point of the South African War in 1900, embattled labor leadership on the East London docks attempted to connect the degradation of dockworker power with a resurgent white chauvinism.[86] The intertwined dynamics of racial and class revanchism may have been far more foundational to the emerging urban expertise of the early twentieth century than canonical historical accounts of the birth of "planning" let on.[87]

But it was across the imperial Indian Ocean that settler populations experimented with urban segregation, from Madras and Calcutta to various colonial hill stations to the "opening of China"; segregationist practice spread across the Pacific to Australia and western North America; and it took radical form to protect white populations from the plague in Hong Kong in 1894 and Bombay in 1896.[88] As the plague spread through shipping, so did "the planetary surge of racist city splitting practices largely under the guise of urban public health reform."[89]

Like the swamp in Merebank, or the mosquito in Egypt, we might announce the "nonhuman agency" of the bubonic plague, but what was crucial was the way in which the plague was interpellated by a circulating imperative to protect European life through new biopolitical means. Paraphrasing

Nightingale, what spread was a hybrid complex of disease and racial fear, along with a proliferating vocabulary and a key concept: *segregación, segregação, segregazione, segregation, segregasie.*[90]

To understand how these terms, and related tools, touched ground, we return to the aftermath of the South African War. In his foundational work, Maynard Swanson argues that the bubonic plague arrived in Cape Town in 1900 in warhorse transports before spreading to other cities; when it arrived in Durban, city hall blamed Indian and African slums, prompting a wave of African flight to the countryside in 1903, followed by a counterwave to the city in the wake of agrarian famine, followed by official fears of a "Native problem" in housing, sanitation, labor control, and "lawlessness."[91] Swanson aptly terms this "the sanitation syndrome": the widespread use of contagion discourse for the expeditious removal of Africans from specific urban locations in Cape Town, Port Elizabeth, Durban, and Johannesburg.

The dynamics in each city were different, and differently violent. The postwar context set the stage for political expediency. Cape Town forcibly moved between six thousand and seven thousand Africans to Uitvlugt in 1901; Port Elizabeth followed by attempting to move Africans to New Brighton in 1903.[92] Natal passed a Native Locations Act in 1904, but its cities refused to shoulder the cost of getting "the government into the locations business."[93] Johannesburg feared the arrival of the plague through returning migrants from port cities rather than through fleas on infected rats in goods trains; the city council could compel Africans to move to a "Kaffir Location," while Coloureds were afforded stands in a "Malay Location," but when the plague hit in March 1904, the council razed to the ground the "Coolie Location" in today's Newtown, forcing its predominantly Indian but also African and Coloured population first to Klipspruit (later Pimville) near a proposed sewerage treatment farm. Indians and Coloureds could not be legally forced to live in a particular place and so moved on, while Africans were compelled to remain in what Swanson calls the "first detached African location" in Klipspruit.[94]

The parallels between violent forced removals of Africans and the violence of concentration camps could not have escaped contemporaries. Swanson adds a crucial rhetorical question: "Was there more than coincidence in the tendency for locations to be established or proposed in the vicinity of rubbish depots and sewage farms, for example at Uitvlugt (Ndabeni) near Cape Town, Klipspruit for Johannesburg, and "on the Umgeni [River] side of the rubbish depot" for Durban?"[95] This rhetorical question resonates in the toxic valley of South Durban more than a century later.

Proximal Remains: Commemorating Afrikaner Suffering, 1913

The former president of the Orange Free State unveiled a monument outside Bloemfontein in 1913, in memory of women and children who died in the camps. Hobhouse sent a letter, read out loud in the context of the new Union of South Africa. She was cautious and precise:

> Do not open your gates to those worst foes of freedom—tyranny and selfishness. Are these not the withholding from others in your control, the very liberties and rights which you have valued and won for yourselves.... We in England are ourselves still dunces in the great world-school, our leaders still struggling with the unlearned lesson, that liberty is the equal right and heritage of every child of man, without distinction of race, colour or sex. A community that lacks the courage to found its citizenship on this broad base becomes "a city divided against itself, which cannot stand."[96]

Omitted from the oration were lines written specifically about forgotten Black inmates: "Does not justice bid us remember today how many thousands of the dark race perished also in the Concentration Camps in a quarrel that was not theirs? ... Was it not an instance of that community of interest, which binding all in one, roots out racial animosity?"[97] These censored words on Black suffering, perhaps her own mea culpa, find an uncomfortable counterpoint in the forgetting of the camps in Merebank, Wentworth, and Jacobs today. What exactly is "that community of interest" that is anti-racist while acknowledging African participation in a war "that was not theirs"? There is a curious, portentous similarity here with the problem of coalitional Black politics at the century's end, in which various non-Africans signed up in solidarity for a Black politics, a struggle that to many "was not theirs," to abolish the grounds of racial animosity. Hobhouse's question might be asked yet again in postapartheid times still structured by Black suffering and white bourgeois privilege. What is also portentous is that her words were read out in 1913, the annus mirabilis of South African dispossession.

Distant Resonances, 2002–2007

The form of a camp is unmistakable in today's Merewent Cheshire Home off Eksteen Road in Wentworth (figure 1.5). When the Wentworth Concentration Camp was dismantled, wood and iron structures came down, and new

FIGURE 1.5 Merewent Cheshire Home, 2007. © Sharad Chari.

military buildings took their place and form. The South Durban camps had a short afterlife in the period of Chinese indenture, when they were briefly used as transit camps, and subsequently as part of housing for the Royal Navy during World War II.[98] The former camp became a training school for Indian police during apartheid and the site where the first Indian policewomen were sworn in during in the turbulent early 1980s (see chapter 8). Today part of it is a massive Pentecostal ministry, but the section that resembles a camp is now a refuge for disabled people in many ways forgotten by the present. The Merewent Cheshire Home makes no reference to the South African War, but it forces us to engage resonances between camp inmates at the dawn of the twentieth century and township residents in the twenty-first.[99]

The Cheshire Foundation Homes for the Sick was registered in London in 1948 by retired Group Captain Leonard Cheshire and "Mrs. Bunny" Cheshire, both of whom served in World War II and who married in Bombay. Mrs. Bunny had worked with survivors of Nazi death camps. On his retirement from the Royal Air Force (RAF), where he was a British observer in the atomic bombing of Nagasaki, Cheshire's focus turned to disability, which he saw as a means to "recapture something of the sense of purpose and comradeship" lost after the war.[100] The dialectics of war and humanitarianism in his account resonates strongly with concern for the South African camps, though the gender dynamics differ. Cheshire's reminiscences are entirely about men taking care of other men, initially all English; his origin tale is of a much junior RAF man entrusting his dying years to Leonard and repaying the debt by leading him to Catholicism. India became his imagined gateway into realizing that people from other parts of the world may also suffer from the social abandonment that can accompany advanced disability but that they may also be entrusted with the work of care.

Cheshire Homes were started with private funds and run by members of surrounding communities to attend to permanently or substantially physically disabled people who did not need hospital treatment but could not for various reasons be cared for at home either.[101] The first Cheshire Home set up in South Africa, the Queensburgh Cheshire Home in a working-class area in Durban, established in 1965, was meant to convey notions of Christian charity and brotherhood among less fortunate (white) people.[102]

When I first visited the Merebank Cheshire Home in 2002, it was something like a residential workshop for disabled Black people from various parts of the country. I was shown handicrafts and met people working on various crafts on their own in a large, dimly lit room. There was also something hopeful in the way in which people showed off the crafts they were working on. The person showing me around spoke in the language of individual achievement, of industry and self-reliance. When I returned in 2008, I found a very different situation. Their state subsidies had been cut, and the manufactory now hired in labor from surrounding Wentworth. On later visits I did not see much going on in the workshop. The disabled inmates sat in the yard. They told me that without work they have nothing to do.

There are several such places, pockets of forgotten people. I visited the Ark at the top of Austerville Drive with a very sensitive community activist with whom I walked around Wentworth. Careful with his words, he cautioned me that this was a place for people in a particularly terrible state. We spoke to a friend of his, a woman who lived in one corner, who told us she was always fearful of her safety, of the loss of her possessions, and of the terrible hygiene at the Ark, but that this was the only option she had left.

Conclusion: Portents of Segregation

When I told an activist friend from Wentworth that I was interested in the concentration camp in the neighborhood he had grown up in, he laughed in embarrassment. Like others, he had never heard of it. What is to be explained here is not memory but forgetting.

A palimpsestic reading of the camp as a site of forgetting requires considerable care. On the one hand, the camps were used to reinforce a selective renovation of Afrikaner dispossession to differentiate an Afrikaner past from the rest. We might presume the improbability of widespread Black solidarity for Afrikaner dispossession given that the camps were used to signify Afrikaner nationalist trauma. We might take as self-evident the implausibility that the remains of Afrikaner camps in recent Indian and Coloured townships might become meaningful sites of historical consciousness. We would be wrong to think that this is where possibilities end.

On the other hand, the specter of the camp allows us to see continuities in the production of sympathy and intervention in the lives of camp inmates, and the deployment of biopolitical concern in places and times far beyond late-Victorian "social imperialism."[103] The forgetting of the camp and its articulations with other carceral forms—the hostel, the prison, the township, the care home for people with special needs—might make Wentworth seem different from other townships, its Coloured people different from others. Wentworth's men seem unlike African migrants, despite their similar trajectories of migrant work and the attendant risks and pleasures of absconding from household responsibilities.[104] The idea of Wentworth's uniqueness, however, holds in negation a set of resonances. Forgetting the camp perpetuates a particular structure of feeling, a frustrated sense of being besieged by the present. This is why bringing the camp back into the frame of historical consciousness is not a quirky aside in this book.

Discursive circulation through the camps and their aftermath creates what Foucault calls "a dense transfer point" connecting circuits of expert and disqualified knowledge in the past with poverty talk and "community work" in South Durban today.[105] Forgetting prevents what appears as resonance from being apprehended as a spatiotemporal dialectical relation. Forgetting the camps reinforces the forgetting of various people today. Hence, community workers in Wentworth today unwittingly reproduce Victorian distinctions between the deserving and undeserving poor, between township residents and those who live in places like the Ark or the Merewent Cheshire Home, or who are in conditions of multifaceted poverty and suffering.

Apart from an unnoticed plaque, partitioned historical consciousness allows the forgetting of what might be a profoundly moving public site of suffering. Forgotten camps conceal a set of experiments with biopolitics, but they also reveal the limits of our segregated consciousness. In the chapters to come, we will see the biopolitical expertise that entered this landscape through the

South African War increasingly drawn into a segregationist frame. In the next chapter, we turn to the possibilities latent in early twentieth-century "peri-Durban." An object of fear and loathing, Durban's *black belt* would become a thorn in the side of what was hoped to be a white city in a "white man's country" but has always remained far more unruly.

Settlements of Memory

Forgeries of Life in Common, 1900–1930s

The production of race is chaotic. It is an alchemy of the intentional and the unintended, of known and unimagined fractures of cultural forms, of relations of power and the power of social and cultural relations. . . . The covering conceit of a racial regime is a makeshift patchwork masquerading as memory and the immutable. Nevertheless, racial regimes do possess history, that is, discernible origins and mechanisms of assembly. . . . Racial regimes are commonly masqueraded as natural orderings, inevitable creations of collective anxieties prompted by threatening encounters with difference. Yet they are actual contrivances, designed and delegated by interested cultural and social powers with the wherewithal sufficient to commission their imaginings, manufacture, and maintenance. This latter industry is of some singular importance, since racial regimes tend to wear thin over time.

—CEDRIC ROBINSON, *Forgeries of Memory and Meaning*

Remembering Racialized Dispossession and Settlement, 2004

The Durban Depot of the South African National Archives is like other archives in several respects. Academics use their charms on archive staff to access material, including files in a protracted state of recataloging.[1] At other moments, this archive is the site of a different kind of industry, to use Cedric Robinson's term, as when members of the public come for the archive's genealogical holdings. On one instance, I was touched to see a man with a video camera filming his great-grandfather's entry in the ship's list on his arrival from India, to celebrate the centenary of his ancestor's passage to Africa. He propped the ship's list against the wall as he patiently filmed the relevant pages. Over subsequent years archive users like this man became more frequent as the Government of India extended new visa categories to people of Indian origin. At the inception of this scheme, veteran Durban activist Fatima Meer visited New Delhi in 2003. Fiercely critical of a distinction between Indians settled in "dollar and pound nations," who were regarded as worthy of dual citizenship, as opposed to those in poorer countries, who were not, Meer refused global Indianness. "We are not a diaspora," she proclaimed. "We have struggled long and hard to be called South African."[2]

What is striking is the difference of view between this stalwart and Indian South Africans at the archives. When I asked one man why he was so eagerly collecting evidence for his application to become a "Person of Indian Origin," he asked me why only white people should have the possibility of moving. Provision of British passports on the basis of ancestry had long been a racial mechanism for sorting white "patrials" from former settler colonies from their brown counterparts.[3] However, Indian citizenship was realizable only by a small minority of Durban Indians. Some people who visited India with such hopes admitted that travel confirmed that South Africa is home. As we will see, Indian nationalism in India had turned full circle from an early twentieth-century abrogation of its working-class emigrants to chasing their money in the early twenty-first.

On another occasion, in 2005, I was chatting with an old bartender at a venerable revolving restaurant overlooking Durban harbor. Jobs in Durban's elite hotels and restaurants like his offered prized careers to some Indian men. When I asked him about his familial past, he grew wistful. Then, raising his voice, he pointed out to the harbor and exclaimed, "Just here, we landed! Just here!" There was no ancestry tracing necessary, just an immediate identification with his ancestor's arrival as an indentured laborer more than a century earlier. What was remarkable was his triumphant tone.

While racialized dispossession haunts Southern Africa, these vignettes remind us that dispossession and its twin, unfree migration, always presume settlement, unless they are genocidal.[4] Generations after the trauma of unfree labor migration, descendants hold on to ways of forging life in common, even under duress. Even the camps of the South African War were not just sites of imperial humanitarianism but also of survival of wartime devastation. The dispossessed often attempt to remake life in common, only to find that it is at the expense of others. This is compounded by the fact that of South Africa's many dispossessions, official historiography has accorded the Land Act of 1913 such a primal importance that it has relegated other histories of enclosure and resettlement to the margins. This is one reason that the subaltern forms of space-making explored in this chapter remain outside the realm of critique. Yet, as we will see, submerged histories of dispossession and the valorization of Indian Durban are twin sides of the same coin.

In his study of systematic misrepresentations of Black life on film, Robinson argues that "forgeries of memory" reveal that "racial regimes tend to wear thin over time."[5] The memory conventions I explore in this chapter grapple with forgeries of life in common as they literally settle in interconnected histories of dispossession and subaltern place-making, revealing the fragility of racial capitalism. Affirmations of Indians surviving indenture and forging communal life contrast sharply with adjacent memories of subalterns whose lives remained perpetually unsettled.

The argument of this chapter is that during the first three decades of the century, Durban's subalterns produced a slow and steady transformation of space that began to distinguish a geography of Indian habitation forged in the peripheries and interstices of a putatively white city from a mixed Black landscape that included those who would later be classified Coloured.[6] As a consequence of this history of space-making, memory conventions of Merebank Indians and Wentworth Coloureds diverge as people recall landscapes of the past in substantially different ways. People racialized as Durban Indians can recall family histories of diversified livelihood and petty accumulation after indenture spread across an archipelagic space still recognizable as Indian Durban. In contrast, people racialized as Coloureds, for the most part, arrived in Durban as dispossessed proletarians whose primary relation to urban land was as perennially insecure tenants. With no recourse to a history of space-making that remains at hand for Merebank Indians, Wentworth Coloureds have a different relationship to the notion of an urban commons. The effects of this difference ramify throughout this book, despite their shared repression of Indian Ocean pasts.

Consider this divergence through David Graeber's provocation that debt is the relation between groups who "cannot yet walk away from each other, because they are not yet equal," while, he adds hopefully, "in the shadows of eventual equality."[7] This formulation helps us consider modes of engagement with "eventual equality" in Indian Merebank and Coloured Wentworth. People from Merebank, like many other South African Indians, can assume that descendants of indentured Indians have overcome a particular structure of debt, so that the hope of equality is quite literally their genealogical legacy. This is indexed by both the bartender pointing out to an imagined ship and the man filming an inert ship's list. In marked contrast, Wentworth's working-class Coloureds cannot as easily claim histories of unfree labor, Indigenous dispossession, or Indian Ocean slavery even though these processes have shaped their personhood. Unable to attend to the debts that their difficult lives have incurred, they carry a different genealogical burden of nonrecognition akin in many ways to the Black American predicament.

Disentangling modes of engagement with the possibility of equality is part of the work of decolonizing historical knowledge. Catherine Burns proposes that we consider "history in chords," attentive to distinct narrative traditions across coercively separated trajectories and also across professional and public uses of history, all of which echo, resonate, and coproduce polyphonies that bear careful listening.[8] When we hear consonance in certain chords and dissonance in others, the music of history calls attention to many forms of critical expression. Moreover, like music, social memories are multidirectional, as Michael Rothberg puts it; they draw laterally in partially cited ways on the experiences and memory conventions of others.[9]

After years of listening in chords, I represent dispossession in Merebank and Wentworth in dialectical counterpoint and spatial interconnection. Merebank Indians appear to participate in processes of emplacement that their memories can literally settle into. Wentworth Coloureds appear to have little recourse of this kind. Merebank Indians can affiliate to a broader geography of Indian Durban. Wentworth's working-class Coloureds, including its long-distance migrants, find home in Wentworth's square mile. While a minority from Wentworth have sought land restitution and, in one instance, chieftaincy, these frustrated exceptions prove the rule that this is an extremely urbanized population cut off decisively from countrysides of the past. As we turn to divergent memory conventions from today's Merebank and Wentworth, we do so with caution, beginning with the colonial transformations that brought Indian Ocean people to Durban's racial shores and that made South Durban a specific kind of liminal zone.

FIGURE 2.1 *Banana Plants Imposed on a View of the Point from the Bluff, 1880–1900.*
© Local History Museum, Durban.

Indenture and After: Forgeries of Racial Capitalism

The Commission found conditions prevailing in certain portions of the peri-Durban area with regard to . . . non-European housing, which it can only describe as deplorable in the extreme. . . . These conditions originated as a result of the inadequacy of housing provision within the Borough. That and the high cost of land had . . . the effect of driving men to migrate across the boundary, and a considerable Indian population established itself as close to their occupations and markets in Durban as they could. In this area there was, of course, no municipal control or supervision. So, has grown up Durban's "black belt," hemming it in on nearly every side, and sometimes within a stone's throw of some of its best residential areas. In the main, the population of this belt is still Indian; but in comparatively recent years the overspill of Durban's native population has streamed into it, for the most part as tenants and lodgers, often under very unsatisfactory conditions, of Indian property-owners; and still more recently Europeans of the poorer classes, unskilled labourers brought into Durban and the like, have followed suit. —BOROUGH BOUNDARIES COMMISSION, 1930

This imaginative photograph (figure 2.1), ambiguously dated 1880–1900, provokes a series of quandaries.[10] The central image of the harbor was likely taken at a dock on the southern edge, with banana palms "imposed" on it, as the caption puts it. Studio touching up was common practice at the turn of the century, but there is an obvious theatricality to this view of boats gently rocking on a placid bay, seen through a jungle canopy. The foreground is the urban fringe, lush and tropical, with an African woman leaning on the bottom of the frame and, behind her on her right, a less discernible person holding something, perhaps a baby. The curtain comprises plantation crops, banana plants that were actually "imposed" on this landscape. The period surrounding the South African War, the time of this photograph, was a time of yearning for imperial certitude in the wake of widespread racial capitalist uncertainty. If there was resolve in a white gaze looking through lens and darkroom, juxtaposing tropical hinterland and lazy harbor, it was quite at odds with the bustle of everyday life for most people in early twentieth-century Durban.[11]

Contrast this photograph with the anxious tone of the Borough Boundaries Commission of 1930, which replaces this sylvan idyll with a "black belt" ridden with disease and disorder, desperate for municipal incorporation, particularly with the appearance of "Europeans of the poorer classes." This is also a forgery in Robinson's sense: it points to a blind spot in colonial thought, the lived world of the urban periphery. In this space marked by official neglect, people forged the spatial integuments of subaltern life, whose material remains are still with us in fruit trees, fruit and vegetable trade, the century-old Victoria Street Indian Market, smaller markets across the city, temples, mosques, processions, and public rituals.[12] Rather than being regarded as inevitable or a product of grit and determination, these spaces of Indian settlement were surrounded by antipathy, and not just from descendants of colonial settlers. Some Africans in mission reserves saw these subalterns *as Indians* with suspicion.[13] In this light, the African woman who stares out of the frame of the image carries an insurgent demand to attend to the profoundly unsettled experiences of Africans. I hope to show that what this staged photograph of a city across the bay completely evades is an actual subaltern occupation of space that effectively evaded colonial power and knowledge.

In fact, both these forgeries of racial capitalism rely on a dominant fantasy of colonial Durban as a modern, white city that used "non-European" labor while denying these people hospitality.[14] Myths of colonial masculinity and conquest had upheld the land grab, rendered in the colonial episteme as a gift of nature. Colonial historiography posits a group of British "1820 Settlers" sent to colonize the frontier with the eastern edge of the Cape Colony, who moved on to Natal and were followed by others, particularly after Natal was annexed to the Cape in 1845. By the time Durban became a municipality in 1854, it defined its natural territorial boundaries as the Umgeni and Umbilo Rivers, the Indian Ocean and Bay of Natal, and the Berea Ridge, natural boundaries evident on map 4.[15]

Early twentieth-century Durban sought to naturalize the history of colonial occupation by recasting the conquest of space as a grant of 6,096 acres, an endowment that was the basis of the municipality's phased land sales and, after 1866, land lease as a source of revenue. The Borough of Durban's preference for short-term leaseholds encouraged people working in Durban to invest in freehold property beyond the city boundaries in Sea View, Bellair near Cato Manor, and South Coast Junction near Clairwood on map 4. When the borough eased up on the leasehold system, its monopoly of land continued to encourage white settlement on cheaper peripheral land exempt from municipal rates, or charges for municipal services. Affluent white people followed suburbanization along rail or tramlines with access to the city at a remove from "Indian penetration," the scare term for Indian propertied presence in the inner city. The borough's monopoly of land pushed "non-European" settlement to the periphery, where working-class whites often saw Indians as competitors for land within reach of work, markets, and routes to the city center.[16]

To understand this urban periphery, we have to backtrack to nineteenth-century questions of race, labor, and capital. After early nineteenth-century wars between Afrikaner Voortrekkers and the Zulu Kingdom, the midcentury ascendancy of British occupation of Natal, the Anglo-Zulu War of 1879, and the destruction of the Zulu Kingdom that followed, British settlers brought sugarcane expertise from Mauritius to the coastal areas north and south of Durban. Since the 1850s sugar interests had lobbied hard for Indian indentured labor recruited through British imperial networks. This would leave a lasting imprint on Durban and its peripheries. Importantly, plantation capital was not a fetter to industrialization but became part of the accumulation regime through the phased release of land and labor for other uses.

People from specific parts of British India were recruited into indenture through processes of dispossession that remain undocumented. The indenture system brought approximately 150,000 people from Bihar and the Madras Presidency to Natal between 1860 and 1911. Descendants of these migrants reimagined their differentiation in ethnolinguistic terms, as "Hindis" and "Tamils," the latter including "Telugus" from the Madras Presidency. They took on last names, a practice unheard of in the contexts they came from. Many of these appear to be the names of dominant castes from their areas of origin; hence, Naidoo, an unlikely caste for an indentured migrant from South

India, became a common last name in the phone book. Plausibly, people experimented with mobility through renaming, but this is now forgotten as it was probably futile in a context in which nobody around them knew, or indeed knows, the finer details of caste in India, for instance, that the -*idoo* suffix in Naidoo is an honorific. In another act of forgetting, many Durban Indians continue to refer to their indentured forebears as "1860 Settlers," implicitly referencing the British "1820 Settlers," but this colonial mimesis goes entirely without comment, not even as a footnote to colonial nostalgia.[17]

Indenture and its aftermath are complex topics. As in other plantation regimes, the historical record is written through planter simplifications. Some sources are blithely sanguine, as a manager of Merebank Estate reports to the Coolie Commission of 1872 that relations with "coolies" on his estate were so amicable that some asked why others were not arriving from India, where "this estate was reported most favourably of."[18] There are clues on the edges of racial common sense that other processes were afoot. When a former manager of Reunion Estate reported to the commission that "coolies" refused accommodation in barracks and "preferred to build their own . . . that by so doing they could get a patch of garden-ground in close proximity or surrounding their house," he could not imagine an emergent subaltern transformation of space that would endure for over a century and a half.[19]

Indentured migrants were followed after the 1870s by "passenger Indians" who paid their passage and were differentiated by class, religion, and region of origin, including Hindu and Muslim Gujarati merchants and shopkeepers. Former indentured and passenger migrants of modest means forged livelihoods in peri-urban areas and in the interstices of colonial towns and cities, often against the odds.[20] Relatively stable access to peripheral land allowed many to engage in complex rural-urban livelihoods as petty traders, hawkers, shopkeepers, horticulturalists, and peasant-workers engaged in periodic waged labor.[21]

Some sugar planters in Merebank in the 1860s and 1870s rented out ten- to twenty-acre plots to former indentured laborers to access their labor in times of shortage as well as to benefit from their labor of clearing land for plantations.[22] The Report of the Indian Immigrants Commission (Wragg Commission) of 1885–87 suggests that ex-indentured small-scale farmers were converting "waste and unproductive land" into "gardens planted with vegetables, tobacco, maize [and] fruit trees."[23] Stallholders at the Indian market in town complained about being undercut by "coolie" street hawkers connected to "Indian gardens" (map 4).[24] In time, the entirety of the city became reliant on cheap produce from "Indian gardens" proliferating throughout Durban's neglected interstices. The importance of the slave plot has been noted by historians of slavery and indenture, but what was happening in Durban was that the slave plot and its produce were extending across the city. Excluded from Crown land grants, denied rights to Crown land in contravention of indenture contracts that promised land after indenture, and neglected by municipal housing, former indentured laborers were engaged in nothing less than a concerted subaltern production of space.[25]

Antipathy and suspicion surrounded this process of space-making. Heather Hughes argues that by the 1890s there was growing anti-Indian sentiment among African convert families in the Inanda Mission Reserve areas to the northwest of Durban, along with a perception that Indians were prone to self-exploitation and dense habitation unsuitable to African homesteads, which were spatially dispersed to support cattle as bridewealth; one convert reported to the Natal Native Commission of 1881, "Three Coolies could live in a space that one Kaffir would want. Natives like cattle; Coolies do not," and, it follows, Africans would be "elbowed out of the country."[26] Although racial categories should give us some pause on how to interpret this source, ideas of Indian "Coolies" prone to Chayanovian self-exploitation recur with a specific frequency across registers, as in this extract from the late 1930s or early 1940s: "Vegetables are being sold very low, in fact at ruinous prices to the grower, excepting the Coolies. The requirements of an Asiatic are so small that the very smallest profit of his productions will suffice to keep the body and soul together, so, where an Englishman would literally starve, he would be in a thriving and prosperous condition. This being the case, and seeing that all garden produce is selling so low, it will not surprise any to hear that the vegetable market is almost completely supplied by the coolies."[27] Ideas of economic and biological threat swirled around the figure of the Indian at the turn of the century. As Jon Soske argues, European anti-Semitism made these lateral citations possible.[28] Durban had already attempted in the late nineteenth century, unsuccessfully, to establish an Indian "location."[29] The Dealer's Act of 1897 empowered the municipal licensing officer to use sanitation to control Indian trade and to contain Indian merchants in the Grey Street enclave, the area that its twentieth-century organic intellectuals, photographer Omar Badsha and novelist Aziz Hassim, call "the Casbah."[30]

When the bubonic plague hit South African cities in 1903, official discourse portrayed a public health menace emerging from Indian and African "slums" (see chapter 1). Cities responded differently. Durban responded from a playbook in which Indian "slums" and the inner-city Casbah besieged a white city.[31] In contrast to anxiety about urbanized Indians, Natal's administrators considered themselves exemplars in financing the coercive exclusion of Africans from urban life. The Shepstone System, a pass system for African day labor devised by Theophilus Shepstone in 1873–74, framed the schizophrenic way in which authorities in the early 1900s saw African labor as a police problem, and urban migration as a health problem.[32] Postwar debates on the pass system for African day labor stoked fears of vigilantism, threats to white women's security, and moral dangers of Indian immigration.[33] But unlike Johannesburg's violent urban removals, Durban did not yet endorse segregation to resolve its "Native question." When Natal passed the Native Locations Act in 1904, employers resisted financing workers' barracks.[34] Durban's unique solution was to use a municipal monopoly on the brewing and sale of sorghum beer to finance the building of "locations," schools, hospitals, and other minimalist "welfare."[35] This "Durban System" received praise as an innovative form of municipal self-financing of "Native control" and was cited as a lesson across South Africa, as it brought Victorian Progressivism into a racial and urban frame.

Crucially, officialdom propped up the fantasy of a white city through racialized transformations in land, labor, and capital. Racial government had to contend with the exigencies of plantation capital and with the immigration not just of Indian indentured laborers but also of mercantile and working classes whose urban presence disrupted the white city. Obsessed by the look of central Durban, city hall did not notice subaltern space-making in the urban peripheries and interstices. In what follows, we turn to the geographies in which many people's recollections settle, as we consider, in counterpoint, settlements of memory from Indian Merebank and Coloured Wentworth.

The Making of an Indian Commons

Dhani. Immigrant No. 37750
Arrived from India about the year 1889. medium built. Light comp toward darker colour. Fine personality. Very energetic. Extremely honest. Lover of annimals—cows used to follow him like pet dogs. Religious, not a keen beliver in Devthas, but later in life was dragged into it [by] his wife. (who used her power to gain almost anything.) Grandfather, having had numerous friends enjoyed the privilege of being a desider between two quarrelers.

Ind. Imm. 625. Juggernath—800–475527A. (Blackburn). 13th Sept 1891.
—"The Diary of Balbhadur Juggernath"

This remarkable précis on the arrival of Dhani, presented as if copied from an official document, is the first page of "The Diary of Balbhadur Juggernath," actually a retrospective memoir written in the 1990s by pensioner and

Merebank Ratepayers Association (MRA) leader Balbhadur "Billy" Juggernath.[36] "The Diary" begins with his grandfather Dhani's passage from India and recounts the Juggernath family's movements from indenture to social prominence through segregation and apartheid; it is an indispensable source on memory conventions afforded to some Indians in Merebank.[37]

The précis intersperses documentary authenticity with obvious fabrication, an act of subaltern forgery. The last statement recalls M. N. Srinivas's classic ethnography on the arbitration of disputes in village India, perhaps transmitted through Indian film to Juggernath's conception of exemplary character.[38] After this unusual start, "The Diary" offers an imaginative reconstruction of Dhani's journey on the SS *Congella*, his life under indenture in Natal, and his arrival in 1914 with a group of similar families in the area that would become Merebank. These "pioneers," the grandson imagines, created something that "resembled village India," with cows, poultry, and vegetable farms on the banks of the Umlaas River; they took produce to the Indian market, sold milk in Merebank, and built a large home on Duranta Road facing what would become the Engen refinery.[39]

Dhani's wife, Surjee, joined a religious group of sadhus, followers of the syncretic Indian mystic Kabir, and these "Kabir *panthees*" (travelers) lived along today's Tara Road. Juggernath writes that each "member of the clan cultivated a piece of land and quite a number had cows" and that they would meet in the evenings to play music on a *kanjri* (perhaps the South Indian frame drum, *kanjira*), sing songs, eat "sweetmeats made of boiled and sour milk," and smoke "ganga cheelum" (marijuana), apparently flouting the intense restriction on indentured laborers' cultivation, possession, and use of cannabis after 1870. These Kabir *panthees* rejected caste and affirmed "the equality of mankind," a remarkable possibility of radically altered forms of life after indenture.[40] The imagination here is wonderfully syncretic, as North Indian medieval poetry is sung with a South Indian drum, aided by South African marijuana, to claim radical equality: a creole poetics of marronage in an African Indian Ocean city.

When Juggernath embellishes family stories to construct a narrative of the refashioning of "the Indian village," what is striking is its distance from social institutions in early twentieth-century India. He finds the "caste system" almost obsolete, but conspicuously absent are the various things that caste indexes in India, including prohibitions on exchanges of things, prayers, food, sex, and labor among various *jatis*, or subcastes, and with various outcasts. What we have in contrast are suggestive forms of mutuality, an anti-caste ethics without the social forms of caste domination. Other aspects of caste probably survived in new form, in restrictions on marriage, but also in forms of networked support. Consider that in a 1906 letter from indentured laborer Vamu Reddy detailing the mistreatment of himself and his wife, Muniammah, he ends with a request for transfer to "a master where a caste man of mine worked."[41]

Retired apartheid-era politician K. Lalloo, ninety-three years old when we spoke, offered a vivid account of his parents' lives a century earlier, of their journey as indentured laborers on the ss *Congella*, after which they were "dished out" to work for farmers north of Durban. Lalloo narrated his parents' leasing of a large farm of twenty-five acres near Pietermaritzburg, where they planted beans, potatoes, rice, *mielies* (maize), and tobacco and were so successful that the white landlord gave them notice. They then moved to Ifafa on the South Coast, where his father secured a large piece of fertile land on annual rent. With a curious turn of phrase, Lalloo said they "cut the bush and made a garden colony." The last phrase could refer to the Indian English "colony," as in state- or company-provided housing estates, harking back to nineteenth-century Anglo-Indian Railway Colonies, but the resonance with the Latin *colonia* as a settled farm is uncannily apt.

Lalloo's parents forged relations of mutuality among "Guru bhais," or devotees of the same guru who participated in labor exchanges called *peti*. Lalloo waxes poetic about the productivity of this farming system, which allowed the family to save and to move to what is now Merebank so that his siblings might attend school. When the family arrived there around 1920, when Lalloo was ten years old, they leased land from one of the large landowners, E. M. Paruk, who rented out land on one side in "the white area, and other side the Indian people . . . we had demarcation, each group must stay on their own," he repeated in the prose of segregation. This remarkable piece of evidence speaks of subaltern forms of mutuality alongside Indian large landlords segregating tenancies in apparent complicity with officialdom.

By the early 1900s, "Indian squatters" occupied land owned by speculators, north and west of the city, and in the southern flatlands labeled "Indian Gardens" on map 4.[42] Importantly, this was not an "illegal" seizure of space but one that worked through the cadastre and land market. Land had been surveyed and cleared, farms had been registered, and some white people moved to Wentworth and the Bluff, where land values were rising.[43] In 1906 only three blocks of land had been subdivided for residence on the Bluff, the first one sold off largely to Indians through the Lokhat brothers, while Wentworth and Fynnlands farms were divided into forty-acre blocks.[44] Robert Dunn held one of the early nineteenth-century land grants from Bayhead to Merebank; "Dunn's Grant" was sold to the Woods family and subsequently sold to Indian buyers.[45] E. J. Paruk and M. A. Karim were major speculators in property in the early twentieth century; Paruk purchased much of Wentworth from Dunn's Grant and resold small lots through the 1920s and 1930s.[46]

Another white landowner, Winn, sold to E. J. Paruk, the Lokhat brothers, and S. M. Jhavary, who leased land annually to Indian farmers.[47] Annual tenancies were an important mechanism for people like Juggernath and Lalloo's forebears to farm on a relatively stable basis. In a curious twist in "The Diary," a former white landholder returns to an Indian home as a ghostly "deity of the immediate environment, called Dee," propitiated through offerings of "choice fruits, liquor (cane spirit) and the sacrifice of a Pig."[48] This ritual propitiation of a former white landholder through pig sacrifice suggests further syncretism in Indian habitation rather than unmediated passages from India.

In fact, we know very little about how farming practices and skills from agrarian Madras or Bihar may have been grafted onto farming maize, sweet potatoes, and tobacco for African markets; fruit and vegetables for the general market in town; or aubergine, garlic, yams, and spices for Indian consumption.[49] People adapted food practices, as fermented *mielie* (maize) meal replaced fermented rice from the Tamil country as "sour porridge" in Natal. Indian farmers found a niche in the rural-urban periphery, and the products of their labor permeated the regional food system. Bill Freund argues that typical Indian smallholdings depended on family labor, but this presumes too much about gender and kinship regimes and what made them "Indian," given differentiated kinship systems in late nineteenth-century North and South India, broadly divergent on dowry and bride-price and differentiated and adapted further in Southern Africa.[50] We might rather presume that colonial ideology shaped realities more fundamentally, as in Françoise Vergès's notion of "colonial family romance" in Reunion Island, Robert Morrell's discussion on the Natal settler elite, or Nafisa Essop Sheik's analysis of colonial regulation of sex, gender, and marriage in Natal.[51]

Juggernath's "Diary" is a treasure trove both for its details of peri-urban social life and for its reiteration of a colonial romance of Indian family, complete with a love of cows and the reassurance of class mobility:

> We lived as a joint family, working in the farm and tending to cows. The farm produce were taken to the Durban Indian Market and the milk were sold locally at 3 pence a quart. Grandfather was very devoted to his cows, a habit I believe he acquired in India. . . . By this time there

was some progress as a result of father working in the Surprise Soap factory at Jacobs. . . . Everybody helped in everything. . . . It was at this period that an acre of land was bought in Duranta Rd for £60 (R120) by instalments. . . . In 1923 we . . . built a large house in Duranta Rd sufficient for the entire family.[52]

Sometime around Dhani's death in 1928, the family acquired more farmland near the Umlaas canal and expanded their range of work and accumulation. While affluent Hindu men like Juggernath and Lalloo could retrospectively recollect family stories of determined petty accumulation, most people in Merebank today recall the past as a set of labored landscapes connecting dispersed peasant-worker settlements. One man spoke in vague terms about his ancestors' indenture "for many, many years" but was certain that they did not receive the allotments promised in indenture contracts but rarely if ever delivered. The late Mrs. Marie spoke in similarly general terms, and her narrative settles in the precise landscapes in which ex-indentured and other working-class Indians forged peasant-worker livelihoods.

Another woman spoke of peri-urban subsistence farming with limited marketing of produce, and she recalled speaking fluent isiZulu. "Tamil I know, but not so good," she said. "We were born and brought up with Africans." When I asked her about caste, she responded through discussion in her family about whether or not to give Africans separate drinking cups, implicitly indexing untouchability in India and its restrictions on interdining, utensil sharing, and physical contact. The separate cup, hated symbol of struggles against untouchability in twentieth-century India, may have been grafted onto relations with Africans, reinforcing similar anti-African practice in the homes of white Durbanites.[53]

In her foundational work on South Durban, Dianne Scott argues that Indians shaped their own landscapes in "Clairwood and District," where "small paths connected the maze of small homes" and where intensive small farming and shack settlement "gave rise to the distinctive pattern of a colourful mosaic spreading across the low-lying flats." They coined place-names like "Wireless," Bodha's Gardens, Bob's Place, and Mowat's Quarry as Clairwood became the hub of Indian social life linked to the Grey Street Indian commercial enclave in town.[54] Scott helps us see beyond the turn-of-the-century colonial scopic regime that looked across the bay to marshlands denuded of settlement and labor, or what Shula Marks called "the myth of the empty land."[55] While the landscape that became Merebank and Wentworth was flood prone and mosquito infested, unsuitable even for concentration camps, it was being fundamentally transformed by subaltern labor and habitation.

Africans appear to have been tenants and brewers on Durban's southern periphery, though on increasingly insecure terms following the 1913 Land Act. Hence, an unmarked white resident of Merebank complained of Indian landlords leasing land to African tenants, who, the complainant insists, must be brewing "Native beer." "You know what class of Natives live in this locality—They are the 'riff raff' of every part of Natal and Zululand," he rants, arguing that they "do no legitimate work" and that "as a consequence the drunkenness and immorality is a perfect nuisance to the neighbourhood."[56] The judgment in this case was a fine or hard labor for the Indian landlord and African tenants, but we should note the moralizing racial discourse that made its first appearance in discourse surrounding the concentration camps.[57] In another instance, when Edward DaSilva, an African veteran of the Great War, attempted to secure a beer license in 1919, his solicitors argued that a licensed beer hall might stem widespread illicit drinking.[58] The request was denied. The Durban chief magistrate argued that "the reference to illicit Beer drinking in and around Merebank is hardly justified" as other agencies were "suppressing the evil."[59] What is striking is that the magistrate refuses the African veteran any moral authority. Both events clarify official antipathy reserved for Africans.

Africans are conspicuously absent from Juggernath's "Diary." There are a few mentions of controlling "Native labour" at the Clairwood Turf Club or on the family farm in Merebank, as well as mention of a Native eating house in Tongaat and of a chauffeur employed by an Indian "gentleman." Racial mixing may have been limited in the rural-urban periphery, but we should be careful about interpreting this as African banishment from urban life. In her foundational study on "the ambiguities of dependence," Marks shows how municipal authorities in Durban sought to co-opt African leadership to attempt to regulate African presence in and around the city.[60] Marc Epprecht extends this argument to show how the Pietermaritzburg municipality sought African Christian *amakholwa* elites in Progressivist initiatives like "model African villages."[61]

Importantly, the 1920s in Durban were a time of heightened African mobilization through the Industrial and Commercial Workers Union and its dynamic provincial secretary, George Champion; this was a time of resistance to the "Durban System" and its monopoly of beer as a means of limiting African petty capital. The 1927 dockworkers' strikes were another sign of continued, militant African presence. In this context liberal mayor Archibald

Lamont became an advocate for a village for "respectable Africans," and co-optation of African *amakholwa* was key to the model village named for him, Lamontville.[62] Juggernath is blithely indifferent to these events in South Durban, as his narrative slips into a segregationist historiography that celebrates Indian familial settlement while Africans remained in a state of flux.

Municipal racism was more aleatory than methodical in its relationship to African tenants as well as to Indian peasant-workers with secure access to land. Renditions of Indian peri-Durban market gardening communities combine the sylvan and idyllic with harsh realities of poverty after indenture. Peri-urban farming was crucial for these subalterns to survive the Great Depression. Yet these were no halcyon days of communal poverty. People recall houses made of wood and iron, material that signifies hardship and self-determination; rooms were added as joint families grew. One man contrasts these houses to the shacks of today, to distance his past from today's Black shack dwellers.

A mixed population squatted on low-lying swampy Crown lands adjoining the bay and inland at Happy Valley.[63] This farming appears to have been largely subsistence and locality oriented, and it reached a peak in the 1920s when the possibility of an Indian peasantry on the urban fringe was squeezed out by segregationist and market forces.[64] Proletarianization pulled Indians out of the possibility of making a living from farming alone, as they took jobs in the municipal corporation, the Natal Government Railways, hotels in town and on the beachfront, domestic servitude, and the early workshops springing up between Congella, Rossburgh, and Jacobs and southward to Merebank.[65] De-peasantization was not, for many, a tragedy. Rather, under the auspices of a progressive Indian middle class, young people were drawn to access education and resources denied by the general poverty of peri-urban life. Many continued as peasant-workers, holding on to market gardens, dairy, poultry, and fishing as sources of livelihood. There is a profound erasure in the historical record of the labor and expertise that made South Durban not just a worked landscape but an incipient urban commons.

Consider Jaya's account of his grandparents' arrival from Travancore on the SS *Umzinto*. He surmises that his grandfather was educated and perhaps even involved in anti-colonial politics in Travancore, which may have determined his deployment not to sugarcane plantations but to Addington Hospital as an indentured orderly. "Obviously he must have had some literacy skills," Jaya recounted, adding with a flourish, "He was reputed to be the first person of colour to have a motorcycle!" Importantly, his grandfather was the founding principal of a Malayalam-Tamil school, precursor to the venerable

Merebank Tamil School Society. Jaya's maternal great-grandmother was "a passenger Indian from somewhere in Tamil Nadu," a traditional healer with skills in childbirth and infertility, perhaps as a *maruttuvachi*, or midwife. This remarkable woman secured property near the river, and after the death of her husband, she married a Welshman called Powers, converted to Methodism, and presided over a large interracial family in a great house on Mere Street.

There is a utopian quality to Jaya's narrative of a racially mixed extended family destroyed by the forces of segregation, but it also shows how some people could invest in communal improvement at some remove from the borough. A slow process of spatial change was connecting the dispersed practices of ex-indentured market gardeners, harnessing them to the project of improvement. The Powers family shows that a key element was the slow and steady building of religious infrastructure, and we know from the work of Goolam Vahed that subaltern Indian religiosity was extremely syncretic.[66]

Early Hindu temples in South Africa were built of wattle and daub with thatched roofs. Believers saw organic deities emerging from sugar estates. In time, temples were constructed of wood and iron, and they became permanent structures through the masonry of master builders blending South Indian and North Indian temple styles.[67] Sugar planters sometimes donated land and building material to secure consent from plantation workers, as in the Ganesha Temple at Mount Edgecombe in 1898.[68] Temple building accelerated with the arrival of master temple builders like bricklayer Kistappa Reddy of North Arcot in South India, who built the first temples at Mount Edgecombe and Umbilo, followed by temples in Pietermaritzburg and along the Natal coast from the 1910s to the 1930s; Reddy also ran the Ganesa Printing Press in Durban, the first bus service from Cato Manor, a taxi business, a grocer shop, a tearoom, and a dairy farm, encapsulating the way in which temple building linked to wider possibilities.[69]

Three temple builders from the Tamil country—Kothanar Ramsamy Pillay of Pudukotai, Barasakthi Naiker, and Tamil scholar Alaga Pillay of Madurai—and a Gujarati called Ramjee built most of the great temples of Natal in the 1920s and 1930s.[70] These "permanent temples" brought priests, teachers, vernacular schools, community halls, and festivals celebrated in the open air, as temple compounds became important public spaces.[71] This astonishingly fast development aided the immigration to South Africa of a multiplicity of Hindu gods consecrated in temples across the city, from Sea Cow Lake and Mount Edgecombe to Cato Manor and Jacobs, from Esperanza and Pampanyoni to Magazine and Railway Barracks, from Sometsu Road and Umgeni Road to Bellair and Umbilo: in other words, in areas proximal to Indian working-class habitation.[72] Even the gods seemed to sanctify the infrastructure of Indian settlement.

A powerfully poignant event clarifies this collective sacralization of settlement. The grave of an unknown indentured Indian was retrospectively recast through a set of circulating rumors as that of a wandering Sufi mystic, so that it could become a *mazaar*, a shrine for an emplaced saint vital to the cosmology of South Asian Islam.[73] The Mazaar of Hazrat Badsha Pir remains a key site in Muslim Durban and a silent tribute to an unknown indentured laborer at the heart of today's city. Rather than repressing a painful past, this event shows how homage to indentured labor was sacralized and worked into the infrastructure of Indian settlement.

The 1910s were an important moment in which reformers from India appeared on the scene to stamp out this syncretic public religiosity, for instance, to dissuade Hindus from participating in the Muslim festival of Muharram.[74] These reformers connected dispersed devotees and encouraged associational life across market gardening communities. Swami Shankeranand established Hindu associations in Sydenham, Mayville, and Sea Cow Lake; he urged devotees to invest in cooperatives, education, and political representation; and he started the Indian Farmer's Association in 1908.[75] He subsequently led the 1912 conference on systematizing Hinduism, which led to the formation of the Hindu Maha Sabha, one of twelve Hindu organizations formed between 1905 and 1915.[76]

Many of the reformers' goals remained unrealized. Most people did not aspire to upper-caste notions of Hindu virtue from a distant India. South African Hinduism remained marked by what one writer problematically calls its "remarkable blend of both non-brahmanical and brahmanical elements."[77] In effect, subaltern forms of popular religiosity persisted, including fire walking, the "six-foot dance" or *therakoot*, worship of mother goddess Draupadi as Garon Gon, the *kavadi* ritual involving spirit possession and body piercing, and the Mariamman "porridge festival," held on Good Friday since 1910.[78] The following exoticized report on a *kavadi* procession at Umbilo Temple in 1935 shows how festivities brought together dispersed devotees:

> The approaches of the Temple were gaily decorated with multi-coloured bunting and vegetation, and vivid splashes of colour. . . . The chanting of the priests, the piping of Indian flutes, and the beating of the nagarars (drums fashioned like tom-toms) mingled with the subdued

hub-bub of conversation as the devotees, bearing on their shoulders "kavadies," marched in procession round the exterior of the Temple prior to concluding their penance within. Altogether between 30 and 40 Hindoos went through this ritual yesterday. They were drawn from all over the Borough. Each community arrived in procession on their own, accompanied by one or more sacred images drawn on low wagons or carts.[79]

Indian Opinion notes in 1931 that a fire-walking ceremony for the goddess Draupadi drew "all sections of the community, Hindus, Christians and Mohommedans."[80] In effect, religious reformers had enabled the spatial connection of dispersed market gardeners, who in turn rejected much of their reformism while taking space through multisensory Tamil traditions like carrying the *kavadi*, fire walking, and "six-foot dance."

This was, I contend, part of a wider subaltern production of space. Indian market gardeners went from hawking produce outside the Grey Street Mosque to securing a covered "early-morning market" on Victoria Street.[81] When the mayor responded to the Indian Farmer's Association's call for a market "for Hindus" by announcing a council-controlled market, Indian farmers boycotted the new Victoria Street market.[82] The city council had to concede to the early-morning "squatters market," for sellers who squatted on the ground, and it has remained an institution, threatened periodically with removal in 1968–71 and 2009–10.[83] Stallholders and hawkers occupied space in the city in ways that defenders of a putatively white city found jarring, as in this anxious report: "The way coolies have accomandeered this thoroughfare one would believe they had assumed military control, the road being completely blocked with carts and boxes. At night no lights are bout and the men make camp fires to sleep. . . . To complete the picture we have a miniature coolie temple, with its tom-toms, the halt, the lamps, the blind, and, during the last season, there was a band."[84] A band! Visceral overload was typical of white complaint, so much so that city hall conceded to building enclosed markets at Warwick and Victoria that allowed marginal hawkers and traders to transact in the popular heart of Durban.[85] These measures did not prevent hawkers from plying the streets, but they did restrict their movements. White Durbanites across the city saw these "Sammys" and "Marys" with a combination of desire and revulsion, as Prinisha Badassy carefully demonstrates, because they relied on this mobile workforce to provide cheap fruit and vegetables on their doorsteps.[86] When white traders protested the presence of hawkers, their movements were prohibited in 1930, 1931, and 1944.[87]

Many African traders were also unsympathetic to Indian hawkers for the preferential treatment afforded them, and also because Indian hawkers had protested against Africans' use of the market lavatory, another indicator that casteist anti-Dalit ideology may have added ballast to anti-African racism.[88]

While temple building followed the spatial interconnections that Indian market gardeners made, mosques with more prosperous mercantile beneficiaries located near sites of commerce and residence. The Grey Street Mosque complex led a confident merchant class to invest in property, trade from Victorian arcades, and renovate art deco facades, much to the consternation of city hall. The city tried to contain Indian presence in central Durban in designated barracks and through racial restrictions on land titles and leases through the Land Alienation Ordinance of 1922, and it withdrew the municipal franchise from Indians in 1925, but it was slow to note that subaltern Indians had begun to root themselves in Durban's peripheries.[89]

This subaltern history of space-making is all the more important because it was surrounded by official antipathy. The official Indian question of the 1920s jostled between encouraging repatriation and attempting segregation. At first, the state focused on induced voluntary repatriation because compulsory repatriation required both finance and the cooperation of the government of India.[90] Following the Round Table Conference in Cape Town, with representation from the government of India, the Cape Town Agreement charged the state with supporting "standards of living" for permanently settled Indians, while those who could not conform to "western standards of living" would face "assisted emigration" back to India or to other countries in which such "standards of living" were not a norm.[91] "Assisted emigration" presumed the biopolitical differentiation of "standards of living" in settler colonies where the state expected "Western" norms, as opposed to places still controlled by the Colonial Office, where it did not.

Indian organizations did not respond with one voice. The South African Indian Congress accepted repatriation, but the Natal Indian Vigilance Association and the South African Indian Federation protested vehemently, the latter distributing pamphlets in Tamil.[92] Rumors circulated about ships with false bottoms disgorging hapless return migrants into the Indian Ocean, about people landing in India only to be dispatched elsewhere, about repatriation to other colonies altogether, and about people being forced by Brahmans in their home villages to submit to expensive purifying rites for crossing the "dark waters."[93] By the Second Round Table Conference of 1932, official discourse had shifted from voluntary repatriation to segregation, as representatives of the Union Government realized that 80 percent of Indians were South African born and unlikely to "return."[94] Something else had changed between the 1910s and 1930s. A window of opportunity emerged when M. K. Gandhi persuaded Jan Smuts to negotiate on "Indo-European relations," but this window closed as Smuts moved to the Imperial War Cabinet and Gandhi faced intensified critique from indentured Indians.[95]

By the 1930s diasporic Indians were also no longer necessary to the swadeshi cause in India. Many Indian elites saw the "colonial-born" Indian through discourses of degeneration in the tropics, as a figure so altered by colonialism as to be destined to remain in the "tropical colonies" to which it had acculturated.[96] The report of the "Independent Commission" on Indians repatriated from South Africa, written by Bhawani Dayal Sannyasi and Banarsidas Chaturvedi and published in 1931, drew authority from various figures, including an astonishing extract written by Gandhi in 1926 on returned emigrants to Calcutta:

> The fact that the majority of these men are Colonial born aggravates their misery. The reader will not appreciate the full meaning of being "Colonial born." These men are neither Indian nor Colonial. They have no Indian culture in the foreign lands they go to, save what they pick up from their uncultured half-dis-Indianised parents. They are not Colonial in that they are debarred access to the Colonial, i.e. Western culture. . . . Here they are social lepers, not even knowing the language of the people. . . . The tropical Colonies must be glad to have them in preference to raw recruits who have to be initiated.[97]

Gandhi's antipathy to indentured laborers stemmed from his failure to draw them under his tutelage in the quest for rights through empire.[98] Indeed, on his return to India from South Africa, he threw his ideological weight into the cause of an Indian nationalism centered on the motherland. This abrogation of Indian working-class diasporas came just as indentured migrants were becoming "Indians" in racial and quotidian terms, well before their counterparts in colonial Bihar or Madras, but with the capacity for antiracist critique.[99] John Kelly and Martha Kaplan locate these dynamics in "the didactic public culture of the Indian National Congress," within which "indenture colonies moved from a cause for intervention, uplift, and rescue to a tragic political problem" centered on the abjection of the returned colonial-born Indian.[100] Indian nationalism's fixation with "sons of the soil" was perhaps an artifact of the early twentieth-century twilight of empire.[101] But what of the diasporas dispossessed again by this eugenic nationalism? How might we attend to their ways of remaking selves and environs through the transformative possibilities of the *kala pani* ("dark waters"), as Sheik asks?[102]

Writing on the Tamil country of South India that most subaltern Indians came from, Anand Pandian argues that the cultivation of "an agrarian civility" drew on late nineteenth-century colonial histories of moral and environmental "improvement" as well as older Tamil conceptions of cultivation (*pàṇpádu*) of soil (*màṇ*) and mind/heart (*màṇàsu*).[103] This elemental sensibility, recast in the eugenic crisis of empire, might be the precise articulation through which former indentured Indians, principally of Tamil origin, could affirm a mutual cultivation of self and of the interstitial lands they so carefully farmed, inhabited, sacralized, and settled as if indefinitely. This ingenious spatial praxis remains uncommented on because it leaves a trace in bodies and landscapes, not in the archival record.

Consider, in this light, that Gandhi sought to save his newspaper *Indian Opinion* from financial ruin by moving to a farm in Inanda on Durban's northern periphery, where settler-workers at Phoenix Settlement built wood-and-iron homes in exchange for a modest salary.[104] As we have seen, wood-and-iron construction indexed notions of auto-construction and self-making that served Gandhi's emerging ideology well. However, rather than simply disseminating his "experiments with truth," might Gandhi have been educated by the slow and steady praxis of ex-indentured market gardeners around him? Perhaps they were the inspiration for Gandhi to say that "Phoenix is intended to be a nursery for producing the right men and right Indians."[105] To put it differently, was Phoenix a market garden?[106]

Crucially, this ethic of cultivation became the basis of a dispersed geography of communal welfare, a mimetic form of Victorian progressivism committed to Indian political, economic, and moral improvement, sometimes with tacit support for segregation. As Indians came to being as a corporate group committed to their communal welfare, affluent sections provided the funds, and quite rapidly a host of organizations emerged, including the Arya Vavuk Sabha (1914), St. Aidan's Hospital (1915), the Parsee Rustomjee Home (1920, following the 1918 influenza epidemic), the Aryan Benevolent Home (1921), the Durban Indian Child Welfare Society (1927), Sastri College (1929), the R. K. Khan Hospital and Dispensary Trust and its satellite clinics (1930s), the Indian Women's Reading and Educational Circle (1935), the Indian Women's League (1938, formed by the radical doctor Kesaveloo Goonarathnum Naidoo, known as Dr. Goonam), the Natal Indian Blind Society (1945), and the Indian Social Service Committee, focused on the sanita-

FIGURE 2.2 Merebank market, Nataraj Shopping Centre, 2007. © Sharad Chari.

tion and housing conditions of poor Indians.[107] This was nothing less than a deepening landscape of Indian progressivism.

Despite the dramatic decline of an Indian peasantry in and around Durban, several households continued to farm the land. A 1940 survey shows "Indians farmed 2,326 acres in Clairwood, Springfield, Mayville, Sea Cow Lake, Riversdale, Umhlatazana and Bayhead on land leased or bought from private landowners, the South African Railways and the DCC [Durban City Corporation]."[108] As late as 1949, at the onset of apartheid, this class provided 75 percent of Durban's vegetable produce.[109] But focusing on a dying peasantry misses the bigger story. The Indian progressive middle class had accomplished the making of a far-reaching infrastructure committed to the social reproduction of Durban Indians. Artifacts of this process are everywhere to be seen, including in the small covered market at the heart of Merebank's Nataraj Shopping Centre, a prosaic monument to subaltern space-making (figure 2.2).

In the context of deepening segregation and apartheid, and in its aftermath today, this contradictory Indian commons remains a space of labor, livelihood, habitation, and association for Durban Indians across ethnicity, gender, and class. Their memories literally settle into this landscape because of a largely forgotten subaltern production of space.

However, settlement in a landscape of multiple dispossessions is fraught with contradiction. For this reason we cross the road from Merebank to Wentworth, and to histories of perennial movement and dispossession.

Permanently Unsettled: Colouredness as Irreconcilable Loss

This account of subaltern Indian settlement finds no parallel with respect to working-class Colouredness in Durban. For the latter, there is no convergent narrative of settlement, no iconic event like indenture, no culturally marked means to mark Coloured pasts, and no archive to research familial gene-alogies. These negations condense in a structure of feeling in Wentworth as a bittersweet *kasie*, a township suffused with singular beauty and suffering.

This is partly a question of constituency: a small population of limited political and economic significance to Durban or Natal.[110] "Durban Coloureds" encapsulate an incredible diversity of trajectories that evade summary except in the general language of tenancy, disfranchisement, forced removal, or migrant labor, none of which hinge on Coloured cultural competence. As Grant Farred puts it, Coloured affiliation is legible only in Southern Africa, but national belonging and racial mixture are not easy to affirm together in post-apartheid times, and this ambivalence pervades routine talk about not belonging then and now.[111] The limited evidentiary means by which Coloureds can authenticate their pasts limit the ways in which they might, in contrast to Indians, affirm ethno-racial and spatial difference. I argue that without a communal sense of security with respect to land, housing, or work, Went-worth's working-class Coloureds conceive of their pasts in widely divergent terms, through claims to the loss of land, ethnicity, or particular forms of life, and that in doing so, they encounter the painful repression of submerged histories of slavery and of gendered forced labor that continues to haunt the present.

First, let us consider a few instances in which people have carefully col-lected material to make claims on landscapes of the past. When we met, the late Morris Fynn had retired from many years as a politician, after which he had left Wentworth to run a school in a shack settlement south of Durban. I sat next to this pensioner, surrounded by maps, photocopied documents, and newspaper clippings, each encased in plastic and filed in a dedicated briefcase.

As he narrated his complex story of transition from the agrarian South Coast of Natal to Durban in the era of segregation, Morris stressed his

deep roots in what he considers his ancestral lands. He gestured to photocopied documents on his famous ancestor, Henry Francis Fynn, an early
nineteenth-century English adventurer who negotiated with multiple sov-
ereignties between the last years of King Shaka, whose consolidation of the
Zulu Kingdom prompted shock waves of conquest and interethnic warfare
in the Mfecane of 1815–40, and the early years of British annexation of Natal
after 1843 which saw the making of "tribal" authority through the Shepstone
System.[112] In this turbulent period, the ancestral Fynn received a chieftaincy
and nine wives from the royal family of Shaka, as well as a land grant from the
British Crown. Fearing war with Shaka's successor, Dingane, H. F. Fynn left
for Cape Town, entrusting these titles to his brother Frank's wife, Ma Vund-
lase, who has a prominent place in his descendant's remembrance of things
past. Fynn returned to Natal as magistrate, offering his knowledge of Nguni
custom to British indirect rule, and he retired on the Bluff, next to today's
Wentworth, apparently in sight of but not possession of his lands. This is how
Morris concludes the myth of his colorful ancestor.

Approximately 150 years later, in 1995, Morris was chosen as "incumbent
chief" by a group of Coloured Fynn descendants, and he has since fought for
recognition as heir to the land grant and chieftaincy, against a Zulu-exclusive
notion of chieftaincy in today's KwaZulu-Natal.[113] He has painstakingly collected evidence to back up his historical claims. As we spoke, he drew out
carefully preserved papers and extracts from books, pointing to photographs
of his uncle, Chief Colin Fynn, and of the lineage leading to him. There is a
mythic quality to Morris's grasping toward a receding past of entanglement,
an allegory of evasive attachment to territory in a century increasingly committed to racial segregation, in which Coloureds were meant to become a
distinct racial group that could not have a share in African custom.

When I interrupted him while he was telling me about his childhood in
Umtulumi to ask if his family were isiZulu speakers, he swiftly refused the
articulation of Zulu nationalism to chieftaincy, recasting the notion of "tribe"
in broader terms. "It was a tribe, just like the Fynns are a tribe. The whole
world is telling us now that Morris Fynn wants to be a Zulu chief. I don't
want to be a Zulu chief; I want to be a Fynn chief!" Denied a university education, he could not "dig into the archives" on these issues earlier in his life.
The importance of archival authority in the making of historical knowledge
was not lost on this pensioner with his carefully maintained collection of
documents.

Looking out at the landscape around us, he insisted that the rural coast-
line south of Durban was fundamentally diverse. When I asked whether

people who would be classified as "Coloured" emerged from histories of sub-sistence farming and migrant labor in the mines, much like other Africans, he responded sharply: "Let me say that at that time there was no such thing as Coloured or Native. We were all natives of the country." He continued in this revisionist vein: "History books" have it that "the Fynns were lawless people" in possession of "illegal arms" while in fact they were "chiefs [who] had to mo-bilize people and [who] wanted to drive the British out of the South Coast. According to history, we were gun smuggling. No, we were preparing a war with the British." The tense change is key in his tunneling through the past.

As we spoke, Morris fished out various things from his portable archive, including maps and documents attesting to his right to land and chieftaincy, and a newspaper clipping in which he dons traditional garb as the incumbent Fynn chief. He once confronted the Zulu chief in the area that he claims is his ancestral right and demanded to see this competitor's historical evidence to weigh it against his own. He even phoned the doyen of Zulu social history, the late professor Jeff Guy of the University of KwaZulu-Natal, to ask him to authenticate his claim, to which Guy politely apologized that this was a matter not of history but of politics.

Another lady, whom I call Louise, like Morris, supplemented her con-versation with me with a carefully preserved personal archive of documen-tary evidence, including her land title and photocopied chapters from books on the mixed Griqua people who trace their migrations to the early Cape Colony. Louise had made an unsuccessful claim on her ancestral property as a direct descendant of Adam Kok, founder of the town of Kokstad. Like many people who identify as Griqua, Louise placed her life in a communal narrative of dispossession in the Orange Free State in the 1850s, followed by a great trek across the Drakensberg, the reconstitution of the short-lived polity of East Griqualand, alienation of land after Adam Kok's death in 1875, and the failed rebellions in the last decades of the nineteenth century.[114]

Despite her evident interest in Griqua history, Louise did not make much of her status as an indigene. Her main concern was to show how colonial-era dispossession remains difficult to redress. As in other cases, like the Dunn clan's land claims case on Durban's North Coast, documentary authority had been disqualified by the cutoff date for land restitution claims, 1913, the in-augural year of the Land Acts that legalized mass African dispossession.[115] Included in Louise's personal archive was the polite official letter from the Land Claims Court that affirmed her history but refused her inheritance on the basis of the 1913 cutoff. To add insult to injury, Louise also showed me an advertisement for a farm called Die Kroon that invites tourists to experience a real Afrikaans outdoor experience on what she considers her ancestral property.

Most people in today's Wentworth do not have similar means to claim land. Dispossessed before 1913, if they had land at all, working-class people who were later classified as Coloureds in places like Wentworth see landed attachment and related notions of ethnic belonging as never having been theirs to lose. What might dispossession mean to them?

When I asked most residents about their origins, I was told wildly divergent spatial stories. A mother and daughter from Kokstad also claimed descent from Adam Kok. I had first spoken to Jane, the daughter, to record her key role in a militant strike in 2000. When Jane explained, "Adam Kok is my mother's great-great-grandfather. . . . He was a Griqua . . . something like a Bushman," her mother refused the pejorative term: "Not really!" to which the daughter countered, "I say *something* like a Bushman. But a Griqua were pure race, unlike us today, who are Coloured, Indian, Black, White. I could say they were the purest Coloured people, so to speak." Ambiguities about Griqua and Coloured affiliation emerge from multiple changes in the legal categories of race over the twentieth century that have left people with more questions than answers about how to talk about the past.

While some Wentworth memories settle in Kokstad and other borderlands of today's KwaZulu-Natal and Eastern Cape, others focus on the center of Durban's Casbah. A woman whom I call Margaret owns her own home and a fleet of taxis and sits on the community policing forum. I realized while interviewing her that she had to fend for herself from a very early age, when her mother's household was "split down the middle." Margaret's sister, mother, and grandmother were classified as white, while she and her brother were classified as Coloured and had to live separately. She began our conversation by relating her interview with an uncle in her own quest to understand how segregation had divided her family ever since British efforts at segregation after a smallpox epidemic in the late 1880s. Against the backdrop of suffering, deepening through the Great Depression, Margaret highlights the determination of her "very proud family heritage," mixed and yet connected to the putatively white city. On one side, her great-grandparents "were descendants from the island of St Helena," of British origins. When they came to Durban, they "lived on Lorne Street in town, where everybody lived." When their family was being torn apart, her white, French-speaking mother from Mauritius had divorced her father and had lived as "European" in Greyville, a mixed area that was later cleared of Indians and Coloureds, including her and her brother.

Margaret signals a history in chords, of Black interconnections with white Durbanites. The loss of whiteness is important for those, like her, who saw friends and family pass into a world of privilege. Coloureds circulate jokes and stories about encounters with those who passed, fleeting exchanges of glances with "play whites" through restaurant windows, and the decision to let them be. The deeper issue for Margaret concerns responsibility for segregation, and the story from her uncle allows her, effectively, to link racial biopolitics to the loss of conviviality. Margaret also conveys a sense of movement, of constant transformations in location and in senses of self. In this maelstrom she has cultivated a persona as a fiercely independent woman, capable of controlling a fleet as a leading township businesswoman and power broker.

Yet another narrative comes from a man with strong connections to neither the rural hinterland nor the city but the ocean. When we met, Hector Henry was a very colorful and insightful pensioner. In addition to having been, like Morris, a whaler and apartheid-era local politician, Henry boasted of being the first person to bring the white supremacist National Party *into* Wentworth in the first democratic elections of 1994. When I asked about his familial past, he said he was the "third generation of a Mauritian family." This was the tip of the iceberg.

Hector related that his grandparents were in "that convoy that landed at King's Rest station." I asked if they were the famous Zanzibaris who settled in King's Rest on the Bluff until it was zoned white.[116] He balked at the term: "Zanzibaris! It's a mixed concept. The Zanzibaris hail from the Muslims who *trekked* up to the top of the hill there from the docks and founded a settlement. . . . There might have been one or two Zanzibaris on the same ship with them, but most of them were the Blacks who lived there, who became the Zanzibaris of King's Rest." Despite the slips between Muslim, Black, and Zanzibari, Hector's view is close to what historians make of this event, in which a ship of emancipated slaves, probably a minority from Zanzibar, docked on the southern side of Durban harbor and formed a Muslim community on the bluffs above, in an area known as King's Rest. Their descendants were later forcibly moved to the shacks of Happy Valley in Wentworth. Threatened with removal once again under apartheid, they petitioned to be moved as "Asiatics" to the new Indian township of Chatsworth for the right to practice Islam alongside their brethren. But not everyone followed this trajectory.

From the Bluff, his "granny and them . . . *trekked* to Clairwood" and "lived on the riverbank there, and eventually they moved over onto Sirdar Road with other Muslim families." Some got into trading, "one or two of them did sheep or goat farming," and his grandparents became tailors. "There was a lot of fruit trees, and they were dealing and selling off fruit," and they managed to own a bit of land until they were dispossessed in the building of the Southern Freeway. Hector's narrative moves through the space of the Indian commons, with its fruit trees and multiple livelihoods. As with a lot of working-class South Africans, there are multiple trajectories of forced movement here, from a slave ship to a Zanzibari neighborhood to the contradictory Indian commons to a Coloured township. There is no sense that Hector's memories settle in any of these places, but rather they remain in movement.

Affirming his Mauritian, Muslim, Black African, Irish, and Zanzibari ancestry, Hector said, "I would grade myself as an indigenous plant." But what does "indigenous" mean if tethered to movement and mixture, not land and autochthony? Henry became a seaman like his father. He traveled the world, and his oceanic career confirmed his polyglot sense of self and place. His invocation of the *trek* is a form of multidirectional memory that references the Afrikaner *trek*, stripping it of its sense of mobile colonization. Instead, he offers a narrative of constant movement, insecurity, poverty, and mixture, perhaps not unlike poor Afrikaners. Hector offered an intuition that all selves and situations are actually fluid, polyglot, and precarious. To name himself the "indigene" is subversive, even hopeful.

One person who really struggled with these questions and lived a similar hope was the late Skido Joseph. Skido was a charismatic man, full of heart, as anyone who knew him would attest. He said to me, "My mother was originally from Mayville; my father was from Overport; my mother's people were from the Basotho tribe; my granny married my grandfather, who had an Irish background; my father's father was an Indian. We've got a *helluva* potpourri or *masala*! That's what I've got in my veins. So I'm a true African!" Skido's narrative skims through areas like Mayville and Overport associated with Durban Indians, while slipping across places and identities, resisting the stickiness of racial classification. His celebration of an Irish-Indian-Basotho Africanity, *not Colouredness*, remains defiant and vital.

Settlements of memory across Wentworth and Merebank appear discrete, and sometimes converge in illuminating ways. Consider Adam's Shop, a landmark at the bottom of Austerville Drive in Coloured Wentworth run by a family considered by its neighbors as Indian. The shop is run by the family of Ismail Adam, eighty-three years old when we spoke. Adam's father was from India, but his mother was from Kokstad. "She was Coloured, then she was married to *this* Indian and came *this* side." Adam knew nothing about his father's family. "Nothing, nothing. No connections. We were not introduced." Adam's father was a hawker in the municipal barracks in Ladysmith, which witnessed a process of subaltern space-making similar to that which I have described in Durban, at a more modest scale. Adam's recollections settle in a Muslim space of circulation in early twentieth-century South Africa that made some room for some Indian men to marry Coloured women while retaining a place in Muslim public life.

Adam's memories strike chords with those his life was supposed to be segregated from. What makes his narrative like those of other Indian Muslims is his work history in a dispersed geography of Indian shopkeeping across the country, including near Kruger National Park. When he moved to Durban, he accessed residence and work through Indian Muslim networks rather than through his wife's Coloured family, which slips out of view in his account. Ironically, this Indian-identified family settled in the Indian-Coloured borderlands of Sydenham and had spent decades, since the mid-1960s, working in Coloured Wentworth. As one son said, "We sleep in an Indian area but have spent every day, morning till late in the night, in Wentworth . . . Sunday to Sunday, service to the community from half past five to half past nine." What is striking is that "community" for this business family meant Wentworth.

Adam's hybrid family history weaves through the ways in which Wentworth Coloureds diverge from Merebank Indians. I have suggested that when Coloureds had access to land and petty farming, it was in the areas of the South Coast where dispossession had taken place since the colonial period and had accelerated in the process of making the Transkei a nominally independent "homeland" under apartheid legislation that culminated in the Bantu Homelands Citizenship Act of 1970 and Bantu Homelands Constitution Act of 1971. By 1981, four homelands were declared fully independent, and by 1984, ten were declared self-governing. From the perspective of liberation movement thinkers, this sham independence and self-government was meant to enshrine the denial of African claims to the franchise in the rest of white South Africa. However, many mixed-race people were also dispossessed through this process of homeland formation. Most Coloureds faced dispossession prior to arriving in peri-Durban, and few have memories of it. In marked contrast, Indian trajectories kept open the possibility of peasant-worker livelihoods in the urban periphery as a basis of familial diversification into industrial employment, with some security of residence. Petty accumulation allowed Indians to stake place and identity in ways effectively denied to Coloureds.

The boundary-crossing trajectory of Adam's family clarifies the distinctiveness of Wentworth's working-class Coloured trajectories. Reliant on a dominant male labor regime of migrant industrial artisanship, and on impermanent tenancies across the city, they have had no recourse to a stable history of space-making and few possibilities for creating a substantial petty bourgeoise class invested in communal settlement. Their lot has been one of constant change and movement in senses of self and belonging. Morris and Louise are a minority in their attempts to claim land and personhood, and the frustrations in these claims followed Fynn to his grave.

Several people have tried to affirm life in Wentworth as a vibrant township, a place of mixture, creativity, suffering, and, as we shall see, militancy. However, several problems present themselves to Wentworth's residents. First, unlike the vibrant neighborhoods that were destroyed by apartheid, a vibrant place that is a *product* of apartheid's forced removals remains difficult if not impossible to affirm. Second, Colouredness as a problem space is haunted by a repression of deeper histories of slavery, unfree labor, and loss of indigeneity, wrapped into complex forms of racism and misogyny encoded in the racial discourse of Colouredness. Distanced from middle-class and Muslim Coloured urbanity in Cape Town, working-class Colouredness as it concentrates in Wentworth is a complex web of silences and partial tales. I turn next to a subaltern narration of this history that begins in a heroic mode but quickly reveals something more enduring about working-class Colouredness in Durban.

* * *

When I met the late Derrick McBride, or Mr. McBride, as he was respectfully called, he was running a *spaza* shop, or convenience store, adjoining his home, and, more important, he was a community activist and neighborhood critic living in a perpetual state of defiance. Over the years we met, he continued to find new issues to engage his irascible intelligence. Ostensibly narrating his life story to me, he begins 140 years before the arrival of Jan van Riebeeck, with an imagined "first contact with the aboriginals of this country, the Khoisan," and colonial settlers. With this flourish he quickly shows how impossible it is to find origins in a historical geography of mixture. "The first child of mixed descent must have died, and his children must have died, and his grandchildren must have died," he says ruefully. The first protagonist in his account is "a person much maligned in South African history books, Herrie die Strandloper . . . the first freedom fighter." Mischaracterized as a stock thief, "he only went to fetch what was taken from him." And McBride adds with a little twist that indexes his own imprisonment in South Africa's notorious island prison, "He was the only person that ever escaped from Robben Island and came to tell the tale." When the freedom fighter and colonizer meet in this parable, Herrie die Strandloper confronts van Riebeeck directly: "You know, how can I go to Holland and put up a fort, and [he raises his voice dramatically] *you come here*! You know, you must *voetsek* [get lost]!" In hushed tones, the orator adds, "And this was the first case of political murder in South Africa."

What is brilliant about this parable is that it begins with colonial violence, political murder, and the denial of mixture as the origin narrative of both Colouredness and South Africanness. McBride continues with an elaborate account of "importation of slaves from Asia, from the East Coast of Africa, from slave vessels that were captured," of interaction between various subject peoples, and of the use of race to discipline and exploit. He then refers to a paper he had written titled "Coloured Landlessness," in response to a landmark land claim made by the Richtersveld community in the Northern Cape to reclaim land lost in the colonial era.

"Coloured Landlessness" is a remarkable pastiche of past and present, a fragment of popular historiography like Juggernath's "Diary," but with quite different insights. The piece begins with a call to "visit the factors that have contributed to this landlessness with unflinching candour and determination to rectify this inequality of the past." This means reckoning with the notion that Coloureds are descendants of slaves. Abolition of slavery turned slaves into apprentices, which mean that "a 60-year-old slave who had been tramping grapes for over 50 years had now to be taught for three to five years how to tramp grapes." In other words, "for Coloured people, freedom always meant further enslavement," and "freed slaves were hundred percent landless." Telescoping into the present in Wentworth, he writes, "Ex-slaves were seasonal workers. . . . The ex-slaves had to pay for shelter and other necessities of life for one year from only a few months' pay, like Engen construction workers of today."

"Coloured Landlessness" is an activist text built on resistance and marronage: "There is nothing that an oppressor can propose that the oppressed cannot dispose of. Some escaped, worked and earned money and freed some of their relatives." What happened to these "freed slaves"? Those "who managed to free themselves of debt invariably worked in the building industry and other industries connected with agriculture, shipping and the sea." Seasonal employment meant "long periods of unemployment and poverty" and a continuing inability to acquire assets or attain security of tenure.

Then the account shifts to Natal, to the making of a condition in which "very few Coloureds owned any fixed property"; they were more often tenants. As the narrative focuses on Durban, it turns to complex histories of insecure jobs, inadequate land, and impermanent housing that became the mainstay of working-class Coloured life. At first, legal Coloured residential property in Durban was confined to Melbourne Flats and Sparks Estate; then, in 1960, Red Hill and Greenwood Park became Coloured residential areas, but the exorbitant prices meant that Durban's Coloured working class could not afford them. The Coloured Group Area in Wentworth allowed homeownership of former military barracks that were sixty years old, again at exorbitant prices. Colouredness in Wentworth therefore retains the legacy of slavery in a constant state of insecurity that does not lead to the acquisition of property except when it is decrepit.

McBride's analysis is a claim about Colouredness in Wentworth as a historically produced form of insecurity that does not lead to either property or propriety. His identification across Khoisan, slave, worker, and tenant is a practice of "multidirectional memory," of lateral moves when "Coloured history" is as impossible to retrieve as land that was never owned, displacement that could not be seen as dispossession. His use of the mythic mode turns into a critique of all settled pasts. The urban periphery was never his, and he is completely unsentimental about it. Implicit in this deep rootlessness born of enslavement is an affirmation of the subject of negation that compelled him to become an anti-apartheid militant (see chapter 9). What is clear is that restitution through "land" alone will never be enough. Nothing except complete freedom will do. This is what Jacques Rancière calls the demand for the "share of the shareless" (*la part du sans part*) from an old retired militant.[117]

McBride's analysis echoes Patric Tariq Mellet's powerful revision of South African history as a series of processes of "de-Africanization," including the coercive assimilation of the San and the Khoe into "Coloured" identity and the coercive de-Africanization of more than 245 streams of people into "Coloureds" and "Natives" in 1911; Mellet calls the effect nothing short of "cultural genocide," but what is striking is that, like McBride's, his militant refusal of Colouredness prompts a fundamental rethinking of South African decolonization.[118]

In a text of great insight, Gabeba Baderoon argues that almost two centuries of slaveholding in the Cape are bound to have lasting effects on South African social life, and yet the legacy of slavery is at best narrowly considered as pertinent to the history of the Cape Colony.[119] Building on Pumla Dineo Gqola's foundational work on slave memory in South Africa, Baderoon argues there has been very little reflection until recently on what remains of the subjection, violence, and humiliation of more than sixty thousand enslaved people, of their domination through a pass system and through forced prostitution and sexual violence against female slaves.[120] The historiographies of slavery, Islam, and race have rendered slavery "a 'Malay' or, at most, a

'Coloured' issue . . . exceptional to broader South African history," a "minoritisation" of slavery exacerbated by apartheid's segregated order of things; in response, Baderoon works with a range of cultural, aesthetic, and literary artifacts to show how slavery fundamentally reshaped South Africa, not least in its pervasive and ongoing gender-based violence.[121]

Subaltern oceanic histories are at the heart of this conundrum. As Baderoon argues, "The fact that two-thirds of the enslaved people at the Cape came from Asia, have made slavery subject to the problem of exceptionalism, in the sense that South Africa's experience of slavery appears to be an Asian rather than an African phenomenon. . . . As a result, it has been hard to show that slavery is an integral and fundamental part of the country's history."[122] Inadvertently, the intensity of the cultural archive that Paul Gilroy names in *The Black Atlantic* makes this submergence of histories of Indian Ocean slavery and forced labor particularly prescient in Durban, whose articulations to the Indian Ocean remain palpable, yet difficult to express.

Gendered sexual violence is at the heart of the forgetting of slavery, intertwined as it has been in rendering "black women's bodies the bearers of the marks of sexual violence during slavery, making them responsible for their own violation and rendering invisible the *systemic sexual violence of slavery*"; the inability by descendants of the enslaved to attend to this gendered historical trauma has left powerful traces in "South African popular language . . . strewn with oaths and vulgar phrases based on derogatory terms for black women's bodies," markedly with respect to Coloured girls and women.[123] Baderoon's powerful argument allows us to read McBride's "Coloured dispossession" through the racial/sexual violence at the heart of slavery and its aftermath. Gqola's and Baderoon's Black feminism attends to the ways in which Black women's praxis becomes the medium and the message, in a painful unraveling of intimate wounds that call an end to a long history of racialized and sexualized dispossession.

Conclusion: Ruins of Memory, Remains of Settlement

Sethe: "It's so hard for me to believe in [time]. Some things go. Pass on. Some things just stay. I used to think it was my rememory. . . . But it's not. Places, places are still there. If a house burns down, it's gone, but the place—the picture of it—stays, and not just in my rememory, but out there, in the world."
Denver: "If it's still there, waiting, that must mean that nothing ever dies."
Sethe: "Nothing ever does."
—TONI MORRISON, *Beloved*

Toni Morrison's Sethe is the slave woman who liberates herself while yearning to break with the past decisively so that her reproductive labor might enable new forms of life.[124] Denver, her daughter, is the part of her who walks out into the street affirming this futurity boldly and relentlessly. Their conversation, also a debt relation between slave mother and free daughter, is about pasts that cannot die fast enough while their legacies are "out there, in the world."

Settlements of memory in Merebank and Wentworth point to debts that remain beyond the mythic restitution of land or autochthony. These debts can never be entirely settled. I have sought to evoke precise vectors of loss as retrospective claims on the future. But there is more to rememory, as Sethe calls it, than getting the past right. Rememory sits with lingering debts, of uncompensated dispossession or unrequited attachment. What Denver yearns for, Sethe pulls back into the heavy presence of the past. Through this dialectic, social memory carries an insurgent demand as people bear unpaid debts of dispossession and racialized belonging literally on their person, at once weighed down and bearing an openness to an actual future. These debts are deeply gendered, transferred intergenerationally in conceptions of damaged personhood and in demands for a just future in which, as Denver hopes, some things can die.

In this light, the contrast between settlements of memory from Merebank Indians and Wentworth Coloureds is striking. The latter are not marked by their debts, in contrast to the descendants of indentured Indians. Yet a shiftless, nomadic proletarianism sticks to these working-class Coloureds through their lives as seafarers, farmworkers, impermanent industrial artisans, and insecure tenants. McBride's insight is that the long afterlife of slavery links these seemingly disparate trajectories as they converge through landlessness and insecurity of work and housing. The injuries, as he sees it, are pervasive and difficult to redress, except through revolutionary change.

Consider in sharp contrast the many official and popular commemorations in 2010 of the 150th anniversary of the arrival of the first Indian indentured laborers, remembered as the "1860 Settlers," without comment on the implicit citation of the British "1820 Settlers," let alone what it might mean to mark indentured laborers in this way; and consider that these commemorations repeat, as they did at the 160th anniversary in 2020. Circulating through these events was a discourse of communal survival and persistence. One may be forgiven on these occasions for thinking that indentured labor was a test of fire to prove the mettle of "Indian community." At the all-too-plausible limits of kitsch in 2010, there were plans for a state-sponsored wax museum in former cane fields showing Indians in their indentured habitat. Forgeries of memory have their own protracted half-life.

Against the twin dangers of nihilism and eternalism, I have sought to think relationally with "settlements of memory" from Wentworth and Merebank. Early in the century, between white supremacy, African exclusion, and anti-colonial nationalism in India, working-class diasporic Indians could draw on Tamil traditions to forge the spatial basis of subaltern Indian life in common. On this subaltern geography, a tradition of Indian progressivism could invest in communal welfare, livelihood, and belonging, as it still does. Consequently, Indians in Merebank, as elsewhere in Durban, can continue to maintain a sense of ethno-racial mutuality in the remains of this settled landscape, its banal built forms and habitual routines, its fruit trees, prayer calls, and strains of music. I have provocatively called this an Indian commons.

However, an Indian commons is a contradiction in terms, a forgery in Cedric Robinson's sense, as it presumes that life-in-common can be separable in space and time from dispossession that happens to other people, elsewhere. From the perspective of Colouredness in Wentworth, such consolations do not work, and the failure of land claims highlights the limits of a juridical approach to the authentication of historical and spatial belonging. Without similar means to valorize attachment to self and place, Coloured imaginations remain vagabond, unruly, and ceaselessly imaginative. Read in dialectical relation to forms of Indian subaltern attachment in hostile times, Coloured settlements of memory point to a revolutionary critique of racial space beyond claims to autochthony or land. These unsettled and unsettling memories point to gendered yearnings for a different, planetary life in common.

As Morrison's Sethe reminds us, "places are still there . . . nothing ever dies." Entangled with this tapestry of memory are traces in the land, obstinate remains of the past. During my years of research, the airport adjacent to Merebank was abandoned in favor of a new airport built on plantation lands north of Durban in time for the 2010 World Cup. Aerial maps of the old airport show that layers of other land uses persist alongside those of capital that would fundamentally alter this landscape. In the lie of the land, we might still encounter farmers and laborers whose lives have been disqualified but not obliterated. A living trace of early twentieth-century peasant-workers persists in a handful of farmers who continued to farm next to what was the airport runway during the years of my fieldwork, an area subsequently slated to be dug out in a massive planned expansion of the Port of Durban. A principle survives this conjuncture: settlements of memory are never innocent of the legacies of dispossession that surround them.

Ruinous Foundations of
Progressive Segregation, 1920s–1950s

The development of the forces of production shattered the wish symbols of the previous century, even before the monuments representing them had collapsed. In the nineteenth century, this development worked to emancipate the forms of construction from art.... A start is made with architecture as engineered construction. Then comes the reproduction of nature as photography. The creation of fantasy prepares to become practical as commercial art. Literature submits to montage in the feuilleton. All these products are on the point of entering the market as commodities. But they linger on the threshold. From this epoch derive the arcades and *intérieurs*, the exhibition halls and panoramas. They are residues of a dream world.... Every epoch, in fact, not only dreams the one to follow but, in dreaming, precipitates its awakening. It bears its end within itself and unfolds it—as Hegel already noticed—by cunning. With the destabilizing of the market economy, we begin to recognize the monuments of the bourgeoisie as ruins even before they have crumbled.
—WALTER BENJAMIN, "Paris, the Capital of the Nineteenth Century," 1938

Infrastructure Dreams, 1923–1952

Something took durable form in the decades between the Urban Areas Act of 1923 and the construction of apartheid's racial townships in 1952: the infrastructural foundations of an industrial landscape forged in the ruins of

FIGURE 3.1 *Congella Reclamation*, circa 1920s–1930s. © Local History Museum, Durban.

Durban's rural-urban *black belt*. This chapter "lingers on the threshold" of the capitalist transformation of space at a moment of deepening segregation. Coeval with this event, we might see Benjamin in Paris on the wrecked shores of Vichy France. Might his thought have resonated more widely, if only it were possible?[1]

With this proximal Benjamin, we might read the photographs that bookend this chapter, figures 3. 1 and 3.3, as dialectical wish images of capitalist infrastructure that foretell eventual obsolescence. As wish images, these photographs are speculative: they splay the veins of infrastructure in the service of critique. While Benjamin may not have seen forced obsolescence as also central to state racism, he took his own life in the face of state racism for which he was an abstract enemy. This "Durban Diary" points to a Black Benjamin who never was either but who might yet help clarify the disastrous interplay of state racism and ruination, now and then.

As white supremacies ricocheted and mirrored each other at the turn of the century, drawing lessons across the globe, participants in communist internationalism and Black radicalism sought to piece together socio-spatially disconnected critiques of racial capitalism.[2] Conjuring a Black Benjamin is possible only in the sense that Cedric Robinson poses "Black Marxism" not as a supplement to a white canon but as its anterior in theory and struggle, and as a political necessity for radicalism beyond Eurocentrism.[3] This possibility was real in the first decades of the twentieth century, when racial capitalist states violently suppressed revolutionary forms of interracial solidarity like the International Workers of the World in the United States, the Industrial Workers of Africa in Johannesburg in the 1910s, and the Industrial and Commercial Workers Union which emerged from the docks of Cape Town and spread across the country in the 1920s.[4] Interracial communist solidarity had to contend with the racial discourse of official Comintern policy, which posed "the world Negro movement" as emanating from the United States, "the center of Negro culture and the crystallization of Negro protest," with Africa positioned as a "reservoir of human labor for the further development of Capitalism."[5]

A second proximal theorist reformulated his thought precisely to refuse the racial frame of the Comintern. Trinidadian Marxist C. L. R. James slowly shifted his conception of Marxist praxis, particularly during his years in the United States, from 1938 to 1956. His archivist Anna Grimshaw notes that the first shift in James's thought came in the wake of Stalin's betrayal of communist internationalism in his 1924 doctrine of "Socialism in One Country," followed by the suppression of proletarian movements across France, Germany, and Spain.[6] The second shift followed James's meeting with the exiled Leon Trotsky in 1939, when he realized their differences on "the Negro Question." Trotsky's defense of the vanguard party's relationship of tutelage with respect to insurgent Black workers was fundamentally at odds with James's interest in the cultural politics of Black radicalism, whether in cricket, calypso, Black American churches, the Cotton Club, his readings of Shakespeare, or his dramatic interpretation of the Haitian Revolution.[7]

James's intuition was that interracial and internationalist proletarian movements had prompted counterrevolution through statist planning and industrialization on both sides of the Iron Curtain. This meant that Black radicalism could not be reduced to "the Negro Question" but had implications for the fate of humanity and, at the dawn of a nuclear age, for life itself. When James joined with Raya Dunayevskaya and Grace Lee Boggs, their Johnston-Forrest Tendency build on this insight, refusing the separation of the First and Second Worlds in Cold War thought, to argue that "total planning is inseparable from permanent crisis."[8] In our post–Cold War age of periodic capitalist crisis, their generalization of Black radical critique is a necessary supplement to Benjamin's critique of ruination, as it takes us back to the ruined hopes of social engineering through industrial transformation in the photographs that frame this chapter.

Conventional historiography might consider photographs like these as drawing authority from a British tradition of fact generation for efficient administration, as Bernard Cohn famously argued of the census and the survey.[9] In Natal, as elsewhere in the world, photography of the feats of industrialization had developed a visual grammar through images of dams, highways, pipes, and other infrastructural marvels. Occasionally, this genre shows people, as in *Congella Reclamation* (figure 3.1); other photographs show habitation in the distance. Jeremy Foster notes of early twentieth-century photography from the South African Railways and Harbours that scenes from the railway carriage envisioned the *veld* as immense, emptied of people, linking older notions of exploration with bourgeois interiority and an emerging national space across an imagined "white man's country."[10] These industrial images have a similar implicit spectator, but we cannot be sure that they were convincing evidence of an industrious white nation, or what they mean when what is meant to be a progressive landscape decays and falls into disrepute.

Photographers Bernard and Hilla Becher and their students comment on the end of this photographic tradition in their "industrial typologies," matrices of nearly identical images of water towers, gas tanks, and other industrial forms; these matrices index colonial ethnology in a dialectical gesture that points to the interplay of imperial mastery and ruination. After the industrial disasters of Chernobyl and Bhopal, these neat photo matrices become graveyards of typological form, legible alongside the brutal intimacies of life in the shadows of oil refineries in the photographs by Peter McKenzie, Cedric Nunn, and Jenny Gordon in the prelude. These works return us to Benjamin on the ways in which the still life of the photograph is perfectly suited to refocusing critique on the smoldering debris of imperial power.[11]

So might we now think with a Black Benjamin in Durban, smoking Durban Poison, extending our imaginative and critical possibilities about the three decades from 1923 to 1952 as centered on the making of South Africa's racial welfare state but also of distinctively twentieth-century ruins that are impossible to avoid in the twenty-first?

What we know with certainty is that industrial infrastructure is never just *there*, obvious and inert, captured for posterity in the mute frame of photography. As we wait with James and Benjamin, this wish image forces us to "linger at the threshold" of industrialization and segregation to consider the disastrous promise of capitalist development. Braced for irony, we descend into the turbulent production of a contradictory space of industry and residence in South Durban during the three decades between the legalization of urban segregation in 1923 and the construction of racialized townships in 1952.

The central argument of this chapter is that while the state sought to bring together progressivism and segregation between the 1920s and the 1940s, it did so on the basis of minimal knowledge of ground realities. Through a series of commissions, the state kept up the pretense of enlightened hegemony while shifting registers in various ways. In its turn to the visual, and particularly to the racial zoning map that prefigured the model of the ideal apartheid city, the state did not demonstrate the certainty of its hegemonic apparatus but rather its protracted decay.

Progressive Segregation and Biopolitical Struggle, 1920s–1940s

Capital relies on labour, right! But you had intertwined with this, the practice of racism initiated by successive governments. Take 1922, the Mineworkers Strike, where they wanted to get African workers. The [white] mineworkers union conducts a strike against the Smuts-Botha regime, to actually attack this. Then, Smuts loses out, mines were closed. He even loses the election! . . . One of the things they pass immediately, in 1924, was the Industrial Conciliation Act. It was then revamped in 1937, building into it racial clauses, segregating, making sure that trade unions were divided into racial compartments, with whites in control of the trade unions. African labour unions were not allowed to form. So, what you have now was that instead of accommodating a Black worker into skilled positions in the labour market, you had them constantly closing because of pressure from white workers. There was accommodation by the ruling class always to ensure voting support from the white worker. . . . Successive governments, whether it was Smuts or Botha [complied]. So, when the Nats come to power, it becomes more pronounced. They now tighten all the gaps, so you had racism built into labour relations, residential segregation. As for accommodating Blacks into any sphere, they were to be third class. —BILLY NAIR

1925 Hertzog initiates legislation to solve the poor white problem. Let me repeat and emphasise, *to solve the poor white problem.* . . . Hertzog also brought in the Wage Act in terms of which a commission was formed to ensure that no white person received below a certain minimum wage because he or she had to maintain standards according to which whites were supposed to live in South Africa and they made four fifths of the population live below those standards unprotected by the Wage Act. —GOVAN MBEKI

The nature of influences changed greatly during the thirty years before 1954; the Coloured people became much more fully recognized as a special people with their own value and needs. —RUBY YATES, *A Garland for Ashes*

These are varied renditions of the conjuncture that I call *progressive segregation*, in which the tools of Progressivism became instruments of segregation.[12] Billy Nair and Govan Mbeki, aging militants interviewed in 2010 and 1996 respectively, look back after apartheid at the three-decade period that preceded it. For both, the mid-1920s was a turning point in South African racial capitalism in which the state harnessed the tools of liberal biopolitical government to the fate of the urban white working class. At this moment, segregation was the price, or payoff, for what former school principal Ruby Yates, reflecting from apartheid's heyday, calls Coloureds becoming "a special people." Each saw these dynamics as part of wider tectonic shifts, but how wide, exactly?

In an important study, Timothy Mitchell argues that early twentieth-century South Africa was a site of innovation to limit democratic forces within an imperial frame and that figures like Jan Smuts defined the "self" in the "self-governing state" in such a circumscribed way as to fundamentally undermine anti-colonial "self-determination" to come.[13] However, it is important to distinguish this will to undermine democratic impulses from the differentiated capacity to do so. Billy Nair's perspective troubles Mitchell's argument. This Durban militant suffered torture, imprisonment, and banning for a commitment to struggle against such a telos. Following on Nair's commitment to struggle, I offer the contradictory term *progressive segregation* for a protracted and anarchic process that sowed the seeds of more contradiction and strife.

Indeed, Nair and Mbeki agree that the specter that haunted the new Union of South Africa of 1910 as a "white man's country" was interracial working-class solidarity.[14] In response to the upsurge of Black worker militancy on the Rand in 1917–20, the state encouraged the emergence of a distinctive South African liberalism at a time when explicit endorsement of "segregation" remained anathema to many.[15] Hence, the Durban Town Council of the early 1920s explicitly denied an intent "to segregate any section or class entirely" wherever "any section has property or interests."[16] As the city turned to incorporate its unruly peripheries, however, it began to find a virtue in segregation.

Through a close reading of the annual Mayor's Minutes and the reports of the Borough Boundaries Commission, the Carnegie Commission of Investigation on the Poor White Question in South Africa, and the Provincial Post-War Works and Reconstruction Commission, we will see how the Durban Town Council and its 1935 successor, the Durban City Council, saw fit to respond, or not, to perennial problems of poverty, housing, health, and work, and to crises provoked by the Great Depression and World War II.

We can now pose the central argument of this chapter more precisely: despite the local state's will to territory, its attempts at biopolitical territoriality remained dogged by limited knowledge, and yet this would be opportune to the making of a local developmental state and to coercive spatial planning through new visual forms of authority. The prose of officialdom reproduced racial fantasies of populations to be policed, reformed, or banned from a port city on the verge of massive industrial expansion. The council's fitful experiments in biopolitical territoriality kept the Black majority in a perpetual state of insecurity while consistently making space for industrial capital. Rather than containing popular struggle, progressive segregation set the conditions for a new terrain of popular politics that I call *biopolitical struggle*.

Will to Territory: Not-Seeing Like a Mayor in the 1920s

Territoriality is built on the sovereign will to territory, in Durban forged through a colonial land grab bolstered by the ideology of an ideal white city. Transatlantic Progressivism had given this sovereign right a particular sheen, while also making possible the use of biopolitical expertise not just to ban but to incorporate people and places into capitalist territoriality. As Bill Freund argues crisply, city hall became expert in the purchase, sale, and lease of land, also to attract industry with the capacity to absorb labor, particularly in the industrialization of land south of the harbor in the photographs that bookend this chapter.[17] The council began to see "peri-Durban" as central to its industrial strategy as early as 1913, and by 1929 it forecast future "industrial districts of South Coast Junction, Merebank, Jacobs and Wentworth."[18] However, territorial mastery does not guarantee that people, place, capital, state, and resources will cohere in capitalist industrialization, which is why a dialectical understanding of biopolitics and capital remains necessary. Without knowledge about populations and territories, the Mayor's Minutes of the 1920s project a fantasy of biopolitical regulation of subaltern life on the *black belt* on the verge of incorporation. This fantasy white city was shaped by fear and suspicion to such an extent that what was at stake was not "seeing like a state" but a willful statecraft of not-seeing.

Consider the variance in how the council saw Coloureds, counted among Asiatics in the 1921 borough census and simultaneously as Europeans in matters of public health.[19] The Department of Health estimated a massive decline in the Coloured population from 4,760 to 1,881 between 1923 and 1926, but at the moment of incorporation of its peripheries in 1932, the council counted no Coloureds at all.[20] While Coloureds were not yet a governmental abstraction, Africans were seen in order to be expelled from urban residence through discourses of contagion. With no knowledge about African forms of life, the Mayor's Minutes repeat Victorian frustration with "the mode of living of Natives in the meaner quarters where so much demoralisation takes place."[21] Contrasting this distanced anxiety, the mayor announces "a bold policy in connection with the housing of the people."[22] White people of modest means, untainted by moral and medical contamination, are the implied subjects of acceptable housing in this biopolitical fantasy of a white city. Between repression of "Natives in the meaner quarters" and "housing of the people" lies the particular fate of South Durban.

In the 1920s the council saw these and other peripheries as unruly and wild. In a significant shift, the Public Health Committees Ordinance of 1923 called for committees to enable "sanitary control" in various areas in South Durban.[23] In today's parlance, this legislation responsibilized white property holders as vanguards of incorporation as long as their actions accorded with the interests of the state.[24] Stephen Sparks shows how South Durban in the 1920s witnessed heightened debate over the use of public health knowledge by the council and by civic groups who routinely conflated ideas of public health, crime, and moral deprivation in making the case for incorporation, but when Indians organized similar committees, they found that, as Sparks puts it aptly, they were not the "public" presumed in *public health*.[25]

There is a hint, in the 1924 minutes, of hopes for stronger territorial mastery of "an Indian residential area" or "a native village" so that "the hordes of Natives living indiscriminately on the outskirts could be better supervised and controlled," but with no decisive steps to realize this.[26] Instead, the minutes turn to roads and footpaths, stormwater drainage and sewerage, tramways, ocean beach works, and the draining of "low-lying, swampy areas on either end of the Borough" where malaria is rife, as it was just decades earlier in the concentration camps (see chapter 1).[27] Blind to the praxis of subalterns who had transformed an inhospitable landscape into "Indian gardens," the council was building the infrastructural basis for *potential* biopolitical territoriality.

What is clear is that this territorial fantasy was responsive to the needs of capital. Industrial capital staked claim to the productive potential of South Durban early on through the Natal Manufacturers Association (NMA) of 1905 and its successor, the Natal Chamber of Industries (NCI) of 1923. The NMA advocated in 1913 for the development of Congella as an industrial area, and it became Durban's first industrial area by 1930, Maydon Wharf, the "chief industrial area" shaded northwest of the Bay of Natal on map 4.[28] In 1925 the NCI pressured the council to purchase 194 acres at Wentworth in 1925 for housing and industrial development, and an additional 425 acres of the Woods Estate in 1931, to form the industrial areas of Jacobs and Mobeni.[29] The incorporation of "Added Areas" was an invitation to capital to reclaim the swamps and mangroves of Bayhead, as is seen in the opening photograph (figure 3.1).[30] However, the alluvial flats remained the preserve of "Indian gardens" in the 1950s, one indicator of the mismatch between territorial ambitions and ground realities (map 4).

Presumptions of whiteness pervade the mid-1920s minutes on indigent relief and housing "within the reach of the poor man's pocket" in white working-class Umbilo.[31] When the mayor appeals for poor relief on the grounds that charitable organizations were overstretched in subsidizing the low wages paid by the South African Railways under the Union Government's white labor policy, it is the white poor who are the main concern.[32] Nascent in this vision is a biopolitical argument for the central government to take on the responsibility of providing living wages for white workers to stabilize relations between capital and white nationhood.

The minutes also begin to frame concern for white working-class men's living wages in the language of "scientific planning with foresight," with the specter of interracial labor organizing on the recent horizon.[33] Ideas of scientific planning and the "city beautiful" enter a racial imagination in which Durban's peripheries wait for relief from "unsightly and insanitary conditions" so that future suburbs might join "a city of beauty, freedom and health."[34] Whiteness and capital were central to this aesthetic discourse, as the borough encouraged unmarked-white committees to focus on urban aesthetics, including uniform balconies and verandas, controls on shops and outbuildings in residential areas, discouragement of overhead wires, and tree planting. Indian merchants investing in art deco facades throughout central Durban were not valorized for their efforts at beautification precisely through these aesthetic norms.

Indians continued to be cast in the Mayor's Minutes as vectors of "unhygienic, insanitary, ugly features" in urban life, apparently visible in "dilapidated tin huts, with neither ventilation nor light, and regardless of air, space or sanitary conditions."[35] The narrowing of deprivation to the housing question had been a persistent theme in Victorian biopolitics across the Metropole and multiple colonies. Durban's repetition of these themes shows how the racial state sorted its approach to housing as it began to advocate for white working-class people in ways that might be considered biopolitical if only for the state's concerted practice of not-seeing the lives of others.

Some of these others were organizing. While Indians became "settlers" in their own eyes (see chapter 2), they faced intense animosity, crystallized in the failed Class Areas Bill of 1923 and the Areas Reservation and Immigration and Registration Bill of 1925, which focused on segregation and limits to land-ownership.[36] As an index of the openness of anti-Indian racism, the mayor refers with openly xenophobic vitriol in 1926 to "the evil of the Asiatic in our midst."[37] Durban Indians appealed to the colonial Government of India, and the latter sent representatives to the first Round Table Conference in Cape Town in 1926 to focus on the Indian question in Durban. Representatives of white Durban argued for residential segregation on racial grounds bolstered by the specter of unsanitary working-class Indian habitation.[38] The delegation from India used the Public Health Act of 1919 to argue for improvement in Indian sanitation and housing, turning biopolitical expertise against racist ends. As a result, the nonstatutory Cape Town Agreement of 1927 proposed voluntary repatriation to India as well as the raising of the "standard of living" of Indians who remained behind, standards that would conform to "Western" norms. While the Natal Provincial Council was loath to finance all that this would entail, the Cape Town Agreement forced the Areas Reservation Bill to be re-voked, and it broadened discursive space for the consideration of "standards of living" beyond the white poor.[39] In effect, this clarified that biopolitics is a matter of struggle.

In practice, the Durban City Council ignored the Cape Town Agreement, focusing concertedly only on "European standards of living." With no hint of irony, the Mayor's Minutes caution that "it is obviously illogical to preach the principles of either physical or moral well-being to people living under con-ditions which militate against those principles."[40] What does not strike the council is that it preaches this illogic indiscriminately to Black people while deepening their inhumane living conditions.

The Mayor's Minutes of the late 1920s follow biopolitical discourse as it shifted focus from epidemiological control to "scientific area planning."[41] The council increasingly wielded this language for coercive ends, for instance, in posing areas under Black occupation in Cato Manor, Springfield, and Went-worth as sites for "town planning layouts" and "garden suburbs," premised on dispossession, though still without clarity about how it would do so.[42] The 1927 minutes present a desire to plan and house people in relation to industrial transformation along the harbor and, "with its logical implication, the indus-trial expansion of Durban."[43] It does not say that this would require destroy-ing the Indian commons that made this space habitable and productive in the first place.

Precisely on the basis of this subaltern infrastructure, Indians imagined fighting on their own terms to become insiders in a progressivist transformation of the city. Some African leaders like John L. Dube and George Champion tried to do so as well. The state began in the 1920s to create narrow spaces of exception for Africans. The 1923 Native (Urban Areas) Act sorted Africans by those who had to comply with residential segregation and pass laws, versus those who were exempt, and local authorities could compel "unexempt" Africans to live in single-sex "native hostels," rent in "native locations," or build homes on leasehold tenure in "native villages."[44] The Mayor's Minutes of the late 1920s show some concern for "facilities for progressive Natives" in the "erection of a Native Village . . . at Wentworth," upgraded two years later to a "Native Township" under "a comprehensive scheme under which the Natives might have some voice in the government of the township."[45] The idea of racially segregated biopolitical territoriality was entering the realm of possibility.

In the first decades of the century, "the Indian question" remained a thorn in the side of this racial fantasy. The Thornton Committee of 1928 criticized Durban for its neglect of Indian housing promised by the Cape Town Agreement, it mobilized public finance for Indian public housing and homeownership, and it pressed the council to incorporate its peripheries to bring them under municipal control.[46] The Health and Housing Committee recommended exempting freehold land in Cato Manor from legislated limits to Indian property ownership, and it complained that "the Indian community is not inclined to cooperate with the Council."[47] While the racial state attempted to partition what it saw as progressive possibilities, its use of the sovereign exception was often unacceptable from the perspective of denizens fighting neglect and social domination. Indians were unique as they had found the means to express their voice in such matters.

In late 1928 the Health and Housing Committee met a deputation claiming to represent "all sections of the Coloured community," including Malays, Mauritians, and St. Helenians, petitioning for Coloured housing in town and work for Coloured artisans.[48] Their petition shows us that some urban residents had hopes for governmentalization as Coloured, noting official concern for the white working class and also communal organization of Indians. The chairman of this committee reported on a public meeting of "the Coloured community" in which people spoke of "extensive overcrowding, and it appeared to him that this section of the population was being exploited by a certain type of Indian landlord."[49] The anti-Semitic trope of the rapacious Indian landlord was expedient to divide people who might have found common political cause.[50]

Two processes converged in 1929. Claiming to provide limited housing for Coloureds while protecting white Durban from Indian homeownership, the Mayor's Minutes begin to speak of African presence through the language of segregation: "During the year it was evident that many Natives . . . were found to be residing on unauthorised premises, and the council decided that by a process of proclamation, portions of the affected centres could be treated *on the segregation principle*. It is expected that by making it difficult for unlawful residence to be permitted, there would in time be a wholesome population living under conditions of satisfactory housing. A step in the direction of clearing the area was taken."[51] This openness to forced segregation was new, and it followed "serious attacks and rioting" after "a Native boycott of a Municipal Eating House" and "encounters with the Police."[52] In other words, it was probably a response to struggle.

The second process was the council's growing commitment to industrialization. The mayor pledged "to dispose of land at a sacrifice" to attract industrial capital that might generate employment.[53] Freund argues that this was when city hall's developmental role became evident, as in its purchase of the former Woods Estate, invaluable flatlands that would become the Jacobs and Mobeni industrial areas.[54] The mayor invokes this developmental vision in explaining the sale of public land in Wentworth to a Belgian textile manufacturer in 1929.[55]

An important argument emerges from this spatial history of statecraft: the parallel emergence of a developmental state and segregation points to their mutual interdependence. In his last scholarly book, Freund skirts around this while pointing out that the South African state was committed to capital accumulation and segregation from the 1910s well into the first decade of apartheid and that "a (near) developmental state" forged during World War II came apart in the 1970s.[56] The elective affinity between the developmental state and racial segregation becomes clearer as we consider that the former has to attend to the spatial and demographic distribution of the externalities of industrialization. All developmental states have to address who is to bear the brunt of industrial waste, yet the geography of the commodity detritus is never addressed in the theory of the developmental state. Durban's history suggests it should be.

Progressive segregation refers to this emerging racial frame through which Durban sought to incorporate its peripheries, neutralizing potential threats by any developmental or segregationist means necessary. Emboldened by the export of gold that every country in the world wanted at the time of the Great Depression, the dreams of a racial El Dorado at home appeared to become a reality, and the incorporation of Durban's peripheries a site for a biopolitical utopia to come.

Fantasies of a Biopolitical City: The Borough Boundaries Commission, 1930

The culmination of this racial fantasy was the council's manifesto of incorporating Durban's peripheries, the report of the Borough Boundaries Commission, firmly on the basis of "not-seeing like a mayor." Recall that as a concept and social technology, "segregation" emerged in 1890s colonial Hong Kong and Bombay and quickly spread across the Indian, Pacific, and Atlantic Oceans with public health as a pretext (see chapter 2). The Boundaries Commission provides its own variation of this fin de siècle global history, as the term became thinkable in relation to unruly ground realities. The polyvalent perversity of Durban's *black belt* and its inventive transformation of space was the other side of the racial state's concerted ignorance of ground realities.

The report of the Borough Boundaries Commission is a fantasy text of racial, biopolitical, and territorial mastery, combining elements of the British colonial gazette, artifact of a fading documentary state, with the new expertise of town planning. The text begins with Durban's ambitions, since 1914, of territorial expansion.[57] The narrative shifts quickly to a representation of a dual city, one planned, the other with substandard infrastructure provided by Indians and inhabited by a racially mixed population. Infrastructural differentiation is key to this split city: "the attractive modern suburb of Durban North, with its neatly-laid-out plots, its artistically designed dwellings served with Durban light and water, and its smooth winding roads" contrasts with the "Indian area known as Paruck's Barracks, where over five hundred people, mostly non-Europeans, live in a most constricted space, for the most part under grossly dirty and insanitary conditions in very wretched wood and iron buildings."[58] While there is some recognition of proletarian rural-urban life, sweeping dichotomies juxtapose unmarked-white with unruly Indian space.

Since the latter is precisely the periphery to be incorporated, the Boundaries Commission details means and costs but also aesthetic and epidemiological risks. Whether those risks are threats to water systems, "improper receptacles" in personal sanitation, or widespread tuberculosis and typhoid, incorporation is colonialism redux:

At Mayville, beyond the ridge near the brickfields, the Commission visited a valley largely occupied by non-Europeans. Over an area of about one square mile it is fairly thickly populated, and in different parts of the valley are to be found numerous facilities of non-Europeans living under very insanitary conditions. Many of the dwellings are of ancient and defective construction, and of wood and iron. The family water supply is invariably derived from a shallow well or water hole, generally improperly covered so that surface contamination is unavoidable. Some form of earth closet is usually to be found. Those inspected were filthy internally, and, as is apparently common with this class of inhabitant, the pail was a rusty paraffin tin. In several instances the disposal site was a piece of disturbed ground in the immediate vicinity of the dwelling. The immediate surroundings of the dwellings inspected were equally filthy, and in several instances adjacent gardens or *mielie* [maize] patches were found to be strewn with patches of human refuse.[59]

The preoccupations of what Warwick Anderson calls "excremental colonialism" are familiar from contemporaneous settler colonies.[60] Recall wood-and-iron construction in descriptions of the concentration camps, in the spread of Indian homes in neglected and peripheral spaces, and in the first Hindu temples (see chapters 1 and 2). For residents, wood and iron stood for low cost, easy assembly, and pride in auto-construction under conditions of hardship. From the perspective of power, wood and iron signified easy destruction.[61]

The very next section, on "trade effluents," portrays the southern periphery as "an important industrial area which promises to expand," admitting that "industrial development brings problems all its own," including effluent disposal, which confounds the South Coast Junction Health Board to such an extent that the chief inspector of factories poses "a general question of sanitation, which becomes more pressing as the areas gradually become industrialized."[62] This passage is remarkable for showing how, as Michel Foucault would have it, the incitement to discourse is uncontrollable, and biopolitical expertise holds the possibility of exposing the predatory aspects of racial capitalism. The text continues to disclose the problem of environmental contagion and the inattention of the offenders, particularly sugar mills unwilling to properly dispose of the noxious dunder produced by refining. Multiple forms of contagion conceal and reveal competing social interests, and the long-term problem of disposal of industrial wastes becomes a "general question of sanitation." Effectively, the Boundaries Commission employs a biopolitical caesura to exempt capital from official critique.

Indeed, the Boundaries Commission exposes the contradiction between contagion and segregation while ignoring its consequences. The medical officer of health attests that "the whole of the Durban and peri-Durban area constitutes one hygienic unit, the health of the community being at the mercy of the weakest part hygienically."[63] Reference is made to Johannesburg town clerk and Victorian Progressive par excellence Lionel Curtis, who had argued for Johannesburg's boundary extension in 1901 for "reasons of unity in sanitary matters."[64] However, on bringing "the coming industrial area" in South Durban under the control of city hall, the commission is silent on who will bear the brunt of industrial pollution.

Responding to various critiques, including Indian deputations vehemently against segregation, the commission draws on colonial comparisons for the merits of municipal unification under liberal government.[65] Against those who argued that incorporation would result in "dumping of Durban's Indian and Native population" in white areas, it argues that incorporation would more effectively control migrant labor, meaning that it would continue to treat Africans as migrants.[66] Responding to classic liberal critique on financial viability, it shifts registers to the biopolitical, to argue that "municipal government [of a 'greater Durban'] is not just a matter of commercial bargaining . . . [but] rather a question of human welfare—a question also of human life."[67] Presciently, the commission poses tighter regulation of movement and integrated municipal government as a response to the potential critique that incorporation might simply create new *black belts*, as critics of the housing question had long argued.[68] In other words, the Boundaries Commission proposes the abstraction of an integrated biopolitical city constituted through economic interdependence in shipping, services, and amenities, a unified "centre for business, amusement and intellectual life," and it projects this abstraction into a policy future in which the Black majority need not matter.[69]

The Boundaries Commission works through the incorporation of peri-Durban with a fine-tooth comb as it details areas that resisted incorporation, like "predominantly rural," unmarked-white Westville and Pinetown, which posed no public health threat and could remain unincorporated, in contrast to the Bluff ridges extending around Wentworth and Jacobs, which had to be incorporated as they "abut an area marked for rapid industrial expansion," where "adjoining ridges must be marked for rapid residential expansion in growing interdependence with it."[70]

On Indian market gardeners, the commission recommends differential rates for agricultural holdings; it commends the council for supporting owner-occupiers as a bulwark against peri-urban rack renting; and it assures that these problems would be resolved by the "comprehensive town planning" that incorporation would usher in.[71] When representatives from the Natal Indian Congress (NIC) and other organizations endorsed incorporation along with restoration of the municipal franchise to Indians, the commission blandly reports that these matters lie "outside the scope of the enquiry."[72]

The Boundaries Commission includes the foundational cadastral map of Durban's Added Areas (map 5). The city center is shaded, and the focus is on peri-urban property of relevance to this commission. The starkness of this "plan," its property demarcations and arcs radiating from the central train station, contrasts sharply with Victorian city maps that paralleled nineteenth-century initiatives of social reform in Manchester and London.

The Ordnance Surveys in Victorian Britain, in Patrick Joyce's reading, brought together civilian and military cartography in the "'liberalism' of state space . . . understood in terms of the sheer plenitude of the information provided," a mass of knowledge that acted as "a positive invitation to interpretation" for both the governing and the governed.[73] The new tool produced through liberal governmentality was the "social map," innovated between 1835 and 1855 to show various aspects of living standards, stretching from medical to moral aspects of "the health of the city."[74] In contrast to these metropolitan expectations, Durban's incorporation was founded on improving health and sanitation, yet the founding map of the Boundaries Commission did not need to convince anyone. Rather, map 5 demonstrates simply and powerfully that the only form of land use that matters is that recorded by the cadastre.

Map 5 names some prominent farms like Dunn's Grant in South Durban, with land cultivated by peasant-workers marked by the generic label "small lots." Much of South Durban, including Wentworth, was parceled in neat rectangular lots, in contrast to the large, irregular lots at the bottom of the map, which would become Merebank. However, the vision projected by the Boundaries Commission did almost nothing to forge consent over an integrated vision of biopolitical territoriality. As is evident in this map, the council knew very little about who Durban's denizens were, let alone how they ought to live. The notion of "standards of living" did make discursive space for some Indian and Coloured elites to project communal visions of "improvement" under conditions of subjection. Yet, the state's territorial ambitions were fundamentally shaped by emboldened attempts to protect white life, which takes us to the second commission that was key to statecraft in the 1930s.

Of "Poor Whites" and "Standards of Living": The Carnegie Commission, 1933

City hall in the late 1920s increasingly pressed for national government support for white workmen's family wages and housing, particularly as the South African Railways had committed to provide permanent jobs for the advancement of "the unskilled white man."[75] These concerns were clarified, amplified, and centralized through the enormously influential Carnegie Commission of Investigation on the Poor White Question in South Africa, commissioned in 1929 and published in five volumes over 1932–33. Tiffany Willoughby-Herard argues that the Carnegie Commission produced white vulnerability and anti-blackness in relation to global circuits of white nationalism, segregationist philanthropy, and scientific racism, which should make it difficult to consider "poor whites" in equivalence with Black suffering.[76] However, official discourse traffics precisely in the fear of equivalence, or more precisely interracial solidarity, whether through labor unionism or the demand for universal "standards of living." While Durban remained largely out of its purview, the Carnegie Commission provided authoritative means to further the fantasy of a white city in a specific way, through the infrastructuralization of racially segmented labor markets that would make it harder still to forge anti-racist working-class solidarities. As Jeremy Seekings argues, this was part of the way in which the commission helped erode the nascent welfare state in defense of white supremacy.[77]

The Carnegie Commission frames "the poor white question" as a multidimensional racial problem whose terms were set, Willoughby-Herard notes, by the production of the "Negro" as a problem, as presciently diagnosed by W. E. B. Du Bois.[78] What was distinctive about the Carnegie Commission was the way in which white degeneration and vulnerability were portrayed as exacerbated by capitalism. For instance, E. G. Malherbe, author of the volume on education, argues that a "pathological situation" has been accentuated by general economic depression.[79] Similarly, the *Psychological Report* argues that job reservations are necessary but insufficient for "the poor white."[80] Malherbe's discussion of "poor whites" brings into view an underlying hope of reconciliation of "white races" through the rehabilitation of white migrants from the impoverished countryside:

The poor white is not a class apart in the "caste" sense of class.

... It is circumstances which have in course of time selected traits in him which have marked him for deterioration and impoverishment....

... The Poor White Problem is essentially an agrarian question.... British and Boer were caught in the same economic maelstrom which takes no count of the very arbitrary distinctions of nationality.

Statistically speaking we call a Poor White an impoverished white person of rural origin.[81]

This use of "caste" as an intractable form of class was indebted to the "caste school of race relations" in the United States and to Du Bois's notion of "color caste," which in turn drew on abolitionist citations of missionary views of India's alleged "caste system" (from the Portuguese *casta*); Du Bois's use of *caste* influenced Gunnar Myrdal's 1937 Carnegie-sponsored study of "the Negro problem" in the United States.[82] These are just hints of the circulation of concepts across racial capitalisms from a range of positions.

Malherbe's reassurance of a common whiteness, and the prevention of its degeneration, hinges on the remedial potential of education, but this reassurance was unstable.[83] A 1938 brochure in English and Afrikaans from a "liberal" perspective suggests with alarm that "poor whites" who could not maintain "a standard of living commensurate with the standards of ordinary decency and morality" ran the risk of sinking to "the standard of the native."[84] The author calls instead for tightening racial barriers to semiskilled artisanal labor through apprenticeships.[85] What we see here is a shift from the defense of racially differentiated standards of living to racialized labor market segmentation.

There is only fleeting reference to the poor white question in Durban in "the rural exodus" studied by the Carnegie Commission, although the commissioners visited the environs of Pietermaritzburg.[86] However, "poor white" discourse resonated with debates about standards of living and in the council's consideration of Wentworth among places for "housing for [unmarked-white] people of limited income."[87] The Carnegie Commission notes in passing but with consternation the "competition of non-Europeans" named "Asiatics" and "Coloureds," who "have almost entirely been drawn into the modern industrial system."[88] The fear of competition, with its lateral citation to anti-Semitism, was commonplace in official discourse with respect to Indians, and the council could draw on it without endorsing Afrikaans-speaking "poor white" migration to an allegedly English Durban.

City hall might not have committed openly to preferential labor and housing for the "poor white" descendants of those who had suffered war and concentration camps a few decades earlier. However, the Mayor's Minutes of the 1930s detail how the council engaged in the prosaic work of infrastructural change, including, in South Durban, resurfacing and tarring Marine Drive, reclaiming Fynnlands beach, connecting Merebank Beach Road to the school, and employing "Indian Relief Gangs" for weed and grass cutting, trimming, and drain clearing across newly incorporated areas.[89] The council did not recognize that macadamizing Sirdar Road, hardening Wentworth Road, draining lower Clairwood, surfacing the Umlaas River Bridge, and so on built on the subaltern production of infrastructural space. And while the new infrastructure was not marked "whites only," labor employed in relief work was marked as "fit," "semi-fit," "Coloured," and "Indian," with the largest numbers in the ranks of the "semi-fit" and "Indian."[90] The Carnegie Commission had helped normalize racially segmented labor in infrastructural construction, to employ "poor whites" in the transformation of newly incorporated areas.

* * *

In South Durban infrastructural change fundamentally meant industrialization and the power of manufacturing capital. In 1937 the council's special committee on industrialization recommended expansion south of the bay, from Maydon Wharf and Congella, along reclaimed land at Bayhead and further south along the South Coast Road through the market gardens of Clairwood and Jacobs.[91] This committee recommended integrating industry, railways, and shipping, linked to planned African and Indian housing schemes in Lamontville and Merebank. By 1938 city hall had forged a lasting alliance with the Natal Chamber of Industries (NCI), declaring South Durban a "productive zone"; Mayor Ellis Brown, a "distinguished industrialist" formerly on the NCI's executive committee, symbolized the emerging hegemonic apparatus.[92]

By this point, the Durban City Council had internalized the interests of industrial capital through a facility with buying, selling, and leasing land.[93] While the central government controlled the port and railways, the council continued to acquire land and make it available for industry. The new expertise of "town planning" was instrumental to this task, as South African town planning shifted focus after the 1923 Native (Urban Areas) Act to technical matters of segregation and industrialization, with town plans largely concerned with the layout and efficiency of new infrastructure.[94] When the National Party allied with the Labour Party in 1924, this Pact Government emphasized independence from Britain and helped shift ruling-class power from mining to agricultural and manufacturing capital, ushering in a period of import substitution industrialization (ISI) that allowed town planning to play a facilitative role.

By the late 1930s, the Pact Government cemented its alliance with the urban white working class through state investment in suburbanization and public transport. Urban planners found opportunities in the making of a new object, the planned industrial town. South African Iron and Steel Corporation's (ISCOR) new steel town, Vanderbijlpark, concretized postwar ISI planning, and it was also a testing ground for bridging spatial organization and racial social engineering. A light engineering zone was located as a "buffer" between Black and white residential areas, for instance.[95] Lessons from Vanderbijlpark would inform planned towns like Sasolburg, Richard's Bay, and Saldanha and industrial decentralization in rural areas north and south of Durban in the 1940s.[96]

Another proximal thinker, jailed Italian militant Antonio Gramsci, named the particular hegemonic apparatus emerging around the Ford industrial complex in Dearborn, Michigan, "Fordism"; articulating work discipline on the factory floor with the raced and gendered social reproduction of labor in communities surrounding the plant, Fordism was bolstered by an ideology of Americanism and an expedient mix of consent and police force.[97] Fordism also involved a production of space through the seemingly neutral production of infrastructure.

The archives document a massive, uneven infrastructural overhaul in South Durban at this time. Roads and beaches in the white working-class residential areas of the Bluff were upgraded in the late 1930s, while Indian areas were neglected.[98] The Southern Sewerage Works, authorized in 1938 and built between 1959 and 1969 in the middle of Merebank, would become the main sewage treatment plant for a massive sewage system across industrial and residential areas.[99] The swampy alluvial flats of the South Durban basin were drained; the Umzinto, Umhlatazana, and Umlaas Rivers canalized; and the Amanzimnyama and Mobeni estates cleared of shack dwellers, leveled, and engineered to make way for an ordered industrial geography. Yet the problems this infrastructural overhaul was meant to fix remained.

Biopolitics by Decree: Policing the ABCs of Segregation in the 1930s

The Mayor's Minutes of the 1930s repeat the certainties of "sanitary inspection," "abatement of nuisances," "sewerage," "anti-mosquito sanitation," and "infectious disease," but they supplement contagion talk with "housing and slum clearance" and closing orders through public health bylaws, as well as attention to maternity, child welfare, nursing homes, and Indian midwives.[100] The introduction of coercive means shows that this was not meant to be a consensual form of biopolitical governmentality but a police form using surveillance, dispossession, and destruction. By a police form, or biopolitics by decree, I refer to Jacques Donzelot's conception of policing "the quality of the population and the strength of the nation," with the caveat that in the postcolony, repression was always at hand.[101]

City hall's attempts at territorial mastery remained differentiated and arbitrary, with the long-term interests of capital in mind, but no need to limit state caprice. When white landlords were threatened with expropriation, new possibilities emerged from this seeming anarchy. In 1937 two white landlords in the Bell Street Area of the Point near the harbor mouth entered into a protracted debate with the council's Public Health (Slums) Committee over whether an entire block had to be designated a "slum," what constituted a "nuisance," whether it was a product of construction or of misuse by tenants, and who was to be held responsible for "rehousing" tenants.[102] When the medical officer of health pushed one landlord on his "scheme for improving or for developing that area," the landlord responded impatiently about this "harping on the word 'scheme.' I have no scheme; demolition is not a scheme."[103]

After an elaborate passing of the buck, the representative of the Indian tenants asked the Public Health Department to "take a certain amount of blame" for "slum conditions," to which the medical officer of health deftly argued that "the Public Health Department lacks the authority to tackle it in a radical way" but also that the council had acquired the power to expropriate the area, to "develop it in the public interest."[104] In the subsequent meeting, the officer elaborates that the Slums Act of 1934 made it possible for expropriation "from the point of view of replanning . . . whereby an area can be expropriated by the Municipality, all the buildings razed to the ground and the whole area replanned for roads, sewerage, etc. and then sold back to the original owners plus the cost of that development if they so desired."[105]

"Replanning" could be much more ambitious than the eradication of slums or uplift of the white poor. Needless to say, replanning was not considered in relation to the dire realities of African residences, for instance, in the Merebank Native Men's Hostel, built to house people evicted from the Bell Street Togt Barracks on the Point.[106] Rather, the council sited this hostel adjacent to "land set aside for industrial sites" in the industrializing of South Durban, with the racialized reassurance that "a portion of the industrial land [might] be utilized for recreation grounds for the Natives and at the same time act as a buffer to the housing scheme."[107]

Slum, scheme, hostel, buffer, and so on were becoming familiar terms, an ABC of segregation that had emerged in an aleatory manner rather than as clear and distinct objects of spatial control.

What I refuse here are two shibboleths of South African radical scholarship on apartheid's emergence. First, the dominant view from Marxist social history, following the work of Martin Legassick and Charles van Onselen, poses a process of elaboration of spatial form from the nineteenth-century mining compound to the mid-twentieth-century apartheid township as a system of "total control," using the framework of Erving Goffman. Second, Foucauldian accounts, principally by Deborah Posel, Aletta Norval, and Jennifer Robinson, argue that orthodox Marxists have underplayed the importance of power, discourse, spatiality, and statecraft. Rather than viewing the apartheid state as either a "grand plan implemented by a large and well-coordinated repressive state bureaucracy" or "a haphazard, conflict-ridden and historically contingent outcome of a disorganized state," Robinson poses "an ongoing tension between these views."[108] I am in complete agreement but would alter the last point to a *dialectical relation* that does not presume a logic of power in either Marxist or neo-Foucauldian terms but attends to the aleatory violence of the ABCs of segregation.

When the military eyed the lands south of the bay for encampment during World War II, city hall sought ways to use wartime conditions for its own experiments in coercive urban planning. Learning of military plans to convert the Merebank hostel site into a Native Battalion Camp, the town clerk deftly made the case for the military to build their camp using the council's plans, so that the council might procure it after the war; citing the proliferation of "hutments occupied by homeless families" on the Durban beachfront after the last world war, the town clerk argued that this would "preclude the possibility of Natives, Indians and Coloureds crowding into the vacant hutments at the termination of hostilities and thereby creating a new slum area within the City."[109] *New slums*, referring to the very reason for incorporation of the peripheries, was a potent scare phrase to get the military to do what the council had been trying to do for decades.

By 1943 the Department of Defence did not need many of the camps it had procured; the council suggested repurposing them for civilian residence.[110] The council posed these "temporary camps" as unsuitable for white working-class families but suited to "single Natives employed on Corporation works, . . . gangs continuously employed in the area and in the development of the Merebank-Wentworth Housing Scheme, and Natives employed by private enterprise in the Merebank and Jacobs Areas."[111] The extract concludes that this proposal to house Africans is "a temporary measure designed to meet the exigencies of war-time," as eventually South Durban would be an industrial area.

This was the context in which the council first suggested the Merebank/Wentworth Housing Scheme in a 1939 appeal for central government finance for a "comprehensive scheme" of acquiring over 1,285 acres from Indian and European owners through the Housing Act, "for the elimination of slums and the improvement of housing accommodations for all members of the community, Europeans, Natives, Coloureds and Indians."[112] The lion's share of 82 percent of the acquired land was to be for Indian housing, with 18 percent allocated for Coloured housing, an indicator of the serious underestimate of people forced to classify as Coloured.[113] This scheme would be revived in debates over the third important commission, on postwar planning.

In the interim, the council used "nuisances" to justify widespread demolition, primarily of Indian buildings.[114] The list of "premises scheduled for demolition" names white owners; larger concerns like Trustees R. K. Khan and E. M. Paruk Hospital and Dispensary Trust; and several individuals, with names of different provenance, sometimes reduced to just a word or a number: Paraman 43559, Subban 126595, Bee Sundhai 3350/1911, Packhara 40121, Noyna 70505, and so on, and including a few Africans, like Sibhoze 9716/9717 and Kuzwayo Damgoza Nhlangoti. Their premises demonstrated "defects and other conditions of nuisance," including

premises in a partly-finished state
linings open-jointed and incomplete
inferior construction
exterior woodwork and verandah brickwork in disrepair
roof, gutters, framing and door/unlined and unceiled
wood floors in disrepair
window woodwork in disrepair
detached room in advanced decay
inadequate light and ventilation
premises dirty
premises filthy
brick pail privy in general disrepair
wood and iron privy of inferior construction and in general disrepair
no bathing facilities

detached kitchen and bathroom constructed of scrap iron, in general disrepair and totally unsuitable

drainage from bath defective

premises filthy and bug-infested

premises bug, roach and rodent infested and ridden with white ants

laundry business on this property disconnected from dwellings[115]

The list is notable for its arbitrariness. Walter Benjamin would call it "a processing of data in the fascist sense," the dull work of bureaucratic power in
rubber-stamping state violence.[116] There is no reference to legal principle in
determining "defects and other conditions of nuisance," yet a few months
later, the medical officer of health proclaimed that "having given the owners
and/or representatives an opportunity of adducing their reasons why their
premises should not be declared slums, the City Council is now satisfied that
such nuisances do exist [to] most effectively be dealt with under the Slums
Act."[117] Registered owners were given two weeks to provide a list of occupiers, title deeds of the property, and details of mortgage bonds.[118] The onus
to disprove "slum" conditions had been devolved to owners, and it is fair to
presume that, for most, this was impossible.

Some Indians in South Durban attempted a long and arduous fight
against the declaration of Merebank and surrounding areas as slums to be
redeveloped into a scheme for sale or lease to existing residents. Balbhadur
"Billy" Juggernath narrates the formation of the Merebank Indian Ratepayers Association (MIRA, later the Merebank Ratepayers Association [MRA]) in
1933, soon after incorporation, when it became clear that the municipal corporation had reneged on extending the basic amenities that were the rationale
for incorporation. Juggernath and others suspected that the council's negligence was a prelude to eviction. The northern boundary of the area declared
a slum in 1938 was adjusted from Collingwood Road to Hime Lane, and the
area "released from the slum" was "approved as Industrial Area as a result of
agitation by white industrialists."[119]

Juggernath recalls a slowing of the council's ability to transform space
when World War II was largely in Europe, but when its center of gravity
shifted to the Pacific, postwar planning created new opportunities.[120] This
is an important insight. Despite press reports that the council had declared
Merebank a slum in 1940, the trail of letters between the city medical officer
of health and the town clerk confirms that no premises had been declared
slums.[121] That same year, the municipal corporation resolved "to acquire land

in Wentworth, Merebank and Umgeni North . . . declared slum areas with the object of building economic and sub-economic building schemes."[122]

When the minister of the interior approved the council's plan to convert the Merebank Slum Area into a Coloured and Indian Housing Scheme in 1942, this came as a shock to the MIRA, not just because "the entire area was already sub-divided into approved building plots owned by Indians and a sprinkling few by whites and Coloureds" but also because they "foresaw that the contemplated scheme will be the beginning of the segregatory policy of the government."[123] The NIC and Natal Indian Association had objected at a 1941 hearing "that segregation was the ulterior motive."[124] The Central Housing Board's recommendation in 1942 was that expropriation ought to be a final resort if owners were not prepared to sell at market value, to which the Natal Indian Association protested that this was segregation.[125]

In July 1942 the Durban Expropriation Joint Council wrote to the minister of public health that MIRA "had challenged the accuracy of the statistics submitted in regard to the racial ownership of the land in question."[126] The ratepayers had called the council's bluff in its charade of biopolitical governmentality without reliable statistical information. After a long exchange of letters, the Merebank/Wentworth scheme was referred to yet another commission.[127]

Powers of the Visual: The Postwar Works and Reconstruction Commission, 1943–1944

World War II brought to center stage the dangers of biopolitical sovereignty, or the articulation of biopolitical tools with the sovereign right to administer mass death, whether in Auschwitz, Dachau, Dresden, Hiroshima, or Nagasaki. Achille Mbembe names this death drive of biopolitical sovereignty "necropolitics," but South Africa took a more carefully partitioned route to welfare and neglect.[128] In 1942 the South African government under Smuts explored welfarist forms through a nonstatutory commission of inquiry on "post-war reconstruction."[129] The Fifth Report of the Social and Economic Planning Council, published in 1945, drew on British commissions of this type, but its recommendations of central authority over planning were resisted by the provinces, particularly by Natal. The administrator of Natal, Heaton Nicolls, carried the project to the provincial level in the Provincial Post-War Works and Reconstruction Commission, which sat between 1943 and 1944 to consider how to apply the principles of planning to Durban. In turn, city hall mobilized its own resources to use this authority to speculate on the Durban of the future.[130]

On the eve of this commission, the Durban City Council saw "reconstruction" not as a euphemism for slum clearance but as a "Post-War Development Programme."[131] As Frederick Cooper argues, the keyword *development* carried wider ambiguities of late-colonial reform and welfare in the 1940s.[132] To explicate "planning" and "development," the City and Water Engineer's Department prepared a report on "Post War Development" in a comparative European frame. This text poses key examples of interwar "progressive development" in the Soviet Union, Germany, and Italy through "bloodshed . . . and great suffering," in contrast to the democratic path pursued by the Allies, where "unemployment is solved through a system of social security and complete freedom for every individual brought out as a result of war."[133] In other words, it recasts biopolitical sovereignty in a Cold War frame. Exceeding the ambitions of the Carnegie Commission, the report emphasizes that "potential development opportunities" ought not to be restricted by "unemployment and Poor White problems."[134]

The report likens Durban to an outstretched hand, the gap between the thumb and index finger representing Durban harbor, the fingers "primarily European in character," interspersed by "Asiatic settlement," and a "racially fluid" thumb, South Durban.[135] Against "the baseless accusation of 'racial segregation,'" the text poses the council's interest in "volitional zoning," as people "gather in groups of like origin and outlook," as in American Chinatowns or Swiss cantons.[136] In heated discussion about this text, the deputy city engineer clarifies, "I would not like to live beside a Native. . . . It is not a question of segregation, but provision for volitional zoning."[137] The report senses that African urbanism cannot be forcibly curtailed but that Africans should be "self-contained and largely self-sustained" in "transition zones."[138]

The proceedings of the Post-War Works and Reconstruction Commission offer an ethnographic glimpse into statecraft that would soon be lost in the archives of the apartheid state. The discussion begins with what is to be done, if not outright segregation. Mayor Ellis Brown presses the commission "to just look very far ahead, almost visionary"; Councilor A. L. Barnes of the council's Special Committee on Post-War Development continues in the language of visionaries and visualization.[139] Senator Denis Shepstone, grandson of Theophilus Shepstone, architect of indirect rule in Natal, adds that the future must rest on the problem of the "de-tribalised Native," of urban Africans desiring the amenities of modern life, and after some discussion of

Indian presence, he argues for "economic segregation" as opposed to "domiciliary segregation."[140]

When the representatives of the council are asked squarely whether they can "envision" a city "split up into three sections, Europeans, Natives and Indians," Shepstone suggests, "it all depends on where you are going to divide those three parts."[141] Barnes defends "rehabilitation" rather than "entire segregation" of Indians; his respondents argue that "the cultivated class of Indian" refuses segregation but that "the poor type of Indian is being exploited by the rich."[142] The stock figure of the exploitative Indian landlord recurs in the discussion, alongside the fear of multiplying "little segregated islands in an ocean of Europeans."[143]

Shepstone focuses on what is to them the fundamental contradiction: How is the city to deal with Black urbanization and the need for labor in Durban's industrialization?[144] The ensuing dialogue swirls around a set of maps, and the chairman approvingly requests that they be seen in relation to "the ultimate division of the racial groups in Durban."[145] The idea of a "permanent solution" to "racial islands" recurs, as does the proposal of "self-government" for Indians and Africans in "townships."[146] The discussion is cautious about "planning," citing the difficulty and expense needed to transform a city of hills "on proper Engineering lines."[147]

In a telling exchange, a representative of the commission proposes that "machinery could be devised whereby the whole planning, within and without the Durban area, could be more or less fixed" through "a map zoning for the different races"; he asks the representatives of the city whether such a map of areas "fixed for Asiatics, Natives, Coloureds and Europeans" would aid planning. The answer is resoundingly affirmative, and "zoning for residential areas on a racial basis" takes the rhetorical place of "segregation."[148]

The ensuing discussion of race zoning maps lasts several years.[149] The council's *Racial Zoning, 1944* (map 6) allocates large areas for Asiatic and Native, but not Coloured, residence, turning multiethnic Cato Manor into an Asiatic area. After the election of the National Party, the commission's *Proposed Race Zones, 1951* (map 7) removes the "racial island" of Cato Manor, and it proposes a continuous geography of racial areas "buffered" by "working areas," including a large Coloured area in Durban North and a consolidation of Indian areas in existing white working-class areas along the Old Main Line from Malvern to Pinetown, a recommendation that would have been politically costly for the council. In the final compromise *Race Zoning Plan, 1952* (map 8), the council accepts mass evictions of the Black population at Cato Manor, particularly after the anti-Indian pogrom of 1949 and the aftermath of mass displacement, and the council has retained space for middle-class Coloured and Indian presence in exchange for not disturbing white working-class suburbs along the Old Main Line. The sequence of maps clarifies how working-class Indians and Coloureds are imagined to share space with an oil refinery in what would become Merebank and Wentworth, clearly marked on the final map.

When the *Durban Housing Survey* brought together these maps in a volume authored by liberal professors observing the transition to apartheid with dispassion, the maps were appended as transparencies to be read one on top of the other in a palimpsestic process that mirrored a city looking for stability through the fetish of segregation.[150] At various moments, the commissioners point to the base map over which the other maps are read, *Topography of Durban, 1952* (map 4), to note the usefulness of river boundaries, or to debate whether Indian elites should have sea views, which might make possible an "Indian corridor" to the industrial area of South Durban.[151] What has receded is any recognition of the "Indian gardens" marked on map 4, or the contradictory Indian commons forged through them.

How do we understand this turn to the visual in the Post-War Commission's work? Did these negotiations over the authority of maps help produce an abstract representation of Durban's future? Dianne Scott argues through a perceptive analysis of "modernist planning" that the deepening power of national and city government as well as of industrial capital was enabled by "the comprehensive vision of South Durban as an industrial zone."[152] This might concede too much to the council, which consistently knew very little. We ought rather to ask how the council sought to conceal its limited power and knowledge through the authority of maps.

The use of maps—their construction, interpretation, cross-referencing, overlay, and transformation—assumes cartographic discourse that defines the possible. Cartographic discourse includes referential aspects of maps but also symbolic characteristics, which can be a powerful force in portraying the facticity of maps.[153] Consider again how map 5 from the Boundaries Commission portrays some of South Durban in neat rectangular lots, in contrast to "small lots" held by Indian peasant-workers. What cartographic discourse produced this truth about space? What ambiguities of land tenure are rendered in fixed and firm boundaries while others are deemed unknowable? What do we make of the removal of adornment from these maps, and why do these tools of white supremacy not proclaim their ideological intentions?

We might take a cue from an image (figure 3.2), archived by the Apartheid Museum in Johannesburg, in which a group of suited men, presumably white

FIGURE 3.2 Officials examine a Johannesburg "Native Townships" plan, circa mid-1950s.
© Apartheid Museum, Johannesburg.

and official, appear engrossed in discussion on a bus over a race zoning map labeled "Native Townships." A man points to the map, as others study its contents. The posed scene on the bus is meant to educate the viewer on the usefulness of the map in the hard work of racial zoning.[154]

This photograph of a map in practice points to that which its users take for granted (figure 3.2). What is assumed is what Thongchai Winichakul, writing on another context, calls "the assumed geo-body" in the map, which links a notion of collective life to the territory of the nation, or in this case of the city.[155] Here the assumed geo-body is the enduring fantasy of a white city, fortified by decades of circulation of ideas of contagion, threatened by Black labor and Indian presence, and consistently belied, from bedrooms to courtrooms. Despite what ought to have been a realization by the 1940s that the white city was an impossibility that bore no resemblance to reality, race zoning maps offered the consolation of neutral expert authority on Durban's racial future. That is precisely what these men perform.

Much of what was debated within the Post-War Commission was literally unreal. When the commissioners press the city on its population estimates, the latter concedes that data on Africans are arbitrary. But there is no evidence of data collection about anyone at all. Elsewhere, officials concede that they do not actually know the scale of rehousing that evictions would produce. A representative of city hall suggests that the housing schemes of the future will have to stretch far outside the city: a literal stretch of the imagination but a portentous one.[156]

At other times, the Post-War Commission is obviously ideological. When it turns to zoning "offensive trades," it portrays the southern part of the bay as the obvious area for polluting industry; and when it turns to the regulation of pollution, the focus is on Indian laundries and furniture workshops, not on sugar mills and other corporate polluters.[157] The commission clarifies that in the "Durban of the future," the interests of industrial capital are secure in "the large industrial area absorbing the head of the Bay, . . . taking in all the presently owned Indian property on the Clairwood Flats, and sweeping down and also taking in the Lamont Estate."[158]

The council complains that it cannot both "de-house" people and provide housing "on a scientific basis," but it prides itself on its Wentworth-Merebank scheme of 3,200 houses. But it is clear that without any data, the council has grossly underestimated actual needs. When discussion turns to backyard lodgers in Indian homes, the commission presumes that these must be "married children, the brother's widow and so on"; this error would be magnified by a larger-than-expected mixed-race population dehoused by evictions of Indian homes across the city in decades to come, subsequently called a crisis of Coloured housing.[159] Recognizing the utter lack of data, the commission calls for what would become the *Durban Housing Survey*.

* * *

Alongside the council's deliberations, the horrors of World War II dramatized the dangers of biopolitical sovereignty. Wartime planning turned these dangers into an opportunity for racial capitalism. The power of the visual was key to the sovereign right to distinguish differentiated rights to housing and services in the absence of statistical data on vital matters, and capital took an active part in this process.

The Chamber of Commerce met with the commission to impress on it the importance of considering the aesthetic and material aspects of urban redevelopment.[160] They commended the commission for its "fanlike development" of racially demarcated areas to prevent "racial islands" and offered to "visualize" the main industrial area in South Durban, with the adjacent Bluff as a "European workers area" and the military camp turned into Coloured housing.[161] The Chamber of Commerce also raised the question of whether "to have, in these areas, some form of Local Government."[162] The aesthetics of planning allowed deliberation about limited self-government within the shell of racial liberalism.

In a remarkable memorandum, the town clerk distinguishes Durban, rehearsing its extension of the municipal franchise to white male and female nationals over twenty-one who meet property qualifications as well as to "Coloured and other non-European men" under the same criteria "who are not Natives" nor "descendants in the male line of Natives of countries which have not hitherto possessed elective representative institutions founded on the Parliamentary franchise"—in other words, not to Indians either.[163] In attempting to balance racism with a British ideology of "responsible self-government," the town clerk repeats arguments about limits to democracy in "white men's countries."[164] In the same breath, he affirms the Atlantic Charter and invokes Smuts's arguments that "its principles cannot be applied at once 'en bloc' in this country but must be carefully worked out on the basis of the special situations, racial, economic and cultural."[165] Assuming fundamental dissimilarity in all aspects of life between the "non-European and the European peoples of the Durban Area," he argues that a single elected body is impossible until a hazy horizon of "Westernization of the Non-European peoples may develop to a greater extent." Were the council's proposals for racial zoning to go through, he suggests "a measure of local autonomy within . . . zones." What is on offer is a vision of differentiated sovereignty cloaked as autonomy without the franchise, in segregated zones that institutionalize the political exclusion of Africans, Indians, and "non-European women." All this well before apartheid.[166]

* * *

The council was desperate for the Post-War Commission to endorse its proposed Merebank-Wentworth Scheme for Indians and Coloureds. Since it did not own the area of the proposed scheme, and as of late 1943 could not expropriate numerous small owners, it asked the commission for stronger control over the processes of acquisition and subdivision in the redevelopment to come.[167]

The city engineer shows detailed plans of layouts for plots, with considerations for traffic, proximity to industry, open spaces, an area on higher ground for well-off Indians, and a university that would never come to be. The commission presumes residents in nearby Clairwood would have to be expropriated to make way for industry, while those dispossessed through the Slums Act in Merebank could be rehoused in the housing scheme adjacent to industry.[168] There is deliberation about whether the proposed scheme would create a Coloured "racial island." An expert from Cape Town allays these fears by arguing that "there has never been any difficulty between Europeans and Coloureds, such as you have now between Europeans and Indians."[169]

Councilor Barnes reassures the commission that the city's vision with respect to Indians and Africans is "of radial development . . . which will extend for a considerable number of miles where they are going to be employed and catered for." Once more, aesthetic ideology comes to the rescue. While the Merebank-Wentworth scheme is a "racial island," residents would be "in proximity to the place that would absorb them in employment."[170] The estates manager picks up this line of argument that since South Durban has become the main industrial area, "we must try and surround that with places where people employed can live close to their employment," so that "the lowest paid labourer" is always close at hand.[171]

The ensuing discussion presses for secrecy at the moment of expropriation, to prevent the "unfair" inflation of land prices and to allow the expropriated a "fair market price."[172] Eviction had to be recalibrated to the idea of a progressive city council upholding economic liberalism. The mayor refuses the possibility of compulsion, and the city treasurer clarifies that transfer of properties would be facilitated gradually and within racial limits.[173]

The commission called back Senator Shepstone to question him on "radial development" and on "participation in local government."[174] Shepstone argues that "it is impossible to have segregation industrially and commercially," and the only real alternative is a positive development policy with respect to industry and agriculture.[175] Echoing a position radicalized in the analysis of radical political economist Harold Wolpe decades later, Shepstone argues that the dominant view about Africans presumes a "family anchorage" in the reserves that has been quite substantially eroded, with a large population "absolutely detribalized."[176] The dynamics of African exclusion in the countryside explode the entire exercise.

* * *

In October 1944 the commission published its *Ninth Interim Report*, known as the *Barnes Report*, the key text for racial planning in Durban. The *Barnes Report* has a fascinating dual structure. Part 1 is a general statement on British ideas of planning in South Africa; problems of public health, rack renting, and "black belts" on the urban periphery; and the importance of a "technical, professional and scientific town planning body" in the service of "a strong and virile European civilisation."[177] We can now read its key argument as follows: planning will save white supremacy by any biopolitical means necessary. Part 2 attempts to reconcile racism and liberalism through ideas of "ethnology" and "inter-racial relationship." The text argues that "racial adjustment" in Durban must accord with other parts of Southern Africa and that planning might thereby limit "residential juxtaposition" between

"Europeans" and others, and between "Asiatics" and "Africans." This racial view is then made consistent with the tenets of liberalism in this remarkable passage:

> Your Commission believes that the population of Natal cannot be divided into economic watertight compartments based on racial lines—that is to say, if economic prosperity is to be established for the whole community, then, in its view, the laws of economics must be allowed as free play between the different racial groups as they are between individuals in each group. A European master who pays his Native servant a wage some part of which finds its way back to a European bank through European channels of commerce or industry demonstrates that economics are not divisible on racial lines. This process of economic inter-relationship might be traced further through all the more complex activities and phases of an intricate economic order based broadly on a Western form of civilisation.[178]

In other words, liberalism could not be compatible with what Shepstone had called "economic segregation." Yet the master-servant parable at the center of this formulation ensures that the movement of wages, interest, and profit is not racially "divisible" because "economic order" is firmly in hands that embody "Western civilization."

The *Barnes Report* goes on to argue that Africans must remain subject to employment and residential discrimination "with the European as trustee," that Coloureds will diverge toward "European standards or . . . Native habits," and that Indians "of the labouring, peasant and employee class" are tolerably useful but that "the Indian of the more affluent classes is a menace to European civilisation in Natal" and must be segregated.[179] Councilor Barnes articulates the racial common sense circulating since the dawn of the century: the Indian middle class is most threatening to the fantasy of the white city, and the strongest justification for racial segregation.

The city council responded well to the *Barnes Report*, as it aided its hopes to rehouse people expropriated by the industrialization of South Durban. The Merebank-Wentworth Housing Scheme was to be built quickly, pending discussions with the Admiralty on Assegai Camp, and with the South African Railways and Harbours on its planned airfield. The *Barnes Report* provided expert justification to expropriate areas "occupied intensively" by Indians and other Black Durbanites.[180]

Undeterred by "Indian squatters," the British Admiralty and the Union Ministry of Defence used the exigencies of wartime to acquire over 250 acres of the Merebank-Wentworth Housing Scheme site from October 1942 to May 1944, to set up HMS Assegai, a training and transit camp, hospital, and drafting office for the Eastern and Mediterranean Fleets of the Royal Navy. [181] References to HMS Assegai appear in the memoirs of veterans who spent time in Natal. With the war's end in sight, the government began a long process of negotiation with the council, culminating in a formal lease agreement with the British Admiralty and the Union Government under which "Wentworth Camp" could be used only for military purposes; after the end of the lease, the council could acquire the land and buildings at a reasonable price.[182] This remarkable document shows how confident the council was in securing its interests from federal and imperial governments.

When the Defense Ministry sought to house "wives and families" of ex-volunteers in the transit camp, reassuring the government that military families would be at some remove from the housing scheme, the council countered with a proposal for housing "Indians of better means" near the Ack-Ack Training Station on the ridge.[183] The government secured areas of Wentworth Naval Camp north of Hime Lane as "zoned and treated for European occupation."[184] When the admiralty vacated the premises in December 1945, the Union Government took over the naval hospital in Wentworth and converted it into a specialized hospital for tuberculosis for Europeans, with "86 modern flats for ex-volunteers in employment."[185]

In a remarkably revealing discussion, the minister of public health proposes a major shift in the government's approach from playing "catch up with ill-health" to "combining preventative measures with curative methods" through "health centres" and an "Institute for Hygiene"; what is most surprising is that this was to be located in and around Clairwood around "housing schemes of various racial creeds" and "in the midst of an industrial area." Assegai camp was suggested as one possible site for this institute, but this was also mooted as "non-European" health workers would have to pass through the white part of Wentworth on a daily basis.[186] The appeal to South Durban as particularly suited to this kind of biopolitical expertise was prophetic, as this was exactly what would happen after the war through the work of pioneers in the field of social medicine (see chapter 4).

In its racial tradition, this claim to biopolitical expertise paralleled a ruthless blindness to African suffering. Stuck within a file on the Merebank Native Hostel is a 1945 petition from a group of African men, Philemon Ncongo, Philemon Radebe, Mkunjili Kumalo, Michael Nzimande, and Simon Dhlamini, representing 180 families who had built homes on private land south of Merebank, who relied on employment in the area, and who faced eviction by the Department of Transport's plan to build a new airfield on the site. "Given notice to leave this ground immediately," they had nowhere to go, as "municipal locations are filled to capacity." There was no response from the town clerk. They appear to have met similar deaf ears from the Municipal Native Administration Department and the Native Commissioner. Archived among letters that needed no response, the African working class continued to be subjects of official neglect.[187]

Conclusion: Impossible Fantasies of Segregation

The industrialization of South Durban was built on the fin de siècle alliance of corporate capital and the state in the aftermath of the nineteenth-century minerals boom, to which the Port of Durban was crucially linked. Capital found its representatives and claims to the potential industrial landscape on the flatlands south of the port early on through the NMA and NCI. The Slums Act of 1934 gave local authorities new powers to demolish and replan existing housing, to dredge land for industrialization along Maydon Wharf and south of the bay, and to clear the remains of the *black belt*.[188] The infrastructural photograph that opens this chapter discloses even as it effaces this violent process of spatial change.

As South Durban transformed from a peri-urban landscape of part-time farmers into an industrial landscape, what remains forgotten are the labors *of* primitive accumulation involved in creating a capitalist landscape.[189] An older resident of Merebank pointed to the cut in the hillside where the Umlaas Canal reaches the ocean; he said his father had dug it out with his own hands. We see this cut in the distance in this photograph from 1984 (figure 3.3). The photograph is divided by the Umlaas Canal as it reaches the ocean above, the Southern Freeway cutting across the frame, and, if one waits long enough, an airplane pathway in the air above, leading to the runway just visible on the upper right, just below the SAPREF oil refinery in the far right. Fragments of neighborhoods, industrial areas, and small farms capture a visual cacophony that is far from the planned order of biopolitical territorialization. The view from on high distances the viewer from the labor and pollution of a productive landscape, but there is no reassurance of aesthetic harmony.

The Black Marxist tradition has tried to connect spatial histories of capitalism with pervasive proletarian Black and subaltern radical critique. The Black Benjamin I have conjured holds up the images that frame this chapter as showing us monuments of the bourgeoisie as ruins that hold many forms of submerged revolutionary potential.

FIGURE 3.3 *Intersecting Umlaas Canal,* 1984. © Local History Museum, Durban.

In the period I have attended to here, African exclusion was institutional-ized as the tools of planning were employed to try to keep Africans in the countryside through regional and "Betterment planning."[190] While the state invested in limited spaces for Black middle-class life in places like Durban's Lamontville "African village" and Baumanville, it attacked Black informal housing relentlessly. In other words, these were also forgeries of progressive segregation. Lamontville and Chesterville, funded by the "Durban System" of municipal self-financing, far from met the massive need for decent housing for African shack dwellers, estimated at twenty-seven thousand by 1948.[191] The ambiguous and contradictory nature of state intervention in the means of life made it clear that African lives were expendable. As we will see in the next chapter, Black critique was far from extinguished.

The Birth of Biopolitical Struggle, 1940s

The way slavery was portrayed . . . changes when you take away "the white gaze." All those won-derful writers who wrote after they were freed were writing for abolitionists. They didn't think I was going to read it, and so they had to please or not disturb white abolitionists with their sto-ries, so you read Frederick Douglass, and I can feel the anger that he erases. That's not there. If he knew I was reading it, it might be a very different book. Even Ralph Ellison. I tell people he called the book *Invisible Man.* As good as the book is, my initial response is, "Invisible to whom?" —TONI MORRISON

Visions and Revisions, 1940s

A photograph from 1940s Durban at war tells us something about a white gaze in a period of intensifying ambiguity (figure 4.1). The context is Dur-ban's fear of Japanese invasion from the sea after a submarine, later con-firmed to be a German U-boat, was spotted off the coast. Barbed-wire fences were seen as a necessary deterrent on beaches that were segregated in prac-tice and would soon be marked "whites only." What we see through the lens in this photograph is a kind of bourgeois naivete, a celebration of white virility as a muscled man, perhaps a serviceman off duty, looks back at a white woman leading her children while another woman raises her child onto the fence, just another prop in bourgeois normality. Against the neat lines of midcentury modern buildings, tangled barbs on the beach call the bluff on all that is banal in Durban in the 1940s. At the center of this remarkably ambiguous image is a Black woman in white pulling a pram, her domestic servitude enabling the increasingly baroque reality around her, her body language figuratively refusing the normality of enjoying a barbed beach in an interimperial war. "Invisible to whom?" indeed.

Recall that Durban city hall of the 1940s had become an engine of knowledge production through a profusion of maps, plans, and documents but with very slim knowledge of social relations on the ground. This aesthetics of power was key to a police form of biopolitical government reliant on force while keeping up a fantasy of technocratic intervention in vital matters. Both city hall's racial aesthetics and this photograph are precisely what Cedric Robinson means by reading "forgeries of memory" in relation to the slow decay of racial capitalism.[1] What remains when we remove the presumption of a white gaze?

FIGURE 4.1 Barbed-wire entanglements on Durban's South Beach, circa 1943. © Local History Museum, Durban.

Consider the photograph again as a dialectical image, in light of a far-flung conversation that might have been, between Toni Morrison, Angela Davis, and the Black domestic worker at the center of the image. While the particulars of the Black South African woman's life may not have mattered for the photographer, her centrality to the photograph begs for reflection of the seemingly mute frame of photography that always indexes a more complex lived world. Any figure in the photograph, including the babies, might have lived the rest of their life in steadfast conviction that segregation and apartheid are anathema to mutuality. Any of these actual people may have joined the anti-apartheid struggle or may have lived in quiet solidarity with its purpose. Solidarity with a nameless Black woman refuses the conscription of all that we do not know about her intellectual life for a project of reconciliation in a racial democracy that maintains Black domestic workers in bourgeois homes, the presumption of progressive segregation within the frame of racial capitalism.

This chapter revises the argument about the conjuncture of progressive segregation through the solidarity between a Black woman looking askance and Morrison's rhetorical question "Invisible to whom?" Precisely because the state did not seek popular consent for biopolitical territoriality, it turned to brute power, through mass forced removals of Black denizens across the city of the 1940s. As people remade their lives within this landscape of segregation and forced removal before apartheid, they were compelled to try to make a habitable space beyond the fantasies of racial capitalist industrialization. Crucially, some strands of opposition did in fact cohere as a collective form of biopolitical critique in Durban and its rural hinterlands. Moreover, a radical Black feminist perspective emerged with a particular force in this conjuncture, connecting the political with the apparently apolitical to contest the harsh lived realities of progressive segregation. This critique of the damage wrought by racial/sexual capitalism was forged before apartheid, and it remains with us today.

As progressive segregation played out spatially through this police form of biopolitical government, it clarified the terrain of struggle for many who lived through its despotism. The daily injuries of segregation provided the practical terrain of resistance that led to the Defiance Campaign of 1950–52, as well as to a range of struggles. An important front of refusal of the articulation of biopower to racial sovereignty was the emergence of "social medicine" from South Durban and from the countryside north of Durban, with wide-ranging effects. The main possibility that this phase opens is the critical use of biopolitical tools for popular rather than statist ends. The main remnant of the three decades before apartheid, we will see, was a will to transform biopolitical expertise and intervention into instruments of struggle. I argue that this moment, particularly in South Durban, saw the birth of biopolitical struggle in the collective refusal of the political neutrality of biopolitics, the gathering of multiple critiques of its gendered and racialized deployment, and a growing interest in turning biopolitics into a terrain of struggle committed to universalizing the demand for access to the means of health and vitality.

Inhabiting a Racial Fantasy, and Refusing It, 1930s–1940s

Forms of life in the city remained at odds with official delusion as people sought to dodge official segregation to the extent possible. Hints of critique emerge from sources we have encountered, such as Balbhadur "Billy" Juggernath's "Diary," which shows how about half of Merebank was affected by the malaria epidemic of 1929–31, through lethal neglect by liberal government.[2] White public health committees, which had argued for incorporation of peri-Durban areas, did little to push the municipality to action, and here again we see how the city brought white populations into a project of biopolitical sovereignty to protect their lives at the expense of the Black majority.

Indian peasant-workers, Juggernath's forebears, continued to occupy a niche in South Durban's spatial division of labor of the 1930s and 1940s, with some room for upward mobility. Deeds Office records show several people funneling income as waiters, plumbers, shop assistants, shopkeepers, butchers, or tinsmiths into property in Clairwood and Wentworth in the mid-1930s.[3] Many households continued to engage in part-time farming, livestock rearing, and fishing. Juggernath writes about his family falling back on farming during the Great Depression, as well as keeping market gardens and poultry going until they were expropriated in the 1940s for the building of what he calls the Merebank Housing Scheme.[4] His son Sunjith recounts the general poverty of people in Merebank in the 1940s, as "some of them did gardening," most on rented land, but "some of them had small plots of land" until it was taken over by the Durban City Council, then sold or rented back as homes in a housing scheme.

Sunjith recalls people living "in small wood-and-iron homes," not quite shacks, which were ultimately demolished. Recall the specific pathos that circulates around "wood-and-iron homes" that signify dignified habitation in periods of hardship. Sunjith recalls a sweep of eviction across Springfield, Cato Manor, Wentworth, Umbilo, and Merebank, and the making of the first townships, with homes of brick. "This was a very big forest, where I live now. The [municipal] corporation gave us this land. They destroyed the forest . . . and gave roads to the people." Juggernath's family history crystallizes the loss of peasant-worker livelihoods on the urban fringe, of homes built by people in a city of hills, swamps, rivers, and forests. The phrase "roads to the people" is laced with the price paid as the violence of infrastructural change folded into urbanization.

Geographers Brij Maharaj and Dianne Scott have impressed on us that the bulk of South Durban's forty thousand forced dispossessions were effected in the 1930s and 1940s, for industrial or infrastructural spatial uses, authorized by provincial and local legislation well before the Group Areas Act of 1950.[5] Removals began in the central ethnic enclaves populated by the Indian middle class, then spread to Cato Manor, Springfield, Mayville, and South Durban, and the city's slim will to rehouse displaced populations deepened the crisis of housing for Durban's Indian and Coloured working classes.[6]

People who had to move continued to be chased by their past in particular ways. In 1944 areas declared slum zones to be removed included Cato Manor, the north bank of the Umgeni River, Karim Lane in South Coast Junction, and Happy Valley between Wentworth and the Bluff. People forcibly moved to Wentworth and Merebank recall areas of multiracial Black residence in the city and its peripheries, including adjacent to the refinery site, with a specific kind of nostalgia. There is a heavy pause, a sigh, or a laugh when people arrive at these remembered spaces, as they mark the narrative rupture of forced removal and the difference from the racial townships to come.

We encountered Jaya's great-grandmother's mixed-race household in early Merebank before the area was zoned Indian (see chapter 2). His great-grandmother had come from the Madras Presidency and may have been a midwife-healer, and while a "traditional Tamil," she remarried to a Welshman called Powers, converted to Methodism, and ran preschools across Merebank while presiding over an interracial extended family from a house on Mere Street near the canal. I had suggested that this family was exemplary of an Indian progressivism in Durban whose possibilities were sharply curtailed as Merebank became an apartheid township.

Jaya's narrative breaks at this moment of racialization. As in other parts of South Africa, narratives of forced removal dwell on sentimental details about pretownship residence, but what is different here is the memory of others moving out while Indians remained. The Tamil-Welsh joint family stands for something else, what should have been. We will return to Jaya's political journey in part 2, but there were ways of refusing the eventuality of a renewed racial capitalism.

Death of a Peasantry, Birth of Infrastructure

The birth of modern infrastructure meant to support the conditions of life also meant the end of other forms of collective provisioning, most significantly of the last peasantry in this part of the world, the peasant-workers of Durban's *black belt*.[7] To subaltern Indians, like the family of C. A. Govender, who moved from gardening near Sea Cow Lake in the early 1940s to the area called Mobeni, where they continued farming on leased land, periodic expropriations had become a fact of life. Mobeni would later become an industrial area, but the locative eMobeni literally means "the sugarcane place."[8] Govender helped his father transport vegetables to the Warwick Avenue market by horse and cart, but their seemingly stable agrarian life was abruptly transformed in 1948, when the corporation bought their land and told them to move. His father moved to Merebank and leased land from one of the big landholders, E. M. Paruk; the family worked this land with "one-two labourers, Indian ladies." Eventually, they owned an acre near the end of the South Coast Road, where the Umlaas Canal turns to enter the ocean. After standard 6 (the eighth grade), Govender remembers waking up at 2 a.m. every morning, getting to work at 2:30 a.m., loading vegetables to take to the market by 6 a.m., and going to night school after a day's farmwork.

This difficult routine was shattered once again: "Somewhere in 1960 the Durban City Council expropriated the land. They bought all land owned by the Indians at a very cheap price, to build houses and factories, and freeways. And that's where we Indians lost out. That was the second blow to the Indian farmers down here. First one was in 1948; the second was round about 1960. We carried on, carried on." Contrasting this forcible transformation of a mixed-use landscape into townships and industrial zones, Govender emphasizes improvements of the land undertaken by marginal farmers like himself in the face of willful negligence by the city's planners. Apart from expropriations, the key events of his life were two major floods, in 1958 and 1987, for which he blames the poor planning of the Umlaas Canal as it bends at the future site of the Mondi Paper Mill. At this point, high tides would force down the barrier next to his plot. After the second flood, Govender was evicted yet again, and he was told that the land was no longer safe to farm, as toxic waste had traveled downstream in the flood and had contaminated the soil. Once more, a prior act of poor urban planning, and the failure to sensibly dispose of toxic waste, forced Govender to move and remake the conditions of his livelihood yet again.

Govender's life's work has involved unrewarded improvisation and innovation, which he described to me in great detail. His anguish was that he faced expropriation once more. We spoke near the land that he has farmed since 1988, on lease from the Airports Company of South Africa. People like Govender have never been recognized for the labors of infrastructural improvement they have been forced to undertake. His intervention with respect to the means of life never attained the status of biopolitical expertise, nor could it successfully articulate with authorized forms of management of land and labor to make it viable in the longer term. This is lost praxis, subaltern expertise that remains silent in the lie of the land.

Land cleared and transformed by peasant-workers was now becoming something else. When the council negotiated the return of Assegai Camp from the admiralty in the late 1940s, it entertained a series of possible names for Assegai Government Village—Haganville, Woodhouse, Rockingham, Cleveland, Harold Davey Town, Harold Daveyville—derived from the names of white residents with claims to historical attachment.[9] The expectation was that this area would become part of white Wentworth. The three-hundred-acre camp was returned to the city to become Assegai Government Village in 1954. Neighborhoods in Wentworth continue to take their names from the naval past: Assegai, SANF for the South African Naval Force, and Ack-Ack, from the sound of a machine gun (map 3). Ironically, these place-names reference the centrality of World War II in the decisive transformation of the mixed-race peasant-worker periphery into a racial township.

The Merebank-Wentworth Housing Scheme was built between 1942 and 1962, with 1,050 acres for Indians and 235 acres for Coloureds, on a new cadastral layout with roads, sewage, stormwater drainage, and pavement.[10] The Natal Indian Association and the Merebank Indian Ratepayers Association (MIRA) (later the Merebank Ratepayers Association [MRA]) protested against the housing scheme as a form of covert segregation, and mass protests were held under the banner of the Durban Expropriation Joint Council of Action, delaying the Central Housing Board's approval.[11] The MRA waged a campaign for about a decade, and when they lost the battle in the courts, they were forced to fold. The council used section 11 of the Housing Act of 1920 as a legislative means to expropriate 656 acres from whites and 629 acres from Indians, purportedly for productive purposes.[12] Community activists reorganized as a coordinating committee, concerned that the council was expropriating homes to provide space for industry. They soon found their expectations confirmed when the informal settlement called Wireless became the site for factories for the Frame Textile Group and for Beacon Sweets.

The more dramatic contrast between industry and residences was yet to be built. At the close of this period, 285 acres in Wentworth became the site of the Stanvac Oil Refinery in 1953, today's Engen refinery. One of Engen's brochures represents the history of this space as a wild, sparsely peopled landscape festering with snakes, caught by a Mexican snake catcher before the construction of the refinery. This mythology of white men taming the landscape is reinforced by photographs of engineers surveying a seemingly unpopulated landscape, more racial forgeries of infrastructural change.

Africans continued to find it difficult to gain a foothold in this geography. This infrastructure, it would seem, was not for them. In 1948, the year the National Party was elected into government, Oliver Maza wrote to the town clerk in extremely respectful longhand, requesting permission to set up a table to sell cooked food at an eating house planned by the city adjacent to the new S. J. Smith Hostel in Merebank; he wrote again four months later as there had been no response.[13] Around the same time, Sipho Shalane requested the opportunity to set up a hairdressing or barber's shop.[14] There are no responses in the archive, a silent roster of official neglect.

The archives do, however, detail an anxious exchange about whether Wentworth Hospital would become a "European" general hospital, as the council wished, or a more specific hospital for tuberculosis patients that would allow "non-Europeans" in but where, the minister of health reassured the mayor, "European" patients "will be segregated within a security fence."[15] At meetings on the fate of South Durban's hospitals, doctors Drummond and Alan Taylor expressed the view that Clairwood could be the site of a unique institute of hygiene and a medical school, both portents of things to come.[16]

The Consolidation of Biopolitical Critique

The 1940s and 1950s saw the emergence of Black politics, galvanized by the mineworkers' strike of 1946, by young militants challenging the leadership within the African National Congress (ANC), and by the Communist Party of South Africa (CPSA) that saw nationalist organizations as allies.[17] Heightened transportation burdens precipitated the bus boycotts of the 1940s, particularly in Johannesburg's Alexandra in 1943. New legislation following the National Party electoral victory in 1948 forced struggles over Black presence in the putatively white city. The Native Laws Amendment Act of 1952 sought to stabilize a section of the African working class who had been born in a city and had lived there since, who had lived there for fifteen years, or who had worked for a specific employer for ten years; Africans who did not meet these criteria faced expulsion.[18]

At this time, the ANC transformed into a mass organization mobilized "nonracially" through its leadership of the Congress Alliance, a coalition with Indian, Coloured, and white political organizations, which also offered cover to underground communists. The CPSA had been dissolved days before the passing of the Suppression of Communism Act of 1950 to reemerge underground in 1953 as the South African Communist Party (SACP). This alliance bore fruit in the mass mobilizations of the Defiance Campaign of 1952, in which the deployment of Gandhian "passive resistance" appeared to be evidence of Afro-Indian solidarity presaging the 1955 Afro-Asian Conference at Bandung, Indonesia. Formed in 1954, the South African Congress of Trade Unions (SACTU) and its underground communists, with initial strength in the largely Indian Textile Workers Industrial Union, was intent to harness Durban's "proletarian populism."[19] Organizers in Durban, including Billy Nair, Moses Mabhida, Stephen Dlamini, and Curnick Ndlovu, created a new style of "political unionism" centered on factory committees. Battles were uphill. During the 1957 strike at the Frame Group of textile factories, African workers did not forge solidarity with their Indian counterparts; this marked the end of the Indian Textile Workers Industrial Union and widened space for SACTU. With strong support from ANC president Albert Luthuli, Africans joined their Indian counterparts in SACTU unions on the docks and in the railway yards and dairies of Durban; major victories for SACTU followed, including in the 1958 stay-away, in which workers in the South Durban industrial area of Mobeni were key participants.[20] In the next few years, SACTU suffered challenges in the railways and on the docks, and the question that remains is how SACTU might have been an effective force for wider political unionism.[21]

Connections among the SACP, SACTU, and the Congress Alliance were close and at times tenuous. The Communist International (Comintern) debates since the 1920s hinged on how proletarian and national-bourgeois movements relate to each other in anti-imperialist struggle. Lenin's position was that "national revolutionary movements" should separate worker and national political organizations; however, the postwar Communist Information Bureau (Cominform) moved toward Stalin's two-stage theory, which argued that national movements would usher in a period of national capitalism to expand the working-class basis for a future socialist revolution.[22]

This two-stage theory of revolution repeats in ANC-SACP thought. However, underground SACP members in the early 1950s argued for working-class organizations to help determine the politics of the ANC-led Congress Alliance, a position they argued was enabled by South Africa's "colonialism of a special type," its "characteristics of both an imperialist state and a colony within a single, indivisible, geographical, political and economic entity."[23]

In late 1950s Durban, women's and labor struggles were only tenuously articulated to the ANC. When approximately twenty thousand people attended a "mass prayer and protest meeting" at Curries Fountain in June 1958, their resolution "against the Group Areas Act and Group Areas Development Act whose implementation will inevitably result in the economic ruin of our people" carefully straddles a nonracial, Charterist appeal to "all South Africans of all races who believe in fair play and justice" with specific appeal to the "Indian community."[24] Indian progressivism was both an instrument of and a fetter on anti-racist working-class solidarity.

Billy Nair, a young boy who grew up in Sydenham and had to work from an early age while studying at night, was quickly drawn into the nascent labor movement of 1940s Durban. When I interviewed the aging militant in his modest home north of Durban over several meetings not long before his passing in 2008, he was particularly interested in revisiting the struggle years for what could have been. Before being drawn into the Congress movement, the Communist Party underground, and uMkhonto we Sizwe (MK), the nascent armed wing of the ANC, for which he would spend twenty years on Robben Island, Nair's primary work was as a labor organizer for the Dairy Workers Union across the city, and subsequently as an organizer for SACTU, an important legal space of activism when the CPSA was dissolved. Members of SACTU and SACP like Nair played a key role alongside Congress activists in the 1955 "Congress of the People" in Kliptown, at which he apparently made submissions to the Freedom Charter on the nationalization of land and industry. Nair insisted that the Congress of the People drew on mass mobilizations across the country, drawing on the praxis of rural Africans imagining a different future.

The banning of the ANC, and the mythology around imprisonment, exile, and underground activism, had, in his view, overshadowed the unprecedented social mobilization of the 1950s. Nair also recalls Black frustration with respect to National Party support for working-class Afrikaner migrants coming to Durban from the *platteland,* the countryside, pushing for stronger labor market segmentation and housing segregation. He notes the state responding in fits and starts to the poor white question in the 1930s and

1940s but becoming much more resolute by the 1950s. In his analysis, the conjuncture of the 1940s was central to the entire architecture of segregation and apartheid, a play of forces between impoverished Afrikaner migrants to the city seeking support from a racial state, and an emerging rural-urban tide of working-class mobilization.

There are other ways to recall this moment, with the Black radical feminism that this chapter begins with. For this, I turn to Poomoney "Poo" Moodley, sister of Mrs. Marie (see chapter 2), who grew up in Clairwood and like many young people was drawn to the political rallies at "Red Square" in 1940s Durban. During the Passive Resistance Campaign, she became part of the door-to-door canvassing efforts that prefigured the organizational work of the 1950s through the trade union movement, the transformation of the Natal Indian Congress by young militants like herself and Nair, the Defiance Campaign, and the historic Women's March on the Union Buildings in Pretoria in 1956, with its central focus on radical anti-racist and feminist unity: "[Prime Minister] Strijdom! *Wathint' abafazi, wathint' imbokodo, uza kufa!*" (You have struck a woman, you have struck a rock, you will be crushed!)

Moodley had been on the executive committee of the Hospital Workers Union. She joined the leadership of the Natal Indian Congress (NIC) in the mid-1950s but remained committed to worker education through SACTU. She had also been a "freedom volunteer" knocking on people's doors to engage popular views on a South Africa to come. She had also become a nurse. When she and others lost their jobs for leading a strike at King George V Hospital, she found work at the Friends of the Sick Association. Moodley was arrested and detained multiple times in the repressive 1960s, including for ninety days in 1963.[25] There are many things to say about the mixed gendered and racial milieu of the ANC, communist, and SACTU organizing that Moodley was part of alongside her comrade Phyllis Naidoo, but it is important to note that her radicalism emerged through a combination of worker and community struggle and also, crucially, through her professional life as a nurse. Indeed, to be a nurse with a political conscience, and by all accounts a daring personality, meant that she could radicalize the notion of care work, to turn very crucially to the fundamental problem of modern segregation: how to critique the racialization of biopolitical tools without giving up on the radical hope of universal access to the means of life. This is the fundamental question concerning biopolitical struggle.

The historiography of Black politics in the transition to apartheid is worth revisiting precisely with this attention to struggle on the terrain of biopolitics. In the 1950s people from Merebank appear to have participated in the labor activism that Billy Nair was involved in, but the records are few and far between. Jaya describes his father's years as a worker in industrial Durban and the intensity of labor organizing. He also describes his mother's involvement in the Passive Resistance Movement of the 1940s, and her work to establish a cooperative to provide cheap provisions to the neighborhood, a practice he and others would return to in the 1970s (see chapter 6).

However, one of the most significant aspects of the consolidation of biopolitical critique is usually left outside this historiography, partly because its full effect was nipped in the bud despite people like Moodley. This centers on the work of Sidney and Emily Kark, pioneers in what would become the fields of community health and social medicine. They were white Progressives who used their expertise for the radical demand for universal access to health and medicine.

Along with their associates, workers, students, and patients, the Karks developed a critique of demographic and epidemiological approaches to fertility, mortality, and natural hazards, drawing on ethnography, sociology, and psychology and connecting primary care to "community health" by building local capacities in vegetable gardening and dietetics; they helped recruit and train community health workers and built comprehensive health centers.[26] The work of the Karks and their associates was crucial to the recommendations of the 1944 National Health Services Commission for a national health service built on local health centers connected to national hospitals, and forty of the planned four hundred health centers were built before the National Party was voted into government in 1948.[27]

Looking back at their career from Pholela in rural Zululand, and to the approach they developed in the 1940s and 1950s, which they would later call *community-oriented primary health care*, the Karks emphasize their own process of learning as they confronted multiple epistemologies of ill health and sought to combine epidemiological, behavioral, and clinical approaches to preventive and curative service rooted in communities.[28] The Karks brought together an early critique of segregation with a critique of Nazism both in Europe and among South African whites; they drew from the liberalism of some of the academic staff at the University of the Witwatersrand (Wits) as well as the new South African Institute of Race Relations, helped form the Society for the Study of Medical Conditions among the Bantu at Wits, and later studied social anthropology at the University of Oxford with Evans Pritchard, Meyer Fortes, and Max Gluckman, which reinforced their education at Wits.[29]

When the liberal minister of the interior, education, and public health, Jan Hofmeyr, supported a survey of children's health and nutrition and a proposal to initiate "health units" in the "Native Reserves," the Karks became involved in the survey and in the Pholela health unit in rural Zululand, the only one to be formed after the onset of World War II. In 1942 Henry Gluckman was appointed chairman of the National Health Services Commission, which would also support their work. Vanessa Noble argues that this group of "forward-thinking public health doctors," including Gluckman, the Karks, and George Gale, "advocated something different"; a report to Hofmeyr in 1942 puts forth "that "doctors should be trained as preserver[s] of health rather than as mender[s] of diseased bodies"—that is, as biopolitical experts.[30]

Gluckman was later appointed minister of health, and between 1945 and 1948, he launched forty health centers across the country. The Karks' work in Pholela was fundamentally communitarian and committed to finding the causes of poverty, malnutrition, and disease. They used "epidemiological surveillance" to diagnose malnutrition, communicable diseases, and psycho-social disorders in a way that refused what they saw as a mind-body split endemic to medical orthodoxy. In 1945 the Karks were transferred to Durban to train health personnel and to start the Institute of Family and Community Health (IFCH), headquartered in the former World War II military hospital in Clairwood in South Durban. Areas proximal to the IFCH were selected for neighborhood family and community health centers, in Lamontville, Merebank ("an urban slum area with a mainly Indian Hindu population who had settled there some three generations earlier. This bordered on an area with a number of Coloured families and adjacent shack dwelling blacks, known as the Clairwood-Jacobs area"), Woodlands ("a white housing estate, recently developed for WWII ex-servicemen and their families"), and Mobeni Industrial Zone, the site of the Industrial Health Centre of the IFCH.[31] Gale, about to become dean of the new University of Natal, Durban Medical School, in 1951, wrote to Sidney Kark to suggest that the "non-European doctor, with his more intimate knowledge of the outlook and language of his own people, will be able to make his most valuable contribution to their health needs" as a kind of general practitioner working inside/outside a hospital environment.[32]

In South Durban the Karks sought this complex approach to community health with teams of doctors, nurses, and health educators providing services to neighborhoods. Health centers ran community health programs for curative and preventive health, including prenatal and postnatal care for mothers and babies. They encouraged school health programs. A preschool center in Merebank formed "milk clubs" to take advantage of municipal delivery of free milk to volunteer homes, and mothers were organized to supervise the program along with a community health educator. Finally, they envisioned an Industrial Health Centre in rapidly industrializing Mobeni, working through clinics within factories and providing health examinations for all and health care specifically to Black workers who did not have the medical and insurance schemes afforded to white workers.[33]

The Karks argued for new kinds of medical practitioners and localized experts in their holistic approach to health care and education. Their notion of "community health educators" met considerable opposition from public health nurses on the British model. In response, they argued that community health education required a class distinct from doctors, nurses, midwives, and social case workers—that is, people who were part of the community but not involved with the urgency of care for the sick. They began training for community health educators in Pholela and then in Clairwood, envisioning a university program, which collapsed when the idea of a national health service was shut down in the late 1950s.[34]

Interpreting their research in South Durban, the Karks saw a "stability of family living" with "three or four generations of family living in Merebank," a startling indication of the settled nature of at least some Indian families in the area. Corroborating Jaya's recollections of his grandmother, they note the importance of "traditional Indian midwives" and comment that Durban City Council's Health Department "supervised these midwives by routine inspection . . . and basic instruction in hygienic methods." Contrasting this with the absence of midwives in rural and urban African settlements in Pholela and Lamontville, they also show that neonatal mortality rates in Indian Merebank and Springfield (7 and 13 per 1,000 live births, respectively) were considerably lower than in "better-off" African Lamontville (35 per 1,000) and poorer rural Pholela (60 per 1,000).[35]

When Sidney Kark was invited by Alan Taylor in 1946 to be part of the committee of the Durban Medical School, his main contribution was to include family practice and community medicine, with the IFCH as a satellite department supported by the Rockefeller Foundation. The notion of "health centers" circulated through these networks from Durban to various parts of the world. However, the Karks recall obstacles, beginning with the fact that the Durban Medical School was segregated from its inception. Rockefeller funding kept the IFCH going in its last five years, until 1955, after which the IFCH and the family medicine clerkship for students at the medical school ended. As they put it, "The many excellent men and women health educators, health recorders and statisticians and laboratory workers who had been trained and worked over a number of years at the IFCH, had also received no official professional recognition of their status. . . . The loss to South Africa of this highly trained and motivated cadre of health professionals was a tragic outcome."[36]

Durban's experiment with social medicine had been reliant on Rockefeller funding. When the Karks left, these people and places remained.[37] Noble writes that doctors and nurses were moved to curative facilities and that "Community Health Workers were either retrenched or used as hospital orderlies."[38] The Karks departed for the United States in 1958, to Chapel Hill, North Carolina, and then on to Israel, to a joint World Health Organization–Israel project in social medicine, and then on to rural community health with the Navajo in the United States. Like the Karks, Mervyn Susser also left the increasingly repressive context that was apartheid's first decade (see chapter 5). However, as the Karks point out, people trained to think about public health remained in South Durban, a landscape increasingly dominated by toxic ill health.

Parallel to these events, the possibility of anti-racist unity through biopolitical or other means was challenged by an event remembered simply as "1949."

The 1949 "Durban Riots": Racial Sovereignty Strikes Back

On the evening of Thursday, January 13, 1949, in the busy Grey Street enclave in the heart of the city, a young African man and a young Indian shop attendant got into an altercation.[39] On the face of it, to see two young men in conflict is unremarkable. Nor would it have been unusual to see Africans subject to racism from shop employees, traders, bus conductors, and other Indian plebeians who worked in what Jon Soske calls the Indian-owned and -run "ersatz infrastructure" of the segregated city.[40] Then the Indian youth threw the African into a window and cut open his head. The space and time of this event are important: "at the end of the day amidst the crowds of Victoria Street, near the central bus depot where thousands of Africans and Indians queued for a bus home. This was the heartland of the Indian commercial center, and the site of Durban's largest 'Native' beer hall and market stalls."[41] Several Africans confronted the shop assistant. Others, among them Indians, came to his defense. Rumors circulated about an Indian crowd killing a young African man, and more people arrived on the scene. Some Indians in balconies above threw bottles and bricks onto Africans below. A street fight between groups of Indians and Africans using sticks and stones spread across the Casbah. Some Africans, later called a "mob," shifted out to attack Indian people, vehicles, and shops late into the night.

Things escalated dramatically on Friday, as groups of African men and women joined a more violent and directed anti-Indian effort, drawing on others through hostels, dance troops, boxing clubs, and other social networks.[42] Police intervention was slow, and some white onlookers goaded people to raid Indian shops. When the military was called in to contain the Casbah, the violent attacks shifted to Cato Manor and Jacobs. In Soske's reading, "rampaging crowds burnt houses and stores, raped Indian women and girls, and viciously bludgeoned Indians of all ages, sexes, and social classes. Particularly in the outlying areas, the pogrom targeted the Indian poor and working class—the only target readily available. The goal was clear: to drive Indians out."[43] The military and police responded violently into the night, with reports of machine guns firing into crowds "for five minutes at a time."[44] Official figures reported "87 Africans, 50 Indians, 4 unidentified, and 1 European killed; 1,087 people injured; 40,000 Indian refugees; over 300 buildings destroyed; and more than 2,000 structures damaged"; African and Indian newspapers reported higher numbers.[45]

Soske follows Bill Freund's characterization of a melee that turned into a pogrom, refusing the term used by the white press and subsequently by popular and scholarly historiography: "the Durban Riots."[46] The transposition of the "race riot" from the United States, Soske argues, was a thin euphemism for racial violence in response to Black assertion in response to racism, and it ignores the complexity of race, the context of segregation, and the targeting of Indians. Freund's explanation makes more of Iain Edwards's focus on the event's epicenter in Mkhumbane, Cato Manor, where a "proletarian populism" was forged through a mixture of migrant labor, Zulu ethnic chauvinism, and an ideology of a "New Africa" built on decisive "war against Indians," which in turn referenced all the ways in which Indians were the proximal oppressors in the landscape of everyday racism in Durban.[47] "Proletarian populism" in Mkhumbane was a rejection of Victorian Progressivism propagated by mission schools and Christian reform; Freund calls it a struggle for "a new sort of patronage."[48] But what kind of patronage would be effective in dismantling everyday racism?

In the aftermath of the event, commentators, particularly African nationalists, struggled with engaging the conditions of possibility of violence without condoning it. An emergent Congress "nonracialism," particularly from ANC-aligned intellectuals like Ismail Meer, Fatima Meer, and Dr. Goonam, posed the 1949 pogrom as an aberration. Dr. Goonam writes, "Many [Africans], in fact, in Cato Manor, Mayville, Second River, Briardene, Sea Cow Lake and Springfield protected their Indian neighbours and sheltered them in their home against attacks by [other] Africans."[49]

Soske looks across the Indian and African press to argue against this Congress scripting of the violence as a wakeup call for a politics of nonracial alliance.[50] The Indian press aligned to the Congress posed the "Durban Riots" as incited by the state, a conspiratorial line that spoke to an Indian public that had long been on the receiving end of official racism. The African press, in contrast, highlighted everyday indignities of life in the segregated city, peppered by acts of Indian arrogance and exploitation; these charges of rack-renting, usury, overcharging, and black marketing, however, echoed a long history of white anti-Indian racism that recycled anti-Semitic tropes of the rapacious trader-moneylender-landlord.

In a lucid and spatially attuned account, Vivek Narayanan argues that "1949 . . . can be read as a parable of the flow and divergence of information," with possibilities of public transgression and racialized privacy across the spaces of a segregated city.[51] The effects of "1949" were just as spatially varied. In the Congress tradition, the aftermath prompted a rearticulation of Indian middle-class activism, heir to the tradition of Indian progressivism, in the form of the Transvaal ANC and the Natal ANC Youth League, and also in underground SACP cells within these organizations. However, membership in the ANC expanded dramatically across the country in the late 1950s except in Natal.[52] Freund's explanation is that the conditions for radical political consciousness were weak in Durban in contrast to the Witwatersrand, but this is a negative explanation.[53] Narayanan's spatial sensitivity is important in this regard.

The whirl of sentiment circulating around "1949" was also notably gendered and sexualized. From its inception, Soske notes that "on the first evening of the 1949 Durban Riots, a crowd of African men gathered outside the Grey Street Women's Hostel, demanding the delivery of women who associated with Indians."[54] The specter of Indian men seducing African women returns in testimony about participating in the riots, and in subsequent writing about the events, echoing National Party fearmongering about miscegenation as well as wider imperial discourses of sexuality, but also the real threat of sexual violence that accompanied African women's domestic labor.[55] Dr. Goonam writes of attending to young girls fourteen and fifteen years old who were raped during the violence in Clairwood, Jacobs, and Merebank; Soske situates this violence against women, and forced and consensual sex across the color line in historical processes that include the expulsion of African women from the city followed by their entry into urban waged work in the 1940s, their movement without passes for a period of time, the gendered shift in domestic labor in white and Indian homes from African "kitchen boys" to African women domestic workers, shifting gender politics in Indian and African nationalisms of the early twentieth century, widespread fear and loathing of the "modern" African woman, and various conflations of African women's employment with assertiveness and promiscuity.[56]

The accusation that Indian men systematically seduced African women was ubiquitous, and it centered on specific places: Indian shops, buses, and domestic spaces.[57] In Indian domestic space, African servants were in relations of apparent intimacy and yet racial distance through restrictions on interdining and sharing of utensils in ways that, at least in Indian homes, indexed anti-Dalit racism in India (see chapter 2). African women's domestic labor was a cipher for broader anxieties about the persistence or adaptation of African social institutions in the context of racial capitalism. The defense of African women from sexual degeneration was a sign of actual, forced and unforced, sexual interaction across the color line, which would soon be recognized in an unexpectedly large Coloured population emerging from the forced removals of Indian homes across the city.

The figure of the Black woman in domestic servitude—whether African, Indian, or Coloured—demonstrated something else, which is that however much the apartheid state might pursue a system of residential segregation, the interiors of homes would remain spaces of variously forced intimacy that held the possibility of something other than racial sovereignty. These itineraries are part of the figure of the Black domestic worker looking away from the camera in the photograph at the beginning of this chapter.

What Remains? Critical Infrastructure

The most obvious forgotten remnant of this period is the contradictory industrial-residential built environment of South Durban, forged between the imperatives of industrialization and segregation, disclosing while effacing the labors of those who made and maintained this productive landscape. Infrastructural maintenance widens the arena of unwaged or unvalorized care work, as feminists have long argued. We have seen that the local state's aleatory territorialization of South Durban into an industrial landscape foisted industrial pollution on those who shared space with manufacturing capital.

From the perspective of people in this environment, habitation was always untenable, and they sought various ways to mark the effects of industry on health long before the language of environmental justice (see chapter 9).

Many scholars have turned to the 1940s in South Africa as a decade of possibility.[58] What we see from South Durban in this period is that some saw possibilities in forging a better welfare state responsive to the Black majority, while others, like the young Billy Nair and Poo Moodley, were forging a militant critique of the social formation. They were engaged in what thinkers from André Gorz to Ruth Wilson Gilmore call "non-reformist reform" or "abolitionist" reform that turns the critique of health injustice into the dismantling of the racial biopolitical infrastructure that sustains capitalism itself.[59]

Consider how the late Phyllis Naidoo, irascible political activist from Durban, found her way at the age of seventeen (around 1945–46) to a settlement run by the Friends of the Sick Association, formed in 1941, which ran a tuberculosis clinic in Newlands. Naidoo recounts how a group of people centered on Paul and Nell Sykes "got together and established a tent and got donations to build a little facility," which she then joined as "a nurse of sorts without any training." The situation was so grim that, as she put it, "We just filled these buggers up," meaning that they could only patch up people's wounds. At some point, she recounts a fundamental disagreement "when one of the fellows who was so sick and we had made him well again was discharged to go home and of course home was unemployment, and in two weeks' time he was back and he died on us. I got the hell in to Paul. I said, 'What are we doing? What are we doing? We're spending our energies here and they come back again.' I was about 17 then. And he said, 'Look, that is politics.'"[60]

This was the turning point for Naidoo, as she turned to the passive resistance movement of 1946, joining Poo Moodley, and subsequently to the Non-European Unity Movement, a Trotskyist organization with deeper roots in the Cape, and particularly in the Pondoland revolts of the early 1950s. In 1956 she became actively involved in support for the 156 Congress leaders imprisoned for two weeks during what would be called the Treason Trial.

When we met in her modest home in the borderlands of middle-class Durban, she sat in a room covered with boxes containing material on these activists, most of whom she thought had been forgotten by the struggle pantheon. Much of the work she continued to do was to document in a series of books the "footsteps" people took, along with her, in the long struggle against apartheid.[61] Antoinette Burton thoughtfully reads Naidoo's writings as "a radical form of biographical and autobiographical memory, and a re-markable archive of Afrindian solidarities and frictions."[62] What is crucial is that her critical imagination, like that of Moodley, took shape in relation to social medicine emerging from regional landscapes of injustice and ill health. As she put it, every footstep in these struggles matters.

Community Health Today, 2002–

Life next to an oil refinery has made Wentworth a hub of interest in vari-ous kinds of private investments in development and social welfare. This and the mobilization around environmental and labor concerns have led the city and corporations to try to engage community representatives through the technocratic language of stakeholder management. Finance for social proj-ects through corporate social responsibility programs has been the topic of fierce debate in community meetings. The South Durban Community En-vironmental Alliance (SDCEA) refuses what it sees as tainted money, while other groups and individuals have taken a more pragmatic perspective, mak-ing every crumb from corporations count for something meaningful to the lives of residents. Despite these risks, a significant number of Wentworth's residents put their bodies and minds to community work.

I spent considerable time with George Ruiters, who also introduced me to the late Aunty Tilly. An unpaid community health care counselor who is largely self-taught, George has been a wellspring of insight that I return to throughout this book. When we met, George had worked across various organizations, on environmental issues, public health, domestic violence, and children's rights, but he has steadily built an expertise in sexuality and HIV/AIDS.

George's family came to Wentworth from the Eastern Cape environs of Kokstad, where, he adds poignantly, "My grandmother used to take in mentally retarded patients. . . . Maybe that's where I got it from . . . I'm not too sure . . . helping others. My aunt and granny used to do a lot of that."[63] George's narrative is one of linguistic fluidity and constant movement, and it offers a powerful argument about the intergenerational transmission of gen-dered caregiving. If Black women have been specific bearers of stigma and pain, they have also been powerful figures in reworking the politics of care.

Like Naidoo and Moodley more than half a century earlier, both George and Aunty Tilly felt their calling as community health workers. Both of them pieced together their training and education in informal ways, as passion-ate professionals who worked carefully around the conservatism and self-interest surrounding them. Both put their time and energy, unfailingly, into the health of people in the community. Careful about the stigma surrounding AIDS, they worked as informal advisors to people on antiretroviral and other time-sensitive medication to ensure compliance. Most important, they worked to make South Durban a place not just of suffering but also of advocacy for the right to dignified conditions of life. In these endeavors they index a longer set of struggles over biopolitical expertise, including those of the unnamed Black participants working with the Karks, and many others since. In their daily practice as community health counselors, both George and Aunty Tilly have kept active the remains of biopolitical struggle forged in South Durban in the 1940s.

Remains of Racial/Sexual Capitalism

In light of the turbulent emergence of biopolitical struggle in the 1940s, how might we return to the conversation among Toni Morrison, Angela Davis, and the Black woman at the center of the photograph at the start of this chapter? How might we take seriously the many visible and invisible dimensions of the praxis of the domestic servant, her arms taut as she pulls a pram, glancing down at the children or possibly at the white woman behind her? We might think with Morrison's reminder about audiences, to imagine all possible ways that she might be read. A simple act of looking back and down, at the center of the frame, captures that human praxis as embodied is never simply legible by any "gaze."

As we read her in this way, she takes over the photograph and its possibilities. We might now read the photograph as a commentary on the impossibility of erasure of the essential labors of raced and gendered care work that are not always but typically, in racial capitalist societies, the provenance of Black women, women of color, and the gender nonnormative. Her literal centrality in the image returns us to many forms of raced/gendered labor essential to the reproduction of labor power, and, by extension, to the biopolitical critique of racial/sexual capitalism. Aunty Tilly's praxis as a wise woman, a fierce African critic of racism and sexism in Wentworth, is part of a wider world of Black women's praxis that has been a red thread through the Black radical tradition, also in South Africa.

In the proximal years of the postwar period, in the lead-up to the surprise electoral victory of the National Party in 1948, white women's virtue was deployed as an electoral fetish detached from the praxis of gendered survival across the color line. Just as the specter of "mixed marriages" had been key to the 1934 election, the protection of the purity of the white race returned in 1948 in a multifaceted desire to keep work, home, community, city, and nation from the contamination of entanglement.[64] While a seemingly ungendered politics between men spoke for the nation, the actually sexed and gendered reality of life was not quite submerged around it.

This is the milieu in which Shireen Hassim powerfully argues that Indian women in the 1940s began to make common cause in public politics with African women in opposition to white supremacy and in defense of women's rights, and they faced routine repression from political organizations; in response, women from the ANC Women's League, the Communist Party, and trade unions formed a nonracial Federation of South African Women.[65] The following excerpt from their "Women's Charter" is a powerful expression of the simultaneity of multiple struggles as foundational to a future of universal rights:

> The law has lagged behind the development of society; it no longer corresponds to the actual social and economic position of women. The law has become an obstacle to the progress of the women, and therefore a brake on the whole of society. This intolerable condition would not be allowed to continue were it not for the refusal of a large section of our menfolk to concede to us women the rights and privileges which they demand for themselves. We shall teach men they cannot hope to liberate themselves from the evils of discrimination and prejudice as long as they fail to extend to women complete and unqualified equality in law and practice.[66]

The federation subsequently accepted the ANC's leadership for pragmatic reasons, Hassim argues, but this did not prevent its autonomous organization of the militant march of two thousand women to the Union Buildings in Pretoria on August 9, 1956, led by a multiracial group of four women, carrying twenty thousand petitions protesting the extension of pass laws to women; this was the historic Women's March that Moodley had attended.

Hassim adds a cautionary point to this much-memorialized moment, that it was not just the ANC Women's League or the Federation of South African Women who were behind the emergence of women's critique. Rather, the gendered praxis of survival in a segregated society pointed to an emergent conception of biopolitical struggle exemplified well in 1940s South Durban. Dealing with the damage of segregation in the years before apartheid, the praxis she points to runs through this book. Here is Hassim's radical Black feminist critique of our collective past and present:

In addition to the overt political organization of women, many other forms of associational life provided solidarity networks for newly urbanized women, functioned as women's forums within religious communities, or performed economics support roles (savings clubs—"stokvels"—and burial societies). These organizational forms need to be recognized if we are to use a more fluid understanding of politics than that defined by male-centered political organizations. In their everyday life within these nonpolitical structures women often develop a collective consciousness that can be mobilized when the survival of communities is at stake. . . . In South Africa the everyday organization of women around their roles as mothers and community members by far outweighs the number of women engaged in overt political activities. Yet, a deeper analysis of women's political organizations suggests that the strategic links and cultural affinities between those organizations and the "apolitical" women's groups are more extensive than is generally credited.[67]

The Science Fiction of Apartheid's Spatial Fix, 1948–1970s

The most important practical issue in race zoning is: Where will the people go who are now living in areas zoned for another race, and how will they re-establish themselves? Our illegal shack areas demonstrate only too clearly how ineffective segregatory laws can be when they merely prohibit a group from living in a certain place but do not provide adequately for them elsewhere. Effective implementation of the Group Areas Act must go even further than providing alternative accommodation. It should strive to make the alternative accommodation so attractive that people will voluntarily try to secure it.

—UNIVERSITY OF NATAL, *Durban Housing Survey*, 1951

Simply this: that race is the tomb wherein the historical consciousness is interred, alive; that try as it might, the empire can never wholly erase intimations of possibilities native to the very idea of humanity; that there is life after apartheid—no, that there is life, human, all-too-human life, palpitating within the peculiar institution of apartheid.

—ATO SEKYI-OTU, *Fanon's Dialectic of Experience*

Fictions of a Racial-Spatial Fix

Omar Badsha, photographer of the iconic image in figure 5.1, is a hinge between the political effervescence of the 1950s as witnessed from Durban's

Casbah, and the revolutionary uprisings of the 1970s. Badsha's praxis is also a hinge in another sense. Thus far, the photographs in this book have been akin to Cedric Robinson's forgeries of racial capitalism.[1] Badsha's photography sought something else. His pioneering work as an engaged photographer and artist-activist helped nurture a Black photographic tradition steadfastly focused on fugitive forms of conviviality necessary for the persistence of struggle.

Shaped by the cultural and political life of the Casbah, Badsha's most powerful influences were his artist father, Ebrahim Badsha, member of the Bantu, Indian, Coloured Arts Group, and his photojournalist uncle, Moosa Badsha. In the 1960s Omar Badsha was recruited into the African National Congress (ANC) underground, where he worked with A. K. M. Docrat and Phyllis Naidoo. In his public life as an artist, Badsha worked with watercolor, printmaking, and photography. He was close to artist Dumile Feni and writers Mafika Gwala and Mandla Langa, each transformed by the Black Consciousness Movement of the 1970s. He enabled connections among independent Black trade unions, the Natal Indian Congress (NIC), Black Consciousness (BC), and university student movements in the 1970s and is remembered by former youth as a living link across generations of dissident politics and art.

Turning back to the photograph (figure 5.1), the backdrop is the Grey Street Mosque, object of many decades of official loathing of Indian presence in town, and a silent reminder that Durban would never be a white city. The caption tells us that the occasion is the celebration of Badsha Pir, the unknown indentured laborer retrospectively recast as a Sufi saint in the settlement of South Asian Islam (see chapter 2). Some versions are titled *Rathi Players*, implying that the taut, bare-chested man holds a dagger aloft while engrossed in ritualized public flagellation to lament the death of Ali, the Prophet's nephew. This ritual from the festival Ashura during the month of Muharram was part of syncretic religious life under indenture, then was pushed into the margins as reformist Islam has sought to stamp out South Asian aspects of religious expression since the 1990s.[2] The photograph captures the persistence of demotic Muslim ritual in postindenture Durban; it is a reminder that this is an Indian Ocean city.

Consider this photograph in relation to this chapter's opening epigraph, an anticipatory forgery from the *Durban Housing Survey* assembled by the Department of Economics of the University of Natal following the *Barnes Report* on racial zoning (see chapter 3). When this excellent volume was

FIGURE 5.1 Badsha Pir birthday celebrations, Grey Street, Durban, 1980. © Omar Badsha.

published, apartheid's forced removals had begun, and the authors make
the same point that I make here, that dispossession implies resettlement
elsewhere. However, dispossession is one instrument in the multifaceted
processes of racism as "state-sanctioned or extralegal production and exploitation of group-differentiated vulnerability to premature death."[3] This is
why the last line of the paragraph is pure liberal delusion, which switches
to the normative when popular consent to forced removal is utterly implausible. Instead, "effective implementation" required an intensification of
a police mode of biopolitical government.[4] Badsha's photograph captures
exactly what escapes its grasp.

Contrast this with the statement from Ato Sekyi-Otu's lucid reading of
Frantz Fanon that "race is the tomb wherein the historical consciousness is
interred, alive," but also that "there is life, human, all-too-human life, palpitating within the peculiar institution of apartheid."[5] This precise, dialectical formulation marks the impossibility of apartheid's attempt to fix racial
capitalism so effectively that it might extinguish all-too-human life. That
the photograph ritually disinters the unknown indentured mystic Badsha
Pir adds a particular pathos to life that survives attempted entombment. As
we encounter the Black photographers mentored by Badsha in chapters to
come, we will see that they have focused exactly on the problem of life that
survives apartheid.

Returning to Badsha's image, we might also ask why some places demolished under apartheid's Group Areas Act of 1950 are memorialized as iconic sites of multiracial conviviality—Cape Town's District Six, Johannesburg's Sophiatown, and Durban's Cato Manor and Casbah—while places produced *by* apartheid cannot be seen as also possible sites of transgressive political culture.[6] Yet this is what Merebank and Wentworth became as racial townships that were also places of conviviality that would support vibrant political cultures in decades to come. While the Merebank-Wentworth Housing Scheme and subsequent apartheid townships of Merebank and Wentworth would soon be surrounded and permeated by polluting industry, its denizens have never submitted to apartheid's deadening certainties.

The argument of this chapter is that even in apartheid's heyday, everyday practice was never entirely overwhelmed by legislative, administrative, or police power. City hall could never make Durban conform to its racial-spatial fictions. Instead, forms of conviviality long constitutive of Durban's interstices became increasingly apparent as apartheid's geographies entered a prolonged political and economic crisis beginning in the late 1960s. This is what the figure of the *rathi* player in Badsha's photograph proclaims. Reading archives of the apartheid state in relation to people's recollections, we will see many dimensions of complicity and contradiction in apartheid's statecraft. Rather than fixed racial worlds, we see dialectical townships that unfix people from their presumed slots in racial space, in many moments of refusal.

Apartheid in History and Theory

For all its familiarity, apartheid resists easy definition. It is . . . even more elusive . . . as a totality.
—SAUL DUBOW, *Apartheid, 1948–1994*

After its 1948 electoral victory, the National Party (or the Nationalists or "Nats") had to turn an imprecise electoral slogan fueled by racial fears of *swart gevaar* (black peril), *oorstrooming* (swamping), and *bloedvermenging* (miscegenation) into policy.[7] Apartheid's ascendant phase, 1948–59, centered on deepening hegemony through "petty apartheid," or the everyday segregation of services and amenities; its second phase, 1959–66, deepened "grand apartheid," or the attempt at nominal independence and "separate development" in ethno-racial-linguistic areas, linking "separate but not equal" segregation in the US South to notions of "development" co-opted from continental decolonization; and its third phase, after 1966, was marked by prolonged political and economic crisis.[8]

In its heyday, apartheid promised an overtly racist variation on the mid-century golden age of welfare capitalism upheld by energy self-sufficiency, global demand for South African gold, anti-communism, and administered segregation of work, housing, welfare, and leisure. Mirroring this complexity, the historiography of apartheid is a treasure trove and a hornet's nest.[9] Apartheid was singular in some respects, an exceptionalism that helped galvanize a global movement to end it. Apartheid statecraft sometimes aided capital's quest for a racial-spatial fix, but it was also "a fix" as an intoxicant and "in a fix" in its protracted last decades, prompting progressive strands of capital to seek a political transition.

Intensified policing and organization in apartheid's first phase spurred the 1960 mass protest against pass law arrests, organized by the Pan Africanist Congress in Sharpeville and Langa. Police violence was followed by the declaration of a state of emergency and the banning of the ANC and Pan Africanist Congress. The underground South African Communist Party (SACP) helped the Congress Alliance to respond. The SACP leadership abstracted from the peasant revolt in Pondoland "a generalized popular susceptibility for revolutionary violence," and the party conference of 1960 committed to "a campaign of economic sabotage to precede a guerrilla war," despite disagreement from Durban communist lawyer Rowley Arenstein, who had defended the Mpondoland insurrectionists, as well as ANC president Albert Luthuli, recipient of the Nobel Peace Prize awarded close to the launch of uMkhonto we Sizwe (MK), literally "Spear of the Nation."[10]

Two years later, a police raid of Liliesleaf Farm in Rivonia unearthed "Operation Mayibuye," a schematic document laying out a strategy for armed struggle.[11] Almost the entirety of the MK High Command was arrested, including key ANC and SACP leadership with the exception of Oliver Tambo and Joe Slovo, both abroad. Nelson Mandela, traveling underground, was arrested on the road in Natal through a tip-off from the Central Intelligence Agency (CIA). The 1963 Rivonia Trial marked a turning point after which the top leadership would languish in jail or in exile for almost three decades.

The tragedy of this moment occludes other possibilities, like mass agrarian mobilization and rural-urban organization. As in the 1940s, resistance in Natal and Zululand towns and the countryside in 1959 was led by women and centered on "issues that affected women's livelihoods, such as the spreading betterment schemes, new forestry regulations, women's passes, taxes on wives, threatened removals from black spots, stock control enforcement and cattle dipping requirements which intensified their work conditions"; rural women joined in urban protests, as at Curries Fountain in Durban and

Umzinto farther south in July 1959.[12] Cherryl Walker documents a fascinating protest in which twenty thousand women struck in Ixopo for their right to have a Native women's commissioner rather than to have their rights mediated by their husbands and headmen; in a simultaneous wave of action, people destroyed three-fourths of the hated cattle-dipping tanks in rural Natal.[13] A mass meeting at Durban City Hall in February that year focused on a boycott of buses and beer halls and a general strike in opposition to forced removals; from late March to early April, mass strikes and marches in Durban had strong support from migrant workers, culminating in an April 1 march of a thousand people from Mkhumbane in Cato Manor to the central jail, which Bill Freund calls "a prospective storming of the Bastille."[14] What is important is the mosaic of livelihood concerns in these struggles.

The clampdown after April 1960 sought to normalize "torture, solitary confinement, indefinite detention without trial [after the 1967 Terrorism Act], deaths in detention," and regular use of the death penalty.[15] Several key organizers in Durban were neutralized: Luthuli was banished to his rural home; Moses Mabhida exiled; Harry Gwala, Curnick Ndlovu, and Billy Nair imprisoned. The aftermath of this moment is often written off as a period of political quiescence, but the banned, jailed, and exiled male leadership made space for women-led militancy, including that of Winnie Mandela, Albertina Sisulu, Fatima Meer, Amina Cachalia, Phyllis Naidoo, and many others.

Twinned with repression was apartheid law, the two pillars of which were the Population Registration Act of 1950, which sought to classify all South Africans by race "based on appearance, general acceptance and repute" and subsequently also by "descent"; and the Group Areas Act of 1950, reenacted in 1957 and 1966, which sought comprehensive racial segregation of residential, commercial, and work areas to eliminate interracial "friction."[16] When Indian Merebank and Coloured Wentworth became racial Group Areas, their residents had already been electorally disfranchised, but for Wentworth's residents, the injury was as recent as 1956.[17] Another set of laws deepened labor market segregation, limiting African construction labor through the Bantu Building Workers Act of 1951 and deepening job reservations through the Industrial Conciliation Act of 1956.[18] The Western Cape was declared a "Coloured labour preference area," spatially and racially limiting specific jobs to people designated Coloured, with effects in places, like Wentworth.[19]

Nationalist hegemony required placating fractions of capital through new forms of biopolitical statecraft. Tightening influx control, focused on African "migrants" to cities, was a compromise between agrarian capital, keen to control migration out of agriculture, and mining capital, interested in stabilizing labor through rural reserves.[20] Biopolitical imperatives deepened the state's administrative power through what Ivan Evans poses as David Harvey's spatial fix, exemplified by the planned urban location "linked to . . . the racialization of space and the incorporation of modern methods of town planning into urban administration."[21]

Apartheid's coercive spatial biopolitics sought to severely curtail African livelihoods in multiple ways: by limiting trade, slowing construction of "subeconomic" housing, ending urban tenancies, cutting back technical and secondary school expansion, and shifting services for the infirm and the elderly to the homelands. The combined attempt was to restrict African urban life to townships and to homelands with restored chiefly authority. Hendrik Verwoerd's policy of "separate development" used the language of decolonization to provide "self-determination" to African "nations" in homelands, while the Promotion of Bantu Self-Government Act of 1959 laid the basis of homeland "self-government" and the end of minimal representation of Africans in Parliament. The 1960 referendum to declare South Africa a republic was a conscious defection from reformism in the British Commonwealth, signified by the British prime minister Harold Macmillan's "Winds of Change" speech in the South African parliament.[22] Verwoerd's successor, John Vorster, subsequently used alarmist demographics on African presence in urban South Africa to accelerate homeland "independence" in the Transkei (1976), Bophuthatswana (1977), Venda (1970), and Ciskei (1981), which left more than eight million Africans disfranchised in fragmented spaces of deprivation. While less than half of the African population in 1970 lived in homelands, official policy labeled them "temporary sojourners" in white areas, harking back to the Urban Areas Act of 1923 and to Victorian criminalization of vagrancy.[23]

Homeland "independence" is important for South Durban because "de-Africanization," in Patric Tariq Mellet's terms, required the expropriation of uncounted numbers of people of mixed backgrounds from the Transkei and from the coastal areas north and south of Durban, who were compelled to move to the city, many of whom would end up classified as Coloureds in Wentworth.[24] Many of them retained rural-urban lives, sending children to extended families in the countryside or to the Little Flower boarding school in Ixopo. Morris Fynn's attempts at claiming chieftaincy were crucially connected to expropriation through homeland "independence" (see chapter 2).

Explaining these complex and differentiated dynamics was of course no simple task. After his escape from a Johannesburg jail, Harold Wolpe became one of the key theorists for the ANC-SACP alliance in exile. In part to demonstrate the indivisibility of communist and anti-apartheid struggle, Wolpe explained the transition to apartheid as necessitated by the increasing inability of households in the reserves to subsidize superexploited male migrant labor in the mines.[25] The ensuing race-class debate hinged on how apartheid and capitalism were interrelated, whether liberal reform was possible within apartheid, and whether anti-apartheid struggle required radical critique of capitalism.

In response to this debate, Stuart Hall argues for the importance of "articulation" of de jure racism and capitalism under apartheid, where articulation implies both "joining-up" and "giving expression" to the specific form of racial capitalism.[26] In parallel, Marxist historians Martin Legassick and Charles van Onselen pose the compound system for migrant labor as providing the spatial archetype for an intensification of segregation culminating in apartheid. In Legassick's framing, apartheid's townships are "carefully segregated and police-controlled areas that resemble mining compounds on a large scale."[27] Yet the question of how the migrant labor system provided the foundations for what Van Onselen calls a system of *total control* remains a question.[28] What falls out of these formulations is precisely Hall's Gramscian attentiveness to the expressive aspect of articulation in common sense and popular will.[29]

Another important line of argument about South African capitalism emerges from Ben Fine and Zavareh Rustomjee's study of the minerals-energy complex (MEC), the alliance of state and corporate entities in the production and export of minerals central to twentieth-century South African capitalism.[30] The prominence of the MEC in the apartheid period centered on parastatals including the Electricity Supply Commission (Eskom), the Iron and Steel Industrial Corporation (Iscor), and petroleum corporation SASOL (South African Coal Oil and Gas Corporation), which promised the apartheid regime energy independence through technology to transform coal into oil.[31] Afrikaner finance capital's inroads into production in the late 1950s helped bridge English and Afrikaner capital in a densely articulated, capital-intensive political economy linking the state and corporate capital.[32] Apartheid capitalism strengthened this bimodal industrial structure, with private and parastatal corporate giants invested heavily in the MEC, and a consumer goods sector protected through import substitution industrialization. Low-wage work in agriculture and labor-intensive industry in state-subsidized border industries adjoining large rural townships and in the MEC effectively relied on the homeland system to absorb the social and political economic costs of an extremely unequal and exclusionary industrial structure.[33]

The MEC was also built into the spatial landscape, where its incapacity to provide work for all but a small minority of its residential neighbors would become entirely obvious. This is to say nothing of the uncountable harms that communities in MEC landscapes have been forced to absorb. As the apartheid state did not collect data on the residential location of cancer patients or of those with chronic respiratory ailments, the health subsidy to capital in places like South Durban remains entirely opaque. Neighbors of the refineries in South Durban continue to battle what is most painfully obvious to them, that their very lives have subsidized the MEC.

Fixing Capital through the Biopolitics of Urban Planning

From the perspective of construction and finance capital, coercive urbanism was immensely profitable. The construction industry grew by leaps and bounds between 1943 and 1952, from R70 million to R450 million, in a time of rampant inflation and currency devaluation.[34] Transformations in the built environment, also in Durban, brought the role of finance capital to the foreground in the 1950s. A key moment in this process was the shifting of capital from mining into other activities, spearheaded by the Anglo American Corporation's formation of the National Finance Corporation in 1949 and a merchant bank in 1955. Increased circulation of finance capital allowed urban redevelopment without state assistance in the central business districts of Johannesburg and Durban and in white suburbanization.

The main question for industrial capital was how to fix capital and labor in the right places and on the right terms. The Natal Chamber of Industries (NCI) was concerned that the Group Areas Act would put pressure on the wage bill through capital having to bear workers' moving expenses and increased rents and transportation costs as a consequence, and it was loath to bear any direct costs of rehousing.[35] However, city hall had long internalized the interests of capital in its spatial policy.

Oil corporations were key players in midcentury South Durban, connected to the globalization of US petro-capital and the transformations of what was once John D. Rockefeller's Standard Oil Company. Standard Vacuum Oil Company of New York looked toward refining in South Africa in 1946. After years of secret negotiation, the council confirmed in 1951 that the Stanvac refinery would be built in Wentworth. Stephen Sparks details the negotiations with the Board of Trade and Industry as well as with white working-class residents on the Bluff before the refinery became operational in 1954.[36] Reorganization of the parent corporation meant that by 1962 Stanvac assets were transferred to Mobil Petroleum Company, and the Wentworth refinery was run by the Mobil Refining Company. Following prolonged pressure from the global Anti-Apartheid Movement, Mobil subsequently sold it to the Afrikaner corporation Gencor, which established Engen Petroleum. After apartheid, the major shareholder in Engen has become the Malaysian parastatal Petronas. The refinery's own rendition of its construction is a tale of mastery of a wild landscape, tamed by a Mexican snake catcher, a narrative of colonial mastery repeated in newspaper reports.

Public action led by white working-class residents on the Bluff altered the geography of capital's spatial fix through sustained pressure against city hall when it announced in 1958 that a second refinery was to be built, initially on Salisbury Island in Durban Harbor, then shifted down the coast between the Indian areas of Merebank and Isipingo, adjoining the site of the Louis Botha Airport.[37] At stake in these debates was the smell of pollution, a persistent complaint from white residents that the council sometimes took seriously. South African Petroleum Refineries (SAPREF) came into being in 1960 with equal shareholdings held by its parent Shell and BP corporations in London; in two years, the name was changed to Shell and BP South African Petroleum Refineries, and SAPREF was operational at its current site between Merebank and Isipingo in 1963. Official narratives, in newspaper accounts of the time and in the refinery's fiftieth-anniversary commemoration publication, repeat tales of technical mastery of a swampy landscape, this time through high-pressure water cannons used to blast the Bluff ridge to raise the ground level by two meters.[38]

In light of the historical circulation of hygienic discourse in this landscape, what is important is that nuisance talk entered an environmental moment in which various people sought to participate, not all of whom could. Official accounts of the fixing of the Wentworth and SAPREF refineries show how the council sold land allocated to the Merebank-Wentworth Housing Scheme, along with land alongside the Louis Botha Airport that would still have been cultivated by market gardeners, to these new refineries on the grounds that it was farther from white ratepayers on the Bluff, who mattered, and closer to Indians, who did not.[39]

Indian residents fought a long and ultimately losing battle against city and provincial levels of government over the site for the Southern Sewerage Disposal Plant, involving the expropriation of thirty-four properties, in parallel with struggles against the expropriation of land for the new housing scheme.[40] Since its formation in 1954, the Coordinating Committee on Housing (Merebank-Wentworth Area) had watched these developments with concern. This committee frames its objections to the hundred-acre sewerage works on behalf of 250 market gardeners, some of whom faced relocation after having been there for forty years. Failing this, it appeals to the provisions of the housing scheme, which would lose land to the sewerage works; it appeals to Indians who would have to move out of the Coloured section of the housing plan; it appeals to the unpleasantness of a sewerage plant among homes; and, finally, recognizing how little any of this might matter to city hall, it appeals to the "unpleasant sight to [the unmarked-white] passer-by, especially tourists."[41]

The city engineer responds that while the volume of untreated waste let out into the Indian Ocean is not yet a public health threat, the urbanization of South and West Durban requires better waste treatment. Returning to the use of physical geography in the erasure of long-term Black residence in the 1940s, he argues that "conditions of topography dictate" that the proposed sewerage works ought to be "somewhere on the flatlands between Bayhead and the Umlaas River Valley" and that "the Merebank/Wentworth site is more remote from residential areas already well established and populated." He continues that the proposed site is "the least suitable for housing development" as it is "low lying and swampy," echoing discourse surrounding the concentration camps. Defending sewerage works as presumed to be the source of odors that may be from elsewhere, and with the caveat that there can be no "absolute freedom from odour," the city engineer argues that any smell will be "less offensive and less widely distributed" than any industrial odor.[42] This argument encapsulates what residents have faced since, the problem of attributing scientific and moral responsibility in a multiply polluted landscape.

The proximity of the scheme and the new Louis Botha Airport also meant the city council had to expect that residents would face constant noise pollution. The secretary of transport reminds the council of an American commission from 1952 that set down conditions for planning residential and industrial areas adjacent to airports; astoundingly, he adds "with some hesitation[,] . . . I propose that the whole township should be replanned."[43] The suggestion quickly disappears from the archives of city hall, but the appeal to regional and urban planning had begun to take the place that public health had as the state's biopolitical expertise of choice.

Indeed, regional planning had become a handmaiden to apartheid statecraft in its second phase, particularly when it was clear that "Betterment planning" in the Bantustans had failed to stem the flow of Africans to cities.[44] The Tomlinson Commission of 1956 argued that economic development in the reserves was politically crucial, the argument that Wolpe had made in radical terms. The state tried to use regional and metropolitan planning to manage its relations with various fractions of capital in the context of a buoyant economy and under heightened political clampdown.[45] Through the 1960s metropolitan planning paralleled state centralization of African housing through Administration Boards, and industrial location through the Physical Planning Act of 1967.[46] As part of the hegemonic apparatus, metropolitan planning focused on urban accumulation and circulation in relation to whites and elites, leaving the central government to address the reproduction of the Black majority as a matter of national security.[47]

Alan Mabin and Philip Harrison's study of town and regional planning in KwaZulu-Natal returns to the aftermath of Durban's *Barnes Report* and its recommendations for town planning legislation, a new planning commission, and a professional town and regional planner.[48] Eric Thorrington-Smith and Ron Pistorius were recruited from England for their experience in British town and regional planning, not least with Abercrombie's Greater London Plan. Thorrington-Smith was inspired by the Tennessee Valley Authority, which he claimed to want to replicate in the Tugela River basin in the 1950s. In complicity with apartheid's "border industries" policy, he envisioned industrialization proximal to labor reserves in the KwaZulu homeland, as in planning industrial Hammarsdale next to the African township of Mpumalanga. Over the next decade and a half, the planning commission shifted focus from agrarian transformation in an imagined Tennessee Valley Authority to industrial areas in Durban, Pietermaritzburg, and the South Coast. The commission maintained the infrastructure of segregation through rigid separations in land use and planning in the African township of Umlazi.

Expatriate South African architect and planner Denise Scott Brown's searing critique of the planning commission argues that "if the aim is a comprehensive plan, then it is not possible for planners . . . to omit considerations of social change and the political change that goes with it"; to do so, she argues with reference to Adolf Eichmann, is cooperation with totalitarianism.[49] There could be no blind faith in liberal biopolitical territoriality through regional planning under apartheid. Fixing capital through coercive planning, even in liberal guise, was also a forgery, inseparable from dispossessions past and future.[50]

Fixing Group Areas, Unfixing the Indian Commons

Some Africans erroneously suggested that the Group Areas Act was designed to affect Indians and to some extent the Coloured people. Such people must now be getting a rude shock to find that Africans have been the first victims of racial zoning.
—ALBERT LUTHULI, 1956

To the Coloured people of the Union the Group Areas Act comes as a first attack on their land rights. As far as the Indian community is concerned, laws dealing with its land restrictions also go back into history.
—MONTY NAICKER, 1956

In the above epigraphs, the presidents of the ANC and the NIC reflect in anger on the Group Areas Act of 1950.[51] After a year's deliberation, city hall's Technical Sub-Committee proposed to displace 70,000 Indians, 8,500 Coloureds, 40,000 Africans, and 12,000 whites, the last reduced to 3,100 after (white) public outcry.[52] More than half of Durban's population was forcibly evicted and moved through the series of Group Areas Acts.[53] There are differences between Albert Luthuli's "rude shock," with the Congress Alliance's hope of nonracial solidarity, and Monty Naicker's reference to a long history of restrictions on Indian property. While the costs of political exclusion are clear to both, the terms of debate were set for them. Both think of corporate "race groups" facing removals, with Indians doing so in line with their historical experience. Decades of urban segregation and the recent anti-Indian pogrom had taken an ideological toll.

Some Indian property owners organized collectively to defend their interests in overtly segregationist terms. The Sydenham and Overport Property-Owners and Residents Committee argued against their removal for a Coloured housing scheme on the grounds that their area was under 95 percent Indian owner-occupation and that "Indians have of their own volition formed a homogeneous group."[54] A petitioner for Indian businesses in "working areas" argued that "in a multi-racial City like Durban, Town Planning cannot be based entirely on the principles that serve a homogeneous city" but instead "must be more elastic . . . where the authorities seek to separate the racial components."[55]

Sometimes defense of Indian property stood in for the Indian commons. A deputation from the Mayville Indian Ratepayers Association explains its long commitment, since 1938, not just to property and business but to "deep and lasting attachments . . . rooted in emotional association with home, Temples, Churches, Mosques, Schools, Burial Places and with Neighbours";

the document warns that farms and firms "small and large will be ruined," that most of the Indians under threat of eviction are below the poverty line, and that "residential segregation . . . spells Economic Strangulation and therefore RUINATION."[56] In a parallel vein, the NIC writes, "The stark and ugly spectre of ruin, impoverishment, destitution and misery is haunting every Indian in the country; tenants as well as property-owners, traders who are to be condemned to cut each other's throats in over-crowded group areas, youth who are witnessing the opportunity-less future descend upon them like the black night when the tropical sun dips below the horizon, the yet unborn who are promised a bovine future amid rags and filth and disease. Oppressed by this spectre and confronted by the decisions of your Committees, the Indian people have every reason to be alarmed and aroused."[57]

Everyone ought to have been alarmed. All Durbanites had come to know of a subaltern production of space through which "Durban was regularly supplied with fresh vegetables and fruit at reasonable prices."[58] Despite years of neglect, in contrast to peripheral white areas, and despite the building of housing of unknown quality for Africans in Cato Manor after the 1949 pogrom, the document goes on to document Indian private investment in schools, places of worship, welfare associations, cemeteries, businesses, factories, dwellings, transport facilities, and a sports ground, totaling approximately £20,000,000.[59] Investment by a progressive Indian middle class had effectively subsidized the racial state. In this light, what is striking in the following list of removals from the 1960s is its focus on unfixing Indians:

Bell Street: Indians were uprooted to make way for Europeans.

Sydenham: Indians were uprooted and are being uprooted to make way for Coloureds.

Cato Manor: Indians were uprooted from a part of Cato Manor for Africans. The whole of Cato Manor is earmarked for Europeans.

West Ridge: Indians were uprooted to make room for European playing fields and tennis courts.

Duffs Road: Indians were uprooted to make room for Africans.

Durban North & Riverside: Indians to be uprooted to make room for Europeans.

Greenwood Park: Indians threatened with uprooting to make way for European occupation.

Clairwood: Indians to be uprooted for white industrial occupation.

Merebank: Indians to be uprooted to make way for Coloured and Indian Housing Schemes.

Hillary, Seaview and Bellair: Indians to be uprooted to make way for Europeans.[60]

The document concludes that "the entire Indian population of Durban will be uprooted if the Zoning proposals of the Durban City Council are accepted."[61]

A scathing letter from another Indian ratepayers association asks why the events of 1949 justify further segregation and whether conflict between English and Afrikaners should mean that "whites will allow themselves to be grouped separately." Refusing the notion that Indians have "lowered Western Civilization in South Africa," the writer argues that they are "not responsible for the large Coloured population" and that "the Indian is very conscious about the purity of his race."[62] What we have here is a propertied Indian refusal of segregation through a defense of racial purity. In time, the Merebank Ratepayers Association (MRA) would develop more radical arguments as it faced new attempts at unfixing of the Indian commons.

The Merebank-Wentworth Housing Scheme became a test case for justifying forced removals through the technical concerns of racial planning. The archival trail of this housing scheme in the files of city hall is long and complex. The scheme had been approved by the council in 1941, adapted after transfer of land to the Ministry of Defence for the British Admiralty's HMS Assegai camp, and adapted further after the siting of the airport, refineries, and sewerage works. By 1955 the council was restive about this housing scheme.

In July 1956 the council resolved to send out final offers to purchase properties, failing which it would seek expropriation. Residents sought to buy time. Private owners, tenants, and residents held a mass meeting and pressed for a stay on expropriations until a meeting between the administrator of Natal and a Coordinating Committee on Housing that sought to represent existing residents.[63] However, residents' class interests diverged strongly. Some well-off residents sought secure land rights to build private homes. The Merebank Branch of the NIC urged the council to afford these people private land titles within the planned transformations of Merebank and Clairwood.[64] The NIC expressed frustration with the slow pace of council housing for Indians on public land, arguing that the spread of shack settlements in Merebank was a direct consequence.[65] In effect, it sought to represent the dehoused while defending the propertied. When the Ministry of Health consented to the expropriation of a long list of people, residents turned to prominent lawyer Rowley Arenstein to represent their case to provincial and city government.[66]

In 1956 the council approved plans for the first 220 houses for Indians in the Merebank-Wentworth Housing Scheme; by 1960, 262 had been completed, 517 were in progress, and a further 833 approved, with building continuing until 1974.[67] Council records show African residents dispossessed in the making of the housing scheme with no representation from the NIC or the Coordinating Committee on Housing. These memos are paragraphs filed with the director of Bantu administration, recommending the eviction of forty families from the railway siding loop, "suggesting" that the Department of Bantu Administration take care of rehousing them.[68] A letter to the town clerk exclaims that "some 20 Bantu families were being housed in shacks and disused horse boxes under the most appalling conditions" after being "removed from the Indian housing scheme area at Merebank."[69] There is no recorded response. African "unfixing" is assumed.

As a consequence of their representative power, discussions about Merebank Indians, now part of a separate Merebank Indian Housing Programme, centered on how to differentiate the majority of public auction sites, with a depth of 100 to 150 feet, from a dozen larger plots ranging up to an acre. "In order to meet the wishes of the Committee," the council adds, "the lots on the ridge, mostly with sea views, have been increased in size."[70] This signals the successful attempt to buy consent from the committee by offering its leadership homes in sought-after locations on the higher ridge, facing the sea or overlooking Merebank. Hence, people like Billy Juggernath inherited housing on the ridge as a consequence of their roles as intermediaries in building the class-differentiated Indian township. On the other end of the class spectrum, a memo states that Indian tenants evicted from the lands of the Wentworth hospital will not be rehoused in the new housing scheme.[71] The fate of these tenants recurs for several years through the archives, before being lost to the files.

Proclaimed Group Areas had not stipulated the exact boundaries between the Indian and Coloured sides of the Merebank-Wentworth Housing Scheme. In late 1959 the council negotiated the return of a hundred acres in the HMS Assegai Camp from the Royal Navy to the city, then designated as part of a Coloured township.[72] A small but seemingly attractive strip of land rising between the refinery and the sea had not been clearly marked. The provincial official of the Group Areas Board thought it ought to be a Coloured area, and permission had been granted to a Coloured children's holiday home for the Rand Cape Coloured Children's Health Fund.[73] A fierce debate ensued about the racial zoning of this area, Treasure Beach, as a middle-class area similar to Merebank's ridge for more affluent Indians. The nearby Bluff Ratepayers and Burgesses Association voiced vociferous opposition in defense of "European occupation" of that end of the ridge.[74]

In practice, fixing Group Areas brought to the fore contradictions between the council's long-standing racial vision for the city and Group Areas Boards seeking to buy properties and consolidate racial zones. The South African Institute for Race Relations reported that the council and the boards "were working in competition with each other in so far as the Merebank/Wentworth Indian Housing Scheme was concerned."[75] But competition concealed a deeper problem. Despite its resolve to begin proclaiming Indian Group Areas, an internal report confessed that "the Council has no data as to the racial groups into which persons fall, and has no means of making authoritative determinations in that respect."[76] This supports my argument about the foundational contradictions of biopolitical territoriality in apartheid's spatial fix, and it clarifies the anti-Indian racism central to the practice of the Durban City Council. This is precisely why Monty Naicker saw continuities with a long history of official anti-Indian vitriol now mobilized against all Black people.[77]

Recall that the council's *Race Zoning Plan, 1952* emerged from experiments with race zoning maps in conversation with the Post-War Works and Reconstruction Commission (see chapter 3). In 1954 the Group Areas Board announced that the Bluff, Montclair/Woodlands, the Main Line Suburbs, Cato Manor, Sherwood, Durban North, and the Beachfront were to be white; Merebank-Wentworth, Reservoir Hills, and Claire Estate would be Indian; and Wentworth was to be a Coloured Group Area. In public hearings in 1953 and 1957, the little strip of land between the Wentworth oil refinery and the sea, later the middle-class Coloured area of Treasure Beach, was among the areas still up for debate.[78]

Once the new township homes were built, residents expressed concerns about the materiality of construction, the dampness and cracking of walls made of hollow concrete blocks, and the impractical layout of rooms.[79] The council finally sought an "independent" report from a Johannesburg-based civil engineer, which details various defects and complaints and concludes that the housing "at Merebank-Wentworth is of good quality when its speed of erection and extremely low cost is considered."[80] Complaints continued, but it became clear to the council that "a large number of unauthorized structures" had sprung up by 1961, "as prayer rooms, kitchens, tool sheds, car port, shower rooms, etc."[81] The council had not anticipated the profusion of backyard additions to homes across Indian Group Areas, a form of economic involution within apartheid's Indian townships that would in time distinguish Merebank from Wentworth.

A small file documents the long and difficult struggles of a group that fit awkwardly alongside other township residents. Letters from the Merebank Indian Agricultural Association show that most of its members were around fifty years old and had insufficient income to meet their monthly rate payments.[82] Govinden Ramsamy, the long-standing secretary of the Merebank-Wentworth Ratepayers Association, the organization that was usually called the Merebank Ratepayers Association and that eventually became the Merebank Residents Association, writes on behalf of these marginal farmers on the banks of the Umlaas River whose income "hardly helps to keep body and soul together" and who struggle to resolve their arrears.[83] In the dialectics of dispossession and resettlement, this was a defense of the persistence of marginal farmers who had made the Indian commons historically possible.

Perpetual Insecurity and the Proliferation of Shack Life

The Merebank-Wentworth Housing Scheme was small in contrast to African townships planned in the 1950s and 1960s, including KwaMashu and Umlazi, Durban's two biggest African townships.[84] Yet this housing development was far from adequate as a response to the waves of dispossession that it claimed to justify. Emergency camps were constructed for Africans in Cato Manor in 1952 and forcibly removed six years later to KwaMashu, and by 1966 almost all shacks and 82,000 people were forcibly moved yet again. In 1955 the corporation announced a fifteen-year program to build a thousand dwellings per year: three hundred for whites along the Old Main Line white working-class areas, six hundred for Indians in Chatsworth and Merebank, and a hundred for Coloureds near Sparks Road and in the Wentworth scheme.[85] The forced removals of 50 to 80 percent of Indians heightened their class differentiation, leaving few with the means to build their own homes, as some could in places like Reservoir Hills. Many moved to housing schemes. The least fortunate were pushed into shack settlements in areas like flood-prone Tin Town on the banks of the Umgeni River.

For the large shack-dwelling population of Durban, segregated and serviced housing development was a mixed blessing; many appeared to consent to stronger racialization in townships in the hope of better housing and secure tenure. Surveyors from the City Treasurer's Department involved in determining access to formal housing came across several problems in the shacks of "Merebank No. 3 Settlement," where people appeared to have quickly built wood-and-iron shacks, or rooms attached to existing shacks, in areas prioritized for access to formal housing.[86] Often these "ringers" were encouraged by relatives or friends to get on the "affected list" of claimants during the survey process. Mrs. Marie described moving from a backyard tenancy in Clairwood to a shack in Merebank when she heard she could get on the list (see chapter 2). Some people tried to work the cadastral politics of relocation.

The city treasurer and estates manager devised surprise "crash surveys" of priority areas to minimize ringers. People were made to fill out housing application forms that asked for identities and shack numbers but made no mention of either expropriation or rehousing, so as to keep people guessing about whether and when they might expect formal housing. A former city estates inspector pronounced the new system a success, reducing the initial 20 percent of "illegal" applications considerably by the mid-1960s.[87]

Following the dissolution of the interracial extended family presided over by his great-grandmother, Jaya's parents moved to Clairwood (see chapters 2 and 4). When his parents divorced, his mother moved the family to a shack settlement in Merebank when she heard that people were getting places in the new township. Jaya described a "massive movement of people in the late 1950s, early 1960s, trucked in and dropped from areas like Feniscowles" into vacant plots in Merebank in 1958–59, and that "when they started building township homes, residents resisted the entry of outsiders."

Not everyone was as fortunate as Mrs. Marie or Jaya's mother. For many, this was a new era of perpetual insecurity. A group of people dispossessed from the Feniscowles farm in Umbilo had spent scarcely three years in shacks in Merebank when they were served notice yet again.[88] The City Estates Department responded that there was "no alternative," adding benevolently, "Wherever possible, however, these displaced people will be absorbed into the scheme."[89] Another group at the "Marine slum settlement," "caught in the extremes of poverty," met with deaf ears from the city council.[90] When the Office of Health reports further shack demolitions in Merebank, it makes no mention of what becomes of residents.[91] A group of "Indian squatters" alongside Edwin Swales Drive between Wentworth and Bayhead was told that they would not be accommodated at the new Merebank-Wentworth Housing Scheme but that they could await "possible consideration in the Chatsworth scheme," failing which the council might have to reconsider "whether priority should not be given to the removal of shacks from the Council's own industrial areas."[92]

As townships close to the city became saturated, the council turned its illogic inside out, blaming shack dwellers on waiting lists for Indian and Coloured housing for reappearing on the lists, or for delaying their removal from shack settlements in proximity to the city and to industrial employment. Certainly, extended families often found informal settlements cheaper and easier to negotiate, as did widows and very low-income families, but the idea that their appeals for formal and secure housing were the cause of the council's perennial backlog was pernicious.

Evictions did not end when people were rehoused in housing schemes. What became clear in the late 1960s was the large number of evictions *from* the massive new Indian township of Chatsworth because of nonpayment of monthly installments, as well as subsistence fishermen evicted from land owned by the South African Railways at Bayhead, and tenants evicted from the city center. The council decided on a new spatial form for these displaced populations, or rather a new-old one, the "temporary transit camp." As the city engineer puts it, this is "the type of transit camp in which displaced families are required to erect their own sub-standard dwellings for occupation until such time as permanent housing is available"; he adds, "The obvious choice of site . . . would be in the Merebank Wentworth Indian Housing Scheme on a vacant 15.8 acre area opposite the site of the Southern Sewerage Treatment Works on the eastern side of the 'Stanvac' canal. This area . . . was previously used as a temporary shack site (287 shacks), the removal of which were completed on 31st October, 1965."[93] In other words, the council destroyed shacks in order to allow other dispossessed people to build shacks.

The MRA protested vehemently, as it had the previous year, about "unhygienic and revolting" "temporary" shacks on Duranta Road.[94] The class basis of this protest was complex, since many working-class residents in Merebank knew the conditions of shack life all too well. The following year saw a proposal for a new category of housing stock instead of self-built shacks, "'In Transit' Sub Sub-Economic Housing," designed "for the lowest income groups based on a very cheap method of construction, using only the cheapest of building materials"; ratepayers protested again, to no avail.[95]

Multiple removals of shack dwellers increased the vulnerability of the poorest residents of South Durban, with declining incomes and decreasing areas for informal tenancy. Many families became priority cases through forced removals and floods. In 1974, 19,070 families were on the waiting list for the nearly completed Chatsworth housing scheme; some had been waiting for twelve years, and several transferred to waiting lists for new schemes in Phoenix and Newlands, announced in 1973. Between 1963 and 1975, about four thousand families, or about twenty-four thousand people, were moved out of South Durban, not including either those who left voluntarily or the two thousand families removed internally to the Merebank-Wentworth Housing Scheme.[96]

Expropriations continued in the transformation of South Durban in the late 1960s. The construction of the Southern Freeway (N2) forcibly removed fifty-four families and destroyed several market gardens along the Umlaas Canal.[97] Some Coloured families initially removed from the Southern Freeway redevelopment and from expropriations in Duranta Road, Croton Road, and "Brickyard" were provided temporary shacks for married families in Merebank and prioritized for formal housing.[98] The route of the Southern Freeway also required expropriation of forty-two houses recently built under what was now called the Merebank Housing Scheme, and though they resisted, fifty-four families were forcibly moved within Merebank in 1972.[99] In 1973 the municipal corporation removed families living in the Bluff Swamps, to create a bird sanctuary and Coloured sports field adjacent to the Wentworth oil refinery; apparently a third of the residents—forty-nine Coloured and thirteen Indian households—left "voluntarily," and the rest were rehoused in Wentworth and Chatsworth. If this seems dizzyingly confusing, we might imagine the perplexity with which people lived through coercive planning.

The corporation looked beyond the industrial estates of Mobeni and Amanzimnyama and considered transforming residential Clairwood into an industrial area, a perennial danger averted through long-term resistance during and after apartheid. In 1964 the corporation turned to a section of the swamplands of Merebank, where the Anglo American Corporation proposed a paper mill. The MRA refused the loss of land from the housing scheme, but the Mondi Paper Mill was approved and built in three years.[100] From the perspective of the council, fixing capital was the main priority, and the destruction of the means of Black life an inconvenience. Meanwhile, the proliferation of shack life was a growing catastrophe.

Wentworth in the Mirror of Merebank

The city realized its serious shortfall in Coloured housing through what a former city estates inspector called a "game of chess": moving tenants around temporary housing across the city.[101] I have argued that many people forced into the racial category of Coloured when removed to Wentworth were precarious tenants of various backgrounds. A minority of middle-class Coloureds from town saw in Wentworth an opportunity for homeownership, as is evident in a petition from the Durban Coloured Federal Council to the Housing Department in 1961 for the sale of houses before launching a letting scheme.[102]

In October 1963 the council proclaimed the largest Coloured Group Area in Durban in today's Wentworth, covering 690 acres in Merewent, Austerville, and Treasure Beach in four types of housing: a housing scheme with 414 "subeconomic" homes and plans for "economic" and "subeconomic" flats, as well as "sub-subeconomic" dwellings for former shack dwellers; 350 acres of state-owned land administered by the Department of Community Development in Austerville Government Village and Wentworth Police Camp; privately owned land around Quality Street, Genoa Road, and Umbria Road; and a zone including the swampy lands between Tara and Pirie Roads and the ridge rising up to Marine Drive, including Treasure Beach, "for good class economic housing."[103] Through haphazard moves, the council had formed a Group Area with a mixture of housing stock from "Wentworth Government Village, the old SANF camp and abutting area known as Chesterville," renamed Austerville in 1964 and bounded by Quality Street, Tara Road, Marine Drive, Lansdowne Road, and the Jacobs industrial area.[104]

This is the moment, 1964–65, in which the Indian and Coloured sections in the Merebank-Wentworth scheme were pulled apart, as more affluent Indians consented to the terms of a racial township in exchange for privately built homes on publicly auctioned land, while the generally poorer Indian and Coloured sections in both townships would depend on municipal tenancies.[105] Class dynamics were folded into the forgeries of apartheid.

A document from a small group of Coloured men from the Durban South Football Association in Austerville clarifies an enduring way in which Wentworth was differentiated from Indian Merebank. These authors include Morris Fynn (see chapter 2) and Archie Hulley, school principal and civic leader. They write that as of 1965, "600 families have moved into" the Coloured area, but without recreational facilities, "our children use streets as playfields" and "we fear that our peace-loving Community is rapidly being driven to delinquency."[106] What is striking is the discourse of delinquent Coloured youth; it would take two decades for this stereotype to be revised for political ends, inconclusively (see chapter 9).

A discussion through archival files turns to place-names, to whether the Indian area would be called Harrisville or Merebank, the Coloured area Assegai or Wentworth. A resident writes to support the name Merebank and to defend his own Khurja Road, named for a town in Uttar Pradesh; the council responds that that the word has been alleged to be offensive "in other Indian dialects."[107] The irony is that the Indian town's name derives from the Urdu word *kharija*, meaning "condemned" or "canceled," because its agricultural revenues had been canceled because its swamplands, unlike Merebank's, were not fit for agriculture. There is nothing in the files, or in the memories of elderly people I have spoken to, that explains the strange brew of South Asian place-names on Merebank's streets. The parallel is with colonial imaginaries in street naming in white neighborhoods. With their mix of references to villages, cities, districts, regions, rivers, and mountains, the streets of Merebank offer curious crossroads where disparate South Asian places connect like nowhere else, at the corner of Warangal and Gadwal, Bhuj and Himalayas, Chenab and Hooghli, or Mumbai and Dhubri. This kaleidoscopic reimagination might be a curiosity for an outsider, but for residents, the main question was how to reclaim neighborhood.

Separating Wentworth and Merebank meant separating political representation. The council sought representatives through the Indian and Coloured Affairs Advisory Committees in the 1950s, and in the 1960s, it separated North and South Durban Local Affairs Committees (LACs) from the Durban Coloured Affairs Committee, dangling the lure of "autonomy" to figures on these committees as the regime was doing in the homelands.[108] The figures on these committees are fascinating characters in their own right: Indian leaders Amichand Rajbansi, Pat Poovalingam, and A. K. Pillay and Coloured leaders Morris Fynn, C. A. Tifflin, R. A. Landers, and Gertrude Stock from Wentworth. In the highly political 1970s and 1980s, many would be labeled apartheid stooges. Indeed, there is ample evidence that many of them gained personally and professionally by working within apartheid institutions and by helping normalize the violence of apartheid capitalism.

The quotidian demands of these committees were often about shoring up the strangeness of "petty apartheid," the everyday segregation of public facilities and events. Stock fought for steps from the Wentworth ridge to the beach, as "Coloured people wishing to visit the beach had to travel through the Indian Township," which she does not say is just across the road.[109] Stock also argued that lobbying for Coloured toilets in town had resulted in separating facilities for Indian and Coloured men, while Coloured women faced the indignity of sharing a toilet with Indian women.[110] Sometimes class interests were clear, as in Landers's view that "there were more people of the Coloured group requiring economic housing than sub-economic" and that the latter "would only lead to slums."[111]

Sometimes these figures refused demolitions, construction materials, "sub-subeconomic housing," or selling prices, and they argued for better libraries, community centers, and health clinics as well. Pushed by the MRA, the South Durban LAC sought "to clarify and settle amicably" the issue of house prices.[112] These committees played a contradictory political role as apartheid intermediaries who were particularly vital in Coloured areas that did not have the benefit of a long-standing progressive middle class to fight for maintenance of the infrastructure of social reproduction. When, as in Indian areas, they had such middle-class leadership, they were often like their progressive forebears in that they were often complicit with official racism. At a joint meeting of the North and South Durban LACs on the possible creation of an Indian Local Authority granted authority for administration and for provision of urban services, for instance, Poovalingam concurred with the apartheid authorities that "autonomy should be accepted in principle"; he was seconded by Rajbansi, who only asked for clarity of boundaries but accepted the consolidation of separate development.[113]

In contrast, the newly consolidated MRA laid bare the incompatibility between industry and residential well-being, using the discourse of planning:

Prior to 1945 Merebank was a spacious area with scattered homes and shacks extending from the Railway Station to the Bluff Hill. The vegetation was lush, wild flowers and birds plentiful and a swampy mere—not without beauty—was to be found. Wooded patches were familiar landmarks. This, then, was the mental picture the Merebank resident had of his district at that time. The Durban City Council in its desire to serve the residents, decided to establish a well-ordered housing scheme particularly to replace the many shacks in the area. A commendable idea in so far as rehabilitation is concerned: but the residents launched the opposition to the Scheme vigorously. They claimed that they could improve the area on their own initiative and pleaded to the Council to pursue the Scheme on Council owned land. . . . Now that the Housing Scheme is a reality, we are deeply concerned that we are hemmed in by industries. To the north of the Housing Scheme is an oil refinery; to the South is another large oil refinery; to the West are the Mobeni Industrial sites. It is obvious to any visitor that we are a residential island in an industrial area. . . . We object in principle to the siting of any industry in the vicinity of a residential area as not being conducive to the well-being of the residents of the Merewent Housing Scheme.[114]

Just before this, Ramsamy of the MRA had written scathingly on behalf of a group of families evicted from Begonia Road. Refused rehousing in Merebank, "they were asked to move their shacks to an area opposite the Mobil Oil Refinery," a suggestion saturated by racism and injustice.[115] With figures like Ramsamy, something else was coming into view: community organizers who worked arduously in the background to fight the collusion of capital and city hall and to represent everyday concerns. The MRA continued to address shoddy construction, sinking homes, and the lack of leisure and market facilities.[116] Rumors circulated about further encroachment of the refineries onto residential land.[117]

As the joint Merebank-Wentworth Housing Scheme for Indians and Coloureds was pulled apart, people living in intimate proximity to Indians were coercively moved to Coloured townships, and they were presumed never to have had an entangled past. This is ironic since the *Durban Housing Survey* shows that 80 percent of Coloureds in midcentury Durban were tenants, predominantly in Indian-owned dwellings, and its maps show Coloureds living in the same areas as Indians.[118] The council was alarmed by the large numbers of mixed-race people rendered homeless by the waves of expropriation of backyard tenancies in Indian homes. While these people came from close proximity to the living quarters of Indians, there is no outcry of fear and loathing of miscegenation between Coloureds and Indians in official or popular historiography. Indeed, Merebank Indians and Wentworth Coloureds are considered to be so distinct, their racial and sexual lives so separate, as to deserve no comment at all. Consider that, when some new residents in Assegai confronted white subalterns forced out of military housing for the new Coloured township, they describe these white residents leaving in anger, trashing their homes, or throwing feces on the walls, marking the racial and class indeterminacy of Coloured Wentworth.

In marked contrast to Wentworth, Merebank was transformed from part of the Indian commons forged early in the century into a racial township that its elite consented to in exchange for land titles for private homes. Titling, from day one impossible in African townships and possible in time for a small elite in Wentworth, enabled Merebank's multiclass character along with representative bodies that claimed their origins in the early 1930s. Temples, shrines, graveyards, and religious practice drew from the early twentieth-century history of syncretic subaltern place-making, but this was a struggled attachment to place in a time in which people continued to be forcibly removed.

Forgeries of Forced Removal

Apartheid's forced removals are the great Rubicon in popular historiography, before which lies a ruse of normalcy, of interracial life populated by jazz clubs, boxing rings, cricket and soccer matches, and gangsters who were more cool than dangerous. People became Durban Indians in the process of settling the landscape, despite official neglect, ongoing xenophobia, and an acute awareness of the tenuousness of homes, farms, and shops. This remembrance of things past inspires a particular pathos: a sigh of familiarity and loss of multiracial and multiclass settlements like Cato Manor, Springfield, and the Casbah. Documentary photography, historical fiction, and popular plays, including the works of Omar Badsha, Aziz Hassim, and Ronnie Govender, materialize the pathos of the contradictory Indian commons lost through the process of forced removal.[119]

One set of figures who speak clearly of an older sense of durable instability are the many men from Wentworth who worked as whalers from the nearby Bluff whaling station. Hector Henry was one such man (see chapter 2). As we spoke in his little home on a side street not far from the bottom of Austerville Drive, he pulled out newspaper clippings, files, and documents about how he followed his father to become a seafarer, before returning to the multiethnic area of Clairwood in which his grandparents had settled, until, as he put it, "the Southern Freeway ran through our front door [and] split the place in half." Henry speaks of Clairwood as a place where "we had three or four races living in one house"; he pauses and adds, "living harmoniously." Henry appears to romanticize these mixed neighborhoods but then quickly refuses this tendency: "Clairwood was wood-and-iron houses, we had the coal stove, prior to that we had to look for wood. We were still in the Third World then. *It was the cold days.*"

Ramsamy describes the Indian shack settlement he came from as "decent wood-and-iron buildings," unlike *jondolos*, or shacks, built, as he put it, after the unbanning of the ANC. He describes a difficult life in Clairwood South, with no electricity, paraffin lamps, wood and coal stoves, and baths once every week or two. Life changed dramatically when his widowed mother moved the household to the subeconomic scheme in Merebank, where they had a home to pay off over thirty years. He watched wealthier people buying land for individual homes on the "economic scheme," while poorer people rented lower-end subeconomic homes. The implication is that Merebank as a township was at its inception multiclass, shaped by the negotiations between the city and the small group of landed families.

In contrast to this history of settlement, people forcibly moved to Wentworth came to former World War II barracks for subalterns of the Royal Navy. Albert moved from Dundee, in the interior of Natal, to Durban, and he found work at Lever Brothers in the printing works in 1949, at the age of eighteen. He lived with his young wife, Rose, in various parts of town, and as tenants for Indian landlords in Overport, Brickfield, and Springfield. When they were renting in Sydenham, they were told that there was a new township called Wentworth where they would receive a house. Albert's brother had already bought a place in Merewent. They moved to the little area called SANF in Austerville in 1959. Rose speaks of the neighborhood with fondness:

> This area was all white people, ex-soldiers. They had to get out because this was now going to be a Coloured community. We moved here with our children. The house was small, we had one bedroom and a kitchen and a long dining room, but our neighbours were very nice. Fortunately, the washhouse was just across. We had Black men who stoked the fire. It was very, very nice. . . . We could walk with our children. We used to take walks with our prams, and we used to go down to the oil refinery. It was like a ship with the lights, and it was very nice for the children; it amused them.

There is a complexity of class aspiration here, of nice neighbors, walks with prams, and "Black men who stoked the fire." Rose would become one of the first group of women in prayer groups involved in the charismatic renewal that swept Wentworth in the 1970s (see chapter 6). This "nice place" is a contrast to dystopian characterizations that have repeated ever since, of gangs, broken families, and widespread violence against women. Another man, Eric, says:

> Wentworth was violent. It was a ghetto. There were people from all parts of the province dumped here. Whether you were Christian, whether you were Muslim, whether you were heathen, you were just all dumped together. There was no really truly family-community spirit. It was cultivated, through hardship, and determination to survive. It was mainly knives and sticks and stones, but it was tough. This was a transit camp for immigrants coming through from England, just after the war. Hence the military hospital. Then they refurbished the area for Group Areas. This [Assegai] was the officers' quarters: whites, I'm talking about.

This narrative of being "dumped" in a "ghetto," in a repurposed "transit camp," with the "determination to survive" is part of the prose of what I call a

Wentworth blues tradition with its own power and pathos (see chapter 9). Eric also claims that his area was for white officers, a cut above the rest of Austerville. The little neighborhood of Assegai would produce many "respectable" social workers and development intermediaries. As Eric put it, violence would prove instructive for his children, as four of his daughters would go into various kinds of community work: one would become a nurse, another a prominent community worker, two others social workers who would later become political activists. As he put it, "The children saw, being social workers, that poverty and being deprived and being confined: *that* was the cause of the violence. This is what urged them on, in the democratic movement." We will return to the paths these young women took from social work to the armed struggle (see chapter 9).

Eric's wife, Louise, does not like being interviewed about her daughters, but she does like remembering her early years in Happy Valley as a counterpoint to the ills of Wentworth. She describes a poor but cosmopolitan world with all sorts of people, including a Xhosa-speaking *tokolosh*, a diminutive trickster figure with exaggerated sex organs. Her husband adds, "There were Pondos, Xhosas, a lot of Indian families, and of course Coloured families. There was no violence, and children grew up to know one another and respect one another." These are familiar memory conventions of a better time somewhere just beyond the bend.[120]

Memories of the transition to apartheid's townships reveal the struggle with the forgeries of difference and estrangement that people were meant to embody. A major difference between Merebank and Wentworth as products of forced removal was that Merebank would continue to be spatially articulated to the remains of the dispersed Indian commons, while Wentworth became increasingly differentiated from its surroundings, also through racialized labor and social assistance.

Racial Divisions of Labor and Social Assistance

Working-class men living in proximity to industrial South Durban sought industrial jobs, but what began to distinguish Wentworth was its dominant male labor regime of semiskilled industrial artisanship. This labor regime drew from the early twentieth-century exclusion of Coloured men from the construction industry, their further restriction along with African artisans through education qualifications set by the 1922 Apprenticeship Act, further deskilling since the 1930s, and decades of work through which Wentworth's

artisans were sought after in limited-duration labor in building and retrofit-
ting refineries across South Africa, the continent, and beyond.[121]

The Coloured Labour Preference Policy instituted by the National Party
in the Western Cape in 1955 sought to put an end to the indeterminacy of Coloured identity in a landscape in which Coloureds spoke Afrikaans but were
supposed to be racially distinct from Afrikaners, who, bolstered by decades
of white uplift, were meant to consider themselves racially pure. The aim of
Coloured Labour Preference, as Secretary of Native Affairs Werner Eiselen
put it in 1955, was "the ultimate elimination of Natives from this region."[122]
Forced racial segmentation of the labor market was meant to compel Coloured people's identification with a Coloured "nation" located geographically
in the Cape. There were competing views from the Department of Labour,
which insisted that Africans would accept lower standards of living, and
hence lower wages, and that Coloureds were "'work-shy' and unsuitable for
certain jobs."[123] By 1973 Africans gained exemptions in heavy manual labor,
shift work, and cold-storage work, and as night watchmen, in a compromise
that racially contrasted Coloured men as dishonest, unreliable, and unsuited
to manual labor.[124]

In practice, racial stereotypes and employers' circumvention of the law to
hire African men undermined the effectiveness of the Coloured Labour Preference Policy. However, it may have compelled some Coloured artisans to
migrate to other Coloured areas like Wentworth. Responding to the failure
of policy, Erika Theron of the 1976 Theron Commission on Coloured poverty and reform concluded that "the employment prospects for at least the
bottom 30%, in terms of education and social status, are very unfavourable.
There will be no permanent or continuous employment prospects for this
group."[125] Between this hapless bottom 30 percent and the jealously guarded
world of industrial construction, semiskilled artisanal labor became the
prized occupation for Coloured men in Wentworth. This would only deepen
when the shortage of skilled labor in the 1960s led manufacturing capital to
push for the transformation of the color bar, admitting African labor into
the ranks of the semiskilled while safeguarding white workers' wages and
promotions.[126]

Alongside the changing racial division of labor, social assistance was, by
the 1960s, generalized to all citizens, with a welfare department working
through a racial structure of subsidies built around the white working class.
As Francie Lund shows, the National Party protected white families' access
to preferential subsidies for housing rentals, loans for civil servants, and

school attendance as well as job reservations, while nonstate organizations like the Dutch Reformed Church bolstered preferential treatment. Indians, and to a lesser extent Coloureds, had private welfare organizations picking up some of the slack, but there was virtually no such private welfare for African children and families.[127] These differences contributed to the divergence of Merebank and Wentworth.

Deepening Fissures in Biopolitical Territoriality

In 1975 a committee of the Chamber of Commerce reported a massive shortage of housing for Coloured people in Durban but also the differentiation of Wentworth into "economic flats," "sub economic flats," "low-cost sub economic flats," and some middle-class homes.[128] On one edge of Wentworth, the shack settlement at Happy Valley had become a very difficult place.

Five weeks before the Soweto Uprising of 1976, Sister Theresa called a meeting and wrote a memorandum signed by Archbishop Denis Hurley and Gerald Patrick "Paddy" Kearney of the Diakonia Council of Churches, a crucible of community activism in Durban. The memorandum details the "total inadequacy" of life in the shacks, telling of overcrowding and extreme lack of privacy, exposure to cold and rain, obstacles to repair or extension of homes, and problems of alcoholism and drug abuse. "Problems of sanitation" include difficulties in disposing of rubbish, overflowing toilet buckets, inadequate drainage and stagnant pools, and people forced to scavenge for spoiled food thrown by others into this area. Attendant health problems include gastroenteritis, malnutrition, bronchitis, sandworm, ringworm, and scabies. Adding insult to injury in a climate of crime and fear, the memorandum details white youth from Durban "coming out in carloads to buy drugs from some of the residents." The memorandum urges that residents be rehoused, as "the people are very justified for asking for what purpose they are being taxed."[129]

The Diakonia memorandum circulated through several city departments, prompting a flurry of internal letters. The city Health Department reports that the shack settlement at Happy Valley was council owned, that twenty-one shacks were rented out by the city Estates Department at R2.30 a month to thirty-one Coloured and five Indian families but also that "the shacks . . . are of poor wood/iron construction and do not comply with the provisions of the Slums Act." City Estates denies the memorandum's report on stagnant pools and scavenging for spoiled food, pointing instead to "regular surveillance by the District Community Health Nurse," and on the matters of crime, alcohol, and drugs, it points to the South African Police.[130] Then the files go silent. We know that the settlement at Happy Valley was removed, its Zanzibari occupants moved to Indian Chatsworth, and some Coloured occupants to Wentworth.

By the mid-1970s, settled life in city-rented shacks and "sub-subeconomic" flats had become more intolerable and had drawn the attention of a new generation of township activists in Merebank and Wentworth. One such place was the "sub-subeconomic" settlement called Minitown in Merebank, where the Durban Indian Child Welfare Society reported health hazards in unsafe communal toilets, stagnant water, unsuitable garbage disposal, and a general environment of dampness, dirt, and decay.[131] The ensuing discussion across city departments and over years concerned whether to upgrade or demolish Minitown, replacing it with a better class of subeconomic housing.[132] But another factor had entered the mix.

In 1968 the council sold 17 hectares of recreational land in Merebank to the Mondi Paper Company to establish a pulp and paper mill. In the late 1970s, the council added an additional 22.8 hectares. In 1979 Mondi approached the city for some of this land for a housing scheme for its employees, at which point the MRA opposed this once again, on the grounds that people had been suffering in shacks for almost a decade while waiting for council tenancies. The MRA lambasted the council for being more sympathetic to the needs of the corporation than those of people in need. Again, the files go silent. We know that Minitown was demolished, and another dense, flat complex was built in its stead, sarcastically known in Merebank as Beverly Hills.[133]

A few years later, another set of complaints emerged around "sub-human existence" in the "sub-economic flats" directly across the street from the Wentworth refinery, which residents called Rainbow Chicken, with reference to corporate chicken farms in South Africa. Peter McKenzie's photograph captures this deadly proximity (see figure P.9). They write pointedly in 1980:

> The trying conditions and circumstances under which the people of Rainbow Chicken have been compelled to live are of the worst kind found anywhere in Durban and districts. It was quite obvious that the sub-standard dwellings had fostered sub-standard life styles.... The caretaker in charge is powerless during the evenings when off duty, against criminal types who practice vandalism, drink excessively, brawl, assault, use foul language and resort to gang wars at will. The question is how long will the Durban Municipality continue to ignore this sub-human existence under its tenancy... undoubtedly getting worse by the day?[134]

The Health Department's glib response is that their health visit confirmed that the infrastructure and conditions are much better than this, although the deputation "had only visited one of the one hundred and ten flats in the entire complex."[135] With this continued disdain for the life of the poorest residents of Wentworth, the city circulated proposals for improving stormwater drainage and sanitation to "develop" the area of Treasure Beach for an aspiring local middle class.[136] Between these events lie the uses of biopolitical discourse in pointing out gross failures in access to the means of life, and the limits to the state's police mode of response to failures of biopolitical sovereignty.

The council's work continued. While the Wentworth Coloured scheme was expanded to include the government camp and police headquarters, the council began planning for a larger township in the northern periphery, Newlands.[137] A brewing storm in the files records a battle about fixing Clairwood as a mixed-use "working space," an Indian residential space, or an industrial area, but by this time the poaching of land earmarked for the Merebank-Wentworth Housing Scheme by the Wentworth oil refinery and the Mondi pulp and paper mill had laid bare the forgeries of apartheid planning.[138]

An anonymous document tabled at the Indian Affairs Committee in 1959 makes the case for "encouraging as many Indians as possible to work the land in smallholdings in order to stem the flow of Indians into the cities and to ensure the flow of sufficient food supplies." The author recommends leaving the river valleys unzoned for market gardens and encourages Indian trading in small towns and rural areas.[139] Playing on the fears of the white city, some people were learning how to use the forgeries of apartheid capitalism for other ends.[140]

The Return of the Mere

In 1962 three-year-old Dayalan Naicker drowned in the mere behind Moltan Place. The M R A had been writing the council for a while about these swamplands between the housing scheme and the Umlaas River and had appealed for their reclamation. The swamp and a set of pools had become a dump for domestic wastewater and for dumped garbage, as well as a breeding ground for flies and mosquitoes.[141] The city engineer responded that nothing could be done about the existing system of sewerage and wastewater drainage before the construction of the new sewerage treatment plant, near the offensive site; "in the interests of public safety," implausibly, the deputy city engineer suggested fencing the mere.[142] With its violent disregard of Black life, the police form of biopolitics could only imagine a fence.

Conclusion: Unfixability as Fugitive Conviviality

Today's new hatreds arise less from supposedly reliable anthropological knowledge of the stable identity and predictable difference of the Other. Their novel sources lie in the problem of not being able to locate the Other's difference in the commonsense lexicon of alterity. Different people are still hated and feared, but the timely antipathy against them is nothing compared to the hatreds turned toward the greater menace of the half-different and the partly familiar. To have mixed is to have been party to a great civilizational betrayal. Any unsettling traces of the resulting hybridity must therefore be excised from the tidy, bleached-out zones of impossibly pure culture.
—PAUL GILROY, *After Empire*

By the end of apartheid's second conjuncture, the racial-spatial fix was not working to stem conflict through a science fiction reality of forced estrangement.[143] Indeed, it could not. This is particularly so for Indians and Coloureds, whose difference under apartheid was never anthropological enough, always "half-different and partly familiar," as Paul Gilroy puts it in his critique of national melancholia. Gilroy argues that in contrast to official myopia about empire, racism, or Blackness, popular culture often points to futures other than the defense of race and nation. As in Gilroy's Albion, South Africa wrestles with its own denial of convivial cultures that refused certainties of racial difference that apartheid sought to forge.[144]

Despite the work of numerous intermediaries in attempting to build consent for "grand apartheid," perhaps among some middle-class Coloured and Indian families, most people experienced continuities with a longer history of contradictory biopolitical statecraft that unfixed racial selves and geographies. The beneficiary of this racial statecraft in South Durban was industrial capital, which deepened the contradictions etched into racial bodies and spaces. In the tradition of progressive segregation, city hall remained steadfast in its support for capital above all else. Group Areas Board discussions remained radically inconclusive about whether particular areas ought to be led by "white determinations" or "Indian determinations," whether to keep certain areas "unzoned," who Coloureds were as a group and how big this population was, let alone how its housing needs should be met. This contradictory racial statecraft leaves us with thorny questions about how to understand forms of life produced in its wake.

Two recent texts propose quite different engagements with apartheid statecraft and its effects.[145] Thomas Blom Hansen diagnoses what he poses as the melancholia entailed in working-class Indian self-identification as the *charous* of Chatsworth, the massive Indian Group Area built in apartheid

Durban.[146] While recognizing that apartheid statecraft did not work as intended, Hansen asserts that people lived under a gaze that was so "panoptic, disciplining, and regulative by making objects and bodies visible and intelligible in the full sense of biopolitical rationalities that were entirely structured by racial categories" that they were compelled to adapt to its "complex cultural economy."[147] After apartheid, he asserts, South African racial space is so determinative that "every act and individual utterance is always/already doubled as a representation of a racial category" and that racial stereotypes "provided the script and the interpretive grid within which individual action—and anxiety—was situated."[148] These claims of uniqueness seemingly leave no act, anxiety, person, or corner behind. Apartheid's racial gaze was ineffective, and, inexplicably, it also shaped space and perception so inexorably that people cannot but submit to racial stereotypes.

Unable to discern effective critique of this dilemma from his interlocutors, Hansen proclaims that "it is quite obvious that colonial rule and apartheid in Freudian terms performed two forms of metaphorical castration: violent subjugation of Zulus and the effeminization of Indians. In both cases it was the phallus, white power, presence, and gaze that regulated social practices of mutual intelligibility."[149] In an illuminating moment, Hansen clarifies "mutual intelligibility" while making common cause with "older white working-class men who had married Indian women and had settled in the township during the 1980s"; he remarks with one such man that they are seen by the *charous* around them as public service employees.[150] The easy assumption of shared whiteness might be precisely the perspective that enables Hansen to reproduce the notion of a South Africa of neat racial categories and practices reinforced through the certitudes of a "white gaze." This contrasts sharply with my argument that both Colouredness and Indianness are products of entanglement denied their poetics and presence by the foibles of statecraft.

The second text is Jacob Dlamini's short reflection on familial memories from the township of Katlehong near Johannesburg, which launches an important critical engagement with nostalgia, not just for what is said by his subjects—on law and order, or control of young people—but also for lived and felt "bonds of reciprocity and mutual obligation . . . that made it possible for millions to imagine a world without apartheid."[151] Dlamini draws on Svetlana Boym's distinction between a "restorative" nostalgia focused on heritage and patrimony and a "reflective" nostalgia attentive to "shattered fragments of memory" and to spatial, embodied, and individual difference, often through irony and humor.[152] His diagnosis of reflective nostalgia asks how the senses were inculcated not so much to discipline Katlehong's residents, but at various moments to heighten class consciousness or to spur militancy. Dlamini helps us consider attachment to the past as nostalgia not for apartheid in general but for ways in which people made life meaningful beyond segregationist conventions of thought and practice.[153]

I would like to offer a different way of considering the apartheid past and its remains, as works of science fiction, or attempts at forced alienation that did not quite work as planned.

Accumulating Remains as Science Fiction

Race is the ultimate science fiction.
—ADILIFU NAMA, *Black Space*

While apartheid statecraft failed to produce a stable racial-spatial fix, how might we understand its attempts to produce a science fiction reality of forced estrangement?[154] Consider Neill Blomkamp's 2009 film *District 9*, which begins with a malfunctioning UFO that has disgorged its malnourished aliens into a dystopian Johannesburg of the future ruled by corporate-state Multi-National United. Derided as "prawns," the aliens occupy the shantytown of District 9, where drugs, guns, and interspecies sex are rife. A small multiracial band is tasked with slum clearance and rehousing in District 10, well outside the city. The film was read as an allegory of resurgent xenophobic violence, but it is also an allegory of the dynamics explored in this chapter.

There is much to say about apartheid archetypes in the film. The anti-hero, Wickus van de Merwe, is the bumbling apartheid bureaucrat reliant on white affirmative action, stumbling toward empathy with the prawn. By the film's end, Wickus transforms into a prawn but still yearns for the comforts of home as he fashions a crude valentine for his wife. Despite inhabiting a prawn body, his heart is safely white and human. Human/animal/monster hybrids are staple fare in science fiction, but what is overt here is its gendered racialization. Adilifu Nama poses normative science fiction's imagination of race as "structured absence and token presence," with "nonwhites [as] primitive simian predecessors of modern humanity."[155] Wickus's transformation recalls "blaxploitation" films like Franklin Schaffner's *Planet of the Apes*, in which white men "symbolically trade places" with animalized Black people to "vicariously experience the stifling impact of American racism."[156] But vicarious thrills in *District 9* stop short at a crucial moment; when Wickus helps a prawn take the spaceship to return to a millenarian future, he does not join the prawn revolution. Some things stay black and white.

Blind to the convivial basis of Black politics that explodes, as we will see, in Durban in the 1970s, the film conforms to a dominant sci-fi theme of longing for white space in an era of global Black and subaltern freedom movements, in which Black people are always-already distorted and marked by corporeal excess and the "phallic prop."[157] In this light, "prawns" and "Nigerians" are once and future Black people, doomed to be centered on the phallic power to kill and copulate. These are the aesthetics that follow the promise of Black sovereignty, as Achille Mbembe cautions.[158] The apology for this racial fantasy is the emasculated white male, shadow of the rescuing Tarzan of yesteryear, bumbling defender of apartheid capitalism. This is where satire cannot confront its replication of racial form.

Fredric Jameson argues that science fiction often evades grasping the future directly, offering in its stead "mock futures" whose purpose lies in "transforming our present into the determining past of something yet to come."[159] But counterstrategies can also be racist. By evading the space-times of Black politics in its most capacious forms, *District 9* represses the dream of another South Africa, a Mzansi—to use the colloquial term for this land from the isiXhosa word *uMzantsi*, "the south"—beyond racial capitalism.

As an alternative that conserves a future beyond race, W. E. B. Du Bois's "The Comet" stages the last two survivors in a postapocalyptic New York City. A working-class Black man and wealthy white woman suddenly have the space for solidarity and attraction. This revisionary Eden falls apart when the woman is rescued from interracial, cross-class love by her father and, by extension, by racial capitalism. Du Bois's short story inspires Ruha Benjamin's futuristic vision of biological and political regeneration on the event of the fiftieth anniversary of the Ferguson uprising in the United States in 2065, in a call for a collective praxis of storytelling in preparation for other futures than those we think we are destined to repeat.[160]

We might read this engagement with science fiction in counterpoint with the question of why notions of the occult reemerge in the modern world, as Mircea Eliade once asked.[161] Jean and John Comaroff pursued this question in their accounts of "the zombie" in relation to abstract labor and of the return of the occult in a time of spiraling debt and messianic neoliberalism in South Africa.[162] Eliade's interest was also in the fantastic, which Sumathi Ramaswamy picks up in a spellbinding account of yearning for the mythic lost continent of Lemuria in the Tamil Indian Ocean through specific "labors of loss" at the end of empire.[163] Might this inspire a reconsideration of the fantasy of a white city or a white country as fabulations that circulate despite their unreality? Consider the jazzlike, polysemic quality of the "unreal city" in T. S. Eliot's epic poem *The Waste Land*.[164] Jeffrey Arp reads it as London's war poem that brings the trenches to the city, linking the poet's personal grief to a cultural archive drawn from the wreckage of war, and yet recasting traditions as mutable, open, and attentive to devastation.[165] Eliot's "unreal city" collapses war and peace, combatant and civilian, the elsewhere of the battlefield and the everydayness of the mass of commuters on London Bridge, in a dialectical imagination oriented to a future beyond grief.

With these meditations in mind, the apartheid city becomes a kind of labor of loss of an ideal of a white man's country, besieged by Black people with variously temporary forms of residence who sought to make place meaningful, with a view to a future after the low-intensity race-gender-class war. What remains when these forgeries slowly die, as they must, still?

Memories of everyday life from Wentworth mirror the utopia of the apartheid capitalist city slowly revealing its dystopic character. Wentworth has always been a vibrant place of transgressive conviviality, but by the 1979s, decades of social domination had taken their toll. By this time, self-conceptions of Wentworth had become more sharply introverted. As in many other places during apartheid's last two decades, this sense of introversion seemed particular to Wentworth, feeding heightened sexual and gender-based violence and abuse, a silent history of suffering that remains largely unsaid, and ample material for a "Wentworth blues." Half a century later, residents live with the difficulty of affirming a vibrant community that still struggles with many dimensions of poverty and suffering.

What was ruined in Wentworth and in working-class sections of Merebank through the first two phases of apartheid was any expectation of stable Fordist work and family life, belied by the trajectories of industrial migrants and their shattered families. What was ruined was the spatial fix to capital itself and, in its wake, widespread resignation to decay explained in raced, sexed, and classed terms (see the introduction). Returning to "community work" in Wentworth since the early 2000s, what remains is an attempt to attend to suffering in terms of the bizarre and the alien. "Mutations of the half-familiar," in Gilroy's apt phrasing, these ruined forms of mutuality point to means of survival that remain painful and just about livable. Grasping the decay of apartheid's racial capitalist order, radical popular imaginations in both Wentworth and Merebank point to the abolition of not just apartheid but the social and spatial forms of racial capitalism that support it. Part 2 shifts to these space-times of struggle.

Remains of Revolution

6

The Theologico-Political
Moment, 1970s

Black man, you are on your own.
—STEVE BIKO, "Black Consciousness and the Quest for a True Humanity," 1978

It becomes more necessary to see the truth as it is if you realise that the only vehicle for change are these people who have lost their personality. The first step therefore is to make the Black man come to himself; to pump back life into his empty shell; to infuse him with pride and dignity, to remind him of his complicity in the crime of allowing himself to be misused and therefore letting evil reign supreme in the country of his birth. —STEVE BIKO, "We Blacks," 1971

Black Consciousness, therefore, takes cognizance of the deliberateness of God's plan in creating Black people Black. It seeks to infuse the Black community with a new-found pride in themselves, their efforts, their value systems, their culture, their religion and their outlook to life. The interrelationship between consciousness of the self and the emancipatory programme is of paramount importance. Blacks no longer seek to reform the system because so doing implies acceptance of the major points around which the system revolves. . . . The surge towards Black Consciousness is a phenomenon that has manifested itself throughout the so-called Third World. —STEVE BIKO, "The Definition of Black Consciousness," 1971

Commemorative Repetitions, 2005/1972, 2007/1981

In 2005 I attended a commemoration of an event that many South Africans call their moment of *conscientization,* or coming into political conscious-ness: the 1972 murder in a Johannesburg prison of a thirty-year-old member of the South African Communist Party (SACP), Ahmed Timol, who had left the country for London, received training, and returned to operate under-ground for more than a year before his capture and assassination.[1] At the Durban launch of his biography by his nephew, a prominent African Na-tional Congress (ANC) politician at the podium named people to stand up to be recognized for their contributions to the struggle, in particular for en-during torture.[2] The audience was encouraged to applaud their sacrifice. In his very next breath, the politician promised that he would not rest until the body of "stalwart of the struggle" Moses Mabhida was brought home from Mozambique. In sequence, these gestures relate dead and violated bodies in an economy of exchange in which the countergift for revolutionary sac-rifice is the postapartheid nation-state, with the ANC securely at its helm. The message was: you suffered so that we can be here now, with the ANC as guarantor of the ongoing revolution.[3]

The stakes of this wager were clearly visible in a more modest event in South Durban in 2007, for a foot soldier of the struggle, Krish Rabilal, held in the Merebank Community Centre. Rabilal had been murdered in 1981 in a cross-border raid of ANC and South African Congress of Trade Unions (SACTU) safe houses in the Matola suburb of Maputo, Mozambique, by South African commandos and Rhodesian mercenaries, in blackface, no less. After an hour of sustained fire, twelve militants had been killed, and Rabilal's body revealed the use of napalm. When he heard of the viciousness of the at-tack, ANC president Oliver Tambo said, "The corpses of the comrades should be left as they are . . . to show the barbarity and brutality of apartheid."[4] In a strange echo, this notion of defiled bodies bearing witness recurs in the video recording of the 2007 commemoration, as the emcee introduces the Rever-end Michael Lapsley as "maimed in a parcel bomb attack in Harare; both arms had to be amputated and he lost an eye," adding with comradely dark humor, "His other eye is apparently not too good either," to which Lapsley laughs squarely into the camera.[5]

As is soon apparent, the laughter is laced with irony. Lapsley speaks about "the extraordinary range of memory in the hall today," and with a raised eye-brow, he asks plainly for many stories to be shared: as he puts it, "stories of struggle, stories of sacrifice, stories of pain, stories of endurance, stories of hope, stories of courage." Combining church oratory with what Elaine Scarry calls the retrospective reconstruction of "the body in pain," the minister summons memories of suffering yet to be voiced.[6] He also signals that "revolution" is always multiple, its claim to fundamental change often belied by the actuality of continuing suffering. After a detour through an imagined postrevolutionary Cuba, Lapsley's oratory dwells on widespread poverty, joblessness, homelessness, and lack of access to antiretroviral medication, bringing the politics of struggle commemoration squarely into the present. Perhaps the most agile thinker on the stage, the disabled veteran proclaims, "We need to be renewed in strength and vigour to build the country of our dreams."

What is striking is the contrast between Lapsley's narration of apartheid-era suffering in order to claim a South Africa yet to come and the well-worn themes of the nation's debts to revolutionary martyrs. Ronnie Kasrils, a veteran of uMkhonto we Sizwe (MK) who had encountered Rabilal at a camp in Angola, has less to say about him than about his trip to Vietnam to meet the venerable General Võ Nguyên Giáp (see chapter 7). With local government elections around the corner, Kasrils turns Giáp's statements about unity in struggle into an argument for the hegemony of the ANC. Returning to the "Matola martyrs," Kasrils insists that many acts of memory "must fit into the monument that the government is building . . . a place of commemoration that will bring us all together in unity." Even the dead are not safe from the party of the revolution.[7]

The very act of commemorating revolution is contradictory; its staging of repetition and dramatization of authority is antithetical to the idea of a break with power. Turn-of-the-millennium revolutionary commemorations in South Africa, and perhaps generally, enact wider evasions, of actual national self-determination, let alone social or sexual liberation. Commemorations are a particular kind of remains that, while seemingly trapped in repetition, can reveal multiple space-times of struggle. As Lapsley reminds us, commemoration can be a site to remind audiences of a future beyond repetition.

In a reading of Paris 1968 and commemorations of it, Alain Badiou argues that there remains an ambiguity in "1968" as understood through the idioms of class struggle, proletarian leadership, and communist parties and that "this common language, symbolized by the red flag, was in fact dying out"; in his view, this blurring of the receding and the emergent "gives May '68 its mysterious intensity."[8]

Anti-apartheid commemorative rituals carry a similar burden. Consider a lone activist at the Merebank function, a long-standing critic of the ANC who was given a slot to speak late in the evening while people were busy eating dinner. Over the din of biryani and conviviality, he reeled off lines about revolutionary martyrdom with a clear look of exhaustion, a desperate plea to an audience as unconvinced as he appeared to be himself. In his tired persistence, he personified the irresolution of receding and emergent political times, lending an auratic quality to what the many-stranded struggle actually was, if not what the political elite has enshrined.

Part 2 of this book turns to the actual multiplicity of struggles, their evasions and continuing challenges.

Conjunctural Moments in a Dialectical Genealogy of Revolution

In Durban of the turbulent 1970s and 1980s, with most liberation movement leadership jailed and exiled, Indian and Coloured neighborhoods not subject to the intense surveillance and proxy violence in African townships became crucibles of multiple forms of political creativity. This is why the dialectics of revolution in Merebank and Wentworth can tell us something about what remains of the idea of revolution itself: the real and imagined radical transformation of state and society; of the accumulation regime and its knowledge effects; and of values of life, labor, art, sex, kinship, and death that might escape the chains of subjection to capital and sovereignty.

With the benefit of hindsight, we might see the compromised idea of Leninist revolution in the wake of the global shifts of the early 1970s through David Graeber's characterization of a dissociation of political equality from economic security across a range of midcentury formations, from Keynesian welfare states to national liberation and feminist movements.[9] In this light, the tragedy of the ruling alliance is that one of the last great twentieth-century national liberation movements resigned itself to liberal dissociation of the political and the economic and to hegemony without radical change. There is a germ of insight in Graeber's formulation if one considers the way in which this national liberation movement so quickly, between 1989 and 1996, put in place a set of compromises that entailed sacrificing a large share of the Black majority to poverty, inequality, and the AIDS pandemic, and that made its own show of populism a screen for what later became clear as private accumulation through state capture. In retrospect, the dialectics of revolution in Durban in the 1970s and 1980s demonstrate many moments of ferment whose political forms might yet be resurgent.

Part 2 turns to the period from the early 1970s to the late 1980s as the opening and partial closure of South Africa's revolution, to refuse both a melancholy leftism that can only bemoan the betrayal of revolution in neoliberal times and a Eurocentric utopianism about communism that does not learn from the global anti-colonial, anti-racist revolution of the long twentieth century.[10] Metropolitan radical traditions repeat this myopia neurotically, as does contemporary radical geography, even when it draws on Henri Lefebvre, the polymath with so little to say about race or colonialism.[11] A host of Black diasporic and Southern or "Third Worldist" radical critics push beyond this occlusion of anticolonial revolution in ways that we might yet read with Lefebvre.

The four chapters in part 2 assemble spatiotemporal conjunctures in a dialectical genealogy of revolution. Recall Stuart Hall's notion of conjunctural diagnosis as assembling moments in their contradictory, ruptured, spatial and temporal complexity (see the introduction). These conjunctural moments are relational and overlapping, and they recruit political lives in Merebank and Wentworth differently. The "theologico-political moment" in this chapter involves various ways of reaching beyond the present, through strike waves, the Black Consciousness (BC) Movement, and a charismatic revival that swept Wentworth's churches. The "insurrectionist moment" in chapter 7 involves underground networks, furtive journeys, and a trail of bodily violence and masculine bravado that drew the mythology of "armed struggle" into Wentworth and Merebank in different ways in the 1970s and 1980s. The "moment of urban revolution" in chapter 8 sought to articulate legal urban organization to illegal and underground networks to work within and beyond the gears of urban government. This moment seems to "resolve" the first two moments in an attempt to forge hegemony, crucially by deploying biopolitical expertise in urban struggle; but the idea of dialectical resolution is always a mirage. This takes us to "the moment of the disqualified" in chapter 9 in sites of revolutionary exclusion in places like Wentworth, where people express enduring aporia in varied ways, in a spectacular sabotage cell that rejected a "proper politics" and in forms of documentary photography that "shot back" from the ruins of apartheid's last decade.[12]

Keeping in mind that these are coterminous and relational moments, we begin with the confluence of a set of emergent revolts in Durban beginning in 1972, which in many ways mark the beginning of an unstoppable urban revolt in South Africa that was one of many reasons for apartheid's end.

The "Durban Moment" as a Theologico-Political Moment

Unless we think in utopian terms about South African society we will not really come to understand how it works today. . . . The fact that something exists is no guarantee that it should exist. A glance at some of the institutions that other societies have taken unquestioningly for granted—cannibalism, slavery, polygamy, communal property ownership, non-competitiveness, nudity, vegetarianism, male supremacy, matriarchy, promiscuity, Puritanism, the rule of divine emperors or the rule of hereditary aristocracies, and even, on occasion, democracy—should make us a little more hesitant in taking absolutely for granted such institutions as private ownership of the means of production, social inequality, monogamy, the school system, "national growth," war, and racial oligarchy in South Africa.
—RICHARD "RICK" TURNER, *Eye of the Needle*, 1972

A number of whites in this country adopt the class analysis, primarily because they want to detach us from anything relating to race. . . . They find it more comfortable. And, of course, a number of them are terribly puritanical, dogmatic and very, very arrogant. They don't know quite to what extent they have to give up a part of themselves in order to be a true Marxist.
—STEVE BIKO, "Interview," 1972

Rick Turner arrived in Durban fresh from the events of Paris in 1968, with its revisionist Marxism and utopianism in the street.[13] Like Steve Biko, Frantz Fanon, and C. L. R. James, Turner was particularly drawn to Jean-Paul Sartre's attempt at bridging Marxism and existential phenomenology.[14] Like Fanon and Biko, Turner saw fundamental transformation of the self as necessary for social justice. All these thinkers struggled in parallel with undoing race in their lived Marxism, to paraphrase Biko.

Turner was a mild-mannered person but a firebrand lecturer, and people flocked to hear him at the art deco Memorial Tower Building towering over the University of Natal on Durban's Berea Ridge.[15] Several who attended were engaged with burgeoning Black trade unions and with student groups working on the Durban Student Wages Commission to help institute living wages.[16] After the outbreak of strikes in 1972–73, Turner and his trade union associates at Bolton Hall conducted important research on the causes of militancy. This research continued when he was banned and wrote under cover of collective authorship.

Biko is posed as Turner's Black activist-intellectual counterpart, adversary, and comrade. Biko's thought represented a fresh voice of Black political self-expression and refusal of white liberal tutelage in the student movement, and more generally in the internal struggle for liberation.[17] Ian Macqueen's research shows how productive the intellectual relationship between Turner and Biko was, as it expressed and engendered deeper questioning of the nature of politics in an intensified period between 1970 and 1974, drawing from New Left Marxism, existentialism, Africanism, and utopian Christianity.[18] When both figures were banned and then murdered at the hands of the apartheid state, Biko in 1977 and Turner in 1978, the brevity of their time added to the intensity of their distinct and interrelated legacies. As intriguing and fresh as these two charismatic men remain, they also magnified a wider collective effervescence, from brewing struggles emerging from the port that spread across industrial Durban, to Black student assertion that ramified through communities, to a surprising set of eruptions within churches.

This conjuncture is referred to in scholarly and popular historiography as "the Durban Moment," although there were many "Durban Moments," as Myron, a former youth from Merebank, cautioned me: "Things were happening on different layers, not necessarily connected, but they did become connected, and disconnected. There's no linear, chronological way of looking at these types of things. It was a kind of situation where networks or weblike formations about information and experiences touched different political notes, so that various people start to get connected in different levels of intensity and involvement." What is clear is that across "political notes," a beautifully musical metaphor, this was a time of questioning distinctions, classifications, theories, and styles of struggle. Participants drew on connections and resonances with the US Black freedom movement, with Black and radical Christianity, and with the youth and countercultural revolts of "the 1960s" across Europe and the Americas. An initial reason for calling this a "theologico-political moment" is the role that radical and Black Christian theology played in political imaginations. As we will see, figures moving through this moment from different traditions and directions forged journeys that in varied ways involved relentless existential questioning. We might interpret this, as historian Macqueen does, through the proximity of various political imaginations in Durban that made this place and time singular, so much so that Tony Morphet could coin the name "Durban Moment."[19] In this interpretation, "the Durban Moment" was *Durban's* moment, an assertion of political singularity.

But there is more to these events than a claim to singularity. An implicit citation in my renaming of this conjuncture is Walter Benjamin's enigmatic "Theologico-Political Fragment." Cautioning against an interpretation of this text that expects the messianic to be revealed in history, Judith Butler argues that the hyphen between the two terms "names a way that the messianic operates as the flashing up of one time within another, or [as] . . . a timelessness within the domain of time."[20] In this interpretation, messianic time traverses historical time, marking the "failure of the historical to signify the divine," but allowing the general condition of transience to be expressed through the worldly "in a more oblique way."[21] As prophetic hopes reveal their transience in Durban of the 1970s, including in the expectation of ghostly divinity, we shall see that many sides of the Durban Moment express what the Benjamin of the 1940s calls the flashing up of the traditions of the oppressed.[22]

The Indian Ocean Strikes Back: The 1972–1973 Strikes

Durban's port was and remains of immense material value as a key hub on the African coast of the Indian Ocean.[23] As C. L. R. James put it in his analysis of the Haitian Revolution, it is the collective and critical will of subjugated workers at a site of significant accumulation that makes for a revolutionary situation.[24] Ralph Callebert shows that dockworkers struck repeatedly, as far back as 1874, periodically in the 1880s, with the nonracial Industrial and Commercial Workers Union in the 1920s, with the Communist Party underground in the 1930s, and through complex rural-urban, multiclass, and ethnic nationalist relations in apartheid's late 1950s.[25] When a thousand stevedores went on strike in late 1972, David Hemson insists that they had launched "the beginnings of mass opposition to apartheid."[26]

Early the following year, the conflagration was reignited at the Coronation Brick and Tile Company in the north of Durban, and a spiraling wave of strikes spread, particularly through the Frame Textile Group, across industrial Durban and the peripheral industrial areas of Pinetown and Hammarsdale—in other words, in South Africa's second most important industrial area.[27]

From the perspective of the group of local radical researchers centered on Turner, these events were extremely fortuitous. Turner had published *The Eye of the Needle* in 1972, as a plea against dystopian conformism.[28] Rejecting the statist communism of the party as another form of dogma, he argued that "the only real alternative is to ensure popular participation, based on workers' control, in a context of political freedom."[29] The 1973 strikes seemed confirmation that this opportunity had arrived. The book's 1973 postscript, "The Present as History," argues that it is surrounded by evidence that the Black working class had come to see their potential power through industrial action.[30]

Banned in February 1973, Turner continued to work with his equally brilliant wife and intellectual partner, Foszia Fisher, and their comrades at the Institute for Industrial Education (IIE), including Halton Cheadle and David Hemson (both banned), Gerhard Maré, and others; they drew in youth researchers, including Shamim Meer.[31] The IIE study on the strike, which could not name Turner as a coauthor, attempts under conditions of repression to explain the causes of the strikes and to carefully dispel the notion that they were impelled by agitators, including the underground ANC and SACP. There certainly were influences on striking workers' demands, including from those at the IIE. As Grace Davie argues, connections forged through the wages commission among students, academic staff at the University of Natal, and workers who attended Wage Board meetings spread ideas of a poverty datum line that striking workers perhaps used to claim authority.[32]

The IIE study insists that the strikes were a form of mass "spontaneous" action, organized to some degree but led by workers who used highly visible forms of street and workplace protest to spread across the city; for instance, the rumor of a train boycott had apparently heightened a sense of crisis across the industrial region, creating the conditions for state and capital to capitulate to the severely deprived working class, who were essential to the conditions of accumulation.[33]

Several factories in the industrial areas of Jacobs and Mobeni in South Durban participated in the strikes of 1973. Worker militancy did not lead to the politics hoped for by Turner; worker struggles were instead drawn into a series of bargains and attempts at institutionalization that may have disarticulated workers' concerns from communities. This may have been the case in Wentworth and Merebank, but the archives are as silent as popular memory about connections in these neighborhoods to the 1972–73 strikes, even though the research in the IIE study shows significant support from Merebank.[34]

In the ensuing years, manufacturing grew considerably, but as John Saul and Stephen Gelb argue, "The balance of class power, at least at the point of production," shifted "decisively and permanently," as expressed through the revival of independent Black trade unionism.[35] A paradox persists, which is that after the great strike waves across the city crested, workplace politics remained marginal to the community activism that emerged in Merebank and Wentworth in the 1970s and 1980s.

In a revealing moment, the IIE study cites a worker with thirty-five years of "service" who refutes the suggestion of a Durban *Daily News* reporter that intimidation was involved in his decision to strike; his answer is "No, sir, this thing comes from God. I am not afraid; nobody told me to go on strike."[36] There is no further commentary. We know nothing more about the worker's utterance, or the complex rural-urban lives and forms of consciousness that it emerges from. We might see the worker's utterance as resonant with

Barney Pityana's gendered phrasing that BC emerged "within the womb of religious societies and organizations."[37] But if we return to the IIE book's full title, *The Durban Strikes 1973 ("Human Beings with Souls")*, what is striking is that the parenthetical phrase is a literal flashing of one time in another.[38]

Conscientization as Praxis: The Black Consciousness Movement

The formation of something called the Black Consciousness Movement is often dated to 1969, when a group of Black student activists walked out of the white-led National Union of South African Students (NUSAS) to form the all-Black South African Students' Organisation (SASO). However, it was neither a movement then nor just a product of this event. Other influences shaped Black youth who around 1972 began to speak in terms of Black Consciousness, capitalized, as their central concern. In a short and intense period, this group formed the Black People's Convention (BPC) and Black Community Programmes (BCP) and began to see themselves as a movement that had stepped into the political space evacuated by the ANC, Pan Africanist Congress, SACTU, and other banned organizations. But BC was more than a response to a "political vacuum," as has been repeated in movement discourse. Rather, it was a collective affirmation of dignity and Black personhood. As several people, including many within its currents, argue, BC rested on practices of critical thinking, reading, writing, and teaching, which would demand the liberation of the thinking Black subject from the protective mantle of white liberalism.[39]

Crucially, this was a prophetic tradition, drawing from progressive Christianity and Black theology, supported by Beyers Naudé and the Christian Institute and by the University Christian Movement (UCM), formed in 1967; it was inspired by Paulo Freire's thought as well as his active support through the World Council of Churches and the South African Council of Churches. South African activists recall their moment of "conscientization," drawing on Freire's *conscientização*, which drew from Frantz Fanon's neologism *conscienciser*, in a South Atlantic circuit, asking what it means to come into consciousness as part of the work of decolonization.[40] Anne Hope, a white woman from Johannesburg, studied at Rhodes University, then at Oxford, and then, on a fellowship from the World Council of Churches, in Boston, where she was steeped in Freire's critical pedagogy. After her return to South Africa in 1971, she then worked with Biko and BC leadership on linking Freirean conscientization with anti-racist participatory methods.

Biko was dismissed from the University of Natal Medical School in June 1972 and joined the staff at BCP at 86 Beatrice Street in town.[41] Many young people received material and intellectual support through these means. Before we turn to one such cohort, it is important to stress that these connections and practices formed the social basis for the formation of Black critical philosophy in close engagement with radical and Black Christianity.[42]

These transformations clarify the central argument of this chapter, that the theologico-political moment was an interconnected set of leaps of faith into the political unknown. Radical Black theology is not incidental; it is fundamental to a conception of political faith in the possibility of dismantling the deep material inequalities and moral injustices sown by apartheid's spatial fix. Consider that in the relation between the three epigraphs that open this chapter, Biko stages a condition of Black personhood ("you are on your own"), the need to "pump life" into it to inculcate pride and dignity, and a declaration that these techniques of the self are not just key to a "programme of emancipation: this is God's plan.[43] This is precisely an argument about political faith.

What distinguished the political faith emergent in this conjunctural moment is that it was steadfastly disinterested in sovereignty and focused on racial justice in the concreteness of Black life. Political faith in this sense is crucial for commitment to an unknown future of Blackness as constitutive of a new human and a new earthliness.[44] After the worker strikes subsided, and after radical Christianity was disciplined by the firm hand of church leadership in a time of intensified repression, this political faith has remained in the praxis of former BC activists.

Between 1970 and 1972, while Biko studied at the medical school, the de facto headquarters of SASO was in his room at the Alan Taylor Residence for Black medical students, adjoining the oil refinery at the center of Wentworth.[45] This would prove fortuitous for a young group of people who had forged something elsewhere, in the basement of a Presbyterian church in Merebank.

The Community of St. Stephen, or Black Action Group

The members of this group—Jaya, Bobby, Willie, Betty, Rishi, Ingrid, Roy, Carmel, Shamim, and Rubin—are still good friends, some in regular contact. As young people from Merebank and Wentworth, with the exception of Shamim, they were drawn to BC thought and to Biko while he was in Wentworth. In turn, Biko appears to have been drawn to their engagement with parallel experiments with Black solidarity through theater and community organization. While their trajectories diverged in the ensuing years across the Unity Movement, the political underground, the exiled MK, Black trade unions under the Federation of South African Trade Unions (FOSATU), Black feminism, and the Anglican Church, they remain friends, and they remain fundamentally shaped by the experiments of their utopian youth. The endurance of their youthful conviction is striking.

All members of this cohort had been shaped by experiences of forced removal in Durban in the 1960s. The slightly older ones, Jaya and Rishi, grew up in Clairwood in the shadows of the earlier generation of ANC activists and their supporters. Jaya remembers the principal in Clairwood High School making them sing the national anthem; he clarifies, "The Indian national anthem!" After moving to Merebank, both participated in high school pranks like sabotaging the float made by their school to celebrate Indian cultural identity on the fifth anniversary of the Republic of South Africa, in 1966. Bobby and his cohort would do something similar on the tenth anniversary of the republic in 1971. These young people remember schools as disciplinary sites but also as places where progressive teachers could sow the seeds of refusal. Myron has a fantastic story about a teacher who had made a memorial to M. K. Gandhi: "Mr. Singh had all these things of Gandhi's: Gandhi's desk, Gandhi's jewels, Gandhi's pen, and he had it in the school." I stopped him to ask, "You mean things like these?" and he continued, "No, no, actual things of Gandhi. He brought all of that stuff and put it in one room of that high school. We would go in and see his stuff: his desk, his writings, his bangles, and that door will always be open and you could always see it. 'What did Gandhi do?' 'He did this' and 'He did that' and so on."[46] Whatever we make of the didactic significance of this Gandhi on display with jewels and bangles (Gandhi in drag?), this childhood memory points to an early moment of questioning.

Bobby had influences at home connecting him to the earlier generation of Congress activists, particularly through his boisterous aunt Poomoney "Poo" Moodley (see chapter 4), who all of them later realized had been a "hard-core communist" along with veteran activist Billy Nair, ready to discuss the ideas of the ANC and Communist Party. Bobby had grown up in this atmosphere of questioning, with this larger-than-life, cigarette-smoking aunt taking on the men in arguments that went late into the night. When this group of friends came together around Bobby, they often met at his home, and they often got into discussions with Aunty Poo that they could later put into political terms. Much later, they would realize that she was also a member of the first MK cell in Durban. While the older generation of Nair and Moodley represented connections to labor, communist, and ANC-allied activism that had led to the arrests and bannings of the early 1960s (see chapter 5), these youth of the 1970s turned their sights elsewhere.

Jaya had been in the Methodist Church when he became involved in 1967 with the recently formed UCM, one of the sites from which Black students relegated to apartheid's racially exclusive universities sought to connect and organize.[47] Facing opposition to this involvement from his church, Jaya shifted to the Merebank Presbyterian Church, a pioneering Presbyterian church started by Joseph Prakasim, whose son Calvin would be drawn into the next wave of youth activists. Importantly, the church was across from Bobby's home. The UCM connection enabled the Merebank youth to forge relationships in Cape Town, connecting them to a group of young women, including sisters Algonda and Carmel. The sisters would later marry Jaya and Roy.

In 1969 this Cape Town Presbyterian church group visited Merebank. That same year, the Presbyterian Church decided to send a representative of their South African Black youth membership to the United States, and as Bobby puts it, they decided not to take someone from an African Presbyterian church because "we were in the middle, so we were acceptable." Bobby's circle was quickly contacted by the white student political organization, NUSAS, "alerting us to demand certain things," but the youth's response was that these "whites were treating us differently, and we want to be equal."[48] This experience is parallel to the formation of SASO, which had also rejected NUSAS on the grounds of white liberal tutelage, an incident that points out that in all likelihood many talented young Black people experienced similar insults. A young man called Tony from the Presbyterian church in Merebank was sent to America, where he went to Berkeley and other places and came back with the idea of "coffee bar ministry" as "churches in the US were trying to engage youth in the rebellion through coffee bars." Bobby pauses while recounting this, then exclaims that they knew nothing about coffee!

What made this grouping around Jaya, Rishi, and Bobby distinct before they met Steve Biko was something they forged in this coffee bar in the basement of the Presbyterian church. They called themselves the Community of St. Stephen. Their basement was painted dark, with psychedelic lights and hippie posters; they had long hair, funky T-shirts, and interracial relationships; and their coffee bar sold music, hot dogs, and coffee to fund trips and activities.[49] Members of this group speak about the incredible sense of possibility they felt in the church basement, with a theological warrant to support their faith in the possibility of change. The coffee bar drew in youth from

Coloured Wentworth, including Willie, Betty, Ruben, and Tys. Effectively it was a racially mixed Indian-Coloured group that refused racial identification precisely at the time of heightened debate about whether the Natal Indian Congress (NIC) should open its doors to "non-Indians."[50] The group changed its name in 1972 to the Black Action Group; they had intense discussions and listened to music and read books, through which they felt connected with what Bobby calls the wider revolt more directly associated with white youth.

Other things were happening simultaneously that did not quite fit into the theologico-political moment but that were also part of the moment of insurrection and the moment of urban revolution, and yet these events are crucial to understand the possibilities afforded to the Community of St. Stephen / Black Action Group in Merebank. In 1970–71 Mewa Ramgobin, Ela Gandhi, George Sewpersadh, and others decided to relaunch the moribund NIC, which, unlike the ANC and SACP, had never been banned. This renewed NIC could give the Congress Alliance a new lease on life, providing legal cover for ANC-related work and for movement activity more generally. Merebank's Nataraj Cinema—an established meeting place where, Myron recalls, "the old *ballies* [older generation of men] would argue, and we'd listen"—was the site of a campaign led by the renewed NIC, an appeal for clemency for political prisoners imprisoned on Robben Island for a decade on the occasion of the 1971 anniversary of the republic.

While youth groups in Merebank were divided on many things, they came together for this clemency appeal and brought several political activists to the township, including George Sewpersadh of the NIC, Norman Middleton of the Labour Party, and NUSAS activists from the University of Natal. Something else seems to have been happening in the late 1960s and early 1970s, which was that, as Jaya describes it, associational life in Merebank—across the ratepayers association, child welfare associations, sports organizations, soccer clubs, and a range of smaller groups and youth clubs including the increasingly active Merebank Ex-Students Society—began to take a political orientation, whether in the clemency appeal or in the nascent critique of racialized sport.

In this time of apparent change in the community, the coffee bar provided the youth group with a space for meeting, reading, talking, and hanging out. Roy calls it a "base." Like others in the BC movement, Bobby stresses the importance of reading. He read the prayers of Michel Quoist for "ideas of homosexual equality" and feminist reordering of intimate life. He insists that

unlike Communist Party cultures, including another youth group in Merebank (see chapter 7), "we would talk about sex and sexual relationships," and
in the process they were self-consciously forming a critical subculture disconnected from the township around them. As a mark of being from Merebank but not *of* it, Bobby recalls that he and Jaya "would listen to jazz; I was
schooled in Miles Davis and John Coltrane, which was completely not logical
for Merebank." This reference to music, and of jazz in particular, is crucial to
signify aesthetic difference as part of a distinctive style of politics attentive to
improvisation and creativity.

How do we understand this marginal site of political awakening? I take
from Fredric Jameson the importance of distinguishing utopian programs
and projects from utopian impulses in everyday life.[51] While utopian programs existed with varied resolution in the background, for instance, as re-
newing ideas in the Freedom Charter, utopian impulses permeated everyday
life in the crisis-ridden 1970s and 1980s. Bobby stressed to me that these
young people were a product not so much of their neighborhood but rather
of an exasperation with what it symbolized: Indianness, convention, orthodoxy, and stasis. The theologico-political moment spawns precisely such
"what-if" space-times, in which time and space collapse into a break with the
"course of events" in Rick Turner's epigraph. The very notion that a group
of young people racialized Indian and Coloured could affirm Blackness was
precisely a product of this utopian impulse. That this utopian impulse was
forged in the basement of a church charges its affirmation of rupture with
political faith.

In 1971 the youth of the Community of St. Stephen started doing "guerrilla
theatre in the churches and out in the open in Merebank and Mobeni." As
a church theater group, they did variants of the passion play, one called *The
Son of Man*, with Jesus "dressed up as an African worker," which white priests
witnessed with some consternation. When these priests tried to counter by
holding camps to win over Black youth, Jaya and Bobby went to disrupt the
camps, to tell the youth to refuse the paternalism of the priesthood—all this
while both aspired to join the priesthood as well. They went on to perform
plays in Chatsworth and KwaMashu, and even as far away as Cape Town,
and Myron and Bobby would later train people in guerrilla theater.[52] One
play called *The Wall* was about breaking down an imaginary divide; another
centered on the murder of Ahmed Timol, which begins part 2 of this book.
As Rishi puts it in the ethos of BC, "We found that in the process we were
also forming ourselves."

Self-Determination and the Turn to "Communities"

Through Jaya's connections, the group approached the student-run Theatre Council of Natal, headed by BC activists Sathasivan "Saths" Cooper and Strinivasa "Strini" Moodley, and Sam Moodley, to perform one of their plays at the SASO conference at the Alan Taylor Residence in Wentworth. While Saths, Strini, and Sam represented activists from "town," the Merebank youth group apparently caught Biko's attention as an organic group of township Indian youth engaged in exactly the kind of project he and others had brought from the Eastern Cape to Durban; unlike Saths and Strini, they were also primarily Christian, and this made the meeting fortuitous for all concerned.

Was there more to this mutual identification than meets the eye? Daniel Magaziner argues that Biko's journey through the existentialism of Jean-Paul Sartre, Albert Camus, Frantz Fanon, and Aimé Césaire led to fundamental questions of being.[53] Lewis Gordon argues much more expansively of Africana philosophy that Christianity was the hinge between existential interiority and the Black quest for liberation.[54] The critical use of Christian tropes would return in the suffering and martyrdom of Biko himself, and this adds a retrospective aura to talk about the charismatic Biko. Even though some members of the Community of St. Stephen were not Christian, radical Christianity gave them a shared vocabulary for existential questioning. Mabogo More refuses the view that US Black Power thought played a determinative influence in this regard, while noting the importance of James Cone's Black theology of liberation; More argues that Biko's existentialism is one strand in an open and diverse South African tradition of Black philosophy.[55] More's and Gordon's formulations are prescient when we consider that Cedric Robinson's notion of a "Black radical tradition" derived from his early work on the African continent.[56]

Emerging from BC, Barney Pityana argues for a deeper engagement with what he characterizes as Biko's Hegelian dialectics. When I pressed him on this argument in relation to the complexities of the Durban Moment, he responded that BC was dialectically engaged with Turner as with the "Gandhians" of the renewed NIC, and when the latter revived Gandhi's Phoenix Settlement as a camp for training young activists across the color line, he said they encouraged BC to participate in this work.[57] Pityana's view is that dialectics exist in the world as a Hegelian motor of history. This contrasts with the approach I take through Stuart Hall, for whom dialectics are a diagnostic means to engage the unruliness of reality, as well as to assemble genealogies to represent this unruliness. However, Pityana does point, in my terms, to differentiated moments within a conjuncture that we can understand as fragile, changing, and struggled over. What is also interesting is that he points to particular sites of praxis like the Phoenix Settlement, transformed by the turn to organizing communities through youth groups across the city.

At their moment of confluence, both Biko and the Community of St. Stephen had begun to experiment with radicalizing "community" in ways that parallel the shift in the US Black Panther Party as it turned to securing community autonomy over the means of survival. Consider Alondra Nelson's argument that under conditions of heightened state repression, the Black Panther Party shifted from "self-defense" to a Third Worldist call for "self-determination" and that community-run health clinics were a key front for this work in a "Maoist" tradition of barefoot doctors. The Panthers held an important Community Survival Conference in 1972 that showcased community health programs that "serve the people, body and soul," turning a popular Panther rallying call into concrete action.[58] Nelson argues that this work built on a longer tradition of Black critique of medicine, drawn into the internal critique of the Black Panther Party in turbulent times, and while it was portrayed as a "reformist" turn, Bobby Seal's sharp response was that "fascists also carry guns."[59] In other words, there had to be a form of revolutionary action beyond the militarized form, and a form of popular mobilization that might take control of the biopolitical tools monopolized by racial capitalist sovereignty.

In Durban, and South Africa more generally, the militarized form would remain primary within the self-conception of the dominant liberation movement organizations for some time. However, places like the Alan Taylor Residence and Phoenix Settlement point to something more like the Panthers' turn to the prefigurative work of building revolutionary community through a popular biopolitics. As one indication of this shift, Biko and others formed a community health project from the Alan Taylor Residence, and they set out to actively engage the neighborhoods around them.

When the Merebank theater group came to perform at Alan Taylor, they caught the attention of Keith Mokoape and Steve Biko. Jaya recalls their excited response at meeting his friends: "This is special, where did these guys come from!" When the slightly older activists from town, Saths Cooper and Strini Moodley, were shocked at Biko's enthusiasm, he apparently responded with a desire to engage more closely with this young group from Merebank and Wentworth.

The meeting between Biko and the Community of St. Stephen / Black Action Group was fortuitous because the latter were also embarking on community work across racial divides in Merebank and Wentworth, recalling older experiments in bulk purchasing and cooperative sales of provisions in Merebank during the passive resistance movement of 1946 (see chapter 4). They also tried to connect young people on both sides of Duranta Road by holding youth camps at Camp Jonathan on the South Coast and also at Port Shepstone, with workshops on "breaking down the racial barriers" that youth had become used to in apartheid's neighborhoods.[60]

In a short time, the youth group became part of almost all the strands of BC. Some were already engaged in what BCP, formed in 1971, sought to do, inculcating community self-reliance.[61] They went on to form the Association for Self-Help (ASH) in 1973. Bobby, Roy, and Myron started their university studies in 1972 at the segregated Indian university, the University of Durban-Westville (UDW), and became active in the SASO walkout from the university, effectively sacrificing their college education for the protest. After the younger group called the strike, a slightly older group of student activists took it over in the background. These men, including Pravin Gordhan, Yunus Mahomed, and Zakeria "Zak" Yacoob, went on to become major political operatives for the Congress movement, and they secured their future in the moment of urban revolution without sacrificing their college educations (see chapter 8).

Some followed the lead of Saths Cooper, who took over the BPC. Roy took this path for a while, playing a key role in the Merewent chapter of the BPC. The group from Merebank connected with Rubin Philip when he was a curate in Wentworth and an established activist in SASO. When I met him, he was the Anglican bishop of Natal. When SASO and the BPC diverged, and with heightened surveillance and repression of their leaders, two among this group, Jaya and Terence, became SASO vice presidents, to which Bobby laughs and says, "I don't know how, because Jaya wasn't even a student!"

After the 1972 SASO conference, Biko asked Jaya if he had a passport, which he did because he and Bobby had hitchhiked to Swaziland. Jaya went on a campaign tour for SASO/BCP to Europe and the United States in 1973, to speak about their projects and raise funds. On the way, he met Black Power, Black theology, student, and exiled ANC, Pan Africanist Congress, and other anti-apartheid groups. He spoke to a Black theology group at Columbia University, attended a conference just after the release of Angela Davis, met people from the American Council of Churches in New York City, encountered Bobby Seal on the campaign trail for mayor of Oakland, and met the Black student caucus at the University of California, Berkeley. After a second international trip, to Malawi, he was detained and banned in 1973, the same year Biko was banned and restricted to his hometown in the Eastern Cape.

In the short and intense period between 1972 and 1973, the youth group from Merebank had spent time with the BC leadership in an atmosphere of nonhierarchy and intimacy: "Barney Pityana, Steve Biko, Harry Nengwekhulu, we knew all of them and we partied together and they would come over" to Bobby's home. Bobby describes a "seminar with Steve on the beach" in which "we took one of those bushes and we were all sitting on branches and on the floor, in the bush, and Steve would explain to us things like 'what is the Third World?' They were introducing concepts to us. They were telling us where the struggle would go, and how whites control the communists. SASO was always thinking about where they're going to go next. We were going to build power bases." I would like to pause here to think about this idea of a power base as a place of refuge and reflection, a site of modern-day marronage.[62] This space of intimacy afforded young men the ability to rethink concepts and to strategize where to go next. It is not clear that the young women in this circle could occupy space in quite the same way, but in the case of the Merebank group, the coffee bar had begun a process of experimentation with gender and sexual freedom as well. What is interesting is the strategy they decided to pursue.

The group of critical and recently evicted students, including Bobby, Roy, and Myron, who were either kicked out or "voluntarily" left UDW, had to put their praxis into new arenas of productivity. The opportunity emerged in the formation of ASH in June 1973, with the expressed aim of "making people 'develop a pride in themselves and their potential—to show the relationship of their environment to themselves,' so as to increase self-reliance and interdependency," with "initial projects in the Merebank-Wentworth area."[63] With its focus on community programs, ASH was meant to be a "power base" within communities that these youth in many ways had sought to reject. An extract from ASH's 1973 Progress Report elaborates on the analytics employed as ASH confronted various problems as simultaneously material and cultural: "poverty, illiteracy, crime, etc. militate against the true humanity of black people" and intensify the "dearth of dynamic cultural expression."[64] Self-help, in this context, is the quest for a human to come, as Richard Pithouse puts it in his reading of Fanon's revolutionary humanism.[65] But was the self in self-help also the self of the Third Worldist quest for self-determination that Timothy Mitchell argues had been fundamentally compromised early in the twentieth century?[66] Could this notion of the self be reappropriated, as these young people presumed, through ecumenical

Christian, Freirean, and Fanonian tools? This was a motivating question in ASH's quest for self-reliance.

One of the ways in which ASH set out to secure self-reliance was through a social survey. The Merebank group conducted a survey of "subeconomic housing" in the valley of the Old Marine Drive. They found that 60 percent of families, most with more than eight members, earned less than R60 per month; the remaining 40 percent of families had maximum monthly earnings of R110. A staggering 80 percent of families had expenditures twice their incomes; families in an a "transit camp" called Minitown expressed "intense dissatisfaction with living conditions." Adult illiteracy was at 35 percent, and slightly more than half of school-age children were going to school.[67] In their analysis, self-reliance in a context of deprivation and proletarianization could be bolstered through bulk purchasing of essential commodities like rice, oil, and sugar, sold to families at fair rates. In addition, ASH set up a "communal bank box," or a rotating fund for families in desperate circumstances, and they planned to raise funds for a nursery school and for adult literacy classes.[68]

Parallel to this work, medical students at the Alan Taylor Residence also became involved in "community projects" in 1971.[69] Vanessa Noble's careful study of this "school of struggle" shows that SASO medical students at Alan Taylor volunteered on a weekly roster, offering primary health care services in the neighboring Happy Valley Clinic.[70] Farther afield, the BCP's New Farm project on preventive medicine at Phoenix Settlement was initiated through house-to-house questionnaires "to determine the extent and effects of the well-known poor conditions, and . . . to define what priorities of a community . . . and what our relevance in the situation could be in terms of action."[71] The language of BCP speaks of "rallying common aspirations," of "a quest for identification as blacks living within a reality of domination," and of "articulation of the black experience" through "an association to deal with programmes involving welfare, culture, black theology, education and literacy, black arts, self-help and other relevant projects."[72] This was nothing short of prefiguring a different organization of subaltern collective will by working through the lived inequalities of segregated urbanism.

Moreover, BCP also saw itself as connected to a wider world of welfare that included the Durban Indian Child Welfare Society, the Cheshire Homes for the infirm, the Aryan Benevolent Home, the M. A. Motala Indian Lad's Hostel in Wyebank, the Darul Yatama Wal Masakeen in Durban, and places of safety and detention for Coloured children, like St. Monica's in Wentworth.[73] There appears to have been an openness to coalition with varied groups allied to the cause of self-help and self-reliance considered broadly, and an openness to legitimization of this work through the National Welfare Act of 1965 to access public funds.[74] While doing this work, Mafika Gwala is painfully aware of the differentiation of services with respect to health and education, as he highlights a commonality of Black neglect.[75] In comparing the Bantustans with the South African Indian Council and the Coloured Representative Council, and in detailing debates within the NIC about their representation of Indians as opposed to all Black people, the BCP pushed the boundaries of groups adjacent to them a bit farther against acceptance of apartheid norms.[76]

There were critiques of BCP on the left, certainly, including Neville Alexander's searing indictment of BCP for seeking self-reliance and conscientization through "continuous financial support from capitalist-imperialist sources."[77] More sympathetically, Rick Turner saw the political novelty of rethinking fundamental values and of organizing to build new forms of mutuality, but he argued that "both the ideological work of articulating and propagating a new black culture and the organizational work of developing community organizations seem for the moment not to have progressed very far" because of a focus on middle-class experiences of rejection from white society.[78] I suspect both Alexander and Turner would have appreciated the attempts to retool biopolitics to question racial selves and landscapes.

In this vein, Bobby says he had to make a break from the Congress and communist traditions, embodied in his aunt, because he felt that it was "too much a European, a white thing that never answered questions of psychological oppression." But he also came into conflict with the Presbyterian Church hierarchy, who did not want to support his interest in becoming a priest, when it became clear that his goal as a priest would be "to break the institution down, because the problem with the church and with theology was that it had been institutionalized." Bobby recalls vague ideas of setting up a Black church in solidarity with African people, and that rather than pursuing formal theological training, he then studied theology on his own and "began having discussions with Steve Biko and Ben Khoapa," another bridge that brought him closer to the communitarian Christianity of BC.

When former members of ASH recall these years, they speak of its lasting imprint even when they had "outgrown" BC as ideology. I suggest that the praxis of Black solidarity and community self-determination contributed something intangible yet crucial to the wider spirit of anti-authoritarianism: a sense of political embodiment forged in the fault lines between political Blackness and racially defined neighborhoods. In this contradictory praxis,

ASH and BCP brought biopolitics out of workplace demands for a poverty datum line circulating around the 1973 strikes and into the domain of the person and the neighborhood, to question the death-dealing articulation of racial embodiment and urban space, to think with Ruth Wilson Gilmore.[79] Focus on the logic of the concrete—on commodity prices, child care, adult literacy, and community health—allowed BCP and ASH to imagine everyday articulations to the struggle for Black welfare. In these myriad everyday acts, they self-consciously sought to draw out the politics in *biopolitics*, to imagine urban life for all.

Transformations of the Durban Moment: Repression

Through these twists and turns, the Durban Moment was becoming much more than a worker uprising. I call it a *biopolitical uprising*, fueled by a conjunctural potion of ecumenical Christianity, worker unrest, BC thought, and the utopianism of youth. If there is a missing citation here, it is to the dockworkers who launched the event, not just as workers in a highly productive industrial port city, but also as multiracial oceanic proletarians bringing the radical traditions of the maritime world to bear on the hidebound terrestrialism of many decades of segregation.[80]

While dockworkers punctured everyday life in apartheid's main port city, there are no archival traces of radical traditions revived by Indian Ocean peoples classified as Indian and Coloured in South Africa's racial formation. There is no interpretive means comparable to the archive of the Black Atlantic ready to hand. The militancy of this moment is legible differently through Gabeba Baderoon's recasting of the submerged histories forcibly coded "Coloured," "Muslim," or, I would add, "Indian" in South African forms.[81] The practice of existential questioning inculcated by BC made space for some young people to wrestle with these questions, in intimate and embodied ways, within limits not of their making.

For the young people from Merebank and Wentworth engaged in this moment, repression came in waves. First, the Community of St. Stephen / Black Action Group was evicted from the basement of the Presbyterian church. Some rented premises on Sambalpur Road that were something like a commune, though they appear not to have fully moved there; they sensed that theirs would not be a utopian experiment with middle-class resources.[82] Another strand turned its activities to underground work; we return to them in the next chapter. Waves of SASO leaders were banned, including Jaya and Rubin in 1973, at the age of twenty-five.[83] Bobby was banned soon after. The state's extrajudicial "banning orders" restricted residence, movement, and communication through published writing, public speech, or "meetings" with more than one person; violation could result in up to five years' incarceration.

State repression came down hard after SASO and the BPC used the independence of Mozambique and the installation of a communist regime there under the Frente de Libertação de Moçambique (FRELIMO) to organize a pro-FRELIMO rally at Curries Fountain in town in 1974.[84] The rally was seen as a direct political provocation, and the leaders of the BPC and SASO were tried in 1975 on charges under the Terrorism Act of 1967. In 1974–75 several BC activists were surveilled, detained, banned, killed, or forced into exile. Roy attempted to work underground for the BPC in 1973 for its first national conference since the bannings. He and Carmel went out of the country to "scout" and to meet exiled leader Abram Onkgopotse Tiro, a week before he was parcel-bombed in Botswana. When Roy received a subpoena to be a state witness in the BPC/SASO trial, he and Carmel, now his wife, and Jaya and Algonda, now also married, left the country on an arduous journey by foot to Lobatse, Botswana.

All those whom I have interviewed recount the details of journeys into exile in painful detail. A cloud of fear and uncertainty followed them as they became exiles. Narratives typically slow down at the moment of departure, each painful step of the journey remembered in excruciating detail: the arrival at a border fence, a passing car, the forest at night, the feared encounter with border guards or dangerous animals, the long night of walking, a final exchange with security police at the airport, and, most important, the last sight of a beloved parent, child, lover, or trusted friend left behind. The mind retains these bodily memories, too hard to express in measured prose. The most difficult thing about recalling the journey into exile is the impossibility of saying goodbye to those who will be interrogated first. What remains in this narrative failure? A gesture. A hidden clue that might later be deciphered as a sign that this is not forever. A hope that separation will be temporary. A touch, to say that this is not your fault. Impossible desires. Deliberately incomplete departures that take a lifetime to repair. These are the fragments that frame the unknowable horizon of exile.[85]

Bobby was detained in 1976 and banned in 1977, and a new chapter emerged as he and Shamim moved to the more middle-class and Muslim neighborhood of Overport on the Berea Ridge. Rubin had a mini-banning order. Jaya was banned under Section 6 of the Terrorism Act. Terrence received a full banning order. When Willie received a banning order, he decided to leave the country.

The others probably did not know that between 1972 and 1976, Willie had begun working with some BC activists from the Alan Taylor Residence who had gone into exile and had joined the ANC and the armed struggle. As he puts it, "Unbeknownst to me, I started working with MK." He was the Natal contact for the first group of medical students from Alan Taylor who had gone into exile, ostensibly for military training, including Gwaza, Shabalala, McDonald, and the Mokoape brothers. He took people to them for military training, and he picked up messages through "dead letter boxes," or hidden sites for caches of arms or propaganda. At some point, he "received an instruction to leave the country and join Gwaza in Lesotho," but it wasn't until he reached there, and after he was met by Gwaza and MK leader Chris Hani, that he realized he had been working with the ANC. When his wife, Betty, joined him, through another arduous journey, she was shocked to find that he had already shifted his allegiances from BC to the rival ANC.

Some from this group, like Jaya and Rishi, found their way to the ANC eventually and became part of the next two moments. Others, like Bobby and Shamim, worked secretly with ANC-allied aboveground and underground groups in supportive ways from about 1977 to 1982, at which point they found that the democratic socialist and fundamentally creative politics of their youth was being disciplined by a secretive and masculinist organizational style that was not what they had bargained for. Several others felt similarly by 1982–83, when the moment of urban revolution revealed its difference from the utopianism of the theologico-political moment (see chapter 8). Others, like Roy and Carmel, remained steadfastly anti-ANC; they became Trotskyists, and though they also left the country with the intention of taking up arms, they did not become part of the moment of insurrection but rather remain resolute critics of the social inequalities bequeathed and fostered in postapartheid South Africa. Repression, exile, and a shifting center of gravity of struggle quelled the Durban Moment, but its utopian impulse persisted.

Charismatic Renewal as Gendered Strike in the Church

At the same time as the strikes, BC, and the countercultural revolt, Wentworth was in the throes of a widespread charismatic renewal that swept its mainline churches. Pentecostalism had been spreading in Durban since the 1960s, but just as the worker strikes were sweeping across Durban in 1972–73, something shook the high-Anglican church of St. Gabriel's in Wentworth. Ross Cuthbertson, the priest of St. Gabriel's at the time, recalls women's prayer groups as part of a brewing storm, a movement of moral regeneration that in his view fundamentally transformed the experience of religion and community in Wentworth.

Ross tells a poignant story of being stuck in a rut as a high Anglican invested in Roman Catholic ritual, the discipline of priestly authority, and the drama of sacramental ritual, with no idea about what it all meant. He was initially fearful of Pentecostalism. When we met in his retirement years, he still saw it largely as a divisive movement. Yet he recalls being drawn into providing "unction" or healing prayer for a woman from the Indian township of Chatsworth. He describes, as soon as he laid hands on her, having an "objective experience" of a terrible force possessing her, running from her body to his. Then, through the power of prayer, he felt a counterforce banishing this evil, which he took to be "an objective experience of God." This turning point in his own life led him to accept that a charismatic renewal was in fact taking hold of his church and that people would now be moved to interrupt the service with their own proclamations, and in time they would prophesy and speak in tongues, just like the Pentecostals.

Importantly, charismatic renewal in Wentworth began with women's groups, and the priests followed their "slain" congregations. If this was a demand from his female congregation, Ross recasts this moment of gendered struggle within the church in quite a different way. He recalls women who had formed prayer groups in 1972–73 coming to him to say that "they were convinced that God had spoken to them to say that the women of St. Gabriel's must allow the men to lead in the life of the church." In the context of male migrant work in whaling, engineering, and construction, Ross's view was that men had been leading lives of silent desperation, subordinate to the women of Wentworth, and that as a result of this collective decision by women empowered by the charismatic renewal, "the men of St Gabriel's came out of the woodwork . . . and it was a beautiful thing to see because the men were leading. . . . God had said the men must lead; give them dignity." Ross argues that this empowerment of men alongside women was far from a retreat into "patriarchalism." Rather, it meant that the community as a whole was entering a phase of moral regeneration.

This minor history of religious effervescence is not easy to square with the Durban Moment, which it is recounted as almost willfully separate from. Indeed, in the memory of Rubin Philip, a young BC activist and curate under Ross in Wentworth who was the Anglican bishop of KwaZulu-Natal when we met, charismatic Christianity was an uneasy fit with BC. Neither Ross nor the bishop at the time was entirely comfortable with Rubin or could reconcile faith and anti-apartheid politics in the 1970s, precisely when Durban was entering a popular revolutionary situation. However, in Rubin's imagination, the radical roots of charismatic renewal were in the traditions of the Black Atlantic. The imagined pull of the Black radical traditions of the Atlantic, again, become a necessary site for the imagination of the human to come, with the Indian Ocean as a mute backdrop.

We might consider charismatic experience as a directly embodied utopian impulse in which the body is immediately "infilled" by the ghostly element of the Christian trinity, capable of penetrating all people. When the Holy Spirit inspires speech, it is glossolalia or authoritative babble, an apostasy of in-communicability. The uncontrollability of bodily response to the Holy Spirit means that priests have to effectively take the pulse of their congregations, as Cuthbertson attempted to, steering the interpretation of demotic religiosity back to the patriarchalism of the primary dyad of God and Son, mediated by the priesthood.

Whatever we make of the charismatic renewal, it offered an experience that might have enabled a powerfully embodied radical politics. Rubin argues that Steve Biko and Black theology were particularly critical of the relationship of church and society and that Black theology "was interrogating what was happening in the charismatic renewal, which was spiritualising the situation at the expense of being involved in its transformation." In contrast, "the leaders of the charismatic renewal countrywide were doing their darndest to bring Black leaders with a sharp political awareness into charismatic awareness and to say *this* is the way." While they were not active agents of the apartheid state, "they were afraid of a Black uprising."

While revivalism at St. Gabriel's may have been many things, in other words, it was also a strike within the church, prevented by the theocratic hand of church leadership from articulating the kind of liberationist political culture that was possible in the psychedelic basement of the Presbyterian church in neighboring Merebank. Keeping in mind Butler's reading of Benjamin on messianic time as traversing historical time, what is striking is are the different ways in which political faith left its trace across Wentworth and Merebank.[86]

Remains of Black Consciousness

What survived the repression of this moment of possibility was a communitarian current that included individuals and their utopian imaginations but also the practical support of ecumenical Christian groups concentrated at Durban's Diakonia Council of Churches. The turn to communities pervaded a wider world of civic mobilization that, by the late 1970s, set the conditions of possibility for the moment of urban revolution.

Many figures who would be active in the 1980s, like Jo Beall, came to political consciousness in ways not unlike the youth of Merebank. As we will see, Jo became part of the mobilizations in 1983 around the Tricameral Parliament, and in the work of canvassing neighborhoods in a mixed group of activists, she and others with her felt a sense of possibility of a grassroots movement against apartheid that was soon disciplined by democratic centralism under conditions of secrecy and suspicion (see chapter 8). A close comrade of Jo's in her youth, Shireen Hassim emerged from a similar praxis of grassroots organization, in her case of autonomous feminism that took her back as a scholar to the history of the Women's Charter.

Something else survived the theologico-political moment and persisted in the repressive period to come. This was the practice of reading and reflection central to BC. In the period that Myron calls the time of repression and intensification of local struggles in the late 1970s, people across political groupings read and thought in comparative ways in order to learn from the succession of defeats and rebellions, including the mass student uprisings of 1976. He recalls, "We were reading Amilcar Cabral, Kwame Nkrumah, Julius Nyerere. We read Frantz Fanon like hell. We were also questioning what is our economic program [since] BC never had an economic program. A lot of us were also reading Marxism. Anything that was banned, we read." They read about Russia in 1917, about Chile in 1973, and about the Vietnam War; they read "between the lines" of a book by a notorious informer, Bruno Mtolo; and when they read official critiques of communism, they thought, "We're reading about our chaps!" This was a remarkably creative practice of subaltern reading that was steadfastly internationalist. In time, they read Antonio Gramsci, Louis Althusser, Paul Baran, and anything they could get access to through a bookshop called Bookmarks, before its owner, Govin Reddy, went into exile in 1980. This yearning and active praxis is very much a fruit of the first moment, and it steered the theologico-political imperative back to struggles in this world, while maintaining political faith in a different future.

Disciplining Critique: "Colonialism of a Special Type"

The fact that the popular rebellion did not become an insurrection pointed up limitations in Black Consciousness ideology. There had been a lack of political direction to guide the outbreak of collective anger in the townships and, although there was some solidarity between

the youth and workers, the gulf had not been bridged. Among the youth there arose an aware-ness that revolution required organisation and comprehensive policies capable of guiding struggle through different phases. Whatever the strengths of the upsurge of 1976 they lacked a strategy and tactics which could only be found in the leadership of the ANC.
—OLIVER TAMBO, on the 1976 Soweto Uprising

The South African National Liberation movement, the ANC and its allies, characterise the South African social formation as a system of "internal colonialism" or "colonialism of a special type."
—Statement of the Lisbon Conference, March 1977

In a perceptive reading of the passage between these texts, Premesh Lalu points to a different kind of remain of Black Consciousness from its primary political rival.[87] Lalu argues that ANC thinking in the wake of BC acknowl-edges BC as a galvanizing force while noting its "limitations" that the ANC could "correct." Consider how the 1977 statement above, just before Biko's murder, attempts to harness the language of "internal colonialism" and "co-lonialism of a special type" in order to co-opt BC's political energies.[88] This attempt drew on a reductive reading of BC thought reproduced by impor-tant works like Gail Gerhart's *Black Power in South Africa*, for which Biko's thought was obsessively "psychological," its focus on the personal interior *rather than* on an exterior of politics and political economy; or as John Saul puts it ungenerously, BC was "more psychological than political."[89] For these perspectives, "correction" comes through an "exterior" promised by state sovereignty. Refusing this metaphysics of internality/externality, or "reading like a state," Lalu offers Biko's *I Write What I Like* as a form of Achille Mbem-be's "African mode of self-writing" premised on a specific postcolonial "ap-paratus of reading" that does away with the idea of correction altogether.[90] In Lalu's hands, Biko emerges as committed to a disintegrating subjectivity focused on the apparatus of reading.

For many ANC-allied thinkers, the BC movement offered an opportunity to theorize apartheid South Africa as a particular form of colonial state that could be overcome by a regime in waiting. But for people shaped indelibly by BC thought, many of whom moved on to other things, the "disintegrat-ing subjectivity" of their detour through BC allowed them to inhabit Black-ness without ontologizing it. Refusing ideological correction by the ANC, the theologico-political moment comprised a set of leaps of political faith in the hope of fundamentally transforming selves and environs. At their most radi-cal extreme, these leaps of faith had no ambition for sovereignty or capital and were antithetical to the quest for another racial capitalist hegemony.

FIGURE 6.1 Site of the Alan Taylor Residence for Black medical students, Wentworth, 2010. © Sharad Chari.

"Alan Taylor," 2010

A photograph shows the Alan Taylor Residence, adjacent to the Engen oil refinery (figure 6.1). There are no commemorative rituals to mark what happened here. In light of a long history of African exclusion from the city, cemented by the Durban System and reinforced by a battery of segregationist legislation and racial practice, this residence for Black medical students, next to an oil refinery, provided a place in the city for an aspiring progressive Black middle class of experts in proximity to a suffering population, as well as a place of mixing across race, class, and gender. There are no plaques for the intimacies of young people in debate around the charismatic Steve Biko, nor for his de facto headquarters when in Durban.

In 2010 the building became a training center for industrial artisans working at the oil refinery. The entire zone in front of it is was securitized under the National Key Points Act of 1980, apartheid-era legislation used to prevent striking refinery workers from assembling at the refinery fence. I stood across the street at the parking lot of the Asherville municipal swimming pool contemplating the meaning of "Alan Taylor" and of other ephemeral sites of solidarity oriented to creative and radical arts of Black endurance.

Black Pride, 2016

Speaking to a packed audience in Pretoria on September 9, 2016, Black Marxist feminist revolutionary Angela Y. Davis ended her Steve Biko Lecture by calling to the stage a young woman called Zulaikha Patel. Earlier in the year, thirteen-year-old Patel had courageously worn her hair natural to Pretoria Girls School, defying the school's regulations against Afros and the taunts that Black girls face. Once a bastion of white privilege, Pretoria Girls School has been part of the dance of racial recalibration in South Africa's school system that geographer Mark Hunter has argued is a key site in the twisting contours of South African hegemony, where new articulations of race, class, and gender are at stake.[91] Two key points stand out in Davis's talk, and they came together when Davis embraced the young Patel along with her entourage.

Davis insisted that the older generation of Black radicals ought not to correct young Black activists, even when they think the youth of today might repeat the mistakes of the past. She quickly destabilized a misreading of Black Lives Matter by insisting, "It is because all lives do not matter that Black Lives Matter becomes necessary."[92] Pausing, Davis argued that we cannot know whether we live in a revolutionary situation but that we cannot afford not to explore the possibility, pointing to the Haitian Revolution as a foundational event for an inclusionary and political notion of Blackness. The Haitian Constitution made the powerful argument that anyone who wanted to stay to rebuild the postrevolutionary society could do so, but they would have to subscribe to a notion of Blackness in service of an emergent, inclusionary humanity.

The theologico-political moment in Durban in the early 1970s was one instance in which these elements came together in a specific way. Similar elements reemerge in new forms, in new articulations of race, class, and gender. And so a young girl who defied her school and proclaimed her proudly Black hair wore on herself the spirit of prior struggles with much wider raced, gendered, and classed interests than her own. Her Gujarati Muslim name, Zulaikha Patel, reminds us of the oceanic histories that converge in South Africa's racial formation. Her raised fist makes Black Power her own. Certainly, the question of whether and how the politics of this event might encompass the broader Black poor remains very much a question. In the video that went viral, she confronts a group of white male police officers who threaten her and other thirteen-year-old Black girls with arrest. She responds, "They want to take us to prison. Take us all!"[93]

The Insurrectionist Moment

Armed Struggle, 1960s–1980s

It must not be forgotten, My Lord, that by this time [1961] violence had, in fact, become a feature of the South African political scene. There had been violence in 1957 when the women of Zeerust were ordered to carry passes; there was violence in 1958 with the enforcement of Bantu Authorities and cattle culling in Sekhukhuneland; there was violence in 1959 when the people of Cato Manor protested against pass raids; there was violence in 1960 when the Government attempted to impose Bantu Authorities in Pondoland. . . . Each disturbance pointed clearly to the inevitable growth amongst Africans of the belief that violence was the only way out. . . . Already small groups had arisen in the urban areas and were spontaneously making plans for violent forms of political struggle. There now arose a danger that these groups would adopt terrorism against Africans, as well as whites, if not properly directed.
—NELSON MANDELA, "I Am Prepared to Die," 1964

Concerning Violence, 1960s

Delivered neither under oath nor subject to cross-examination, Nelson Mandela's statement from the dock is a work of rhetorical genius. Scarcely three years earlier, he had embarked on a secret pan-African tour in which he met future presidents Julius Nyerere in Tanganyika and Kenneth Kaunda in

Northern Rhodesia, Emperor Haile Selassie in Ethiopia, Gamal Abdel Nasser in Egypt, Habib Bourguiba in Tunisia, Ahmed Sékou Touré in Guinea, and Ahmed Ben Bella of Algeria; he toured Morocco, Mali, Sierra Leone, Liberia, and Senegal; and he visited the exiled Front de libération nationale (FLN) in Morocco. Elleke Boehmer notes that Frantz Fanon is strikingly absent from this pantheon.[1] Mandela had not read Fanon's *Les damnés de la terre* (the damned of the Earth), which was translated into English in 1963 after Mandela's incarceration, but their fates were linked. Fanon was transported to the United States in 1961 by the Central Intelligence Agency (CIA) to receive treatment for leukemia and would die there. Mandela was captured on a CIA tip-off in 1962 and would spend twenty-seven years in prison.

Whether the formation of uMkhonto we Sizwe (MK) and the turn to violence was necessary is a complex issue, fueled by the prose of Cold War insurgency and counterinsurgency.[2] In one perspective, the Algerian exiles in Morocco had convinced Mandela that the FLN had realized that they had no chance of a military victory against the French occupiers and that the primary aim of guerrilla warfare should be to force the enemy to negotiate; and this position would have been completely at odds with what the majority of his comrades in South Africa thought.[3] Indeed, the leadership hiding at Liliesleaf Farm had been devising a plan of coordinated armed struggle outlined in "Operation Mayibuye," the document that would imprison much of the MK High Command for decades (see chapter 5).

In light of a lack of consensus concerning armed struggle, Mandela's genius in his statement from the dock is in his dramatization of his "African background," before he turns to address how to direct the popular will. He describes his African tour as political education on military strategy from a wide variety of perspectives.[4] What remains latent is that he had not been able to engage the militants in Sekhukhuneland, Mpondoland, and Cato Manor with a similar ethic. Might he have been surprised by what he found there? Might it have added support to the FLN's caution concerning violence?

Andrew Nash argues that Mandela's political ideology modifies an earlier notion of a "tribal model of democracy," particularly from Anton Lembede, as the site for the development of democratic virtue and harmony between the courageous, sacrificing leader and contentious African communities, and as a rapprochement of African and Western liberal democratic forms. With the African National Congress (ANC) legitimized as the vehicle for courageous leadership, embodied in Mandela's person, this contradictory "tribal model" persisted in the transition to a democratic order that sidestepped the Marxist critique of racial capitalism; the ANC's alliances with Indian, Coloured, and white organizations were transformed through this "tribal model" into "four nations" seeking to build a harmonious future.[5] The colonial origins of "tribalism," particularly in Natal, as well as its afterlife, are well studied.[6] What is interesting in Nash's diagnosis is the way it is harnessed in the politics of multiracial alliance.

My argument in this chapter is that the call to arms diverged across Merebank and Wentworth. While some young people were drawn to Black Consciousness (BC), a group consisting primarily of young men from Merebank took a different path through the revived Natal Indian Congress (NIC), underground political and military networks connected to the External Mission of the ANC, and various attempts at infiltration into the country, including the highly secretive Operation Vula. This Congress-aligned group could tap into the longer history of Indian progressivism to attend to Mandela's caution to "properly direct" grassroots militancy. However, in doing so, they had to contend with what they experienced directly, that the External Mission had in no way "directed" the revolts of the 1970s, including the Durban Moment, the BC movement, or the Soweto Uprising.

Indeed, just as part 1 of this book details the long history of the state's concerted ways of not knowing, the External Mission rested on not knowing the actual landscape of struggle within the country. Instead, the moment of insurrection drew the External Mission into a thicket of fear and suspicion of internal enemies. The originality of Merebank's activists is that they wore many hats, remaking political and military activity in unique ways that grappled with the limitations of militancy orchestrated by remote control.

Indeed, people participated in the struggle under conditions not of their making, which is why the dialectics of abstract and concrete struggle played out differently across Wentworth and Merebank. Indian Merebank built an elaborate multitiered world of activism through traditions of community uplift with deep roots in Durban's social fabric, nurtured by the quiet and generative political work of relatively unknown activists, while life in Wentworth became increasingly introverted in a carceral space in which the boundaries of the criminal and political became increasingly blurred (see chapter 9).

Understanding the changing geographies of struggle, particularly for those not steeped in anti-apartheid struggle history, requires briefly turning to the broader canvas on which the exiled movement held to a conception of armed struggle despite internal debate on its efficacy as well as deepening infiltration by the apartheid security apparatus.

Antinomies of Armed Struggle

Anticipating repression after the Sharpeville massacre in 1960, in which police opened fire on people protesting the pass system, Oliver Tambo had left the country with suitcases filled with ANC files, effectively into political asylum, to lead the ANC's External Mission for three decades.[7] What is unbelievable today is the suitcases of files, a sign of revolution in analog times. Even for the times, this detail betrays an innocence about information that would quickly give way to pervasive infiltration, betrayal, secrecy, and internal repression.

The External Mission's conception of armed struggle under conditions of exile was shaped by a set of comparisons. While the movement imagined revolution on the model of Algeria, Cuba, and Vietnam, would-be combatants languished for decades in camps and underground cells across the Frontline States of Angola, Tanzania, Zambia, Botswana, Lesotho, and Mozambique. Exiled comrades witnessed changing conditions of decolonization in Southern Africa, from a first phase of relatively peaceful transitions in Zambia and Malawi in 1964, Lesotho and Botswana in 1966, and Swaziland in 1968, to a phase of protracted and violent transitions in Rhodesia after 1965, and long civil wars following independence from Portugal in Angola and Mozambique in 1976.[8]

In the first phase, decolonized states related differently to liberation movements. Kaunda's Zambia hosted the External Mission's headquarters in Lusaka from 1969, but safe houses, secrecy, and military details at ANC conferences continued to be necessary. Hastings Banda's Malawi negotiated with the Nationalists as early as 1967 and remained hostile to liberation movements. Lesotho, Botswana, and Swaziland provided space for ANC cells until they were pressured not to in the mid-1980s through South African Defence Force (SADF) cross-border raids, targeted assassinations, and technological, fiscal, and trade deals under Prime Minister John Vorster's "Outward Looking" policy.

During the second phase, ANC-allied movements were embroiled in protracted armed combat on their own soil in Rhodesia, Mozambique, and Angola, which accentuated the different realities of MK soldiers as well as leadership committed to military results.[9] Campaigns of armed incursion into South Africa in the late 1960s were important to demonstrate this commitment. Key among these was the 1967 Wankie Campaign, in which the Luthuli Detachment crossed the Zambezi River, one flank of which intended to build what one commander, Chris Hani, called "a Ho Chi Minh trail to

South Africa."[10] Both flanks met security forces from Rhodesia and Botswana, backed by the SADF; some died, and others were captured. Hani distinguished himself as an exceptionally articulate defender of the common soldier, and his commitment through suffering added to his growing acclaim as a popular hero of MK, rival among the movement's rising stars to Thabo Mbeki's seemingly patrician and unmanly interest in détente rather than combat.[11]

Wankie was followed by the Sipolilo Campaign in 1967, which also ended in capture and imprisonment of MK soldiers in Rhodesia for as long as twelve years. To critics within the ANC, these campaigns were adventurist.[12] Mbeki lectured to an ANC school, "We shall not repeat the Wankie-type operation. . . . The force we have is a force of political educators and military trainers and cannot be used as a striking force"; anticipating what I call the moment of urban revolution, he added that operatives ought to infiltrate South Africa to engage struggles over "wages, taxes, house rents, educational costs, health, land, etc."[13] Hani maintained that the leadership ought to have reflected on Wankie and Sipolilo to rethink the importance of political work to support advancing combatants. These debates echoed in the guarded internal critique by Ben Turok in 1968 that "given the present lack of a friendly border, the one absolutely essential pre-condition for armed activity is a soundly organized structure with real mass support" but also that "in an era when wars of national liberation are no novelty. . . . It will surely not be long before South Africa itself catches fire."[14]

Another fire had been stoked in MK camps. The "Hani memorandum" criticized the lack of democracy and accountability in the movement, deepening classism and corruption, and extreme forms of discipline, including secret trials and executions of suspected spies; it concluded that "the ANC in Exile is in deep crisis as a result of which a rot has set in."[15] The memorandum also objected to exclusion of non-Africans from ANC membership and critiqued the political strategies and "mysterious business enterprises" of MK commander in chief Joe Modise as well as ANC youth leader Thabo Mbeki and head of security Duma Nokwe.[16] Devastatingly, it described the External Mission as "an end unto itself" with no "account of the functioning branches inside the country," no credible information on "the existing political situation inside the country," and no will to risk the lives of leadership by sending them home.[17] Memorandum signatories, including Hani, were removed from and then reinstated back in the ANC. By some accounts they came close to being executed.

The ANC National Executive Committee (NEC) faced other stresses as well, as the movement was in deep financial crisis in the late 1960s, both

Tanzania and Zambia were wary of ANC presence after SADF incursions, and the Zambian government asked for a list of operatives in 1969, a very dangerous thing for an increasingly infiltrated movement.[18] These challenges compelled the leadership to hold its First National Consultative Conference in Morogoro, Tanzania, in 1969, which produced the first comprehensive program for the armed struggle.

The document adopted at Morogoro, "Strategy and Tactics," marks a shift from armed incursions by small, elite MK groups to guerrilla warfare and, in a concession to critics, to the rebuilding of the political underground and to mobilization of "the African masses" but also of Coloured and Indian people who "suffer varying forms of national humiliation, discrimination and oppression" and "a large and growing working-class" who might ensure that the outcome of struggle is "a real people's South Africa."[19] This text also reiterates a founding fiction of MK, the separation of political and military activity, which spoke to competing strands of the External Mission. One of the conference organizers, ANC and SACP leader Joe Matthews, a year before his own disillusionment with the SACP, saw his and Nokwe's roles as dampening Che Guevara's conception of guerrilla warfare sparked by elite groups, to draw in Indian and Coloured communities.[20] "Strategy and Tactics" delicately recognizes the "primary role of the most oppressed African mass" but also "those belonging to the other oppressed groups" as well as "white revolutionaries."[21] This was important for places like Merebank and Wentworth as they encountered the moment of insurrection in the early 1970s.

Morogoro opened ANC membership across race; while the NEC remained closed to non-Africans, a new subcommittee called the Revolutionary Council (RC) was open to all, a significant concession to the "nonracial" MK. The RC was tasked with fusing political and military operations, but this would only be the case at the top of the External Mission hierarchy and not yet on the Eastern Front (Mozambique, connected to Natal) or the Western Front (Botswana, connected to the Transvaal).[22] The incisive Tambo sent rivals Hani and Mbeki to lead the post-Morogoro drive for internal political reconstruction in Botswana, Lesotho, and Swaziland at the same time as the Durban Moment.[23]

There was a degree of openness in the External Mission of the early 1970s, as the ANC's official journal *Sechaba* published profiles of key BC and South African Students' Organisation (SASO) figures, as well as anonymous pieces by Steve Biko and by Mangosuthu "Gatsha" Buthelezi. Before launching his Inkatha movement in 1975 and well before it became a state-supported rival to the ANC, Buthelezi visited Lusaka and met Kaunda and ANC members, as did the director of the Christian Institute, Beyers Naudé, who was also close to BC.[24] The ANC's financial situation improved considerably after Swedish prime minister Olaf Palme visited Lusaka in 1971, and by 1976 Sweden's contributions to the ANC outpaced financial aid from the Soviet Union.[25] The ANC was becoming a potential hegemonic force.

The period from 1975 to 1984 offered a window for some in the liberation movement to find common cause with Marxist regimes of the Frente de Libertação de Moçambique (FRELIMO) in Mozambique and the Movimento Popular de Libertação de Angola in Angola. Ruth First chose to live in Maputo from 1977 as director of research at the Centro dos Estudos Africanos at Universidade Eduardo Mondlane. Her charisma and brilliance attracted remarkable figures until her assassination by a letter bomb from the Security Branch of the South African Police, also known as the Special Branch, in 1982. Slovo had followed her to Maputo to head the new Special Operations Unit (Special Ops).[26] As an indication of imagined solidarities between Mozambican and South African struggles, many Durban activists recall "Viva FRELIMO" rallies on the eve of Mozambican independence as defining their politicization.[27]

The late 1970s to the early 1980s offered exiled MK combatants, including from Durban, the opportunity to operate from Frontline States, before deadly attacks including the Matola Raid pushed regimes into nonaggression pacts with the apartheid regime, beginning with the 1984 Nkomati Accord with Mozambique; a secret pact with Swaziland in 1984; treaties with Lesotho, Botswana, Zimbabwe, and Mozambique in 1986; and with the Islamic Republic of the Comoros in 1987.

This period also made possible various attempts to link MK's political and military machineries. Military operations were divided into the Western Front, led by Joe Modise in Lusaka, and the Eastern Front, led by Slovo in Mozambique, assisted among others by Jacob Zuma. Hani and Lambert Moloi commanded political, military, and intelligence operations in Lesotho. There were four regional military machineries working from Mozambique and Swaziland. Krish Rabilal from Merebank and Sunny Singh (a.k.a. Bobby Pillay) from Durban were part of "Natal Urban." Glory Sedibe, later revealed to have been an *askari*, or turned operative, was part of "Eastern Transvaal Rural."[28] On his release from Robben Island, Sathyandranath Ragunanan "Mac" Maharaj says he was tasked with reestablishing the political underground in the country; he was later made secretary of the Internal Political Reconstruction Committee (IPRC, or "the Internal") of the RC between 1976 and 1980. This was the same period of operation of the Swaziland Internal Political Committee, which focused through two arms on the political underground in the Transvaal and Natal; the latter included Judson Kuzwayo, Visvanathan "Vis" Pillay (Ivan), and Terrence Tryon, the latter two from Merebank and Wentworth. The Maputo Internal Political Committee included Zuma, Sue Rabkin, and Sunny.[29]

After intense debate about how to respond to the 1970s struggles in the country, the External Mission reshuffled political and military operations in Regional Politico-Military Councils (RPMCs) in 1983–85, including Slovo, Zuma, and Siphiwe Nyanda (Gebuza). After the Nkomati Accord, a coordinating mechanism in Swaziland took over from the Mozambique RPMC, including Ronnie Kasrils, Ebrahim Ismail Ebrahim (Ebie), Muziwakhe Boniface Ngwenya (Thami Zulu), and Gebuza; they could operate with relative autonomy for a period of time, with Ivan, Terrence, and Zulu leading the Natal Urban Politico-Military Committee. Most of these figures would be drawn into Operation Vula (see chapter 8).[30]

As part of the overhaul of ANC structures in 1979, Tambo established Special Ops to focus on high-profile sabotage of strategic or economic installations. In 1982 a new Military Headquarters (MHQ) formalized MK on military lines along the Western and Eastern Fronts. Two years later, Special Ops was brought under MHQ, reporting directly to Slovo; this was crucial to an underground unit emerging in Wentworth in the 1980s, connected to Mozambique and Botswana (see chapter 9).

In 1983, in a deeper overhaul, the RC was replaced by the Politico-Military Council (PMC) with a secretariat and representation from the National Executive Committee (NEC) of the ANC, the MK Military Headquarters (MHQ), the Internal Political Committee (dealing with the underground, propaganda, mass mobilization, and data processing), and National Intelligence (NAT, dealing with intelligence, counterintelligence, and security); the PMC was chaired by the president of ANC, Oliver Tambo, but it included the secretaries-general of the three main allied organizations, the ANC, the South African Communist Party (SACP), and the South African Congress of Trade Unions (SACTU). This was an extremely comprehensive approach to overall planning.

Despite this centralized coordination, front areas were given more leadership autonomy through Regional PMCs, with the authority to form Area PMCs, as we will see in Operation Butterfly in Wentworth. Finally, although it was conducted with extreme secrecy, secret even to many in the leadership of the PMC, Operation Vula was meant to infiltrate high leadership into South Africa to coordinate a national politico-military structure (see chapter 8).[31] We revisit these structures and operatives as we return to Merebank and to a renewal of the Congress movement.

Congress Revival in Merebank

While one group of young people from Merebank and Wentworth went from a church basement to the BC movement, another group became part of the NIC, revived in June 1971 at Bolton Hall in Durban with Mewa Ramgobin, Gandhi's granddaughter Ela Gandhi, George Sewpersadh, and Florence Mkhize prominently present.[32] This group was tapping into Merebank's long histories of mobilization, including the Passive Resistance Movement. Recall that the Merebank Ratepayers Association (MRA) had taken the council to court on the question of selling prices for homes (see chapter 5). A new generation of activist youth was emerging from this milieu.

Vis Pillay (later with the nom de guerre Ivan), Kambadesan Govender (Coastal), Krish Rabilal, and brothers Satish and Munmohan (Spider) Juggernath of Billy Juggernath's family (see chapter 3) were the main members of this group connected to Congress politics, to communist thought through Coastal, and to tireless political work for the underground through Spider and his future wife, Usha. Ivan and Krish ascended the ranks of the ANC and MK, and Ivan became a key figure behind Operation Vula. The journeys and fortunes of this Congress-allied group diverged considerably from their counterpart in the theologico-political moment.

These young people shared with their BC counterparts a background of forced removals and community mobilizations in the late 1960s and early 1970s. Ivan describes his parents coming to live in wood-and-iron shacks before the Merebank housing scheme, then living on Bhuj Road across the street from Bobby as well as the Presbyterian church (see chapter 6). He attended Hillside School, which he thought was built on an old Anglo-Boer War concentration camp, now demolished, a detail that adds to the drama of his story. Ivan's older brother Dhayiah had been part of a youth group trip to London, where he later reported being recruited into MK, a detail Ivan seemed not to know when we spoke. Their uncles R. A. Pillay and R. R. Pillay had been involved in the politics of the 1950s, the first arrested in the Treason Trial and the second a trade unionist right into the 1980s; both were banned and unable to engage these young people. Ivan, Coastal, Satish, and Krish became involved in the Durban Indian Child Welfare Society and the Friends of the Sick Association, the latter a seedbed for an earlier generation of activists like Phyllis Naidoo (see chapter 4). They also became involved in a local soccer association that became part of struggles for nonracial sport, through which they met Archie Hulley, a school principal and a major figure in the South African Council on Sport, the organization that led the movement to deracialize sport.

Coastal apparently had a copy of *African Communist* from the late 1960s and could recite Mandela's statement at the dock verbatim. They tried to connect with people in the Non-European Unity Movement, a Trotskyist movement tracing back to George Padmore and C. L. R. James in London as well as to Cape Town of the 1930s and 1940s. In 1971 they participated in the relaunching of the NIC and started a Merebank branch. They held an anti–Republic Day meeting at Nataraj Cinema in Merebank on the tenth anniversary of the declaration of the Republic of South Africa, to which they invited Morgan Naidoo of the South African Council on Sport, lawyer Pius Langa, and Paula Ensor of the National Union of South African Students (NUSAS).

This was the period of release of political prisoners who had served a decade on Robben Island. Activist lawyer and member of the SACP, ANC, and MK, M. D. Naidoo, was prominent among those from Durban; Ivan met him several times. The two African activists Ivan would work with, Judson Kuzwayo and Shadrack Maphumulo, were among those released from Robben Island; both were veterans in labor organizing. In the early 1970s, Ivan became the secretary of the Southern Durban Civic Federation, which tried to connect Indian civics in 1971–72. When I asked him why it was only Indian civics, he responded, "You hardly had any civic formations anywhere else," including in the neighboring African areas of Lamontville and Umlazi, "because the repression was stronger there, but you had recruitment for MK going on in the early 1970s." Ivan confided to M. D. Naidoo that he wanted to make contact with the ANC "as an individual." Naidoo told him to wait and handed him a copy of John Eaton's *Political Economy: A Marxist Textbook*, with the innocuous title "political economy" on the cover.

Before someone from the ANC made contact, this youth group did something novel. From 1972 to about 1975, they typed, copied, and distributed a free broadsheet newspaper called the *Sentinel*, some copies of which Ivan carefully kept through years in exile. Satish owned a typewriter, and work began in Ivan's garage and moved into secretly rented premises on Sambalpur Road. Material saved by Ivan lists "Sentinel patrons," with the names and addresses of fifty-four supporters, and there is a "Secretarial Report to the Second Annual General Meeting, June 1971 to June 1974." In late 1974 or early 1975, Sunny, on his release from Robben Island, recruited Ivan to establish an underground cell of the ANC, after which such records would be impossible. The 1972–75 period represents an early attempt to connect community organizations and to use the public sphere to articulate the Congress Alliance with popular political will, before being driven underground.

Between articles on issues ranging from the activities of youth groups to temple construction, the *Sentinel* acknowledges sponsors from general stores, tailors, jewelers, pawnbrokers, the local soccer club, and the MRA as representative of the community. The editors clarify a political agenda cautiously when they lament poor attendance at an MRA meeting or when they report on the Merebank branch of the Black People's Convention (BPC).[33] A telling editorial from June 1973 rejects the capitulation of the South Durban (Indian) Local Affairs Committee (LAC) to the council's plan to make Indian areas "autonomous," arguing that meaningful autonomy should ensure the "economic viability of the Indian areas."[34] These young people were grappling with racial liberalism and apartheid reformism meted out to Indian communities, a debate that would return in the early 1980s on the question of participation in the Tricameral Parliament (see chapter 8).

The *Sentinel* from 1973 and 1974 documents young people turning to community concerns, including those of residents of the Dinapur Road barracks, bus passengers faced with rising fares, and neighbors of the Mobil Refining Company complaining about noise pollution; a fascinating discussion centers on whether Indian workers joined in the 1973 strikes in solidarity with African workers or in fear of antagonizing them.[35] The last copy, from December 1974, focuses on inflation and the rising cost of bread, and it speaks of "Black South Africans" as being at the mercy of "a sick 'white' society and its economic system."[36] This is one indicator that some young people were in fact moving between BC and Congress circles in a shared sphere of youth and community upheaval indebted to the existential questioning central to BC. The paths between these young people diverged strongly when some in the Congress group were forced to go underground.

Underground: Uncertain and Compromised

Sunny Singh had been arrested in 1963 at the age of twenty-one, among the first group of MK recruits in Durban. He was also among the first political prisoners released after ten years on Robben Island, along with Zuma. In Durban between 1974 and 1976, before leaving for exile, Sunny found ways to circumvent house arrest to meet young people to revive what he described as a moribund underground. He recalled Zuma driving a truck for the municipality and attempting in African townships what he sought to do in Indian areas, including in town, where he sought recruits ideologically committed to "the Congress way of thinking." When he encountered the BC youth of Merebank, he tried "penetrating" their activities at the Association for Self-Help (ASH): no easy matter with this group of freethinking youth (see chapter 6). He also began similar activities in the new Indian township of Chatsworth. In Merebank, Coastal introduced Sunny to Vis Pillay (not yet called Ivan). Sunny had financial means for underground activities through the NIC. He linked with pharmacist Pravin Gordhan, who had been part of the student group that had taken over the lead of the protests spearheaded by BC youth at the University of Durban-Westville (see chapter 6), and they started a clinic in impoverished Mayville.

Things happened quickly over a short period. Terrence from Wentworth was a member of the BC youth group pulled into the SASO leadership. Like some others during and after the intense repression of BC, he slowly shifted to the ANC camp. He remembers encountering Sunny through Govin Reddy's bookstore in town, where he found books by Paul Sweezy and Leo Huberman. Terrence says Sunny "was like a faith healer" who nurtured young minds. After the SASO bannings, Terrence was called into the Durban office. He describes getting social worker Nkosazana Dlamini into SASO and negotiating with the Mobil oil refinery to get a *kombi* (shared van taxi) to take nurses and medical students to the African townships of Inanda and KwaMashu on weekends to operate clinics, much as the BC activists had done. They had law students like Jeff Radebe offer legal clinics in KwaMashu. Terrence cites Biko on building infrastructure for the people: "Black man, you are on your own!"

Terrence's fate was tied to the quickening pace of banning SASO members, which shot people like him up the hierarchy; "I was a *lightie* [youth], and I was a national leader!" Increasingly harassed in 1976, he was faced with a situation in which, as he narrated, Nkosazana was on the run from the police after returning from Swaziland with banned literature, and he was tasked with taking her and others across the border to Botswana. He had no idea yet about border crossings; little did he know that for the next decade and a half he would move in and out of the country illegally multiple times. Imprisoned for three and a half months in 1976, he met hardened activists who were part of ANC veteran Harry Gwala's second trial. Imprisoned again in 1977–78, Terrence met "the big teacher in prison," recaptured Robben Islander Shadrack Maphumulo. In 1978 he left the country when he received a message from Mac in Swaziland, and from this point, he joined the political wing of MK and came in close contact with the group from Merebank centered on Ivan.

Through this intense period, Terrence had transitioned from the theologico-political moment to the moment of insurrection. Nithianandan "Elvis" Govender, whose family moved to Merebank in 1976, took a parallel path from SASO to the ANC when he went on a secret six-week trip to Maputo to meet Ivan, Maphumulo, and Kuzwayo.[37]

Before leaving for exile, Maphumulo and Kuzwayo had formed a unit around the same time that Ivan was recruited by Sunny. Ivan approached his brother Dhayiah (Joe), who, neither Ivan nor Sunny seemed to acknowledge may have already been recruited by Kasrils in London in 1973; Joe later recounts procuring a farm to begin armed activity with Ivan.[38] But Sunny describes being shocked to meet Joe in exile, confusing him with his brother. Ivan recalls his brother having been involved in BC networks, and going to London on a holiday with messages from the BC movement to the International University Exchange Fund. The fund was at the time headed by Craig Williamson, later uncovered as an apartheid spy implicated in the murders of Ruth First and the family of Marius Schoon. Ivan did not know much about what transpired with his brother in London, but he recalls him coming back and experimenting with bucket bombs. Elsewhere, Ivan describes Sunny's surprise when Ivan arrived at the MK camp in Funda, Angola, where Sunny and Joe were being trained in urban guerrilla warfare by two Irish Republican Army (IRA) commanders, implying that Joe did indeed take a different route than Ivan.[39] These discrepant accounts of recruitment are part of the murkiness of knowledge in and of the underground.

Ivan recruited a couple whom he had worked with in the BC-aligned Black Allied Workers Union, Petrus (Pat Msomi) and Jabulile "Jabu" Nyawose. One day, they opened the newspaper to find that Maphumulo had fled the country. They immediately realized that there was a paper trail that could be traced to a car rented by Joe and that Pat and Jabu were implicated as well. They left that night, and Sunny quickly followed.

When I asked Ivan whether his unit in Durban was supposed to engage in sabotage, he responded:

It was all a muddle. There were no clear instructions about what to do. We got some pamphlets that we distributed. We were asked to buy some vehicles. Money was provided for that. It would have been easier for my brother and myself to do some of these things than our African comrades. Pat was used to go to Swaziland quite a few times. We were asked to take Mac Maharaj out of the country. When Sunny left the country, eventually, our cell was involved in taking him out of the country. Beyond that, it was not actually clear what one was doing. Nobody had to ask us to paint ANC slogans around town.

What is interesting is the way in which Ivan's views about the underground transformed in exile:

> To my surprise, it was only when I went into exile, only around 1978–79, that there became greater clarity about what should be done inside the country. What you had up to then was only "Let's go and recruit for the ANC," "Let's take arms into the country," and "Let's carry out attacks." That's all. It's after some of us came out of the country and started this debate that said, "Look, you've got no links to the mass struggle that's going on. You've got to be involved in the mass struggle. How do you recruit people that you know nothing about?"

Two weeks after Joe left the country, he came back in with instructions to take Ivan out. Unusually, Ivan briefed three comrades in Merebank: Coastal, Krish, and a slightly younger Rayman Lalla. Ivan would come back into the country illegally three times. The first time was just two months later. He laughed and said he just walked through the Golela border. He then came back to get Krish, leaving for Botswana via Johannesburg, where they were arrested and reported to the authorities as political refugees and members of the ANC. At this point, they diverged, Krish becoming part of MK while Ivan became part of the political underground.

When I pressed Ivan on the relationship between the political underground and MK, he said I could think of it as the political wing of MK, even though that was not quite correct. Ivan's struggle to explain this pointed to the way in which his network would go on to make some of their own political decisions, including linking political and military activity, as well as his work alongside Kuzwayo in the new Internal Political Reconstruction Committee tasked with forming ANC underground units within the country, to which he could bring his trusted networks in Merebank.

What became clear in conversation with Ivan and others is that the ANC underground did not conform to a neat pyramidal order of formalized recruitment and advancement through the ranks. This was not the imagination enshrined in Gillo Pontecorvo's iconic film *The Battle of Algiers*, in which the French military mastermind cracks the pyramidal cell structure and breaks the movement. In practice, cells in the ANC underground were often semiautonomous, and problems of knowledge were legion. This situation was common to late twentieth-century underground movements centered on semiautonomous cells, as someone who was probably an IRA militant living in South Africa in the 1980s explained to me. There may have been more to this than meets the eye. Ivan explained to me that at their moment of recruitment, the model was precisely formulated with the IRA's notion of semiautonomous cells in mind. As time went on, by the late 1970s, the importance of linking political and military activity, and of connecting exile and underground and aboveground civic and labor mobilization, would make it necessary to shift to a more relational, weblike form, with very different implications for political praxis.

After the movement of large numbers of youth of 1976 into exile along with an unknown number of plants by the state, problems of knowledge underground heightened. As the movement became more attentive to security, it became clear that the porosity of information was unavoidable owing to torture and espionage. The implication for the historiography of the underground is that no narrative is clear and that all truths are convenient fictions. What I assemble here are accounts from a large number of interviews with participants, triangulated to some extent by secondary sources, marking ambiguities as they appear. Perhaps what is most interesting is the nature of knowledge as the armed struggle became more evasive, and boundaries between combatant and spy increasingly difficult to discern. This was the enduring problem that Operation Vula sought to respond to by forging a clean *and knowable* network of underground operatives (see chapter 8).

Cross-Border Raids and Deepening Problems of Knowledge

In Swaziland, Joe joined the military wing of the ANC and was captured, by some accounts mistaken for Ivan, in a cross-border raid by the infamous Security Branch commander Dirk Coetzee. He was subjected to punishing interrogation at the paramilitary torture farm Vlakplaas, established by Coetzee in 1979 as a paramilitary base, or an operational combat unit, as described by Eugene de Kock, dubbed "Prime Evil" by the press, who took over in 1982. Ivan recalls his brother's sense that if he had gone through this without being politically active, he would have had to leave, as he did for Canada in 1986. We know the extent of infiltration of this group by the security police through Jacob Dlamini's biography of the *askari*, or MK operative turned by the Security Branch, Glory Sedibe.[40] Sedibe had been in Matola with Ivan and Krish and played a role as an *askari* in the cross-border raid that culminated in the 1981 Matola Raid, in which Krish and others were slaughtered.

At the Merebank commemoration for Krish and other victims of the Matola Raid that opens chapter 6, Ivan acknowledged people in the audience, including Coastal and Spider, as well as fallen comrades Pat and Jabu. He recalls taking Krish out of the country; his training in the MK camp at Kibash, Angola, under the nom de guerre Ashok; and his subsequent journeys to the GDR and on to "the front" under the name Goodwin. Ivan and Krish worked separately underground, "both illegal, but we met from time to time." Ivan apologized that he could not say very much that was personal about Krish except that there was no drink and no girlfriends and that he was soft-spoken and self-effacing. In Ivan's rendition, he was an everyman of the struggle.

Kasrils spoke at the commemoration about his first encounter with Krish in Kibash camp. He recalls looking at two young men lying under lemon trees, chatting. Kasrils had trepidations about lecturing to South African youth politicized by the struggles of the 1970s about a country he had left in 1963. He remembers the scent of lemon as the young men told him about what Durban was like when they left. There is something poignant about this moment of yearning for home across generations in exile, and of the seasoned activist realizing the limits of his knowledge. Several figures remembered Krish for his softness, a conception of revolutionary masculinity at odds with the dominant gendering of the MK insurrectionist. Krish stands for a masculine militant marked by self-effacement and sexual restraint, all the more striking as he had emerged into political consciousness in a place and time surrounded by youthful questioning of race, gender, and sexuality.

Ivan and Joe were joined in exile by a woman, Rajaluxmi "Rajes" Pillay (later Rae), with a fascinating story of her own. Rajes had grown up in a modest family in Kimberley; her father was a greengrocer, and when he died, her mother took the children to England when they were ready to go to college. As a young girl, she was struck by the cosmopolitanism of London. She had a circle of Black friends from South Africa, Nigeria, Kenya, and other countries. Whether at parties or in rallies, it was the mixed character of student life in London that she found most striking. In the book that commemorates her life, there is a particularly beautiful photograph of her dancing with abandon with a mixed group of young people in London.[41] Things started changing when she attended meetings at the flat of communist exile Yusuf Dadoo, at which she and about eighteen other young people were drawn into anti-apartheid politics.

Leaving London meant the end of these relationships. When she came back to the University of Natal, Durban, in 1963, "it was at the height of political trials . . . all the main students had been banned," and the colleges were segregated. She attended the University of Natal Non-White Campus near the market in town, became secretary of the Student Representative Committee, and had her first run-in with the Security Branch in 1967 when she helped organize the funeral of ANC president Albert Luthuli, who had been banished to his rural home north of Durban. After the formation of SASO in 1969, she went to their conferences and to political meetings and films at the Alan Taylor Residence in Wentworth, but she says she did not take to BC. Neither did she join Congress activism as did many young Indians. Working at a bank and at a supermarket in town, Rajes used volunteer work through the ecumenical Diakonia Council of Churches to assist families of political prisoners. When white colleagues at work asked her why she knew so many Black people, she would innocently respond that it was just volunteer work. In many ways, Rajes's political trajectory had already proven to be unique, drawing from multiple currents while maintaining an independent critical perspective.

While working through these networks, Rajes was recruited into the underground by Kuzwayo, who sent her a postcard from abroad under a pseudonym. Recruitment by postcard was another anachronism that would soon become impossible. Rajes circulated propaganda from abroad, including books by Che Guevara and Cuban and Chilean films about revolution. She sent someone out of the country to meet Kuzwayo and received instructions to procure topographic maps of various parts of the country. Using the pretext of starting women's groups across the country, she managed to secure maps from the government printers and sent them out under the carpets of a car. Then, she says, the demands to dispense money and procure personnel increased, and in the process, in her view, care for operatives was often compromised.

At one point, a nurse sent to her workplace turned out to have been working for the Security Branch. Soon after this, she received a message that she had to leave and that someone was going to take her out of the country. Like many people who went into exile, she had to do so in stealth. She could not tell those she loved most, who would certainly be harassed by the Security Branch. When she contacted her mother a few months later, her mother wept because she had known nothing about her daughter's plans. This is the point in narratives of exile at which affect marks the deep intimate costs of the decision to be political, often with the presumption that exile would only be for a little while.[42]

Rajes lived underground in Swaziland from 1979 to 1991, as Rae. From her moment of arrival at the External Mission, Rae was advised to find a place to live along with two Indian male exiles, as if it were obvious that she ought to live with other Indians rather than with other women. This is how she met Ivan and Joe; soon after this, she married Ivan and was with him for many years. Like Ivan, she joined the political wing. As she put it, "Right when you came in, you had to make a choice between the two wings of the organization: the political and the military wing. I chose the political wing because by that time there was a dearth of any political presence of opposition. The military wing is the bomb squad, and it was easier for women to get into the political wing anyway." She laughs as she says she chose the nom de guerre Rae to confuse the cops about her gender. She also had to try to make it in what she knew was an extremely masculinist and hierarchical organization.

Rae did not speak much about going to Angola for military training, but her comrade Phyllis told me was that Rae was deemed unfit for military service when a grenade went off in her hand, that she then had to be sent to Cuba for arduous medical treatment, and that she carried the physical and psychic trauma with her. We discussed the gendered division of labor in the struggle, which she speaks of with piercing clarity in her interview for the Gandhi-Luthuli Documentation Centre; in both her conversation with me and the interview, she details how women were expected to clean up the mess of the armed struggle, by literally mopping up the remains of bombed comrades, as she had to do after the Matola Raid.[43] This unvalorized, unrecorded, and deeply traumatic revolutionary labor was singularly foisted on women combatants.

Rae described her underground political work as "setting up cells inside the country, sending in personnel, handling arms, handling propaganda, seeing to communication, and getting safe houses for people." When I asked her where she was in the underground structure in Swaziland, she responded, "You don't get a hierarchy like in a firm; you become an all-rounder. I had to help smuggle in arms, literature, transfer of cars for personnel, receiving messages, and decoding communications. General all-round activity. Keeping in contact with the rear bases in Maputo, which is where we were controlled from, until Maputo fell with the Nkomati Accord, after which we established direct contact with Lusaka." Rae provided recruits basic political education about how to avoid giving away comrades, or how to decode information. These were becoming standard political techniques, for which some people were sent to Moscow for training on the forging of passports, the use of disguises, or ways of evading detection. In retrospect, these were dying arts of secrecy, and people like Rae and Ivan were already seeing the limits of analog forms of security.

From 1979 to about 1987, Ivan and Rae handled about sixteen cells in South Africa from abroad, while a section working in African areas in the Durban central district handled another set of cells; the implication is that they were to focus on Indian areas. Rae was told she would not be sent into the country, because the work she was doing was too sensitive and she knew too much. Ivan, in contrast, was sent in on numerous covert missions, even though he posed a greater risk to networks.

Rae also describes an internal critique that emerged in a conference in Maputo in 1982 or 1983, when a commander was talking about infiltrating personnel into South Africa, and Rae and Ivan responded that there were people inside the country but no established routines or structures. The dominant view of the External Mission in the early 1980s was still that cells would be contacted from outside, through messages or furtive crossings of people like Terrence and Ivan. This notion of external political control of internal cells was at odds with the work of activists who had been nurtured in the theologico-political moment and with that of people like Rae who had been operating as "all-rounders" all along. These issues, debated in the ANC since the Morogoro conference in 1969, would reemerge in the ANC's 1979 *Green Book*.

Rae's political life followed Frontline States' buckling under pressure from South Africa to close ANC camps: "When the crunch came, they chose to chuck the ANC out of the country, Swaziland in 1984–85, Lesotho around then, Botswana as well." Rae left Swaziland for Maputo in 1986 and thereafter went to Lusaka in 1989. She was one of many internal critics of the model of incursions into the country and of the separation of politics from internal sabotage. These debates led to the complex reorganization of structures detailed earlier and to the formation of PMCs to oversee political and military work in frontline countries. "That," she said to me, "was what led to Vula."

What is clear from Rae's accounts is that exile life was constantly traumatic. "For one thing, you couldn't sleep in your house" for fear of the Special Branch knowing locations, potentially through the torture of captured comrades. Like others, Ivan and Rae always met people in hotel rooms or third locations. Others were not as careful. Zweli "Oscar" Nyanda took activists home to debrief them, some of whom divulged where people were living: "The very next night they were assassinated." Rae kept "a reserve of friends to spend the night with."

When Joe was kidnapped from his house in 1981 and taken to Vlakplaas, Ivan and Rae and their supporters used the print media and the international Anti-Apartheid Movement in Brussels, London, and Amsterdam to keep up the pressure, particularly because the kidnapping happened on foreign soil. Crucially, they found that one of his kidnappers had dropped a passport and that he was a member of the Renamo counterinsurgency in Mozambique, funded by South Africa with support from the United States. When the embarrassed South African government intervened to ask the prosecutor not to oppose bail, Joe was quickly dumped back in Swaziland, and his captors disappeared. After ANC activists were expelled from Swaziland in 1982 and 1985, Joe emigrated to Canada.

What was clear was that "one of the chaps that Joe worked with defected, and was noted in many trials as Mr. X." Rae and Ivan became increasingly wary of people coming in from South Africa, as they discerned that their networks were being infiltrated. They realized that people like Joy Harnden, later exposed as a spy responsible for at least one death, had gone through the ranks to reach fairly high levels. "You get people working in Zuma's office, with all the code names, and one day you find that he's gone home," in other words, as an agent of the security apparatus all along.

The murkiness does not end here. Muziwakhe Boniface Ngenwa (Thami Zulu) had been a member of the ANC Internal and of the SACP, and he had been invited to join the MK High Command, backed by Hani. After becoming commander of the Natal Machinery in Swaziland from 1983 to 1988, he was abruptly withdrawn to Lusaka along with most of the Natal Machinery. After nine MK activists under Zulu's command had been murdered by cross-border raids by a South African hit squad, Zulu's deputy Edward Lawrence (Ralph Mgcina, Fear, Cyril Raymonds) was detained and interrogated by the ANC. Zulu was then arrested and detained for seventeen months by the ANC in its notorious security camp, iMbokodo, where Zuma had become deputy director. He was released in 1989, suffering with tuberculosis and AIDS, five days before his death. The autopsy shows he was poisoned while in the care of a senior ANC medical officer, son of a Durban NIC stalwart and mentor to Jacob Zuma. Yet Joe Modise and Chris Hani of MK wrote an obituary celebrating Zulu as "a giant and gallant fighter."[44] The murkiness surrounding Thami Zulu pervades the moment of insurrection.

Rae quit the political underground in exile around 1986 "because things got too hot." The Swaziland structures were demolished, and people redeployed. Ivan was seconded to Operation Vula. Rae was sent to Russia for political training for four months in 1988. In Moscow she came in contact with liberation movements from across the world at the Institute for Social Sciences, but language differences made social interaction difficult. She contrasts this experience with her youthful time in London. The political education was grim: "Gramsci they made mention of, but their main emphasis was Marx and Lenin." She had to prepare a paper on the struggle inside the country, with the emergence of the United Democratic Front (see chapter 8), and her analysis was that "no mass movement can exist for any length of time unless it is backed up by a military formation, and therefore it is necessary for a politico-military structure to be formed inside the country." While it is unlikely that Rae was privy to Vula, she had come to realize its precise aim. Indeed, the embers of this formulation had been in circulation since at least the Hani memorandum of the late 1960s.

While in the political wing, Rae was clearly committed to the idea of armed struggle. She told me she assumed that she would return to South Africa in military uniform with her machine gun in the back of a truck, like Che entering Havana—even though she had been deemed unfit to be a soldier and had suffered laborious surgery and post-traumatic stress. Denied the right to be a soldier, yet needed for cleaning up the front line, Rae points to the powerful pathos of the insurrectionist moment. Rae was sent home in 1990 because she had a medical breakdown, allowed to return before other exiled comrades. She went straight to her mother, by then frail and old. When I met her, she was a gracious older lady who spoke to me patiently over cups of tea. She made it very clear that she remains a revolutionary.

A Spider's Web of Organization

Something else was happening below the radar in Merebank in the 1970s and 1980s. Through the quiet work of Spider and Usha, Merebank saw the emergence of a dense web linking legal organizations like the NIC and MRA to safe houses, with supporters providing resources. They protected furtive figures like Ivan moving in and out of the country, and they connected underground work in South Africa with ANC groups in the Frontline States. While the underground was clouded in secrecy, problems of knowledge only multiplied in the wider sphere of support work. There are no records of membership, and considerable murkiness as people think back through clouds of secrecy and mythmaking. One person joked to me about a friend of his who says he did underground work in the 1980s: "He must have been *so deep underground* that none of us had any idea!" And yet this activist apparently walked around the township in full revolutionary outfit, in fatigues, boots, and a beret. This was possible because the incredible multiplicity of forms of legal and illegal activism in Merebank meant that nobody was quite sure whether someone was what they appeared to be.

The nephew of the venerable community leader Billy Juggernath was nick-named Spider, particularly appropriate for the web of connections through which he and Usha forged a crucible for young Congress activists, some of whom went into exile and many of whom became part of the growing internal civic movement. I locate this activity within the moment of insurrection, al-though it is another bridge with the first moment and the moment to come.

When I spoke to Spider and Usha, he began by locating his own political activity from around 1967. His classmates at school were the next wave of students to question the apartheid order of things. Spider's father was a link, along with G. Ramsamy (see chapter 5), to the older tradition of ratepayers activism in the MRA, including people who refused the LACS and wanted universal franchise. Spider and Usha met at university in 1972. They listened to Crosby, Stills and Nash; Joan Baez; and Jimi Hendrix: "Protest music! They all spoke about peace." They married in 1978 and set up their own flat at Narbani Mansions, opposite the Nataraj Shopping Centre, as an oasis in a time of political repression. They contrast the space they created with the intellectualism of the BC group and their coffee bar. They recall their differ-ence in doing "door-to-door work" and in working resolutely in Indian areas as part of a broader "nonracial, multiracial" Congress movement. But this door-to-door organizing labor also distinguishes them from the insurrec-tionist mode; it marks a communitarian tradition within the Congress fold that drew in several young people who were drawn to grassroots political work that needed to be done.

After working at a library and then in labor unions connected to the Trade Union Advisory and Coordinating Council and subsequently to the Federa-tion of South African Trade Unions (FOSATU), Spider came into contact with labor activists Alec Erwin, Johnny Copelyn, Chris Albertyn, Alpheus Mthethwa, and Omar Badsha. We saw that Badsha had linked older ANC figures and traditions to new generations of BC, Congress, and trade union activists and that although he maintained a Congress position, he remains to this day fiercely supportive of youth activists, intellectuals, artists, and critics of the status quo. He supported Spider's work with the unions after 1974, in the chemical and then textile sectors. After this, Spider's work shifted from labor unions to libraries, part-time study, and some teaching. "Dismissed due to politics," interjected Usha, laughing.

Speaking to Spider and Usha was a treat, as they spoke in tandem, com-pleting each other's thoughts, and laughing in the interstices. When he an-swered my question about the constraints of working through racial networks, as Indians committed to nonracialism, Spider turned to her and asked, "Did I get that right?" "Totally," Usha adds, "it had to be like that. If in those days an African and Indian were driving together, the police would stop you." Spider narrates a story about accompanying a group of young Indian activists at the Phoenix Settlement activist camp who had decided to go into the nearby African township of KwaMashu. As soon as they got there, "a policeman followed us right through and [*both laugh*] escorted us until we were right out of the area! We were totally controlled." This was particularly the case after the repressions of the late 1970s.

Spider and Usha are remarkable for having kept a low profile as enablers of multiple forms of struggle. Their work is not easily contained in the insurrectionist moment, but they provided essential support to MK through people like Ivan and through another Merebank recruit active in Chatsworth, Sydney Moodley. They didn't ask questions and turned a blind eye when their car was borrowed to go across the border. At some point, Spider says that they were playing such an important role with community activists that "decisions were taken that, look, Spider mustn't know about the underground." Their function was to "carry on your rabble rousing, throw up activists; guys much younger than me would be called from Swaziland and just taken away, see?" As connectors between forms and levels of struggle, they also prefigured in practice what the movement sought for in various ways.

On Concrete and Abstract Struggles, and
a Mythic Trip to Vietnam

I have spoken to a large number of peripatetic figures to understand the texture of life in exile and underground, through the web of secretive and public activity, within and across national borders, in and out and across apartheid's fractured geographies. Actual activists were always more compromised than the abstractions of the Third World militant they held up. Imagined comparisons with victorious Cubans, Algerians, or Vietnamese provided a ruse of normalcy that rarely confirmed certainties about insurrection. While speaking to former members of the underground and their kin, the most poignant moments emerged in asides and breaks in the narrative, in moments of pause in remembrance of loves lost and intimacies denied. These gestures are made with reference to necessary secrecy in the underground, to habits of revolutionary discipline, or to the violence of forced exile. There are no easy consolations, and yet these structures of feeling are powerfully revealing.

In all these instances, sentiment indexes the limits of power and knowledge in the moment of insurrection. Indeed, the bitter irony is that just as the history of statecraft from city hall demonstrates the racial state's dogged disinterest in ground realities, the same could be said of the movement in exile, albeit for different reasons. The urban eruptions of the 1970s made this clear. The lack of knowledge is evident in the way in which some ANC figures recall touring the country on release from Robben Island "to get a sense of things" before leaving for exile, as if realities could be gleaned through a quick reconnaissance. The underlying problem was the certainty with which some ANC leaders assumed that there was a political vacuum in their absence, an underground that had been dismantled and was waiting for their intervention.[45]

When Mac was released from Robben Island, spiriting out the document that would become Mandela's autobiography, he went to his brother's home in Merebank.[46] He recounts a series of underground journeys to, as he puts it, see things for himself. The lesson he gleaned from these travels was that the model of armed incursions into the country was fundamentally flawed because of the lack of political leadership within the country. From his perspective, the urban movements of the 1970s had been fundamentally rudderless without the directive role of the ANC and SACP. But, like others before him, Mac was also questioning official movement ideology enshrined since the 1960s in Operation Mayibuye, the Wankie and Sipolilo Campaigns, and the Morogoro conference, all of which called for leadership, subsequently the External Mission, to direct a rural guerrilla movement, but without agrarian mobilization.[47] An activist in the Swaziland underground spoke of the weakness the External Mission faced in reaching rural areas, and of the urban focus of armed incursions. While the urban-centric ANC missed its opportunity to connect to the agrarian movements of the 1950s and 1960s, it was surprisingly ill equipped to learn from the urban rebellions of the 1970s. This led to further questioning of strategy, including of the cherished idea of armed struggle itself.

In response to debates within the ANC, a small group of the RC led by Tambo went on a study tour to Vietnam in October 1978, culminating in an oracular meeting with the legendary ninety-five-year-old General Võ Nguyên Giáp, who has an iconic status in the cultural politics of the Cold War left, not unlike Che Guevara, for defeating the French in Điện Biên Phủ and the US-backed South Vietnamese as well. In this revolutionary parable, repeated on several occasions, as in the commemoration that begins chapter 6, Giáp caught the South Africans off guard by impressing on them the importance of building a mass political base at the center of their revolutionary strategy.[48] Giáp offered a communist strategy for building hegemony not through conventional military combat but through political and military activity to weaken both the enemy and rival political organizations, through blurred boundaries between civilians and combatants, as well as a strengthened underground linked to a united front of grassroots organizations.[49]

The meeting with Giáp was interpreted in varied ways and for various ends, with implications for divergent political cultures in Merebank and Wentworth. For one strand, it was the decisive argument for working with the resurgence of mass politics and for bringing together political and military activity.[50] This is where the ANC's 1979 *Green Book* is important as a text that bends Marxism-Leninism to recognize the importance of a united front for the ANC to command and direct mass mobilization.[51] This strand fit well with what was already happening in the dense and multilayered web of activism in Merebank, where the networks around Spider and Usha had clarified the politics of alliance to reach the imaginations of ordinary people.

For the militarist strand led by Slovo, the *Green Book* and the trip to Giáp pointed to the importance of building a "national liberation army" in the country to spur the conditions of "people's war." This position emphasized the importance of armed struggle for socialism. Even Tambo, by no means a Marxist, seems to have been drawn toward socialism by his trip to Vietnam. Special Ops was formed as a concession to the militarists, initially under Tambo but eventually under Slovo and MHQ, tasked with spectacular "armed propaganda" in the country.[52] This strand fit well with developments in Wentworth (see chapter 9).

The IRA appears to have provided expertise in reconnaissance for the attack on three South African Coal Oil and Gas Corporation (SASOL) petroleum plants in June 1980: an event that was apparently crucial for morale in ANC exile camps after years of waiting and unrest.[53] The image of a burning oil refinery circulated as vindication of an insurrection that had in fact begun. Slovo apparently stayed up on the night of the SASOL attack, looking at the sky from Maputo, imagining that he might finally *see* revolution in South Africa.[54] A parallel event in Durban, a botched operation to blow up the Mobil oil refinery at the center of Wentworth, would be cited by Robert McBride as "armed propaganda" that drew him into the South African revolution (see chapter 9).

The varied lessons from the trip to Vietnam take us back to the dialectics of abstract and concrete struggles, articulated differently through Wentworth and Merebank. The next two moments magnified these differences. In Merebank the multilayered form of praxis exemplified by Spider and Usha mirrored the making of an urban movement on the scale of metropolitan

Durban (see chapter 8). In an increasingly introverted Wentworth, a Special Ops cell one person removed from Slovo inhabited the tense dialectics of the criminal and the political in sabotage, including a spectacular car bombing (see chapter 9).[55] This takes us to the third and fourth moments, the moment of urban revolution, which created the conditions of possibility for the hegemony of the exiled ANC in Durban, and the moment of the disqualified, which marked the aporias that would remain in this search for revolutionary hegemony.

Remains of Insurrection: Operation Butterfly

The sublation, both preservation and cancelation, of the moment of insurrection in the emerging moment of urban revolution was foreshadowed in South Durban in Operation Butterfly, an attempt to bring the political and the military together within the country through an integrated Area Political Committee structure in Durban that mirrored the PMC structures in Frontline States. The two wings in Swaziland got together and wrote up an organizational chart and plan, which they sent to Lusaka for confirmation. When they received no response, they continued with the operation, "encouraged after . . . decisions at the Kabwe conference favoring a closer political-military relationship in operational structures."[56] The timing was fortuitous. Mozambique's signing of the Nkomati Accord in 1984 meant the effective end of overt support to the ANC and the movement of arms and personnel into Swaziland, where several leaders, including Hani, Slovo, Siphiwe Nyanda, and Kasrils, were stranded for a time. Several of them had been critical of the inadequacy of parallel structures instituted by the RC to link political and military operations. Under Kasrils's command, this group effectively used the post-Nkomati political crisis to integrate political and military leadership in Swaziland.[57]

Ivan and Ebrahim Ismail Ebrahim (Ebie) had made illegal trips into South Africa in preparation and were in contact with an underground intelligence unit in Durban led by Moe Shaik (see chapter 8). This was the political side of what was meant to be a merger of political and military activity. Through a separate set of networks, erstwhile pharmacist Gordhan was also attempting to connect the political underground with civic and labor politics. On the military side, an MK unit connected to the Swaziland machinery was active in Wentworth at the Alan Taylor Residence, centered on Vejaynand "Vejay" Ramlakan, later surgeon general of the postapartheid South African National Defence Force.

Alan Taylor had remained a political crucible since its BC heyday, but its valence had shifted to this group of ANC-aligned figures, who continued outreach to surrounding neighborhoods through weekend community clinics. They also continued the parties that brought a lot of people into contact with activists. What was unusual about Ramlakan's unit was that it centered on a mixed-race group of charismatic figures, many of whom had open political lives and many of whose activities appear to have been quite open to surveillance.

Rayman, from Merebank and a few years younger than Ivan, had worked with him in Swaziland until he "got blown" when an envelope found at the Matola Raid was traced back to communication between him and Krish (Goodwin) through Joe's school. Rayman had already begun to operate as a kind of unofficial underground activist, but he never told anyone that he was in MK, nor did he ever tell people whom he recruited for "political or operational work" who exactly they were working for. Rather than create the possibility of figures who might turn state witness against him, he said, "You make it appear like a small anarchist grouping over there which is thinking on its own." In other words, Rayman embraced the reality of working with semiautonomous groups and partial information. He recruited people not just in his neighborhood but also in Wentworth and in Indian areas, including Chatsworth and on the South and North Coasts.

After he was exposed as an activist, Rayman had to leave the country, where he joined MK military structures in Swaziland. By this time, Swaziland networks had been quite seriously contaminated. Nevertheless, Rayman kept moving in and out of the country, "ten to twenty times a year, sometimes legally, sometimes with false passports." He made trips to various places in western and eastern Europe and the Americas. For many of these trips, he said, "There are no traces," another sign of a receding analog world of identity surveillance and subversion. Around 1982 Rayman describes debates about the dispersion of cells and the problems with reliable safe houses. This was when Sue Rabkin and Terrence Tryon had been proposing Operation Butterfly to Lusaka.

From Rayman's perspective, Operation Butterfly emerged in 1982, first in a "military phase," where it "was able to network and train and develop a lot of people," and "at a particular stage, we decided that Butterfly should link with politics" at the same time that Swaziland operatives "were merging politics and military." He mentions Operation Crow in rural northern Natal, and Operation Butterfly, centered on Ramlakan's cell in Wentworth. Howard Barrell documents Ramlakan using the telephone to communicate with underground operatives and holding important operational meetings at his home: extremely risky forms of conduct.[58] In one comrade's view, Butterfly was exposed because of a few "loose tongues" at Alan Taylor, and "it was the first arrests for terrorism based in the community since Rivonia." But "several Butterfly operatives escaped detection" and could later be brought into Operation Vula. The latter appears to have some truth, as some Vula operatives I have spoken to were also part of Butterfly but have never openly spoken of their involvement in either operation.

Terrence left Wentworth to go into exile in 1978 for his open work in SASO, but he continued to connect ANC and BC networks. In contrast to Rayman's rendition, Terrence argues that Butterfly became necessary because the "underground was growing, but needed coordination, and Swaziland was too far." In other words, this was a repudiation of the External Mission's attempts at orchestrating insurrection by remote control. Terrence characterizes the tendency at Special Ops to continue to "make an operation and go back to have a beer in Swaziland or Mozambique, and go back to the camp; they were hit men and they had the money to do it." Butterfly was something quite different, he adds; "military fellows are military fellows: they look at a military target and forget that there's a political struggle." On the other hand, life for the ANC operative in Swaziland had become increasingly lethal, or, as Terrence put it, "In Swaziland you go to bed and wait for De Kock to come."

One of the things Terrence had to contend with was that "the military fellows would like to steal people" from the inside, whether a prominent community activist or promising student activist. "We would say leave that fellow, the SRC [Student Representative Council] president is going to give you two hundred fellows. Let him do his work properly. The ANC fellows were always in a hurry: quick things, a screw in the park!" In contrast, he saw Ivan and the former BC activists he worked with as engaged in a slower and more patient game: "It will take longer, but the results would be better." When Butterfly was organized, it was a combination of political, military, security, and intelligence operations, with more than 150 people involved. Terrence came into the country in 1985, along with Andrew Zondo, who was conducting completely separate military operations further south in Isipingo: "He went wherever, and I went elsewhere; it was a case of separation of activities." Apparently Ramlakan made a phone call to Swaziland to congratulate the Natal Machinery on Zondo's bombing of a shopping center in Amanzimtoti on the South Coast, where five civilians were killed. Testimony to the Truth and Reconciliation Commission (TRC) shows that this phone conversation was monitored by the Special Branch, who reported, "Within two days we apprehended about 80 percent of the persons who were involved in Operation Butterfly."[59]

Both the Ramlakan unit and Butterfly were blown in late 1985. The main arrests were of military figures, primarily through lax security. One of the deputies of the head of the Natal Machinery in Swaziland, Cyril (Ralph or Fear), who had been part of drafting the operation, revealed himself in 1988 as an agent of the Special Branch. Cyril had apparently been tapped to rise much higher in the ranks of MK, another indication of how little people actually knew about what and whom to believe. On learning this, Sue Rabkin and others suspected that the whole operation had been "drawn up by the enemy."[60]

Several people uncontaminated by the official networks escaped arrest, including Nozizwe Madlala. All the exiles who had infiltrated into the country had been arrested, except for Terrence, who pretended he was going to the shop in his shorts on a motorbike and instead went to a comrade in Sydenham Heights and on to Abba Omar in Johannesburg before leaving the country, followed by Abba. Several networks on the political side that remained uncontaminated were picked up again by Vula, a much better-resourced operation that learned considerably from Butterfly's mistakes. "But Vula wouldn't have been nothing to Butterfly if we had the money then," Terrence said, laughing, "Fuckin' arseholes!"

Operation Butterfly pointed clearly to the importance of coordinated activity in the country as well as to deep problems of security, probably to the highest levels. One of the reactions to Butterfly from the External Mission was that leadership coordinating activities in the country was "not sufficiently mature." This prompted the view in Operation Vula that it was necessary to infiltrate the very highest levels of leadership into the country, including Mac, Kasrils, and Nyanda. From other directions, the insurrectionist mode was slowly being recognized as insufficient or obsolete.

Unbeknownst to most of these operatives, other moves were afoot. The External Mission had begun to imagine the possibility of a return to South Africa without revolution. An important step was taken with Thabo Mbeki's conversations with fractions of South African capital. Apparently, Tambo expressed frustration to venerable London exile Vella Pillay that Thabo Mbeki had begun to operate outside official policy. Mandela had also begun to hold secret meetings and was apparently incensed that he was not the only one doing so on behalf of the movement. Whatever we make of these moves, it is clear that in the early to mid-1980s, some people were beginning to imagine their roles in a postapartheid order. While both the theologico-political and insurrectionist conjunctural moments were still active in some form into the 1980s, a third conjunctural moment offered the possibility of articulating them, with the ANC as the hegemonic force of the future.

The Moment of Urban Revolution, 1980s

Specters of Hegemony

The images that open this chapter frame the moment of urban revolution in Durban in the 1980s. A flyer from 1980 (figure 8.1) portrays groups of people, some in saris, marching from Indian and Coloured townships and uniting as the Durban Housing Action Committee (DHAC). The late 1970s witnessed a renewal of community struggles focused on bread-and-butter concerns: high rents, transportation costs, inadequate public housing, the price of food, the introduction of value-added tax, and continued forced removals. Many found access to the means of life under apartheid nonviable, and DHAC sought to give direction to this discontent. Gregory Houston argues that this was a concerted Gramscian "war of position" spreading revolutionary consciousness; Bernard Magubane's Gramscian analysis of the 1980s posed this revolutionary consciousness as transformed through the revolts of the 1970s into an unstoppable "Black offensive."[1]

Quite quickly, the state responded with a 1983 referendum on constitutional reform through "power sharing" in a new Tricameral Parliament with

FIGURE 8.1 *Mass Rally*, October 5, 1980, Durban Housing
Action Committee, SPA.

a white House of Assembly, a Coloured House of Representatives, and an
Indian House of Delegates. To many activists, this would institutionalize
complicity with African exclusion; to others, it was a pathway to power; and
to some, it was an opportunity for "rejectionist participation," as formulated
in debates preceding the 1980 South African Indian Council elections.[2] The
United Democratic Front (UDF) was launched in 1983 to link, connect, and
coordinate mobilization against the Tricameral referendum that continued
to deny universal franchise.[3] Members of DHAC, like the Merebank Ratepayers Association (MRA), were drawn into its mantle. There is a craft quality to
the poster, a collage of hand-drawn and typed elements that mirror an urban

FIGURE 8.2 Newly elected ANC leaders, Durban, 1991. © Omar Badsha.

movement fabricated through streams of people, like five fingers coming together in a fist led by DHAC.

In contrast, Omar Badsha's photograph (figure 8.2) of the National Executive Committee (NEC) of the unbanned African National Congress (ANC) at its first national conference in thirty-two years in Durban in July 1991 shows six movement leaders, three of them future state presidents; four exiles are at the center (Jacob Zuma, Chris Hani, Thabo Mbeki, and Joe Slovo), flanked by National Union of Mineworkers and Congress of South African Trade Unions leader Cyril Ramaphosa on the far left, and UDF leader Mosiuoa "Terror" Lakota on the far right. Reflecting on this photograph, Badsha notes that their tense body language was reflective of different political currents in 1991.[4] Unlike the 1980 poster, this is far from a demonstration of unity. Only Lakota looks directly at the photographer, a comrade in the internal struggles, as if they share the discomfort. The conference had resolved to suspend armed activity but not abandon uMkhonto we Sizwe (MK), which was to deepen its combat readiness across the country. Tellingly absent in the photograph are leaders of the highly secretive Operation Vula, short for *vul'indlela*, or "opening the way." After months of silence, Nelson Mandela had only ten days earlier delivered a press statement on the indemnification of ANC members involved in Vula.[5]

The passage between these images reflects the trepidation with which the External Mission eyed the brewing urban movements of the 1980s. The idea that mass mobilization was one of "four pillars" alongside the underground, armed activity, and international solidarity did not resolve how exactly exiled leadership would be directive. The ANC's inability to respond creatively and quickly to events like the Vaal Uprising of 1984 showed its communication systems across exile and underground to be slow and compromised. Importantly, the political culture of the UDF made space for debate across constituencies and issues. In Durban decisions were close about whether to call for a boycott of the 1983 whites-only referendum, or what the position ought to be on a possible Indian and Coloured referendum. Prominent figures in the Natal Indian Congress (NIC) supported entry into Tricameral structures. The Million Signatures Campaign allowed the UDF to revive an open, public form of activism reminiscent of the era before the banning of liberation movement organizations in 1961.

In Durban the moment of urban revolution was a concerted effort to link the communitarianism of the theologico-political moment with the democratic centralism of the insurrectionist moment to forge the conditions for the exiled ANC to become a hegemonic force. The small group of men who had taken over the Black student strike at the University of Durban-Westville (UDW) a decade earlier had become skilled political operatives with complex underground and aboveground political lives. They sought to make themselves indispensable to the External Mission. Using the revived NIC as cover, they tried to link and direct Durban's civic and workers' struggles through DHAC, and as the latter became a UDF affiliate, urban mobilization in Durban became part of a seemingly unstoppable force.

The charismatic figure at the helm of this urban movement was Pravin Gordhan (PG), later twice deposed as finance minister, then embroiled in a protracted political battle with the faction protecting Zuma in the latter's multiple attempts at evading lawsuits on sexual violence, state capture, and evasion of justice. When I met him, PG was commissioner of the South African Revenue Service, which had made massive inroads in tax compliance while facilitating the export of capital from the country. PG is a man of energy and contradiction, much loved by the South African middle class, by capital, and by many of his former comrades. As I waited for him in the hallway, imagining what would be the impressive office of the taxman, someone unexpectedly appeared on the seat next to me and spoke to me as if an old friend, telling me exactly what I needed to know. This was PG; his form of interaction fit perfectly with what people he worked with called his unique organizing style as he managed to infiltrate and connect disparate personalities and networks in a carefully planned strategy to build hegemony.

The group around PG, including Yunus Mahomed, Zak Yacoob, Alf Carrim, Farouk Meer, Jerry Coovadia, and veteran Billy Nair (see chapter 4), were collectively and ungenerously characterized as an "Indian cabal," notably by Winnie Madikizela-Mandela in 1997 and also by rival factions jostling for supremacy in the last years of apartheid.[6] Yet the Durban UDF included African stalwarts like Curnick Ndlovu, who had been released from Robben Island in the mid-1980s along with Nair, as well as Archie Gumede and several African activists from Lamontville.

Ari Sitas provides a vivid account of the mobilization in the mid-1980s of "comrades" tenuously connected to vanguardist leadership.[7] African comrades were subject to a distinct regime of violence from Indian activists, without the resources or support of anything like the long history of Indian progressivism. The brutal murders of Griffiths and Victoria Mxenge by apartheid death squads in 1981 and 1985 made this clear. While the characterization of an "Indian cabal" was racist, it did have a social basis in simmering hostilities between different fractions in the struggle, and in the historical contradictions of Indian settlement in Durban (see chapter 2).

A rival group to PG's centered on the charismatic Moe (sometimes "Mo") Shaik, who transitioned from the heady days of Black Consciousness (BC)–influenced student activism at UDW to join his brother Yunis, recruited to the ANC by Ivan Pillay (see chapter 7), along with Jayendra Naidoo to form an underground ANC unit called the Mandla Judson Kuzwayo (MJK) Unit. After one of their torturers from the Security Branch turned into their informer, dubbed "the Nightingale," the MJK Unit ran a highly productive security operation called Bible.

From Wentworth, a third underground unit formed around Robert McBride, another key operative in Durban in the 1980s (see chapter 9). In Mac Maharaj's view, PG, Moe, and Robert were fighting for supremacy in the political landscape of Durban in the 1980s. Whatever we might make of this, the presumption is that hegemony should be built through an enlightened vanguard, despite the communitarian currents in BC, Congress, and youth activism of the 1970s and in various strands of feminism and workerism, including independent Black labor unions.

The argument of this chapter is that the attempt to direct the urban revolution also involved a set of closures and routes not taken, signaled by feminist and worker critique, new forms of urban militancy, and the wide gap between experts and a differentiated working class. Moreover, multiple moves were afoot. Some in the leadership began to meet with fractions of capital and state.[8] In the shift from secret talks to open negotiations after 1990, a strand of insurrectionists hoped for a revolutionary alternative to negotiated settlement, either because it would serve as an insurance policy in case negotiations failed or because they felt that a socialist path had been too quickly discarded after the fall of the Soviet Union. This was Operation Vula, with strong connections in Merebank as well as to other areas in Indian Durban, including Overport, Reservoir Hills, and Tongaat. Yet another strand imagined building on the coalition of civic organizations in a 1991 call for popular determination of urban governance, the Campaign for a Democratic City. Despite very different politics, both Vula and the campaign were too distant from the negotiated settlement that brought a democratic racial capitalism in which many of the political elite sought a hegemonic role; both Vula and the campaign were also distanced from the lives of most Black people, as feminists and workerists pointed out in different ways.

Something else had emerged through the remains of the theologico-political moment. Many young people in the NIC fold were drawn to radical communitarian work to alleviate conditions in shack settlements in Merebank's Minitown or Tin Town on the flood-prone banks of the Umgeni River.[9] While they attended workshops on poverty in the revamped Phoenix Settlement, they were reviving biopolitical expertise in social work, public health, and social medicine. By the late 1970s, they were not alone. These DHAC networks encouraged the expertise of sociologists, lawyers, doctors, social workers, planners, economists, historians, and geographers to document dispossession, produce research for housing struggles, and provide expert opinion in court cases. In so doing, they renewed the challenge laid down by BC to fight for the life of communities and for the conditions of their vitality.

This civic biopolitics is all the more remarkable for emerging at a time of intensified states of emergency in which the terrain of struggle was changing quickly and in uncertain ways. Widespread intimidation, arrests, and torture dramatized the stakes in multiple strands that people traversed in different ways. Some imagined linking labor and community struggle to the underground. Others engaged raced and gendered class struggles over social reproduction. Yet others sought to use biopolitical expertise in urban planning to resist new rounds of dispossession. Across these strands, the moment of urban revolution relied on yet never came to grips with the political labor of women comrades, as well as critiques from South African Black feminists. The UDF sought connections across urban civic and labor struggles, but the precise role that the independent Black trade union movement would play remained unclear, as events in Merebank indicate. Finally, the movement faced serious limits to intelligence and security, which the electronic communications system set up by Vula sought to fix decisively. But if Vula focused on the problem of knowledge, it did not adequately question the problem of articulating subaltern will in building hegemony. We begin with the possibilities that had emerged from the remains of the Durban Moment.

Gender and the Disciplining of Grassroots Struggle

The late 1970s and early 1980s witnessed a groundswell of activism in workplaces and communities. Multiple strands of communitarian, women's, labor, and civic struggle reached for the tools of biopolitics to question the lived infrastructure of racism, building on histories of rural and urban struggle by ordinary women and men in Durban since the 1940s and during the effervescence of the early 1970s.

Jo Beall's activism was forged in the remaking of the communitarianism of the theologico-political moment after the repressions of the BC movement, after which she was drawn into the contradictory dynamics of the political underground. While working on her honors thesis at the University of Natal, she was drawn to Marxist feminism. An invitation to a weekend sleepover with an NIC women's group took her to Gandhi's former Phoenix Settlement, which had become a center of political education. Jo describes the intensity of the experience of "feeling as if I'd come home to people who talked the same language." The group bridged political traditions, and it drew her into community activism in the early 1980s protests against the proposed Tricameral Parliament.

In the interim, Jo had finished her master's degree and had begun teaching African history at UDW, where she ran an honors course and came into contact with Zac Yacoob, Abba Omar, Shireen Hassim, and Shaheen Bawa, as well as Heather Hughes and Jeremy Grest at the University of Natal, Durban (UND). They were involved in various ways with the banned ANC, the Congress of South African Students (COSAS), and feminist groups. Some of them worked across Moe's and PG's networks. However, it was the work of organizing against the Tricameral Parliament that Jo describes as absolutely energizing. She and others canvassed neighborhoods in mixed white, Indian, Coloured, and African groups in a form of grassroots mobilization reminiscent of the Women's March of 1956. "The presence of a white person," she explained to me, "meant that people who were not political, quite justifiable under apartheid, were less threatened." This was a conscious effort at knitting together the political and the apparently apolitical, as her comrade Hassim put it.[10]

Working across racially segregated neighborhoods, Jo was offered a geographic education that shaped her lifelong commitment to urban politics. Importantly, she recalls the challenges of organizing across Durban. "Wentworth was very on top of the issues," but not everyone could be drawn in; "there was a lot of fear in Phoenix; Chatsworth felt very organized." Jo had spent time in African townships doing Christian outreach as a girl, but these working-class Indian areas were new to her. She also realized that political apathy was not a racially exclusive phenomenon: "I remember the other really shocking thing is how I realized for the first time that there were apolitical Black people in South Africa, because I figured that all Black people were political and militant and opposing apartheid; Black being African, Coloured, Indian."

The other main thing that stayed with her was the quality of grassroots mobilizing across the city. "A lot of people were politicized," she said, and in retrospect, "it was all a buildup to the UDF. There were huge meetings with all the NIC women coming out with huge big pots of *breyani* and curry in halls all over." What had emerged was a popular articulation of frustration without a manifesto or a vanguard, organized through patient canvassing by people like Jo and her comrades.

Then, quite abruptly, a small group of NIC men decided to seek refuge in the British consulate in Durban in the spring of 1984. Earlier that year, Billy Nair (see chapter 4) had been released from Robben Island. He immediately joined the anti-Tricameral campaign and was detained under Section 29 of the Internal Security Act of 1982, which had expanded the apartheid state's repressive powers; Billy quickly went into hiding. He resurfaced later that year along with Archie Gumede, Mewa Ramgobin, Paul David, George Sewpersadh, and M. J. Naidoo when they entered the British consulate and announced that they sought protection from the apartheid state. To the consternation of the British government, three stayed for three weeks, the others for three months, and they called it an occupation. All but Nair were charged with high treason. Nair insisted that *they* had mobilized the whole country against the Tricameral system but that when the state hit back by charging them for treason on foreign soil, this "magnified detention without trial, made it a worldwide affair."[11]

For people involved in the day-to-day canvassing against the Tricameral system, who experienced, as Jo put it, "a huge swell at the grassroots and a lot of both inter- and intraracial mobilization," the occupation came as a shock. "We were told, that's where you put your energy. The British embassy hostage thing happened, and all the energy was taken away from grassroots mobilizing, and we had to campaign for this thing." A small, elite group of Congress men had hijacked the grassroots movement, turning the focus on themselves. The contradiction between resurgent communitarianism and masculinist vanguardism was crystal clear.

Several years later, when Jo was arrested by the security police and detained without trial, it appeared that they had gained access to a document that she had written about the campaign against the Tricameral Parliament. "I wrote this blazingly critical piece which basically said that Pravin Gordhan and Yunus Mahomed and all of them had dominated this campaign, and they had taken the wind from the sails of what had been a really important grassroots movement, and all the momentum was lost with them running doing this *high jinks* at the embassy . . . and I said there is a tendency in the NIC for some of the people to control the sources, to control decision-making, and if I didn't know better, I'd worry that there was a using of people in the African population." This document, meant for the External Mission and lost to public archives, seems to have instead been through multiple security screens, including perhaps both ANC operatives and the Security Branch. She later received corroboration that the message had reached African comrades on Robben Island, who thanked her for courageously speaking out at a crucial time.

A few years later, Jo Beall, Shireen Hassim, and Alison Todes published a foundational critique of the movement's tendency to see women's struggles and the insights of South African feminism as "a bit on the side" rather than as central to praxis and to future socialist policy.[12] Against the dominant view of feminism as a Western bourgeois import, the authors refuse a genderless rendition of the South African struggle. They show that the mass mobilizations that followed the 1973 Durban Moment took on a specific character in struggles over rent and transportation costs at a time of declining standards of living, and that while women were in the lead in some campaigns, "political leadership ultimately fell into the hands of men."[13] What is to be done, they argue, is to actively transform women's skills, confidence, and linguistic fluency.

"'A Bit on the Side?'" indicts the leadership for using "high-publicity political strategies" like the occupation of the British consulate to shift "attention away from political issues founded on material needs." The article concludes that "in retrospect, it seems that the material demands expressed in the campaigns in the townships in the early 1980s were lost."[14] But the disciplining of women was never quite as secure as the masculinist leadership may have imagined. Meanwhile, the political landscape had been transformed by the Zulu-nationalist Inkatha movement led by Gatsha Buthelezi, which had moved from being close to the ANC in the late 1970s to becoming its deadly rival, supported by the apartheid state to effectively wage low-intensity war with the ANC-allied UDF in the 1980s. This is the context in which the authors argue that Black women had revolutionized their conception of motherhood in collective and political terms, particularly in African townships like Lamontville.[15]

Envisioning a socialist South Africa, the authors argue that women's struggles bring a fundamental materialist perspective to the demand for a radical redistributive policy that would benefit women by raising the social wage and by reducing reliance on undervalued care work. This formulation mirrors the vision of the Combahee River Collective a decade earlier, which had argued for a Black radical feminist vision that was socialist and Third Worldist.[16] South African feminists wrote from the trenches of 1980s struggles to refuse the masculinist default position of a leadership that sought to actively intimidate and silence the praxis of militant women who ought to have assumed the leadership of a widening movement built on the community struggles of the 1980s.

As Pregs Govender and many others have attested, the leadership's *choice* was to relegate women and feminism to "a bit on the side," to enable the spectacular, racialized, phallocentric form of class power that continues to occupy the state today.[17] The socialist materialism powerfully defended by Beall, Hassim, Todes, and many others in the trenches of struggle around sexuality, gender, health, and social welfare remains the only real alternative because of its focus on biopower beyond masculinist, capitalist sovereign power. The emergence and erasure of this feminist critique is a key part of the urban movement of the 1980s.

Agitprop for a Different City

When the city council announced rent increases across Durban in March 1980, it spurred a wave of civic organization across the city, and DHAC took the lead in this political work. The leadership of DHAC was active in the NIC and in the ANC underground, and several became key intermediaries in the ANC's hopes of hegemony in Durban, but these urban concerns provided its political foundation. While DHAC's base was entirely in Indian and Coloured areas, the affiliated Joint Rent Action Committee (JORAC) worked in parallel in African areas, with a presence in the limited spaces afforded to a "respectable" African middle class, such as Lamontville and Chesterville, and with an ambition to spread across African townships and hostels adjacent to Durban and formally part of the fragmentary geography of the KwaZulu homeland.

A group of NIC leaders in Durban met occasionally in the home of the late Hassim Seedat, who had become active in anti-apartheid politics while studying for the bar in London in the late 1950s and who was detained in the country in 1965. When we met, he had become an inveterate collector of Gandhian, South African Indian, and anti-apartheid material. Active in the revival of the NIC in 1971, he appears by the 1980s not to have been seen either by activists or by the Security Branch as of any political significance, and this was fortuitous. During the raids of the late 1980s, people dropped boxes marked "DHAC" at Seedat's home, and they lay untouched in a basement room until he was kind enough to let me work through them. What is striking in this personal archive is that it contains key manifestos from DHAC and JORAC, as well as DHAC's routine and persistent correspondence with the city, records of disturbances and protests, flyers and calls to action, movement-related academic studies of urban politics and inequality, and material on how to conduct underground work.

Of these documents, "A Brief History of the Durban Housing Action Campaign (DHAC) and the Joint Rent Action Committee (JORAC)" is a work of rhetorical genius that links the 1970s development discourse of "basic needs" to people's demands for the means of survival, or what I call *biopolitical struggle*.[18] In other words, its focus is squarely on struggles over social reproduction, the domain that feminists had been arguing could no longer be ignored. Neither women thinkers nor the gendered nature of struggle is recognized, even though they are its condition of possibility. The document encodes key aspects of Congress thought in its call for a new society, and it admonishes forces of division, broadly phrased to include anyone critical of the Congress tradition, in defense of "communities." But the ambiguous category *community* could mean apartheid's racialized communities as well as communities of resistance built through conscientization in the tradition of BC.

What is quickly apparent from this text is that while both DHAC and JORAC worked under conditions of repression, African affiliates of JORAC felt the power of the apartheid police state brutally, as in the 1983 assassination of Harrison Msizi Dube, one of the founders of JORAC from Lamontville.[19]

While the everyday activism of DHAC received considerable support from the circuits of Indian progressivism, into which it neatly fit, JORAC had to contend with the state-sanctioned violence of Inkatha as well, particularly after struggles against the 1983 decision by the Department of Co-operation and Development to incorporate Lamontville and Hambanathi into KwaZulu, and into the ambit of Inaktha.[20] Its base in Indian and Coloured Durban gave DHAC some insulation from the conflicts in rural-urban African life in 1980s Durban and its KwaZulu hinterland, although underground militants connected to DHAC did become involved in the growing war between UDF and Inkatha groups. Plausibly, DHAC could present itself as an urban movement with ambitions for wider hegemony because its base was with urbanized Indian and Coloured populations, with solidarity with the rural-urban lives of Africans through JORAC.

The division between DHAC and JORAC was a consequence of residential apartheid, certainly, but also of mobilization against the Tricameral Parliament. The groundswell of mobilization of Indian and Coloured people to refuse sham representation in a racist parliament that denied universal franchise helped DHAC's expansion. Once the Tricameral system was in place, DHAC kept up the pressure on the alleged representatives of Indians and Coloureds, continuing to show that it was a travesty even in meeting their livelihood needs.

The DHAC files show how the organization pushed against on multiple levels of government, while also crafting political propaganda, or agitprop for a different city. On the one hand, in a steady stream of petitions and a bureaucratic dance of letters, DHAC followed the illogic of the state to unveil the violence of apartheid urban government in Indian and Coloured areas. In one trail of correspondence, DHAC pushed chief minister of the Indian House of Delegates Amichand Rajbansi on a new rent formula, to no avail; on the heels of this, the Security Branch raided the DHAC office, and what follows is livid correspondence between DHAC and the minister of housing. Across the letters, DHAC ingeniously uses a technical argument about a rent formula as a ruse to unveil the brute force that underpins the liberal mirage of Tricameral government.[21]

In its correspondence with the city on the new rental formula, DHAC argues on behalf of eighteen thousand tenants across Durban's housing schemes.[22] A 1988 letter to the Town Clerk's Department lists seventeen affiliated organizations from Tongaat, Phoenix, Newlands East and West, Asherville, Sydenham, Wentworth, Merebank, Isipingo, and across areas in Chatsworth: that is, from across Durban's main Indian and Coloured areas.[23]

But a 1988 clipping from the *Daily News* shows concern for white tenants of public housing as well.[24] A 1989 clipping of a political advertisement from the *South Coast Herald* calls for a boycott of the general elections that perpetuate the Tricameral system; it boldly uses the nonracialism of the Congress tradition, and it insists, "If You Do Not Vote, You Cannot Be Charged. You Will Not Lose Your Pension, Grant or Subsidy."[25] A research report from Michael Sutcliffe of the Town Planning Department at UND argues of Local Affairs Committee (LAC) elections that Indians and Coloureds in Durban and Pietermaritzburg had largely rejected these structures.[26]

The affiliate organizations in DHAC encouraged pamphleteering oriented to radicalizing communities. Some pamphlets call for developing expertise in urban struggle. For instance, the Newlands Advice Centre details evictions in the shack settlements between Newlands East and KwaMashu and offers a detailed discussion on the council's attempts at raising rents; it argues fiercely that the Tricameral committee tasked with tenancy "relief" through a "new rental formula" offers "no significant relief for the hard-pressed tenants and homeowners."[27] When the council pressed ahead with the new formula after an income survey conducted in 1987, housing activists carried out their own survey and continued to press against the blunt illogic of the new housing policy.

Visual means are key to this agitprop, including careful layout and the use of photographs, cartoons, and drawings to illustrate arguments in novel ways. A pamphlet from the Sydenham Committee of Concern, member of the United Committee of Concern (UCC) across Coloured areas, uses satirical cartoons to show the president engaged in a puppet show with Coloured and Indian representatives in the proposed Tricameral structure (figure 8.3).[28] When Bobby was under banning orders (see chapter 6), he turned to drawing political cartoons as a form of engagement. In an age before computers, pamphlets like this showcase the importance of manual artistry in engaging common sense.

The cartoons show that the Tricameral system would enshrine Indian and Coloured second-class citizenship, harden urban apartheid, and enable the conscription of Indian and Coloured men. This last argument is a stroke of genius, as it shows that defending apartheid requires putting young men in the line of fire. The final images in the sequence printed in the pamphlet show the president wearing the mask of the Labour Party leader (figure 8.4), while the only real alternative is the UDF, represented in the very next image in the pamphlet by a photograph of UCC activist Virgille Bonhomme.

FIGURE 8.3 "The President's Council Proposals," Durban, 1983. Sydenham Committee of Concern, Durban Housing Action Committee, SPA.

Among DHAC's files are pamphlets designed to circulate within townships. The four-page pamphlet of the Wentworth Advice Centre clearly identifies people, including Skido Joseph (see chapter 2) alongside Myrtle Beaunior. In a tie, a typewriter by his side, Skido is ready to provide paralegal and other forms of advice on wide-ranging issues (figure 8.5). What is striking, again, is the artisanal quality of the pamphlet, its local sponsors, and the wide range of issues dealt with, including education, identity documents, and substance abuse. The issue ends with a drawing of Skido with a deadpan expression that contrasts with the charismatic and friendly community activist much beloved in Wentworth (figure 8.6).

A cursory "History of the W.R.C." (Wentworth Rent Committee) in the same pamphlet simply states that "high unemployment, cuts in earnings, high inflation rate and increased evictions have caused a number of problems to emerge in the Wentworth area" and that these material concerns had led this committee "to establish themselves as a base" in the Wentworth Advice Centre; the word *base* is a gentle reminder of the war of position in apartheid communities.[29] In contrast to this pamphlet from Wentworth

FIGURE 8.4 "Apartheid has a new face," Durban, 1983. Sydenham Committee of Concern, Durban Housing Action Committee, SPA.

oriented to the community, other pamphlets were meant for wider circulation. These pamphlets announce a public movement with people demanding "Houses, Security and Comfort for All!" or "Bring Rents Down." In a time of intensified repression, photographs of crowds are a testament to the courage of the common person to be seen.

The use of photography in agitprop also meant that photographers and their negatives became objects of evidence for counterinsurgency, as the state was desperately trying to show that DHAC and the UDF were linked to the ANC underground. Black documentary photographers responding to lived inequalities also faced police repression; they were sought after for testimony of events they photographed, and their negatives were raided as evidence for political trials (see chapter 9).

The documentary trail in the DHAC files accelerates around 1988. The UDF had been banned the previous year, and many leaders had been arrested. A press statement from April 1988 announces the first occasion in the history of South African cities in which Black and white residents "joined hands" to

WENTWORTH ADVICE CENTRE

NEED ADVICE...

Legal Aid
Rent
Evictions
Pensions
Grants
Alcohol and Drug Abuse
I.D. and Other Documents
Education

Myrtle & Keith interviewing clients.

WE WANT TO HELP

a project of

Wentworth Rent Committee

FIGURES 8.5 AND 8.6 Wentworth Advice Centre pamphlet, early 1980s, Durban Housing
Action Committee, SPA.

demand affordable rents.[30] In a press statement from late 1988, Bonhomme
applauds "Candlelight Night" across Durban, in which 70 percent of residents of Wentworth, Merebank, Chatsworth, and Phoenix, and to some extent Mariannridge, Newlands East, Tongaat, and Isipingo, turned off their
lights in solidarity with municipal tenants under threat of eviction. "In
areas such as Wentworth, Merebank, and Chatsworth residents lit candles,
marched down the street singing hymns and prayed openly and unasham-
edly," reports the statement, along with mosque prayers by candlelight in
Phoenix and "prayer meetings held in the yards."[31] While DHAC relied on
the ecumenical Diakonia Centre and its leading figures, Father Gerald Patrick "Paddy" Kearney and Archbishop Denis Hurley, it also appealed to other
forms of popular religiosity. Periodically, DHAC could claim small victories,
for instance in the council's consent to review its new rental formula, to stop
evictions, or to provide relief to the poorest tenants; but it continued the
ongoing work of representing widespread suffering as a consequence of the
council's continued electricity cutoffs.[32]

A memorandum from "the Mothers of Sydenham Heights, Eland House,
Phoenix, Chatsworth, Melbourne Flats, Wentworth and Newlands East"

argues that the council cannot increase rents when existing rents are un-affordable given frozen wages and the burden of food, transport, and education costs.[33] The use of "motherhood" to drive home the costs of social reproduction and to demand "a direct say in all matters that affect our lives" recalls Beall and colleagues' argument about the radicalization of motherhood in struggle.[34] By creating a platform to broaden the terrain of struggle in all these ways, inadvertently, DHAC was taking the urban struggle to the terrain of biopolitics. However, multiple strands of struggle also intensified the limits to this kind of urban revolution, drawing in Merebank and Wentworth in different ways.

Populists, Workerists, and Urban Expertise

Vish Supersad was working with the Tongaat Child Welfare Society in the late 1970s and became involved in DHAC and the UDF at their inception. Simultaneously, he joined the political underground linked to Swaziland in 1979. Supersad was one of the NIC leaders who once posed the idea of working within the South African Indian Council, a position that took PG to London to debate with movement leadership about the possibility of working within apartheid state structures. He also started working with former BC activists Bobby Marie and Shamim Meer (see chapter 6), who retained relative independence as people openly aligned with labor and feminist groups.

In 1980 Supersad and others formed the Community Research Unit (CRU) at the University of Natal, Durban (UND), with Jerry Coovadia, Paulus Zulu, Francie Lund, Noddy Jinabhai, and others on the board. Supersad recalls social research at the CRU as an alibi for explicit political work.[35] In time, the CRU grew into the Centre for Community and Labour Studies, connecting with the work of Ari Sitas and Astrid von Kotze, linking community theater with independent trade unions.

Dan Smit had been in the United States in the late 1970s, studying planning and economics at the University of Oregon and the University of Washington. He returned in 1981 to do a PhD at UND, where Michael Sutcliffe was in urban planning, and Jeff McCarthy and Dianne Scott in geography, the latter connected to struggles in Clairwood. Smit connected with PG, Supersad, and Vidhu Vedalankar at the CRU, where he organized a reading group on Manuel Castells's *The Urban Question*. "Castells was a fairly major theoretical inspiration for how to put the UDF together," he insisted. "We started to apply theory, although that was driven by real material issues on the ground: rents and transport." When DHAC came into being as an umbrella organization, Dan argues that the people around him found a theory of urban movement in Castells's *City, Class and Power* for its "linking urban social movements mobilizing around bread-and-butter issues, mobilizing around the social wage, around housing, rates, transport, industrialization and then trying to link organizations to each other into some kind of umbrella structure; the thinking behind the UDF was precisely that."

I asked him how he engaged Phil Harrison's suggestion to me that Northern debates between Castells and David Harvey played out in South African urban struggles of the 1980s. Dan clarified, "It was a question of where you organized, and a question of where 'class' was in all of this." He pointed to the distinction between "populists" aligned with the Congress tradition and "workerists" aligned with independent Black trade unions, and he noted that while he was in the populist camp, he had strong connections to workerists.

What was at stake in these debates, from Dan's perspective, was not an abstract position on the workplace versus the community as the primary locus of struggle. When community struggles attempted to bring unions into boycotts, for instance, they met strong resistance; "key players in the community were SACP [South African Communist Party] members [with] a strongly vanguardist orientation, whereas the union movement tended to stress a New Left grassroots form of organizing." He paused to emphasize the irony. "Populists were vanguardists, actually! That vanguard was referred to as 'the cabal,' and they were largely in the SACP: Pravin, Vish, Billy, Lechesa Tsenoli from Lamontville." Opposing SACP vanguardism were grassroots workerists and African nationalists, but with the latter weak in the particular milieu of 1980s Durban, the main opposition to the emerging hegemony of the ANC came from workerists. There was more nuance to this still, as Steven Friedman argues, in the importance of "left workerists" committed to radical social change through the independent political voice of the Federation of South African Trade Unions (FOSATU), which never allied with the UDF and were wary of the class politics of the ANC.[36]

On the face of it, what activists appear to have read through Harvey was a commitment to class struggle over the built environment that had to be engaged in its specific articulations. In contrast, populists appear to have read Castells for a general theory of urban community struggles as "essentially class struggles over the social wage," which allowed the vanguard to think they had the key to link and orchestrate dispersed struggles. What appear to be South African readings of Harvey and Castells reflect different understandings of the spatial articulation of urban struggles. The SACP view, at a time when party leadership was doggedly Stalinist, was that the vanguard knows through a generic theory of Marxist praxis how to articulate "class struggles over the social wage." Articulation in that case is entirely abstract, legible to the enlightened leadership. Workerists, committed to a grounded notion of articulation, had to attend to concrete material and ideological expressions of struggle, legible through grassroots pedagogy inherited from the 1970s, whether legible through Paolo Freire or Antonio Gramsci. Neither Harvey nor Castells provided the framework for most rank-and-file activists, but the contrast between these conceptions of praxis is striking.

We have encountered the critique of vanguardism from socialist feminists who saw it also as a form of patriarchalism, of silencing actual raced and gendered labors behind struggles over the social wage. Unlike most populists and workerists, feminists were also transforming their own understandings in relation to the lived struggles of Black women with whom they sought to forge solidarity through rather than despite the multilingual South African landscape.

Smit, Sutcliffe, McCarthy, Scott, and others who were part of CRU and subsequently of the Built Environment Study Group also turned their critical gaze to the state in a period of urban reform. As Smit put it, "Where the regime moved money, the tactic was to engage it and to change the terms of reference." This would prove complicated in some places, as in the upgrading of the S. J. Smith, Glebelands, and Mobeni Hostels in South Durban. "Those were an interesting terrain of struggle where Inkatha–ANC/UDF tensions were strong." S. J. Smith Hostel was next door to Lamontville, where a strong civic culture had emerged under conditions of severe repression. Smit was appointed in the late 1980s to a UDF-Inkatha steering committee for the upgrading of this hostel; he said, "I was there as a technocrat. The reality was that within six months of the formation, two members on both sides had been killed in the conflict. We abandoned that particular project." The Built Environment Study Group also became involved in the community struggles against the rezoning of Indian Clairwood in South Durban as an industrial zone. In Smit's view, they "won the battle, and through the process the community became highly mobilized." The urban experts connected to the UDF could win these kinds of battles in Indian and Coloured areas where they did not face the township wars with Inkatha.

The upgrading of Austerville, the official name of the Coloured area of Wentworth, was one such instance, which Dan called "highly participative." Seymour Bedderson's study helps us see the redevelopment of Austerville, beginning with its objectives to improve services and "the public environment" and to promote homeownership, job creation, broad-based benefit from the project, "alleviation of social pathologies," and the coordination of community organizations toward these contradictory ends.[37] The reporting of social pathologies resonates with the circulation of late-Victorian moral discourse in Wentworth decades earlier (see chapter 1). The text carries liberal hope that "successful" revitalization might turn Austerville into a "decent socially acceptable neighborhood with a viable housing market" that need not displace poor people; citing Roland Graser and Sheldon Rankin, the author makes much of their argument that crime and poverty in Austerville are inseparable.[38] The town planner responsible for the project clarifies that transformations in urban form would facilitate tenant associationism and surveillance, that removing pedestrian routes cutting across areas would maximize surveillance, and that all this will minimize "mischief and crime."[39] Upgrading replayed the fantasies of urban apartheid.

Bedderson's study does show improved stormwater drainage in the former naval barrack areas of Drake and Frobischer, as well as new potable water and electrical services from the city council, with individual meters to facilitate the sale of public housing. On the other hand, state-owned flats on Woodville Road, the place from which this book begins, continued to have "ineffective" sewer and freshwater systems, "resulting in unsafe living conditions." On the other side of the class spectrum, the council sold ninety-eight sites at R10 per square meter to first-time homeowners to construct dwellings in Treasure Beach on the hillside across from the refinery and with access to the sea, a scheme that privileged more well-off residents who could finance building their own homes. Subsequently, the city opened up an additional thirty-nine sites for Coloured people from beyond Austerville, and then further sites in Austerville, many for people from the barracks and flats.[40]

Given class differences in the redevelopment process and the presence of a civic organization, we should expect Austerville's upgrading to have become a target of movement critique. Sixty percent of the labor for the project was locally procured. The project set up the Committee for the Redevelopment of Austerville, including representatives from provincial and city government, the Tricameral House of Representatives, and the Coloured Local Affairs Committee. The Committee for the Redevelopment of Austerville was dissolved in 1990 following serious critique from the Auswent Civic Association, which split into the Auswent Civic Association and the Austerville Residents' Co-ordinating Forum.[41] Does this mean that an attempt to secure consent from the majority was met with community resistance? One former activist recalls that upgrading provided an opportunity for a key family of power brokers connected to the copresident of the UDF, Albertina Sisulu, to negotiate access to prime housing in Treasure Beach. Others recall politically conservative school principals and teachers gaining access to housing as well.

The timing of the Austerville redevelopment initiative is important. The state under P. W. Botha had initiated the National Security Management System, rolled out in the 1980s as part of a "total strategy" with coordination across departments of the state, designed to respond to heightened activism in the country including through the infiltration of civics, encouragement of vigilantes and "warlords," and other forms of intimidation and violence. The National Security Management System worked through Joint Management Centres (JMCs), divided into regional Sub-JMCs and Mini-JMCs. There was a South Durban Sub-JMC and a Wentworth Mini-JMC. The Austerville redevelopment program must have been connected to this "total strategy." And yet a major underground cell would emerge in Austerville from precisely the spaces transformed through the redevelopment process (see chapter 9).

Independent Black Labor Unionism in Merebank

Pat Horn had been involved in the University Christian Movement (UCM) as a student at the University of the Witwatersrand in Johannesburg in the early 1970s and was strongly influenced by BC and Paulo Freire. Pat agreed with the line that Black students should work in their communities and that white students should do something else, so she worked on adult literacy in factories. Soon after the 1973 strikes, she was approached by Johnny Copelyn, instrumental in the South African Clothing and Textile Workers Union at Bolton Hall in Durban. After 1973, workers had been joining the General Factory Workers Benefit Fund and were starting to form small industrial unions in the industrial areas of Jacobs and Mobeni in South Durban as well as in Pinetown. Pat describes the formation of a textile union and a metal union that was the precursor of the National Union of Metal Workers of South Africa, and also attempts by the state to "hit the unions" by showing they were connected to the underground.

Pat was asked to run the Pinetown office and to train workers from the textile and chemical factories, which she did alongside adult literacy classes. The state's repression continued, as did state reformism through industrial conciliation structures, liaison and works committees, and the formation of parallel Trade Union Council of South Africa (TUCSA) unions for white, Coloured, and Indian workers. In contrast to these parallel unions, the "independent" trade union movement tried to expand workers' actual voice and power. The state branded them communists. Pat says, "Communist was a broad category: everybody who was against the state was called 'communist'!" This led to the banning in 1976 of Pat as part of about twenty-seven trade unionists including Copelyn, Christopher Albertyn, and Alpheus Mthethwa in Durban; and Moses Ndlovu, Mike Murphy, and Jeanette Murphy in Pietermaritzburg. "This thing of being banned," Pat adds, "makes one more determined."

In 1981 her banning order expired, and FOSATU formed to federate independent trade unions. Pat worked in Empangeni organizing paper factories under the Paper Wood and Allied Workers Union. In 1982 she began working with Moses on the southern Natal region, and their first major drive, in 1983, was at the Mondi Paper Mill in Merebank. At its inception, the paper mill had an agreement to provide jobs in Merebank and to keep the majority of its workforce Indian. This agreement seemed to have been forgotten when Pat arrived, but the workforce consisted of about eight hundred Indian workers (not all from Merebank), some Coloureds, and four hundred African workers. Pat's view was that Mondi had largely escaped the strike waves of the 1970s because wages were better there than in many other places, and also because the Indian workforce was difficult to organize, in part because they were in a TUCSA union with some benefits, like pension schemes. The TUCSA unions generally collaborated with management and the state, and many of them had negotiated closed-shop agreements to which African workers were sometimes bound against their will.

The main TUCSA union in Mondi, as in the refineries, was the boilermakers' union. This is what the Indians and some white workers belonged to, but the general view was that it had done nothing for them. Pat found considerable mistrust between African and Indian workers, and she and her comrades decided to organize them separately. Through BC connections to Bobby Marie and Myron Peter (see chapter 6), Pat arranged meetings with Indian workers. Separately, she and Moses worked to win support among African workers. This is when Anand Govender became active. They initially had a problem accessing workers because the land around Mondi is owned by the company, and they could not meet workers at the factory gates. Instead, they got on Mondi buses from Chatsworth via Lamontville, talked to workers on the bus, and hid under the seats when the bus stopped at Mondi. They had an insider from a political family in the managing director's office who would share minutes of managerial meetings about how to break their union drive. They also reached out to the liberal spokesperson of the Anglo

American Corporation that owned Mondi at the time, Bobby Godsell, on complaints of racial discrimination in the company.

Mondi, in turn, launched a massive intimidation campaign with the view that no factory had organized large groups of Indian workers. The organizers stepped up their efforts as well in a six-week joint campaign across paper, metal, and sweet-food unions and three major factories. "We joined forces and worked together, and this thing hit Mondi by storm." They organized Indian workers and African workers, with a mixed shop steward committee, and in six weeks they had a majority, with almost equal numbers of African and Indian members. "Then the intimidation really started inside the factory." The union became much more vigilant. When a white production manager "just let out his venom" at an Indian worker, the union averted going public and managed to get a written apology. This event galvanized the workforce so that they could then have a ballot and election for mixed shop stewards, and the racially segregated liaison committees were dismantled. "After that," says Pat, "it was an irreversible thing."

What was the relationship between these remarkable events at Mondi and the long tradition of community organization in surrounding Mere-bank? Pat's analysis was that Indian workers had admirable working-class consciousness but did not see common cause with the political organizations active in Merebank. They saw the NIC figures as "a bunch of intellectuals who don't understand worker issues." Despite the UDF's interest in forging connections between civics and labor unions, activists "were always going into hiding; it was impossible to find them. Workers couldn't go into hiding, so they considered it a luxury that these activists had no responsibilities!" On the other hand, she recalls that UDF activists often perceived workers as trapped in economism, without an interest in community struggles.

A slightly different perspective emerged from Merebank resident Gordon, who joined Mondi in 1979, the same year FOSATU was formed, when he "couldn't just see the injustice going on." He recalls the struggles of 1987–88, which he says "might be the first recognition agreement in the apartheid period." The main barrier, in his view, was that Indians were not politicized; most Indians supported the National Party, while a significant share of African workers supported the state-aligned Inkatha. The organizers persuaded workers by saying they had nothing to do with politics, which meant that they could have active Inkatha shop stewards. However, the ANC-aligned civic activists in Merebank may not have understood this complexity and may have cast workers as not politically aligned at all. As a consequence, some community activists supported worker actions, including the MRA's

G. Ramsamy, Siva Chetty, or Mrs. Marie, but in general it appears that workers and community members were not usually active supporters of each other's struggles.

In 1985 Pat moved on to work with the Chemical Workers' Industrial Union, which had not managed to organize the refineries and had not been successful in organizing Indian workers. The boilermakers' union at the time was barely active, and working conditions were better than what Pat had found at Mondi at the inception of their organizing, despite significant casualization. Pat started organizing at SAPREF (South African Petroleum Refineries), where she and her comrades managed to get access to workers on-site. They also had some access to some in management who were political, and they used a similar strategy as at Mondi to slowly build a majority at SAPREF as well as at the Wentworth refinery. They fought the subcontracting of security services at Mondi, but only, as it turned out, succeeded in delaying it.

What is striking about this period of independent industrial union organizing is that it was so separate from the organizational culture around it, despite the density of activism in Merebank. Pat had relied on personal connections with former BC activists "who had become more Marxist and had drifted into the labor movement." She maintains, "We were able to build democratic structures independently of the ANC and the underground. Many of us believed that the ANC was a bourgeois nationalist movement. There were people among us who were in the underground. We were trying to avoid what had happened to SACTU [South African Congress of Trade Unions]," which had been smashed in the 1950s when trade unionists like Billy Nair were arrested for sabotage. "We believed strongly that the unions had to develop strongly and independently with worker-controlled leadership." In effect, this was a different kind of critique of the insurrectionist moment and its fetishism of the underground at the expense of mass organizing on material concerns. If, as Johnny Copelyn argues, "the ANC had been absolutely contemptuous of unions in the 1970s," on the grounds that armed struggle was the only way to fight a police state, its volte-face in the 1980s would prove fraught in some places.[42]

Project Bible

In the 1980s it was clear that the movement had been thoroughly infiltrated by the state security apparatus. An important response emerged from another charismatic operative, Moe Shaik. Moe had grown up in a relatively poor, mixed-race, Malay-Indian family in Greenwood Park; he was registered

Malay while his brothers were registered as either Indian, Malay, or "other Coloured." He recalls that he was never quite Indian, never quite Coloured, and this bizarreness of race lodged in his consciousness early on. Moe was also fundamentally shaped by the world he saw through his father's shop on Albert Street in town, where he encountered communist activist and inveterate book collector A. K. M. Docrat and where he could walk over at an early age to political gatherings at Curries Fountain, including the 1974 "Viva FRELIMO" rally.

Despite growing up in a segregated Indian area and going to Gandhi-Desai School, Moe was first refused admission to UDW because he was registered Malay; he chose a subject that required him to be at UDW and participated in its vibrant political culture. Despite the banning of BC leadership, he recalls BC opening their minds in a new way. Abba Omar describes the early years of their political work in the vein of the theologico-political moment and its commitment to questioning everything.

On a trip to Swaziland in 1977–78, Moe's brother Yunis had met Judson Kuzwayo, Ivan Pillay, and Rajes Pillay (Rae) (see chapter 7), who asked him to start an underground unit. He recruited Moe and Jayendra Naidoo to form the MJK Unit; they describe their commander outside the country as Ivan, who reported to the head of the Swaziland Regional Politico-Military Council (RPMC), Ebrahim Ismail Ebrahim (Ebie), who in turn reported to Jacob Zuma in Maputo. From about 1980 to 1985, they were tasked with propaganda, surveillance, recruitment, and operations—an all-round unit entrusted to receive leadership like Ebie infiltrated into the country prior to the ANC Kabwe Conference in June 1985.

Kabwe was an important turning point for the External Mission and its exploration of multiple avenues. Oliver Tambo requested clearance for "talks" with "important people," making space for a new area of tactical work.[43] He also renewed a commitment to mass action and armed struggle in a time of heightened state repression, as the NEC statement put it, to "make apartheid unworkable, render the country ungovernable"; importantly, he equivocated on the legitimacy of "soft targets" caught in the crossfire.[44] Kabwe delegates voted overwhelmingly to endorse "nonracialism" in the entire ANC, bringing Slovo, Mac, and others into the NEC. Importantly, Kabwe began deliberations about the future Constitution and Bill of Rights.

In December 1984 Ebie conveyed an instruction from Tambo that the unit was to be ready for a new phase in which leadership would relocate to fight from within the country.[45] Ebie came into the country in order to have a set of consultations underground in advance of the Kabwe Conference, and the

MJK Unit took care of security and logistics. Ebie had been meeting with Klaas de Jonge and Hélène Passtoors, a Dutch-Belgian couple who had been recruited into Special Ops in Mozambique and had been involved in sabotage campaigns; they had been living in the country for six months. Unbeknownst to them, they were under surveillance. When the Security Branch discovered an arms cache, and Ebie had been seen at the airport with Passtoors, the trail quickly led to the unit. Under instruction, Moe and Yunis acted as decoys to get Ebie out through PG's network, and as a result Ebie escaped and did in fact get to Kabwe. As a consequence of this forced exposure, the brothers were arrested; Moe faced a very difficult nine months of solitary detention under Section 29 of the Internal Security Act. In December 1986 security forces kidnapped Ebie in Swaziland, and they came back to look for Moe. But at this point his own security network had prepared him and Yunis to operate underground for the next two years. Perhaps at this point he also decided not to concede to direction from exile but rather to reverse the relationship by seeking knowledge on the ground. What transpired was unusual.

A member of the Security Branch whom Moe and Yunis had encountered in prison, and who had witnessed Yunis's torture by Lieutenant "Hentie" Botha, was so disgusted by their humiliating mistreatment that he decided to turn and work for them. He approached Moe slowly in detention, and when they were out, he arrived at Moe's optometry practice with the latest Security Branch file on the ANC. Moe called this man the Nightingale, for singing the enemy's secrets, and his identity remains unknown to this day. In his memoir Moe describes his first encounter with the file vividly, including its detailed intelligence reports on surveillance in the country as well as in other countries with an ANC presence; it included an account of Lieutenant Botha's contact with an agent in Swaziland concerning Ebie. In the flush of this encounter, Moe realized that the Security Branch "was a sophisticated operation" and that in contrast "the ANC was amateurish."[46]

Emboldened, Moe took a copy of the file to Yunis and Yunus Mahomed. He says that the principle of democratic centralism required him to make the case to them as his superiors; they agreed to put it to "the Monna," Billy Nair. They also suggested that if leadership agreed, Moe should lead a specialized intelligence unit while the rest of the MJK Unit would shift focus to unions and the mass movement. Nair was impressed with the breakthrough but advised not letting the information go through Swaziland but rather taking it directly to London to get it to Tambo.

In the interim, Mo began meeting the Nightingale regularly, often at the Overport Centre parking lot. He describes every meeting with the

Nightingale as beginning in a very tense way, as each of them assessed whether the other had been turned.[47] In effect, both might have been playing the enemy, in a delicate balance that could only be legible through the painful intimacy of a torture cell turned into a site of solidarity. There is a gendered aside in the Nightingale's story of transformation; he recalls his political turn when he witnessed Moe and Yunis suffer while their mother was dying. There is a strange symmetry between the argument that the Durban social-ist feminists were making about the centrality of gender and of revolution-ary motherhood in overt political struggle, and this abstract "mother" as a precondition for highly secretive underground work. Interestingly, the unit would be reliant on the intelligence work of a group of highly skilled women operatives.

In January 1987 Moe secured a flat where Reservoir Hills meets the Um-geni River, where he set up a computer coding system with a searchable database of information from the Nightingale's files. He brought in student activists "Zoe" and "Rebecca" to work on the complex coding process, and subsequently "Catherine" to head the analysis section and then "Milla" to work on economic intelligence. "Wally," an MJK Unit member in London, be-came a link between their unit and the ANC in London. The cross-referenced data could now help trace sources back to their handlers, and Moe reports identifying "at least three high-ranking sources within the ANC" and "signifi-cant leads to many others."[48]

Moe traveled with a false passport to London and met several in the lead-ership, including the new head of intelligence, Jacob Zuma, who took the reports to Tambo. Apparently, when he saw the reports, including on meet-ings with him, Tambo replied, "I believe they are as true as the Bible," and thus was born "Project Bible." Criticism from the rank and file about the ANC's security department at Kabwe prompted Tambo to transform intelligence, and Project Bible was drawn into this process. Tambo authorized training and resources for the unit, with secure communication from Johannesburg, via Wally in London directly to Zuma as head of intelligence. Moe was sent to East Germany for intelligence training from the Stasi. Now that there was indication that the ANC might have been infiltrated all the way to the NEC, the Nightingale would become crucial to counterespionage. Around this time, intelligence from the unit was key to identifying an infiltrator in the Botswana MK machinery in a plot to murder Aboobaker Ismail ("Rashid") or his associates in Special Ops (see chapter 9).[49]

When the Security Branch realized that they had a mole among them and began to interrogate their members, beginning with "nonwhites," Moe's unit fed the Nightingale ANC information to help him rise up the ranks and maintain his trustworthiness. This was a complex operation that required some amount of information sharing along with "false flagging," or providing disinformation about identities and events, so as to throw off the other side. The relationship between Moe and the Nightingale remains shrouded in mystery; it carries the ruse that individuals engaged in a dance of misinformation might hold the keys to unlock corruption at the highest levels of the ANC.[50]

Sometime between 1985 and Ebie's capture in 1986, an underground operative handled by Moe and known to Ebie was tasked with taking a toothpaste tube filled with information from Durban to the ANC in London. After three days in a safe house, expecting to meet Ebie and with a vivid sense of being watched, the operative was led to King's Cross Station and was utterly surprised to meet Zuma openly at Burger King, completely undisguised. There is a possibility that the toothpaste tube conveyed views from the political underground to the ANC leadership, which had opened itself to critiques of various kinds in advance of the Kabwe Conference. Another possibility is that it confirmed some of the material that Moe would later take over in person to London. What remains baffling is the highly exposed interaction involving an underground operative who had already been detained and Zuma, soon to be the head of ANC intelligence.

To manage the flow of cross-border finance for Project Bible, Moe's brother Schabir turned to the *hawala* system of long-distance finance that had been the mainstay of Indian Ocean Muslim finance.[51] In his book, Moe says he had recruited Sandy Africa of Operation Butterfly (see chapter 7), Claudia Manning and Clifford "Cliffie" Collings from Wentworth, as well as Selina Pillay, Kammila Naidoo and Shaheen Bawa. They specialized in political and economic intelligence and counterintelligence, and they recruited other sources in the Special Branch, whom they called the Owl and the Sparrow. In 1988 Billy Nair arranged a meeting with Moe, living underground, and Mac, who had come into the country illegally with Siphiwe Nyanda (Gebuza), and Moe's unit took a new turn. Claudia, Selina, and Kammila were sent to Moscow as part of the External Mission's most daring and innovative mission.

Operation Vula

Recall that Ivan had left Merebank in 1977 and worked in the Internal Political Reconstruction Committee (IPRC, or the Internal), tasked with forming ANC underground units inside the country (see chapter 7). After experiencing infiltration in Mozambique and Swaziland, the loss of close comrades, the abduction of his brother, and the capture of Ebie, Ivan recalls questioning the model of warfare drawn from the Irish Republican Army. "Our thinking began to change in the early 1980s; we now needed to create not independent units but networks, preparing the ground, guiding the mass movement, and recruiting for MK." In fact, he had already been engaged with the many-layered activism in Merebank centered on Spider and Usha Juggernath (see chapter 7). Mac stressed to me that the task was to understand the movement from the inside out rather than from the outside in, and from his perspective as secretary of the IPRC, this meant locating within South Africa.

Former ANC intelligence operative Howard Barrell's research at the time shows continuing debate over bridging political and military operations, cutting redundancies, and learning from the limits of models of revolution, including Che Guevara's notion of armed incursions, Võ Nguyên Giáp's emphasis on building bases to foment a people's war, or indeed Operation Butterfly's attempt at coordinating political and military action. Little had changed in ANC operations since the 1960s despite organizational change through the Revolutionary Council (RC), the Internal, and RPMCs.[52] With a high failure rate of operations and losses of life through *askaris* and cross-border attacks, the military strategy had not proven sustainable.[53]

Ivan argues that after 1981 there was an emboldened sense that "we couldn't continue to try to direct this thing by remote control from outside the country; the time had come to actually locate the leadership in the country." He and others communicated this to leadership in early 1982 at a conference in Maputo, just as activists were evacuated from Mozambique to Swaziland after the 1984 Nkomati Accord. The report to Lusaka was "lost," but the remarkable group continued under conditions of relative autonomy with Operation Butterfly (see chapter 7).

As former operative Janet Love puts it, the imperatives that prompted Operation Vula are impossible to rank: locating high leadership within the country, rebuilding underground networks, conserving the means of insurrection, hiding caches of arms, and providing a directive role to "all clandestine domestic political, military, ordnance, logistics, communications, security and intelligence work at regional level," to be slowly scaled to the national level.[54] Mac was the mastermind, although others would play key roles, particularly Ivan in Lusaka and Tim Jenkins in London. Only after I pressed him did Ivan admit, "I coordinated the Vula project. I reported to Joe Slovo and O. R. Tambo."

After a 1986 meeting in Lusaka at which the idea of locating NEC members in South Africa was raised, and after careful persuasion of Tambo, Slovo, Zuma, and Chris Hani, the NEC gave Tambo a "blank check" to form a highly secretive special committee concerning the movement of unspecified NEC members into the country, without the need to report back to the NEC. That evening, Tambo and Slovo went to Mac's house and tasked him with a concept paper, which they debated, particularly on the communications system. In late 1986 or early 1987, they asked him to enter the country with Gebuza as his deputy; Ronnie Kasrils would follow in 1990, and Hani would take a similar path to the Western Cape. The "legend" in the NEC was that Mac was in the hospital in Moscow for the next few years, Gebuza was on a Soviet military training course, and Kasrils was in a cast in a Vietnamese hospital. Much to his consternation, Joe Modise, head of MK, was among those kept in the dark.

Mac described to me his last meeting with Tambo in Lusaka. He and Gebuza stood at attention as Tambo reportedly said, "I'm appointing you [Mac] commander, and I'm appointing you [Gebuza] deputy commander. This is your task. And the only failure I'm going to accept is that you return to Lusaka alive." After accepting, Mac asked to see Tambo privately; they went into an alcove, where Mac recalled saying, "I don't want you to answer this question. You have a thirty-man NEC with twenty-six Africans, but you're sending *me* to Natal and Gauteng. Natal is riddled with the Indian-African problem. Why didn't you pick an African? Whatever answer you give me is going to be the wrong answer. . . . But are you really grappling with the problem?"[55]

The story of Vula is exciting because in many ways it was a success. After building a new set of underground networks to spirit arms and exiles into the country, including Mac, Gebuza, Kasrils, Love, and others, it established a rudimentary electronic messaging system with first-generation laptop computers brought into the country by an airline stewardess connected to the Dutch Anti-Apartheid Movement, then upgraded to calculators held up to pay phones relaying encoded messages across South Africa, London, and Lusaka. One of Vula's greatest feats was to connect the imprisoned Mandela to Tambo during the delicate period of negotiation, through messages spirited out by Mandela's lawyer, encoded by Mac, and relayed electronically to Tim in North London, who then conveyed decrypted messages to Tambo in Lusaka. Tim and Ivan, subdued men under intense pressure, were at the heart of the entire enterprise.

Ivan went into the country first for three months in 1986 "to understand what is going on, create units." This was during the second state of emergency, so he had to be extremely careful. "Tees" had set up a safe house in a basement in Reservoir Hills, their "main base." Ivan recalls going into Merebank a few times at night to meet people. He recalls quite a bit of underground political activity in the Indian areas of Tongaat and Merebank, as well as in Pietermaritzburg, and in Coloured areas of Newlands East and Asherville. He speaks of "scores of cells in different parts of the country," some set up independently and then linked to Mac later, for instance, in the Cape. Parts of earlier units that had not been exposed, for instance, from Operation Butterfly, were pulled into what almost nobody knew of as Vula.

Tim Jenkins had been recruited by Kasrils while the former was on a family vacation to London in 1974. Back in Cape Town, Tim and his friend Stephen Lee planted leaflet bombs for two years before they were captured and sentenced in 1978. Before arriving at Pretoria Central Prison, Tim had quietly planned his escape; at the workshop, just by looking into keyholes, he made working wooden keys not just for his cell but for practically every keyhole he and his coconspirators might encounter, using a device to look into a keyhole from the outside. They had to work cage door by cage door, decoding each one, returning to their cell each night to begin again. One day, they simply walked out, then walked across the border. In London, Tim was a natural at training underground operatives, and the ideal person to fashion an encryption system for Vula at the dawn of the digital age.

When I met him, Tim was presenting a paper on cryptocurrencies at Keith Hart's human economy workshop at the University of Pretoria. He thought he still had the Vula computer with all the material on it, another indication of a passing era. In February 1987 Mac and Tim met in Lusaka and found themselves in agreement about the importance of means of communication. Old means of deciphering code messages were painstakingly slow and difficult in conditions of hiding. Personal computers were becoming programmable, and Tim experimented with using touch-tone phones to relay sounds internationally. Mac brought Tim into Vula.

Conny Braam, central in the Dutch Anti-Apartheid Movement, met Mac in Amsterdam to discuss Vula and to begin recruiting fresh operatives, including air hostess Antoinette Vogelsang, who could carry material like the first-generation portable computer without being screened at the airport. In her account of Vula, Braam describes meeting Ebie in Lusaka in 1986 after the capture of Passtoors and de Jonge, when he and Kasrils asked her whether she could find "foreign" people who might move to the Frontline

States to provide cover for them and arrange safe houses.[56] She then went to Mozambique to await Ebie's arrival from South Africa, where law professor and activist Albie Sachs took her and Zimbabwean African People's Union cadre Jeremy Brickhill to swim in the sea at a beach free of land mines; she also met Joy Harnden, who was unmasked as a spy in 1989. In 1987 Brickhill was seriously injured by a car bomb in Harare; in 1988 Sachs was maimed in a similar attack at the same beach. Braam traveled back via Lusaka to get plaster imprints of activists' teeth to make disguises; the plaster imprints were stolen in a Rome transit lounge. Before the end of the year, Ebie was captured. Braam's implication is that Ebie's 1986 movements were related to Vula, but Mac disagrees. In April 1987 Mac contacted her and went to Amsterdam to discuss disguises that might allow leadership to survive unrecognized in South Africa for long periods, perhaps for years.

In August 1987 Mac and Gebuza entered South Africa illegally. Gebuza describes walking in disguise past security police at the airport in Swaziland. Antoinette smuggled various things undetected through both Amsterdam's Schiphol airport and Johannesburg's Jan Smuts airport; she passed the laptop on to Mac, and a couple of weeks later, the first messages reached Tim in London. In a short time, the system was automated, and information could be sent directly from the South African underground through Tim on to Lusaka. Tim remembers messages going back and forth each day, and then "day in and day out; everything had to be filtered through London." When the message went through, Love recalls, you would have to wait for a confirmation on a pager, which could take "three-quarters of an hour to two and a half hours." For the first time, dispersed activists could communicate fairly instantly. Public phones and Telcom phone cards, Mac recalls, allowed them to convey messages without creating a pattern. Tim describes his "grandstand view" of operations, including "the requirements, the dangers, the plans that people had for smuggling weapons or people into the country, the passwords that people were using" in his hub of connectivity.[57]

Mac thought it imperative to link Tambo in Lusaka as directly as possible with Mandela, who had been moved in 1988 from Robben Island to Victor Verster Prison near Cape Town, partly to isolate him from the networks on Robben Island. Tambo was extremely cautious, as it could jeopardize the long-term mission of Vula. Mac sent a small message through Mandela's lawyer, and he took the response to mean that Mandela understood that he was in the country. Tim says of the very first report from Mandela transmitted through digital covert means, "There was no warning that this kind of message was going to come." Janet recalls, "When I was retyping the handwritten notes of Madiba [Mandela's clan name used with respect], the reality of that just was so incredibly strong." The importance of this channel, Tim explains, was that while the apartheid regime may have presumed that it was engaging in "talks" with an individual, Mandela was now talking on behalf of the organization. Mac puts it more strongly: "Without this communication system, the apartheid regime was sitting on an issue where they could divide the movement into fragments, and set us at war with each other. Mandela would have been seen as a sellout. And we would have bedlam in the struggle ranks."[58]

Mac left South Africa in late July or early August 1989, advised by Tambo to meet him, Ivan, and Slovo in Moscow, and then went to Lusaka to discuss Kasrils's return. While Mac was in London, Tambo had a stroke. Meanwhile, Walter Sisulu and other key political prisoners were released and went to Lusaka to discuss what release meant. Mac returned to South Africa early in 1990. On February 2, 1990, F. W. de Klerk unbanned the ANC, Pan Africanist Congress, and SACP. On February 11, Mandela was released. Kasrils entered South Africa illegally at the end of the month. Vula operatives remained underground, deepening networks and hiding caches of arms around the country because, according to Tim, "most of us didn't trust what was going on. We thought this was a ruse to get us all back into South Africa, and then they'd just arrest us all. So, we continued."

Kasrils's perspective was that weapons remained important as the regime continued to foment proxy wars against ANC-aligned activists. In contrast, Mac emphasizes that Vula's key role was "to convince the underground by political discussion" of the importance of shifting tactics in a time of negotiation.[59] In other words, there were internal tensions about Vula's imperatives. Mac spoke to me about Tambo's advice: "In the past, Mac, we have been trying to run before we crawl. I do not want Vula to do that. Stick to your mandate; root yourself politically; create the conditions for military." Others thought otherwise. Mac recalls, "Billy Nair drove me around [Durban] and showed me the torture room at C. R. Swart [police station]; he said 'that's what you need to blow up,' and I said that's not what I'm here for." A few years later, "Ronnie [Kasrils] sends a request within one month of being here" for the release of a certain number of AK-47s to attack Inkatha warlords at a mass march. Mac refused and instead asked for details of where the information was gathered. Billy Nair went to Mac and said, "What are you doing here? Why are you in the country? Fuck off!" Mac responded that he could stop the march without killing innocent lives and that if instead he had released arms, the police could "clean out the area, all your snipers are dead before the march starts," and what will be remembered is the tragedy that ensues. He had Ronnie and Gebuza meet with the Durban RPMC, and they stayed up all night debating the politics of his return.

Anthea Jeffery argues that Mac read Vietnamese revolutionary theory from Giáp, as well as Hoàng Văn Thái and Văn Tiến Dũng, which is why Mac states that Vula's primary aim was "to build the long-term capability of MK to fight a protracted people's war" and that the massive stockpiling of matériel and the escalation of political killings, also of Inkatha leaders, in KwaZulu and Natal between 1988 and 1990 support this objective.[60] There were internal debates about the role of the insurrectionist moment, to be sure. Yet the ANC's disinclination to disband MK after the onset of negotiations meant that the legal return of combatants combined with the smuggling of arms through Vula offered MK what Jeffery calls a Trojan horse, a continued means of waging war under the cover of its end; this was also consistent with Giáp's strategy.[61]

Moe thinks back to this period as one of "jostling for power within the ANC" as decisions about leadership were made without recognition of underground structures, which was probably extremely disconcerting to the activists who were continuing to risk their lives. In May 1989 twenty senior members in the SACP, including Vula leadership, convened an underground conference at Tongaat. Moe's view was that Operation Eagle was undetected by the state.[62]

Between May and June, Mac and Kasrils, now granted indemnity, were instructed to leave the country and return legally, having recovered from their ailments in Moscow and Vietnam. Gebuza, as Mac's deputy, was left in charge and began to connect with Vula operatives in the Western Cape.

Dipak Patel (Taps) was twenty-five years old in 1989 and had finished two years of university, had qualified as an engineer, and was working at South African Breweries alongside life underground since the age of sixteen or seventeen. At this point, he became a full-time activist and was tasked by the Durban RPMC headed by PG to shelter a courier, Mac, posing as Dipak's uncle Lara, and to make all necessary arrangements for him. Dipak perceived about twenty-eight independent lines of communication from political and military underground cells out of the country and thought that "Vula's mandate . . . was to rationalize these lines of communication and command to ensure that whatever strategy was chosen . . . there would be a coherence in command." In his view, this was consistent with Gebuza becoming the head of Vula military in Natal, and Dipak shifting to work with him to prepare for insurrection. He is open and articulate about the difficulties: "We had a political sense that MK and the political underground together would take this country," though it was less clear what their relationship to the mass movement would be. To add to this, he describes a deep sense of contradiction as he arranged for the movements of weapons and of Soviet-trained combatants at the precise moment that de Klerk announced the unbanning, and again when Mac, commander of Vula, disappeared and reappeared openly, indemnified and on television.[63]

Around July 8, 1990, two Vula operatives in Durban, Mbuso Shabalala and Charles Ndaba, were captured, probably tortured, killed, and thrown into the Tugela River; this was not known at the time, and much remains murky, but five members of the Security Branch received amnesty under the Truth and Reconciliation Commission (TRC) process for their unlawful arrest, detention, and murder and for unlawful disposal of remains and failure to report these deaths.[64] Whether Ndaba was an informer, as alleged by the Security Branch, or whether he cracked under torture, as Mac argues, the Security Branch came to know of a set of safe houses, as well as the car in which they arrested a disguised Gebuza. On July 11, Tim in London lost contact with Gebuza and was worried about the key disks and files. Through more interrogation the Security Branch found another safe house on July 14, with a treasure trove of unencrypted key disks, codes, passwords, phone numbers on an acoustic modem, and links to pagers and voicemails. The entire operation was blown open. Tim quickly shifted to damage control, salvaging the network in twenty-four hours, changing codes and passwords. Mac and Kasrils, back in the country legally, rushed to Durban, thinking matters had been contained.[65]

Meanwhile, a section of the Vlakplaas torture camp was transformed into a counterintelligence site as the apartheid regime came to understand the enormity of Operation Vula. De Klerk's government turned to familiar tropes of red-baiting, and it tried to turn Mandela against Mac by insinuating that this was a communist plot to eliminate him; they did not realize that Mandela had known about Vula for quite a while. Arrests continued. Mac's indemnity was flouted, and he was arrested on July 25 and physically interrogated. Kasrils went back underground; Janet went deeper underground, keeping Vula communication going. Mac and seven comrades faced the court, charged with terrorism, on October 29; they were released on bail that November, and the following March, nine trialists along with Ronnie were indemnified against prosecution.[66] Finally, on June 22, 1991, Mandela released a statement recognizing Operation Vul'indlela, naming Ronnie Kasrils, Vuso Shabalala, Charles Nqakula, Janet Love, Christopher Manye, Moe Shaik, Solly Shoke, Mpho Scott, Ivan Pillay, and Jabu Sithole; he demanded to know the fate of Ndaba and Mbuso Shabalala; and he named Mac internal commander of the External Mission's last operation.[67]

Tim recalls the crucial lesson of Vula as being about strong communications. The communications network continued to function until mid-1991, but much of this heroic work remains unrecorded. And yet the pressure of this extraordinary event was perhaps felt in the civic movement.

"We Unbanned the ANC on the Street"

After the banning and repression of the UDF in 1987, its affiliates, including DHAC, joined forces with the Congress of South African Trade Unions to form the Mass Democratic Movement in 1989.[68] While DHAC had been forced to work through Indian and Coloured civic organizations, the Mass Defiance Campaign provided an opportunity to plan a joint action with civic organizations from African townships. The 1989 march for "Housing For All in a People's City" along with "A Non-Racial Democratic City Council" was in keeping with Congress ideology, and it was explicit in its call: "Away with Apartheid." The march was banned at the last moment, but the crowd marched down West Street all the same, confronting riot police with tear gas and batons, and DHAC and other civic structures announced the formation of a new movement called the Durban Civic Movement.[69] Bonhomme, who had signed many of DHAC's press statements and remains visually present in pamphlets while also working underground, said to me unequivocally, "We unbanned the ANC on the street. That huge march was full of ANC flags and banners, in 1989, *before* the unbannings!" This flyer (figures 8.7 and 8.8) portrays the Freedom March of September 1989 as testimony to this popular unbanning of apartheid.

Rejecting apartheid—"Away with the Racist City Council," "Away with Apartheid"—the flyer grounds anti-apartheid politics in urban struggles against squatting, homelessness, rents, and rates. The timing is important, in the wake of the fall of the Berlin Wall, at a time of possibility in Poland, Hungary, Czechoslovakia, and Hungary, and before the dissolution of the Soviet imperium. In this interregnum, the pamphlet poses an anti-apartheid politics that is also an early critique of neoliberalism—"Privatisation Is Not the Answer"—while it leaves the door open for a "People's City" to come.

The work of DHAC continued after the unbanning of the ANC in 1990; it wrote against the government's Co-ordinating Council for Local Authorities, which sought local government restructuring without consultation with communities or the democratic movement. The uncertain future of

DURBAN CIVIC MOVEMENT

JOIN THE MARCH FOR

HOUSING FOR ALL
IN A
PEOPLE'S CITY

THOUSANDS ON THE FREEDOM MARCH - SEPTEMBER 1989

MARCH ON 2 DECEMBER 1989
FROM: ST EMMANUEL CATHEDRAL
10:00 AM

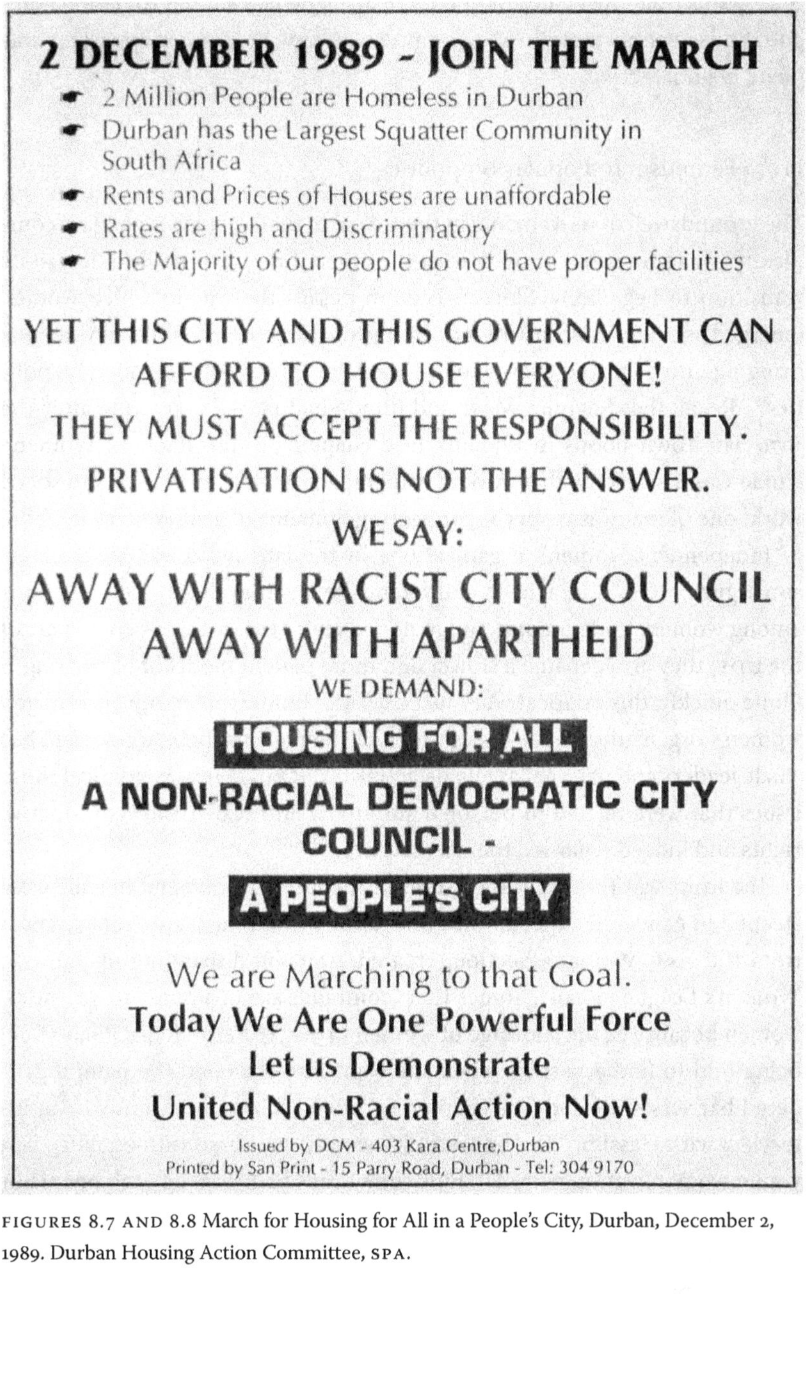

2 DECEMBER 1989 - JOIN THE MARCH

- 2 Million People are Homeless in Durban
- Durban has the Largest Squatter Community in South Africa
- Rents and Prices of Houses are unaffordable
- Rates are high and Discriminatory
- The Majority of our people do not have proper facilities

YET THIS CITY AND THIS GOVERNMENT CAN AFFORD TO HOUSE EVERYONE!

THEY MUST ACCEPT THE RESPONSIBILITY.

PRIVATISATION IS NOT THE ANSWER.

WE SAY:

AWAY WITH RACIST CITY COUNCIL
AWAY WITH APARTHEID

WE DEMAND:

HOUSING FOR ALL

A NON-RACIAL DEMOCRATIC CITY COUNCIL -

A PEOPLE'S CITY

We are Marching to that Goal.
Today We Are One Powerful Force
Let us Demonstrate
United Non-Racial Action Now!

Issued by DCM - 403 Kara Centre, Durban
Printed by San Print - 15 Parry Road, Durban - Tel: 304 9170

FIGURES 8.7 AND 8.8 March for Housing for All in a People's City, Durban, December 2, 1989. Durban Housing Action Committee, SPA.

local government occupied DHAC as its members debated the "redefining of [metropolitan] boundaries" and the "redistribution of wealth of the city."[70] But by this time the center of gravity of struggle had shifted to national negotiations over postapartheid government. A new hegemonic apparatus was being negotiated.

From Feminism to Popular Biopolitics

The groundswell of movements in the 1980s, in their gender/race/class complexity, was somewhat at odds with the aims of the External Mission in its transition to hegemony. Shireen Hassim details the way in which women emerged as a political constituency alongside the civic and labor movements, bringing unrecognized energy to the quest for "grassroots" democratic politics.[71] Recall that Shamim Meer and others had played a key role after the 1976 Tin Town floods in Phoenix (see chapter 6). The Phoenix Women's Circle was inspired by this work of bringing feminist commitments to social work, one of many attempts at connecting domains of gendered oppression.

Independent women's organizations in the late 1970s and 1980s, Hassim argues, were "nonracial in a different way" as they debated the relations among women, trade unions, and male-led civics that would become part of the UDF; they also debated a slower and more patient model of organizing.[72] Quite quickly, this political work faced a set of limits: leadership encouraged women's organizing under the strategy of the path to "people's power," but "male leaders and nationalist female activists did not define as political those issues that were related to personal autonomy and sexual and reproductive rights and indeed regarded them as divisive."[73]

The irony was that activist cultures in the underground and in exile were steeped in gendered expectations, obligations, and injustices. A 1987 report from the ANC Women's Section, created after the disbanding of the ANC Women's League in exile, argues that "comrades are in a hurry to 'privatize' women because of the shortage of women in MK."[74] Recall Rajes Pillay (Rae) being told to find a partner when she went into exile and the painful gendered barriers she faced (see chapter 7). Albie Sachs put it bluntly in an interview with Hassim: "The line was 'it's simple, we agree with equality.' But young women wanting scholarships sometimes had to sleep with people or could be given tasks on the assumption that women are available as sexual partners."[75] One woman in the underground describes how a group of female comrades put their stories together and realized that they all shared experiences of rape or near-rape violence. She also recalls the sense that certain women had to be available when senior members of the ANC came through the country illegally. In the light of pervasive gender-based violence within movement culture, the role of autonomous and nonracial women's activism was crucial to the 1980s conjuncture, pulling it away from the militarism and masculinism enshrined in the moment of insurrection.

This is the context in which the Durban Women's Group, in which Shamim was active, rejected the division of grounded community struggles from the broader political struggle; in doing so, Shamim, Phumelele Ntombela-Nzimande, and other women were self-consciously challenging the division of political and apolitical activity. These debates continued after the formation of the Natal Organisation of Women (NOW) in Durban in 1981; one side favored building up from communities with strong working-class leadership and women's agendas, and another side, with support from the ANC underground, favored explicit political organization of women in the national liberation struggle; the latter view prevailed. Some, like Hassim, noticed that NOW's mobilizing strategy was quite similar to the efforts of the Inkatha Women's Brigade. The strategic decision of NOW brought it closer to the dynamics of the Durban UDF, and its leadership were subject to extreme repression as a consequence.

Multiple strands of women's activism persisted in the country through this period. An important moment was the UDF Women's Congress of April 1987, convened by Pregs Govender, which articulated a comprehensive gendered critique and plan for rehabilitation of the UDF, were it to take women comrades and gender politics seriously. The External Mission had a parallel set of internal struggles for the recognition of women as equals in the movement, with an important submission from the Women's Section to the Kabwe Conference. However, these currents battled against a shared hierarchical, militarist, and masculinist form of organization central to the political imagination of many in leadership.[76]

I have suggested that UDF networks drew on biopolitical expertise when expedient. Some militant women thinkers were doing this in a different, more organic, and more radical way. Francie Lund arrived in Wentworth in 1970. She had grown up with some politicization through her mother, who had been involved in the Liberal Party and in Black Sash, and whose friends had been detained. Francie finished a degree in social work but was not drawn to clinical social work as it did not attend to the causes of health injustice. Instead, she spent time in "a very radical community health hospital" in Scotland. Eight months in Wentworth in 1970–71 was her first time engaging community health in the context of "something called 'the gangs.'" She left for further study in community development at Manchester, after which she returned to Cape Town as a community organizer. This is when she embarked on something quite remarkable: the first community self-survey in South Africa, centered on Coloured housing, in 1978, "using a data collection exercise for mobilization . . . it was Saul Alinsky and Paolo Freire, these were the gurus who sat on our shoulders."

While involved in the early learning movement, connected to mass democratic organization, Francie "interviewed a whole lot of community leaders: political activists under the guise of being community workers." She also began to see the difference between Coloured townships in Cape Town and Durban and why the issues surrounding the 1976 Theron Commission did not travel to Durban. Named for lead investigator Erika Theron, a professor at the University of Stellenbosch who began her career with a master's thesis that was background research for the Carnegie Commission on the poor white question (see chapter 3), the Theron Commission looked in parallel ways at Coloured deprivation in the aftermath of the Tricameral system. Francie saw connections between places like Wentworth and Zululand, as the 1970s saw people dispossessed by the homeland system, de-Africanized, classified as Coloured, and moved to Wentworth and to other parts of working-class Durban (see chapter 2).

When Francie returned to Durban in 1981, she found "every single day a shock in terms of the difference in the politics." One thing that struck her was the starkness of racial discourse, with terms like *kaffir* and *coolie* used within activist circles, but also "a much more pragmatic politics." Her assigned guide to community groups, who would become an important friend, was Vish Supersad, an important connection to the External Mission with a much lower public profile than others in leadership around him. Francie started teaching at UND, where she met Lawrence Schlemmer, once a part of the Rick Turner night university, who had also been part of a community survey in Sparks Estate with Foszia Fisher and Henry Africa. Schlemmer had just been appointed to the Buthelezi Commission on the future of the Kwa-Zulu homeland; Gatsha Buthelezi had asked him to head the Inkatha Institute in 1975, but in the 1980s the divide between those working with Inkatha, supported by the regime and sharply against the ANC, and those allied to the Congress tradition was widening; as Francie puts it, "The polarization [at UND] was made as Sutcliffe on one side and Schlemmer on the other."

The major issue, in Francie's view, was what to make of the question of international sanctions against corporations in South Africa: "Should they disinvest or stay and leave behind a big fund for liberation or African betterment;

Buthelezi would have been on the side of capital." Schlemmer constructed a survey that set up questions as centered on the loss of jobs, "and Lawrie was a better researcher," she says regretfully, noting that the interests of sugar and timber capital were very strongly behind social science that might refute the case for sanctions. But Sutcliffe "did a survey at KwaMashu and turned the questions around, which was very clever." On the heels of this battle of surveys, Schlemmer's office was firebombed.

Francie also became involved in the Phoenix and Tongaat Health Screening Programmes, which she describes as "community mobilization for the movement outside the country for beginning to try and build a real grassroots platform with real participation of really poorer people, to move away from the elite politics" of the NIC leadership. She provided support for an independent community health self-study in Lamontville in 1982, she worked in neighboring Umlazi, and she worked with the prominent Ntsebeza family in Cala in the northern Transkei with what she calls "the only completely African grassroots primary health care project in the country," near the famous Ntsebeza bookshop and library. She describes long conversations with Lungisile Ntsebeza, who explained the "centralism" in "democratic centralism" that she had found so difficult in UDF leadership. She remembers "a stand-up fight with one of them at a workshop in Shepstone" Building at the University of Natal; when she refused to toe the line, the leader said, "You will be disciplined, Francie," to which she responded, "Discipline me, then," and walked out. Francie's view was that they were simply authoritarian with respect to rank-and-file activists, but in Cala, Lungisile got her to see that this was the centralism in democratic centralism, and she understood, "It's a whole approach, a whole ideology," which she rejected.

In 1986 Francie's mother called from Edendale Hospital in Pietermaritzburg, after the armed rescue of a captured comrade; as it turns out, this was the McBride unit from Wentworth (see chapter 9). Her mother had said, "I can't go to work anymore; there's blood everywhere." Francie took this metaphorically as well; Buthelezi had sent messages to the hospitals, and it seemed like a turning point in the political violence between the ANC and Inkatha. In retrospect, she thought "Edendale was a crucible for the worst that was coming down." By the late 1980s, one of Francie's friends had been murdered, and Francie's home was being used as a meeting place, a safe house, and a place to take affidavits on political violence. She was becoming vulnerable to the violence around her in new ways, and she had movement support to go to the London School of Economics to gain skills for reconstruction. In 1988 she was taken by Nkosazana Dlamini-Zuma to Lusaka to come up with the ANC's AIDS program. While she effectively moved to working at the national level in the late 1980s, taking her feminist insights to broader realms of social policy, she says, "What was really important for me was understanding that part of the success of the struggle was in the democratization, the learning that was going on in the trade unions, from the organizers to the shop stewards."

What is ingenious about Francie's thought is the way in which it pulls together the lessons of praxis in the domains of the independent unions, feminist groups, and community health work, gathering together a radical approach to a popular biopolitics. This commitment to expanding universal access to the means of life refuses the violent subordination of the tools of biopolitics to racial capitalism and sovereignty. This radical and popular bio-politics was the path not imagined, far from the masculinism and militarism at the forefront of the conjunctural moment of urban revolution.

Conclusion: Revolutionary Surplus

They were infiltrating everything. It was a very systematic organization, and very powerful to the point where it began to steer the NIC, it began to steer community movements, and then at some point began to formulate a strategy.
—BOBBY, on "the collective" in Durban in the 1980s

Bobby and Shamim had come of age in the theologico-political moment. Despite Bobby's banning order, they moved out of Merebank and worked with ANC-allied underground and aboveground groups in supportive ways, from about 1977 to 1982. Under surveillance, they met members of "the collective" steering the urban movements secretly at night. Bobby describes trying to read Stalin to fit into this group, but his prior education in liberation theology and BC thought made it impossible. At an everyday level, he felt "I'm dealing with conservative people."

Bobby's understanding of revolution was fundamentally different. "For me the question of democracy and openness was a principal issue. We were involved in theater and poetry and music." "The collective" just could not relate. Their political imagination was built through the tools of the insurrectionist conjuncture, with its blend of Cold War politics, masculinism, and vanguardism. In 1982 Bobby and Shamim broke away from "the collective" and concentrated their efforts on independent workers' and women's organizations. What remained in the aftermath of the urban movement was autonomous critical voices who sometimes made common cause with the political underground and the UDF but who also rethought communitarianism in the turbulent 1980s.

On the surface, 1980s Durban might seem to exemplify Henri Lefebvre's struggles for "the right to the city": "a cry and a demand [for] a transformed and renewed right to urban life."[77] The Campaign for a Democratic City might support this reading, and indeed geographer Jenny Robinson makes a brief appearance in DHAC records of this event. In the late 1980s, waves of young people turned to the Merebank Ex-Students Society, the MRA, the Wentworth Advice Centre, and a nascent environmental movement, in new formations of the urban movement. And while the urban movements did not fully articulate a vision of a different city, the fragments of this possibility remain present in struggles for spatial and environmental justice in Durban ever since, including in the alliance of the South Durban Community Environmental Alliance (SDCEA) and groundWork in the 2000s (see the introduction).

However, Lefebvre's notion of a right to urban life must be pried open for its internal tensions. While cities as socio-technical assemblages facilitate the movement of finance, people, things, and imaginations, they are also machines for social differentiation, exploitation, surveillance, and control. That urban formations might be primarily oriented to sustaining life is fundamentally utopian. Such cities do not exist. The question is how people imagine taking over the means of life, or the tools of biopolitics, for all urban denizens and for the environment. "Right to the city" does not adequately grasp this work of renovating the tools of biopolitics used to build the infrastructure of racial capitalism in order to dismantle it. Yet the critical renovation of biopolitics also requires democratizing the raced, gendered, and classed monopoly on biopolitical expertise. Black women who entered politics through social work, nursing, environmental advocacy, and related professions have been key agents of this work. They are the real secret agents of the democratic future.

South Africa of the 1970s and 1980s reminds us that the urban struggles in the context of racial capitalism also contained a demand by the oppressed to be human, a case that BC made early on and that feminists and workerists picked up in different ways. But these future rights to egalitarian selves and space have also at various moments been interpreted as the right to negate and destroy alongside the right to build or participate. For one group emerging from Wentworth, acts of sabotage and an infamous car bombing of two beachfront bars were part of this decidedly illiberal assertion of a right to destroy, but without the clear consolation that violence might be the midwife of a postracial order. This takes us to the fourth moment, and to Wentworth in the 1980s.

The Moment of the Disqualified, 1980s–2000s

A colonized people is not alone. In spite of all that colonialism can do, its frontiers remain open to new ideas and echoes from the world outside. It discovers that violence is in the atmosphere, that it here and there bursts out, and here and there sweeps away the colonial regime. . . . The great victory of the Vietnamese people at Điện Biên Phủ is no longer, strictly speaking, a Vietnamese victory. Since July, 1954, the question which the colonized peoples have asked themselves has been, "What must be done to bring about another Điện Biên Phủ? *How can we manage it?"* —FRANTZ FANON, *Wretched of the Earth*

Car Bomb on the Beachfront, June 14, 1986

Robert McBride and Matthew Lecordier drove the blue Ford Cortina from Wentworth. Greta Apelgren followed in her sister's Mazda, dressed for the evening. When they hit a bump along the coastal highway to the central business district, Robert slipped to Matthew that there were sixty kilograms of explosives in the boot. They stopped in town at West Street, outside the glass-fronted Hyperama House and Home. In her rearview mirror, Greta could see the young men in discussion. She assumed they were leaving the

Cortina there for other comrades to pick up. As they operated on a need-to-know basis, she had not felt it necessary to ask. Robert then joined her and asked her to drive the Mazda to the Marine Parade. They drove back and forth along the Durban beachfront, then returned to West Street. Robert got back into the Cortina, and they drove both cars to Pine Street, within walking distance from the beachfront. Robert then asked Greta to drive him back to the Marine Parade. Greta questioned Robert when he asked her to park the Mazda in a tight corner space next to the Parade Hotel across from the Why Not and Magoo's bars. When he insisted, she parked the car, and Robert left her, asking her to wait for him to return. A young man going into the Parade Hotel commented on the parked cars before realizing he was staring at a stern woman inside. Two other men tried to make small talk with her, to no avail. Fifteen minutes later, Robert returned with Matthew in the Cortina and signaled with his lights for her to leave her spot, which she did. Not knowing where to go, Greta parked on the next road. Robert and Matthew joined her a few minutes later, and Robert said, "Drive; we're going back home." A young flower seller crossed the street.[1]

Robert and Greta had come back into the country from Botswana three days earlier, just before President P. W. Botha's declaration of another state of emergency on June 12, 1986; like the state of emergency from July 20, 1985, to March 7, 1986, mass arrests of civic activists followed. The police had picked up Greta's brother and sister and were looking for her in her guise as a community activist. They were not looking for Robert, who had no activist profile. On leaving the beachfront, Robert realized that he had forgotten to fill the getaway car with petrol. They stopped at a petrol station on Beatrice Street, and Robert asked Greta to take a circuitous route up the steep Sydenham Road. At a clearing on the Berea Ridge, Robert asked Greta to stop, at which point she asked him, "Why, and why *here*?" He responded that from here they would be able to see the flames from the explosion. As it dawned on her that they had just set off a car bomb, Greta's first response was to ask whether they had time to get back down there. "As crazy as it sounds," she recalls, "you do get crazy in that situation." She looked back at Robert and Matthew and saw the two men were "totally drained, like they couldn't make any more decisions. They couldn't *do* anything. I took over from him and said, 'We are going home now.' And I decided which route and everything."

This is one of many versions of the event of June 14, 1986. By the next morning, the bombing of the Magoo's and Why Not bars at the Parade Hotel had made national headlines. Quickly, the event propelled a set of shapeshifting narratives: testimonials of injured survivors confronting the idea of enjoying a segregated beachfront in a state of emergency, statements from captured militants extracted through torture and intimidation, and changing versions of events repeated differently by members of the cell in trials, court-room appeals, Truth and Reconciliation Commission (TRC) hearings, and other postapartheid retrospections, including in interviews with me. The media barrage placed the members of this unit, particularly Robert McBride, in a singular state of infamy. Yet, through various controversies, he has been periodically supported from the highest echelons of the African National Congress (ANC).

Over the short period between 1984 and 1986, a self-organized anti-apartheid unit comprising young people from Wentworth had, through various twists of fate, become a Special Ops unit one person removed from Joe Slovo, head of the SACP. Members of this cell conducted furtive trips to Botswana to courier weapons, returning to conduct infrastructural sabotage, the booby-trapped murder of a high-ranking security policeman, the daring rescue of a captured comrade, and the car bombing of two beachfront bars. Oliver Tambo had made a statement following the Kabwe Conference of 1985, building on Võ Nguyên Giáp's advice in Vietnam, that distinctions be-tween "hard" and "soft" targets would disappear but that the ANC, unlike the South African Defence Force (SADF), would strive to avoid civilian casual-ties.[2] Responding to this call to intensify the struggle, multiple self-organized combat units began to spring up within South Africa; some, though not all, were recruited by trained cadres from outside who brought small caches of weapons to "dead letter boxes" (secret hiding places) to enable acts of "armed propaganda."[3] Locating their actions on this broader terrain, members of the McBride cell refuse the infamy they are consigned to for actions that the media reduce to "the Magoo's bombing," linked to white civilian casualties, while Black casualties of other attacks, including car bombs and cross-border attacks, are not remembered with the same pathos. Modes of reckoning with "Magoo's" remain hopelessly racialized.

The emergence of this cell goes also back to a specific milieu in Wentworth, to its street gangs and outlaw cultures, and to a different set of processes and citations. While the underground tried to make militants by circulating banned literature and by teaching Cold War technologies of countersurveil-lance, a distinct political tendency in Wentworth drew on the theologico-political and insurrectionist moments while refusing to be disciplined by the leadership of the urban revolution. This is when Merebank's and Went-worth's articulations to the struggle took decisively different paths. While Merebank's networks converged in a concerted strategy of urban revolution, from the United Democratic Front (UDF) to Operation Vula, the Wentworth cell was part of a conjuncture that I call *the moment of the disqualified.*

My argument is that the moment of the disqualified cut through the visceral boundary between politics and crime in diasporic Blackness, demanding a more encompassing freedom than that envisioned by the urban revolution. Wentworth's history of racialization prepared some residents to engage struggles for social justice through the psychic wounds of racism in a way that pushed against Congress nonracialism as well as coalitional Black politics to confront the philosophical problem of ontologizing Blackness, even for ostensibly militant ends. For some young people, the only way to confront the racial ontologization of space and personhood was through spectacular sabotage: by literally blowing this racial reality to smithereens. For others, it was a figurative shooting back with a camera, to produce aesthetic objects for critical reflection about the enduring problem of racial ontology that persists in postapartheid times.

Unlike the other three moments, I name this *the moment of the disqualified* not for what it lacks but for what it faces directly, the relation among Blackness, negation, and revolution. Indeed, if the point of revolution is to abolish, it is important to consider these saboteurs and photographers in relation for their divergent but interrelated engagements with forms of praxis that remain, for the most part, forgotten and unvalorized. Yet both forms reflect painful modes of reckoning with enduring racial and spatial injustice in South Africa today. By turning in different ways to the blurring of crime and politics, both forms stretch the revolution beyond the fight over sovereignty, capital, and territoriality, to embodied and psychic decolonization.

I will argue that photographers Cedric Nunn and Peter McKenzie in particular return to their negatives to show us the enduring power of critique from those who refuse to be disqualified. In the process, these photographic critics construct an audiovisual blues form that helps us see beyond the nihilist specter of a self-and-other-destroying race war. I conclude with environmental justice as also a part of this attention to slow violence in the lived environment, an attention that remains both widely recognized and powerfully disqualified, as witnessed in the opening lines of this book.

After a period on the run, most members of the cell linked to Robert McBride were captured and tried. On receiving a death sentence, twenty-three-year-old Robert turned to the gallery with these astonishingly bold words, reminiscent of Nelson Mandela's statement at the dock: "I have taken you quite a distance along the road. Freedom is just around the corner. I am leaving you at the corner, and you must take that corner to find freedom on the other side." Led out of the courtroom, Robert raised his fist and shouted, "The struggle continues till Babylon falls!"

Prelude to Infamy, or Stretching the Revolution

Babylon system is the vampire
Sucking the children day by day.
Babylon system is the vampire
Sucking the blood of the sufferers.
Building church and university
Deceiving the people continually . . .
—BOB MARLEY, "Babylon System"

When I spoke to him, Robert had a high-profile job at the South African Department of Home Affairs.[4] As we approached the event of the car bomb, he turned to the leadership's mythic 1979 trip to Vietnam, where, as he put it, they received "the blueprint for people's war," beginning with politicization through "armed propaganda" to "give people hope that there is a resistance, and it's right here in Wentworth." Following this script, Robert thought, "We were at the stage between armed propaganda and arming the masses; so, it's hit and run, it's clandestine, it's confrontation with the enemy; that's basically what we were up to." He reeled off the lessons of Vietnam, the formation of Special Ops, the *Green Book*, and the Kabwe Conference. By the time we spoke, he was seasoned in responding to strangers about his actions. He thought he had answered Frantz Fanon's question in the epigraph: "'What must be done to bring about another Điện Biên Phủ?'" What is not clear is how the movement "managed" his cell and its actions.

Importantly, when the twenty-three-year-old was led out of the court with his fist raised, his precise words, "The struggle continues till Babylon falls," cited other "ideas and echoes." Robert and the young men around him had looked to the most important diasporic Black intellectual engaged with African decolonization, Bob Marley.

In a thoughtful reading of Marley's oeuvre, Grant Farred poses him as the Black vernacular intellectual who spoke most closely to diasporic African suffering and solidarity, particularly in the intense years of 1977–80, in which he released the trilogy *Exodus*, *Survival*, and *Uprising*.[5] Marley had been exiled from Jamaica, and after his trips to Gabon and Ethiopia, with anticolonial and anti-apartheid struggles in Southern Africa in mind, his *Survival* abandons his earlier dichotomy of debauched Western "Babylon" contrasting a romanticized African "Zion."[6] Instead, he poses a dialectical, vampiric "Babylon System" "sucking the blood from the sufferers," the last word referencing the "rude boys" or petty gangsters of Kingston's Trenchtown, who had "redefined Kingston street life into a phantasmagoria of insolence."[7] Fanon famously argues that "Marxist analysis should always be slightly stretched every time we have to do with the colonial problem."[8] Marley stretches and internationalizes Black "sufferers" from Jamaica to Southern Africa. Hence, "Africa, Unite" sings Pan-Africanism while "moving right out of Babylon."[9] Youth in a Coloured township in Durban could hear the dialectical strains of *Survival* as meant for them, pulling them out of their carcerality in imagined articulation with a wide world of Trenchtownian sufferers. Robert had a banned copy of *Survival* that he acquired in 1982, the same year his mother gave him a licensed gun. He knew it well when he raised his fist to the "Babylonian" courtroom.

Robert had been part of a group of young men who sought refuge from the turf battles between small-time gangsters in Wentworth in the early 1980s. These young people experienced their neighborhood as saturated with Catholic, Anglican, and Pentecostal churches that for the most part toed the apartheid line, as did prominent schoolteachers and principals, several of whom had joined the Labour Party or supported the Tricameral Parliament. Marley's *Survival* sang precisely of Black solidarity to these young people in a township still reeling from the effects of apartheid's forced removals, saturated by the painful repression of actually vibrant histories of movement.

Wentworth's population grew after the construction of flats in the 1970s and through waves of people forced to move from various parts of Durban. In the wake of dispossession, young men forged what Clive Glaser calls "overlapping personal and territorial familiarity" in street gangs tied to microterritory.[10] Map 9 reconstructs the gang turf of the 1970s and 1980s, including that of the Drain Rats of Assegai and the K-1 Trucks of SANF (the former housing of the South African Naval Force, extending down to Adam's Shop; see chapter 2), and their archenemies, the Woodstock Vultures, across Austerville Drive and down to Woodville Road. Wentworth's street gangs were in some ways like their counterparts in the Cape Flats, or Soweto's *tsotsis* who participated in the 1976 rebellion, but Wentworth gangs are remembered only on one side of the boundary between crime and politics.[11]

According to local lore, the Vultures and the Trucks were once one gang that split in 1976–77. Former Vulture Allan recalled, "The fight actually started by the Trucks coming [to Woodstock] and interfering with the people," and someone "slept with some of the guys' sisters." I asked Allan about the legendary Sly, who terrorized people with a sword. Allan laughed, "He broke it in a fight!

But we all had swords or bush knives [large hunting knives]. We made some, bought some, some were found; [garbage] bin lids were our shields! Little bricks, bottles, those were the weapons." There were petty intrigues: "The Destroyers aligned themselves with us 'cause they were fighting the Drain Rats, who were aligned with the Trucks." Terrence describes "gangsterism" in Wentworth of the mid-1970s as so bad that when "a terrible gangster" called Abu died, "everybody came to the funeral to make sure he was dead, the bastard!" Robert grew up in Drain Rat territory, and his early memories are of perilous journeys through Destroyer territory to get to Fairvale High School, down by the oil refinery, or through Vulture territory to get to his dad's workshop.

Wentworth stories of the 1970s center on street gang skirmishes with swords or bush knives and intimidation of residents. These violent attacks included routine sexual violence against women in the community. And as money poured in from Wentworth's industrial migrants employed in building the SASOL II (1980) and SASOL III (1982) oil refineries, gangs invested in guns and became part of Durban's lucrative drug trade. Ivan recalls looking from exile at a newspaper with a "headline that said that Wentworth was the most violent place in South Africa at the time, in 1979–80. And it's a very small place!"

The remembrance of gangsterism past is permeated by forced removals, itinerant industrial labor, conflict over disposable earnings, fractured families, violence against women, the deepening drug economy, and the emergence of powerful drug lords. Causal lines crisscross in a powerful web of explanation that conveys that there was no way out. Explanation mimics the form of a carceral space as if cut off from the rest of the city, which afforded 1980s Wentworth a quasi-sovereignty bolstered by news accounts of a lawless place ruled by gangs, ripe for the petty authoritarianism of school, church, and police: agents of the "Babylon System."

This was in marked contrast to Merebank, where Indian progressivism and intergenerational civic activism drew in Indian youth into various forms of organizing work, through which they could perceive their everyday spatial practice as part of a postapartheid city and country to come. As we have seen, some Wentworth youth joined these networks through the United Committee of Concern (UCC) and the UDF, through figures like Virgille Bonhomme, Jean Manning ("Mrs. Manning"), Pravin Gordhan (PG), and Moe Shaik. Some young women from prominent local families became activists through professional lives as social workers or university students. The absorption of some into the moment of urban revolution clarifies those who took a different path.

The tendency I identify here centers on young people in Wentworth drawn into struggle networks while facing the long and painful legacies of working-class Coloured life in Durban. Reading Wentworth in the mirror of Merebank clarifies the way in which this milieu was shaped by an experience of transience and rootlessness, not as racial or anthropological essence, but rather as a philosophical problem that residents have had to face. The consequence has been a distinctive set of political innovations forged through the experience of exclusion or negation, with much wider significance.

Returning to the group around Robert, Allan moved from Woodstock to Ogle Road, from Vulture to Young Destroyer territory. He befriended Matthew, Antonio, Robert, and three others, including "the guy that spilled on them." They met in the backyard shack of Allan's relative's home on Ogle Road, where "the guys used to come just for the pleasure of sitting, smoking, music." This is where they met Bob Marley and the Wailers and honed their refusal of the Babylon System. As Wayne put it, "Growing up in the area, you could see the racism and thuggery, it was coming from *somewhere*. There were people who were responsible for socioeconomic problems that were caused by the state. They were responsible for *everything*."

A year after Robert obtained the album *Survival* and a licensed gun, in 1983, Ricky shared with Robert, and others in the group, US Black revolutionary George Jackson's prison letters, *Soledad Brother*. Little did they know that Robert would mastermind an operation to free a captured comrade not unlike Jonathan Jackson's attempt to free George Jackson from the Marin County courthouse. Robert had had a few run-ins with gangs in the late 1970s, but in 1983 he got into more intense altercations, including one in which he shot another young man dead. These events established the group of young men around Robert as a countergang, not immune to the violence of street gangs, but with space to dwell through Marley and Jackson on a different set of possibilities. This was a rougher version of the countercultural space forged in the basement of the Presbyterian church in Merebank a decade prior (see chapter 6), quite different in class, gender, and race, and it would alter the lives of this cohort of young people.

Meanwhile, school boycotts and organizing associated with the urban movements of the 1980s were drawing in many young people in Wentworth. Vincent, Marcel, Wayne, Kevin, Marson, Gaster, and others became part of the student movement; they formed Wentworth's chapter of the Congress of South African Students (COSAS) and came into contact with student activists from across the country. Vincent also connected with underground operatives involved in a failed attempt at sabotaging a polling station for the Tricameral Parliament elections; two uMkhonto we Sizwe (MK) activists were killed when a limpet mine went off early, and one bloodied comrade went directly to Vincent's home. One would think that this would have exposed him to the police, but this would give too much credence to surveillance.

Things happened quickly between 1984 and 1986. Renditions vary widely, sometimes of necessity. Wayne said to me: "The activities of what happened where are still a mystery to some of us. We done what we had to do, and that's it. It's not beneficial to me that you know everything that I know. It's a hard thing just talkin' about because . . . some people are living in that whole setup where they believe that what they fought for they've achieved, and others believe what they fought for they never achieved. And there still might have to be another struggle to get what people initially set out to achieve. For different people, it's different things." This is precisely what a spatiotemporal dialectical method helps illuminate, that "for different people, it's different things." Some young people drawn from Wentworth's outlaw culture found opportunities to tap into the moment of insurrection seemingly on their own terms, a proclamation of popular sovereignty made possible by Wentworth's isolation as a carceral geography. Others took routes similar to young people in Merebank. Several young women forged key roles in social and community work, particularly through the Wentworth Improvement Programme (WIP) in Assegai. Sisters Greta and Jeanette Apelgren, and their brother Eric, became active in church-affiliated work that drew in and inspired a lot of young people in the township to start youth groups, a very important moment for a lot of young women and men, and also a way of shifting focus from the territorial power of gangs.

Greta went to the University of the Western Cape to study social work, where she became involved with Black Consciousness (BC) and anti-apartheid political culture in Cape Town. She went out with "a Muslim guy [who] was part of a military group that went to blow up offices and burn down classrooms." When she came back, she worked as a social worker across "the length and breadth of this township, but mostly in the poorest areas, the flats and the semidetached houses," and she describes "the drinking to cope with the sadness and anger" of torn families in Wentworth in the 1970s, but also "violence and aggression, all the sexual abuse, physical abuse." From family casework, she moved to community work in 1981, and after a year of health education in the new Coloured township of Newlands East, she moved to the child abuse unit at Addington Hospital.

Greta's politicization at Addington Hospital recalls Fanon's experience at Blida, with a gendered twist.[12] She recounts an incident when an African woman had a baby with a white man, and she was forced to give up "the very Coloured-looking child" while she was still breastfeeding him. Greta was put in the situation of facilitating the separation of mother and child; when the mother was resistant, she tried to help her relocate and keep the child, even helping her with food and clothing. A couple of months later, she found out that the mother had been imprisoned for killing a woman who tormented her for having a *boesman* ("bushman," or Coloured) child, after which she had to give up the child. "For some reason," Greta laughs nervously, "it affected me so badly, the child's screaming. . . . It was a turning point in my life. I said I will never be a human being if I don't burn apartheid, burn the system, destroy it. I was so, so [*pauses*], I want to say inspired, but I was so affected. There was no turning back." The pause is important. Greta cannot quite glorify violence, but she sees the systemic violence shaping the fraught relations of racialized motherhood, and she finds in this a moment of profane illumination about what is to be done if she is ever to "be a human being," which, in this context, she most certainly did not think she was.

Greta became involved in the anti-Tricameral movement, along with Jeanette and Eric. She worked on "alternative structures for the youth" as Wentworth of the early 1980s was "overtaken by the youth gang violence and the drug scene and the deaths every day." In time, youth leaders "used those structures to deal with the false consciousness of being 'Coloured.'" They organized interracial youth camps, connected with progressive figures in the church like Father Kerry, and became involved with the UCC (see chapter 8). In the last six months of 1985, with the repression and infiltration of the UDF, Greta "backed out of politics entirely." That is when Robert recruited her to be a "commissar." She laughed: "I think *commissar* is just a title given to people who move information and weapons; it sounds like a title like *general*, but it's not!"

Another group became involved in a communist-inspired youth structure called Youth Forum. Glen and Claudia, children of local Congress leader Jean Manning, had been part of the UCC, and Glen became the national treasurer of COSAS. When COSAS was banned in 1986, several of them went into hiding. Former COSAS activist Marcel said to me, "Our schooling wasn't that bad, Sharad. We had laboratories where we could do experiments. We were kept second class to the white man; it wasn't really as bad as the African schools. That's why COSAS couldn't grow here." When COSAS was banned, these young people regrouped as the Congress of Austerville Organised Students, abbreviated CAOS; he laughed, commenting, "It sounded like *chaos!*"

Meanwhile, the group listening to Marley, including Robert, Nazim, Allan, Matthew, and Marson, formed into a self-organized anti-apartheid unit. They trained on Highbury grounds by the oil refinery photographed by Cedric Nunn (figure P.1). At some point, some of them decided to set fire to a part of their high school, Fairvale. Robert had started at Bechet teachers' college, where he connected with Gordon Webster, who had taken a trip out of the country, made contact with the ANC, and become part of Special Ops. He recruited Robert formally, and they conducted several acts of industrial sabotage. Robert then recruited Greta to work with him to courier arms and other material from Botswana either for their own use or to hide in "dead letter boxes" (secret locations for caches) to use in future missions.

While the External Mission was trying to infiltrate the country to set up its own political infrastructure, militant groups like Robert's cell within South Africa were piecing together operations in their own ways. The event that captured the imaginations of many young activists in Durban and across the country was when Robert and his father, Derrick, orchestrated a daring rescue of Gordon, who had been shot and captured and was being held under military guard at Edendale Hospital outside Pietermaritzburg.

The group met at Derrick's Factorama workshop and planned the entire operation, with some in disguise and the theatrical Derrick dressed as a priest. They describe nurses cheering as they wheeled Gordon out of the hospital. But there were also Black casualties, as Inkatha's Buthelezi quickly noted. Some in the External Mission, including Chris Hani, supported the bravado of the escape; it was talked about in the MK camps as well as in activist circles around the country. Others found the adventurism too much of a break in the ranks, and a sign of missing leadership within the country; this was how some in the leadership also saw the car bombing.

Mike Davis argues that the car bomb is "the poor man's nuclear weapon," relatively inexpensive, yet surprisingly destructive and loud, as indiscriminate as the aerial bombs used by advanced democracies, leaving little forensic evidence while providing a voice for marginal and even ad hoc groups.[13] This formulation fits the McBride cell well, as a group of young men with tenuous connections to the exiled movement and sporadic political education pulled off an event with lasting emotional effects in South Africa. Certainly, semiautonomous cells in modern revolutionary movements interpret messages and act on them in ways that the movement has to account for retrospectively. Tambo had repeated the call to make South Africa "ungovernable" while cautioning that he had "no wish to celebrate liberation day surrounded by a desolate landscape of destroyed buildings, and machines reduced to scrap metal."[14] If the leadership could cover their ideological tracks, young men from a Coloured township stigmatized as gang-ridden had already been interpellated as prone to crime and willing to fight by any means necessary.

When I interviewed Robert and Greta, separately, their lives having taken very different turns, both referred to the records of their trials and to various submissions to the TRC, including the harrowing fifteen days of testimonies from all members of their cell and its exile network in 1999, at which many of them met all the others for the first time. Unlike Robert, Greta refused to testify at her trial in an apartheid court: "I believe we were prisoners of conscience and that we should be given prisoner-of-war status, and unless I'm tried in a military court, I'm not participating in a criminal court." Vincent and Allan pleaded guilty and were imprisoned on Robben Island; Gaster was among those who were released for lack of evidence, but he could no longer walk around Wentworth with his comrades in prison.[15] I turn to the aftermath of their sentences in postapartheid times, and to truth telling in a new age of corruption, still haunted by many returns to the boundaries between politics and crime among the political elite as well as the most deprived. In Wentworth this boundary zone has become an indispensable critical vantage on the difficulties of transforming the racial capitalist palimpsest of the Babylon System.

TRC Tales: Problems of Knowledge after Apartheid, 1997–2007

I will never be judged by the same standards as those who maintained and supported apartheid.... Those who committed offences in the interests of apartheid did so to perpetuate it. My actions were to destroy it. I ask the public and the TRC members to consider what their attitude would have been to the establishment of a court, or quasi court, which judged the actions of the Nazis in the same way it judged the actions of those who resisted in the concentration camps.... I therefore, with no prejudice to my son Robert John McBride, or any other applicants to the amnesty committee, withdraw from all proceedings relating to this committee. I will take no part in them—either as a witness, an applicant, a bystander, a civilian or a concerned South African.
—DERRICK MCBRIDE, withdrawing his application for amnesty to the TRC

Look, besides the three women who died there, there were eighty-three who were injured, and out of that eighty-three, about forty or fifty were quite seriously injured. They underwent major operations, and with some of them no matter how many operations they had, shrapnel in various parts of their body.... The way Robert put that bomb together, it wasn't just normal TNT in those limpet mines.... He put bullets and pieces of steel that he cut up. So, when it exploded, the force of it, besides bringing the building down, it lodged into people. And the bomb was placed by the window of the bar, near the dance floor. So those in clear proximity got major, major injuries.
—GRETA APELGREN

Greta details the design of the car bomb, which TRC testimony focuses on at great length, as if the materiality of the bomb answers a series of questions.[16] Did Robert follow procedure in making a car bomb? Did he mean to hurt with a particular intensity? What did this have to do with his ability, or lack thereof, to prove his contrition within the redemptive arc of the TRC? Was the choice of target legitimate per ANC policy? Or was it purely an act of racial anger? Was the bombing sanctioned by the External Mission? Was there a "Kabwe test" in the determination of acceptable loss of civilian life?[17] Gordon's statement at his trial following his capture upon returning illegally to South Africa, ostensibly to free Robert from death row, was that their commander, Rashid, was "bloodthirsty." Was this his personal view or a difference in military strategy? Gordon did not respond to the call to bear witness at the TRC; his disappearance from public view and his death in 2022 add to the sense that the full story will never be told.

The individual whose testimony has changed quite dramatically through various tellings is Robert. In a retrospective explanation of his changing testimony, he explains to the TRC that he had to present himself in an apartheid court as if he was acting of his own will, so as not to implicate the banned ANC, but that he could now be more open about acting on instruction from his commander, Rashid. He also discloses that Gordon had been instructed to prepare a car bomb, that they had discussed this together with ANC operatives in Botswana, and that he had been tasked with taking over this operation after Gordon's capture and escape.[18] Robert maintains the position, in his Section 29 evidence to the TRC, that on one reconnaissance trip to the beachfront bars, he was turned away at the door and overheard a man leaving the bar saying, "May the force be with you."[19] Not knowing the line from the recent hit movie *Star Wars*, Robert interpreted the man's statement as a reference to the Special Forces, and this convinced him that the bar was frequented by off-duty members of the SADF's Special Operations unit. Robert takes issue with the way his Section 29 evidence was used in the TRC *Final Report*, which argued that this exercise had been conducted in an extremely amateurish and naive manner. His argument that the two bars were targeted as places frequented by security policemen from the nearby C. R. Swart Square could not be substantiated. None of those killed or injured appeared to have had any link to the military or the Security Branch.[20]

The choice of target is a point that Robert returns to in various testimonies. He points to policemen torturing him with a particular vengeance because they could have been there that night, and says that someone in prison confirmed that the target was frequented by off-duty servicemen of the

South African Defence Force. He asks for a list of people his cross-examiner represents. Testimonies at TRC hearings provide adequate evidence that Robert had been formally recruited to the ANC, that he had met operatives in exile, that he and Gordon were trained there, and that he was given room to make his own judgments, some of which may have been at odds with some in the ANC leadership. Indeed, his claim to take on a role of political and military leadership was precisely what figures like Mac Maharaj found impossible, requiring exiled leadership to return to the country.

At a few points, Robert and his attorney point out that the "Why Not" police docket had gone missing. Their implication is that some details, particularly the names of the injured, including perhaps people who could be traced to the police and security forces, are lost to history.[21] The missing docket adds a particular twist to this tale of elusive knowledge, but it also stands for the aporia at the heart of the moment of the disqualified, a sign of enduring irresolution after apartheid.

Robert's father, Derrick, refused to testify to the "quasi-court" of the TRC as part of his distaste for a narrative of redemption in a time of continued political and economic injustice. While Greta did not testify in the amnesty hearings either, she did testify in the TRC special sessions on apartheid's prisons. In a complicated twist that she has recounted elsewhere, also to me, she says that she was consigned to solitary confinement after refusing the advances of another operative in prison and that it was the racialized betrayal from a comrade that was particularly brutal. There are many layers to this vignette of a comrade refusing coerced sex from another comrade in apartheid's prison, an event prefigured in a long and repressed history of sexual violence in South African society. Greta remains proud of her action as an MK soldier, but she also recognizes that violence damages both perpetrator and victim, and she lives with the damage and faces it directly.

After his release from prison, Robert connected with Winnie Mandela, Ronnie Kasrils, and others to distribute what he later realized were caches of arms from Operation Vula to Self Defence Units in Katlehong, east of Johannesburg, in the war with Inkatha militias.[22] In Robert's view, ANC weapons, communications equipment, and leadership and alliances with the Pan Africanist Congress, the Azanian People's Liberation Army, and the Azanian National Liberation Army helped forge the largest ANC branch in the country, a key site of popular power in the transition period. Robert has been the subject of several controversies after apartheid, including charges of cross-border gun running, drunk driving, and defeating the ends of justice; when we spoke, his response was that he continues to have enemies from the old order. He has also been, at various points, a voice of reason against corruption and state capture.

Two individuals clarify the peculiarity of Robert's origins, and of the particular form of politics his unit represents. Both are white, of dramatically different class backgrounds, and both threw themselves into African liberation struggles in completely different ways. The first is an unlikely comparison, because he could not come from a more diametrically opposed position; the second was crucial to Robert's release from death row.

John Mulligan is an aging irascible community figure in Wentworth, like his friend Derrick McBride. His story is so complex that it is hard to imagine he could make it up, and it is absolutely unverifiable. John was born in Bulawayo of an Anglo-Irish farm family and, after his schooling, was drawn from military training into the wars of 1966–67: "*We* called them terrorists; *they* call them freedom fighters. . . . The first terrorists were ANC terrorists on their way to South Africa." From the Rhodesian light infantry, he went on into the Rhodesian Air Rifles, and over several years he went into combat with the Frente de Libertação de Moçambique (FRELIMO) in Mozambique, the Zambian paramilitary, and the Botswana paramilitary led, astonishingly, by his former classmate Ian Khama, the son of the president of Botswana between 1966 and 1980, Seretse Khama. In 1971 John became active in cross-border wars across Zambia and Mozambique and in South Africa into Kruger National Park. "Let me tell you," he said in his booming voice, "the Rhodesian army were probably the best bush fighters in the world. We fought an army in a war with fuck all; half the time we didn't get paid."

After 1967 meager wages brought him periodically to work as a fitter and turner in South Africa's oil refineries. At one point, "we used to go six weeks to the war, six weeks to the economy." Through the late 1960s, "I used to time my leave for the shutdown. I'd come down and work three to four weeks, get enough money, I'd have a good fucking job, make as many babies as I can, and try to get back for the same shit again." Over his periodic trips, John saw the transformation of South Durban into an industrial landscape dominated by oil refineries. In 1981 he moved to Warner Beach, just south of Durban; "one day at the shutdown, I saw this *stekkie* ['a piece'], this Coloured girl, so I started *charfing* [flirting with] her, and thought, fuck, man, why must I pay, and I moved in with her in Wentworth." John continued military contract work on and off between work on the refineries.

One day, he ran into his old Rhodesian commanding officer, who called him to a meeting on the Bluff, where he "saw a lot of old faces there from the army, from the Thirty-Second Battalion; they asked him whether he would like to be part of a little 'sleeping team' to do a little bit of research, a little bit of spying." He accepted and became part of what he describes as a high-level sleeper cell of Rhodesian and South African military personnel. He insisted in 2007, "They're still on the go today; I went to a meeting about a year ago, and they've got a big graph, and they are actually running a comparison of Rhodesia and South Africa year by year."

At the same time as his friend Derrick was becoming active with his son in Special Ops, John began to infiltrate Inkatha on behalf of his new unit. "When I went into [Inkatha], because I knew a lot of Black soldiers who had been trained in Rhodesia, [it] was to recruit them and put them into the KwaZulu police. My whole job was to train fuckin' Self Protection Units for Inkatha." In 1989 he was seconded to military intelligence, and at some point, the Security Branch turned on him and tried to kill him off. He went underground for two years; "I stayed in Wentworth *one-way* [at length, intensely], didn't even go to town."

John's story is too bizarre to be discounted. He is open about all the people he thinks were spies among activists in Wentworth and Merebank and right up to the presidency. As a white "Rhodesian," his political idiom, with its commitment to rough masculinity, sexual domination, hard work, and militant action, was not unlike that of people from across the political spectrum in Wentworth. This might explain why he could slip into obscurity and retirement in this particular place, where his right-wing radicalism could take cover in the blurred boundaries of crime and politics that characterize the moment of the disqualified.

The second figure who helps clarify the conditions of possibility for the McBride cell was a young white woman from an affluent background, whose father was an executive of the Anglo American Corporation. Paula Leyden, later Paula McBride, became Robert's girlfriend while he was on death row at Pretoria Maximum Security Prison. Paula became central to his legal defense and to an international campaign to free Robert. In her testimony to the TRC, she speaks about her daily visits to "the head office of hangings," where, between 1987 and 1990, she witnessed what she describes as a procession to the execution chamber.[23] When we spoke, she was living with her partner, the writer Tom O'Neill, on a farm outside Kilkenny, Ireland.

We began by discussing how Robert's MK cell came apart and why one of its members cracked and turned state witness. Tom added, "When the pressure came on, they didn't have the ideological framework to support them, so it doesn't appear to have taken much pressure for him to crumble." Clearly, Gordon and Robert had political training on their trips out of the country, and Derrick was an autodidact with a strongly independent political sensibility, but some of the younger activists in the cell may not have had a similar political education. When I asked them more about the workings of the cell, Tom interjected again with a very precise statement that semiautonomous underground cells "operate autonomously in most modern guerrilla movements anyway, within the very broad framework, and the driving forces within the cell will have a big influence on the kind of direction, whether it is indefinite politicization, which can in some cases be just avoiding doing anything, or maybe the other extreme, just rushing it when people are not sufficiently politicized to bear the subsequent strain that's going to come on them." Tom was not certain that the specificity of the event had much to do with the car bomb; after all, there had been prior car bombs like the Church Street car bomb of 1983 or the car bomb in Durban in 1984, for which Rayman Lalla from Merebank was granted amnesty. Tom added again, "It was extensively used in the North and one of the more efficient ways to deliver your goods somewhere. . . . The thing is how civilian is the area. Was this too soft a target or not? By the standards of the PLO [Palestine Liberation Organization] or the IRA [Irish Republican Army]: not at all, but by the standards of the ANC, it probably was." Paula nodded, continuing that this was not the case for the military leadership, like Chris Hani: "Not a shadow of a doubt remained in his mind, I know that."

What is striking is that in the last years of apartheid, Paula appealed to the ANC leadership in Lusaka for Robert's conviction to be commuted to a term sentence, and in the process, she became part of the internal critique of the movement's conceptualization of the boundary between criminal and political prisoners. She found herself profoundly moved by her visits to Robert: "Death row was, for me, a real microcosm; everything intensified. It was like looking at the cauldron of South Africa, in a very real way. I became like a person possessed on that issue. I couldn't believe that here was this place constructed for death."

The External Mission distinguished political prisoners from people on death row, while Paula's argument to them was that the death penalty is inhumane, "in South Africa in particular, because there were very few people on death row who you could not make a political case for." The task was to get them to see it as a political matter, and a key figure in shifting movement opinion on this point was Phyllis Naidoo. With others, particularly Brian Currin from Lawyers for Human Rights, Paula also lobbied the National Party. As a consequence of this pressure, on February 2, 1990, when de Klerk announced the unbanning of movement organizations and the release of political prisoners, he also announced a moratorium on the death penalty. The death penalty was abolished by the newly created Constitutional Court in 1995.

Against the enduring ambiguities surrounding the car bomb, the abolition of the death penalty was a clear victory that would not have seen the light of day had the ANC and the National Party not been pressured by a well-organized lobby. The clarity of this mobilization takes Paula outside the outlaw culture that McBride's cell emerged from and, in many ways, remains connected to. None of the activists from this cell have become struggle heroes, even if their fates have been very different. Unlike Paula, none of them have been able to move on from their past.

How might we look again at this milieu in Wentworth as a site of political improvisation parallel to the basement of the Presbyterian church in Merebank? I take a cue from Nunn's photograph in the prelude of a young Robert engrossed in conversation in 1983 (figure P.7). At first glance, this image, perhaps of a Wentworth Improvement Programme meeting, shows young people who may have been participants in civic organizations linked to the urban movement of the 1980s (see chapter 7). But we know that this was the tip of the iceberg and that something else was at work in the lives of many of these young people. We cannot, of course, speculate about their internal lives. However, what distinguishes the moment of the disqualified is the way in which it looks directly into the psychosocial wound of racialization, forcing open the illegitimacy of the order of things. No "innocent" conception of Congress nonracialism or coalitional Blackness would be adequate to the task of attending to these wounds.[24]

I deliberately pose this moment as *looking into the wound*, because ways of seeing have been crucial, and photography has a critical role to play in this book. Photographs enter as testimony in multiple courtrooms surrounding the McBride cell, as well as in other retrospective narrations. In the TRC amnesty hearings, Robert discusses a photograph of the decoy he and Greta's sister Jeanette placed at the Pine Street Parkade; he responds to a newspaper photograph of a police sergeant, "clothes ablaze," staggering out of the Wentworth Substation; and he brings up photographs in the aftermath of the car bomb in its proximity to the two bars.[25] Robert engages photographs to illustrate the truth content of his actions and their effects. And one of the most striking things Greta said to me of their police mug shots and of photographs in the press was that these images presented them as unkempt Coloureds. Greta prided herself on always being well dressed and put together. She could not abide representations of her and Robert as wild and ungroomed, photographic representation meant to convey that their actions were uncivilized and not the product of revolutionary reason.

Jacob Dlamini's reading of the security police's "terrorist album" includes a beguiling photograph of "captured" ANC insurgent/apartheid spy Peter Mokaba, handcuffed and in a leather jacket, pointing to the section of barbed wire where he and a comrade had crossed the border from Swaziland to South Africa.[26] Dlamini reads Mokaba's gesture into the bush both as choreographed and as indexing complex histories embodied in compromised personhood. The only thing that is clear is that photography provided a crucial means of critical discourse. This is particularly the case in places like Wentworth and Merebank where the visual appears to disclose something about the nature of suffering. This is even more the case for those who came of age in the 1970s and 1980s and who, as one of them put it, reached for a Canon AE-1 rather than an AK-47 as an instrument of critique. Turning to this minor history of photography, we find a different attention to the moment of the disqualified that wrestles, as Mokaba did not publicly, with the vexed boundary between crime and politics during and after apartheid.

Shooting Back

The history of photography in Southern Africa, as Patricia Hayes carefully diagnoses, condenses in specific conjunctures, in nineteenth-century traffic in daguerreotypes across the Indian Ocean via Mauritius to Durban; in iterations of imperial photography in Southern Africa that we have seen vividly in the first four chapters; and in resistance traditions since the 1950s in the work of Eli Weinberg or the photographers of *Drum Magazine*, including of pioneering photographers Alf Khumalo, Ernest Cole, Peter Magubane, and Jürgen Schadeberg, followed in the 1970s by David Goldblatt with his geographic sensitivity to "the structure of things then," including the brittle sides of whiteness.[27] Hayes calls the 1980s photographic conjuncture a "'rising up of surfaces' that link mourning and uprising"; drawing from Georges Didi-Huberman's *Uprisings*, Hayes refers to a set of gestures—embodied, photographed, printed, circulated, consumed—that, for particular collectives and particular times, leave an impression of upliftment and departure from the impossible condition of being penned in, pinned down, or politically prone.[28]

Hayes turns to the key figure linking art and politics across generations from the 1960s to the 1980s, and indeed into the twenty-first century: Omar Badsha, organic intellectual of Durban's Casbah (see chapter 5). Since the 1960s Badsha has taken the question of "Black Arts" seriously, working with the provocation that social critique and aesthetic experimentation are inseparable. This sharpened in a particular way through his work with the ANC underground and exile networks while the leadership were jailed, and his engagement with BC, independent Black trade unions, the revival of the Natal Indian Congress (NIC), and Black artists and writers.

In 1979 Badsha published a photobook dedicated to his daughter, *Letter to Farzanah*, which explicitly links photography and anti-apartheid critique; it was immediately banned. In 1982 he and Paul Weinberg founded the photographers' collective Afrapix. The magazine *Staffrider*, launched in 1978, named after township slang for fare dodgers hanging onto suburban trains, published and circulated Black cultural production. Afrapix drew in leading photographers of the times, including Paul Weinberg, Santu Mofokeng, Cedric Nunn, Peter McKenzie, Myron Peter, Jeeva Rajgopaul, Rafs Mayet, Graham Goddard, Lesley Lawson, Guy Tillim, Chris Ledochowski, Wendy Schegmann, Anna Zieminski, Gille de Vlieg, Gisèle Wulfsohn, and Deseni Moodliar. They called themselves "documentary photographers" as opposed to photojournalists and held exhibitions, most notably at Johannesburg's Market Theatre. Several participated in Culture and Resistance Symposium/ Festival in Botswana in 1982 and the exhibitions *Nichts wird uns trennen* (Nothing will separate us) in West Germany in 1983, *The Hidden Camera* in Amsterdam in 1987, and *Culture for Another South Africa* in Amsterdam in 1989. These were sites of political work with the global Anti-Apartheid Movement, and they demonstrated the crucial role of the cultural front and its aesthetic critique. In figure 9.1 we see photographer Peter McKenzie from Wentworth at the Culture and Resistance Symposium/Festival in Botswana July 5–9, 1982, lost in reverie before speaking.[29]

The political economy of anti-apartheid print culture was slowly transforming Afrapix, whose photographers were engaged in many things as politically conscious artists. They experimented with slide shows in organizing workers. They sought and trained new generations of political photographers. Afrapix grew alongside the multifaceted urban struggles of the mid-1980s. As Hayes aptly puts it, "There soon emerged a palpable need to supply photographs to agencies and organizations supporting (and often funding) the struggle against apartheid from outside, especially in Western Europe," with demands for weekly packages of photographs mailed to as many as ten destinations.[30] An employee of the London-based solidarity group International Defence and Aid Fund describes the need for particular kinds of visual simplifications, and they were "looking for blood," for "hard, hard-assed pictures," particularly for campaigns against state executions.[31] When the

FIGURE 9.1 Peter McKenzie (center, seated) at the Culture and Resistance Festival, Botswana, 1982. © Tim Besserer, www.TimBesserer.com.

fund transformed and edited photographs to make them conform to these expectations, Hayes asks, How documentary must documentary photography be? Ledochowski says to Hayes, "We were propagandists for the struggle and yet the demands to produce iconic images were intense"; he jokes, "You wait two hours for one *Amandla!* And maybe by then you might have nodded to sleep and you miss the shot. The main shot, the Badsha or Weinberg type photo. Because we were all influenced by those archetypal shots."[32]

There were also security concerns in producing propaganda. Both Afrapix and the associated film collective started by Weinberg, Afrascope, were routinely subject to police raids. The state saw their archives as ripe for political trials. When Calvin moved from Merebank to Johannesburg in 1982, he joined Afrascope and became its director in 1983; he was also politically connected to COSAS. Calvin was detained for five months in 1984–85 under Section 29 of the Internal Security Act of 1982 and then released, only to be called to be a state witness in the Delmas Treason Trial of 1985–89. He then left the country, to his lasting regret.

The Delmas trial judgment notes his absence from the country before entering a long discussion on whether videos of public meetings are reliable evidence, what videos actually are ("not a photograph or cinematograph film"), whether they are alterable, and whether the soundtrack synchronized with a roving camera can be trusted; the judge proclaims, "Having sat through two weeks of video viewing, I am convinced that the video can be a helpful tool to arrive at the truth. It does not suffer from a fading memory as do witnesses. . . . The best word artist cannot draw his verbal picture as accurately and as clearly as does the cold eye of the camera."[33]

Not everyone shared this idiosyncratic view. Afrapix photographers questioned the certainties of anti-apartheid visual culture in the late 1980s and went different ways before its dissolution in 1991. The photographers often also continued projects that were not obviously functional to the simplifications of anti-apartheid markets. Chris Ledochowski and Cedric Nunn pursued long-term engagement with specific locales, the Cape Flats and the KwaZulu-Natal North Coast, respectively; Santu Mofokeng developed haunting explorations of ephemerality and irresolution in apartheid's dying decade and, later in his life, focused on spirituality and environmentally fragility.[34]

Early 1980s Afrapix photographers may have had to attend to the strictures of anti-apartheid visual simplification, but as Hayes suggests, "Their photographs leave behind a sediment of the 1980s to which we will doubtless repeatedly return."[35] This precise formulation is important to think with. *What is this sediment that we return to, or for?*

Many of these documentary photographers have returned to the sediment of the 1980s quite literally by going back through their negatives, considering their possibilities for telling other stories precluded by the imperatives of anti-apartheid narrative. This is powerfully demonstrated in Nunn's retrospective photobook *Call and Response* and in Paul Weinberg, David Robbins, and Gcina Mhlope's *Durban: Impressions of an African City*. Before focusing on Peter McKenzie as exemplary critic in the moment of the disqualified, to engage his practice of looking yet again, I turn to a set of evocative amateur photographs from his micro-neighborhood that offer one response about what a particular cohort returns to, and for.

The Lanes of SANF, 1970s, 2002

I encountered these evocative photographs (figures 9.2–9.8) of young people in the lanes of SANF, named for the former homes of the South African Naval Force, in a 2002 exhibition at Durban's KwaMuhle Museum called *Cycle of Violence*. Curated by Wayne Tifflin from Wentworth, *Cycle of Violence* narrated the rise and fall of street gangs through four phases: from the "unplanned mistake" in the making of Wentworth, to social conditions in the apartheid township, to gangs as "a search for identity?" with a thoughtful question mark, to the activation of the community with the church in the lead. When an outspoken Wentworth resident asked the curator why it was necessary to endure yet another presentation on gangs in Wentworth, he responded, "We want to show how people in Wentworth came out of it, how people survived it."

The most vivid element of Tifflin's curation is drawn from personal photographs from SANF, where semidetached homes are arrayed on a hillside with little lanes running between them. The lanes recur in accounts of gangs ducking from each other and of activists evading the police, and also in the Austerville Redevelopment Project in the 1980s. These amateur photographs taken in the 1970s are a record of being in the lanes, whether as groups of young people sitting together, sometimes posing with a baby, or a young couple next to their home, or a young man crossing a field. Sometimes the group is in the street, sometimes posing for the photographer who playfully enters the frame as a shadow, and sometimes the photographer catches them in the midst of dancing. Some photographs record style, as young men pose with a leg outstretched and a hand in a pocket, often with their signature hats and *kasie* (township, from the Afrikaans *lokasie*, "location," for Black township) style.

The photographs make no reference at all to gang turf. Indeed, we cannot say anything about what the lanes mean. Their significance is entirely indexical. We can see that the lanes were important to the young people who made this intimate record of belonging in SANF. We might read these amateur photographs as expressions of camaraderie and creativity among young people. For some of the most striking photographs, however, there is a specific visual convention in the way in which young people photograph themselves dancing, posing, or sitting in the lane. The last image (figure 9.8) conveys this visual convention most vividly; the image is framed perfectly to give the lane its due. In sharing the frame with their beloved lane, these young people record an ethic of spaciousness, a yearning beyond their exhaustion with the interiors of township homes, with parental authority and the summer heat of Durban.

I mean *spaciousness* in the specific sense invoked by Frantz Fanon. *Les damnés de la terre* (*The Wretched of the Earth*) has been powerfully read as a text about a human to come, but it is also about an earthliness to come, a text concerned with geography in three senses: as *la terre* in the revolutionary struggle for land, bread, and dignity; as *la terre brulée*, or scorched earth, in the critique of all forms of racial-spatial ruination; and as an index

FIGURES 9.2–9.4 *Cycle of Violence* exhibition, Local History Museum, Durban, 2002. © Local History Museum, Durban.

of an emergent Earth that the damned will inherit after the abolition of this capitalist-imperialist world. Before his famous statement, "Marxist analysis should always be slightly stretched every time we have to do with the colonial problem," Fanon dramatizes "a colonial world . . . cut in two, with two zones, two towns, two peoples."[36] Ato Sekyi-Otu helps us read these and other passages not as ontological axioms but as part of Fanon's dramaturgical dialectic that reels the reader in before unraveling their expectations.[37] When Fanon characterizes "the native town, the Negro village, the medina, the reservation . . . [as] a world without spaciousness," he forces the reader to reflect on how these variously colonized figures might make space.[38] Precisely in a situation meant to be claustrophobic, spaciousness can be the most militant demand possible.

Consider Katherine McKittrick's thoughtful reading of the life of Harriet Jacobs (pseud. Linda Brent), the slave woman who hid for two years in a little

garret built into the attic of her grandmother's home, where she could easily be recaptured by her slave master, who presumed that she has run far away.[39] McKittrick poses the garreted slave woman in the process of freeing herself— biding her time for the moment at which she might leave with her children—as signifying a politics and poetics of Black feminist endurance. This is a tactical space-time, a spatial expression of subaltern political will to lead the collective to an Earth to come. Through Fanon and McKittrick, the photographs of the lanes of SANF, with their gestures to friends, lovers, family, children, dance, music, and liveliness, become much more than they seem. From the carceral landscape of Wentworth in the 1980s, these images are a poetic call for a spacious world to come and a determination to wait for it.

When the police, church, and community organizations converged to eradicate street gangs, they enclosed the lanes in private walls, with narrow gaps to mark a lost commons (figure 9.9). Walter Benjamin comments on Eugène

FIGURES 9.5–9.8 *Cycle of Violence* exhibition, Local History Museum, Durban, 2002. ©
Local History Museum, Durban.

FIGURE 9.9 Remains of the lanes of SANF, Wentworth, 2008. © Sharad Chari.

Atget's photographs of deserted Parisian streets that "he photographed them like scenes of a crime . . . for the purpose of establishing evidence."[40] The walled lanes are also the scene of the crime. The saved photographs remain evidence that these young people refuse to desert the scene. The crime remains racial capitalism. We turn next to a photographer who lived in SANF and knew it intimately as a young person in the 1970s and early 1980s and who turned to photography as a medium of Black cultural politics.

Peter McKenzie: Photographer of the Disqualified, 2000s

Peter McKenzie left the township, as did many others, following the currents of anti-apartheid cultural politics through Badsha's mentorship in Afrapix. He described to me what it was like to return to his corner at Pascal Place, which he had felt compelled to leave as a young man:

> There was a corner you could go to, always people you could talk to. There was help if you needed, to go and fuck someone up on the other side of town. You learnt about sex on the corner. . . . Everybody walks up and down 'cause it's too hot to stay inside. You got this continuous mobility of people going "Ey, howzit?" The life of those gullies was also about being in Durban, and the heat of summer. You could not stay in your house. It was too crowded. It was too hot. So, life was to be lived on the streets outside.

Peter contrasts the gullies with being stuck at home, but unlike others around him, he found the means to leave. Yet his photography kept bringing him back to his *kasie*, to capture the melancholic afterlife of apartheid's townships. He spoke of his choice to turn to photography as self-consciously parallel to his peers' turn to the armed struggle. And despite leaving for Johannesburg, and later Marseille, and returning to Durban in his final years, he maintained an insider/outsider relationship to Wentworth; as he says of his 2005 exhibition *Vying Posie* (Going Home), "I am from Wentworth but not of Wentworth."[41]

Peter's work engages with the dialectics of past and present in a particular way, as he steers between revolutionary expectation and reflection on lost possibilities. Resisting easy consolation, his photographs rest in fleeting intimacies within the contradictions of township life. Revisiting negatives from the 1970s and 1980s, he reaches for recent means of critique of the durability of apartheid's forms. This is not nostalgia that might turn the photographs of the lanes into objects of reverie but rather a politically charged melancholy that disavows the past while engaging its active presence.[42]

Consider his 2007 documentary film with Sylvie Peyre, *What Kind...?* ("What's up?") The film focuses on Peter's childhood friends, former members of the κ-1 Trucks, who received exemplary sentences in 1983 for the alleged murder of a man from rival Vultures turf. His friends say they were framed. As Piet Usher repeats ruefully, his hat pulled low over his eyes, "We paid the time; they did the crime." These young men started coming out of prison in 1994, and the coincidence with the democratic elections gives Peter the opportunity to question these intersecting freedoms.

Following Fred Moten's polyphonic reading of "the sound of a photograph," I read the film as an audiovisual blues text with multiple, braided strands.[43] One strand starts with handheld video from a moving car and a montage of everyday life in Wentworth, with industrial smokestacks as an occasional backdrop. Another strand brings together Peter's photographic portraits since 1994 (see the prelude). A third takes the form of interviews with recognizable community and environmental leaders from Wentworth's civil society of the 2000s (see the introduction). Peter's friends speak to his handheld camera with an intimacy, sometimes in rhyme, with laughter and township slang. In contrast, the experts look directly into the camera, speaking in measured tones and standard English to an audience that might already watch documentaries. Peter moves between these worlds as translator and shapeshifter, sometimes narrating, sometimes hanging out in the *shebeen* (local bar) with his friends. Terrence "Terrible T's" Fynn laughs as he playfully lifts his shirt to show off his tattoos: "When I *vyied* in [went in], I was a young *laaitie* [youngster], *check*, I'm like a drawing board!" The narrative pauses as background music invites the viewer into the spaciousness of the *shebeen*, where the men do not have to explain anything.

When they recount the scene of the crime from 1983, their alibis, and their subsequent hardship, they speak in generalities. Terrence says, "Wentworth was *bad*, my *bru*. They didn't even have doctors and nurses to stitch the holes up. They had to bring soldiers in to stitch the people up that time, for about two to three years, they had to bring the army-*ous* [guys] to stitch them up, that's how *blind* it was, it was *bad*!" Piet says young men didn't have a choice but to associate with gangs; being from a particular area in Wentworth meant guilt by association: "Wherever you went, they included you. They said you come from that area, you're part of that place, so you're a gangster from that area.... There wasn't people that were gangsters; they just *made like* [pretended to be] gangsters.... I didn't even see the guy who died on that particular day, but I was put in this case because of the enemy.... I don't know if they feared me or what, but they just put me in this case, in fact all of us." But who was "the enemy," exactly?

The absence of a recognizable anti-apartheid idiom brings an anticlimactic character to Peter's exploration of his friends' "freedom." Terrence Fynn repeats a stock racialized lament: "All that time in jail, nothing's changed . . . *ey*, but even like now, it was still like the same, *nevermind* things is changing and *whatwhat*, it's like the same, my *bru*. Like me, I don't even vote, because the *witous* [white guys] were doing things that time, the *darkie-ous* [black guys] are doing the same thing. I'll tell you *waaruit* [straight], it's *darkie* for *darkie*, *witou* for *witou*, *charou* [Indian] for *charou*, my bru." He does not say *bruinou* (Coloured man) for *bruinou*.

Despite repeating the racial common sense pervasive in Wentworth, these young men make no reference to community leaders as their representatives. Nor do they claim the redemption arc that the *Cycle of Violence* exhibition tried to do for "gangsterism." They make no reference to anti-apartheid militants like Robert and Greta. Piet, the most discerning figure, expresses the collective sentiment of the five men: "We tried to put our past behind us . . . but you can see what's happening to us, the people is bring our past forward. We're marked with our past, for things what we never even *do*."

The film does not adjudicate guilt or innocence; it dispenses with the forensic exercise that haunts the former members of the McBride cell. However, it does give these former young men from SANF the space to present the damaging effects of living with their sentences. They do not name the "enemy," but they indict apartheid's police and court as much as the rival gang, as well as the discourses that frame them as irredeemably dangerous. They display their despair viscerally, their raced and gendered frailty completely unlike the heroic masculinity of the armed-struggle militant.

The film also represents these damaged men as adjacent to and not quite legible to the experts who speak for biopolitical struggles that continue to shape life in Wentworth. *What Kind . . . ?* is an audiovisual blues text through which we can see, hear, and feel the pathos of life in a toxic sink that continues to differentiate experts, who can be heard, from those who embody continued degradation, the vanguard of the disqualified.

From the edges of the McBride cell, we might return to Wayne said to me's words that the world of the saboteurs and of alleged gangsters is "still a mystery to some of us," but also that: "You see, there still might have to be another struggle to get what people initially set out to achieve." The documentary photographers of the 1980s anticipated this in the photographic archive they have left us, as well as in their own attempts at wrestling with its demands. Peter died in August 2017, but he remains an organic intellectual of the moment of the disqualified. He put his political faith in relationships with people and place, in their actual, damaged form, with no judgment except of the political elite. And he left us that laugh we remember all too well, to remind us who will have the last laugh.

At apartheid's end, as we see in *What Kind . . . ?*, the emerging form of biopolitical expertise that held some hope of galvanizing political will was environmentalism.

Environmentalism in the Remains of Biopolitical Struggle, 1989–2008–2023

In 1989, in response to changes to US tax law through pressure from the Anti-Apartheid Movement, Mobil divested from South Africa, including from the Wentworth refinery. The beneficiary was Gencor, which ran the Engen refinery until 1996. In the interim, from 1991, Engen began to take environmentalism more seriously. Simultaneously, the Merebank Ratepayers Association (MRA) marked the unbanning of liberation movements by surveying residents' experience of atmospheric air pollution and respiratory ill health. The results were striking. The MRA proclaimed a "pollution crisis." The survey was quickly disqualified by the refineries and the Health Department as lacking scientific evidence.[44] The refinery attributed ill health to a generic industrialization and urbanization in which there were no culpable agents. This, as we know, was a sign of things to come.

An opportune moment arose in 1995 when President Mandela stopped en route to the Engen refinery to listen to protesters, an encounter that led to the formation of the South Durban Community Environmental Alliance (SDCEA) in 1997. Young militants in Merebank were key to bringing radical environmental politics to bear on the civic organizations working across South Durban's racial divides. Recall that the SDCEA, groundWork, and local civics including the Wentworth Development Forum (WDF) and MRA linked environmental activism with urban, provincial, national, and international environmental politics, simultaneously pressuring the state, working the courts, conducting militant research, and demonstrating in the street (see the introduction). This complex geography of activism recalls anti-apartheid struggles but with a new premium on transparency and publicity.

In the early 2000s, the key law regulating air pollution was still the Atmospheric Pollution Prevention Act of 1965, largely unenforced with respect to Black communities during apartheid.[45] This contradicted the environmental clause in the constitutional Bill of Rights, which enshrines the right "to an environment that is not harmful to . . . health or well-being; and . . . to have the environment protected, for the benefit of present and future generations."[46] GroundWork and its allies availed themselves of the environmental clause, the right to information, the protection of whistleblowers, and the right to representation in the public interest.[47] After a protracted struggle, Durban was chosen in 2003 as the site to pilot the eThekwini Municipality Air Quality Management System under the auspices of the Multi-Point Plan, and the new Air Quality Act of 2004 was signed into law in 2005. Ground-Work remains vigilant about legal compliance and has fought for a broader list of hazardous chemicals, strict enforcement of pollution standards, and popular participation in monitoring enforcement. Siva Chetty had emerged through Merebank's civic struggles to become a key figure in the city's pollution control unit, until its restructuring in 2011, precisely the moment that the city put forth plans of expanding the petrochemical-industrial hub in South Durban. Chetty moved into the private sector at around this time as well.

A second legal struggle concerned the 2007 renewal of the National Key Points Act of 1980, apartheid legislation to protect places of strategic national interest from sabotage. In 1984 the Wentworth refinery was subject to a failed attack with rocket-propelled grenades by MK, an event that inspired Robert McBride's politicization.[48] In the 2000s the area around the refinery was important in a different way for environmental activists collecting evidence of pollution, as well as for limited-duration industrial artisans engaged in strike action (see the introduction). Access to the perimeter was key to exercising the democratic rights to information, as well as for demonstrations.

In 2002, after the militant strike led by the Chemical, Engineering and Industrial Workers Union (CEIWU) found broad support across local civic and welfare organizations, the Ministry of Defence extended the National Key Point around Engen refinery, encroaching on a local mosque and nearby homes. When I met CEIWU workers on strike at the time, they had been pushed out to the grounds by the swimming pool. At this moment, activists had forged a militant labor, community, and environmental alliance against the forces that insulate the oil refineries as occupying powers over an industrial-residential landscape. Unlike the Air Quality Act, which replaced its predecessor with a potentially more democratic legal form, the draft National Key Points and Strategic Installations Bill of 2007 sought to renew this remnant of apartheid's security apparatus to criminalize labor and civic groups employing constitutional rights, while protecting corporate power under the guise of security.[49]

Meanwhile, SDCEA, WDF, and groundWork were also trying to build community expertise through a "bucket brigade" system of air sampling, to document the effects of long-term exposure to toxic pollutants. They were running up against the limits to this strategy as well. As a groundWork report put it, "The struggle is really against official silence and the willful ignorance that serves to frustrate . . . demands that industry must clean up and compensate those it has harmed."[50] Community activists were critical of the municipality's devolution of regulatory responsibility to civic "stakeholders" without resources for effective regulation. The result was widespread dissimulation about pollution knowledge.[51] The alliance of organizations continues working on multiple fronts, fighting injustice in fence-line communities as well as in metropolitan spatial planning and national infrastructural policy.[52]

A few geographic quandaries came to light through these struggles. First, in the struggle against toxic waste dumping in the neighboring African township of Umlazi, groundWork realized that a victory in one place can mean a dump is simply moved elsewhere. The challenge that SDCEA faced was to forge an alliance across townships, since air pollution does not discriminate by race. To paraphrase groundWork founder-activist Bobby Peek, environmental struggles are bittersweet; they require ongoing door-to-door organizing.

A second quandary concerns relocation. Living next to refineries does not make any sense. Yet, when the municipality has suggested that people relocate, residents have been unequivocal that they do not want to relive apartheid's forced removals. I began this book by arguing that Wentworth diverges from Merebank in that its residents do not feel connected to a broader geography of Coloured Durban; most do not affirm being Black but instead affirm stigmatized racialization as working-class "Wentonians." Relocation in democratic times typically means ending up in a home in the far reaches of African township sprawl, distanced from the city center, the prospect of industrial work, and ties of community. South Durban residents know they cannot assume that they will ever be moved to the beautiful, leafy neighborhoods of former white areas on the Berea Ridge or north of the city, nor that industry would relocate either. This takes us back to the geographic quandary that moving the polluter is never a satisfactory solution either.

The problem that activists confronted in the first democratic election was that despite the vibrant histories of activism that have circuited through Wentworth and Merebank, the majority of residents voted for the Nationalists or for racially marked political parties, rather than for the political alliance that claimed to be the agent of liberation. These racialized populations did not sign up en masse for Black liberation, nor did they generalize environmental struggle by building on medical, feminist, and worker activism in this very landscape. Residents in a toxic valley refuse to *be* disqualified in new ways today.

In December 2020, after a terrible explosion at the Engen refinery, the causes of which have not been conclusively disclosed, refinery operations were halted by the Department of Environmental Affairs pending investigation. Between 2000 and 2016 SDCEA recorded fifty-five explosions in the South Durban Industrial Basin, eighteen of them at Engen and two at the SAPREF (South African Petroleum Refineries) refinery. In April 2021 Engen decided to shut down its refinery by 2023. The CEO's rationale is that it is unsustainable in the long term. By this revelation, he means that it is unsustainable to the accumulation strategy of the Malaysian parastatal Petronas, which in early 2023 decided to sell its 74 percent share in Engen to Vivo Energy, with the Phembani Group continuing to stay as the Broad Based Black Economic Empowerment partner. A long struggle seems to have ended. Or has it? Community residents and activists in groundWork and SDCEA remain vigilant of the conversion of the refinery into a petroleum storage facility that will continue to foist burdens of ill health on its Black neighbors. They remain mobilized, as they must, until they end corporate occupation conclusively and for all and attend to its accumulating burdens in people's lives and in their lived environs.[53]

Accumulating Remains

Rhythms of Expectation

Repetition cannot long escape the ironies it bears within it.
—EDWARD SAID, *The World, the Text, and the Critic*

I really believe that the work is done by historical specificity, by understanding what is specific about certain moments, and how those moments come together, how different tendencies fuse and form a kind of configuration—never one that's going to last forever, hegemony never does, it always has unruly elements and it's always struggling to master a terrain etc. And those forces are going to produce a shift to another conjuncture. . . . I have to feel the kind of accumulation of different things coming together to make a new moment, and think, this is a different rhythm.   —STUART HALL

Consider, again, Cedric Nunn's haunting photograph of soccer players in the shadows of the Wentworth oil refinery (figure P.1). Through Fred Moten's multisensory notion of "the sound of the photograph," I have suggested that Nunn and Peter McKenzie are artisans of an audiovisual blues tradition that pulls Black Atlantic cultural forms to Indian Ocean shores.[1] As an intellectual and aesthetic tradition, the blues tarries with the power of ontologization, or with the ways in which people and places refuse being fixed as racial things with essences.[2] Ponder this, and the soccer players in Nunn's image will have already run off the frame, into lives that are never fixable by racial capitalism or biopolitical sovereignty.

Throughout this book racial capitalism and biopolitics are haunted by their own fantasies of productivity and vitality. The tenuous articulation of race, sovereignty, biopower, and capital can never guarantee full employment, perpetual growth, or universal access to the means of life.[3] Karl Marx's notion of capitalism, with its dialectical play of appearance and reality, presumes that capitalism's contradictions are immanent, that capital is haunted by its form. Jacques Derrida's homage to Marx reads his method as presuming to throw off the veils of fetishism while welcoming the specter of a coming communism, leaving behind a set of questions about how we might engage the spectral as part of critical diagnosis.[4] I have sought to keep this in mind while working through apartheid's remains.

The power of the spectral helps us understand why Black documentary photographers have emerged as the key organic intellectuals in this book. As photographic intellectuals like Nunn and McKenzie work patiently through the medium of film, they provide a corpus of evidence that helps us consider how people strive to outlive the ruinous articulation of biopolitics, sovereignty and racial capitalism. At various moments, some people have tried to repurpose the tools of public health, urban planning, social work, or environmentalism as instruments of biopolitical struggle. The political imaginations in these attempts range from liberal reform to radical abolition because, I argue, biopower can express a variety of politics. The political hope I end with is that we might find in such eruptions of biopolitical struggle, now more than ever, a biopolitics for an actual planetary future.

This political task has to engage what Edward Said calls the irony of repetition, his reading of Marx's theatrical opening of *The Eighteenth Brumaire of Louis Bonaparte*, in which history repeats itself first as tragedy, then as farce.[5] Marx's object of critique is the tragedy that precedes the farcical autocratic nephew who calls himself Bonaparte. In doing so, Marx is at pains to distinguish his own approach to repetition from that of the pretender king. We might pause to consider the postapartheid political elite calling on anti-apartheid rhetoric when expedient, seemingly impervious to deepening inequality and Black suffering after apartheid. In Said's reading of Marx,

> Louis Bonaparte legitimizes his usurpation by appeal to repetition in natural sequences. Marx, on the other hand, repeats the nephew's rep-

etition and so deliberately goes against nature. In *The Eighteenth Brumaire* repetition is Marx's instrument for ensnaring the nephew in a manufactured world of analyzed reality. From the work's opening sentence, the celebrated citation from Hegel, Marx's method is to repeat in order to produce difference, not to validate Bonaparte's claims, and to give facts by emending their apparent direction. Just as the pretender son turns into a clearly revealed nephew, so even Hegel, who had considered the repetition of an event a strengthening and confirmation of its value, is cited and turned around. . . . Repetition cannot long escape the ironies it bears within it.[6]

Apartheid Remains has sought to diagnose apartheid's prolonged end as an accumulation of ironies, remains that cannot quite repeat the past. What do we make of this accumulation of contradictory remains of multiple pasts?

The rhythms of expectation have perhaps never been so destabilized as in our current era of resurgent authoritarian-phallocentric-xenophobic populism, grotesque inequality, and planetary ecocide. For a time, one of the last great anti-colonial national liberation movements of the twentieth century held out a global beacon, as it sought allies for its just critique of apartheid capitalism. The scope and complexity of this far-flung movement are comparable to movements for the abolition of the transatlantic slave trade. We must hope for a similar global movement against capitalism, imperialism, and climate injustice attentive to their many forms and fronts. Many people I interviewed for this book gave a part of themselves for the struggles to end apartheid. With their praxis in mind, how might we conceive of the postapartheid present by facing its contradictions squarely?

Apartheid Remains begins and ends with livelihood struggles in Wentworth and Merebank in the early 2000s, where people living in conditions of multifaceted injustice struggle against their plight. Refusing to concede defeat, people confront the remains of multiple pasts as limits to the world they imagine.

Part 1 of *Apartheid Remains* offers a method for diagnosing the historical geography of racial capitalism as a palimpsest. From the turn-of-the-twentieth-century arrival of late-Victorian biopolitical fantasies of gendered whiteness and racial government in Anglo-Boer War concentration camps, what remains are fantasies of differential government of "the poor" (see chapter 1). From remembered histories of dispossession and settlement, I argue for a dialectical reading of "Indian" and "Coloured" personhood and territoriality as continuing to shape divergent forms of political life while remaining in the aporetic space of submerged Indian Ocean histories in South Africa's seemingly intransigent racial geographies (see chapter 2).

From an account of "progressive segregation," I have sought to show how racial biopolitical statecraft was forged through concerted not-knowing, to produce a specific toxic landscape that mirrors of our planetary condition (see chapter 3). Reconsidered through radical Black feminism and in relation to gendered struggles before apartheid, the foibles of statecraft were fertile grounds for the emergence of biopolitical struggle (see chapter 4). Part 1 ends with the "golden years" of apartheid, which remained frustrated in remaking reality in the image of its science-fictional fantasies. The remains of coerced estrangement are also of planetary significance in the return of xenophobic-phallocentric authoritarianism in the slow degeneration of racial capitalism and biopolitical sovereignty, differently, everywhere (see chapter 5).

Part 2, "Remains of Revolution," offers a disaggregation of the anti-apartheid revolution that was and was not, depending on where and how one looks. Events circuiting through Wentworth and Merebank suggest four intertwined conjunctural moments that played out differently across lived geographies. To avoid the presumption that the first two moments come together in the third, leaving the fourth behind, let us consider them differently.

The moment of insurrection might seem to be the real thing, with the parable of Joe Slovo imagining he could see the burning refineries in Sasolburg from Mozambique. The expectation of revolution *as* insurrection was fanned by Cold War politics, literature, and popular culture and by a train of personal sacrifices for this conception of political community. Yet the resolutely militarist and masculinist expectations of this moment remain clouded in secrecy, intrigue, and post-traumatic suffering. At the high point of the moment of urban revolution in the 1980s, despite the uprising of civic and labor activism, activists faced pervasive difficulties in sustaining and connecting people's struggles in relation to the secretive and militarist traditions of the insurrectionists; while Operation Vula sought to fix this contradiction, it did so on terms set by the moment of insurrection. The sidelining of the politics of gender, sexuality, and intimacy in these two moments meant that the democratic government was completely unprepared, indeed neglectful, as the HIV/AIDS pandemic ravaged the social fabric, heedlessly deepening Black suffering.

What remains of the urban and insurrectionist moments are suspicions and intrigues of struggle lineages reaching from these neighborhoods to the leadership of the African National Congress (ANC), drawing in several people in this book. The uses of uncertainty have shifted to subterfuge around the lives of the power elite, and the protection of state capture by politically connected fractions of capital. What also remains of the urban moment are civic organizations and struggles for medical, gender, sexual, labor, environmental, and housing justice in relation to the tenuous hegemony of the ANC and its allies. The intrigues in civil society in both Wentworth and Merebank are legible in this light, as are the broader challenges faced by organizations defending people's livelihoods during the multifaceted crises of our time.

The failures of articulating popular hegemony in the decade of transition, from the mid-1980s to the mid-1990s, left a specific regret in the lives of activists who gave much of themselves to the struggle. This is particularly so in the moment of the disqualified, in spaces akin to what Fred Moten and Stefano Harney call the *undercommons*, from which the militant act carries the risk that "this will be regarded as theft, as a criminal act."[7] Units like the Robert McBride cell took this risk and effectively provided political muscle for the movement, but they did so because of the historical processes that racialized them in a particular way, unlike the activists of the Alan Taylor Residence or both the Congress and Black Consciousness (BC) groups from Merebank, who could tap into the long history of Indian progressivism built on an exclusionary Indian commons.

The moment of the disqualified reflects the failures of dominant left political discourse and of democratic government to meaningfully represent the movements of the poor, whether in anti-eviction protests or in the shack dwellers movement. In this extremely unequal society with tremendous promise, new militant subjects refuse social domination cloaked in radical discourse, proposing new forms of politics of and for the undercommons. The moment of the disqualified therefore remains.

Finally, the theologico-political moment emerged in a crucible of dock-worker, industrial labor, student, community, and feminist struggle in the early 1970s, when it seemed to some that everything could be transformed. I pose this moment as a leap of political faith that many activists took through BC and other communitarian currents. What remains of the theologico-political moment are utopian impulses that pervade today's environmental and labor struggles in neighborhoods around oil refineries, which have forged inspiring community-based and globally connected forms of environmental protest. And yet this utopianism is deeply limited if it cannot speak to the psychic burden of racial ontologization so carefully borne by the activist-artists of the moment of the disqualified.

The notion that popular communitarianism and insurrectionism could be turned into ballast for a new hegemonic apparatus led by a movement

FIGURE C.1 *George Ruiters*, Wentworth, 2003. © Jenny Gordon.

in exile proved to be a powerful illusion, one that has been hijacked to narrower ends than many imagined. Indeed, the events of the 1980s should have been the death knell of vanguardism everywhere. This does not mean that Leninist democratic centralism suffered a world-historical defeat to a new horizontalism but that demotic forces unleashed globally and in different ways at other moments may be impossible to repress. The question is, still, what their political direction might be.

There are powerful reasons to imagine how the theologico-political moment might recognize its kinship with the moment of the disqualified, to ensure that the terrain of biopolitical struggle is not inevitably co-opted by racial liberalism, sovereignty, and capital. Indeed, of the four moments, figures from the theologico-political moment, including some who participated in the moment of urban revolution and the moment of the disqualified, continue to identify with the radical praxis through which they forged visions of social change not beholden to capture by capital or the racial state.

I conclude in solidarity with two exemplary organizers in the realm of health advocacy, George Ruiters and the late Aunty Tilly. Both worked across the length and breadth of Wentworth, on issues including environmental pollution, public health, domestic violence, children's rights, and compliance with antiretroviral medication. Their tireless advocacy for decent conditions of life remains one of the best examples in this book of a communitarian and popular biopolitics that we cannot do without. A last photograph of George, taken by Jenny Gordon (figure C.1), shows us that the time beyond apartheid's remains is always here, spatialized and embodied in the work of conserving political hope.

Black Atlantic to Indian Ocean

Afrofuture as the Common

A mystery lies at the heart of this book: we will never know what spark lit the Durban dockworkers' strike of 1972–73. We only know that what followed was an uncontrollable set of struggles that, along with other forces, brought down apartheid and might yet help bring down its successor. We do not know whether this spark was carried by militant seafarers, conscripts of our fragile world. We only know the slow and painful repression of Indian Ocean histories of racial and sexual violence palpable in South African forms and structures of feeling. I have sought to follow this cue through little, expansive windows from Merebank and Wentworth.

As multiple strands of struggle amplified through South Africa's fitful revolution, the resources of the Black Atlantic offered specific hopes. To some, Black Power promised a seizure of the gears of sovereignty. To others, it offered the tools of biopolitics to disassemble the infrastructure of state racism. Thinking Black Power oceanically from Durban might have held the possibility of freeing it from enslavement to sovereignty and capital. In the face of such hopes, the prison house of racial capitalism reasserts its presence. And so the last great twentieth-century national liberation movement to gain state power in the name of the people slowly degenerated into a captured and corrupt machine that dangles the lure of class mobility for some as the few gorge on the public coffers. Many characters in this absurdist postcolonial situation find their way through this book, connecting what were never just township histories to the question of how to refuse apartheid's remains.

But the oceanic spark in Durban's dockworker strike stands for something other than a lost Indian Ocean subalternity or a lapsed Black politics. At the confluence of the Black Atlantic and the Indian Ocean, the palimpsestic record of racial capitalism and struggle in Durban points to a different conception of "the common" from that of the Euro-American avant-garde.[1] The fastest demographic growth by the middle of this century will be on the African continent. In the long aftermath of the twentieth-century anticolonial revolution, our burning Earth is becoming an increasingly oceanic and Black planet. If and when a hypothetical humanity faces its planetary kin with compassion, it will have to do so in relation to Africa's diasporas, including its internal ones. The prospect of a poetry of the future depends on the solidarities that Black politics and poetics might conjure in the present.[2] Afrofuture *is* the common.

ACKNOWLEDGMENTS

This book has accumulated many debts over time and space. My greatest thanks go to many people from Merebank and Wentworth, and across South Africa, who shared time and insight over many years. I try to name them all in the bibliography. Of those no longer with us, Peter McKenzie, Aunty Marie, Derrick McBride, Skido Joseph, and Marcel Andrews are greatly missed. Particular thanks to George Ruiters, Greta Apelgren, Patricia Dove, Jambo Solomons, Des D'Sa, Bobby Peek, Mrs. Perumal, Jo Beall, Bobby Marie, Shamim Meer, Cedric Nunn, Jenny Gordon, Omar Badsha, and Neefa McKenzie.

Three crucibles of creativity nourished this project: the University of Michigan at the turn of the millennium; the University of Natal, Durban (UND), which became the University of KwaZulu-Natal (UKZN) in the early 2000s; and the University of the Witwatersrand (Wits) in the early 2010s. What made each place and time so exciting is difficult to condense, but each gave me a proper reeducation. I have thanked the Michiganders profusely already, and I wish I could share this with Fernando Coronil.

Of the Durbanites, this book comes too late to thank Vishnu Padayachee and Bill Freund. I remain grateful to many, and in particular to Caroline Skinner, Richard Ballard, Catherine Burns, Keith Breckenridge, Stephen Sparks, Nafisa Essop Shaik, Vashna Jagarnath, Prinisha Badassy, Anesh Naidoo, Richard Pithouse, Monique Marks, Bernard Dubbeld, Deepak Mistrey, Rakesh Patel, Yogesh Naidoo, Ketan Parbhoo; and a Durban diaspora that includes Vasu and Sudeshan Reddy, Kerry Chance, Niren Tolsi, Shannon Walsh, Jon Soske, Upjeet Chandan, Mark Hunter, Gill Hart, and David Szanton.

At Wits in the early 2010s, I am grateful to the Anthropology Department, the Centre for Indian Studies in Africa, and the Wits Institute for Social and Economic Research, and to many people, including Isabel Hofmeyr, Reshmi

Singh, Dilip Menon, Melanie Samson, Shireen Hassim, Lucy Allais, Kelly Gillespie, Zen Marie, Naadira Patel, Matthew Wilhelm-Solomon, Srila Roy, Sarah Nuttall, Achille Mbembe, Najeebha Deshmukh, Adila Deshmukh, Charne Lavery, Pamila Gupta, Juan Orrantia, Nolwazi Mkhwanazi, Joel Quirk, Stacey Sommerdyck, Loren Landau, Caroline Kihato, Claudia Gastrow, Kirk Sides, Chris Lee, Sarah Duff, Lenore Manderson, and many exciting undergraduate and postgraduate students. And then there was this bus, with Dhammamegha, Angela Davis, Gina Dent, Françoise Vergès, Gabeba Baderoon, Neo Muyanga, Ruha Benjamin, Ghassan Hage, David Theo Goldberg, Casey Golomski, and many others. From London to Jozi, Anokhi Parikh, and Thandiswa Mazwai. Beverly Palesa Ditsie for the gift of collaboration. Across continents, Alok, Mathew, Arkaja, and Gautam. Capetonians, including Ute Kuhlman, Craig Mason-Jones, Ruchi Chaturvedi, Suren Pillay, Erin Torkelson, Premesh Lalu, Patricia Hayes, Sue Parnell, Owen Crankshaw, Andy Tucker, Patrick Rivers, and Kai Wood Mah. A residency at the Stellenbosch Institute for Advanced Studies with wonderful comrades helped me in the final stages.

Particular gratitude for Dharmagiri, Mvuleni mountain, Kittisaro, Thanissara, Maia, Niel, Phumla, Annika, Jenny, Joanne, Dürten, Thenjiwe, and many others (each with their own retinue).

In London, I am grateful for Stuart Corbridge, Claire Mercer, Gareth Jones, Henrike Donner, Hendrik Wittkopf, Deborah James, Andrea Gibbons, Simón Uribe, Edyta Materka, Taneesha Mohan, Jayaraj Sundaresan, Dorothea Kleine, Jo Beall, Rashmi Varma, Subir Sinha, Shabnum Tejani, Tariq Jazeel, Laleh Khalili, and Jenny Robinson. Thanks to Mina Moshkeri at the London School of Economics for the beautiful maps. Life in London was complete with Rashmi, Subir, Lila, Shabnum, Riz, Srinivas, Erik, Philippe, Monica, Jaime, David, Subham, Neeta, Chandra, Asher, and Preetha, and, a hop away, Milena. Not quite perpetual succor, Graeme Napier afforded me an unknown number of years at Westminster Abbey.

Warm gratitude to all my colleagues at the Berkeley Geography Department, and in particular to Jovan Lewis, Josh Mandel, Ambrosia Shapiro, Eron Budi, Clancy Wilmott (and Emma Fraser), Jake Kosek, and many wonderful undergraduate and graduate students. A few groups make Berkeley more politically and intellectually exciting: the Berkeley Faculty Association defends the public university, and the *Critical Times* crew practices critique as thoughtful solidarity. In these and other things, particular thanks to James Vernon, Leslie Salzinger, Samera Esmeir, Natalia Brizuela, Colleen Lye, Paola Bacchetta, Michael Burawoy, Breana George, Ramsey McGlaser, Lawrence

Cohen, Fumi Okiji, Poulomi Saha, Aarti Sethi, Courtney Cox, Eric Stanley, Donald Moore, and many other wonderful colleagues.

Thanks to Ruthie Gilmore (and Craig) for changing what is possible in geography. Thanks to fellow travelers on the good ship *Antipode*, and in particular to Andy Kent (skipper), Katherine McKittrick, Nik Theodore, Vinay Gidwani, Wendy Larner, Melissa Wright, Jenny Pickerel, Tariq Jazeel, and a host of others at the journal and foundation. Gratitude for James McCarthy, Amy Ross, Wendy Wolford, Scott Prudham, Aaron Bobrow-Strain, Paul Amar, and Charmaine Chua.

This project has benefited from support from the Michigan Society of Fellows, the Rackham Faculty Grant and Fellowship, the National Research Foundation of South Africa, the National Institute for Humanities and Social Sciences in South Africa, the Institute for International Studies at Berkeley, a Mellon Humanities Research Fellowship, and a residency at the Stellenbosch Institute for Advanced Studies. I am grateful for research support from all the departments I have been affiliated with.

Archives and libraries have been central to anything of value here. The Durban Archives Repository of the National Archives of South Africa remains an outstanding resource, and I am in debt to the archivists for allowing me to access material in the process of reclassification. The provincial repository at Pietermaritzburg was similarly very helpful. The Local History Museum in Durban is a gold mine, particularly for its photographic collections. Thanks to the Killie Campbell Africana Library, Wits Historical Papers at the University of the Witwatersrand, the University of Pretoria Institutional Repository, and the library of the Stellenbosch Institute for Advanced Studies. Activist histories would be impoverished without collections at the Gandhi-Luthuli Documentation Centre at the UKZN Westville Campus, the Padraig O'Malley Heart of Hope Collection at the Nelson Mandela Centre of Memory, South African History Online (SAHO) with thanks to Omar Badsha, the South African History Archive (SAHA), and Truth and Reconciliation Commission (TRC) material from the Department of Justice. In London the Women's Library, now at the LSE, is an exceptional resource. The British Library is a haven that has nourished this work. I am very grateful to archive and library staff at all these institutions who make our scholarly work possible.

Several people afforded access to personal archival collections as well. I am grateful to the Juggernath family and to Derrick McBride, Hector Henry, Ivan Pillay, Morris Fynn, and Hashim Seedat for sharing their collections generously.

Intrepid readers worked through the manuscript, helping me beyond measure. Prema Chari has always been the first reader. Gill Hart gave me careful comments on a memorable walk. Keith Breckenridge, Shireen Hassim, and Lucy Allais came to Berkeley to read and think together. Paola Bacchetta, Michael Watts, James Vernon, Phil Campanile, Keith Hart, Matthew Shutzer, Kavita Phillip, Chandan Reddy, Ashwin Mathew, Mukul Kumar, Ward Smith, Mike Kirkwood, Richard Pithouse, Zachary Levenson, Asher Ghertner (and his wonderful graduate seminar), and two referees offered invaluable insights on the manuscript, as did many others on various parts, including a passing *tohfa* of great value from Geeta Patel (and Kath). Gabeba Baderoon is a gift who helps me finish books. Sibahle Ndwayana and Adam Hasan aided greatly with the *graft* of citation.

I am grateful to audience responses at multiple talks at meetings or colloquia under the auspices of the American Association of Geographers, the American Anthropological Association, and the Association of Southern African Anthropology; geography departments at Berkeley, Rutgers, Minnesota, Cambridge, Liverpool, Royal Holloway, Queen Mary, LSE, and Toronto; anthropology departments at Michigan, Wits, CUNY, Chicago, and Goldsmiths; history and African studies at UKZN; the African studies workshop at Chicago; the Unit for Humanities at Rhodes; the African Centre for Cities at the University of Cape Town; Development Studies at UKZN; the Johannesburg Workshop for Theory and Criticism; the Centre for Indian Studies in Africa at Wits; History Workshop at Wits; the Eisenberg Institute at Michigan; the Urban Democracy Lab at New York University; the Center for Humanities at Tufts; cultural studies at the University of California, Santa Cruz; "Markets and Modernities" at Toronto; "Henri Lefebvre Today" at the Delft University of Technology; "Scarred Landscapes / Imperial Debris" at the New School; "Historical Materialism" in London; "BIOS: Life, Death, Politics" at the Unit for Criticism and Interpretive Theory, the University of Illinois at Urbana Champaign; "Space, Capital and Social History" at the Centre for Modern Indian Studies, Göttingen; "Ontological Insecurity" at the African Centre for Migration Studies at Wits; HUSS lab at the American University of Cairo; and "RAI2020: Anthropology and Geography" by the Royal Anthropological Institute and the Royal Geographical Society. Particular thanks to all who asked difficult questions.

Elizabeth Ault at Duke has been a very supportive editor from our first interactions, and especially during revision in the time of a pandemic. The honor of being in a series edited by Katherine McKittrick, Deb Cowan, and Simone Browne is compounded by their exemplary scholarship. I remain thankful to all of them, as well as to patient project editor Michael Trudeau, careful editorial assistant Benjamin Kossak, eagle-eyed copyeditor Kim Miller, and to all on the Duke production and marketing team who bring this book into the world.

Life in the Bay is enriched by Yasmin, Thu-ha, Winter, Dan, Mona, Priya, and Musa. Through fire and brimstone, bubbly and cake, Ros and James and Alice and Jake. Across space-times, Simona, Milena, Jasbir, Anand, Sanchita, Tahir, Ananya, Eric, Scott, and MBF Padmini.

As always, gratitude for Ma and Pa, Arvind and Jeannie, Nikhil and Maya; and for Sara Jazbhay, as well as for the warm memory of A. H. M. Jazbhay, who always asked me with interest and a smile how the book was coming along.

Words slow as I contemplate this journey with Ismail Jazbhay. Between all lines, this is for him, and for what we found at a city by the sea.

INTRODUCTION. DETRITUS IN DURBAN, 2002–2008

Epigraph: Gilmore, "Forgotten Places," 35–36.

1　I use pseudonyms if I can discern any potential negative consequences from information I present. I do not cite interlocutors, dates, or locations to protect subjects or because some conversations were across multiple dates during ethnographic fieldwork. Any quotation in this book that does not have a citation in the notes is from my interview recordings, currently in my possession. I sometimes use actual first names so that people might see themselves in the text, without making their full names searchable through the index. I usually use first names for people I interviewed or know personally and last names for people I did not interview or when, for reasons of respect, I would not call them by their first name. These are imperfect decisions. A full list of the people I was fortunate to interview is in the bibliography. Some of these are partial names, because that is the name I was given. Most interviews were conducted between 2002 and 2008 across South African cities.

2　*Coloured* and *Indian* are South African racial categories, which means their use is never innocent. See the section in this introduction "On Racial Risks and Spatial Histories" for more on these terms and also on the anti-racist political term *Black*.

3　In the context of depreciation of the South African rand compounded by a currency crisis in early 2001, I use 2007 exchange rates, similar to those in 1998–2000, when the census data were being collected.

4　Wentworth's annual household incomes were between $3,000 and $14,000; Merebank's were in the next range, up to $23,000. Statistics South Africa, Census, 2001.

5　Statistics South Africa, Census, 2001. I accessed digital data on CD-ROMs, not published print or online digital versions.

6　On Durban, see Pattman and Khan, *Undressing Durban*. KwaZulu, literally "place of the Zulus," was given quasi-independence by the apartheid state from 1972 until 1994.

7 Gilmore's crisp formulation in "Fatal Couplings": "Racism, specifically, is the state-sanctioned or extralegal production and exploitation of group-differentiated vulnerability to premature death" (16).

8 Undated recording from early 2003 meeting at Austerville Community Centre, Wentworth.

9 W. Benjamin, *Illuminations*, 249.

10 Fanon, *Wretched of the Earth*, 39. Garner's phrase was picked up by many Black people subject to US police violence and became a slogan of Black Lives Matter movements.

11 Chari, "Post-Apartheid Livelihood Struggles"; Chari, "Detritus in Durban."

12 Tony Carnie, "The Poison in Our Air"; Wright, "Living and Dying."

13 T. G. Robins et al., "Respiratory Health."

14 Wiley, Root, and Peek, "Contesting."

15 Peek, "Doublespeak in Durban."

16 Desai, *We Are the Poors*.

17 Pithouse, "Solidarity, Co-optation and Assimilation"; Comaroff, "Beyond Bare Life"; Chance, *Living Politics*; Figlan et al., *Living Learning*.

18 Care work beyond the household is a well-studied topic; in geography, see K. Mitchell, Marston, and Katz, *Life's Work*; on dignity, Richard Pithouse, "Hit the Tire," and Vincent Lloyed, *Black Dignity*.

19 Philip clarifies that South African cooperatives have been largely producer cooperatives, as in Wentworth, but that about 40 percent were unviable for reasons of low skill levels (particularly in financial management), an oversupply of labor, limited markets, and "an expectation of a high level of direct democracy and worker control" without consensus about collective practice or the mandate of elected management, leading to ongoing conflict. Philip, *Co-operatives in South Africa*, 19–23.

20 Pithouse, "Politics of the Poor"; Pithouse, "'Our Struggle'"; Pithouse, "Struggle Is a School"; Chance, *Living Politics*; Von Schnitzler, *Democracy's Infrastructure*.

21 Hart, "The Provocations of Neoliberalism," 680; Makhulu, *Making Freedom*, xv.

22 S. Hassim, *Women's Organizations*; Jayawardena, *Feminism and Nationalism*.

23 Farred, "Not-Yet Counterpartisan," 589–94.

24 Samera Esmeir, "The Palestinians and the Struggle."

25 This is not to say that this is how Gilmore arrived at her formulation. Gilmore, *Abolition Geography*, 252–54. Epigraphs to this section: Harvey, *Justice*, 295; Gilmore, *Golden Gulag*, 26–27.

26 In his 1881 letters to Vera Zasulich, Marx recasts his method as explicitly multitemporal and open to the possibility that the Russian rural commune, the *obschina*, might be shorn of its inegalitarian (in particular, patriarchal) elements to help shape a communism of the future. See Marx, "Drafts"; see also K. Anderson, *Marx at the Margins*; Tomba, *Marx's Temporalities*.

27 Harvey, "Dialectics of Spacetime."

28 Lefebvre, *Production of Space*, 372–74, 395–97.

29 For a generous reading of Lefebvre, see Kipfer et al., "Globalizing Lefebvre?"

30 Harvey, *Justice*, 295.

31 Harvey, *Justice*, 295–96.

32 Harvey, *Justice*, 296.

33 An important exception is Harvey, *Paris, Capital of Modernity*.

34 Gilmore, *Geographies of Racial Capitalism*.

35 C. Robinson, *Forgeries of Memory*, xiii–xvi.

36 C. Robinson, *Forgeries of Memory*.

37 W. Benjamin, "Hashish in Marseilles," 673–79.

38 Gilmore, *Golden Gulag*.

39 Swanson, "Sanitation Syndrome"; Foucault, *"Society Must Be Defended."* Epigraphs to this section: Marx, *Capital*, 325, with thanks to Arvind Narrain for pointing me to this passage; Foucault, *History of Sexuality*, 140–41.

40 There are now several important books doing this work, including Dubow, *Commonwealth of Knowledge*; Beinart, *Rise of Conservation*; and McCulloch, *Asbestos Blues*.

41 Foucault, *Birth of Biopolitics*, 317; Foucault, *Security, Territory, Population*; Foucault, *History of Sexuality*, 138–45; Foucault, *"Society Must Be Defended"*; Stoler, *Race*.

42 Foucault, *Security, Territory, Population*, 10.

43 Lake and Reynolds, *Drawing the Global Colour Line*; Stoler, "Racial Histories."

44 Sunder Rajan, *Biocapital*.

45 Chari, "Blues."

46 Wolin, *Wind*, 289–90, 317–49; Chari, "State Racism"; Chari, "Blues."

47 Breckenridge, "Biometric Obsession"; Breckenridge, "Progressivism Unleashed"; Breckenridge, *Biometric State*, 206–7.

48 Rodgers, *Atlantic Crossings*; McGerr, *Fierce Discontent*; Breckenridge, "Progressivism Unleashed," 9–10.

49 Breckenridge, "Progressivism Unleashed," 10.

50 Breckenridge, "Progressivism Unleashed."

51 Berry, *No Condition Is Permanent*, 22–42.

52 Stoler, *Race*; W. Anderson, *Colonial Pathologies*; Breckenridge, *Biometric State*; MacDonald, "Durban-Bound."

53 Stoler, *Race*; Stoler, *Carnal Knowledge*.

54 Lake and Reynolds, *Drawing the Global Colour Line*.

55 Matthew Hannah, in *Governmentality and the Mastery of Territory*, proposes that biopolitical governmentality entails the mastery of territory and the ability to generate and use comprehensive statistical information about people and resources with popular consent; and that the latter, in turn, presumes techniques of observation and means of communication, the ability to differentiate populations and resources, and the centralization of regulation and enforcement of governmental knowledge. In much of the postcolonial world, if not everywhere, this is a tall order.

56 See Rabinow and Rose, "Biopower Today," on differentiating expert knowledge, intervention, and subjectivation; Breckenridge, *Biometric State*, on

disaggregating the tools of biopolitics; and Rodgers, *Atlantic Crossings*, for demonstrating why these differences matter in the different domains of "social politics," urban planning, public health, or rural reconstruction.

57 Mbembe, "Necropolitics"; Mbembe, *Necropolitics*.

58 Comaroff, "Beyond Bare Life"; S. Robins, "From 'Rights' to 'Ritual'"; Fassin, *When Bodies Remember*; Pithouse, "Solidarity, Co-optation and Assimilation"; Pithouse, *Writing the Decline*; Hart, "Provocations of Neoliberalism"; Hart, *Rethinking the South African Crisis*; Gibson, "What Happened."

59 Foucault, *"Society Must Be Defended"*; Fassin, *When Bodies Remember*, 49.

60 Petryna, *Life Exposed*; McCulloch, *Asbestos Blues*; Klawiter, *Biopolitics of Breast Cancer*; Gould, *Moving Politics*.

61 Taylor, *How We Get Free*.

62 Key works on the geography of segregation include Swanson, "Sanitation Syndrome"; J. Robinson, *Power of Apartheid*; Parnell, "Creating Racial Privilege"; and Western, *Outcast Cape Town*. On instabilities of labor control, see Breckenridge, "Verwoerd's Bureau of Proof," and MacDonald, "Durban-Bound."

63 Key works on the political economy of transition that inform this book include Fine and Rustomjee, *Political Economy*; Padayachee and van Niekerk, *Shadow of Liberation*; Marais, *South Africa*; Bond, *Elite Transition*; Hart, *Disabling Globalization*; Padayachee, *Development Decade?*; and Von Holdt, *Transition from Below*. On activism, some key texts that inform this one include Barchiesi, "Classes, Multitudes" and *Precarious Liberation*; Desai, *We Are the Poors*; Gibson, *Challenging Hegemony* and *Fanonian Practices*; Pithouse, "Solidarity, Co-optation and Assimilation"; and Ballard, Habib, and Valodia, *Voices of Protest*. On urbanism, some key texts that inform the analysis here include Freund and Padayachee, *(D)urban Vortex*; S. Nuttall and Mbembe, *Johannesburg*; Simone, *For the City Yet to Come*; J. Robinson, "(Im)mobilizing Space"; Pieterse and Simone, *Rogue Urbanism*; Parnell and Mabin, "Rethinking Urban South Africa"; Mabin, "Comprehensive Segregation" and "Labour, Capital, Class Struggle"; Maharaj, "Apartheid, Urban Segregation" and "The Local State and Residential Segregation"; and Pieterse and Parnell, *Africa's Urban Revolution*. Key texts on agrarian change that inform this study include Bundy, *Rise and Fall*; Beinart, Delius, and Trapido, *Putting Plough to the Ground*; Van Onselen, *Seed Is Mine*; Walker, *Women and Resistance*; Ntsebeza and Hall, *Land Question*; Ntsebeza, *Democracy Compromised*; A. Du Toit and Neves, "Rural Livelihoods"; and a large body of work from the Institute for Poverty, Land and Agrarian Studies at the University of the Western Cape.

64 Marais, *South Africa*. Texts that have taken on this charge include Hunter, *Love*; Hunter, *Race for Education*; Mosoetsa, *Eating from One Pot*; Skinner, "Struggle for the Streets"; Skinner and Dobson, *Working in Warwick*; Gibbs, *Mandela's Kinsmen*; Samson, "Not Just Recycling," "Trashing Solidarity," and "Whose Frontier"; Veriava, "South African Diagram"; Veriava and Naidoo, "Predicaments"; Sparks, "Apartheid Modern"; Sheik, "Customs in Common"

and "Entangled Patriarchies"; Badassy, "'Is Lying a Coolie's Religion?'"; and Reynolds, Fine, and van Niekerk, *Race, Class*. On memory, heritage, and the cultural politics of the aftermath, see S. Nuttall, *Entanglement*, "Upsurge," and "Afterword: The Shock of the New Old"; S. Nuttall and Coetzee, *Negotiating the Past*; and Hamilton et al., *Reconfiguring the Archive*.

65 T. Sithole, *Black Register*; Farred, "Where Does the Rainbow Nation End?"; Farred, "Black Intellectual's Work"; Farred, *Martin Heidegger*; Gqola, *What Is Slavery to Me?*; Gqola, *Renegade Called Simphiwe*; Baderoon, *Regarding Muslims*. Other works in this vein, with important differences among them, include Mangcu, *Biko*, "Liberating Race from Apartheid," and *Colour of Our Future*; Ndlovu-Gatsheni, *Coloniality of Power* and *Empire*; Ndlovu-Gatsheni and Ndlovu, *Decolonization*; Collis-Buthelezi, "Case for Black Studies" and "Requiem"; Modisane, Collis-Buthelezi, and Ouma, "Introduction: Black Studies, South Africa, and the Mythology of Mandela"; Veriava and Naidoo, "Remembering Biko"; L.-A. Naidoo, "Role of Radical Pedagogy"; Pillay, "Problem of Colonialism"; and Mellet, *Lie of 1652*.

66 S. Hall, *Selected Writings on Race*; S. Hall, *Selected Writings on Marxism*; Kundnani, "What Is Racial Capitalism?"; Kundnani, *What Is Antiracism?*

67 S. Hall, "Race, Articulation," 234–36.

68 S. Hall et al., *Policing the Crisis*.

69 S. Hall, "Race, Articulation," 239. There are strong echoes in this fight on the terrain of consciousness with the work of E. P. Thompson; see E. Thompson, "Eighteenth-Century English Society."

70 James, *History of Pan-African Revolt*, 24–25, 77; James, *Black Jacobins*; James, "Haitian Revolution"; Chari, "Mysterious Moves of Revolution."

71 Centre for Contemporary Cultural Studies, *Empire Strikes Back*.

72 S. Hall, "New Ethnicities," 165; Ferguson, "Lateral Moves."

73 S. Hall, "Black Diaspora Artists," 3.

74 *Oxford English Dictionary*, s.v. "moment," accessed July 31, 2012, http://www.oed.com/view/Entry/120997.

75 Everatt, *Origins of Non-racialism*; Frederikse, *Unbreakable Thread*; Suttner, "Understanding Non-racialism."

76 Collis-Buthelezi, "Case for Black Studies," 8; Sharpe, "Black Studies."

77 Mangcu, "Liberating Race from Apartheid"; Collis-Buthelezi, "Case for Black Studies."

78 Mbembe, *Critique of Black Reason*, 2–6, 182–83; see also Mbembe, *Out of the Dark Night*, 41.

79 Glissant, *Poetics of Relation*; Gilroy, *Black Atlantic*; McKittrick, *Demonic Grounds*; Trouillot, *Silencing the Past*; and in Southern African space, in addition to all the thinkers in note 65 of this introduction, Simone, *For the City Yet to Come*; Mbembe, *Critique of Black Reason*; Mbembe, *Out of the Dark Night*; Vergès, *Monsters and Revolutionaries*; Lalu, *Deaths of Hintsa*; Baderoon, *Regarding Muslims*.

80 Erasmus, *Race Otherwise*; Levenson, *Delivery as Dispossession*.

81 C. Robinson, *Forgeries of Memory*.

82 Posel, "What's in a Name?"; Lee, *Unreasonable Histories*, 24.

83 Erasmus, "Introduction: Re-imagining Coloured Identities in Post-apartheid South Africa"; Erasmus, *Coloured by History*; Reddy, "Politics of Naming"; Adhikari, *Burdened by Race*; Adhikari, *Not White Enough*.

84 Farred, "Where Does the Rainbow Nation End?," 186.

85 For a critical treatment of this trope, which is not a quotation, see Adhikari, *Not White Enough*.

86 Ebrahim-Vally, *Kala Pani*; Vahed, "Making of Indian Identity"; Vahed, Desai, and Waetjen, *Many Lives*.

87 Bonner and Nieftagodien, *Alexandra*; Bozzoli, *Theatres of Struggle*; Desai and Vahed, *Chatsworth*; Desai, *Wentworth*; and a large body of popular writing including, from Wentworth, Lottering, *Winnifred and Agnes*.

88 Desai, *Wentworth*, 27.

89 Hunter, *Race for Education*.

90 For her insights on "relational comparison," see Hart, *Disabling Globalization*.

91 Chari, *Gramsci at Sea*, chap. 1; Gilmore, *Abolition Geography*, 260.

92 Chari, *Gramsci at Sea*; Chari, "'Interlocking Transactions.'"

93 Steedman, *Landscape*, 144; Coronil, "Beyond Occidentalism," 81; Eley, *Forging Democracy*, ix, quoting Morris, *Dream of John Ball*, 722: "I . . . pondered how [people] fight and lose the battle, and the thing that they fought for comes about in spite of their defeat, and when it comes turns out not to be what they meant, and other [people] fight for what they meant under another name."

CHAPTER 1. REMAINS OF A CAMP

Epigraph: Hobhouse, *Brunt of the War*, 317–18.

1 Foucault, *History of Sexuality*, 130; Stoler, *Along the Archival Grain*, 63; Hunter, *Love*.

2 I am grateful to Keith Breckenridge for this insight over many years of productive debate about what he calls "power without knowledge."

3 On urban informality as improvisational, see Simone, *For the City Yet to Come*, which echoes the historical argument in Berry, *No Condition Is Permanent*; see also the precise arguments about African urban informality in Frederick Cooper, "Urban Space, Industrial Time," and Luise White, "A Colonial State."

4 On the difficulties of narrating pain, see Scarry, *Body in Pain*; and Daniel, *Charred Lullabies*.

5 Thanks for the company and keen insight of Richard Ballard on August 9, 2010.

6 B. Roberts, *Those Bloody Women*, 68.

7 B. Roberts, *Those Bloody Women*, 68.

8 I use the term *Anglo-Boer War* when I discuss texts that use this term and *South African War* when thinking from the present, with some skepticism about what it means to make the name of a war inclusive.

9 Pierre Nora, "General Introduction: Between Memory and History," in Nora and Lawrence Kritzman, *Realms of Memory*, the translation of the multivolume editions of Pierre Nora, *Lieux de Mémoire*, which posed "sites of memory" alongside the decline of lived collective memory in the wake of national historiographical consciousness and its sharpening archival imperative; see also Nora, "Between Memory and History: Les Lieux de Mémoire." There are too many texts to cite on the "archival turn" of the 1990s. In geography, Jeremy Foster pushes beyond Nora to "non-declarative forms of memory" or "memory through things"; Stephen Legg roundly critiques Nora's nation-centrism and nostalgia for collective memory. Foster, "From Socio-nature to Spectral Presence," 183; Legg, "Contesting and Surviving Memory."

10 Stoler, *Carnal Knowledge*; Stoler, *Race*.

11 I use the term *Victorian* loosely in a time after Victoria's reign to consider biopolitical expertise as a late nineteenth-century transatlantic and colonial knowledge/power project.

12 Hyslop, "Invention of the Concentration Camp," 273.

13 Forth, *Barbed-Wire Imperialism*, 4–5.

14 Forth, *Barbed-Wire Imperialism*, 9.

15 Stoler, "Colony," 47, 55.

16 Hyslop, "Invention of the Concentration Camp," 252–53.

17 See Yurchak, "Soviet Hegemony of Form," 485–86, on the "hegemony of form" in the last years of the Soviet Union; and Stoler, *Along the Archival Grain*, 37–38, 98, on "grids of intelligibility" and the argument that "affective knowledge was at the core of political rationality in its late-colonial form . . . in the cultivation of compassion, contempt and disdain."

18 Baucom, *Specters of the Atlantic*, 121–22.

19 Following a cue from Stoler (*Along the Archival Grain*, 106), fantasies are key to statecraft. I poach Jacques Derrida's "hauntology" to refer to fantasies that are not simply about "ontical" things but rather make claims to their own potential ontology, to that which patently *is not* but which *could be*; see Chari, "Blues"; Derrida, *Specters of Marx*.

20 Thanks to Geeta Patel on the "past-perfect subjunctive"—see chapter 3, note 1.

21 Stoler, *Along the Archival Grain*, 144.

22 Among the vast scholarship on the South African War, key texts are Pakenham, *Boer War*; Warwick, *Black People*; Nasson, *South African War*; Nasson, *War for South Africa*; Van Heyningen, *Concentration Camps*; and B. Roberts, *Those Bloody Women*.

23 Hyslop, "Invention of the Concentration Camp."

24 Several texts point to Black involvement in the South African War, including Warwick, "African Labour"; Warwick, *South African War*; Warwick, *Black People*; Cuthbertson, Grundlingh, and Suttie, *Writing a Wider War*; and works by Bill Nasson, Brian Roberts, Shula Marks, and Helen Bradford.

25 S. Marks, "War and Union," 160; S. Marks, "Before 'the White Man Was Master,'" 3–4; S. Marks, "White Masculinity," 219.

26 Texts in British gender history that I have relied on include Davin, "Imperialism and Motherhood"; Ware, *Beyond the Pale*; C. Hall, *White, Male and Middle Class*; Rose, *Limited Livelihoods*; Burton, "States of Injury" and *Burdens of History*; Sinha, *Colonial Masculinity*; Poovey, *Making a Social Body*; Clark, *Struggle for the Breeches*; Midgely, *Gender and Imperialism*; Clark, "New Poor Law"; Levine-Clark, "Engendering Relief"; Steedman, "Fictions of Engagement"; and Koven, *Slumming*.

27 For instance, Krebs, "'Last of the Gentlemen's Wars'"; Burton, "States of Injury"; Denness, "Women and Warfare"; S. Marks, "White Masculinity."

28 B. Roberts, *Those Bloody Women*, 3.

29 War Office, Reports of the Working of the Refugee Camps in the Transvaal (Cd. 819); War Office, Further Papers Related to the Working of the Refugee Camps in the Transvaal (Cd. 853); War Office, Concentration Camps Commission (Cd. 893); War Office, Further Papers Relating to the Working of the Refugee Camps in South Africa (Cd. 902); War Office, Further Papers Relating to the Working of the Refugee Camps in South Africa (Cd. 934); War Office, Further Papers Relating to the Working of the Refugee Camps in South Africa (Cd. 936); War Office, Return of Farm Buildings, etc., in Cape Colony and Natal Destroyed by the Boers (Cd. 979).

30 T. Mitchell, *Rule of Experts*.

31 Stedman Jones, *Outcast London*; Koven, *Slumming*. Epigraph to this section: Hobhouse, *Report of a Visit*, 4.

32 Despite this astonishing life, Paula Krebs summarily labels her an upper-class woman. Krebs, "'Last of the Gentlemen's Wars.'"

33 For instance, Lord Roberts's letter to General Botha, September 2, 1900:

> Sir, I beg to address your Honour in regard to the actions of the comparatively small bands of armed Boers who conceal themselves in the neighbourhood of our lines of communication, and who constantly endeavour to destroy the railroad, thereby endangering the lives of passengers, both combatants and non-combatants, travelling by the trains.
>
> I address your Honour on this subject because, with the exception of the districts occupied by the army under your Honour's personal command, there are now no properly organized Boer armies in the Transvaal and the Orange River Colony, and the war degenerates into the actions of irregular and irresponsible guerrillas. This would be detrimental to the country, and so regrettable from every point of view that I feel compelled to do all in my power to prevent it.
>
> In order to put these views into practice, I have issued instructions that the Boer farmhouses near the spot where an effort has been made to destroy the railroad or to wreck the trains shall be burnt, and that from all farmhouses for a distance of ten miles around such a spot all provisions, cattle, etc. shall be removed.
>
> (quoted in Hobhouse, *Brunt of the War*, 29)

34 Hyslop, "Invention of the Concentration Camp."
35 Hobhouse later noted that only the Port Elizabeth camp was known of in England when she began her investigation. B. Roberts, *Those Bloody Women*, 120–21, 135.
36 B. Roberts, *Those Bloody Women*, 135.
37 B. Roberts, *Those Bloody Women*, 139–40.
38 On the latter point, see Hyslop, "Invention of the Concentration Camp," 259.
39 Hobhouse, *Report of a Visit*.
40 Hobhouse, *Brunt of the War*, 46.
41 Hobhouse, *War without Glamour*, 33, 36.
42 Hobhouse, *War without Glamour*, 40.
43 Hobhouse, *War without Glamour*, 96.
44 Hobhouse, *War without Glamour*, 90.
45 Hobhouse, *War without Glamour*, 112.
46 Krebs, *Gender, Race*.
47 Fischer, *That Miss Hobhouse*, 152.
48 Quoted in Fischer, *That Miss Hobhouse*, 152–53.
49 Quoted in Fischer, *That Miss Hobhouse*, 154.
50 S. Marks, "Before 'the White Man Was Master,'" 12.
51 Van Heyningen, *Concentration Camps*, 82–99.
52 Quoted in Fischer, *That Miss Hobhouse*, 169.
53 Forth, *Barbed-Wire Imperialism*, 184, 293n179.
54 Quoted in Fischer, *That Miss Hobhouse*, 170.
55 S. Marks and Trapido, "Lord Milner," 56–58.
56 Harvey, *New Imperialism*.
57 Spivak, "Can the Subaltern Speak?," 296; on the racialization of "Boers" through the war, see Denness, "Women and Warfare."
58 B. Roberts, *Those Bloody Women*, 188.
59 B. Roberts, *Those Bloody Women*, 192.
60 Russell, *A-B-War*.
61 B. Roberts, *Those Bloody Women*, 193.
62 War Office, Concentration Camps Commission (Cd. 893).
63 Quoted in B. Roberts, *Those Bloody Women*, 64–65.
64 Van Heyningen, *Concentration Camps*, 206.
65 T. Mitchell, *Rule of Experts*, 19–53.
66 Quoted in B. Roberts, *Those Bloody Women*, 65; Van Heyningen, *Concentration Camps*, 357.
67 B. Roberts, *Those Bloody Women*, 66.
68 B. Roberts, *Those Bloody Women*, 66–67.
69 War Office, Concentration Camps Commission (Cd. 893), 1.
70 B. Roberts, *Those Bloody Women*, 204–5.
71 War Office, Concentration Camps Commission (Cd. 893), 8.
72 Quoted in B. Roberts, *Those Bloody Women*, 206.
73 B. Roberts, *Those Bloody Women*, 206.

74 Quoted in B. Roberts, *Those Bloody Women*, 208.

75 B. Roberts, *Those Bloody Women*, 210.

76 B. Roberts, *Those Bloody Women*, 211.

77 B. Roberts, *Those Bloody Women*, 212.

78 Fischer, *That Miss Hobhouse*, 201–6.

79 B. Roberts, *Those Bloody Women*; Gilmore, *Golden Gulag*, 247.

80 Hyslop, "Invention of the Concentration Camp," 259.

81 Forth, *Barbed-Wire Imperialism*, 203.

82 Forth, *Barbed-Wire Imperialism*, 207–8.

83 Linebaugh and Rediker, *Many-Headed Hydra*; Rodgers, *Atlantic Crossings*; Nightingale, *Segregation*.

84 Nightingale, *Segregation*.

85 Rodgers, *Atlantic Crossings*.

86 On London's restrictive covenants, see Nightingale, *Segregation*, 78; on docker leader Ben Tillet, see Schneer, *London 1900*, 60; on urban biopolitics, ostensibly, see Stedman Jones, *Outcast London*.

87 The urtext on the history of urban planning that sees no need to engage with racism is P. Hall, *Cities of Tomorrow*; on the "revanchist" city, see N. Smith, *New Urban Frontier*.

88 Nightingale, *Segregation*, 14, 16.

89 Nightingale, *Segregation*, 16.

90 Nightingale, *Segregation*, 159–60.

91 Swanson, "'Durban System,'" 171; Maylam, "Explaining the Apartheid City," 24–25; la Hausse, "Struggle for the City."

92 Swanson, "Sanitation Syndrome" 391, 393, 401.

93 Swanson, "'Durban System,'" 172.

94 Swanson, "Sanitation Syndrome," 388; see Beavon, *Johannesburg*, 75–78, on the "Destruction of 'Coolie Location,'" in which he estimates that 1,600 Indians and 1,400 Africans had been in the area in late 1903; for a Benjaminian engagement with this violent past, see Malcomess and Kreutzfeldt, *Not No Place*, 150.

95 Swanson, "'Durban System,'" 172.

96 Quoted in B. Roberts, *Those Bloody Women*, 252.

97 Quoted in B. Roberts, *Those Bloody Women*, 252.

98 MacDonald, "Durban-Bound"; see also chap. 3 of this book.

99 See Anand Pandian's dazzling play of juxtaposition and resonance in *Crooked Stalks*.

100 Cheshire, *Hidden World*, 13.

101 Cheshire Foundation Homes for the Sick, *Cheshire Homes*.

102 Cheshire, *Hidden World*.

103 S. Marks and Trapido, "Lord Milner," 55.

104 On the absconder, see White, "Tempora et Mores."

105 Foucault, *History of Sexuality*, 103.

CHAPTER 2. SETTLEMENTS OF MEMORY

Epigraph: C. Robinson, *Forgeries of Memory*, xii–xiii.

1 I remain grateful to Marijke du Toit and Goolam Vahed, who cracked this archive, and to Marijke for sharing the secret code to changing box numbers that made navigation possible.

2 Fatima Meer, in Baruah, "Gandhi." As in other chapters, I rely on several interviews for quoted text and also for unquoted material, but I do not cite sources, places, or dates of these interviews. All quotations not cited are from my own interview material. A full list of people I interviewed can be found at the beginning of the bibliography. This is an imperfect attempt at protecting sources. My rationale is in the first note in the introduction.

3 Sivanandan, *Catching History*, 76.

4 Hart, *Disabling Globalization*; Moore, *Suffering for Territory*.

5 C. Robinson, *Forgeries of Memory*, iii.

6 See the section "On Racial Risks and Spatial Histories" in the introduction for my use of *Black*. "Mixed Black" is a way of acknowledging that people lived entangled lives that were harbingers of a tenuous coalitional Black politics to come.

7 Graeber, *Debt*, 122.

8 Burns, "Useable Past," with thanks for further thoughts on "history in chords," Johannesburg, September 12, 2010. The implicit debt is to Mikhail Bakhtin.

9 Rothberg, *Multidirectional Memory*.

10 Epigraph to this section: Durban Archives Repository (DAR), National Archives of South Africa, Durban Borough Boundaries Commission 1929, p. 13, 3/DBN ANN A4.11 14.4.1.

11 Thanks to Zen Marie on "looking back through the lens" at whiteness in photographic ways of seeing, Cape Town, August 18, 2010.

12 The classic studies are Scott, "Communal Space Construction"; and Vahed, "Making of Indian Identity."

13 Hughes, *First President*, 24.

14 Freund, *African City*, 109.

15 Umbilo River is just north of Sea View on map 4.

16 Mayor's Minutes, 1931, pp. 2, 13, DAR, 3/DBN ANN A4.11; Durban Borough Boundaries Commission, 1929, DAR 3/DBN ANN A4.11 14.4.1.

17 Thanks to Isabel Hofmeyr for conversations on this.

18 Joel Lean, Merebank, June 17, 1872, National Archives of South Africa, Pietermaritzburg Archives Repository (NAB), Attorney General's Office (AGO) 1/9/2 8A/1872; and evidence of Joel Lean in Natal (Colony), *Report of the Coolie Commission*, in Y. S. Meer et al., *Documents*, 133–34. Fatima Meer was banned at the time and is not listed among the team of authors, although she had begun the ten-year project of compiling these documents at the Institute for Black Research that she had founded and led.

19 Evidence of Thomas Warren Lamport, in Natal (Colony), *Report of the Coolie Commission*, in Y. S. Meer et al., *Documents*, 130–31.
20 Padayachee and Morrell, "Indian Merchants."
21 Scott, "Communal Space Construction," 32.
22 Bhana and Brain, *Setting Down Roots*, 47.
23 Quoted in Bhana and Brain, *Setting Down Roots*, 64.
24 Bhana and Brain, *Setting Down Roots*, 64.
25 Former indentured laborers were excluded from Crown land grants near proclaimed townships, by abolition of ex-indentured rights to Crown land in 1891 in contravention of indenture contracts that promised land on completion, and by ongoing municipal neglect. Scott, "Communal Space Construction," 32.
26 Quoted in Hughes, *First President*, 24.
27 Undated, anonymous document, probably authored by Ian Gordon Halliday, midcentury authority on Indian market gardeners, University of the Witwatersrand, Historical Papers, AD843RJ, Records of the South African Institute of Race Relations, pt. 2, Mc2.7.1.
28 Soske, *Internal Frontiers*.
29 Maharaj, "'Spatial Impress'"; Swanson, "'Durban System'"; Swanson, "'Asiatic Menace'"; Maylam, "Rise and Decline," 62.
30 Scott, "Communal Space Construction," 32; Badsha, *Imperial Ghetto*; A. Hassim, *Lotus People*.
31 Swanson, "'Durban System,'" 171.
32 Swanson, "'Durban System,'" 66.
33 Swanson, "'Durban System,'" 167.
34 Swanson, "'Durban System,'" 169.
35 Swanson, "'Durban System,'" 174.
36 Thanks to Sunjith Juggernath for access to his father's "Diary," to Stephen Sparks for sharing the excitement of finding it, and to Dianne Scott for pointing to it in her work.
37 From a vast field of oral history and memory, see Portelli, *Death of Luigi Trastulli*; Trouillot, *Silencing the Past*; Foster, "From Socio-nature to Spectral Presence"; Legg, "Contesting and Surviving Memory."
38 Srinivas, "Caste Dispute."
39 S. Meer, "Juggernath Family."
40 For a parallel argument from the dispossessed of the Atlantic world, see Linebaugh and Rediker, *Many-Headed Hydra*.
41 Vamu Reddy to Protector of Indian Immigrants, Durban, 1906, NAB, Protector of Indian Immigrants (II), 1/148 14099/1906.
42 The number of Indians owning land in Durban County was 4,018 in 1910, and almost 80 percent of Indian agricultural land was coastal. Scott, "Communal Space Construction," 82.
43 Scott, "Communal Space Construction," 135.
44 Scott, "Communal Space Construction," 155.

45 Scott, "Communal Space Construction," 166.

46 Scott, "Communal Space Construction," 167.

47 Scott, "Communal Space Construction," 168.

48 Juggernath, "Diary," 20. William Dalrymple reports on a grave of a James Stewart of the East India Company in Bombay killed during the Anglo Maratha War in 1779, shot from his hiding place in a tree by a Maratha marksman, and his transformation into a Tantric deity called Ishtur Phadka to whom police officers offer weekly blood sacrifices and who is commemorated in three sites including at the Wadgaon police station. Dalrymple on Facebook, March 3, 2019, with photographs, https://www.facebook.com/WilliamDalrympleTheAnarchy/posts/d41d8cd9/1051111425073853/.

49 Scott, "Communal Space Construction," 169.

50 Freund, *Insiders and Outsiders*, 171.

51 Vergès, *Monsters and Revolutionaries*; Morrell, *From Boys to Gentlemen*; Sheik, "Customs in Common"; Sheik, "Entangled Patriarchies."

52 Juggernath, "Diary," 15–16.

53 Richard Pithouse cautions that this has been common practice in white homes, with the use of specific enamel plates and cups; perhaps multiple racist forms added ballast to racist practice. Personal communication, April 24, 2022.

54 Scott, "Communal Space Construction," 138–39.

55 S. Marks, "Myth of the Empty Land," 8; Scott, "Communal Space Construction," 127–33.

56 Payet, Merebank, to Sgt Margotts, Magistrate's Office, February 3, 1915, appended to letter from Margotts to Public Prosecutor, Durban, February 5, 1915, NAB, Chief Native Commissioner (CNC), 193 1915/173 Natives Land Act, 1913 Re Contravention of by Indians and Others at Merebank.

57 Attorney General, Natal, to the Chief Native Commissioner, Pietermaritzburg, May 3, 1915, NAB, CNC, 193 1915/173 Natives Land Act, 1913 Re Contravention of by Indians and Others at Merebank.

58 Messrs. Henwood and Britter to Chief Native Commissioner, Pietermaritzburg, September 5, 1919, NAB, CNC, 383B 1919/2185, Application for Beer License by Retired Soldier.

59 Chief Magistrate, Durban, to the Chief Native Commissioner, Pietermaritzburg, September 13, 1919, NAB, CNC, 383B 1919/2185, Application for Beer License by Retired Soldier.

60 S. Marks, *Ambiguities of Dependence*.

61 Epprecht, "Native Village Debate"; Epprecht, *Welcome to Greater Edendale*.

62 Zondi, "First African Township"; Torr, "Lamontville-Durban's 'Model Village'"; Torr, "'Better-Class Native'"; Torr, *History of Lamontville*.

63 Scott, "Communal Space Construction," 168.

64 Freund, *Insiders and Outsiders*.

65 Padayachee, Vawda, and Tichman, *Indian Workers*; Scott, "Communal Space Construction," 217.

66 In 1936, 79.64 percent of Durban Indians were Hindu and 14.74 percent Muslim. Vahed, "Making of Indian Identity," 181.

67 Mikula, Kearney, and Harber, *Traditional Hindu Temples*, 9–15.

68 Mikula, Kearney, and Harber, *Traditional Hindu Temples*, 13, on Mount Edgecombe, Sawoti, and Darnall.

69 Reddy built the Umbilo Temples (1903, 1905) and the Newlands Narainsamy Temple (1906–8). Mikula, Kearney, and Harber, *Traditional Hindu Temples*, 14.

70 Kothanar Ramsamy Pillay built temples in Port Elizabeth (1893), Park Station Road, Umbilo, Mount Edgecombe (1912), Columbine Road (1924), Umgeni Road (1910), Dundee (1910), Pietermaritzburg (1915), and Railway Barracks (1924). Alaga Pillay, trained as a temple builder and Tamil scholar in Madurai, South India, built temples in Umgeni Road (1911), Ladysmith (1916), Park Station Road (1930), Umzinto (1931 and 1932), and Magazine Barracks (1937). Barasakthi Naiker built temples in Sirdar Road (1924), the Cato Manor (1932), Dromore Road (1930), Kwadabeka (1946), Brickfield Road (1938), Clairwood (1945), and Coughlan Crescent (1942). The last major temple builder, Ramjee, built temples in Verulam (1913), Isipingo Rail (1912), Sea View (1904), Sirdar Road (1920), and Randles Road (1923). Mikula, Kearney and Harber, *Traditional Hindu Temples*, 14–15.

71 Mikula, Kearney, and Harber, *Traditional Hindu Temples*, 9.

72 Mikula, Kearney, and Harber, *Traditional Hindu Temples*, 47.

73 Green, *Bombay Islam*.

74 Vahed, "Making of Indian Identity."

75 Vahed, "Making of Indian Identity," 183.

76 Vahed, "Making of Indian Identity," 184.

77 Kumar, *Hindus in South Africa*, 15.

78 Kumar, *Hindus in South Africa*, 55; F. Meer, *Portrait*, 155; Vahed, "Making of Indian Identity," 197–98.

79 Quoted in Vahed, "Making of Indian Identity," 196.

80 Quoted in Vahed, "Making of Indian Identity," 197–98.

81 Vahed, Desai, and Waetjen, *Many Lives*, 16.

82 Vahed, Desai, and Waetjen, *Many Lives*, 17.

83 Vahed, Desai, and Waetjen, *Many Lives*, 255; Vahed, "Making of Indian Identity," 75.

84 Quoted in Vahed, "Making of Indian Identity," 77.

85 Vahed, "Making of Indian Identity," 77.

86 Badassy, "'Is Lying a Coolie's Religion?,'" 481; Vahed, "Making of Indian Identity," 77.

87 Vahed, "Making of Indian Identity," 79.

88 Vahed, "Making of Indian Identity," 76, 80.

89 Scott, "Communal Space Construction," 64–65, 90; Vahed, "Race or Class?"

90 Since 1895 indentured laborers had been subject to a £3 tax to stay on in Natal as "free Indians," the consequence of which was high rates of reindenture and repatriation; Gandhi's Satyagraha campaign had this tax as one of its targets.

When it was revoked in 1914, the Indian Relief Act encouraged repatriation by providing free return passage to India on the condition of surrender of domicile rights in South Africa. Mesthrie, "Reducing the Indian Population," 36–37, 39.

91 Quoted in Mesthrie, "Reducing the Indian Population," 40.
92 Mesthrie, "Reducing the Indian Population," 49.
93 Mesthrie, "Reducing the Indian Population," 49–50.
94 Mesthrie, "Reducing the Indian Population," 51–52.
95 Breckenridge, "Gandhi's Progressive Disillusionment."
96 W. Anderson, *Colonial Pathologies*; Stoler, *Race.*
97 Gandhi, quoted in Sannyasi and Chaturvedi, *Report*, 9; see also Kelly and Kaplan, "Diaspora and Swaraj," 318, 316–20.
98 Breckenridge, "Gandhi's Progressive Disillusionment."
99 Kelly and Kaplan, "Diaspora and Swaraj," 315.
100 Kelly and Kaplan, "Diaspora and Swaraj," 207, 326.
101 Kelly and Kaplan, "Diaspora and Swaraj," 327.
102 Sheik, "Words on Black Water."
103 Pandian, *Crooked Stalks*, 17–22; citing A. K. Ramanujan, *Interior Landscape*, on the intertwining of interior and exterior landscapes (*thinnai*) in the Tamil country. On colonial improvement, see R. Drayton, *Nature's Government*, and Grove, *Green Imperialism.*
104 Hughes, *First President*, 108–9.
105 Hughes, *First President*, 109.
106 Thanks to Isabel Hofmeyr for this generous question, Johannesburg, August 1, 2011.
107 Vahed, "Making of Indian Identity," 118–29.
108 Vahed, "Making of Indian Identity," 75.
109 Vahed, "Making of Indian Identity," 75.
110 Mayor's Minutes 1922, p. 4, DAR 3/DBN ANN A4.11. Natal Coloureds were counted among Europeans in the census until 1902 and in the statistics on registration of births and deaths until 1924; the Borough Census of 1921 includes Coloureds under Europeans with the proviso that public health statistics count them under "Indians & other Asiatics." Kuper, Watts, and Davies, *Durban*, 76.
111 Farred, "Where Does the Rainbow Nation End?"; Farred, *Midfielder's Moment.*
112 Wylie, "'Proprietor of Natal'"; Guy, *Theophilus Shepstone.*
113 Meyers, "Descendents."
114 Beinart, "Anatomy of a Rural Scare."
115 Section 25(7) of the South African Constitution and the Restitution of Land Rights Act set June 19, 1913, as the cutoff date for land restitution claims because of its historical significance as the beginning of the series of Native Land Acts that authorized African dispossession.
116 Vahed, "The 'Other Asiatics'"; Kaarsholm, "Zanzibaris or Amakhuwa?"

117 Rancière, *Disagreement*.
118 Mellet, *Lie of 1652*.
119 Baderoon, *Regarding Muslims*.
120 Gqola, *What Is Slavery to Me?*
121 Baderoon, *Regarding Muslims*, 8–11, 14, 16–17.
122 Baderoon, *Regarding Muslims*, 21.
123 Baderoon, *Regarding Muslims*, 86–88.
124 Epigraph to this section: Morrison, *Beloved*, 36.

CHAPTER 3. RUINOUS FOUNDATIONS OF PROGRESSIVE
SEGREGATION, 1920S–1950S

Epigraph: W. Benjamin, "Paris," 44–45.
1 Thanks to Geeta Patel for her thoughts on the past-perfect subjunctive, the subjunctive mood in Hindi, June 20, 2012; Steedman, *Landscape*, 144.
2 Lake and Reynolds, *Drawing the Global Colour Line*; Baldwin, *Beyond the Color Line*; Featherstone, *Solidarity*.
3 C. Robinson, *Black Marxism*.
4 Johanningsmeier, "Communists"; Bradford, *Taste for Freedom*; Callebert, *On Durban's Docks*.
5 Johanningsmeier, "Communists," 165.
6 Anna Grimshaw, in James, *C.L.R. James Reader*, 7.
7 Paul Buhle, introduction to *State Capitalism and World Revolution*.
8 James, *State Capitalism*, 113.
9 Cohn, *Colonialism*, 4.
10 Foster, "Capturing"; Foster, *Washed with Sun*.
11 W. Benjamin, "Little History of Photography"; W. Benjamin, *Illuminations*, 166–95; W. Benjamin, "Work of Art."
12 Epigraphs to this section: Billy Nair, author interview, 2010; Govan Mbeki, interview by Padraig O'Malley; Yates, *Garland for Ashes*, 7. On the Industrial Conciliation Act, see Lever, "Capital and Labour"; Davies, "Class Character"; Legassick, "Legislation, Ideology and Economy."
13 T. Mitchell, *Carbon Democracy*.
14 Bradford, *Taste for Freedom*.
15 Tim Couzens, "Moralizing Leisure Time," 315 (citing Martin Legassick and Baruch Hirson); Cell, *Highest Stage*.
16 Mayor's Minutes, 1922, p. 20, DAR, 3/DBN ANN A4.8.
17 Freund writes that "Durban itself became a large-scale, effective speculator in property, organising the lease and sale of property in such a way as to profit while creating jobs and building up the economic weight of the city." Freund, "City Hall," 14.
18 Memo for Consideration by Council-in-Committee. Durban Borough Boundary Commission, p. 3, and Annexure A, p. 3, DAR, 3/DBN ANN A4.11 14.4.1 Durban Borough Boundaries Commission, 1929.

19 The borough census of 1920 counted "Europeans" at 46,113, "Natives" at 29,011, and "Indians & Other Asiatics (Including Coloured, Mauritians, St Helena, &c.)" at 18,391; however, "for Public Health statistics, the 'Coloured' population is included in the 'European,' the estimated number in Durban being reckoned about 4,200." Mayor's Minutes, 1921, p. 4, DAR, 3/DBN A4.8.

20 University of Natal, *Durban Housing Survey*, 19, 35.

21 Mayor's Minutes, 1923, p. 11, DAR, 3/DBN ANN A4.8.

22 Mayor's Minutes, 1923, p. 19, DAR, 3/DBN ANN A4.8.

23 Mayor's Minutes, 1924, p. 5, DAR, 3/DBN ANN A4.8.

24 This is Stephen Sparks's perceptive observation. Sparks, "'Playing at Public Health,'" 6.

25 Sparks, "'Playing at Public Health,'" 4–6.

26 Mayor's Minutes, 1924, pp. 4, 24, DAR, 3/DBN ANN A4.8. The minutes go on to report dissatisfaction with the press for reporting on "passive resistance" to the "dipping" of Africans for typhus prevention, which the council maintains should rather be called "cleansing"; the imperative here is not "biopolitical" but rather a humiliating form of domination in which subjects are neither enlisted in their own vitality nor enumerated and regulated as a population.

27 Mayor's Minutes, 1924, pp. 19–23, DAR, 3/DBN ANN A4.8.

28 Scott, "Communal Space Construction," 239.

29 Scott, "Communal Space Construction," 241.

30 Scott, "'Creative Destruction,'" 245, citing the Natal Chamber of Industries, 26th Annual Report, 1932–33, p. 19.

31 Mayor's Minutes, 1925, p. 10, DAR, 3/DBN ANN A4.9; the quote is from Mayor's Minutes, 1926, p. 5, DAR, 3/DBN ANN A4.9.

32 Mayor's Minutes, 1926, p. 17, DAR, 3/DBN ANN A4.9.

33 Mayor's Minutes, 1926, p. 6, DAR, 3/DBN ANN A4.9.

34 Mayor's Minutes, 1926, p. 7, DAR, 3/DBN ANN A4.9. On nuisance law in Delhi today, see Ghertner, *Rule by Aesthetics*.

35 Mayor's Minutes, 1926, p. 7, DAR, 3/DBN ANN A4.9.

36 Smuts's Union Government had prepared the Class Areas Bill of 1923 for the compulsory restriction of trading and residence of "classes," in particular Class Areas in the coastal belt; Indian activists continued to mount a response to the threat of segregation in Durban. Scott, "Communal Space Construction," 62; Desai and Vahed, *Monty Naicker*.

37 Mayor's Minutes, 1926, pp. 12–13, DAR, 3/DBN ANN A4.9.

38 Papers related to the Round Table Conference, 1926–27, D. F. Malan Collection, Library of the Stellenbosch Institute for Advanced Study, South Africa.

39 Scott, "Communal Space Construction," 62–63, 82. See University of Natal, *Durban Housing Survey*, for the view of liberal economists persuaded that the Union and British Indian governments had affirmed the right to maintain Western standards of life and that Indians should, if they could, conform to these standards. The liberal-racial presumption here is that white people across class "conform" by nature, without support.

40 Mayor's Minutes, 1927, p. 9, DAR, 3/DBN ANN A4.9.

41 "The problem is one of scientific area planning in the suburbs, housing, and the rigid observance of public health regulations." Mayor's Minutes, 1927, p. 4, DAR, 3/DBN ANN A4.9.

42 Mayor's Minutes, 1927, p. 5, DAR, 3/DBN ANN A4.9. The idea of the "garden suburb" had emerged by compromising Ebenezer Howard's "garden city" ideal of rural-urban anarchist cooperatives as an alternative to capitalist urbanism, which instead produced middle-class commuter suburbs. P. Hall, *Cities of Tomorrow*.

43 Mayor's Minutes, 1927, p. 6, DAR, 3/DBN ANN A4.9.

44 Crankshaw, "Class, Race and Residence," 367–68. Owen Crankshaw and Susan Parnell argue with respect to Johannesburg that this provision of class-differentiated housing for Africans only became a priority in the 1940s and that the Urban Areas Act of 1923 was implemented slowly in this regard, with the main focus on slum clearance. Parnell, "Racial Segregation in Johannesburg."

45 Mayor's Minutes, 1927, p. 29, DAR, 3/DBN ANN A4.9; Special Committee re Housing, July 19, 1929, p. 2, DAR, 3/DBN 1.3.3.1.1 Health and Housing Committee, 1927–29.

46 Scott, "Communal Space Construction," 65.

47 Meeting on Visit of Central Housing Board (circa late 1928), p. 32, 3/DBN 1.3.3.1.1 Health and Housing Committee, 1927–29.

48 "Housing of Coloured Community" (circa late 1928), p. 32, 3/DBN 1.3.3.1.1 Health and Housing Committee, 1927–29.

49 Special Meeting Re Housing, October 31, 1928, pp. 2, 32, 3/DBN 1.3.3.1.1 Health and Housing Committee, 1927–29.

50 Soske, *Internal Frontiers*.

51 Mayor's Minutes, 1929, p. 16, DAR, 3/DBN ANN A4.10 (emphasis in original).

52 Mayor's Minutes, 1929, pp. 16–17, DAR, 3/DBN ANN A4.10.

53 Mayor's Minutes, 1929, p. 12, DAR, 3/DBN ANN A4.10.

54 Freund, "City Hall," 15.

55 "Sale of Land for Manufacture," 1929, DAR, 3/DBN 4.1.2.1268.

56 Freund, *Twentieth-Century South Africa*, 62–81.

57 Province of Natal, *Report of Commission Appointed to Consider and Report upon (1) the Extension of the Boundaries of the Borough of Durban or (2) the Better Government of the Local Areas Adjacent Thereto* (henceforth *Borough Boundaries Commission Report*), 1930, reprinted in Mayor's Minutes, 1931, p. 3, 3/DBN ANN A4.10.

58 *Borough Boundaries Commission Report*, 8–9.

59 *Borough Boundaries Commission Report*, 13.

60 W. Anderson, "Excremental Colonialism."

61 Thanks to Prema Chari for pushing me on wood-and-iron construction.

62 *Borough Boundaries Commission Report*, 15.

63 *Borough Boundaries Commission Report*, 19.

64 *Borough Boundaries Commission Report*, 19.

65 The Kenya Commission argued against multiple municipalities governing a common social and economic region. *Borough Boundaries Commission Report*, 24–25.

66 *Borough Boundaries Commission Report*, 28, 30.

67 *Borough Boundaries Commission Report*, 30.

68 *Borough Boundaries Commission Report*, 36.

69 *Borough Boundaries Commission Report*, 25.

70 *Borough Boundaries Commission Report*, 36–37.

71 *Borough Boundaries Commission Report*, 46–47, 48, 54–55.

72 *Borough Boundaries Commission Report*, 55–56.

73 Joyce, *Rule of Freedom*, 100.

74 Joyce, *Rule of Freedom*, 101–2.

75 Mayor's Minutes, 1927, pp. 10–11, DAR, 3/DBN ANN A4.09; Johann Friedrich Wilhelm Grosskopf estimates that 95 percent of "white labourers" in 1926 were Afrikaners from rural areas, many of whom were quickly promoted to train conductors. Grosskopf, *Economic Report*, 195–96.

76 Willoughby-Herard, *Waste*.

77 Seekings, "Carnegie Commission," 537.

78 Willoughby-Herard, *Waste*.

79 Malherbe, *Educational Report*, 3–4.

80 Wilcocks, *Psychological Report*, 177.

81 Malherbe, *Educational Report*, 6 (italics in original).

82 Visweswaran, *Un/common Cultures*, 110–20.

83 Malherbe, *Educational Report*, 7. Volume 4 on health similarly concludes that "no evidence has been found during the investigation to show that either epidemic or endemic disease, underfeeding or ill-feeding, or the climate of South Africa so deleteriously affects the physique or nutrition of the well-to-do sections of the European population as to bring about their poverty. The primary causes which have resulted in the Poor White Problem have not been physical. But poverty and ignorance lead to malnutrition and so weaken the poor white's resistance to disease, lessen his physical efficiency and thus accentuate the problem." Murray, *Health Factors*, 127.

84 Touleier, *Poor White Problem*, 6.

85 Touleier, *Poor White Problem*, 27.

86 Grosskopf, *Economic Report*, 184, on Durban, xiv–xv. Touleier's booklet is written for popular dissemination of ideas from the Carnegie Commission, and it notes that Durban and its environs attracted the attention of the commission. Touleier, *Poor White Problem*, 7.

87 Mayor's Minutes, 1931, p. 7, DAR, 3/DBN ANN A4.10.

88 Grosskopf, *Economic Report*, 164–65.

89 Mayor's Minutes, 1935, pp. 2–4, DAR, 3/DBN ANN A4.11.

90 Mayor's Minutes, 1936, pp. 3, 5, DAR, 3/DBN ANN A4.11.

91 Scott, "Communal Space Construction," 249.

92 Scott, "'Creative Destruction,'" 246, citing the Natal Chamber of Industries, 31st Annual Report, 1938–39, p. 28.

93 McCarthy, "Problems of Planning"; Freund, "City Hall," 14.

94 Smit, "Political Economy," 55.

95 Smit, "Political Economy," 79.

96 Smit, "Political Economy," 94; Sparks, "Apartheid Modern."

97 Gramsci, *Selections from the "Prison Notebooks*," 277–318.

98 Scott, "Communal Space Construction," 255–56.

99 Scott, "Communal Space Construction," 256.

100 *Borough Extension Enquiries Commission Report*, pp. 3–9, DAR, 3/DBN ANN A4.11 14.6.1.

101 Donzelot, *Policing of Families*, 6–7.

102 Assistant City Engineer to the Town Clerk, September 17, 1937, enclosed transcript of Public Health (Slums) Committee Meeting, pp. 2–3, 5, 9, DAR, 3/DBN 4.1.3.2146 643J Slum Clearance SJ.8 Point Area.

103 Assistant City Engineer to the Town Clerk, September 17, 1937, enclosed transcript, p. 13.

104 Assistant City Engineer to the Town Clerk, 1937, enclosed transcript, p. 17.

105 Minutes of Public Health (Slums) Committee, September 20, 1937, enclosed transcript of committee meeting, p. 5, DAR, 3/DBN 4.1.3.2146 643J Slum Clearance SJ.8 Point Area.

106 Memo from the Town Clerk (circa late 1939 / early 1940), DAR, 3/DBN 4.1.3.2097 643J MNH Merebank Native Men's Hostel, 1938–45.

107 Memo from the Town Clerk, , p. 6.

108 J. Robinson, *Power of Apartheid*, 28.

109 Town Clerk to Central Housing Board, September 9, 1942, p. 6, DAR, 3/DBN 4.1.3.2097 643J MNH Merebank Native Men's Hostel, 1938–45.

110 Extract from Report of City and Water Engineer, December 21, 1943, DAR, 3/DBN 4.1.3.2097 643J MNH Merebank Native Men's Hostel, 1938–45.

111 Extract from Report of City and Water Engineer, 1943.

112 "Chronological Record of the Merebank/Wentworth Housing Scheme," p. 1, DAR, 3/DBN 4.1.3.2146 643J Slum Clearance SJ.7 Merebank Wentworth Area, 1940.

113 "Chronological Record," p. 1.

114 "Chronological Record," p. 2.

115 "Schedules of Defects and Other Conditions of Nuisance," March 5, 1940, DAR, 3/DBN 4.1.3.2146 643J Slum Clearance SJ.7 Merebank Wentworth Area, 1940.

116 W. Benjamin, *Illuminations*, 220.

117 Town Clerk to W. D. Robertson, August 14, 1940, p. 1, DAR, 3/DBN 4.1.3.2146 643J Slum Clearance SJ.7 Merebank Wentworth Area, 1940.

118 Town Clerk to W. D. Robertson, August 19, 1940, p. 2, DAR, 3/DBN 4.1.3.2146 643J Slum Clearance SJ.7 Merebank Wentworth Area, 1940.

119 Juggernath, "Diary," 73–75.

120 Juggernath, "Diary," 75.

121 Merebank Indian Ratepayers Association to Town Clerk, October 14, 1940; City Medical Officer of Health to Town Clerk, October 25, 1940; and Town Clerk to Merebank Indian Ratepayers Association, October 29, 1940, all in DAR, 3/DBN 4.1.3.2146 643J Slum Clearance SJ.7 Merebank Wentworth Area, 1940.

122 "Chronological Record," p. 3.

123 Juggernath, "Diary," 76.

124 "Chronological Record," p. 4.

125 "Chronological Record," p. 7.

126 "Chronological Record," p. 7.

127 "Chronological Record," p. 7.

128 Mbembe, "Necropolitics"; Mbembe, *Necropolitics*.

129 Hyslop, "Segregation."

130 Mabin and Harrison, *"Imaginative Planning,"* 284–85.

131 City Medical Officer of Health to Town Clerk, May 15, 1943, DAR, 3/DBN 4.1.3.243 Post-War Works and Reconstruction Commission.

132 Cooper, *Decolonization and African Society*.

133 City and Water Engineer's Department, "Post War Development—Durban," May 28, 1943, p. 1, DAR, 3/DBN 4.1.3.243 Post-War Works and Reconstruction Commission.

134 City and Water Engineer's Department, "Post War Development—Durban," p. 2.

135 City and Water Engineer's Department, "Post War Development—Durban," p. 4.

136 City and Water Engineer's Department, "Post War Development—Durban," p. 5. See also Proceedings Resumed, May 1943, p. 86, DAR, 3/DBN 4.1.3.243 Post-War Works and Reconstruction Commission.

137 Proceedings Resumed, 1943, p. 86.

138 City and Water Engineer's Department, "Post War Development—Durban," pp. 5–6.

139 Post-War Works and Reconstruction Commission. Record of Proceedings, May 27, 1943, pp. 51–54, DAR, 3/DBN 4.1.3.243 Post-War Works and Reconstruction Commission.

140 Post-War Works and Reconstruction Commission. Record of Proceedings, 1943, pp. 54–55. Thanks to Stephen Sparks for pointing out that D. G. Shepstone was indeed the grandson of Theophilus Shepstone; he worked closely with Smuts on "the Indian question" at the time of the Pegging Act controversy, and was provincial administrator of Natal from 1948 to 1958. Personal communication, June 8, 2012.

141 Post-War Works and Reconstruction Commission. Record of Proceedings, 1943, p. 55.

142 Post-War Works and Reconstruction Commission. Record of Proceedings, 1943, pp. 56–57.

143 Post-War Works and Reconstruction Commission. Record of Proceedings, 1943, p. 57.

144 Post-War Works and Reconstruction Commission. Record of Proceedings, 1943, p. 58.

145 Post-War Works and Reconstruction Commission. Record of Proceedings, 1943, p. 60.

146 Post-War Works and Reconstruction Commission. Record of Proceedings, 1943, pp. 64, 130–31.

147 Transcript of Proceedings, June 15, 1943, pp. 135, 137, DAR, 3/DBN 4.1.3.243 Post-War Works and Reconstruction Commission.

148 Transcript of Proceedings, 1943, p. 138.

149 Transcript of Proceedings, 1943, p. 138.

150 Thanks to Geeta Patel for the conversation that sparked this, June 20, 2012.

151 Proceedings Resumed, 1943, p. 88.

152 Scott, "'Creative Destruction,'" 237.

153 Hartley, "Maps, Knowledge, and Power," 278–79; Poovey, *History of the Modern Fact*.

154 An unattributed copy is in Mabin, "Reconstruction," p. E6.0. The image is on prominent display at the Apartheid Museum, also without attribution.

155 Winichakul, *Siam Mapped*, 17, 143.

156 Transcript of Proceedings, 1943, p. 139; Proceedings Resumed, 1943, p. 99.

157 Transcript of Proceedings, 1943, p. 143.

158 Proceedings Resumed, 1943, p. 83.

159 Proceedings Resumed, 1943, pp. 101–2.

160 Deputation Representing the Chamber of Commerce, June 17, 1943, p. 184, DAR, 3/DBN 4.1.3.243 Post-War Works and Reconstruction Commission.

161 Deputation Representing the Chamber of Commerce, 1943, pp. 187–88.

162 Deputation Representing the Chamber of Commerce, 1943, p. 193.

163 Memorandum to the Natal Provincial Post-War Works and Reconstruction Commission Submitted to the Durban City Council, 1943, pp. 1, 9, DAR, 3/DBN 4.1.3.243 Post-War Works and Reconstruction Commission.

164 Lake and Reynolds, *Drawing the Global Colour Line*.

165 Memorandum to the Natal Provincial Post-War Works and Reconstruction Commission, 1943, pp. 10–11.

166 Memorandum to the Natal Provincial Post-War Works and Reconstruction Commission, 1943, pp. 11–14.

167 Proceedings Resumed at 2:15 p.m., September 10, 1943, pp. 768–69 (15–16), DAR, 3/DBN 4.1.3.243 Post-War Works and Reconstruction Commission.

168 Proceedings Resumed at 2:15 p.m., 1943, pp. 753–57 (1–4).

169 Proceedings Resumed at 2:15 p.m., 1943, pp. 757–61 (4–8).

170 Proceedings Resumed at 2:15 p.m., 1943, pp. 763–66 (10–13).

171 Proceedings, October 20, 1943, p. 771, DAR, 3/DBN 4.1.3.243 Post-War Works and Reconstruction Commission, box 2.

172 Proceedings, October 20, 1943, p. 761.

173 Proceedings, October 20, 1943, pp. 765–67.

174 Proceedings, November 10, 1943, p. 827, DAR, 3/DBN 4.1.3.243 Post-War Works and Reconstruction Commission, box 2.

175 Proceedings, November 10, 1943, p. 830.

176 Proceedings, November 10, 1943, p. 831; Wolpe, "Capitalism and Cheap Labour-Power."

177 Published and amended *Ninth Interim Report of the Post-War Works and Reconstruction Commission Regarding Provincial and Town Planning*, January 18, 1945, pp. 3–5, DAR, 3/DBN 4.1.3.243 Post-War Works and Reconstruction Commission, box 3. Alan Mabin and Philip Harrison argue that this drew from the social ecology of Patrick Geddes, also part of Smuts's views, but they don't quite theorize why this was consistent with a particular kind of racial ideology of "harmony between races." Mabin and Harrison, *"Imaginative Planning,"* 285–86.

178 *Ninth Interim Report*, 5–6.

179 *Ninth Interim Report*, 7.

180 Extract from "Progress Report on Housing with Special Reference to 9th Interim Report of the Post-War Works and Reconstruction Commission," October 8, 1945, pp. 3–4, DAR, 3/DBN 4.1.3.243 Post-War Works and Reconstruction Commission, box 4.

181 Secretary for Defence to Town Clerk, October 3, 1942; and Memorandum for Finance Committee, October 23, 1942, both in DAR, 3/DBN 4.1.3.1339 284Q Acquisition of Land at Wentworth Merebank, 1942–45.

182 "Land Known as the Wentworth Naval Camp (H.M.S. Assegai), Durban," September 28, 1944, pp. 1–3, DAR, 3/DBN 4.1.3.1339 284Q Acquisition of Land at Wentworth Merebank, 1942–45.

183 Town Clerk's Office, Memorandum for Finance Committee, Wentworth Naval Camp: H.M.S. Assegai, June 26, 1945, p. 2; and Town Clerk's Office, Memorandum (circa August–November 1945), both in DAR, 3/DBN 4.1.3.1339 284Q Acquisition of Land at Wentworth Merebank, 1942–45.

184 Commissioner for Defence Land Titles to Town Clerk, November 26, 1945, DAR, 3/DBN 4.1.3.1339 284Q Acquisition of Land at Wentworth Merebank, 1942–45.

185 "Deputation Sees Gen. Smuts," *Daily News* clipping (circa December 1945 / early 1946), DAR, 3/DBN 4.1.3.1339 284Q Acquisition of Land at Wentworth Merebank, 1942–45.

186 Notes of a Meeting between the Hon. Minister of Public Health, the Hon. Minster of the Interior and His Hon. the Administrator and Council's Representatives Regarding the Future Uses of Clairwood Camp Hospital, November 12, 1946, pp. 2–3, DAR, 3/DBN 4.1.3.1400 284Q Acquisition of Land at Wentworth Merebank, 1942–45.

187 Native Commissioner to Town Clerk, July 26, 1945, DAR, 3/DBN 4.1.3.2097 643J MNH Merebank Native Men's Hostel, 1938–45.

188 Mabin and Smit, "Reconstructing South Africa's Cities?," 202.

189 Linebaugh and Rediker, *Many-Headed Hydra*.

190 Regional planning boomed through the establishment in 1940 of the Natal Town and Regional Planning Commission, with two key experts: Douglas Mitchell, who had been on the Post-War Works, Planning and Reconstruction Committee, and E. Thorrington-Smith, who had also spent time in the military, where he had read about the Tennessee Valley Authority in the US South. "Betterment planning" was a response to the Native Economic Commission of 1932, which concluded that the "native reserves" were in a state of economic decline, which would increase urban migration. Without reforming land tenure, or providing infrastructure or marketing facilities, "Betterment planning" was consistent with keeping Africans out of the city. Smit, "Political Economy," 91–93.

191 University of Natal, *Durban Housing Survey*, 347.

CHAPTER 4. THE BIRTH OF BIOPOLITICAL STRUGGLE, 1940S

Epigraph: Morrison and Davis, "Toni Morrison and Angela Davis."

1 C. Robinson, *Forgeries of Memory*, iii.

2 Juggernath, "Diary," 4.

3 Scott, "Communal Space Construction," 221.

4 Juggernath, "Diary"; Scott, "Communal Space Construction," 221.

5 Maharaj, "Group Areas Act"; Scott, "Communal Space Construction," 118.

6 Scott, "Communal Space Construction," 66–67.

7 Freund, *Insiders and Outsiders*.

8 Thanks to Richard Pithouse for this gem. Personal communication, April 24, 2022.

9 Mabel Bayley to Mayor Ellis and Mrs. Ellis, January 19, 1947; Constance Davey to Mayor Ellis, January 18, 1947; note from Town Clerk John McIntyre (circa 1942–45), all in DAR, 3/DBN 4.1.3.1339 284Q Acquisition of Land at Wentworth Merebank, 1942–45.

10 Scott, "Communal Space Construction," 261.

11 Scott, "Communal Space Construction," 264–65.

12 Scott, "Communal Space Construction," 263.

13 Oliver Maza to Town Clerk's Office, June 23, 1948; Oliver Maza to Town Clerk's Office, October 19, 1948, both in DAR, 3/DBN 4.1.3.2098 643J MNH Merebank Native Men's Hostel, 1947–49.

14 Copy to Manager, Native Administration Department, December 19, 1949, DAR, 3/DBN 4.1.3.2098 643J MNH Merebank Native Men's Hostel.

15 Minister of Health to Mayor Ellis, May 10, 1947; and on the council's position, see also Notes on Interview between Secretary for Health and Representatives of the City Council regarding Hospitalisation Services, June 19, 1947, pp. 4–5, both in DAR, 3/DBN 4.1.3.1400 284Q Acquisition of Land at Wentworth Merebank, 1947–49.

16 Untitled minutes of meeting on the future of Clairwood Camp Hospital, pp. 3–4, (circa 1947–49), DAR, 3/DBN 4.1.3.1400 284Q Acquisition of Land at Wentworth Merebank, 1947–49.

17 Lodge, *Black Politics*; Smit, "Political Economy," 107.

18 Maylam, "Rise and Decline," 69.

19 Freund, "Confrontation and Social Change," 125.

20 Freund, "Confrontation and Social Change," 125–26. Robert V. Lambert reflects on this moment in the late 1970s as a participant in what I call the theologico-political moment (see chapter 6). See Lambert, "Political Unionism."

21 Lambert, "Political Unionism," 208. Bill Freund argues that this was unlikely given SACTU's position on "a fundamentally unreformable capitalism and apartheid" and state criminalization of strikes. Freund, "Confrontation and Social Change," 127.

22 Everatt, "Alliance Politics," 23.

23 Quoted in Everatt, "Alliance Politics," 32, citing South African Parliamentary Papers, SC. 10–53, *Report of the Select Committee on the Suppression of Communism Act Enquiry*, Central Committee Report to the Communist Party of South Africa Annual Conference, January 1950.

24 Resolution, appended to letter from the Sponsors Committee to the Town Clerk, August 27, 1958, DAR, 3/DBN, 4.1.4.1432 Race Zoning, Late 1950s.

25 P. Naidoo, *Footprints in Grey Street*, 172–73. Antoinette Burton perceptively notes that Naidoo recounts Moodley's detention in careful solidarity with the possibility of sexual assault that women in detention routinely faced. Burton, *Brown over Black*, 129–30.

26 Kark and Kark, *Promoting Community Health*, vii.

27 Kark and Kark, *Promoting Community Health*, vii.

28 Kark and Kark, *Promoting Community Health*, xiv–xv.

29 Kark and Kark, *Promoting Community Health*, xvii, 6, 8.

30 Noble, *School of Struggle*, 75, quoting *Report of the Committee of Enquiry on the Medical Training of Natives to the Ministry of Public Health*, June 15, 1942, p. 8, National Archives Repository, Pretoria (NAR), Department of Health (GES) 2957, PN 5, Native Medical Aids.

31 Kark and Kark, *Promoting Community Health*, 45, 82, 91.

32 George W. Gale, "The Functions of the Institute of Family and Community Health (Clairwood) with Particular Reference to the Durban Medical School," November 7, 1951, p. 1, NAR, GES 1831 68/30, Medical and Dental Training for Natives, 1948–58, quoted in Noble, *School of Struggle*, 75.

33 Kark and Kark, *Promoting Community Health*, 98, 103–4, 107.

34 Kark and Kark, *Promoting Community Health*, 120–21, 126.

35 Kark and Kark, *Promoting Community Health*, 134, 142–43.

36 Kark and Kark, *Promoting Community Health*, 177–78, 180, 194–95.

37 Abigail Neely details the afterlives of health and healing in Pholela today. Neely, *Reimagining Social Medicine*.

38 Noble, *School of Struggle*, 89.

39 Soske, "'Wash Me Black Again'"; Soske, *Internal Frontiers*; Edwards, "Mkhumbane, Our Home."

40 Soske, "'Wash Me Black Again,'" 7; Soske, *Internal Frontiers*.

41 T. Nuttall, "'It Seems Peace,'" 16, quoted in Soske, "'Wash Me Black Again,'" 116–17.

42 Soske argues that "however spontaneous the initial melee, a fair amount of evidence suggests that the next day groups of Africans, organized through workers hostels and other social networks (perhaps *ingoma* dancing troops and boxing clubs), sought to take advantage of the situation." Soske, "'Wash Me Black Again,'" 117, citing T. Nuttall, "'It Seems Peace,'" 18; and Hemson, "Class Consciousness," 351–53.

43 Soske, "'Wash Me Black Again,'" 118.

44 T. Nuttall, "It Seems Peace," 23, quoted in Soske, "'Wash Me Black Again,'" 119.

45 Soske, "'Wash Me Black Again,'" 119.

46 Freund, "Confrontation and Social Change," 121.

47 Freund, "Confrontation and Social Change," 121–22; Edwards, "Mkhumbane, Our Home," 7, 12.

48 Freund, "Confrontation and Social Change," 122.

49 Goonam, *Coolie Doctor*, 138, quoted in Soske, "'Wash Me Black Again,'" 122–23.

50 Soske, "'Wash Me Black Again,'" 145–46, on Fatima and Ismail Meer, but also Phyllis Naidoo's more cautious approach to the legacy of the violence that she encountered when speaking to young Indians on the occasion of Luthuli's death.

51 Narayanan, "In Search of 1949," 16.

52 Soske, "'Wash Me Black Again,'" 147.

53 Freund, "Confrontation and Social Change," 123.

54 Soske, "'Wash Me Black Again,'" 149.

55 Stoler, *Carnal Knowledge*; Soske, "'Wash Me Black Again,'" 129.

56 Soske, "'Wash Me Black Again,'" chap. 4; Soske, *Internal Frontiers*.

57 Soske, "'Wash Me Black Again,'" 178, 180–82, 188.

58 Dubow and Jeeves, *South Africa's 1940s*.

59 Gilmore, *Golden Gulag*; Gorz, *Strategy for Labor*.

60 Phyllis Naidoo, interview by Padraig O'Malley, October 26, 2003, Heart of Hope Collection online, Nelson Mandela Centre for Memory, http://www.nelsonmandela.org/omalley/index.php/site/q/03lv03445/04lv03833/05lv03891/06lv03909.htm.

61 P. Naidoo, *Footprints in Grey Street*; P. Naidoo, *Footprints beyond Grey Street*; P. Naidoo, *Enduring Footprints*.

62 Burton, *Brown over Black*, 124.

63 As in other chapters, I rely on several interviews for quoted text and also for unquoted material, but I do not cite sources, places, or dates of these interviews. All quotations not cited are from my own interview material. A full list

of people I interviewed can be found at the beginning of the bibliography. This is an imperfect attempt at protecting sources. My rationale is in the first note in the introduction.

64 Dubow, *Apartheid*, 7–10.

65 S. Hassim, *Women's Organizations*, 24–25.

66 Federation of South African Women, "The Women's Charter," quoted in S. Hassim, *Women's Organizations*, 25.

67 S. Hassim, *Women's Organizations*, 27.

CHAPTER 5. THE SCIENCE FICTION OF APARTHEID'S SPATIAL FIX, 1948–1970S

Epigraphs: University of Natal, *Durban Housing Survey*, 428; Sekyi-Otu, *Fanon's Dialectic of Experience*, 25.

1 C. Robinson, *Forgeries of Memory*. As in other chapters, I rely on several interviews for quoted text and also for unquoted material, but I do not cite sources, places, or dates of these interviews. All quotations not cited are from my own interview material. A full list of people I interviewed can be found at the beginning of the bibliography. This is an imperfect attempt at protecting sources. My rationale is in the first note in the introduction.

2 Vahed, "Contesting Indian Islam."

3 Gilmore, *Golden Gulag*, 28.

4 The Group Areas Act of 1950 was amended almost annually and reenacted in the Group Areas Consolidation Acts of 1957 and 1966. The Group Areas Development Act of 1955, renamed the Community Development Acts of 1955 and reenacted in 1966, was meant to apply Group Areas legislation. Policing is assumed in the administration of these acts, which were repealed by the Abolition of Racially Based Land Measures Act of 1991.

5 Sekyi-Otu, *Fanon's Dialectic of Experience*, 25.

6 But see Ashwin Desai's account of "the beautiful game" in apartheid Wentworth. Desai, *Wentworth*.

7 Epigraph to this section: Dubow, *Apartheid*, v.

8 Welsh, *Rise and Fall*, 52; Dubow, *Apartheid*, chap. 1.

9 Key historical studies consulted include, chronologically, S. Marks and Trapido, *Politics*; L. Thompson, *History of South Africa*; Bozzoli et al., "History from South Africa"; Bonner, Delius, and Posel, *Apartheid's Genesis*; Posel, *Making of Apartheid*; Beinart, *Twentieth-Century South Africa*; Worden, *Making of South Africa*; Beinart and Dubow, *Segregation and Apartheid*; J. Robinson, *Power of Apartheid*; O'Meara, *Forty Lost Years*; Parnell, "Racial Segregation in Johannesburg"; Padayachee, *Development Decade*?; Welsh, *Rise and Fall*; Dubow, *Apartheid*; and Breckenridge, *Biometric State*. Key works of political economy include Wolpe, "Capitalism and Cheap Labour-Power"; Saul and Gelb, *Crisis in South Africa*; S. Hall, "Race, Articulation"; Wolpe, *Race, Class*; Fine and Rustomjee, *Political Economy*; Evans, *Bureaucracy and*

Race; Crankshaw, *Race, Class*; Bond, *Elite Transition*; Marais, *South Africa*; Hart, *Disabling Globalization* and *Rethinking the South African Crisis*; Freund, *Twentieth-Century South Africa*; and Padayachee and van Niekerk, *Shadow of Liberation*. For key urban studies and planning texts, see note 29 of this chapter.

10 Lodge, *Black Politics*, 234; see also Mbeki, *South Africa*; Matoti and Ntsebeza, "Rural Resistance."

11 O'Malley, "Operation Mayibuye."

12 Freund, "Confrontation and Social Change," 129.

13 Walker, *Women and Resistance*, 232; see also Freund, "Confrontation and Social Change," 130; for more on past and present livestock dipping, see Gibbs, "Collapse, Conflict."

14 Freund, "Confrontation and Social Change," 128.

15 Welsh, *Rise and Fall*, 80.

16 Welsh, *Rise and Fall*, 54–55; Posel, "What's in a Name?"

17 Welsh, *Rise and Fall*, 53.

18 Welsh, *Rise and Fall*, 56–57.

19 Goldin, *Making Race*.

20 Marais, *South Africa*, 15–16.

21 Evans, *Bureaucracy and Race*, 8.

22 Cooper, "Parting of the Ways."

23 Welsh, *Rise and Fall*, 67–71, 90.

24 Mellet, *Lie of 1652*.

25 Wolpe, "Capitalism and Cheap Labour-Power."

26 Quoted in S. Hall, "Race, Articulation," 223, citing Aidan Foster-Carter, "The Modes of Production Controversy"; see also G. Hart, "Changing Concepts of Articulation," 90–92.

27 Legassick, "South Africa," 261.

28 Van Onselen, "Crime and Total Institutions," 63.

29 A rich interdisciplinary corpus of South African scholarship engages apartheid and capitalism in compelling ways. Key studies on urban apartheid include, among other works by these scholars, J. Robinson, *Power of Apartheid*; Western, *Outcast Cape Town*; Bank, *Home Spaces, Street Styles*; Van Onselen, *New Babylon, New Nineveh*; Parnell, "Racial Segregation in Johannesburg"; Mabin, "Reconstruction"; Mabin and Smit, "Reconstructing South Africa's Cities?"; Atkins, *Moon Is Dead!*; D. Smith, *Apartheid City and Beyond*; Bickford-Smith, *Emergence*; Makhulu, *Making Freedom*; Malcomess and Kreutzfeldt, *Not No Place*; Bozzoli, *Theatres of Struggle*; Hyslop, *Notorious Syndicalist*; Glaser, *Bo-Tsotsi*; and Bonner and Nieftagodien, *Alexandra*. On the Durban area, see Maylam, "Explaining the Apartheid City"; Edwards, "Mkhumbane, Our Home"; Maylam and Edwards, *People's City*; Hemson, "Class Consciousness"; Freund, *Insiders and Outsiders*; Vahed, "Making of Indian Identity" and "Constructions of Community" (and Vahed's entire corpus); Desai and Vahed, *Chatsworth*; Vahed and Waetjen, *Gender, Modernity*; Scott, "Communal Space

Construction"; Maharaj, "Group Areas Act," "Land Reform Policy," "Segregation, Desegregation and De-racialisation," "'Spatial Impress,'" and "Local State"; Pithouse, "In the Forbidden Quarters"; Dubbeld, "Capital" and "History of the Decline"; Sparks, "'Playing at Public Health'" and "Civil Society"; Soske, *Internal Frontiers*; Skinner, "Struggle for the Streets"; Dobson and Skinner, *Working in Warwick*; Ballard, "Desegregating Minds" and "'Slaughter in the Suburbs'"; Ballard and Jones, "Natural Neighbors"; Hunter, *Love* and *Race for Education*; and Erwin, Marks, and Fleetwood, *Voices*.

30 Fine and Rustomjee, *Political Economy*.

31 Marais, *South Africa*, 19.

32 Marais, *South Africa*, 19.

33 Marais, *South Africa*, 20.

34 Smit, "Political Economy," 114.

35 Natal Chamber of Industries to Town Clerk, August 28, 1958, DAR, 3/DBN 4.1.4.1432 Race Zoning, Late 1950s.

36 Sparks, "'Stink.'"

37 Sparks, "Civil Society"; Town Clerk to Provincial Secretary, Cape Town, May 23, 1962, DAR, 3/DBN 4.1.5.835 Oil Refinery, 1960–64.

38 SAPREF, *SAPREF*, 14; extract from report on 1960 pamphlet *The Shell Co. of South Africa*; extract from "They'll 'Move' the Bluff," *Natal Mercury*, November 7, 1960; extract from "Preparing for Natal's Biggest Industry: Bulldozers in Action on the Refinery Site," *Natal Daily Mercury*, November 5, 1960, all in DAR, 3/DBN 4.1.5.835 Oil Refinery, 1960–64.

39 "Land Negotiations: SA Petroleum Refineries (Pty) Ltd and Standard Vacuum Refining Co SA Pty Ltd" (circa 1960–64), DAR, 3/DBN 4.1.5.835 Oil Refinery, 1960–64.

40 Town Clerk to Provincial Secretary, August 24, 1955, DAR, 3/DBN 5th Correspondence 643.1.6.vol 1. (Please note these files in DAR were to be reclassified and had been sitting in boxes with this older classificatory system.)

41 Town Clerk to Provincial Secretary, August 24, 1955.

42 Memorandum: Re Application for Minister's Approval in Terms of Section 11(1) of the Housing Act 1920 of Expropriation of the Durban City Council of Certain Lots for the Purposes of Carrying Out the Amended Merebank/Wentworth Housing Scheme, n.d., pp. 15–16, DAR, 3/DBN 5th Correspondence 643.1.6.vol 2; this memo draws on City Engineer to the Secretary, Natal Housing Board, September 12, 1955, DAR, 3/DBN 5th Correspondence 643.1.6.vol 2.

43 Co-ordinating Committee on Housing (Merebank-Wentworth Area) to Housing Committee, Durban City Council, January 18, 1955, p. 3, DAR, 3/DBN 5th Correspondence 643.1.6.vol 1.

44 Smit, "Political Economy," 116.

45 Smit, "Political Economy," 151.

46 Smit, "Political Economy," 153.

47 Smit, "Political Economy," 154.

48 Mabin and Harrison, "Imaginative Planning," iv–vi, 92–96, 100–107, 139–42.

49 Scott Brown, "Natal Plans," 163.

50 Stedman Jones, *Outcast London*; Anti-Eviction Mapping Project, *Counterpoints*.

51 Epigraphs to this section: Luthuli, "Some Aspects of the Apartheid Union Land Laws," 71; Naicker, "Paper on the Group Areas Act."

52 Kuper, Watts, and Davies, *Durban*, 192.

53 Smit, "Political Economy," 103.

54 Sydenham and Overport Property-Owners and Residents Committee to Town Clerk, August 18, 1958; "Zoning of Mayville, Cato Manor, Manor Gardens, Candella and Stella Hill for Future European Occupation under the Group Areas Act, 1950, as Amended, Submitted to the Durban City Council," 1958, both in DAR, 3/DBN 4.1.4.1431 Indian and Coloured Affairs Committees, 1959–69.

55 Memorandum by A. B. Moolla Tabled at Committee, February 21, 1958, pp. 4–5, DAR, 3/DBN 4.1.4.1431 Indian and Coloured Affairs Committees, 1959–69.

56 Mayville Indian Ratepayers Association to Town Clerk, March 10, 1958, DAR, 3/DBN 4.1.4.1431 Indian and Coloured Affairs Committees, 1959–69; "Zoning of Mayville, Cato Manor, Manor Gardens, Candella and Stella Hill for Future European Occupation," 1958, pp. 2–3.

57 Natal Indian Congress to the Mayor, November 6, 1958, DAR, 3/DBN 4.1.4.1433 Race Zoning, Late 1950s.

58 "Zoning of Mayville, Cato Manor, Manor Gardens, Candella and Stella Hill for Future European Occupation," 1958, p. 4.

59 "Zoning of Mayville, Cato Manor, Manor Gardens, Candella and Stella Hill for Future European Occupation," 1958, p. 9. South Africa used British pounds in the Union of South Africa from 1910 to 1921 and South African pounds until 1961, when the Republic of South Africa shifted to a new decimalized currency, the rand.

60 "Zoning of Mayville, Cato Manor, Manor Gardens, Candella and Stella Hill for Future European Occupation," 1958, p. 8.

61 "Zoning of Mayville, Cato Manor, Manor Gardens, Candella and Stella Hill for Future European Occupation," 1958, p. 9.

62 Western Indian Ratepayers Association to Town Clerk, May 27, 1958, p. 2, DAR, 3/DBN 4.1.4.1431 Indian and Coloured Affairs Committees, 1959–69.

63 Resolution Passed at Mass Meeting of Residents Held at the Merebank School Hall on Sunday the 14th August, 1955, DAR, 3/DBN 5th Correspondence 643.1.6.vol 1.

64 Natal Indian Congress, Merebank Branch, to Town Clerk, August 13, 1955, DAR, 3/DBN 5th Correspondence 643.1.6.vol 1.

65 Natal Indian Congress to Town Clerk, November 7, 1955, DAR, 3/DBN 5th Correspondence 643.1.6.vol 1.

66 R. I. Arenstein to Provincial Secretary, October 25, 1956; R. I. Arenstein to City Valuator and Estates Manager, November 3, 1956, both in DAR, 3/DBN 5th Correspondence 643.1.6.vol 3.

67 Scott, "Communal Space Construction," 266.

68 "Bantu Residents in the Merebank/Wentworth Housing Scheme," January 20, 1960; "Removal of Native Families from the Merebank/Wentworth Housing Scheme," January 22, 1960, both in DAR, 3/DBN 4.1.5.1392 Wentworth Merebank Housing Scheme.

69 Bantu Affairs Commissioner to Town Clerk, January 9, 1961, DAR, 3/DBN 4.1.5.1392 Wentworth Merebank Housing Scheme.

70 "Merebank Indian Housing Scheme—18th Allocation of Lots—62 Public Auction and 148 Loans to Individuals," signed Acting City Engineer (circa 1960), DAR, 3/DBN 4.1.5.1392 Wentworth Merebank Housing Scheme.

71 Report to Messrs Longtill Limited on an Inspection of the Housing for Indians at Merebank, Wentworth, Natal, February 1961, DAR, 3/DBN 4.1.5.1392 Wentworth Merebank Housing Scheme.

72 Report for Housing Committee Meeting, January 22, 1960, DAR, 3/DBN 4.1.5.1392 Wentworth Merebank Housing Scheme.

73 Town Clerk to the Mayor, September 5, 1956, DAR, 3/DBN 4.1.4.1432 Race Zoning, Late 1950s.

74 Bluff Ratepayers and Burgesses Association to Town Clerk, November 1, 1956, DAR, 3/DBN 4.1.4.1432 Race Zoning, Late 1950s.

75 South African Institute for Race Relations to Town Clerk, July 20, 1959, p. 351, DAR, 3/DBN 4.1.4.1432 Race Zoning, Late 1950s.

76 Draft Memorandum to General Purpose Committee, Durban City Council, "Group Areas etc." (circa late 1956), DAR, 3/DBN 4.1.4.1432 Race Zoning, Late 1950s.

77 On my use of *Black*, see the section "On Racial Risks and Spatial Histories" in the introduction.

78 City Engineer to Town Clerk, May 22, 1958, pp. 6–7, DAR, 3/DBN 4.1.4.1432 Race Zoning, Late 1950s.

79 Co-ordinating Committee on Housing to Chairman, Housing Committee, February 29, 1960; Co-ordinating Committee on Housing to Town Clerk, April 14, 1960, both in DAR, 3/DBN 4.1.5.1392 Wentworth Merebank Housing Scheme.

80 Extract from Minutes of Housing Committee, September 16, 1960, DAR, 3/DBN 4.1.5.1392 Wentworth Merebank Housing Scheme.

81 City Health Department to Town Clerk, September 26, 1962; City Engineer to Town Clerk, October 16, 1961, both in DAR, 3/DBN 4.1.5.1395 Wentworth Merebank Housing Scheme.

82 Merebank Indian Agricultural Association to Town Clerk, July 9, 1963, DAR, 3/DBN 4.1.5.1248 Merebank Indian Market Gardeners.

83 Merebank-Wentworth Ratepayers Association to Town Clerk, September 29, 1963, DAR, 3/DBN 4.1.5.1248 Merebank Indian Market Gardeners.

84 The National Party framed Black housing as part of its paternalistic interest in improvement, but regressive financing was used to keep Black people from affordable routes to homeownership. Black housing was not a major public works program for white artisans; it did offer employment to Black semiskilled

construction labor. Manufacturing capital's need for stable labor provides a compelling rationale for the scale of Black housing provision, as local authorities sought to attract capital in the booming postwar moment. Smit, "Political Economy," 123–28.

85 Bailey, "Origins of Phoenix," 69.

86 Scott, "Communal Space Construction," 322.

87 Scott, "Communal Space Construction," 324.

88 Co-ordinating Committee on Housing to Town Clerk, June 28, 1961, DAR, 3/DBN 4.1.5.1394 Wentworth Merebank Housing Scheme.

89 City Estates Department to Town Clerk, July 31, 1961, DAR, 3/DBN 4.1.5.1394 Wentworth Merebank Housing Scheme.

90 Merebank Municipal Tenants Association to Town Clerk, November 14, 1961; City Treasurer's Department to Town Clerk, November 14, 1961, both in DAR, 3/DBN 4.1.5.1395 Wentworth Merebank Housing Scheme.

91 Extract from City Medical Officer's Health Report, April 4, 1961, DAR, 3/DBN 1.3.3.1.1 and 1.3.3.6.1 Health and Housing Committee.

92 Town Clerk's Memorandum for Housing Committee (circa May–June 1962), DAR, 3/DBN 4.1.5.1395 Wentworth Merebank Housing Scheme.

93 City Engineer to Town Clerk, April 10, 1968, DAR, 3/DBN 1.2.35.6.1 South Durban Indian LAC.

94 Merebank Ratepayers Association to Town Clerk, April 26, 1968, DAR, 3/DBN 1.2.35.6.1 South Durban Indian LAC.

95 City Treasurer to the Town Clerk, August 20, 1969, pp. 1–2; Merewent Ratepayers Association to Town Clerk, October 16, 1969, both in DAR, 3/DBN 1.2.35.6.1 South Durban Indian LAC, 1968–69.

96 Scott, "Communal Space Construction," 346–51.

97 Minutes of South Durban Indian Local Affairs Committee, March 5, 1968, p. 14, DAR, 3/DBN 1.2.35.6.1 South Durban Indian LAC.

98 Scott, "Communal Space Construction," 333–35.

99 Scott, "Communal Space Construction," 335.

100 Scott, "Communal Space Construction," 284.

101 Former city estates inspector, interview by Dianne Scott; Scott, "Communal Space Construction," 347.

102 Acting Town Clerk's Memorandum for Housing Committee, May 17, 1961, DAR, 3/DBN 1.3.3.1.1 and 1.3.3.6.1 Health and Housing Committee.

103 City Engineer to Town Clerk, June 15, 1971, pp. 2–7, DAR, 3/DBN 1.2.38.1.1 Durban Coloured LAC, 1971–72.

104 City Engineer's Department to Town Clerk, September 14, 1964; extract from Minutes of Housing Committee, September 17, 1964, both in DAR, 3/DBN 4.1.5.1397 Wentworth Merebank Housing Scheme.

105 Extract from Minutes of Public Health Committee, September 7, 1961, DAR, 3/DBN 4.1.5.1396 Wentworth Merebank Housing Scheme.

106 Durban South Football Association to Town Clerk, February 22, 1965, DAR, 3/DBN 4.1.5.1396 Wentworth Merebank Housing Scheme.

107 Resident on Khurja Road to City Council, December 17, 1963; City Engineer to Town Clerk, February 26, 1964, both in DAR, 3/DBN 4.1.5.1397 Wentworth Merebank Housing Scheme.

108 The files of the Indian and Coloured LACs are replete with this lure of autonomy. See DAR, 3/DBN 1.2.44.1.1 Indian and Coloured Affairs Advisory Committee, 1953; 1.2.35.1.1 South Durban Indian LAC, 1967–74; 1.2.35.6.1 South Durban Indian LAC, 1967–71; 1.2.38.1.1 Durban Coloured LAC, 1971–75.

109 Minutes of Durban Coloured LAC, June 24, 1971, p. 8, DAR, 3/DBN 1.2.38.1.1 Durban Coloured LAC, 1971–72.

110 Minutes of Durban Coloured LAC, June 24, 1971, p. 8.

111 Minutes of Durban Coloured LAC, November 1, 1973, p. 57, DAR, 3/DBN 1.2.38.1.1 Durban Coloured LAC, 1972–74.

112 Minutes of Southern Durban Indian LAC, November 26, 1971, DAR, 3/DBN 1.2.35.1.1 South Durban Indian LAC, 1971–72.

113 Minutes of Joint Meeting of Southern and Northern Durban Indian LACs, March 21, 1973, DAR, 3/DBN 1.2.35.1.1 South Durban Indian LAC, 1972–73.

114 Memorandum from Merewent Ratepayers Association, December 31, 1964, DAR, 3/DBN 4.1.5.1397 Wentworth Merebank Housing Scheme.

115 G. Ramsamy to Town Clerk, December 31, 1964, DAR, 3/DBN 4.1.5.1397 Wentworth Merebank Housing Scheme.

116 For instance, Merebank-Wentworth Ratepayers Association to Town Clerk, June 29, 1962; October 12, 1963; and November 26, 1963; Merewent Ratepayers Association to Town Clerk, May 25, 1965; and others, all in DAR, 3/DBN 4.1.5.1397 Wentworth Merebank Housing Scheme.

117 Merebank-Wentworth Ratepayers Association to Town Clerk, September 24, 1963; Merebank Municipal Tenants Association to Town Clerk, September 23, 1963, both in DAR, 3/DBN 4.1.5.1397 Wentworth Merebank Housing Scheme.

118 University of Natal, *Durban Housing Survey*, 232–33.

119 Badsha, *Imperial Ghetto*; A. Hassim, *Lotus People*; R. Govender, *At the Edge*.

120 Williams, *Country and the City*.

121 Goldin, *Making Race*, 16–18, 41, 66.

122 Quoted in Goldin, *Making Race*, 88.

123 Quoted in Goldin, *Making Race*, 147.

124 Goldin, *Making Race*, 148.

125 Quoted in Goldin, *Making Race*, 149.

126 Crankshaw, *Race, Class*, 49.

127 Lund, *Changing Social Policy*, 9.

128 The committee estimates Durban's Coloured population at a perhaps implausible fifty thousand in 1973, and Coloured families in need of housing at eight thousand. The Durban Chamber of Commerce, Report and Recommendations of the Social Amenities Sub-Committee on Coloured Housing, March 5, 1975, pp. 1–3; City Treasurer to Town Clerk, December 10, 1975, both in DAR, 3/DBN box 292 Wentworth, Late 1970s.

129 Memorandum from Sister Theresa, Archbishop Hurley, and G. P. Kearney, May 8, 1976, DAR, 3/DBN box 292 Wentworth, Late 1970s.

130 City Health to Town Clerk, June 21, 1976, DAR, 3/DBN box 292 Wentworth, Late 1970s.

131 Hillside Branch to Acting Director, Durban Indian Child Welfare Society, November 28, 1977, DAR, 3/DBN box 322 Housing Merebank Wentworth.

132 Town Clerk's Memorandum for Management Committee, Merebank Indian Sub-Economic Housing Scheme, February 20, 1979, DAR, 3/DBN box 322 Housing Merebank Wentworth.

133 Merebank Ratepayers Association to Town Clerk, August 20, 1979; and October 14, 1979, DAR, 3/DBN box 322 Housing Merebank Wentworth.

134 Report of Relations Committee Delegation and Wentworth Affairs Delegation, February 14, 1980, DAR, 3/DBN box 292 Wentworth, Late 1970s.

135 Health Inspection Report, April 15, 1980, DAR, 3/DBN box 292 Wentworth, Late 1970s.

136 City Engineer's Department, Report for Committee: Redevelopment of Treasure Beach Coloured Area, July 27, 1979, DAR, 3/DBN box 292 Wentworth, Late 1970s.

137 Extract from the Official Record of the Proceedings of the Committee of the Group Areas Board, Sitting in Durban during May, 1957, May 6, 1957, DAR, 3/DBN 4.1.4.1431 Indian and Coloured Affairs Committees, 1959–69.

138 Minutes of Indian Affairs Committee, November 29, 1956, p. 4, DAR, 3/DBN 4.1.4.1431 Indian and Coloured Affairs Committees, 1959–69.

139 The Relation between Employment of Indians and Their Residential Areas, Handed to the Indian Affairs Committee, February 6, 1959, DAR, 3/DBN 4.1.4.1431 Indian and Coloured Affairs Committees, 1959–69.

140 A. B. Moolla of Kingsgate Clothing Manufacturers, later a key Muslim progressive in Durban, similarly makes the case for peri-urban agriculture in Durban's several river valleys and for Indian businesses in "working areas," as supportive of the city's efforts in race zoning. The measured prose of Indian progressivism, supported by the South African Institute of Race Relations, was adapting the forgeries of apartheid capitalism for communal ends. Views of Mr. A. B. Moolla to Be Presented to the Meeting of the Council in Committee on 27th May, 1958, on the Council's Group Areas Proposals, p. 3, DAR, 3/DBN 4.1.4.1431 Indian and Coloured Affairs Committees, 1959–69; South African Institute of Race Relations to Town Clerk, August 27, 1958, 3, DAR, 3/DBN 4.1.4.1433 Race Zoning, Late 1950s.

141 City Health Department to Town Clerk, September 26, 1962; City Engineer to Town Clerk, October 25, 1962; Merebank and Wentworth Ratepayers Association to Town Clerk, August 25, 1962, all in DAR, 3/DBN 4.1.5.1395 Wentworth Merebank Housing Scheme.

142 City Health Department to Town Clerk, September 26, 1962; City Engineer's Department to Town Clerk, February 6, 1963, both in DAR, 3/DBN 4.1.5.1395 Wentworth Merebank Housing Scheme.

143 Epigraph to this section: Gilroy, *After Empire*, 137.

144 S. Nuttall, *Entanglement*; S. Nuttall, "Upsurge"; S. Nuttall, "Afterword: The Shock of the New Old."

145 Many thanks to Jean Comaroff for a question to which I offer this belated response.

146 Hansen, *Melancholia of Freedom*.

147 Hansen, *Melancholia of Freedom*, 6.

148 Hansen, *Melancholia of Freedom*, 7.

149 Hansen, *Melancholia of Freedom*, 140.

150 Hansen, *Melancholia of Freedom*, 126.

151 Dlamini, *Native Nostalgia*, 13.

152 Boym, *Future of Nostalgia*, 49.

153 Dlamini, *Native Nostalgia*, 62, 116, 147.

154 Epigraph to this section: Nama, *Black Space*, 42.

155 Nama, *Black Space*, 12.

156 Nama, *Black Space*, 127.

157 Nama, *Black Space*, 69.

158 Mbembe, *On the Postcolony*.

159 Jameson, *Archaeologies of the Future*, 288.

160 R. Benjamin, "Black to the Future"; with thanks to Ruha for leading me to Du Bois's "The Comet."

161 Eliade, "The Occult and the Modern World," cited in Kripal, *Authors of the Impossible*, 5.

162 Comaroff and Comaroff, "Alien-Nation"; Comaroff and Comaroff, "Occult Economies"; Comaroff and Comaroff, "Millennial Capitalism."

163 Ramaswamy, *Lost Land of Lemuria*.

164 Many thanks to Prema Chari for leading me to Eliot, *The Waste Land*.

165 Arp, "Urban Trenches."

CHAPTER 6. THE THEOLOGICO-POLITICAL MOMENT, 1970S

Epigraphs: Biko, "Black Consciousness and the Quest for a True Humanity," 97; Biko, "We Blacks," 29; Biko, "The Definition of Black Consciousness," 49.

1 In 1966 Timol, a twenty-five-year-old teacher, left South Africa under the pretext of performing the *hajj*, for which he could get a passport. In Saudi Arabia he met Maulvi Cachalia, who had established the African National Congress (ANC) mission in India, and SACP stalwart Yusuf Dadoo, also his childhood doctor. Recruited by Dadoo into the SACP, Timol went to London and onward, with Thabo Mbeki, to the International Lenin School in Moscow. Back in Johannesburg in 1970, Timol communicated by letter to London, detailing mailing lists, the need for political literature, and sites for potential letter bombs; he had started printing pamphlets; and he was picked up with Salim Essop in October 1971. After intense torture Essop was admitted to Johannesburg General Hospital. The police claimed that Timol

had rushed to a window and jumped out of the tenth floor of the detention center at John Vorster Square. The undertaker who prepared his body noted all the marks of torture, but the magistrate ruled that nobody was to blame for his death. In an inquest into Timol's death in 2017, the court determined that he had been tortured and murdered and that the last person to see him, former security policeman João Rodrigues, should be charged with murder and obstruction of justice; he was denied an appeal in June 2021, but died in September without being held criminally accountable.

2 Cajee, *Timol*. As in other chapters, I rely on several interviews for quoted text and also for unquoted material, but I do not cite sources, places, or dates of these interviews. All quotations not cited are from my own interview material. A full list of people I interviewed can be found at the beginning of the bibliography. This is an imperfect attempt at protecting sources. My rationale is in the first note in the introduction.

3 The implicit citation is to Lenin's theory of revolution as the capture of the bourgeois state by the revolutionary party, followed by the second stage of socialist transformation. As we will see, the 1970s were a period of intense questioning of this stagism. The politician, of South African Indian Muslim origin, could acknowledge Timol, ostensibly a member of "his community," only by also invoking a prominent Black African, Moses Mabhida: your African for our Indian.

4 Quoted in Manghezi, *Maputo Connection*, 131.

5 Krish Rabilal commemoration, 2007, DVD, in author's possession.

6 Scarry, *Body in Pain*.

7 W. Benjamin, "Theses"; Coronil, "Beyond Occidentalism," 80.

8 Badiou, *Communist Hypothesis*, 54–55.

9 Graeber, *Debt*.

10 Bond, *Elite Transition*; read in counterpoint to Desai, *We Are the Poors*; but also Pithouse, *Writing the Decline*; Hart, *Rethinking the South African Crisis*; Badiou, *Communist Hypothesis*.

11 Although see Stefan Kipfer et al., "Globalizing Lefebvre?"

12 Many thanks to Kai Bosworth for this apt phrasing following a talk at the Department of Geography, University of Minnesota, April 17, 2014.

13 Epigraphs to this section: Turner, *Eye of the Needle*, 6–7; Biko, "Interview," 34. See also Macqueen, "Re-imagining South Africa," 153–54; Macqueen, "Black Consciousness in Dialogue"; Macqueen, *Black Consciousness and Progressive Movements*.

14 Nash, "Moment of Western Marxism."

15 Lambert, "Eddie Webster."

16 Davie, "Strength in Numbers"; Davie, *Poverty Knowledge*.

17 Biko, *I Write*; Mangcu, *Biko*.

18 Macqueen, "Re-imagining South Africa," 2–4.

19 Dubbed by Tony Morphet, "Brushing History," cited in Macqueen, "Re-imagining South Africa," 144–45.

20 J. Butler, "One Time Traverses Another," 276.

21 J. Butler, "One Time Traverses Another," 273, 278.
22 J. Butler, "One Time Traverses Another," 274, citing W. Benjamin, "Theses."
23 Hemson, "Beyond the Frontier of Control?," 86.
24 Thanks to Keith Hart and Ruth Gilmore for insisting on this point, in James and in general.
25 Callebert, *On Durban's Docks*, 127–51.
26 Hemson, "Beyond the Frontier of Control?," 86.
27 The strike wave began on January 9, 1973, at the Coronation Brick and Tile Company on the northern edge of Durban, where two thousand workers struck for an increase in the minimum cash wage. The Durban Student Wages Commission had been involved in collecting evidence of low wages here. Zulu Paramount Chief Goodwill Zwelethini had apparently spoken to workers in late 1972 and may have left them with the expectation of higher wages the following year. Smaller strikes broke out soon after, on January 10, 1973, at the transport firm of A. J. Keeler and, at the tea blending and packaging factory of T. W. Beckett and Co., where 150 workers stopped work. On January 15, ship's painters and cleaners struck at various firms, including J. H. Akitt and Co. on Point Road and James Brown and Hamer. On January 22, convoy drivers at Motorvia in Pinetown demanded a raise to pay their children's school fees. On January 25, mill workers struck at Frametex in New Germany, and other workers at Frame Textile Group mills followed. On January 29, women garment workers downed tools at S. Pedlar and Co., also in New Germany; sugarcane workers struck at Westbrook Estate; African and Indian workers struck against a deduction in sick benefit funds at the Natal Canvas Rubber Manufacturers; African and Indian women struck at the Consolidated Wool-washing and Processing Mill in Pinetown; and a pipe factory called Hume Ltd. closed down when its workers struck. The strike wave reached South Durban on January 31 when 1,000 African and Indian workers struck at the Frame Group's Consolidated Textile Mill in Jacobs as well as at Frame's Afritex Mill in Jacobs; 300 workers downed tools at National Chemical Products; and several other factories had partial or total stoppages, including the United Oil and Cake Mills at Mobeni, J. Wright and Sons in Jacobs, Tri-Ang Pedigree in Mobeni, and several other sites in Umgeni, New Germany, and Pinetown. On February 1, the strike spread to Colgate-Palmolive Ltd. at Boksburg, 200 African workers struck at Elgin Metal Products on Voortrekker Street in Jacobs, a strike committee was formed at the Blaikie-Johnstone factory in Jacobs, hundreds of African workers struck at Falkirk Iron Co. in Jacobs, and 200 refused the night shift at Hebox in Hammarsdale. On February 2, 1,300 workers struck at Dunlop (South Africa) Ltd., 2,800 stayed away at Ropes and Mattings Pvt. Ltd., most workers at the General Chemical Corporation (Coasted) Ltd. stopped work, and the strike spread to Crossley Carpets, to Airco Engineering in Wentworth, and to several factories in Pinetown, Durban, Madadeni, and East London. More than 3,000 workers for the Durban Corporation struck on February 5; also on that day, 500 Indian and African workers downed tools at

the tin manufacturer Metal Box in Mobeni, and workers struck at King George V Hospital and several other factories. A set of factories in the industrial area of Hammarsdale struck over the next few days; they were followed by workers at Coca-Cola on February 6 and at Clover Diary and Durban Abattoir on February 7; other factory workers followed suit in Pietermaritzburg, Effingham, and Empangeni and at Sappi in Mandini. On February 8, flat cleaners struck at Grosvenor Court on the Durban beachfront. Municipal workers struck in Stanger on February 12, and municipal bus drivers struck in Johannesburg from February 14 to 19. Milkmen struck in Johannesburg on March 15, followed by newspaper workers on March 17; steel workers in Germiston struck on March 21, followed by other large factory strikes at which press were prohibited; following this, 500 workers struck at Alusaf at Richards Bay and 1,000 struck at H. J. Henochsburg at Johannesburg. Strikes spread to Alberton, East London, Tongaat, Vanderbijlpark, and Cleveland and once again to Jacobs on August 9 at Frame's largest blanket factories. On November 28, Durban's municipal "black bus drivers" struck and brought public transport to a standstill. All of this is to say this was a massive and growing general strike. Gwala, *Black Review*, 135–36; Institute for Industrial Education, *Durban Strikes*.

28 This book was part of the set of studies produced in the first phase of the Study Project on Christianity in Apartheid Society (Spro-cas), which was succeeded by an action-oriented project called the Special Project on Christian Action in Society (Spro-cas 2), all of it funded by the Christian Institute and the South African Council of Churches. Ian Macqueen argues that these studies fit into what Adam Ashforth calls a "Great Tradition" of commissions to engage African life in order to bolster state power. Macqueen, "Re-imagining South Africa," 133, with reference to Ashforth, *Politics of Official Discourse*.

29 Turner, *Eye of the Needle*, 71.

30 Turner calls the strikes of January 1972 "perhaps the largest series of strikes that has ever occurred here. Nearly one hundred thousand mainly African workers went on strike in a large number of different factories. Although these strikes are illegal, the government has been forced to accept them, and in many cases the workers have won increases in wages." Turner, *Eye of the Needle*, 132.

31 Thanks to Susanne Klausen for insisting on Fisher's significance.

32 Workers interviewed by Davie in 2004 appear not to have found the role of student activists pivotal, or sustained in years to come. Davie, *Poverty Knowledge*.

33 Institute for Industrial Education, *Durban Strikes*. On rumor in the history of struggle, see Amin, *Event, Metaphor, Memory*.

34 Institute for Industrial Education, *Durban Strikes*, 59–69; S. Marie [Meer], *Divide and Profit*.

35 Saul and Gelb, *Crisis in South Africa*, 106–7.

36 *Daily News*, Durban, February 4, 1973, cited in Institute for Industrial Education, *Durban Strikes*, 100.

37 Quoted in Macqueen, "Re-imagining South Africa," 12.

38 J. Butler, "One Time Traverses Another," 276.
39 Magaziner, *Law and the Prophets*, 3–4, 6; Chetty, "Young, Gifted and Black";
    Pityana et al., *Bounds of Possibility*.
40 Freire, *Pedagogy of the Oppressed*; Fanon, *Black Skin, White Masks*.
41 L. Wilson, "Bantu Stephen Biko," 35.
42 Macqueen, "Re-imagining South Africa," 177; Magaziner, *Law and the Prophets*.
43 Biko, "Black Consciousness and the Quest for a True Humanity," 97; Biko, "We
    Blacks," 29; Biko, "The Definition of Black Consciousness," 49.
44 I have in mind the final lines of Fanon, *Wretched of the Earth*.
45 Macqueen, "Re-imagining South Africa," 141.
46 Myron put it with characteristic flair: "While we were in high school, we
    also got involved politically [with] other guys who had finished their matric.
    Some of them were political." (In South Africa, "matric," short for *matricula-
    tion*, refers to graduation from high school with results that meet minimum
    university entry requirements.) When I asked what they were inspired by,
    he responded, "Basic things," like the demand for equality or for better living
    conditions. He exclaimed, "Not Gramsci," whom he would read later.
47 Macqueen, "Re-imagining South Africa," 35.
48 Bobby, interview in Chetty, "Young, Gifted and Black," 256.
49 Chetty, "Young, Gifted and Black," 135–36.
50 Desai and Vahed, *Colour, Class and Community*. I have not been able to do
    justice to this important book published after my manuscript was under review.
51 Jameson, *Archaeologies of the Future*, 1–9.
52 Jaya, interview in Chetty, "Young, Gifted and Black," 108.
53 Magaziner, *Law and the Prophets*, 8–10.
54 Gordon, *Existentia Africana*.
55 More, "Intellectual Foundations," 187, 191–92; More, "Biko."
56 Richard Pithouse, personal communication, April 24, 2022.
57 Barney Pityana, personal communication, London, October 9, 2012.
58 Nelson, *Body and Soul*, 1–22. The quotation was a widespread Panther expres-
    sion and the title of Nelson's book.
59 Nelson, *Body and Soul*, 62.
60 Betty, interview in Chetty, "Young, Gifted and Black," 270.
61 In January 1972, under the umbrella of Spro-cas 2, BCP was formed with
    Bennie Khoapa as director. Despite the critique of white leadership in the
    first phase of Spro-cas by Biko and others, BCP was spared from this kind of
    critique by conserving its autonomy and leadership. Hadfield, *Liberation and
    Development*, 91–92; Ramphele, "Empowerment," 156, 160. BCP and SASO
    shared offices, and BCP provided Biko employment when he was expelled
    from the University of Natal in 1972.
62 N. Roberts, *Freedom as Marronage*.
63 Gwala, *Black Review*, 1–2.
64 Gwala, *Black Review*, 2.
65 Pithouse, "'That the Tool Never Possesses.'"

66 T. Mitchell, *Carbon Democracy*.

67 Gwala, *Black Review*, 2.

68 Gwala, *Black Review*, 2–3.

69 Gwala, *Black Review*, 3.

70 Noble, *School of Struggle*, 250.

71 "The 'New Farm' Project on Preventive Medicine, Wentworth, Durban," n.d., p. 1, SASO Files, SASO, cited in Sono, *Reflections*, 71.

72 Gwala, *Black Review*, 164.

73 Gwala, *Black Review*, 6–10.

74 Gwala, *Black Review*, 6.

75 Gwala, *Black Review*, chaps. 3, 7, and 8.

76 Gwala, *Black Review*, chaps. 4, 5, and 6.

77 Alexander, under the pseudonym No Sizwe, *One Azania*, 130.

78 Turner, *Eye of the Needle*, 139.

79 Gilmore, "Fatal Couplings."

80 See Callebert, *On Durban's Docks*, 154, on how furtive and difficult it can be to discern the connections between dockworkers and seafarers in the archival record.

81 Baderoon, *Regarding Muslims*.

82 Bobby, interview in Chetty, "Young, Gifted and Black," 259.

83 Gwala details the banning orders not just of the main leadership but also of Mervyn Josie, aged 25, "1st year BA student of UNSA, Was Administrative Assistant at time of banning. Restricted to Durban," banned from August 22, 1973, to August 22, 1978; and Rubin Philip, aged 25, "A former vice-president of SASO. Studied at the Federal Seminary, Alice. Represented South African Anglicans under 28 at a meeting of the Consultative Council in Durban," banned from October 27, 1973, to October 27, 1978. Gwala, *Black Review*, 95.

84 Brown, "Experiment in Confrontation."

85 See chapter 7, note 42. Many former exiles shared these sentiments.

86 J. Butler, "One Time Traverses Another," 276.

87 Epigraphs to this section: Tambo, *Preparing for Power*, 114, quoted in Lalu, "Incomplete Histories," 111; African National Congress, "Colonialism," quoted in Lalu, "Incomplete Histories," 111.

88 Lalu, "Incomplete Histories," 112.

89 Gerhart, *Black Power*; Saul, *Recolonization*, 7.

90 Biko, *I Write*; Mbembe, "African Modes of Self-Writing."

91 Hunter, *Race for Education*.

92 Davis, "Steve Biko Memorial Lecture."

93 Vilakazi, "South African Students Protest."

CHAPTER 7. THE INSURRECTIONIST MOMENT

1 Boehmer, *Nelson Mandela*, 104–9.

2 See Ellis, "Genesis," on Mandela's clandestine membership in the South African Communist Party (SACP) as an indication of communist influence in the

ANC; see also Ellis, *External Mission*. Hugh Macmillan roundly rejects this "conspiratorial view of history." Macmillan, *Lusaka Years*, 10.

3 Jonny Steinberg, *Winnie and Nelson*, 174.

4 Mandela, "I Am Prepared to Die."

5 Nash, "Mandela's Democracy."

6 Mamdani, *Neither Settler nor Native*, 151–52, 190; Landau, *Popular Politics*.

7 Simpson, *Umkhonto We Sizwe*, 21.

8 S. Marks, "Independence and Decolonization," 70–71.

9 Macmillan, *Lusaka Years*, 34.

10 Hani, "Wankie Campaign," also in Karis and Gerhart, *Nadir and Resurgence*, 380–84.

11 Macmillan, *Lusaka Years*, 40; see also Hani, "Wankie Campaign." For a complex portrayal of Mbeki see Gevisser, *Thabo Mbeki*.

12 Macmillan, *Lusaka Years*, 59.

13 Quoted in Macmillan, *Lusaka Years*, 79.

14 Turok, *Strategic Problems*, republished as Turok, *ANC*, 120.

15 Macmillan, *Lusaka Years*, 71–72; the Hani memorandum is excerpted and abridged in Karis and Gerhart, *Nadir and Resurgence*, 389–94; see also the introduced and annotated version in Macmillan, "Hani Memorandum."

16 Macmillan, *Lusaka Years*, 72–73.

17 In Karis and Gerhart, *Nadir and Resurgence*, 390.

18 Macmillan, *Lusaka Years*, 82.

19 "Strategy and Tactics," excerpted and abridged in Karis and Gerhart, *Nadir and Resurgence*, 398–404; the full text is on the ANC Historical Documents Archive at the Marxists.org website, https://www.marxists.org/subject/africa/anc/1969/strategy-tactics.htm.

20 Macmillan, *Lusaka Years*, 78.

21 In Karis and Gerhart, *Nadir and Resurgence*, 402.

22 O'Malley, "ANC Operational Structures."

23 Macmillan, *Lusaka Years*, 107.

24 Macmillan, *Lusaka Years*, 107–9.

25 Macmillan, *Lusaka Years*, 100.

26 Wieder, *Ruth First*, 220–49. On secret SACP meetings within MK from the late 1970s, see Macmillan, *Lusaka Years*, 18.

27 Brown, "Experiment in Confrontation."

28 Dlamini, *Askari*.

29 Truth and Reconciliation Commission, *Further Submissions*. As in other chapters, I rely on several interviews for quoted text and also for unquoted material, but I do not cite sources, places, or dates of these interviews. All quotations not cited are from my own interview material. A full list of people I interviewed can be found at the beginning of the bibliography. This is an imperfect attempt at protecting sources. My rationale is in the first note in the introduction.

30 Truth and Reconciliation Commission, *Further Submissions*.

31 O'Malley, "ANC Operational Structures."

32 Dhupelia-Mesthrie, "Revival."

33 Anonymous, "Editorial," *Sentinel*, 1972, Ivan Pillay private collection, Pretoria.

34 Anonymous, "Autonomy," *Sentinel*, June 1973, pp. 1–2, Ivan Pillay private collection.

35 Anonymous, "Strikes," *Sentinel*, June 1974, p. 5, Ivan Pillay private collection.

36 Anonymous, "Anger over Bread Rises," *Sentinel*, December 1974, pp. 1–3, Ivan Pillay private collection.

37 "Nithianandan 'Elvis' Ganese Govender," South African History Online, April 14, 2021, https://www.sahistory.org.za/people/nithianandan-elvis-ganese-govender.

38 Chetty, "Young, Gifted and Black," 296; Kasrils, *Armed and Dangerous*, 153.

39 Ivan Pillay, "A Tribute to Sunny Singh," November 30, 2019, South African History Online, https://www.sahistory.org.za/archive/tribute-sunny-singh-ivan-pillay.

40 Dlamini, *Askari*.

41 Archary, Moodley, and Qono, eds., *Beyond Borders*, 20.

42 Macmillan begins his account of the ANC in exile with the trauma faced by political exiles from the moment of secret departure, through tortured relationships with those left behind and an indeterminate number of years of inconsolable homesickness, to the ambiguities of return without revolutionary change. Macmillan, *Lusaka Years*.

43 Rajes Pillay, interview by Vino Reddy, May 24, 2002, Voices of Resistance Collection, Gandhi-Luthuli Documentation Centre, UKZN.

44 Trewhela, *Inside Quatro*, 99.

45 See Suttner, *ANC Underground*, for a subtler account of widespread support for the banned movement.

46 Mandela, *Long Walk to Freedom*.

47 Houston and Magubane, "ANC's Armed Struggle"; Houston and Magubane, "ANC Political Underground"; Houston, "ANC's Armed Struggle," 1038.

48 Karis and Gerhart, *Nadir and Resurgence*, 303.

49 Jeffery, *People's War*, 15–39; Giáp, *People's War, People's Army*.

50 Karis and Gerhart, *Nadir and Resurgence*, 303.

51 "The character of the South African ruling class and the nature of its state apparatus dictates that national liberation and people's power can only be won by revolutionary violence in a protracted armed struggle which must involve the whole people and in which partial and general mass uprisings will play a vital role. Such a people's war can only take root and develop if it grows out of, and is based on, political revolutionary bases amongst the people." African National Congress—South African Communist Party, *Green Book*, 729; also Booysen, *African National Congress*, 475n62.

52 Karis and Gerhart, *Nadir and Resurgence*, 305. Special Ops command included Slovo, Montso "Obadi" Mokqabudi (killed in the Matola Raid), and Aboobaker "Rashid" Ismail, who was commissar of Special Ops until 1983, when he re-

placed Slovo as commander. Between 1981 and 1984, Ernest Lekothe Pule and Lester Dumakude were in Swaziland under Special Ops.

53 Karis and Gerhart, *Nadir and Resurgence*, 305.
54 Wieder, *Ruth First.*
55 Houston, "ANC's Armed Struggle," 1044.
56 Barrell, "Conscripts," chap. 9.
57 Barrell, "Conscripts," chap. 7.
58 Barrell, "Conscripts," chap. 9.
59 Examination of Colonel Hendrik Johannes Petrus Botha, "On Resumption: 12th November 1998—Day 4," TRC Amnesty Hearing Transcripts, https://www.justice.gov.za/trc/amntrans/1998/98110919_dbn_981112dbn.htm.
60 Barrell, "Conscripts," chap. 9.

CHAPTER 8. THE MOMENT OF URBAN REVOLUTION, 1980S

1   Houston, *National Liberation Struggle*, 5; Magubane, *South Africa.*
2   Desai and Vahed, *Colour, Class and Community*, 99–132. As in other chapters, I rely on several interviews for quoted text and also for unquoted material, but I do not cite sources, places, or dates of these interviews. All quotations not cited are from my own interview material. A full list of people I interviewed can be found at the beginning of the bibliography. This is an imperfect attempt at protecting sources. My rationale is in the first note in the introduction.
3   Seekings, *UDF.*
4   Hayes, "Seeing and Being Seen," 560.
5   "Mandela's Statement on Vula," June 22, 1991, Heart of Hope Collection online, Nelson Mandela Centre for Memory, https://omalley.nelsonmandela.org/omalley/index.php/site/q/03lv03445/04lv03996/05lv04005.htm.
6   Mac Maharaj's view when we spoke was that the author of the "cabal" formulation was Moe Shaik.
7   Sitas, "Making of the 'Comrades' Movement," 631–32.
8   Padayachee and van Niekerk, *Shadow of Liberation*, chap. 3.
9   Ancer and Whitfield, *Joining the Dots*, 28–32.
10 S. Hassim, *Women's Organizations.*
11 Billy Nair, interview by Dimakatso Shongwe, July 12, 2002, p. 58, Voices of Resistance Collection, Gandhi-Luthuli Documentation Centre, University of KwaZulu-Natal (UKZN).
12 Hassim, Meterlekamp (Beall), and Todes, "'Bit on the Side?'"
13 Hassim, Meterlekamp (Beall), and Todes, "'Bit on the Side?,'" 5.
14 Hassim, Meterlekamp (Beall), and Todes, "'Bit on the Side?,'" 14–15.
15 Hassim, Meterlekamp (Beall), and Todes, "'Bit on the Side?,'" 15, 18–19, citing Beall et al., "African Women."
16 Taylor, *How We Get Free.*
17 P. Govender, *Love and Courage.*

18 "A Brief History of the Durban Housing Action Campaign (DHAC) and the Joint Rent Action Committee (JORAC)," p. 2, Hashim Seedat personal archive (HSA), DHAC box 1.

19 Houston, *National Liberation Struggle*, 207.

20 Houston, *National Liberation Struggle*, 209.

21 For instance, of this stream of letters, DHAC to Chairperson, Health and Housing Committee, March 11, 1988, and DHAC to Minister of Housing, March 11, 1988, both in HSA, DHAC box 1.

22 Letter from the Sectretary, DHAC, to the Director General, Dept. of Local Government, Housing and Agriculture, House of Representatives, Cape Town, June 14, 1988, HSA, DHAC box 1.

23 Letter from the Secretary, DHAC, to the Town Clerk's Department, March 1, 1988, HSA, DHAC box 1.

24 "Over 18,000 Families Cry 'We Can't Afford Rent Increases,'" *Daily News*, June 16, 1988, HSA, DHAC box 1.

25 "Do Not Vote" political advertisement, *South Coast Herald*, August 27, 1989, HSA, DHAC box 1.

26 Michael Sutcliffe, "The Municipal Elections in South Africa: Report on the Indian and Coloured Vote in Durban and Pietermaritzburg," Municipal Elections Monitoring Group, Department of Town and Regional Planning, University of Natal, HSA, DHAC box 1.

27 Newlands East Residents Association pamphlet, 1988, HSA, DHAC box 1.

28 Sydenham Committee of Concern pamphlet (circa 1988), HSA, DHAC box 1.

29 Wentworth Advice Centre pamphlet (circa 1980s), HSA, DHAC box 1.

30 Joint statement of the Durban Housing Action Committee (DHAC) and the Flamingo Court Residents, press statement, April 25, 1988, HSA, DHAC box 1.

31 Virgille Bonhomme, "Candlelight Night," DHAC press statement, September 2, 1988, HSA, DHAC box 1.

32 Virgille Bonhomme, "Victories Achieved by the DHAC Thus Far," DHAC press statement, September 1988, HSA, DHAC box 1.

33 Memorandum Presented to the Durban City Council's Management Committee by the Mothers of Sydenham Heights, Eland House, Phoenix, Chatsworth, Melbourne Flats, Wentworth and Newlands East, April 19, 1988, HSA, DHAC box 1.

34 Beall et al., "African Women."

35 Vish Supersad, interview by Musa Ntsodi, October 17, 2002, Voices of Resistance Collection, Gandhi-Luthuli Documentation Centre, UKZN.

36 Friedman, "From Classroom," 533–34.

37 Bedderson, "Neighbourhood Revitalization," 68.

38 Bedderson, "Neighbourhood Revitalization," 58, 70, citing Graser and Rankin, *Crime in Austerville*; also Rankin, "Socio-Demographic Profile."

39 Bedderson, "Neighbourhood Revitalization," 80.

40 Bedderson, "Neighbourhood Revitalization," 81–82, 86, 104–6.

41 Bedderson, "Neighbourhood Revitalization," 113–14.

42 Copelyn, *Maverick Insider*, 188.
43 Barrell, "Conscripts to Their Age," chap. 9, on "talks" with nongovernmental white groups, independent trade unions, and UDF affiliates, as distinct from "negotiations" aimed at resolution of the struggle under specific conditions: dismantling apartheid, changing the police and security apparatus, securing the unconditional release of political prisoners and the return of exiles, and obtaining complete political freedom.
44 Mac Maharaj, interview by Padraig O'Malley, August 24, 1998, Heart of Hope Collection online, Nelson Mandela Centre for Memory, https:// omalley.nelsonmandela.org/omalley/index.php/site/q/03lv03445/04lv03689 /05lv03697/06lv03698.htm.
45 Yunis Shaik, interview by Padraig O'Malley, May 28, 2004, Heart of Hope Collection online, Nelson Mandela Centre for Memory, https://www .nelsonmandela.org/omalley/index.php/site/q/03lv03445/04lv03833/05lv03915 /06lv03924.htm. The timing is important; from the perspective of Lusaka, this decision may only have been in 1986; see Mac's view later in this chapter.
46 Shaik, ANC *Spy Bible*, chap. 9, p. 66, Kindle loc. 823.
47 Moe Shaik, interview by Padraig O'Malley, May 7, 2004, Heart of Hope Collection online, Nelson Mandela Centre for Memory, https://www. nelsonmandela.org/omalley/index.php/site/q/03lv03445/04lv03833/05lv03915 /06lv03917.htm; Shaik, ANC *Spy Bible*.
48 Shaik, ANC *Spy Bible*, 92–94, Kindle loc. 1171–92, 1487–511.
49 Moe Shaik, interview by Dimakatso Shongwe, July 6, 2002, Voices of Resistance Collection, Gandhi-Luthuli Documentation Centre, UKZN; Shaik, ANC *Spy Bible*, 101, Kindle loc. 1275.
50 Shaik and "the Nightingale," interview by Padraig O'Malley, May 25, 2004, Heart of Hope Collection online, Nelson Mandela Centre for Memory, https:// www.nelsonmandela.org/omalley/index.php/site/q/03lv03445/04lv03833 /05lv03915/06lv03922.htm.
51 Shaik, ANC *Spy Bible*, 101, Kindle loc. 1567–88.
52 Barrell, "Conscripts to Their Age," 450–68.
53 Mac is suspicious of Craig Williamson's boasts about infiltrating the ANC right up to the NEC; for the latter, see Ancer, *Spy*; O'Malley, *Shades of Difference*.
54 Quoted in Barrell, "Conscripts to Their Age," 439.
55 He used the contemporary province names, anachronistically, presumably for my benefit.
56 Braam, *Operation Vula*, 16, 25–27.
57 Edmunds, *Vula Connection*.
58 Edmunds, *Vula Connection*.
59 Quoted in Edmunds, *Vula Connection*.
60 Jeffery, *People's War*, 93–94, citing O'Malley, *Shades of Difference*, 244–45, 247, 248, 262, 272; Giáp, *People's War, People's Army*; Thai and Dung, *Great Spring Victory*.
61 Jeffery, *People's War*, 157–58.

62 Shaik, ANC *Spy Bible*, Kindle loc. 1979.

63 Dipak Patel, interview by Padraig O'Malley, October 16, 2002, Heart of Hope Collection online, Nelson Mandela Centre for Memory, https:// omalley.nelsonmandela.org/omalley/index.php/site/q/03lv00017/04lv00344 /05lv01405/06lv01426.htm.

64 TRC Amnesty Hearing Decision for Hendrik Johannes Petros Botha, Salmon Johannes Gerhardus Du Preez, Laurence Gerald Wasserman, Johannes Albertus Steyn, and Casper Adrian Van Der Westhuizen, AC/2001/099, March 27, 2001, https://www.justice.gov.za/trc/decisions/2001/ac21099.htm; *Truth and Reconciliation Commission of South Africa Report*, October 29, 1998, vol. 3, p. 257, SAHO, https://www.sahistory.org.za/sites/default/files/volume_3_0.pdf.

65 Jenkins, "Story."

66 Jenkins, "Story."

67 Press statement of ANC Deputy President, Nelson Mandela, on the Operation Vulindlela and the Indemnification of ANC Members, June 22, 1991, Heart of Hope Collection online, Nelson Mandela Centre for Memory, https://omalley .nelsonmandela.org/omalley/cis/omalley/OMalleyWeb/03lv03445/04lv03996 /05lv04005.htm.

68 Baskin, *Striking Back*.

69 Undated document, HSA, DHAC box 2.

70 DHAC press statement, May 29, 1990, HSA, DHAC box 1.

71 S. Hassim, *Women's Organizations*.

72 S. Hassim, "Past, Present, and Future."

73 S. Hassim, *Women's Organizations*, 52.

74 S. Hassim, *Women's Organizations*, 98.

75 S. Hassim, *Women's Organizations*, 99.

76 S. Hassim, *Women's Organizations*, 57–60, 66–67.

77 Lefebvre, "Right to the City," 158.

CHAPTER 9. THE MOMENT OF THE DISQUALIFIED, 1980S–2000S

Epigraph: Fanon, *Wretched of the Earth*, 70 (my emphasis).

1 There is no rendition of this event that can get away from its various tellings. The information in this and the next paragraph is from the Section 29 inquiry for Zahraj (should be Zahrah) Narkedien (previously Greta Apelgren), April 21, 1997, South African History Archive (SAHA), B01.5.75.02.13; see also Rostron, *Till Babylon Falls*; Rostron; *Robert McBride*; Mokae, *Robert McBride*. As in other chapters, I rely on several interviews for quoted text and also for unquoted material, but I do not cite sources, places, or dates of these interviews. All quotations not cited are from my own interview material. A full list of people I interviewed can be found at the beginning of the bibliography. This is an imperfect attempt at protecting sources. My rationale is in the first note in the introduction.

2 Gerhart and Glaser, *From Protest to Challenge*, 6:137.

3 Gerhart and Glaser, *From Protest to Challenge*, 6:139.

4 Epigraph in this section: Marley and the Wailers, "Babylon System," from *Survival*.

5 Farred, *What's My Name?*

6 Marley and the Wailers, *Survival*.

7 S. Davis, *Bob Marley*, 49, quoted in Farred, *What's My Name?*, 227.

8 Fanon, *Wretched of the Earth*, 39–40.

9 Farred, *What's My Name?*, 267–69.

10 Glaser, *Bo-Tsotsi*, 726.

11 Glaser, *Bo-Tsotsi*; M. Marks, *Young Warriors*.

12 Fanon, *Wretched of the Earth*.

13 M. Davis, *Buda's Wagon*, 8–11.

14 Goodwin, "Oliver Tambo."

15 Sharpley, *Yesterday*, 88–90.

16 Epigraphs in this section: "TRC: 'A Window Dresser': Derrick McBride," South African Press Association, September 26, 1999, https://www.justice.gov.za /trc/media/1999/9909/p9900926a.htm. Epigraph from Apelgren from author interview. Vejay Ramlakan read out Derrick McBride's statement at McBride's funeral on February 8, 2020: "Derrick McBride Funeral 08 February 2020," SABC News video, 2:28:47, https://www.youtube.com/watch?v=xtJfrA-yONo. TRC Special Report documents are available at SAHA online, including testimony of Aboobaker Ismail, Amnesty Hearings 53734 and 53742, September 29 and October 7, 1999, Durban; testimony of Ernest Lekothe Pule, Amnesty Hearing 53735, September 29, 1999, Durban; testimony of Lester Dumakude, Amnesty Hearing 53737, September 29, 1999, Durban; testimony of Johannes Mnisi, Amnesty Hearing 53736, September 29, 1999, Durban; testimony of Robert McBride, Amnesty Hearings 53738–41, October 4–7, 1999, Durban; testimony of Zahrah Narkedien (née Greta Apelgren), Amnesty Hearing 53743, October 7, 1999, Durban; testimony of Allan Pearce, Amnesty Hearing 53744, October 8, 1999, Durban; testimony of Marcel Trevor Andrews, Amnesty Hearing 53745, October 8, 1999, Durban; testimony of Matthew Lecordier, Amnesty Hearing 53746, October 11, 1999, Durban; testimony on behalf of victims, Amnesty Hearing 53747, October 12, 1999, Durban; testimony of Zahrah Narkedien, Prison Hearings 56365, July 21, 1997, the Fort, Johannesburg; testimony of Paula McBride, Prison Hearings 56359, July 21, 1997, Johannesburg, Department of Justice, accessed November 3, 2023, https://www.justice.gov.za /trc/special/prison/mcbride.htm.

17 Johannes Mnisi refuses a "Kabwe test." Testimony of Mnisi, Amnesty Hearing 53736, September 29, 1999, Durban, Truth Commission Special Report, http:// sabctrc.saha.org.za/hearing.php?id=53736.

18 Testimony of Robert McBride, Amnesty Hearing 53739, October 5, 1999, Durban, Truth Commission Special Report, http://sabctrc.saha.org.za/hearing .php?id=53739.

19 TRC confidential and closed hearings under Section 29 of the Promotion of National Reconciliation and Unity Act of 1995 interviewed individuals under

oath and on camera on events related to gross violations of human rights under apartheid. As of 2015, these are archived at the SAHA. Section 29 of apartheid's Internal Security Act of 1982 allowed for indefinite interrogatory detention of suspected members of the underground, routinely involving torture.

20 Truth and Reconciliation Commission, TRC *Final Report*, October 29, 1998, vol. 3, chap. 3, subsection 29, http://sabctrc.saha.org.za/reports/volume3 /chapter3/subsection29.htm.

21 Testimony of Robert McBride, Amnesty Hearing 53740 and 53741, October 6 and 7, 1999, Durban, Truth Commission Special Report, http://sabctrc.saha .org.za/hearing.php?id=53740 and http://sabctrc.saha.org.za/documents /amntrans/durban/53741.htm.

22 Testimony of Robert McBride, Amnesty Hearing 53741, October 7, 1999.

23 Testimony of Paula McBride, Prison Hearings 56359, July 12, 1997.

24 See S. Hall, "New Ethnicities," 165–66, on the end of the innocent conception of the essential Black subject.

25 Testimony of Robert McBride, Amnesty Hearing 53740, October 6, 1999.

26 Dlamini, *Terrorist Album*, 277–78.

27 Hayes, "Power, Secrecy, Proximity," 144; Goldblatt, *South Africa*.

28 Hayes, "Photographic Publics," 303; Didi-Huberman, *Uprisings*.

29 Hayes, "Photographic Publics," 304–10.

30 Hayes, "Photographic Publics," 307.

31 Hayes, "Photographic Publics," 314–16.

32 Ledochowski, quoted in Hayes, "Power, Secrecy, Proximity," 153.

33 The State v. Mabuha Baleka and 21 others, High Court of South Africa, Transvaal Provincial Section, vol. 100, pp. 4906–07 (1986), Special Collections, Historical Legal Documents, University of Pretoria Institutional Repository, accessed April 19, 2022, https://repository.up.ac.za/handle/2263 /63530.

34 Ledochowski, *Cape Flats Details*; Nunn, *Call and Response*; Mofokeng, *Chasing Shadows*.

35 Hayes, "Photographic Publics," 325. For instance, we might look again at Badsha, *Imijondolo*; F. Wilson and Badsha, *South Africa*.

36 Fanon, *Wretched of the Earth*, 38.

37 Sekyi-Otu, *Fanon's Dialectic of Experience*, 4–8, 76.

38 Fanon, *Wretched of the Earth*, 38.

39 McKittrick, *Demonic Grounds*, 37–63.

40 W. Benjamin, *Illuminations*, 228.

41 "*Vying Posie: Photographs by Peter McKenzie*," Absolutearts.com, May 11, 2005, https://www.absolutearts.com/artsnews/2005/05/11/32995.html.

42 Steinmetz, "Colonial Melancholy," 299.

43 Moten, *In the Break*, 193–97; Chari, "Blues," 154.

44 Sparks, "Civic Culture," 12.

45 M. Butler et al., *Corporate Accountability*, 10.

46 Constitution of the Republic of South Africa, 1996, https://www.justice.gov.za
   /legislation/constitution/saconstitution-web-eng.pdf.
47 M. Butler et al., *Corporate Accountability*, 13.
48 Truth and Reconciliation Commission, Amnesty Committee, decision regarding this special ops unit of MK in Wentworth, AC/2001/128, Cape Town, 2001,
   https://www.justice.gov.za/trc/decisions/2001/ac21128.htm. Vejay Ramlakan
   implies at Derrick McBride's funeral that he had been involved in planning
   this attack. "Derrick McBride Funeral 08 February 2020," at 29:30.
49 The new bill used elements from the Labour Relations Act of 1995—limits to
   strikes and lockouts in *essential services*—to allow National Key Points to be
   declared where provision of *essential services* is in question.
50 Hallowes and Munnik, *Poisoned Spaces*, 149.
51 M. Butler et al., *Corporate Accountability*, 63.
52 M. Butler et al., *Corporate Accountability*, 67; and M. Butler and Hallowes,
   Forging the Future, 168.
53 Makhaye, "Residents Breathe Easier."

CONCLUSION. ACCUMULATING REMAINS

Epigraphs: Said, *World*, 125. S. Hall and Back, "At Home," 665.
1 Moten, *In the Break*, 193–97.
2 Chari, "Blues."
3 Chari, "Blues"; see this book's introduction.
4 See Derrida, *Specters of Marx*; Chari, "Blues," for elaboration of this argument.
5 Said, *World*, 125, citing Marx, *Eighteenth Brumaire*.
6 Said, *World*, 124–25.
7 Moten and Harney, *Undercommons*, 28.

CODA. BLACK ATLANTIC TO INDIAN OCEAN

1 Hofmeyr, "Black Atlantic," rather than Badiou, *Communist Hypothesis*.
2 On the relation between the poetry of the future and the present, see F.
   Coronil, "Beyond Occidentalism," 81.

INTERVIEWS

By the author in Durban, Pietermaritzburg, Park Rynie, Gauteng, Cape Town, and Kilkenny, Ireland, 2002–9. Noms de guerre or polite forms of address are in parentheses.

Ibrahim Adam
Ismail Adam
Marcia Faith Adams
Earl Africa
Henry Africa
Sandy Africa
Frank Alexander
Donny Anderson
Marcel Andrews
Eric Apelgren
Eric Apelgren Sr.
Greta Apelgren
Jeanette Apelgren
Louise Apelgren
Stirling Augustine
Omar Badsha
Yvonne Bassier
Jo Beall
Virgille Bonham
Tayyab Hanif Bonomali
Eugene Brandon
Brenda
George Bridger
Valerie Cartens
Carmel Chetty
Roy Chetty

Siva Chetty
Clifford Collings
Herbert Collings
Ross Cuthbertson
Paul David
Debbie
Cheryl Debruin
Di
Patricia Dove
Des D'Sa
Louis Enock
Shahnaz Essop
Merle Favis
Albert Firman
Winnie Forbay
Matthew Francis
Colin Furie
Morris Fynn
Sharon Fynn
Arlene Glover
David Goldstone
Catherine Gordeen
Pravin Gordhan (PG)
Anand Govender
C. A. Govender
Kumaresan Govender
Mrs. P. Govender
Velli Govender
Viji Govender
Natlene Greaves
Joey Grimett
Mrs. Grimett
Beverly Hapitan
Phil Harrison
Aziz Hassim
Hector Henry
Maureen Henry
Pat Horn
David Isaacs
Vincent James
Wayne Jean-Pierre
Jennifer Johnson
Dennis Jones
Keith "Skido" Joseph

Jaya Josie
Ish Juggernath
Janey Juggernath
Spider Juggernath
Sunjith B. Juggernath
Usha Juggernath
Mr. Kay
Mrs. Kay
Marlene Kay-Greaves
Paddy Kearney
Ben Kingsley
Quinton Kippen
Barry Kistnasamy
Aletta Knipe
Noel Kok
Ingrid Kotze
Colin LaFoy
Roy Laikram
Rayman Lalla
K. Lalloo
Harry Landers
Llewelyn Landers
Niel Larrett
Jenny Lawrence
Cheryl Lawson
Rashaad Leonard ("Ricky")
Betty Leslie
Willie Leslie
Paula Leyden
Karl Linderboom
Lorraine
William Lottering
Francie Lund
Adhir Maharaj
Brij Maharaj
Mac Maharaj
Ram Narain Maharaj
Daramlingam Manickam
Sivagami Manickam
Alfred Manning
Claudia Manning
Jean Manning
Bobby Marie
Lutchmee Marie ("Mrs. Marie")

Leonard Mbokazi
Derrick McBride
Robert McBride
Marlene McClure
Peter McKenzie
Roy McPherson
Ruby McPherson
Shamim Meer
Troy Meyers
Patrick Mkhize
Kubesh Moodley
Alan Moolman
Jeanette Moolman
Chinna Kisten Moonsamy
Mathilda Morolong
John Mulligan
Alan Munn
Phyllis Naidoo
Rajah Naidoo
Rajen Naidoo
Umsha Naidoo
Billy Nair
Gordon Nair
Roy Nair
Cedric Nunn
Abba Omar
Owen
Jeevan Padayachee
Neelavathi Padayachee
Allan Pearce
Pearl
Bobby Peek
Krish Perumal
Mrs. Perumal
Myron Peter
Fred Peterson
Ronnie Peterson
Rubin Philip
Devan Pillay
Ivan Pillay
Rajes Pillay (Rae)
Ramola Pillay
Riedawaan Pillay
Sue Pillay

Tex Pillay
Trevor Pillay
Adrian Poole
Calvin Prakasim
David Pretorius
François Quarrie
Rhodesia Quebekels
Nundilall Rabilal
Jeeva Rajgopaul
Deepchund Ramchurren
Ranjith Ramkissoon
G. Ramsamy
Strini Reddy
Zolla Reddy
Thomas Robins
Roseanna
George Ruiters
Cerigh Samai
Olga Samuels
Sammy Sayed
Hashim Seedat
Sharon
Michelle Simon
Ari Sitas
Rishi Singh
Sunny Singh (Bobby Pillay)
Dan Smit
Jane Smith
Aubrey Snyman
Gail Snyman
Jambo Solomons
Irene Stainbank
Tilly Stewart ("Aunty Tilly")
Michael Sutcliffe
Sammy Syed
Vivienne Taylor
Wayne Tifflin
Terrence Tryon
Stephen van Wyck
Flo Walljee
Charles Walters
Rose Warren
Wayne
Renee Wilson

Archives

National Archives of South Africa, Durban Archives Repository (DAR)
3/DBN Town Clerk Files, Durban
ANN A4.8 to A4.11 Mayor's Minutes, 1921–36
ANN A4.11 14.4.1 *Borough Boundaries Commission Report*, 1929
ANN A4.11 14.6.1 *Borough Extension Enquiries Commission Report*
1.2.7.1.1 Housing (Slums) Committee
1.2.34.1.1 and 1.2.34.6.1 Indian Joint Advisory, 1944–79
1.2.35.1.1 and 1.2.35.6.1 South Durban Indian LAC, 1967–75
1.2.38.1.1 and 1.2.38.6.1 Durban Coloured LAC, 1971–75
1.2.44.1.1 Indian and Coloured Affairs Advisory Committee, 1953
1.3.3.1.1 and 1.3.3.6.1 Health and Housing Committee, 1927–29 and
1960–61
1.3.7.1.1 Special Committee on Indian Affairs, 1944
4.1.3.491 138SJ Encroachment Farm Wentworth, 1935
4.1.2.1268 Sale of Land at Wentworth for Manufacture Purposes, 1929
4.1.3.1339–1400 284Q Acquisition of Land at Wentworth Merebank, 1942–45,
1947–49
4.1.3.2097–2098 643J MNH Merebank Native Men's Hostel, 1938–45,
1947–49
4.1.3.2146 643J Slum Clearance SJ.7 Merebank Wentworth Area, 1940
4.1.3.2146 643J Slum Clearance SJ.8 Point Area
4.1.3.243–46 Post-War Works and Reconstruction Commission
4.1.3.247 *Durban Housing Survey*
4.1.3.1339–1400 284Q Acquisition of Land at Wentworth/Merebank
4.1.3.2097–2098 643J Merebank Native Men's Hostel, 1934–45
4.1.4.1431 Indian and Coloured Affairs Committees, 1959–69
4.1.4.1432–1434 Race Zoning, Late 1950s
4.1.4.1471–1472 Wentworth Merebank Scheme, Late 1950s
Transfer List of Fifth Correspondence System, in transition to 4.1.5.1 to
4.1.5.135
> B2734 Indian Housing Scheme Merebank/Wentworth, 1964
> B2797 Housing for Coloured People Merebank/Wentworth, 1963
> 643.1.6 vols 1–3. 1951–57 (4.1.4.1471) Town Clerk Files
> 4.1.5.835 Oil Refinery, 1960–64
> 4.1.5.1248 Merebank Indian Market Gardeners, 1963
> 4.1.5.1392 to 4.1.5.1397 Wentworth Merebank Housing Scheme, 1960–65
Early 1970s files in the process of being cataloged
> Box 30 Austerville Town Planning Scheme
> Box 80 Smoke Control Air Pollution
> Box 105 Group Areas Race Zoning
> Box 292 Wentworth, Late 1970s
> Box 322 Housing Merebank Wentworth

National Archives of South Africa, Pietermaritzburg Archives Repository (NAB)
AGO Attorney General's Office
CNC Chief Native Commissioner
II Protector of Indian Immigrants

Local History Museum Archive, Durban
Photographic collections, including *Cycle of Violence*

Killie Campbell Africana Library, University of KwaZulu-Natal, Durban
Fynn, Henry Francis, Collection

University of Pretoria Institutional Repository
Special Collections, Historical Legal Documents, including Delmas Treason Trial record of proceedings, https://repository.up.ac.za/handle/2263/63530

University of the Witwatersrand, Historical Papers Research Archive
AD843RJ, Records of the South African Institute of Race Relations

Gandhi-Luthuli Documentation Centre, University of KwaZulu-Natal (UKZN)
Voices of Resistance Collection, https://scnc.ukzn.ac.za/doc/Audio/VOR /Transcript.htm

Nelson Mandela Centre of Memory
Heart of Hope Collection, https://omalley.nelsonmandela.org

Library of the Stellenbosch Institute for Advanced Study, South Africa
Malan, D. F., Collection

Department of Justice
Truth and Reconciliation Commission (TRC) Amnesty Hearing Decisions and Transcripts

South African History Archive (SAHA)
AL 2431, Records of the United Democratic Front
TRC hearings, decisions, submissions, and final reports archived with the South African Broadcasting Company (SABC), https://sabctrc.saha.org.za/documents .htm

South Africa History Online (SAHO)

Political biographies and archival material, https://www.sahistory.org.za

The Women's Library, London (now at the London School of Economics)

Papers of Millicent Garrett Fawcett, 1870–1929: correspondence and papers, 7/MGF

Personal Collections

Fynn, Morris, Durban
Henry, Hector, Wentworth
Juggernath family, Merebank
McBride, Derrick, Wentworth
Pillay, Ivan, Pretoria
Seedat, Hashim, Durban (HSA) (DHAC boxes numbered by author)

Primary and Secondary Works

Adhikari, Mohamed, ed. *Burdened by Race: Coloured Identity in Southern Africa.* Cape Town: University of Cape Town Press, 2009.

Adhikari, Mohamed. *Not White Enough, Not Black Enough: Racial Identity in South Africa's Coloured Community.* Athens: Ohio University Press, 2005.

African National Congress. "Colonialism of a Special Type." Statement of the Lisbon Conference, March 1977. http://www.anc.org.za/ancdocs/history/special.html.

African National Congress—South African Communist Party. *The Green Book: Report of the Politico-Military Strategy Commission to the ANC National Executive Committee.* African National Congress, Lusaka, August 1979.

After Echo Park Lake Collective. *(Dis)Placement: The Fight for Housing and Community after Echo Park Lake.* Los Angeles: UCLA Luskin Institute on Inequality and Democracy, 2022.

Amin, Shahid. *Event, Metaphor, Memory: Chauri-Chaura, 1922–1992.* Oxford, UK: Oxford University Press, 1995.

Ancer, Jonathan. *Spy: Uncovering Craig Williamson.* Johannesburg: Jacana, 2017.

Ancer, Jonathan, and Chris Whitfield. *Joining the Dots: An Unauthorised Biography of Pravin Gordhan.* Johannesburg: Jonathan Ball, 2021.

Anderson, Kevin. *Marx at the Margins: On Nationalism, Ethnicity, and Non-Western Societies.* Chicago: University of Chicago Press, 2010.

Anderson, Warwick. *Colonial Pathologies: American Tropical Medicine, Race, and Hygiene in the Philippines.* Durham, NC: Duke University Press, 2006.

Anderson, Warwick. "Excremental Colonialism: Public Health and the Poetics of Pollution." *Critical Inquiry* 21, no. 3 (1995): 640–69.

Anti-Eviction Mapping Project. *Counterpoints: A San Francisco Bay Area Atlas of Displacement and Resistance.* Oakland, CA: PM, 2021.

Archary, Kogie, Indu Moodley, and Sinthi Qono, eds. *Beyond Borders—From Swaraj to Swailand: Rajes Pillay's Journey from Exile to Freedom.* Durban:

Gandhi-Luthi Documentation Centre, with Digital Innovation of South Africa and SAHO, 2021.

Arp, Jeffrey A. "Urban Trenches: War Poetry and the Unreal City of the Great War in T. S. Eliot's *The Waste Land.*" Master's thesis, Iowa State University, 2005.

Ashforth, Adam. *The Politics of Official Discourse in Twentieth-Century South Africa.* Oxford, UK: Oxford University Press, 1990.

Atkins, Keletso. *The Moon Is Dead! Give Us Our Money!* London: Heinemann, 1993.

Badassy, Prinisha. "'Is Lying a Coolie's Religion?': The Household Sammys and Marys of Colonial Natal, 1880–1920." *African Studies* 77, no. 4 (2018): 481–503.

Baderoon, Gabeba. *Regarding Muslims: From Slavery to Post-apartheid.* Johannesburg: Wits University Press, 2014.

Badiou, Alain. *Communist Hypothesis.* London: Verso, 2015.

Badsha, Omar. *Imijondolo: A Photographic Essay on Forced Removals in the Inanda District of South Africa.* Johannesburg: Raven, 1985.

Badsha, Omar. *Imperial Ghetto: Ways of Seeing in a South African City.* Maroelana: South African History Online, 2001.

Badsha, Omar. *Letter to Farzanah.* Durban: Institute for Black Research, 1979.

Bailey, David Eric. "The Origins of Phoenix, 1957–1976: The Durban City Council and the Indian Housing Question." Master's thesis, University of Natal, Durban, 1987.

Baldwin, Kate A. *Beyond the Color Line and the Iron Curtain: Reading Encounters between Black and Red, 1922–1963.* Durham, NC: Duke University Press, 2002.

Ballard, Richard. "Desegregating Minds: White Identities and Urban Change in the New South Africa." PhD diss., University of Wales, Swansea, 2002.

Ballard, Richard. "'Slaughter in the Suburbs': Livestock Slaughter and Race in Post-Apartheid Cities." *Ethnic and Racial Studies* 33, no. 6 (2010): 1069–87.

Ballard, Richard, Adam Habib, and Imraan Valodia. *Voices of Protest: Social Movements in Post-Apartheid South Africa.* Pietermaritzburg: University of KwaZulu-Natal Press, 2006.

Ballard, Richard, and Gareth Jones. "Natural Neighbors: Indigenous Landscapes and Eco-Estates in Durban, South Africa." *Annals of the Association of American Geographers* 100, no. 1 (2011): 131–48.

Bank, Leslie. *Home Spaces, Street Styles: Contesting Power and Identity in a South African City.* London: Pluto, 2011.

Barchiesi, Franco. "Classes, Multitudes and the Politics of Community Movements in Post-apartheid South Africa." In *Challenging Hegemony: Social Movements and the Quest for a New Humanism in South Africa*, edited by Nigel Gibson, 161–94. Trenton, NJ: Africa World, 2006.

Barchiesi, Franco. *Precarious Liberation: Workers, the State, and Contested Social Citizenship in Postapartheid South Africa.* Albany: State University of New York Press, 2011.

Barrell, Howard. "Conscripts to Their Age: African National Congress Operational Strategy, 1976–1986." PhD diss., Oxford University, 1993. https://omalley.nelsonmandela.org/index.php/site/q/03lv02424/04lv02712/05lv02713.htm.

Baruah, Amit. "Gandhi Was a Phenomenal Success, Says Fatima Meer." *Hindu,* January 12, 2003.

Baskin, Jeremy. *Striking Back: A History of Cosatu.* Johannesburg: Ravan, 1991.

Baucom, Ian. *Specters of the Atlantic: Finance Capital, Slavery, and the Philosophy of History.* Durham, NC: Duke University Press, 2005.

Beall, Jo, Michelle Friedman, Shireen Hassim, Ros Posel, Lindsay Stiebel, and Alison Todes. "African Women in the Durban Struggle, 1985–86: Towards a Transformation of Roles?" *South African Review,* no. 4 (1987): 30–57.

Beavon, Keith. *Johannesburg: The Making and Shaping of the City.* Pretoria: University of South Africa Press, 2004.

Bedderson, Seymour Alistair Benedict. "Neighbourhood Revitalization: The Case of Austerville, Durban, Republic of South Africa." Master's thesis, University of Natal, 1995.

Beinart, William. "The Anatomy of a Rural Scare: East Griqualand in the 1890s." In *Hidden Struggles in Rural South Africa: Popular and Political Movements in the Transkei and Eastern Cape, 1890–1930,* edited by William Beinart and Colin Bundy, 46–77. London: James Currey, 1987.

Beinart, William. *The Rise of Conservation in South Africa: Settlers, Livestock, and the Environment, 1770–1950.* Oxford, UK: Oxford University Press, 2003.

Beinart, William. *Twentieth-Century South Africa.* Oxford, UK: Oxford University Press, 1994.

Beinart, William, Peter Delius, and Stanley Trapido. *Putting Plough to the Ground: Accumulation and Dispossession in Rural South Africa, 1850–1930.* Johannesburg: Ravan, 1986.

Beinart, William, and Saul Dubow. *Segregation and Apartheid in Twentieth-Century South Africa.* New York: Routledge, 1995.

Benjamin, Ruha. "Black to the Future: Rethinking Race, Science, and Subjectivity." Paper presented at the workshop on Histories of the Future: Race, Science, and Subjectivity. Princeton University, February 6, 2015. http://histscifi.com/essays /benjamin/regeneration.html.

Benjamin, Walter. "Hashish in Marseilles." In *Walter Benjamin: Selected Writings,* vol. 2, pt. 2, *1927–1934,* edited by Michael W. Jennings, Howard Eiland, and Gary Smith, 673–79. Cambridge, MA: Belknap Press of Harvard University Press, 1999.

Benjamin, Walter. *Illuminations: Essays and Reflections.* Edited by Hannah Arendt. New York: Schocken, 1986.

Benjamin, Walter. "Little History of Photography." In *Walter Benjamin: Selected Writings,* vol. 2, pt. 2, *1927–1934,* edited by Michael W. Jennings, Howard Eiland, and Gary Smith, 507–30. Cambridge, MA: Belknap Press of Harvard University Press, 2005.

Benjamin, Walter. "Paris, the Capital of the Nineteenth Century." In *Walter Benjamin: Selected Writings,* vol. 3, *1935–1938,* edited by Michael W. Jennings and Howard Eiland, 32–49. Cambridge, MA: Belknap Press of Harvard University Press, 2002.

Benjamin, Walter. "Theologico-Political Fragment." In *Reflections,* edited by Peter Demetz, translated by J. Jephcott, 312–13. New York: Schocken, 1978.

Benjamin, Walter. "Theses on the Philosophy of History." In *Illuminations: Essays and Reflections*, edited by Hannah Arendt, 253–64. New York: Schocken, 1986.

Benjamin, Walter. "The Work of Art in the Age of Its Technological Reproducibility, Second Version." In *Walter Benjamin: Selected Writings*, vol. 3, *1935–1938*, edited by Howard Eiland and Michael W. Jennings, translated by Edmund Jephcott, Howard Eiland, et al, 101–33. Cambridge, MA: Belknap Press of Harvard University Press, 2006.

Berry, Sara. *No Condition Is Permanent: The Social Dynamics of Agrarian Change in Sub-Saharan Africa*. Madison: University of Wisconsin Press, 1993.

Bhana, Surendra, and Joy Brain. *Setting Down Roots: Indian Migrants in South Africa, 1860–1911*. Johannesburg: Wits University Press, 1990.

Bickford-Smith, Vivian. *The Emergence of the South African Metropolis: Cities and Identities in the Twentieth Century*. Cambridge: Cambridge University Press, 2016.

Biko, Steve. "Black Consciousness and the Quest for a True Humanity." In *I Write What I Like*, edited by Aelred Stubbs, 87–98. Oxford, UK: Heinemann, 1987.

Biko, Steve. "The Definition of Black Consciousness." In *I Write What I Like*, edited by Aelred Stubbs, 48–53. Oxford, UK: Heinemann, 1987.

Biko, Steve. "Interview with Steve Biko." By Gail Gerhart. In *Biko Lives! Contesting the Legacies of Steve Biko*, edited by Andile Mngxitama, Amanda Alexander, and Nigel C. Gibson, 21–42. New York: Palgrave Macmillan, 2008.

Biko, Steve. *I Write What I Like*. Edited by Aelred Stubbs. Oxford, UK: Heinemann, 1987.

Biko, Steve. "We Blacks." In *I Write What I Like*, edited by Aelred Stubbs, 27–32. Oxford, UK: Heinemann, 1987.

Blomkamp, Neill, dir. *District 9*. Culver City, CA: Sony Pictures, 2009.

Boehmer, Elleke. *Nelson Mandela: A Very Short Introduction*. Oxford, UK: Oxford University Press, 2008.

Bond, Patrick. *Elite Transition: From Apartheid to Neoliberalism in South Africa*. London: Pluto, 2000.

Bonner, Philip, Peter Delius, and Deborah Posel, eds. *Apartheid's Genesis, 1935–1962*. Johannesburg: Ravan, 1994.

Bonner, Philip, and Noor Nieftagodien. *Alexandra: A History*. Johannesburg: Wits University Press, 2008.

Booysen, Susan. *The African National Congress and the Regeneration of Political Power*. Johannesburg: Wits University Press, 2011.

Boym, Svetlana. *The Future of Nostalgia*. New York: Basic Books, 2001.

Bozzoli, Belinda. *Theatres of Struggle and the End of Apartheid*. Athens: Ohio University Press, 2004.

Bozzoli, Belinda, Peter Delius, Joanna Roberts, and Josh Brown, eds. "History from South Africa." Special issue, *Radical History Review* 1990, no. 46–47 (1990).

Braam, Conny. *Operation Vula*. Johannesburg: Jacana, 2004.

Bradford, Helen. *A Taste for Freedom: The ICU in Rural South Africa, 1924–1930*. New Haven, CT: Yale University Press, 1987.

Breckenridge, Keith. "The Biometric Obsession: Trans-Atlantic Progressivism and the Making of the South African State." Paper presented at the First Network Workshop on the Documentation of Individual Identity: Historical, Comparative and Transnational Perspectives since 1500, University of Oxford, September 26–27, 2008.

Breckenridge, Keith. *Biometric State: The Global Politics of Identification and Surveillance in South Africa, 1850 to the Present*. Cambridge: Cambridge University Press, 2014.

Breckenridge, Keith. "Gandhi's Progressive Disillusionment: Thumbs, Fingers, and the Rejection of Scientific Modernism in *Hind Swaraj*." *Public Culture* 23, no. 2 (2011): 331–48.

Breckenridge, Keith. "Progressivism Unleashed: Reinterpreting Reconstruction." Paper presented at the History and African Studies Seminar, Department of Historical Studies, University of KwaZulu-Natal, Durban, October 28, 2009.

Breckenridge, Keith. "Verwoerd's Bureau of Proof: Total Information in the Making of Apartheid." *History Workshop*, no. 59 (2005): 83–108.

Brown, Julian. "An Experiment in Confrontation: The Pro-Frelimo Rallies of 1974." *Journal of Southern African Studies* 38, no. 1 (2012): 55–71.

Buhle, Paul. Introduction to *State Capitalism and World Revolution*, by C. L. R. James, in collaboration with Raya Dunayevskaya and Grace Lee Boggs, xi–xxiii. Chicago: Charles H. Kerr, 1986.

Bundy, Colin. *The Rise and Fall of the South African Peasantry*. Berkeley: University of California Press, 1979.

Burns, Catherine. "A Useable Past: The Search for 'History in Chords.'" In *History Making and Present Day Politics: The Meaning of Collective Memory in South Africa*, edited by Hans Erik Stolten, 351–62. Uppsala, Sweden: Nordiska Afrikainstitutet, 2007.

Burton, Antoinette. *Brown over Black: Race and the Politics of Postcolonial Citation*. New Delhi: Three Essays Collective, 2012.

Burton, Antoinette. *Burdens of History: British Feminists, Indian Women, and Imperial Culture, 1865–1915*. Chapel Hill: University of North Carolina Press, 1994.

Burton, Antoinette. "States of Injury: Josephine Butler on Slavery, Citizenship, and the Boer War." *Social Politics* 5, no. 3 (1998): 338–61.

Butler, Judith. "One Time Traverses Another: Benjamin's 'Theologico-Political Fragment.'" In *Walter Benjamin and Theology*, edited by Colby Dickinson and Stéphane Symons, 272–85. New York: Fordham University Press, 2016.

Butler, Mark, and David Hallowes. *Forging the Future: Industrial Strategy and the Making of Environmental Injustice in South Africa: The groundWork Report*. Pietermaritzburg: groundWork, 2003.

Butler, Mark, David Hallowes, Chris Albertyn, Gillian Watkins, and Rory O'Connor. *Corporate Accountability in South Africa: The Petrochemical Industry and Air Pollution: The groundWork Report*. Pietermaritzburg: groundWork, 2002.

Cajee, Imtiaz. *Timol: A Quest for Justice*. Johannesburg: Real African, 2005.

Callebert, Ralph. *On Durban's Docks: Zulu Workers, Rural Households, Global Labor.* Rochester, NY: University of Rochester Press, 2017.

Carnie, Tony. "The Poison in Our Air." Special article series. *Mercury*, Durban, September 11–15, 2000.

Castells, Manuel. *City, Class and Power.* Translated by Elizabeth Lebas. London: Palgrave, 1978.

Castells, Manuel. *The Urban Question: A Marxist Approach.* Translated by Alan Sheridan. Cambridge, MA: MIT Press, 1977.

Cell, John. *The Highest Stage of White Supremacy: The Origins of Segregation in South Africa and the American South.* Cambridge: Cambridge University Press, 1982.

Centre for Contemporary Cultural Studies. *The Empire Strikes Back.* London: Routledge, 1982.

Chance, Kerry Ryan. *Living Politics in South Africa's Urban Shacklands.* Chicago: University of Chicago Press, 2017.

Chari, Sharad. "The Blues and the Damned: (Black) Life-That-Survives Capital and Biopolitics." *Critical African Studies* 9, no. 2 (2017): 152–73.

Chari, Sharad. "Detritus in Durban: Polluted Environs and the Biopolitics of Refusal." In *Imperial Debris: On Ruins and Ruination*, edited by Ann Laura Stoler, 131–61. Durham, NC: Duke University Press, 2013.

Chari, Sharad. *Gramsci at Sea.* Minneapolis: University of Minnesota Press, 2023.

Chari, Sharad. "'Interlocking Transactions': Micro-foundations for 'Racial Capitalism.'" In *Ethnographies of Power: Working Radical Concepts with Gillian Hart*, edited by Sharad Chari, Mark Hunter, and Melanie Samson, 49–75. Johannesburg: Wits University Press, 2022.

Chari, Sharad. "Mysterious Moves of Revolution: Specters of Black Power, Futures of Postcoloniality." In *The Postcolonial Contemporary: Political Imaginaries for the Global Present*, edited by Jini Kim Watson and Gary Wilder, 77–94. New York: Fordham University Press, 2018.

Chari, Sharad. "Post-Apartheid Livelihood Struggles in Wentworth, South Durban." In *The Development Decade? Economic and Social Change in South Africa, 1994–2004*, edited by Vishnu Padayachee, 427–43. Cape Town: Human Sciences Research Council Press, 2006.

Chari, Sharad. "State Racism and Biopolitical Struggle: The Evasive Commons in Twentieth-Century Durban, South Africa." *Radical History Review*, no. 108 (2010): 73–90.

Cheshire, Leonard. *The Hidden World.* London: William Collins and Sons, 1981.

Cheshire Foundation Homes for the Sick. *The Cheshire Homes: A Pictorial Record.* Liss, UK: Cheshire Smile, 1963.

Chetty, Carmel T. M. "Young, Gifted and Black: Oral Histories of Young Activists in Cape Town and Durban in the Early 1970s." Master's thesis, University of KwaZulu-Natal, 2005.

Clark, Anna. "The New Poor Law and the Breadwinner Wage: Contrasting Assumptions." *Journal of Social History* 34, no. 2 (2000): 261–74.

Clark, Anna. *The Struggle for the Breeches: Gender and the Making of the British Working Class*. Berkeley: University of California Press, 1995.

Cohn, Bernard. S. *Colonialism and Its Forms of Knowledge: The British in India*. Princeton, NJ: Princeton University Press, 1996.

Collis-Buthelezi, Victoria J. "The Case for Black Studies in South Africa." *Black Scholar* 47, no. 2 (2017): 7–21.

Collis-Buthelezi, Victoria J. "Requiem: Roundtable on Tendayi Sithole's *The Black Register*; An Introduction." *Critical Times* 4, no. 2 (2021): 314–20.

Comaroff, Jean. "Beyond Bare Life: AIDS, (Bio)Politics, and the Neoliberal Order." *Public Culture* 19, no. 1 (2007): 197–219.

Comaroff, Jean, and John Comaroff. "Alien-Nation: Zombies, Immigrants, and Millennial Capitalism." *South Atlantic Quarterly* 101, no. 4 (2020): 779–805.

Comaroff, Jean, and John Comaroff. "Millennial Capitalism: First Thoughts on a Second Coming." *Public Culture* 12, no. 2 (2000): 291–343.

Comaroff, Jean, and John Comaroff. "Occult Economies and the Violence of Abstraction: Notes from the South African Postcolony." *American Ethnologist* 26, no. 2 (1999): 279–303.

Cooper, Frederick. *Decolonization and African Society: The Labor Question in French and British Africa*. Cambridge: Cambridge University Press, 1996.

Cooper, Frederick. "A Parting of the Ways: Colonial Africa and South Africa, 1946–48." *African Studies* 65, no. 1 (2006): 27–44.

Cooper, Frederick. *Struggles for the City: Migrant Labor, Capital, and the State in Urban Africa*. Beverly Hills, CA: SAGE, 1983.

Cooper, Frederick. "Urban, Space, Industrial Time, and Wage Labor in Africa." In *Struggles for the City: Migrant Labor, Capital, and the State in Urban Africa*, edited by Frederick Cooper, 7–50. Beverly Hills, CA: SAGE, 1983.

Copelyn, Johnny. *Maverick Insider: The Struggle for Union Independence in a Time of National Liberation*. Johannesburg: Picador Africa, 2016.

Coronil, Fernando. "Beyond Occidentalism: Toward Nonimperial Geohistorical Categories." *Cultural Anthropology* 11, no. 1 (1996): 51–87.

Couzens, Tim. "Moralizing Leisure Time: The Transatlantic Connection and Black Johannesburg." In *Industrialisation and Social Change*, edited by Shula Marks and Richard Rathbone, 314–37. New York: Longman, 1982.

Crankshaw, Owen. "Class, Race and Residence in Black Johannesburg, 1923–1970." *Journal of Historical Sociology* 18, no. 4 (2005): 354–93.

Crankshaw, Owen. *Race, Class and the Changing Division of Labour under Apartheid*. London: Routledge, 1997.

Cuthbertson, Greg, Albert Grundlingh, and Mary-Lynn Suttie, eds. *Writing a Wider War: Rethinking Gender, Race, and Identity in the South African War, 1899–1902*. Athens: Ohio University Press, 2002.

Daniel, E. Valentine. *Charred Lullabies: Chapters in an Anthropology of Violence*. Princeton, NJ: Princeton University Press, 1996.

Davie, Grace. *Poverty Knowledge in South Africa: A Social History of Human Science, 1855–2005*. Cambridge: Cambridge University Press, 2015.

Davie, Grace. "Strength in Numbers: The Durban Student Wages Commission, Dockworkers and the Poverty Datum Line, 1971–1973." *Journal of Southern African Studies* 33, no. 2 (2007): 401–20.

Davies, Rob. "The Class Character of South Africa's Industrial Conciliation Legislation." *South African Labour Bulletin* 2, no. 6 (1976): 6–20.

Davin, Anna. "Imperialism and Motherhood." *History Workshop Journal*, no. 5 (1978): 9–65.

Davis, Angela. "Steve Biko Memorial Lecture." University of South Africa, Pretoria, September 9, 2016. SABC News video, 43:40. https://www.youtube.com /watch?v=_8t_qxgDF2o.

Davis, Mike. *Buda's Wagon: A Brief History of the Car Bomb*. London: Verso, 2007.

Davis, Stephen. *Bob Marley*. Rochester, NY: Schenkman, 1988.

Denness, Zoë. "Women and Warfare at the Start of the Twentieth Century: The Racialization of the 'Enemy' during the South African War (1899–1902)." *Patterns of Prejudice* 46, no. 3–4 (2012): 255–76.

Derrida, Jacques. *Specters of Marx*. New York: Routledge, 1994.

Desai, Ashwin. *We Are the Poors: Community Struggles in Post-Apartheid South Africa*. New York: Monthly Review Press, 2002.

Desai, Ashwin. *Wentworth: The Beautiful Game and the Making of Place*. Pietermaritzburg: University of KwaZulu-Natal Press, 2019.

Desai, Ashwin, and Goolam Vahed. *Chatsworth: The Making of a South African Township*. Durban: University of KwaZulu-Natal Press, 2013.

Desai, Ashwin, and Goolam Vahed. *Colour, Class and Community—the Natal Indian Congress, 1971–1994*. Johannesburg: Wits University Press, 2021.

Desai, Ashwin, and Goolam Vahed. *Monty Naicker: Between Reason and Treason*. Pietermaritzburg: Shuter and Shooter, 2010.

Dhupelia-Mesthrie, Uma. "The Revival of the Natal Indian Congress." In *The Road to Democracy in South Africa*, vol. 2 *(1970–1980)*, edited by South African Democracy Education Trust, 883–99. Pretoria: University of South Africa Press, 2006.

Didi-Huberman, Georges. *Uprisings*. Paris: Jeu de Paume and Gallimard, 2016.

Dlamini, Jacob. *Askari: A Story of Collaboration and Betrayal in the Anti-Apartheid Struggle*. Johannesburg: Jacana, 2014.

Dlamini, Jacob. *Native Nostalgia*. Johannesburg: Jacana, 2009.

Dlamini, Jacob. *Terrorist Album*. Cambridge, MA: Harvard University Press, 2020.

Dobson, Richard, and Caroline Skinner. *Working in Warwick: Integrating Street Traders into Urban Plans*. Durban: University of KwaZulu-Natal, 2009.

Donzelot, Jacques. *The Policing of Families*. Baltimore: Johns Hopkins University Press, 1977.

Drayton, Richard. *Nature's Government: Science, Imperial Britain, and the "Improvement" of the World*. New Haven, CT: Yale University Press, 2000.

Dubbeld, Bernard. "Capital and the Shifting Grounds of Emancipatory Politics: The Limits of Radical Unionism in Durban Harbor, 1974–85." *Critical Historical Studies* 2, no. 1 (2015): 85–112.

Dubbeld, Bernard. "A History of the Decline of Stevedoring Labour in Durban, 1959–1990." Master's thesis, University of Natal, Durban, 2003.

Du Bois, W. E. B. "The Comet." In *Darkwater: Voices from within the Veil*, 253–73. New York: Harcourt, Brace and Howe, 1920.

Dubow, Saul. *Apartheid, 1948–1994.* Oxford, UK: Oxford University Press, 2014.

Dubow, Saul. *A Commonwealth of Knowledge: Science, Sensibility, and White South Africa, 1820–2000.* Oxford, UK: Oxford University Press, 2006.

Dubow, Saul, and Alan Jeeves. *South Africa's 1940s: Worlds of Possibilities.* Johannesburg: Double Storey, 2010.

Du Toit, Andries and David Neves. "Rural Livelihoods in South Africa: Complexity, Vulnerability and Differentiation." *Journal of Agrarian Change* 13, no. 1 (2013): 93–115.

Du Toit, Marijke, and Jenny Gordon. *Breathing Spaces: Environmental Portraits of South Durban.* Pietermaritzburg: University of KwaZulu-Natal Press, 2016.

Eaton, John. *Political Economy: A Marxist Textbook.* Rev. ed. New York: International Publishers, 1966.

Ebrahim-Vally, Rehana. *Kala Pani: Caste and Colour in South Africa.* Cape Town: Kwela, 2001.

Edmunds, Marion, dir. *The Vula Connection.* Johannesburg: Sabido Productions, 2014. eNCA video, 58:25. https://www.youtube.com/watch?v=29vrvKsKXPI.

Edwards, Iain. "Mkhumbane, Our Home: African Shantytown Society in Cato Manor Farm, 1946–60." PhD diss., University of Natal, 1989.

Eley, Geoff. *Forging Democracy: The History of the Left in Europe, 1850–2000.* Oxford, UK: Oxford University Press.

Eliade, Mircea. "The Occult and the Modern World." In *Occultism, Witchcraft, and Cultural Fashions: Essays in Comparative Religion*, 47–68. Chicago: University of Chicago Press, 2012.

Eliot, T. S. *The Waste Land.* New York: W. W. Norton, 2001.

Ellis, Stephen. *External Mission: The ANC in Exile, 1960–1990.* Cape Town: Jonathan Ball, 2012.

Ellis, Stephen. "The Genesis of the ANC's Armed Struggle in South Africa 1948–1961." *Journal of Southern African Studies* 37, no. 4 (2011): 657–76.

Epprecht, Marc. "The Native Village Debate in Pietermaritzburg, 1848–1925: Revisiting the 'Sanitation Syndrome.'" *Journal of African History* 58, no. 2 (2017): 259–83.

Epprecht, Marc. *Welcome to Greater Edendale: Histories of Environment, Health, and Gender in an African City.* Montreal: McGill-Queen's University Press, 2016.

Erasmus, Zimitri. *Coloured by History, Shaped by Place: New Perspectives on Coloured Identities in Cape Town.* Cape Town: Kwela, 2001.

Erasmus, Zimitri. "Introduction: Re-imagining Coloured Identities in Post-apartheid South Africa." In *Coloured by History, Shaped by Place: New Perspectives on Coloured Identities in Cape Town*, 13–28. Cape Town: Kwela, 2001.

Erasmus, Zimitri. *Race Otherwise: Forging a New Humanism for South Africa.* Johannesburg: Wits University Press, 2017.

Erwin, Kira, Monique Marks, and Tamlynn Fleetwood. *Voices of Resilience: A Living History of the Kenneth Gardens Municipal Housing Estate.* Durban: University of KwaZulu-Natal Press, 2018.

Esmeir, Samera. "The Palestinians and the Struggle of the Dispossessed." *openDemocracy,* May 14, 2021. https://www.opendemocracy.net/en/north-africa-west-asia/palestinians-and-struggle-dispossessed.

Evans, Ivan. *Bureaucracy and Race: Native Administration in South Africa.* Berkeley: University of California Press, 1997.

Everatt, David. "Alliance Politics of a Special Type: The Roots of the ANC/SACP Alliance, 1950–1954." *Journal of Southern African Studies* 18, no. 1 (1992): 19–41.

Everatt, David. *The Origins of Non-racialism: White Opposition to Apartheid in the 1950s.* Johannesburg: Wits University Press, 2009.

Fanon, Frantz. *Black Skin, White Masks.* Translated by Charles Lam Markmann. New York: Grove, 1967.

Fanon, Frantz. *Les damnés de la terre.* Paris: F. Maspero, 1961.

Fanon, Frantz. *The Wretched of the Earth.* Translated by Constance Farrington. New York: Grove, 1965.

Farred, Grant. "The Black Intellectual's Work Is Never Done: A Critique of the Discourse of Reconciliation in South Africa." *Postcolonial Studies* 7, no. 1 (2004): 113–23.

Farred, Grant. *Martin Heidegger Saved My Life.* Minneapolis: University of Minnesota Press, 2015.

Farred, Grant. *Midfielder's Moment: Coloured Literature and Culture in Contemporary South Africa.* London: Routledge, 2000.

Farred, Grant. "The Not-Yet Counterpartisan: A New Politics of Oppositionality." *South Atlantic Quarterly* 103, no. 4 (2004): 589–605.

Farred, Grant. *What's My Name? Black Vernacular Intellectuals.* Minneapolis: University of Minnesota Press, 2003.

Farred, Grant. "Where Does the Rainbow Nation End? Colouredness and Citizenship in Post-apartheid South Africa." *New Centennial Review* 1, no. 1 (2001): 175–99.

Fassin, Didier. *When Bodies Remember: Experiences and Politics of AIDS in South Africa.* Berkeley: University of California Press, 2007.

Featherstone, David. *Solidarity: Hidden Histories and Geographies of Internationalism.* London: Zed, 2012.

Federation of South African Women. "The Women's Charter." April 17, 1954. https://www.sahistory.org.za/article/womens-charter.

Ferguson, Roderick. "The Lateral Moves of African American Studies in a Period of Migration." In *Affinities: The Gender and Sexual Politics of Comparative Racialization,* edited by Grace Hong and Roderick Ferguson, 113–30. Durham, NC: Duke University Press. 2011.

Figlan, Lindela, Rev. Mavuso, Busi Ngema, Zodwa Nsibande, Sihle Sibisi, and Sbu Zikode. *Living Learning.* Pietermaritzburg: Church Land Programme / Abahlali baseMjondolo, 2009. https://abahlali.org/files/Living_Learning.pdf.

Fine, Ben, and Zavareh Rustomjee. *The Political Economy of South Africa: From Minerals-Energy Complex to Industrialisation*. Boulder, CO: Westview, 1996.

Fischer, John. *That Miss Hobhouse*. London: Secker and Warburg, 1971.

Forth, Aidan. *Barbed-Wire Imperialism: Britain's Empire of Camps, 1876–1903*. Berkeley: University of California Press, 2017.

Foster, Jeremy. "Capturing and Losing the 'Lie of the Land': Railway Photography and Colonial Nationalism in Early Twentieth-Century South Africa." In *Picturing Place: Photography and the Geographical Imagination*, edited by Joan M. Schwartz and James R. Ryan, 141–61. London: I. B. Tauris, 2003.

Foster, Jeremy. "From Socio-nature to Spectral Presence: Re-imagining the Once and Future Landscape of Johannesburg." *Safundi* 10, no. 2 (2009): 175–213.

Foster-Carter, Aidan. "The Modes of Production Controversy." *New Left Review*, no. 107 (1978): 47–77.

Foster, Jeremy. *Washed with Sun: Landscape and the Making of White South Africa*. Pittsburgh, PA: University of Pittsburgh Press, 2008.

Foucault, Michel. *The Birth of Biopolitics: Lectures at the Collège de France, 1978–1979*. Basingstoke, UK: Palgrave Macmillan, 2008.

Foucault, Michel. *The History of Sexuality*. Vol. 1, *An Introduction*. New York: Vintage, 1980.

Foucault, Michel. *Security, Territory, Population: Lectures at the Collège de France, 1977–1978*. Translated by Graham Burchell. Basingstoke, UK: Palgrave Macmillan, 2007.

Foucault, Michel. *"Society Must Be Defended": Lectures at the Collège de France, 1975–76*. New York: Picador, 2003.

Frederikse, Julie. *The Unbreakable Thread: Non-racialism in South Africa*. Bloomington: Indiana University Press, 1990.

Freire, Paulo. *Pedagogy of the Oppressed*. Translated by Myra Ramos. New York: Continuum, 1970.

Freund, Bill. *The African City: A History*. Cambridge: Cambridge University Press, 2007.

Freund, Bill. "City Hall and the Direction of Development: The Changing Role of the Local State as a Factor in Economic Planning and Development in Durban." In *(D)urban Vortex*, edited by Bill Freund and Vishnu Padayachee, 11–39. Pietermaritzburg: University of Natal Press, 2002.

Freund, Bill. "Confrontation and Social Change: Natal and the Forging of Apartheid, 1949–72." In *Political Economy and Identities in KwaZulu-Natal: Historical and Social Perspectives*, edited by Robert Morrell and Georgina Hamilton, 119–40. Durban: Indicator / University of Natal Press, 1996.

Freund, Bill. *Insiders and Outsiders: The Indian Working Class of Durban, 1910–1990*. Portsmouth, NH: Heinemann, 1995.

Freund, Bill. *Twentieth-Century South Africa: A Developmental History*. Cambridge: Cambridge University Press, 2019.

Freund, Bill, and Vishnu Padayachee, eds. *(D)urban Vortex: South African City in Transition.* Pietermaritzburg: University of Natal Press, 2002.

Friedman, Steven. "From Classroom to Class Struggle: Radical Academics and the Rebirth of Trade Unionism in the 1970s." *Journal of Asian and African Studies* 49, no. 5 (2014): 526–43.

Gerhart, Gail M. *Black Power in South Africa: The Evolution of an Ideology.* Berkeley: University of California Press, 1978.

Gerhart, Gail M., and Clive L. Glaser, eds. *From Protest to Challenge: A Documentary History of African Politics in South Africa, 1882–1990.* Vol. 6, *Challenge and Victory, 1980–1990.* Bloomington: Indiana University Press, 2013.

Gevisser, Mark. *Thabo Mbeki: A Dream Deferred.* Cape Town: Jonathan Ball, 2007.

Ghertner, Asher. *Rule by Aesthetics: World-Class City Making in Delhi.* Oxford, UK: Oxford University Press, 2015.

Giáp, Võ Nguyên. *People's War, People's Army.* Hanoi: Foreign Languages Publishing House, 1961. https://www.marxists.org/archive/giap/works/1961/peoples -war-peoples-army/1961-pwpa.pdf.

Gibbs, Tim. "Collapse, Conflict or Social Cohesion? Learning from Livestock Dipping Associations in KwaZulu-Natal." PLAAS Working Paper 62. Institute for Poverty, Land and Agrarian Studies, University of the Western Cape, Bellville, South Africa, 2020.

Gibbs, Tim. *Mandela's Kinsmen: Nationalist Elites and Apartheid's First Bantustan.* Martlesham, UK: James Currey, 2015.

Gibson, Nigel C., ed. *Challenging Hegemony: Social Movements and the Quest for a New Humanism in South Africa.* Trenton, NJ: Africa World, 2006.

Gibson, Nigel C. *Fanonian Practices in South Africa: From Steve Biko to Abahlali baseMjondolo.* Basingstoke, UK: Palgrave Macmillan, 2011.

Gibson, Nigel C. "What Happened to the 'Promised Land'? A Fanonian Perspective on Post-Apartheid South Africa." *Antipode* 44, no. 1 (2011): 51–73.

Gilmore, Ruth Wilson. *Abolition Geography: Essays towards Liberation.* Edited by Brenna Bhandar and Alberto Toscano. London: Verso, 2022.

Gilmore, Ruth Wilson. "Fatal Couplings of Power and Difference: Notes on Racism and Geography." *Professional Geographer* 54, no. 1 (2002): 15–24.

Gilmore, Ruth Wilson. "Forgotten Places and the Seeds of Grassroots Planning." In *Engaging Contradictions: Theory, Politics, and Methods of Activist Scholarship,* edited by Charles R. Hale, 31–61. Berkeley: University of California Press, 2008.

Gilmore, Ruth Wilson. *Geographies of Racial Capitalism.* Directed by Kenton Card for the Antipode Foundation. New York: BFD Productions, 2019. Video, 16:19. https://antipodeonline.org/geographies-of-racial-capitalism.

Gilmore, Ruth Wilson. *Golden Gulag: Prisons, Surplus, Crisis, and Opposition in Globalizing California.* Berkeley: University of California Press, 2007.

Gilroy, Paul. *After Empire: Melancholia or Convivial Culture?* Abingdon, UK: Routledge, 2004.

Gilroy, Paul. *The Black Atlantic: Modernity and Double Consciousness.* Cambridge, MA: Harvard University Press, 1993.

Glaser, Clive L. *Bo-Tsotsi: The Youth Gangs of Soweto, 1935–1976*. Oxford, UK: James Currey, 2000.

Glissant, Édouard. *Poetics of Relation*. Translated by Betsy Wing. Ann Arbor: University of Michigan Press, 1997.

Goldblatt, David. *South Africa: The Structure of Things Then*. New York: Monacelli, 1998.

Goldin, Ian. *Making Race: The Politics and Economics of Coloured Identity in South Africa*. London: Longman, 1987.

Goodwin, Peter. "Oliver Tambo: Pretoria's Public Enemy Number One." *Gazette*, July 5, 1986.

Goonam, Kesaveloo. *Coolie Doctor: An Autobiography*. Durban: Madiba, 1991.

Goonewardena, Kanishka, Stefan Kipfer, Richard Milgrom, and Christian Schmid, eds. *Space, Difference, Everyday Life: Reading Henri Lefebvre*. New York: Routledge, 2008.

Gordon, Lewis. *Existentia Africana: Understanding Africana Existential Thought*. New York: Routledge, 2000.

Gorz, André. *Strategy for Labor: A Radical Proposal*. Translated by Martin A. Nicolaus and Victoria Ortiz. Boston: Beacon, 1964.

Gould, Deborah. *Moving Politics: Emotion and Act Up's Fight against AIDS*. Chicago: University of Chicago Press, 2009.

Govender, Pregs. *Love and Courage: A Story of Insubordination*. Johannesburg: Jacana, 2008.

Govender, Ronnie. *At the Edge and Other Cato Manor Stories*. Durban: Manx, 1996.

Gqola, Pumla Dineo. *A Renegade Called Simphiwe*. Johannesburg: Jacana, 2013.

Gqola, Pumla Dineo. *What Is Slavery to Me? Postcolonial/Slave Memory in Post-apartheid South Africa*. Johannesburg: Wits University Press, 2010.

Graeber, David. *Debt: The First 5,000 Years*. New York: Melville House, 2011.

Gramsci, Antonio. *Selections from the "Prison Notebooks" of Antonio Gramsci*. Edited and translated by Quintin Hoare and Geoffrey Nowell Smith. New York: International Publishers, 1971.

Graser, Roland, and Sheldon Rankin. *Crime in Austerville*. Durban: Institute for Social and Economic Research, UDW, 1983.

Green, Nile. *Bombay Islam: The Religious Economy of the West Indian Ocean, 1840–1915*. Cambridge: Cambridge University Press, 2011.

Grosskopf, Johann Friedrich Wilhelm. *Economic Report: Rural Impoverishment and Rural Exodus*. Vol. 1 of *The Poor White Problem in South Africa: Report of the Carnegie Commission*. Stellenbosch, South Africa: Pro Ecclesia-Drukkery, 1932.

Grove, Richard. *Green Imperialism: Colonial Expansion, Tropical Island Edens and the Origins of Environmentalism, 1600–1860*. Cambridge: Cambridge University Press, 1995.

Guy, Jeff. *Theophilus Shepstone and the Forging of Natal: African Autonomy and Settler Colonialism in the Making of Traditional Authority*. Scottsville: University of KwaZulu-Natal Press, 2013.

Gwala, Mafika, ed. *Black Review, 1973*. Durban: Black Community Programmes, 1974.

Hadfield, Leslie Anne. *Liberation and Development: Black Consciousness Community Programs in South Africa*. East Lansing: Michigan State University Press, 2016.

Hall, Catherine. *White, Male and Middle Class: Explorations in Feminism and History*. Cambridge, UK: Polity, 1992.

Hall, Peter. *Cities of Tomorrow: An Intellectual History of Urban Planning and Design in the Twentieth Century*. Oxford, UK: Wiley-Blackwell, 2002.

Hall, Stuart. "Black Diaspora Artists in Britain: Three 'Moments' in Post-war History." *History Workshop*, no. 61 (2006): 1–24.

Hall, Stuart. "New Ethnicities." In *Black British Cultural Studies*, edited by Houston Baker, Manthia Diawara, and Ruth Lindeborg, 163–72. Chicago: University of Chicago Press, 1996.

Hall, Stuart. "Race, Articulation, and Societies Structured in Dominance." In *Selected Writings on Race and Difference*, edited by Paul Gilroy and Ruth Wilson Gilmore, 195–245. Durham, NC: Duke University Press, 2021.

Hall, Stuart. *Selected Writings on Marxism*. Edited by Gregor McLennan. Durham, NC: Duke University Press, 2021.

Hall, Stuart. *Selected Writings on Race and Difference*. Edited by Paul Gilroy and Ruth Wilson Gilmore. Durham, NC: Duke University Press, 2021.

Hall, Stuart, and Les Back. "At Home and Not at Home: Stuart Hall in Conversation with Les Back." *Cultural Studies* 23, no. 4 (2009): 658–87.

Hall, Stuart, Chas Critcher, Tony Jefferson, John Clarke, and Brian Roberts. *Policing the Crisis: Mugging, the State, and Law and Order*. London: Macmillan, 1978.

Hallowes, David, and Victor Munnik. *Poisoned Spaces: Manufacturing Wealth, Producing Poverty; The groundWork Report*. Durban: groundWork, 2006.

Hamilton, Carolyn, Verne Harris, Jane Taylor, Michele Pickover, Graeme Reid, and Razia Saleh. *Reconfiguring the Archive*. Cape Town: David Philip, 2002.

Hani, Chris. "The Wankie Campaign." *Dawn: Journal of Umkhonto we Sizwe; Souvenir Issue* (December 1986): 34–37. Available at https://www.sahistory.org.za/archive/dawn-souvenir-issue-1986.

Hannah, Matthew. *Governmentality and the Mastery of Territory in Nineteenth-Century America*. Cambridge: Cambridge University Press, 2003.

Hansen, Thomas Blom. *Melancholia of Freedom: Social Life in an Indian Township in South Africa*. Princeton, NJ: Princeton University Press, 2012.

Hart, Gillian. "Changing Concepts of Articulation: Political Stakes in South Africa Today." *Review of African Political Economy* 111 (2007): 85–101.

Hart, Gillian. *Disabling Globalization: Places of Power in Post-Apartheid South Africa*. Berkeley: University of California Press, 2002.

Hart, Gillian. "The Provocations of Neoliberalism: Contesting the Nation and Liberation after Apartheid." *Antipode* 40, no. 4 (2008): 678–705.

Hart, Gillian. *Rethinking the South African Crisis: Nationalism, Populism, Hegemony*. Athens: University of Georgia Press, 2014.

Hartley, J. B. "Maps, Knowledge, and Power." In *The Iconography of Landscape: Essays on the Symbolic Representation, Design and Use of Past Environments*, edited by Denis Cosgrove and Stephen Daniels, 277–312. Cambridge: Cambridge University Press, 1988.

Harvey, David. "Dialectics of Spacetime." In *Dialectics for the New Century*, edited by Bertell Ollman and Tony Smith, 98–117. London: Palgrave Macmillan, 2008.

Harvey, David. *Justice, Nature, and the Geography of Difference*. Cambridge, MA: Blackwell, 1996.

Harvey, David. *The New Imperialism*. Oxford, UK: Oxford University Press, 2003.

Harvey, David. *Paris, Capital of Modernity*. New York: Routledge, 2005.

Hassim, Aziz. *The Lotus People*. Durban: Institute for Black Research / Madiba, 2002.

Hassim, Shireen. "Past, Present, and Future of the ANC Women's League, and Implications for Gender Equality." Helen Joseph Lecture, University of Johannesburg, August 18, 2014.

Hassim, Shireen. *Women's Organizations and Democracy in South Africa: Contesting Authority*. Pietermaritzburg: University of KwaZulu-Natal Press, 2006.

Hassim, Shireen, Jo Meterlekamp (Jo Beall), and Alison Todes. "'A Bit on the Side?': Gender Struggles in the Politics of Transformation in South Africa." *Transformation*, no. 5 (1987): 3–32.

Hayes, Patricia. "Photographic Publics and Photographic Desires in 1980s South Africa." *Photographies* 10, no. 3 (2017): 303–27.

Hayes, Patricia. "Power, Secrecy, Proximity: A Short History of South African Photography." *Kronos*, no. 33 (2007): 139–62.

Hayes, Patricia. "Seeing and Being Seen: Politics, Art and the Everyday in Omar Badsha's Durban Photography, 1960s–1980s." *Africa* 81, no. 4 (2011): 544–66.

Hemson, David. "Beyond the Frontier of Control? Trade Unionism and the Labour Market in the Durban Docks." *Transformation*, no. 30 (1996): 83–114.

Hemson, David. "Class Consciousness and Migrant Workers: The Dockworkers of Durban." PhD diss., University of Warwick, 1979.

Hobhouse, Emily. *The Brunt of the War and Where It Fell*. London: Methuen, 1902.

Hobhouse, Emily. *Report of a Visit to the Camps of Women and Children in the Cape and Orange River Colonies*. London: Friars Printing Association, 1901.

Hobhouse, Emily. *War without Glamour; or, Women's War Experiences Written by Themselves, 1899–1902*. Translated by Emily Hobhouse. Bloemfontein: Nasionale Pers Beperk, 1924.

Hofmeyr, Isabel. "The Black Atlantic Meets the Indian Ocean: Forging New Paradigms of Transnationalism for the Global South—Literary and Cultural Perspectives." *Social Dynamics* 33, no. 2 (2007): 3–32.

Houston, Gregory. "The ANC's Armed Struggle in South Africa." In *The Road to Democracy in South Africa*, vol. 4, *1980–1990*, edited by Gregory Houston, 1037–170. Pretoria: University of South Africa Press, 2010.

Houston, Gregory F. *The National Liberation Struggle in South Africa: A Case Study of the United Democratic Front, 1983–1987*. Aldershot, UK: Ashgate, 1999.

Houston, Gregory, and Bernard Magubane. "The ANC's Armed Struggle in the 1970s." In *The Road to Democracy in South Africa*, vol. 2, *1970–1980*, edited by Bernard Magubane and Gregory Houston, 453–530. Pretoria: University of South Africa Press, 2006.

Houston, Gregory, and Bernard Magubane. "The ANC Political Underground in the 1970s." In *The Road to Democracy in South Africa*, vol. 2, *1970–1980*, edited by Bernard Magubane and Gregory Houston, 371–72. Pretoria: University of South Africa Press, 2006.

Hughes, Heather. *First President: A Life of John L. Dube, First President of the ANC*. Johannesburg: Jacana, 2011.

Hunter, Mark. *Love in the Time of AIDS: Inequality, Gender, and Rights in South Africa*. Bloomington: Indiana University Press, 2010.

Hunter, Mark. *Race for Education: Gender, White Tone, and Schooling in South Africa*. Cambridge: Cambridge University Press.

Hyslop, Jonathan. "The Invention of the Concentration Camp: Cuba, Southern Africa and the Philippines, 1896–1907." *South African Historical Journal* 63, no. 2 (2011): 251–76.

Hyslop, Jonathan. *The Notorious Syndicalist: J. T. Bain; A Scottish Rebel in Colonial South Africa*. Johannesburg: Jacana, 2005.

Hyslop, Jonathan. "'Segregation Has Fallen on Evil Days': Smuts' South Africa, Global War, and Transnational Politics, 1939–46." *Journal of Global History* 7, no. 3 (2012): 438–60.

Institute for Industrial Education. *The Durban Strikes 1973 ("Human Beings with Souls")*. Durban: Institute for Industrial Education, 1974.

Jackson, George. *Soledad Brother: The Prison Letters of George Jackson*. New York: Coward-McCann, 1970.

James, C. L. R. *The Black Jacobins: Toussaint Louverture and the San Domingo Revolution*. London: Secker and Warburg, 1938.

James, C. L. R. *The C.L.R. James Reader*. Edited by Anna Grimshaw. Oxford, UK: Blackwell, 1992.

James, C. L. R. "The Haitian Revolution in the Making of the Modern World." In *You Don't Play with Revolution: The Montreal Lectures of C.L.R. James*, edited by David Austin, 51–70. Oakland, CA: AK, 2009.

James, C. L. R. *A History of Pan-African Revolt*. Washington, DC: Drum and Spear, 1969.

James, C. L. R. *State Capitalism and World Revolution*. In collaboration with Raya Dunayevskaya and Grace Lee Boggs. Chicago: Charles Kerr, 1986.

Jameson, Fredric. *Archaeologies of the Future: The Desire Called Utopia and Other Science Fictions*. London: Verso, 2005.

Jayawardena, Kumari. *Feminism and Nationalism in the Third World*. London: Zed, 1994.

Jeffery, Anthea. *People's War: New Light on the Struggle for South Africa*. Johannesburg: Jonathan Ball, 2019.

Jenkin, Tim. "The Story of the Secret Underground Communications Network of Operation Vula. Part 6: Vula Winds Up." *Mayibuye: Journal of the African National Congress* 6, no. 6 (1995). http://www.hartford-hwp.com/archives/37a/043.html.

Johanningsmeier, Edward. "Communists and Black Freedom Movements in South Africa and the US, 1919–1950." *Journal of Southern African Studies* 30, no. 1 (2004): 155–80.

Joyce, Patrick. *The Rule of Freedom: Liberalism and the Modern City.* London: Verso, 2003.

Juggernath, Balbhadur (Billy). "The Diary of Balbhadur Juggernath." Unpublished manuscript, n.d. Juggernath family personal collection, Merebank.

Kaarsholm, Preben. "Zanzibaris or Amakhuwa? Sufi Networks in South Africa, Mozambique, and the Indian Ocean." *Journal of African History* 55, no. 2 (2014): 191–210.

Karis, Thomas G., and Gail M. Gerhart, eds. *Nadir and Resurgence, 1964–1979.* Vol. 5 of *From Protest to Challenge: A Documentary History of African Politics in South Africa, 1882–1990.* Bloomington: Indiana University Press, 1997.

Kark, Emily, and Sidney Kark. *Promoting Community Health: From Pholela to Jerusalem.* Johannesburg: Wits University Press, 1999.

Kasrils, Ronnie. *Armed and Dangerous: From Undercover Struggle to Freedom.* Johannesburg: Jacana, 2013.

Kelly, John, and Martha Kaplan. "Diaspora and Swaraj, Swaraj and Diaspora." In *From the Colonial to the Postcolonial: India and Pakistan in Transition,* edited by Dipesh Chakrabarty, Rochona Majumdar, and Andrew Sartori, 311–31. Oxford, UK: Oxford University Press, 2007.

Kipfer, Stefan, Christian Schmid, Kanishka Goonewardena, and Richard Milgrom. "Globalizing Lefebvre?" In *Space, Difference, Everyday Life: Reading Henri Lefebvre,* edited by Kanishka Goonewardena, Stefan Kipfer, Richard Milgrom, and Christian Schmid, 285–305. New York: Routledge, 2008.

Klawiter, Maren. *The Biopolitics of Breast Cancer: Changing Cultures of Disease and Activism.* Minneapolis: University of Minnesota Press, 2008.

Koven, Seth. *Slumming: Sexual and Social Politics in Victorian London.* Princeton, NJ: Princeton University Press, 2004.

Krebs, Paula M. *Gender, Race, and the Writing of Empire: Public Discourse and the Boer War.* Cambridge: Cambridge University Press, 1999.

Krebs, Paula M. "'The Last of the Gentlemen's Wars': Women in the Boer War Concentration Camp Controversy." *History Workshop Journal,* no. 33 (1992): 38–56.

Kripal, Jeffrey J. *Authors of the Impossible: The Paranormal and the Sacred.* Chicago: University of Chicago Press, 2010.

Kumar, P. Pratap. *Hindus in South Africa: Their Traditions and Beliefs.* Park Rynie, South Africa: Majestic Printers, 2000.

Kundnani, Arun. *What Is Antiracism? And Why It Means Anticapitalism.* London: Verso, 2023.

Kundnani, Arun. "What Is Racial Capitalism?" *Arun Kundnani: On Race, Culture, and Empire* (blog), October 23, 2020. https://www.kundnani.org/what-is-racial -capitalism.

Kuper, Leo, Hilstan Lett Watts, and Ronald Davies. *Durban: A Study in Racial Ecology.* New York: Columbia University Press, 1958.

la Hausse, Paul. "The Struggle for the City: Alcohol, the Ematsheni and Popular Culture in Durban, 1902–1936." Master's thesis, University of Cape Town, 1984.

Lake, Marilyn, and Henry Reynolds. *Drawing the Global Colour Line: White Men's Countries and the International Challenge of Racial Equality.* Cambridge: Cambridge University Press, 2008.

Lalu, Premesh. *The Deaths of Hintsa: Postapartheid South Africa and the Shape of Recurring Pasts.* Pretoria: Human Science Research Council, 2009.

Lalu, Premesh. "Incomplete Histories: Steve Biko, the Politics of Self-Writing and the Apparatus of Reading." *Current Writing: Text and Reception in Southern Africa* 16, no. 1 (2004): 107–26.

Lambert, Robert. "Political Unionism in South Africa: The South African Congress of Trade Unions, 1955–65." PhD diss., University of the Witwatersrand, Johannesburg, 1998.

Lambert, Robert. "Eddie Webster, the Durban Moment and New Labour Internationalism." *Transformation,* nos. 72–73 (2010): 26–47.

Landau, Paul. *Popular Politics in the History of South Africa, 1400–1948.* Cambridge: Cambridge University Press, 2010.

Ledochowski, Chris. *Cape Flats Details: Life and Culture in the Townships of Cape Town.* Los Angeles: Tsehai, 2008.

Lee, Christopher J. *Unreasonable Histories: Nativism, Multiracial Lives and the Genealogical Imagination in British Africa.* Durham, NC: Duke University Press, 2014.

Lefebvre, Henri. *The Production of Space.* Translated by Donald Nicholson-Smith. Oxford, UK: Blackwell, 1991.

Lefebvre, Henri. "The Right to the City." In *Writings on Cities,* edited and translated by Eleonore Kofman and Elizabeth Lebas, 147–59. Oxford, UK: Blackwell, 1996.

Legassick, Martin. "Legislation, Ideology and Economy in Post-1948 South Africa." *Journal of Southern African Studies* 1, no. 1 (1974): 5–35.

Legassick, Martin. "South Africa: Forced Labor, Industrialization and Racial Differentiation." In *The Political Economy of Africa,* edited by Richard Harris, 229–70. New York: Halsted, 1975.

Legg, Stephen. "Contesting and Surviving Memory: Space, Nation, and Nostalgia in Les Lieux de Mémoire." *Environment and Planning D: Society and Space* 23, no. 4 (2005): 481–504.

Levenson, Zachary. *Delivery as Dispossession: Land Occupation and Eviction in the Postapartheid City.* Oxford, UK: Oxford University Press, 2022.

Lever, Jeff. "Capital and Labour in South Africa: The Passage of the Industrial Conciliation Act, 1924." In *Essays in South African Labour History,* edited by Eddie Webster, 82–110. Johannesburg: Ravan, 1978.

Levine-Clark, Marjorie. "Engendering Relief: Women, Ablebodiedness and the New Poor Law in Early Victorian England." *Journal of Women's History* 11, no. 4 (2000): 107–24.

Linebaugh, Peter, and Marcus Rediker. *The Many-Headed Hydra: Sailors, Slaves, Commoners, and the Hidden History of the Revolutionary Atlantic.* Boston: Beacon, 2000.

Lloyd, Vincent. W. *Black Dignity: The Struggle against Domination.* New Haven, CT: Yale University Press, 2022.

Lodge, Tom. *Black Politics in South Africa since 1945.* London: Addison-Wesley Longman, 1983.

Lottering, Agnes. *Winnifred and Agnes: The True Story of Two Women.* Cape Town: Kwela, 2002.

Lund, Francie. *Changing Social Policy: The Child Support Grant in South Africa.* Cape Town: Human Sciences Research Council Press, 2008.

Luthuli, Albert. "Some Aspects of the Apartheid Union Land Laws and Policy as Affecting Africans," Conference on the Group Areas Act convened by the NIC, Durban, May 5–6, 1956. In *Lutuli: Speeches of Chief Albert John Lutuli, 1898–1967,* compiled by E. S. Reddy, 67–65, Durban: Madiba, 1991. Available at https://www.sahistory.org.za/sites/default/files/Lutuli%20 speeches.pdf.

Mabin, Alan. "Comprehensive Segregation: The Origins of the Group Areas Act and Its Planning Apparatus." *Journal of Southern African Studies* 18, no. 2 (1992): 405–29.

Mabin, Alan. "Labour, Capital, Class Struggle and the Origins of Residential Segregation in Kimberley, 1880–1920." *Journal of Historical Geography* 12, no. 1 (1986): 4–26.

Mabin, Alan. "Reconstruction and the Making of Urban Planning in Twentieth Century South Africa." In *blank_____: Architecture, Apartheid, and After,* edited by Hilton Judin and Ivan Vladislavic, E6.1–9. Rotterdam, Netherlands: NAi, 1999.

Mabin, Alan, and Philip Harrison. *"Imaginative Planning with Practical Considerations?" The Contribution of the KwaZulu-Natal Town and Regional Planning Commission to Planning and Development, 1951–1996.* Pietermaritzburg: KwaZulu-Natal Town and Regional Planning Commission, 1996.

Mabin, Alan, and Dan Smit. "Reconstructing South Africa's Cities? The Making of Urban Planning, 1900–2000." *Planning Perspectives* 12, no. 2 (1997): 193–223.

MacDonald, Andrew. "Durban-Bound: Chinese Miners, Colonial Medicine and the Floating Compounds of the Indian Ocean, 1904–7." *Journal of Natal and Zulu History* 23, no. 1 (2005): 107–46.

Macmillan, Hugh. "The Hani Memorandum: Introduced and Annotated." *Transformation,* no. 69 (2009): 106–29.

Macmillan, Hugh. *The Lusaka Years: The ANC in Exile in Zambia, 1963 to 1994.* Johannesburg: Jacana, 2013.

Macqueen, Ian Martin. *Black Consciousness and Progressive Movements under Apartheid.* Pietermaritzburg: University of KwaZulu-Natal Press, 2018.

Macqueen, Ian Martin. "Black Consciousness in Dialogue in South Africa: Steve Biko, Richard Turner and the 'Durban Moment,' 1970–1974." *Journal of Asian and African Studies* 49, no. 5 (2014): 511–25.

Macqueen, Ian Martin. "Re-imagining South Africa: Black Consciousness, Radical Christianity and the New Left, 1967–1977." PhD diss., University of Sussex, 2011.

Magaziner, Daniel. *The Law and the Prophets: Black Consciousness in South Africa, 1968–1977.* Athens: Ohio University Press, 2010.

Magubane, Bernard. *South Africa: From Soweto to Uitenhage; The Political Economy of the South African Revolution.* Trenton, NJ: Africa World, 1989.

Magubane, Bernard, Philip Bonner, Jabulani Sithole, Peter Delius, Janet Cherry, Pat Gibbs, and Thozama April. "The Turn to Armed Struggle." In *The Road to Democracy in South Africa*, vol. 1 *(1960–1970)*, edited by South African Democracy Education Trust, 49–134. Pretoria: University of South Africa Press, 2010.

Maharaj, Brij. "Apartheid, Urban Segregation, and the Local State: Durban and the Group Areas Act in South Africa." *Urban Geography* 18, no. 2 (1997): 135–54.

Maharaj, Brij. "The Group Areas Act in Durban: Central-Local State Relations." PhD diss., University of Natal, 1992.

Maharaj, Brij. "Land Reform Policy in Post-Apartheid South Africa: The Elusive Quest for Social Justice?" In *Geographies and Moralities: International Perspectives on Development, Justice and Place*, edited by Roger Lee and David M. Smith, 165–79. Malden, MA: Blackwell, 2004.

Maharaj, Brij. "The Local State and Residential Segregation: Durban and the Prelude to the Group Areas Act." *South African Geographical Journal* 77, no. 1 (1995): 33–41.

Maharaj, Brij. "Segregation, Desegregation and De-racialisation: Racial Politics and the City of Durban." In *(D)urban Vortex*, edited by Bill Freund and Vishnu Padayachee, 171–94. Pietermaritzburg: University of Natal Press, 2002.

Maharaj, Brij. "The 'Spatial Impress' of the Central and Local States: The Group Areas Act in Durban." In *The Apartheid City and Beyond*, edited by David M. Smith, 76–88. London: Routledge, 1992.

Makhaye, Chris. "Residents Breathe Easier as Engen Refinery to Close." *New Frame*, June 17, 2021. Archived October 1, 2022, at the Wayback Machine, https://web.archive.org/web/20221001110012/https://www.newframe.com/residents-breathe-easier-as-engen-refinery-to-close.

Makhulu, Anne-Maria. *Making Freedom: Apartheid, Squatter Politics, and the Struggle for Home.* Durham, NC: Duke University Press, 2015.

Malcomess, Bettina, and Dorothee Kreutzfeldt. *Not No Place: Johannesburg; Fragments of Spaces and Times.* Johannesburg: Jacana, 2013.

Malherbe, Ernst Gideon (E. G.). *Educational Report: Education and the Poor White.* Vol. 3 of *The Poor White Problem in South Africa: Report of the Carnegie Commission.* Stellenbosch, South Africa: Pro Ecclesia-Drukkery, 1932.

Mamdani, Mahmood. *Neither Settler nor Native: The Making and Unmaking of Permanent Minorities.* Cambridge, MA: Harvard University Press, 2020.

Mandela, Nelson. *Long Walk to Freedom.* New York: Little, Brown, 1994.

Mandela, Nelson. "I Am Prepared to Die: Nelson Mandela's Statement from the Dock at the Opening of the Defence Case in the Rivonia Trial." Palace of Justice, Pretoria Supreme Court, Pretoria, South Africa, April 20, 1964. Transcript of audio recording, Nelson Mandela Foundation, NMS010. Archived December 22, 2022, at the Wayback Machine, https://web.archive.org/web/20221222010405/http://db .nelsonmandela.org/speeches/pub_view.asp?pg=item&ItemID=NMS010.

Mangcu, Xolela. *Biko: A Biography*. Cape Town: Tafelberg, 2012.

Mangcu, Xolela, ed. *The Colour of Our Future: Does Race Still Matter in Post-apartheid South Africa?* Johannesburg: Wits University Press, 2015.

Mangcu, Xolela. "Liberating Race from Apartheid." *Transformation*, no. 47 (2001): 18–27.

Manghezi, Nadja. *The Maputo Connection: ANC Life in the World of Frelimo.* Johannesburg: Jacana, 2010.

Marais, Hein. *South Africa Pushed to the Limit: The Political Economy of Change.* London: Zed, 2011.

Marks, Monique. *Young Warriors: Youth Politics, Identity and Violence in South Arica.* Johannesburg: Wits University Press, 2001.

Marks, Shula. *The Ambiguities of Dependence in South Africa: Class, Nationalism, and the State in Twentieth-Century Natal.* Baltimore: Johns Hopkins University Press, 1986.

Marks, Shula. "Before 'the White Man Was Master and All White Men's Values Prevailed'? Jan Smuts, Race and the South African War." *Studien um Südlichen Afrika* 6 (2000): 1–17.

Marks, Shula. "Independence and Decolonization in Southern Africa." In *The History of Southern Africa*, edited by Amy McKenna, 70–71. New York: Britannica Educational, 2011.

Marks, Shula. "The Myth of the Empty Land." *History Today* 30, no. 1 (1980): 7–12.

Marks, Shula. "War and Union, 1899–1910." In *The Cambridge History of South Africa*, edited by Robert Ross, Anne Kelk Mager, and Bill Nasson, 157–210. Cambridge: Cambridge University Press, 2009.

Marks, Shula. "White Masculinity: Jan Smuts, Race and the South African War." *Proceedings of the British Academy*, no. 111 (2001): 199–223.

Marks, Shula, and Stanley Trapido. "Lord Milner and the South African State." *History Workshop Journal*, no. 8 (1979): 50–80.

Marks, Shula, and Stanley Trapido. *The Politics of Class, Race and Nationalism in Twentieth Century South Africa.* Harlow: Longman, 1987.

Marley, Bob, and the Wailers. *Survival.* Produced by Bob Marley and the Wailers and Alex Sadkin. Kingston, Jamaica: Island Records / Tuff Gong, 1979.

Marx, Karl. *Capital—A Critique of Political Economy: Volume 1—The Process of Capitalist Production*, edited by Frederick Engels. New York: International Publishers, 1979.

Marx, Karl. "Drafts of a Reply to Vera Zasulich." In *Late Marx and the Russian Road: Marx and "the Peripheries of Capitalism,"* by Teodor Shanin, 99–126. New York: Monthly Review Press, 1983.

Marx, Karl. *The Eighteenth Brumaire of Louis Bonaparte.* Translated by Daniel de Leon. New York: International Publishers, 1898.

Matoti, Sukude, and Lungisile Ntsebenza. "Rural Resistance in Mpondoland and Thembuland, 1960–1963." In *The Road to Democracy in South Africa*, vol. 1 *(1960–1970)*, edited by South African Democracy Education Trust, 163–92. Pretoria: University of South Africa Press, 2010.

Maylam, Paul. "Explaining the Apartheid City: 20 Years of South African Urban Historiography." *Journal of Southern African Studies* 21, no. 1 (1995): 19–38.

Maylam, Paul. "The Rise and Decline of Urban Apartheid in South Africa." *African Affairs* 89, no. 354 (1990): 57–84.

Maylam, Paul, and Iain Edwards. *The People's City: African Life in Twentieth-Century Durban*. Pietermaritzburg: University of Natal Press, 1995.

Mbeki, Govan. Interview by Padraig O'Malley (POM). Heart of Hope Collection online, Nelson Mandela Centre for Memory, March 19, 1996. http://www.nelsonmandela.org/omalley/index.php/site/q/03lv00017/04lv00344/05lv00965/06lv00975.htm.

Mbeki, Govan. *South Africa: The Peasants' Revolt*. London: Penguin, 1964.

Mbembe, Achille. "African Modes of Self-Writing." *Public Culture* 14, no. 1 (2002): 239–73.

Mbembe, Achille. *Critique of Black Reason*. Translated by Laurent Dubois. Durham, NC: Duke University Press, 2017.

Mbembe, Achille. "Necropolitics." In *Biopolitics: A Reader*, edited by T. Cambell and A. Sitze, 161–92. Durham, NC: Duke University Press, 2013.

Mbembe, Achille. *Necropolitics*. Translated by Steven Corcoran. Durham, NC: Duke University Press, 2019.

Mbembe, Achille. *On the Postcolony*. Johannesburg: Wits University Press, 2015.

Mbembe, Achille. *Out of the Dark Night: Essays on Decolonization*. Translated by Daniela Ginsburg. New York: Columbia University Press, 2021.

McBride, Derrick. "Coloured Landlessness." Unpublished manuscript, Derrick McBride personal collection, Wentworth, Durban, circa 2003.

McCarthy, Jeff. "Problems of Planning for Urbanisation and Development: The Case of Natal's Coastal Margins." *Geoforum* 17, no. 2 (1986): 267–87.

McCulloch, Jock. *Asbestos Blues: Labour, Capital, Physicians, and the State in South Africa*. Oxford, UK: James Currey, 2002.

McGerr, Michael. *A Fierce Discontent: The Rise and Fall of the Progressive Movement in America, 1870–1920*. Oxford, UK: Oxford University Press, 2003.

McKenzie, Peter, and Sylvie Peyre, dirs. *What Kind . . . ?* Marseille: Les Pas Perdus / Henri's Cabin Films, 2007. SAHO video, 43:01, https://www.sahistory.org.za/archive/what-kind-film-peter-mckenzie-sylvie-peyre.

McKittrick, Katherine. *Demonic Grounds: Black Women and the Cartographies of Struggle*. Minneapolis, MN: University of Minnesota Press, 2006.

Meer, Fatima. *Portrait of Indian South Africans*. Durban: Premier, 1969.

Marie [Meer], Shamim. *Divide and Profit—Indian Workers in Natal*. Worker Resistance in Natal Project, University of Natal, Durban, 1986.

Meer, Shamim. "Juggernath Family." In *Group Portrait South Africa: Nine Family Histories*, edited by Annari van der Merwe and Paul Faber, 204–27. Cape Town: Kwela, 2003.

Meer, Y. S. et al. *Documents of Indentured Labour in Natal, 1851–1917*. Durban: Institute for Black Research, 1980.

Mellet, Patric Tariq. *The Lie of 1652: A Decolonized History of Land*. Cape Town: Tafelberg, 2020.

Mesthrie, Uma. "Reducing the Indian Population to a 'Manageable Compass': A Study of the South African Assisted Emigration Scheme of 1927." *Natalia*, no. 15 (1985): 36–56.

Meyers, Troy. "Descendents of the Founders of Durban: The Fynns Today." Archive and Public Culture, March 14, 2011. http://www.apc.uct.ac.za/apc/projects /ancestral-stories/descendents-founders-durban-fynns-today.

Midgely, Clare, ed. *Gender and Imperialism*. Manchester: Manchester University Press, 1998.

Mikula, Paula, Brian Kearney, and Rodney Harber. *Traditional Hindu Temples in South Africa*. Durban: Hindu Temple Publications, 1982.

Mitchell, Katharyne, Sallie A. Marston, and Cindi Katz, eds. *Life's Work: Geographies of Social Reproduction*. Hoboken, NJ: Wiley-Blackwell, 2004.

Mitchell, Timothy. *Carbon Democracy: Political Power in the Age of Oil*. London: Verso, 2011.

Mitchell, Timothy. *Rule of Experts: Egypt, Techno-Politics, Modernity*. Berkeley: University of California Press, 2002.

Modisane, Litheko, Victoria J. Collis-Buthelezi, and Christopher Ouma. "Introduction: Black Studies, South Africa, and the Mythology of Mandela." *Black Scholar* 47, no. 2 (2017): 1–6.

Mofokeng, Santu. *Chasing Shadows: Thirty Years of Photographic Essays*. London: Prestel, 2011.

Mokae, Gomolemo. *Robert McBride: A Coloured Life*. Pretoria: South African History Online in association with Vista University, 2004.

Moore, Donald. *Suffering for Territory: Race, Place, and Power in Zimbabwe*. Durham, NC: Duke University Press, 2005.

More, Mabogo P. "Biko: Africana Existentialist Philosopher." In *Biko Lives! Contesting the Legacies of Steve Biko*, edited by Andile Mngxitima, Amanda Alexander, and Nigel C. Gibson, 45–68. New York: Palgrave Macmillan, 2008.

More, Mabogo P. "The Intellectual Foundations of the Black Consciousness Movement." In *Intellectual Traditions in South Africa: Ideas, Individuals and Institutions*, edited by Peter Vale, Lawrence Hamilton, and Estelle H. Prinsloo, 173–96. Scottsville: University of KwaZulu-Natal Press, 2014.

Morphet, Tony. "'Brushing History against the Grain': Oppositional Discourse in South Africa." *Theoria*, no. 76 (1990): 89–99.

Morrell, Robert. *From Boys to Gentlemen: Settler Masculinity in Colonial Natal, 1880–1920*. Pretoria: University of South Africa Press, 2001.

Morris, William. *A Dream of John Ball and a King's Lesson*. London: Longman's Green, 1913.

Morrison, Toni. *Beloved*. New York: Random House, 1987.

Morrison, Toni, and Angela Davis. "Toni Morrison and Angela Davis on Friendship and Creativity." Interview by Dan White. University of California, Santa Cruz, Newscenter, October 29, 2014. https://news.ucsc.edu/2014/10/morrison-davis-q-a.html.

Mosoetsa, Sarah. *Eating from One Pot: The Dynamics of Survival in Poor South African Households*. Johannesburg: Wits University Press, 2011.

Moten, Fred. *In the Break: The Aesthetics of the Black Radical Tradition*. Minneapolis, MN: University of Minnesota Press, 2003.

Moten, Fred, and Stefano Harney. *The Undercommons: Fugitive Planning and Black Study*. Wivenhoe, UK: Minor Compositions, 2013.

Murray, W. A. *Health Factors in the Poor White Problem*. Vol. 4 of *The Poor White Problem in South Africa: Report of the Carnegie Commission*. Stellenbosch, South Africa: Pro Ecclesia-Drukkery, 1932.

Naidoo, Leigh-Ann. "The Role of Radical Pedagogy in the South African Students Organisation and the Black Consciousness Movement in South Africa, 1968–1973." *Education as Change* 19, no. 2 (2015): 112–32.

Naidoo, Phyllis. *Enduring Footprints*. Durban: Rebel Rabble, 2009.

Naidoo, Phyllis. *Footprints beyond Grey Street*. Durban: Phyllis Naidoo, 2007.

Naidoo, Phyllis. *Footprints in Grey Street*. Durban: Far Ocean Jetty, 2002.

Naicker, Gangathura Mohambry (Monty). "Paper on the Group Areas Act and Its Effects on the Indian People of Natal, May 1956." Conference on the Group Areas Act convened by the NIC, Durban, May 5–6, 1956. Available at https://www.sahistory.org.za/archive/group-areas-act-and-its-effects-indian-people-natal-may-1956-dr-gangathura-mohambry-monty.

Nama, Adilifu. *Black Space: Imagining Race in Science Fiction Film*. Austin: University of Texas Press, 2008.

Narayanan, Vivek. "In Search of 1949." Paper presented at the History and African Studies Seminar, University of Natal, Durban, 1999. Available at https://abahlali.org/files/Narayanan_1949.pdf.

Nash, Andrew. "Mandela's Democracy." *Monthly Review* 50, no. 11 (1999): 18–28.

Nash, Andrew. "The Moment of Western Marxism in South Africa." *Comparative Studies of South Asia, Africa and the Middle East* 29, no. 1 (1999): 66–81.

Nasson, Bill. *The South African War, 1899–1902*. London: Edward Arnold, 1999.

Nasson, Bill. *The War for South Africa: The Anglo-Boer War (1899–1902)*. Cape Town: Tafelberg, 2010.

Natal (Colony). *Report of the Coolie Commission Appointed to Inquire into the Condition of the Indian Immigrants in the Colony of Natal*. Pietermaritzburg: P. Davis and Sons, Government Printers, 1872.

Ndlovu-Gatsheni, Sabelo J. *Coloniality of Power in Postcolonial Africa: Myths of Decolonization*. Dakar, Senegal: Council for the Development of Social Science Research in Africa, 2013.

Ndlovu-Gatsheni, Sabelo J. *Empire, Global Coloniality and African Subjectivity*. New York: Berghahn, 2013.

Ndlovu-Gatsheni, Sabelo J., and Morgan Ndlovu. *Decolonization in the 21st Century: Living Theories and True Ideas*. London: Routledge, 2022.

Neely, Abigail. *Reimagining Social Medicine from the South*. Durham, NC: Duke University Press, 2021.

Nelson, Alondra. *Body and Soul: The Black Panther Party and the Fight against Medical Discrimination*. Minneapolis, MN: University of Minnesota Press, 2011.

Nightingale, Carl H. *Segregation: A Global History of Divided Cities*. Chicago: University of Chicago Press, 2012.

Noble, Vanessa. *A School of Struggle: Durban's Medical School and the Education of Black Doctors in South Africa*. Scottsville: University of KwaZulu-Natal Press, 2013.

Nora, Pierre. "Between Memory and History: Les Lieux de Mémoire." *Representations*, no. 26 (1989): 7–24.

Nora, Pierre. "General Introduction: Between Memory and History." In *Realms of Memory: Rethinking the French Past*, edited by Pierre Nora and Lawrence D. Kritzman, translated by Arthur Goldhammer, 1:1–23. New York: Columbia University Press, 1996.

Ntsebeza, Lungisile. *Democracy Compromised: Chiefs and the Politics of Land in South Africa*. Leiden, Netherlands: Brill, 2005.

Ntsebeza, Lungisile, and Ruth Hall, eds. *The Land Question in South Africa: The Challenge of Transformation and Redistribution*. Cape Town: Human Sciences Research Council Press, 2007.

Nunn, Cedric. *Call and Response*. Johannesburg: Fourthwall, 2012.

Nuttall, Sarah. "Afterword: The Shock of the New Old." *Social Dynamics* 45, no. 2 (2019): 280–85.

Nuttall, Sarah. *Entanglement: Literary and Cultural Reflections on Post-apartheid*. Johannesburg: Wits University Press, 2009.

Nuttall, Sarah. "Upsurge." In *Acts of Transgression: Contemporary Live Art in South Africa*, edited by Jay Pather and Catherine Boulle, 41–59. Johannesburg: Wits University Press, 2019.

Nuttall, Sarah, and Carli Coetzee, eds. *Negotiating the Past: The Making of Memory in South Africa*. Oxford, UK: Oxford University Press, 1999.

Nuttall, Sarah, and Achille Mbembe. *Johannesburg: The Elusive Metropolis*. Durham, NC: Duke University Press, 2008.

Nuttall, Tim. "'It Seems Peace but It Can Be War': The Durban 'Riots' and the Struggle for the City." Paper presented at Twelfth National Conference of South African Historical Society, Pietermaritzburg, University of Natal, 1989.

O'Malley, Padraig. "ANC Operational Structures." Heart of Hope Collection online, Nelson Mandela Centre for Memory, circa 1985–2005. Accessed September 9, 2023. https://omalley.nelsonmandela.org/index.php/site/q/03lv02424/04lv02730/05lv02731/06lv02802/07lv02803.htm.

O'Malley, Padraig. "Operation Mayibuye" (document found by the police at Rivonia, South Africa, July 11, 1963). Heart of Hope Collection online, Nelson

Mandela Centre for Memory. https://omalley.nelsonmandela.org/index.php/
site/q/03lv01538/04lv01600/05lv01626/06lv01628.htm.

O'Malley, Padraig. *Shades of Difference: Mac Maharaj and the Struggle for South
Africa*. New York: Viking, 2007.

O'Meara, Dan. *Forty Lost Years: The Apartheid State and the Politics of the National Party, 1948–1994*. Athens: Ohio University Press, 1996.

Padayachee, Vishnu, ed. *The Development Decade? Economic and Social Change
in South Africa, 1994–2004*. Pretoria: Human Sciences Research Council Press,
2007.

Padayachee, Vishnu, and Robert Morrell. "Indian Merchants and Dukawallahs in
the Natal Economy, c. 1875–1914." *Journal of Southern African Studies* 17, no. 1
(1991): 71–102.

Padayachee, Vishnu, and Robert van Niekerk. *Shadow of Liberation: Contestation and Compromise in the Economic and Social Policy of the African National
Congress, 1943–1996*. Johannesburg: Wits University Press, 2019.

Padayachee, Vishnu, Shahid Vawda, and Paul Tichman. *Indian Workers and Trade
Unions in Durban: 1930–1950*. Report No. 20, Institute for Social and Economic
Research. Durban: University of Durban-Westville, 1985.

Pakenham, Thomas. *The Boer War*. London: Weidenfeld and Nicolson, 1979.

Pandian, Anand. *Crooked Stalks: Cultivating Virtue in South India*. Durham, NC:
Duke University Press, 2009.

Parnell, Susan. "Creating Racial Privilege: The Origins of South African Public
Health and Town Planning Legislation." *Journal of Southern African Studies* 19,
no. 3 (1993): 471–88.

Parnell, Susan. "Racial Segregation in Johannesburg: The Slums Act, 1934–1939."
South African Geographical Journal 70, no. 2 (1988): 112–26.

Parnell, Susan, and Alan Mabin. "Rethinking Urban South Africa." *Journal of
Southern African Studies* 21, no. 1 (1995): 39–61.

Pattman, Rob, and Sultan Khan. *Undressing Durban*. Durban: Madiba, 2007.

Peek, Bobby. "Doublespeak in Durban: Mondi, Waste Management, and the
Struggles of the South Durban Community Environmental Alliance." In *Envi-
ronmental Justice in South Africa*, edited by David McDonald, 202–20. Athens:
Ohio University Press, 2002.

Petryna, Adriana. *Life Exposed: Biological Citizens after Chernobyl*. Princeton, NJ:
Princeton University Press, 2013.

Philip, Kate. *Co-operatives in South Africa: Their Role in Job Creation and Poverty
Reduction*. South African Foundation, Johannesburg, October 2003. Available
at https://waqfacademy.org/wp-content/uploads/2013/03/Kate-Philip-KP.-10
_2003.-Co-operatives-in-South-Africa-Their-Role-in-Job-Creation-and-Poverty
-Reduction.-South-Africa.-Kate-Philip.pdf.

Pieterse, Edgar, and Susan Parnell, eds. *Africa's Urban Revolution*. London: Zed,
2014.

Pieterse, Edgar, and AbdouMaliq Simone, eds. *Rogue Urbanism: Emerging African
Cities*. Johannesburg: Jacana, 2013.

Pillay, Suren. "The Problem of Colonialism: Assimilation, Difference, and Decolonial Theory in Africa." *Critical Times* 4, no. 3 (2021): 389–416.

Pithouse, Richard. "Hit the Tire: The Strike Mutates into a New Form." *Critical Times: Interventions in Global Critical Theory* 5, no. 3 (2022): 632–44.

Pithouse, Richard. "In the Forbidden Quarters: Race, Space, and the Enduring Rationality of Rebellion in Durban." PhD diss., Rhodes University, 2014.

Pithouse, Richard. "'Our Struggle Is Thought, on the Ground, Running': The University of Abahlali baseMondolo." Centre for Civil Society Research Report No. 40, University of KwaZulu-Natal, Durban, 2006.

Pithouse, Richard. "A Politics of the Poor: Shack Dwellers' Struggles in Durban." *Journal of Asian and African Studies* 34, no. 1 (2008): 63–94.

Pithouse, Richard. "Solidarity, Co-optation and Assimilation: The Necessity, Promises and Pitfalls of Global Linkages for South African Movements." In *Challenging Hegemony: Social Movements and the Quest for a New Humanism in Post-Apartheid South Africa*, edited by Nigel C. Gibson, 247–86. Trenton, NJ: Africa World, 2006.

Pithouse, Richard. "Struggle Is a School: The Rise of a Shack Dwellers' Movement in Durban, South Africa." *Monthly Review* 57, no. 9 (2006): 30–52.

Pithouse, Richard. "'That the Tool Never Possesses the Man': Taking Fanon's Humanism Seriously." *Politikon: South African Journal of Political Studies* 30, no. 1 (2003): 107–31.

Pithouse, Richard. *Writing the Decline: On the Struggle for South Africa's Democracy.* Johannesburg: Jacana, 2016.

Pitkin, Hanna. *The Attack of the Blob: Hannah Arendt's Concept of the Social.* Chicago: University of Chicago Press, 1998.

Pityana, N. Barney, Mamphela Ramphele, Malusi Mpumlwana, and Lindy Wilson, eds. *Bounds of Possibility: The Legacy of Steve Biko and Black Consciousness.* Cape Town: New Africa, 2016.

Pontecorvo, Gillo, dir. *The Battle of Algiers.* Rome: Igor Film, 1967.

Poovey, Mary. *A History of the Modern Fact: Problems of Knowledge in the Sciences of Wealth and Society.* Chicago: University of Chicago Press, 1998.

Poovey, Mary. *Making a Social Body: British Cultural Formation.* Chicago: University of Chicago Press, 1995.

Portelli, Alessandro. *The Death of Luigi Trastulli and Other Stories: Form and Meaning in Oral History.* Albany: State University of New York Press, 1991.

Posel, Deborah. *The Making of Apartheid, 1948–1961: Conflict and Compromise.* Oxford, UK: Oxford University Press, 1991.

Posel, Deborah. "What's in a Name? Racial Categorisations under Apartheid and Their Afterlife." *Transformation*, no. 47 (2001): 50–74.

Rabinow, Paul, and Nikolas Rose. "Biopower Today." *BioSocieties* 1, no. 2 (2006): 195–217.

Ramanujan, A. K. *The Interior Landscape: Love Poems from a Classical Tamil Anthology.* Oxford, UK: Oxford University Press, 1994.

Ramaswamy, Sumathi. *The Lost Land of Lemuria: Fabulous Geographies, Cata-strophic Histories*. Berkeley: University of California Press, 2004.

Ramphele, Mamphela. "Empowerment and Symbols of Hope: Black Conscious-ness and Community Development." In *Bounds of Possibility: The Legacy of Steve Biko and Black Consciousness*, edited by Barney Pityana, Mamphela Ramphele, and Malusi Mpumlwana, 154–78. Cape Town: David Philip, 1991.

Rancière, Jacques. *Disagreement: Politics and Philosophy*. Translated by Julie Rose. Minneapolis, MN: University of Minnesota Press, 1999.

Rankin, Sheldon. "A Socio-Demographic Profile of the 'Coloured' Community of the Durban Metropolitan Area." Report 22. Durban: Institute for Social and Economic Research, 1986.

Reddy, Thiven. "The Politics of Naming: The Constitution of Coloured Subjects in South Africa." In *Coloured by History, Shaped by Place: New Perspectives on Coloured Identities in Cape Town*, edited by Zimitri Erasmus, 64–79. Cape Town: Kwela, 2001.

Reynolds, John, Ben Fine, and Robert van Niekerk, eds. *Race, Class and the Post-apartheid Democratic State.* Scottsville: University of KwaZulu-Natal Press, 2019.

Roberts, Brian. *Those Bloody Women: Three Heroines of the Boer War*. London: John Murray, 1991.

Roberts, Neil. *Freedom as Marronage*. Chicago: University of Chicago Press, 2015.

Robins, Steven. "From 'Rights' to 'Ritual': AIDS Activism in South Africa." *American Anthropologist* 108, no. 2 (2006): 312–23.

Robins, T. G., S. Batterman, G. B. Mentz, B. Kistnasamy, C. Jack, E. Irusen, U. Lalloo, R. Naidoo, N. Baijnath, H. Amsterdam et al. "Respiratory Health and Air Pollution in South Durban: The Settlers School Study." *Epidemiology* 16, no. 5 (2005): S79.

Robinson, Cedric. *Black Marxism: The Making of the Black Radical Tradition*. London: Zed, 1983.

Robinson, Cedric. *Forgeries of Memory and Meaning: Blacks and the Regimes of Race in American Theater and Film before World War II*. Chapel Hill, NC: University of North Carolina Press, 2007.

Robinson, Jennifer. "(Im)mobilizing Space—Dreaming of Change." In *blank_____: Architecture, Apartheid, and After*, edited by Hilton Judin and Ivan Vladislavic, D7.1–9. Rotterdam, Netherlands: NAi, 1999.

Robinson, Jennifer. *The Power of Apartheid: State, Power and Space in South African Cities*. Oxford, UK: Butterworth-Heinemann, 1996.

Rodgers, Daniel T. *Atlantic Crossings: Social Politics in a Progressive Age*. Cambridge, MA: Belknap Press of Harvard University Press, 1998.

Rose, Sonya O. *Limited Livelihoods: Gender and Class in Nineteenth-Century England*. Berkeley: University of California Press, 1992.

Rostron, Bryan. *Till Babylon Falls*. London: Coronet, 1991.

Rostron, Bryan. *Robert McBride: The Struggle Continues*. Cape Town: Tafelberg, 2019.

Rothberg, Michael. *Multidirectional Memory: Remembering the Holocaust in the Age of Decolonization*. Stanford, CA: Stanford University Press, 2009.

Russell, Gilbert. *A-B-War Concentration Camps in Natal: Aug. 1900–Jan. 1903.* Durban: G. Russell (self-published), 1988.

Said, Edward. *The World, the Text, and the Critic.* Cambridge, MA: Harvard University Press, 1983.

Samson, Melanie. "Not Just Recycling the Crisis: Producing Value at a Soweto Garbage Dump." *Historical Materialism* 25, no. 1 (2017): 36–62.

Samson, Melanie. "Trashing Solidarity: The Production of Power and the Challenges to Organizing Informal Reclaimers." *International Labor and Working-Class History* 95 (2019): 34–48.

Samson, Melanie. "Whose Frontier Is It Anyway? Reclaimer 'Integration' and the Battle over Johannesburg's Waste-Based Commodity Frontier." *Capitalism Nature Socialism* 31, no. 4 (2020): 60–75.

Sannyasi, Bhawani Dayal, and Banarsidas Chaturvedi. *A Report on the Emigrants Repatriated to India under the Assisted Emigration Scheme from South Africa and on the Problem of Returned Emigrants from All Colonies.* Bihar, India: Pravasi-Bhawan, 1931.

SAPREF. *SAPREF, 1963–2013 50th Anniversary: Fuelling SA for 50 Years.* Durban: SAPREF, 2013.

Saul, John S. *Recolonization and Resistance in Southern Africa in the 1990s.* Trenton, NJ: Africa World, 1993.

Saul, John S., and Stephen Gelb. *The Crisis in South Africa: Class Defense, Class Revolution.* New York: Monthly Review Press, 1981.

Scarry, Elaine. *The Body in Pain: The Making and Unmaking of the World.* Oxford, UK: Oxford University Press, 1985.

Schaffner, Franklin, dir. *Planet of the Apes.* Century City: Apjac Productions and Twentieth Century Fox Films, 1967.

Schneer, Jonathan. *London 1900: The Imperial Metropolis.* New Haven, CT: Yale University Press, 2001.

Scott, Dianne. "Communal Space Construction: The Rise and Fall of Clairwood and District." PhD diss., University of Natal, 1994.

Scott, Dianne. "'Creative Destruction': Early Modernist Planning in the South Durban Industrial Zone, South Africa." *Journal of Southern African Studies* 29, no. 1 (2003): 235–59.

Scott Brown, Denise. "Natal Plans." *Journal of the American Institute of Planners* 30, no. 2 (1964): 161–66.

Seekings, Jeremy. "The Carnegie Commission and the Backlash against Welfare State-Building in South Africa, 1931–1937." *Journal of Southern African Studies* 34, no. 3 (2008): 515–37.

Seekings, Jeremy. *The UDF: A History of the United Democratic Front in South Africa, 1983–1991.* Cape Town: David Philip, 2000.

Sekyi-Otu, Ato. *Fanon's Dialectic of Experience.* Cambridge, MA: Harvard University Press, 1999.

Shaik, Moe. *The ANC Spy Bible: Surviving across Enemy Lines.* Cape Town: Tafelberg, 2020.

Sharpe, Christina. "Black Studies: In the Wake." *Black Scholar* 44, no. 2 (2014): 59–69.

Sharpley, Gaster. *Yesterday.* Amalinda, South Africa: Bonz, 2004.

Sheik, Nafisa Essop. "Customs in Common: Marriage, Law and the Making of Difference in Colonial Natal." *Gender and History* 29, no. 3 (2017): 589–604.

Sheik, Nafisa Essop. "Entangled Patriarchies: Sex, Gender and Relationality in the Forging of Natal: A Paper Presented in Critical Tribute to Jeff Guy." *South African Historical Journal* 68, no. 3 (2016): 304–17.

Sheik, Nafisa Essop. "Words on Black Water: Setting South African 'Plantation Literature' Afloat on the *Kala Pani.*" *Interventions* 24, no. 3 (2022): 389–98.

Simone, AbdouMaliq. *For the City Yet to Come: Changing African Life in Four Cities.* Durham, NC: Duke University Press, 2004.

Simpson, Thula. *Umkhonto We Sizwe: The ANC's Armed Struggle.* Cape Town: Penguin Random House South Africa, 2016.

Sinha, Mrinalini. *Colonial Masculinity: The "Manly Englishman" and the Effeminate Bengali in the Late Nineteenth Century.* Manchester: Manchester University Press, 1995.

Sitas, Ari. "The Making of the 'Comrades' Movement in Natal, 1985–91." *Journal of Southern African Studies* 18, no. 3 (1992): 629–41.

Sithole, Tendayi. *The Black Register.* London: Polity, 2020.

Sivanandan, Ambalavaner. *Catching History on the Wing: Race, Culture and Globalisation.* London: Pluto, 2008.

Sizwe, No (Neville Alexander). *One Azania, One Nation.* London: Zed, 1979.

Skinner, Caroline. "The Struggle for the Streets: Processes of Exclusion and Inclusion of Street Traders in Durban, South Africa." *Development Southern Africa* 25, no. 2 (2008): 277–42.

Skinner, Caroline, and Richard Dobson. *Working in Warwick: Integrating Street Traders into Urban Plans.* Durban: University of KwaZulu-Natal Press, 2009.

Smit, Daniel. "The Political Economy of Urban and Regional Planning in South Africa, 1900 to 1988: Towards Theory to Guide Progressive Planning Practice." PhD diss., University of Natal, Durban, 1989.

Smith, David, ed. *The Apartheid City and Beyond: Urbanization and Social Change in South Africa.* London: Routledge, 1992.

Smith, Neil. *The New Urban Frontier: Gentrification and the Revanchist City.* London: Routledge, 1996.

Sono, Themba. *Reflections on the Origins of Black Consciousness in South Africa.* Pretoria: Human Sciences Research Council Press, 1993.

Soske, Jon. *Internal Frontiers: African Nationalism and the Indian Diaspora in Twentieth-Century South Africa.* Athens: Ohio University Press, 2017.

Soske, Jon. "'Wash Me Black Again': African Nationalism, the Indian Diaspora, and Kwa-Zulu Natal, 1944–1960." PhD diss., University of Toronto, 2009.

South African Students Organisation. "The 'New Farm' Project on Preventive Medicine." Wentworth, Durban, circa 1972.

Sparks, Stephen. "Apartheid Modern: South Africa's Oil from Coal Project and the History of a Company Town." PhD diss., University of Michigan, 2012.

Sparks, Stephen. "Civic Culture, 'Environmentalism' and Pollution in South Durban: The Case of the Wentworth Refinery." Paper presented at History and African Studies Seminar, Department of Historical Studies, University of Kwa-Zulu Natal, Durban, South Africa, April 19, 2005.

Sparks, Stephen. "Civil Society, Pollution and the Wentworth Oil Refinery." *Historia* 51, no. 11 (2006): 201–33.

Sparks, Stephen. "'Playing at Public Health': The Search for Control in South Durban, 1860–1932." *Journal of Natal and Zulu History* 20, no. 1 (2002): 1–28.

Sparks, Stephen. "'Stink, maar uit die verkeerde rigting': Pollution, Petroleum and Politics in South Africa, 1954–1960." Paper presented at the History and African Studies Seminar, University of KwaZulu-Natal, Durban, November 14, 2004.

Spivak, Gayatri Chakravorty. "Can the Subaltern Speak?" In *Marxism and the Interpretation of Culture*, edited by Lawrence Grossberg and Cary Nelson, 271–313. Champaign: University of Illinois Press, 1988.

Srinivas, M. N. "A Caste Dispute among the Washermen of Mysore." *Eastern Anthropologist*, 7, no. 3–4 (1954): 148–68.

Statistics South Africa. Census, 2001. Pretoria: Statistics South Africa.

Stedman Jones, Gareth. *Outcast London: A Study in the Relationship between Classes in Victorian Society*. London: Penguin, 1976.

Steedman, Carolyn. "Fictions of Engagement: Eleanor Marx, Biographical Space." In *Eleanor Marx (1855–1898): Life, Works, Contacts*, edited by John Stokes, 69–81. Aldershot, UK: Ashgate, 2000.

Steedman, Carolyn Kay. *Landscape for a Good Woman*. New Brunswick, NJ: Rutgers University Press, 1987.

Steinberg, Jonny. *Winnie and Nelson: Portrait of a Marriage*. Cape Town: Jonathan Ball, 2023.

Steinmetz, George. "Colonial Melancholy and Fordist Nostalgia." In *Ruins of Modernity*, edited by Julia Hell and Andreas Schönle, 294–320. Durham, NC: Duke University Press, 2010.

Stoler, Ann Laura. *Along the Archival Grain: Epistemic Anxieties and Colonial Common Sense*. Princeton, NJ: Princeton University Press, 2009.

Stoler, Ann Laura. *Carnal Knowledge and Imperial Power: Race and the Intimate in Colonial Rule*. Berkeley: University of California Press, 2002.

Stoler, Ann Laura. "Colony." In *Political Concepts: A Critical Lexicon*, edited by J. M. Bernstein, Adi Ophir, Ann Laura Stoler, Jacques Lezra, and Paul North, 45–58. New York: Fordham University Press, 2018.

Stoler, Ann Laura. *Race and the Education of Desire: Foucault's History of Sexuality and the Colonial Order of Things*. Durham, NC: Duke University Press, 1995.

Stoler, Ann Laura. "Racial Histories and Their Regimes of Truth." *Political Power and Social Theory*, no. 11 (1997): 183–206.

Sunder Rajan, Kaushik. *Biocapital: The Constitution of Postgenomic Life*. Durham, NC: Duke University Press, 2006.

Suttner, Raymond. *The ANC Underground in South Africa*. Johannesburg: Jacana, 2008.

Suttner, Raymond. "Understanding Non-racialism as an Emancipatory Concept in South Africa." *Theoria: A Journal of Social and Political Theory* 59, no. 130 (2012): 22–41.

Swanson, Maynard. "'The Asiatic Menace': Creating Segregation in Durban, 1870–1900." *International Journal of African Historical Studies* 16, no. 3 (1983): 401–21.

Swanson, Maynard. "'The Durban System': Roots of Urban Apartheid in Colonial Natal." *African Studies* 35, no. 3–4 (1976): 159–76.

Swanson, Maynard. "The Sanitation Syndrome: Bubonic Plague and Urban Native Policy in the Cape Colony, 1900–1909." *Journal of African History* 18, no. 3 (1977): 387–410.

Swanson, Maynard. "Urban Origins of Separate Development." *Race and Class* 10, no. 1 (1968): 31–40.

Tambo, Oliver. *Preparing for Power: Oliver Tambo Speaks*. Compiled by Adelaide Tambo. Ibadan, Nigeria: Heinemann Educational, 1987.

Taylor, Keeanga-Yamahtta. *How We Get Free: Black Feminism and the Combahee River Collective*. Chicago: Haymarket, 2017.

Thai, Hoang Van, and Van Tien Dung. *Great Spring Victory*. Hanoi: People's Army Publishing House, 1976.

Thompson, Edward P. "Eighteenth-Century English Society: Class Struggle without Class?" *Social History* 3, no. 2 (1978): 133–65.

Thompson, Leonard. *A History of South Africa*. New Haven, CT: Yale University Press, 1990.

Tomba, Massimiliano. *Marx's Temporalities*. Chicago: Haymarket, 2013.

Torr, Louise. *The History of Lamontville, 1930–1950*. Durban: University of Natal, 1985.

Torr, Louise. "Lamontville-Durban's 'Model Village': The Realities of Township Life, 1934–1960." *Journal of Natal and Zulu History* 10 (1987): 103–17.

Torr, Louise. "Providing for the 'Better-Class Native': The Creation of Lamontville, 1923–1933." *South African Geographical Journal* 69, no. 1 (1987): 31–46.

Touleier [pseud.]. *The Poor White Problem in South Africa (Die Armblankevraagstuk)*. Johannesburg: Liberty Press (Vrydheidspers), 1938.

Trewhela, Paul. *Inside Quatro: Uncovering the Exile History of the ANC and SWAPO*. Johannesburg: Jacana, 2009.

Trouillot, Michel-Rolph. *Silencing the Past: Power and the Production of History*. Boston: Beacon, 1995.

Truth and Reconciliation Commission. *Further Submissions and Responses by the African National Congress to Questions Raised by the Commission for Truth and Reconciliation*. South African History Archive (SAHA), May 12, 1997. https://sabctrc.saha.org.za/documents/submit/56410.htm#Appendix%201.

Turner, Richard. *The Eye of the Needle: Towards Participatory Democracy in South Africa*. Johannesburg: Study Project on Christianity in Apartheid Society (Spro-cas), 1972.

Turok, Ben. *The ANC and the Turn to Armed Struggle*. Johannesburg: Jacana, 2010.

Turok, Ben. *Strategic Problems of South Africa's Liberation Struggle*. Richmond, Canada: Liberation Support Movement Information Center, 1974.

University of Natal, the Research Section in the Department of Economics and Certain Other Specialists in Other Departments. *The Durban Housing Survey: A Study of Housing in a Multi-racial Community*. Pietermaritzburg: University of Natal Press, 1952.

Vahed, Goolam. "Constructions of Community and Identity among Indians in Colonial Natal, 1860–1910: The Role of the Muharram Festival." *Journal of African History* 43, no. 1 (2002): 77–93.

Vahed, Goolam. "Contesting Indian Islam in KwaZulu-Natal: The Muharram Festival in Durban, 2002." In *The Popular and the Public: Cultural Debates and Struggles over Public Space in Modern Africa, India and Europe*, edited by Preben Kaarsholm and Isabel Hofmeyr, 109–40. Calcutta: Seagull, 2009.

Vahed, Goolam. "The Making of Indian Identity in Durban, 1914–1949." PhD diss., Indiana University, 1995.

Vahed, Goolam. "The 'Other Asiatics' of Bayview." In *Chatsworth: The Making of a South African Township*, edited by Ashwin Desai and Goolam Vahed, 84–92. Pietermaritzburg: University of KwaZulu-Natal Press, 2013.

Vahed, Goolam. "Race or Class? Community and Conflict amongst Indian Municipal Employees in Durban, 1914–1949." *Journal of Southern African Studies* 27, no. 1 (2001): 105–25.

Vahed, Goolam, Ashwin Desai, and Thembisa Waetjen. *Many Lives: 150 Years of Being Indian in South Africa*. Pietermaritzburg: Shuter, 2010.

Vahed, Goolam, and Thembisa Waetjen. *Gender, Modernity, and Indian Delights: The Women's Cultural Group of Durban, 1954–2010*. Cape Town: Human Sciences Research Council Press, 2010.

Van Heyningen, Elizabeth. *The Concentration Camps of the Anglo-Boer War: A Social History*. Johannesburg: Jacana, 2013.

Van Onselen, Charles. "Crime and Total Institutions in the Making of Modern South Africa: The Life of 'Nongoloza' Mathebula, 1867–1948." *History Workshop Journal*, no. 19 (1985): 62–81.

Van Onselen, Charles. *New Babylon, New Nineveh: Studies in the Social and Economic History of the Witwatersrand*. London: Longman, 1982.

Van Onselen, Charles. *The Seed Is Mine: The Life of Kas Maine, a South African Sharecropper, 1894–1985*. New York: Hill and Wang, 1996.

Vergès, Françoise. *Monsters and Revolutionaries: Colonial Family Romance and "Métissage."* Durham, NC: Duke University Press, 1999.

Veriava, Ahmed. "The South African Diagram: The Governmental Machine and the Struggles of the Poor." PhD diss., University of the Witwatersrand, Johannesburg, 2014.

Veriava, Ahmed, and Prishani Naidoo. "Predicaments of Post-apartheid Social Movement Politics: The Anti-privatisation Forum in Johannesburg." *New South African Review* 3 (2013): 76–89.

Veriava, Ahmed, and Prishani Naidoo. "Remembering Biko for the Here and Now." In *Biko Lives! Contesting the Legacies of Steve Biko*, edited by Andile Mngxitima, Amanda Alexander, and Nigel C. Gibson, 233–52. New York: Palgrave Macmillan, 2008.

Vilakazi, Thabile. "South African Students Protest against School's Alleged Racist Hair Policy." CNN, September 1, 2016. https://www.cnn.com/2016/08/31/africa /south-africa-school-racism/index.html.

Visweswaran, Kamala. *Un/common Cultures: Racism and the Rearticulation of Cultural Difference*. Durham, NC: Duke University Press, 2010.

Von Holdt, Karl. *Transition from Below: Forging Trade Unionism and Workplace Change in South Africa*. Pietermaritzburg: University of Natal Press, 2003.

Von Schnitzler, Antina. *Democracy's Infrastructure: Techno-Politics and Protest after Apartheid*. Princeton, NJ: Princeton University Press, 2016.

Walker, Cherryl. *Women and Resistance in South Africa*. London: Onyx, 1982.

Ware, Vron. *Beyond the Pale: White Women, Racism and History*. London: Verso, 1992.

War Office. Reports of the Working of the Refugee Camps in the Transvaal, Orange River Colony, Cape Colony and Natal, 1901, Cd. 819.

War Office. Further Papers Related to the Working of the Refugee Camps in the Transvaal, Orange River Colony, Cape Colony and Natal, 1901, Cd. 853.

War Office. Concentration Camps Commission: Report on the Concentration Camps in South Africa by the Committee of Ladies Appointed by the Secretary of State for War, 1902, Cd. 893.

War Office. Further Papers Relating to the Working of the Refugee Camps in South Africa, 1902, Cd. 902.

War Office. Further Papers Relating to the Working of the Refugee Camps in South Africa, 1902, Cd. 934.

War Office. Further Papers Relating to the Working of the Refugee Camps in South Africa, 1902, Cd. 936.

War Office. Return of Farm Buildings, etc., in Cape Colony and Natal Destroyed by the Boers, 1902, Cd. 979.

Warwick, Peter. "African Labour during the South African War, 1899–1902." *Collected Seminar Papers*, no. 21 (1977): 104–16.

Warwick, Peter. *Black People and the South African War, 1899–1902*. Cambridge: Cambridge University Press, 1983.

Warwick, Peter, ed. *The South African War: The Anglo-Boer War 1899–1902*. London: Addison-Wesley Longman, 1980.

Weinberg, Paul, David Robbins, and Gcina Mhlope. *Durban: Impressions of an African City*. Brixton, South Africa: Porcupine, 2002.

Welsh, David. *The Rise and Fall of Apartheid*. Johannesburg: Jonathan Ball, 2009.

Western, John. *Outcast Cape Town*. Cape Town: Human and Rousseau, 1981.

White, Hylton. "Tempora et Mores: Family Values and the Possessions of a Post-Apartheid Countryside." *Journal of Religion in Africa* 31, no. 4 (2001): 457–79.

White, Luise. "A Colonial State and an African Petty Bourgeoisie: Prostitution, Property, and Class Struggle in Nairobi, 1936–1940." In *Struggle for the City: Migrant Labor, Capital, and the State in Urban Africa*, edited by Frederick Cooper, 167–94. Beverly Hills, CA: SAGE, 1983.

Wieder, Alan. *Ruth First and Joe Slovo in the War against Apartheid*. Johannesburg: Jacana, 2013.

Wilcocks, Raymond William. *Psychological Report: The Poor White*. Vol. 2 of *The Poor White Problem in South Africa: Report of the Carnegie Commission*. Stellenbosch, South Africa: Pro Ecclesia-Drukkery, 1932.

Wiley, David, Christine Root, and Sven "Bobby" Peek. "Contesting the Urban Industrial Environment in South Durban in a Period of Democratisation and Globalisation." In *(D)urban Vortex*, edited by Bill Freund and Vishnu Padayachee, 223–55. Pietermaritzburg: University of Natal Press, 2002.

Williams, Raymond. *The Country and the City*. Oxford, UK: Oxford University Press, 1973.

Willoughby-Herard, Tiffany. *Waste of a White Skin: The Carnegie Corporation and the Racial Logic of White Vulnerability*. Berkeley: University of California Press, 2015.

Wilson, Francis, and Omar Badsha. *South Africa: The Cordoned Heart*. Cape Town: Gallery, 1986.

Wilson, Lindy. "Bantu Stephen Biko: A Life." In *Bounds of Possibility: The Legacy of Steve Biko and Black Consciousness*, edited by B. Pityana, M. Ramphele, and M. Mpumlwana, 15–77. Cape Town: David Philip, 1991.

Winichakul, Thongchai. *Siam Mapped: A History of the Geo-Body of a Nation*. Honolulu: University of Hawai'i Press, 1997.

Wolin, Richard. *The Wind from the East: French Intellectuals, the Cultural Revolution, and the Legacy of the 1960s*. Princeton, NJ: Princeton University Press, 2010.

Wolpe, Harold. "Capitalism and Cheap Labour-Power in South Africa: From Segregation to Apartheid." *Economy and Society* 1, no. 4 (1972): 425–56.

Wolpe, Harold. *Race, Class and the Apartheid State*. London: James Currey, 1988.

Worden, Nigel. *The Making of South Africa: Conquest, Segregation and Apartheid*. Oxford, UK: Oxford University Press, 1994.

Wright, Beverly. "Living and Dying in Louisiana's 'Cancer Alley.'" In *The Quest for Environmental Justice: Human Rights and the Politics of Pollution*, edited by Robert D. Bullard, 87–107. San Francisco: Sierra Club Books, 2005.

Wylie, Dan. "'Proprietor of Natal': Henry Francis Fynn and the Mythography of Shaka." *History in Africa*, no. 22 (1995): 409–37.

Yates, Ruby. *A Garland for Ashes: The Story of St. Monica's Home*. London: Faith, 1960.

Yurchak, Alexei. "Soviet Hegemony of Form: Everything Was Forever, Until It Was No More." *Comparative Studies in Society and History* 45, no. 3 (2003): 480–510.

Zondi, Madoda. "The Creation of a First African Township in Natal: Lamontville." Paper presented at the History and African Studies Seminar, Department of Historical Studies, University of KwaZulu-Natal, Durban, October 23, 2013.

Noms de guerre and polite forms of address are in square brackets.

Everatt, David, 21

expertise, 14–17, 26, 67, 76: biopolitical, 41, 103, 106, 110, 139, 201; camps and, 36, 40–45, 54, 59–60; community health, 152, 337; on film, 332, 334–35; planning, 109, 115, 125, 167; social medicine, 130, 144, 153; in urban struggle, 262, 269, 297, 301. *See also* disqualified knowledge

exile: as problem, 219, 243, 249, 394n42; External Mission debates about, 231, 250–52

existentialism, 203, 212

expropriation, 23, 117, 121, 127–29, 136–39, 163, 166–67, 171, 175–77, 181; *see* dispossession

External Mission of the ANC, 28, 229–34, 282, 285, 293, 319; conception of struggle and, 245, 250, 254–55, 260; women and, 296–97

Fanon, Frantz, 19, 223, 228, 303, 307, 311; Biko and, 202, 206, 212; earthliness and, 207, 325; new human and, 215; Sekyi-Out on, 157, 159; spaciousness and 4, 325, 328; stretching Marxism and, 308

Farred, Grant, 10, 18, 23, 84, 307

Fawcett, Millicent, 44, 49

Federation of South African Women, 154

feminism, 20, 49, 150, 210; Black Marxism and, 10, 17–21, 24–25, 99, 131, 226; Black radicalism and, 94, 135, 154–55, 208, 329, 342; critiques of the movement from, 143, 223, 261–67, 276, 284, 300–301, 343; Third World and, 17, 266; as late-Victorian, 44, 49. *See also* Black feminism; Marxism (Black Marxist feminism); socialist feminism

Ferguson, Roderick, 19

First, Ruth, 233, 239

Fisher, Foszia, 204, 298

food practices, 73

forced labor, 84

forced removals, 55, 84, 162, 171, 176; apartheid and, 91, 159, 174, 182–184, 257, 308–9, 337; prior to apartheid, 135, 137, 150

forgeries, 26, 66, 96, 140; of apartheid, 27, 158, 178, 184, 188, 193; Cedric Robinson on, 61–63, 134

forgetting, 39, 55

form of life, 84, 95

Forth, Aidan, 41, 53

FOSATU (Federation of South African Trade Unions), 208, 248, 275, 279–80

Foster, Jeremy, 100

Foucault, Michel, 14; discipline, biopower and sovereignty, 14; on sexuality as dense transfer point, 34–35, 59; on incitement to discourse, 110

Frame Textile Group, 140–41, 204, 389n27

franchise, 22, 126–27; Coloureds, Indians and, 80, 84, 112, 162; Africans and, 90, 163; universal, 248, 258, 268

Freedom Charter, 142, 211

Freire, Paolo, 206, 216, 276, 278, 298

FRELIMO (Frente de Libertação de Moçambique), 219, 317; Viva FRELIMO rallies, 233, 282

Freund, Bill, 73, 103, 108, 148–49, 162, 368n17

Friedman, Steven, 275

Friends of the Sick Association, 143, 151, 235

Frontline States, 230, 233, 245, 247, 252

futurity, 21, 95, 192, 345–46

Fynn, Henry Francis, 85

Fynn, Morris, 84–86, 88, 91, 163, 178–79

Fynn, Terrence "Terrible T's," 333–34

Fynnlands, 72

Gandhi, Ela, 210, 235

Gandhi, M. K., 81–82, 208; Gandhian passive resistance and, 141

gangs, 3, 13, 182–83, 187, 297, 305, 308–13, 324–25, 329, 333–34

Gelb, Stephen, 205

Gencor, 166, 335. *See also* Engen refinery

gender: Anglo-Boer War and, 43–44, 47; biopolitics and, 136, 301; Durban Riots and, 149–50; photography and, 334; postapartheid livelihood struggles and, 8–10, 152; settlements of memory and, 73, 83–84, 94–96; in struggle, 153–54, 215, 220–21, 242, 244, 262–67, 276, 296–97, 342–43

genealogy, 15–16, 27, 36, 64; dialectics and, 25, 200–201, 212

Gerhart, Gail, 224,

Giáp, Võ Nguyên, 199, 250–51, 286, 291, 305

Gilmore, Ruth Wilson, 1, 3, 11–13, 218; on abolitionist reform, 151; on racism, 53, 159

Gilroy, Paul, 94, 189, 193

Glaser, Clive, 308

Goddard, Graham, 322

gold, 49, 52, 108, 161

Goldblatt, David, 321

Goonam, Dr., *see* Naidoo, Kesaveloo Goonarathnum (Dr. Goonam)

Gordhan, Pravin [PG]: UDW walkout and, 214, 238; underground and, 283, 291; urban movement and, 252, 260–61, 263, 265, 275

Gordon (Merebank resident, former Mondi worker), 280

Gordon, Jenny, 29, 100, 344

Gordon, Lewis, 212

Govender, Anand, 279

Govender, C. A. (Merebank farmer), 138–39

Govender, Kambadesan [Coastal], 235–236, 238, 240, 242

Govender, Nithianandan [Elvis], 239f

Govender, Pregs, 266, 297

Govender, Ronnie, 182

Marxism (*continued*)
164, 228; reading Marx and, 308, 328, 340–41, 354n26; urban struggles and, 263, 276, 281
masculinism, 19–20, 44, 66; armed struggle and, 201, 242, 318, 334, 342; in political organization, 17, 220, 244, 265–66, 297, 300
Mass Democratic Movement, 293
Matthews, Joe, 232
Matola Raid of 1981, 198–99, 233, 241–42, 244, 253, 394n52
Mauritius, 67, 87–88
Maydon Wharf, 104, 115, 131
Mayet, Rafs, 322
Mayville, 78, 83, 89, 110, 137, 149, 169, 238
Mbeki, Govan, 101–2
Mbeki, Thabo, 5, 231–32, 255, 259
Mbembe, Achille, 21, 121, 192, 224
McBride, Derrick, 91–94, 251, 313–14, 316–19, 401n48
McBride, Robert, 251, 261, 303–10, 312–20, 334, 336, 343
McCarthy, Jeff, 274, 276
McKenzie, Peter, 29, 100, 187, 306, 322–24, 332–35, 339
McKittrick, Katherine, 328–29
Meer, Farouk, 261
Meer, Fatima, 4, 62, 148, 162
Meer, Shamim, 205, 207, 219–20, 274, 296–97, 300
Melbourne Flats, 93, 273
Mellet, Patric Tariq, 93, 163. *See* de-Africanization
memory, 26, 152; activism and, 152, 198–99, 205, 219; apartheid and, 160, 184, 190, 193; forgeries of, 61, 63, 134; *lieux de mémoire* and, 38–39, 359n9; multidirectional, 64, 89, 93; partitioned, 40, 56, 58; as settlements of memory, 70, 83, 87, 95–96
Merebank Concentration Camp Memorial Garden of Remembrance, 36, 38, 40, 43
Merebank Ex-Students Society, 210, 301
Merebank Indian Ratepayers Association, 120–21, 139
Merebank Residents Association. *See* MRA
Merewent Cheshire Home, 38, 56–59
MHQ (Military Headquarters of MK), 234, 251
Middleton, Norman, 210
migration, 16, 62, 70, 80, 89, 93, 114, 163
Milla (Project Bible underground activist), 284
Million Signatures Campaign, 260
Milner, Alfred, 43, 46, 48, 51, 53
Mineworkers Strike of 1922, 101
Mineworkers Strike of 1946, 140
Minh, Ho Chi, 230, 250
Mini Town, 187, 216, 262
Mitchell, Timothy, 102, 215
MJK Unit (Mandla Judson Kuzwayo Unit), 261, 282–84

MK (uMkhonto weSizwe), 142, 199, 208, 220, 246, 259, 284; exile and, 199, 230–34; formation of, 161, 228; infiltration of, 245–46; Merebank and, 235–242, 249; Wentworth and, 311, 313, 316, 318, 336; women and, 244, 296. *See also specific operations*
Mkhize, Florence, 235
Mkhumbane, 148, 162
Mobeni: activism and, 141, 211, 276, 278, 389n27; concentration camp and, 36; farming and, 138, 211; industry and, 2, 105, 108, 116, 145–46, 177, 180, 205
Mobil refinery, 2, 166, 181, 237–38, 251, 335. *See* Engen refinery
Modise, Joe, 231, 233, 246, 287
Mofokeng, Santu, 322, 324
Mokaba, Peter, 321
Mokoape, Keith, 213
Mondi Merebank paper mill, 2, 5, 177, 187–88, 279–81
Moodliar, Deseni, 322
Moodley, Poomoney "Poo," 143, 151, 208
Moodley, Strinivasa "Strini," 212–13
Moodley, Sydney, 249
More, Mabogo, 212
Morogoro conference of 1969, 232, 245, 250
Morphet, Tony, 203
Morrell, Robert, 73
Morrison, Toni, 94–96, 133, 135, 153
Moten, Fred, 333, 339, 343
Movimento Popular de Libertação de Angola, 233
Mozambique, 198, 219, 230, 232–34, 252, 283, 317, 342
MRA (Merebank Ratepayers Association): after apartheid, 3, 5, 335; early years of, 71, 120, 171, 174, 176–77, 180–81, 187–88; urban movements and, 235 237, 247–48, 258, 301
Mthethwa, Alpheus, 248, 279
Mulligan, John, 317–18
multidirectional memory, 64, 89, 93
municipal self-financing, 70, 132
Muslim, 68, 78, 88–91, 158, 218–19, 226, 285
mutuality, 11, 71–2, 135, 193, 217; in ethno-racial form, 96
Mxenge, Griffiths, 261
Mxenge, Victoria, 261

Naidoo, Jayendra, 261, 282
Naidoo, Kammila, 285
Naidoo, Kesaveloo Goonarathnum (Dr. Goonam), 82, 148–49
Naicker, Monty, 169, 173
Naidoo, M. D. (Mooroogiah Dhanapathy Naidoo), 236

Pact Government, 115–16

Padmore, George, 236

Palestine Liberation Organization, 319

palimpsest: as form, 27, 54, 314; as historical-geographic method, 10, 25, 36, 341; in photographic practice, 29; as reading practice, 40, 59, 124

Palme, Olaf, 233

Pan Africanist Congress, 161, 206, 214, 290, 316

Pandian, Anand, 82

Paris 1968, 199, 202

passive resistance movement of 1946, 143–44, 151, 235

Passtoors, Hélène, 283, 288

Patel, Dipak (Taps), 291

Patel, Zulaikha, 226

Patricia (community leader, Wentworth), 34–36, 43

Pearce, Allan (former antiapartheid activist from Wentworth), 308, 310, 312, 314

peasant-workers, 23, 26, 68, 74, 76, 90, 96, 112, 124, 136–39

Peek, Bobby, 6, 337

Pentecostalism, 4, 57, 220–21, 308

people's war, 251, 286, 291, 394n51

personhood, 28–29, 64, 91, 95, 207, 306, 321, 341

Peter, Myron, 203, 208, 210–11, 214–15, 223, 279, 391n46

Petronas, 2, 166, 338. *See also* Engen refinery

Peyre, Sylvie, 333

Philip, Rubin, 207, 214, 218–19, 221–22

Phoenix Settlement, 82, 212–13, 216, 249, 262–63

Phoenix Women's Circle, 296

photography: agitprop and, 269, 271; audiovisual blues critique and, 339–340; dialectical image and, 97–98, 100, 135, 150; as documentary photography, 4, 19, 29, 201; as forgery, 39–40, 65–66, 125, 131, 133–34, 140; moment of the disqualified and, 306, 320–334; Omar Badsha and, 69, 158–160, 259

Pietermaritzburg, 46, 72, 75, 77, 114, 168, 269, 299, 313

Pillay, A. K., 179

Pillay, Dhayiah [Joe], 235, 239–42, 244–46

Pillay, Rajaluxmi "Rajes" [Rae], 242–47, 282, 296

Pillay, Selina, 285

Pillay, Vella, 255

Pillay, Visvanathan "Vis" [Ivan], 234–42, 244–49, 252–54, 261, 282; Operation Vula and, 285–88, 290, 292, 309

Pinetown, 111, 123, 204, 278, 389n27

Pistorius, Ron, 168

Pithouse, Richard, 215, 365n53

Pityana, Barney, 206, 212, 215

Plaatje, Sol, 52

planetarity, 17, 21, 54, 96, 340–42, 346

planning: apartheid and, 26, 167–68, 188, 277–78; biopolitics of, 15–16, 54, 111–12, 128, 262; C. L. R. James on, 99; as racial, 26–27, 54, 171; as scientific, 103, 105–6; struggles over, 1, 180, 269, 274–78, 340, 337; as town and regional planning, 109, 112, 115–16, 128, 163, 167–69, 171, 177, 376n190. *See also* Provincial Post-War Works and Reconstruction Commission of 1943–44 (Post-War Commission); Betterment Planning

PMC (Politico-Military Council), 234, 252

political faith, 207, 211, 223–24, 335, 343

political hope, 5, 7, 9, 18, 21, 24, 29, 340, 344

pollution, 3, 111, 126, 131, 150, 166–67, 237; air pollution, 5–6, 335–37, 344. *See also* waste

Pondoland revolts, 151, 161

Pontecorvo, Gillo, 240

poor white question, 40, 101–2, 113–115, 122, 142, 298, 371n83

Poovalingam, Pat, 179

Population Registration Act of 1950, 22, 162

populists, 275–76

Port of Durban, 2, 96, 131, 204

Posel, Deborah, 118

postapartheid (as problem space), 7, 9–10, 18, 56, 198, 256, 340–41

Prakasim, Calvin, 209, 323

praxis: 7, 10, 13, 36, 142, 341; BC and, 206–7, 213, 215, 217, 223; Black women and, 20, 25, 94, 153; Blackness and, 29, 99, 192, 306; photography as, 158; popular biopolitics and, 300, 344; South African feminism and, 154, 265–66; as spatial, 82, 104, 139; urban movements and, 251, 276

production of space, 12, 98, 116; as contradictory, 101; as subaltern, 63, 69–70, 79–80, 83, 90–91

Progressivism: as Transatlantic project, 15, 53, 103; model African villages and, 75–76; urban reform and, 54, 70

progressivism: Africans and, 52, 75–76, 107; as Indian progressivism, 26, 82–83, 96, 137, 142, 149, 170, 229, 261, 268, 309, 343, 386n140; segregation and, 26 102–3, 108–9, 135, 189, 342

Project Bible, 261, 281–85

proletarian populism, 141, 148

property, 67, 73, 80, 92–93, 112, 169–70

Provincial Post-War Works and Reconstruction Commission of 1943–44 (Post-War Commission), 102, 121–128; biopolitics and, 15–16, 167, 262, 340, 344; bubonic plague and, 54, 69; community health and, 145–47, 152; *Ninth Interim Report (Barnes Report)* of, 128–130, 159, 168; public health, 5, 46, 136; racial statecraft and, 103–4, 128, 130; segregation and, 109, 111, 117; standards of living and, 106

Public Health Act of 1919, 106

Public Health Committees Ordinance of 1923, 104

Rabilal, Krish [Ashok; Goodwin], 198, 199, 233, 235, 240–42, 253
Rabkin, Sue, 234, 253, 255
race, 19–24, 54, 61, 159; caste school and, 114; race-class debate and, 164; and national melancholia, 189.
race zoning, 157, 173, 386n140; maps of, 26, 123, 125
racism: anti-African racism as, 74, 80; anti-Dalit casteism as, 80, 150; anti-Indian racism as, 106, 123, 148, 169, 173; anti-Semitism and, 69, 107, 114, 149; as collective intoxication, 13; Gilmore's definition, 1, 53; as municipal racism, 76. See also specific racial categories
racial capitalism. See capitalism
racial islands, 123, 126–28
racial ontologization, 29
racial-spatial fix, 13, 24
Radebe, Jeff, 238
Rajbansi, Amichand, 179, 180, 268
Rajgopaul, Jeeva, 322
Ramaphosa, Cyril, 259
Ramaswamy, Sumathi, 192
Ramgobin, Mewa, 210, 235, 264
Ramlakan, Vejaynand "Vejay," 252–55; 401n48
Ramsamy, Govinden, 174, 181–82, 248, 281
Rancière, Jacques, 93
Rankin, Sheldon, 277
RC (Revolutionary Council), 232–34, 250, 252, 286
Rebecca (Project Bible underground activist), 284
Reddy, Govin, 223, 238
refineries. See individual names
religiosity: BC and, 206; charismatic renewal, 183, 201, 220–22; syncretism of, 77–78, 158; reform and, 78–79; popular forms of, 222, 273
rent struggle, 265–74
Reservoir Hills, 173–74, 262, 284, 288
responsible self-government, 16, 127
revolution, 27–29, 198–204; Blackness, negation and, 306; counterrevolution of planning and, 99; External Mission theory of and, 230–32, 250–52, 255, 286–87, 291, 342, 394n51; Fanon and, 215, 325; gender and, 244, 284; popular biopolitics and, 213, 344; two-stage theory of, 141–42, 388n3; urban movement and, 260–62, 274, 300
Rishi (former Merebank youth activist), 207–9, 211, 220
Robben Island, 91, 142, 210, 265, 289, 314; prisoners released from, 233, 236–38, 250, 261, 264
Roberts, Brian, 52
Roberts, Frederick, 33, 45
Robinson, Cedric, 12–13, 61–63, 66, 96, 99, 134, 158, 212. See also forgeries
Robinson, Jennifer, 118, 301

Rothberg, Michael, 64. See also multidirectional memory
Round Table Conferences of 1926 and 1932, 80, 106
Roy (former Merebank youth activist), 207, 209–10, 214–15, 219–20
Roy, Ananya, 13
Royal Navy, 57, 130, 172, 183
RPMC (Regional Politico-Military Council), 234, 282, 291
ruins, 97–98, 100. See also Walter Benjamin
Ruiters, George, 152–53, 344

Sachs, Albert "Albie," 289, 296
SACP (South African Communist Party), 18, 141, 161, Ahmed Timol and; 198, 234; theories of revolution and, 142, 161, 164, 232, 250, 275; underground 149, 205, 291
SACTU (South African Congress of Trade Unions), 141–43, 198, 234, 281, 377n21
SADF (South African Defence Force), 230, 305, 316; Special Forces of, 315
safe house, 198, 230, 244, 247, 253, 285, 288–89, 292, 299
Said, Edward, 339–40
SANF (South African Naval Force), 139, 178, 183, 308, 324–34
sanitation: 51, 53, 69, 104–6, 186; as "sanitation syndrome," 14, 55; incorporation and, 109–12, 116
Sannyasi, Bhavani Dayal, 81
Sartre, Jean Paul, 202, 212
SASO (South African Student Organization), 206–7, 209, 212–16, 218–19, 232; aftermath of banning of, 238–39, 243, 254
Sasolburg, 6, 116, 342; SASOL bombings and, 251; 342
Saul, John, 205, 224
Scarry, Elaine, 199
Schadeberg, Jürgen, 321
Schegmann, Wendy, 322
Schlemmer, Lawrence, 298–99
Schoon, Marius, 239
Scott Brown, Denise, 168
Scott, Dianne, 74, 124, 137, 274
Scott, Mpho, 292
SDCEA (South Durban Community Industrial Alliance), 3, 6, 152, 301, 335, 337–38
Sea Cow Lake, 77–78, 83, 138, 149
Seal, Bobby, 213–14
Security Branch, 233, 241, 243, 245, 255, 265, 267–68, 292, 315, 318; Project Bible and, 261, 283–85
Sedibe, Glory, 233, 241
Seedat, Hashim, 267